The Official
VIRGINIA CIVIL WAR BATTLEFIELD GUIDE

John S. Salmon

STACKPOLE BOOKS

0 11557 02868 3

Published by
STACKPOLE BOOKS
5067 Ritter Road
Mechanicsburg, PA 17055
www.stackpolebooks.com

The Official Virginia Battlefield Guide was funded in part by a grant from the U.S. Department of the Interior through the American Battlefield Protection Program, National Park Service. Any opinions, findings, and conclusions or recommendations expressed herein are those of the author and do not necessarily reflect the views of the Department of the Interior.

Cover illustration: Fredericksburg and Spotsylvania National Military Park, Virginia. Virginia Department of Historic Resources, John S. Salmon

Cover design by Tracy Patterson

Printed in the United States of America

10 9 8 7 6 5 4 3

FIRST EDITION

Library of Congress Cataloging-in-Publication Data

Salmon, John S., 1948–
    The official Virginia Civil War battlefield guide / John S. Salmon.—1st ed.
        p. cm.
    Includes bibliographical references (p.) and index.
    ISBN: 0-8117-2868-4
    1. Virginia—History—Civil War, 1861-1865—Battlefields—Guidebooks. 2.
Virginia—History—Civil War, 1861-1865—Campaigns. 3. United States—-History—Civil
War, 1861–1865—Battlefields—Guidebooks. 4. United States—-History—Civil War,
1861–1865—Campaigns. 5. Virginia—Tours. 6. Historic sites—Virginia—Guidebooks. I.
Title.

E534 .S27 2001
973.7'3—dc21
                                                                        2001020150
    ISBN 978-0-8117-2868-3

For Emily

CONTENTS

ILLUSTRATIONS

FOREWORD

Why do battlefields arouse such strong emotions in so many people? Why do visitors drive hundreds of miles to see rolling farmlands and forested hills and manicured parks? Why are people still stirred by events that happened more than a century ago? Why do so many regard battlegrounds as hallowed—even sacred—soil?

Perhaps the answer to all these questions is that war, more than any other experience, distills and intensifies what is good and bad, noble and mean, wise and foolish, brave and cowardly about human beings. A battlefield evokes a concentrated human encounter with life and death in a manner that words and images often fail to do. Thus, books and motion pictures are pale substitutes for visiting the spots where great events occurred, and where the fate of our country was decided by individual striving and sacrifice. We stand awestruck in those places, and struggle to comprehend and to learn, and come away profoundly moved, saddened, uplifted, and enriched.

Virginia is blessed with more important Civil War battlefields than any other state. About a fifth of them have been preserved forever in national, state, or local parks, and many of the rest are in the hands of private owners who cherish and protect them. During the decade that this book was researched and written, however, some of the most significant battlefields—from Ball's Bluff to Chancellorsville, from the Wilderness to New Market Heights, from Winchester to Cloyd's Mountain—have come under increased development pressure. Without public support and private stewardship, they may follow Chan-tilly and Salem Church into oblivion. Every acre of battlefield land paved over means that one more window to our national understanding is closed forever.

Yet there have been successes, too. Malvern Hill, once seemingly doomed, is now secure, thanks to federal, state, and local funding, and a supportive developer. Likewise, some of the best earthworks at North Anna River, once threatened, have been saved and are now in a county park. Parts of the Fredericksburg battlefields have been bought for preservation. Land has been donated to Staunton River Bridge Battlefield State Park. The Virginia Military Institute has acquired additional portions of the New Market battlefield. The Trevilian Station battlefield may become a state park. And Wilson's Wharf is now preserved and accessible because of the efforts of the property owner and the assistance of the Virginia Department of Historic Resources and other government agencies.

The secret of such large-scale preservation is partnership. Although the case for history should be obvious and compelling—numerous studies and surveys have underscored the array of benefits from the social to the aesthetic to the economic—it takes landowners, interest groups, and government participation to make it a reality. This is especially true in the case of battlefields, which typically encompass hundreds or thousands of acres, often on the edges of cities or suburbs. To form the necessary partnerships takes hard work, commitment, money, and creative thinking. It takes the vision to see that if we ensure a future for these treasures, they will enrich the future for all of us. This is the essence of heritage stewardship.

The Virginia Department of Historic Resources is a strong advocate of heritage stewardship and the creation of effective partnerships, and we want you, the reader, to become our partner. In the back of the book you will find a list of major organizations that strive to preserve battlefields and other historic resources. I hope that you will support their work—financially as well as through your own efforts—and join with us to save our national treasures. You have already taken the first step by purchasing this book. By visiting the battlefields, you will help raise awareness of their importance among property owners, land-use planners, and prospective developers.

Today, you and your children can stand at Manassas where Jackson once stood "like a stone wall." You can walk the path inside Fort Pocahontas at Wilson's Wharf and peer over the earthworks, and wonder how outnumbered black Union troops held off repeated charges by Fitzhugh Lee's cavalry. You can visit Belle Grove in the Shenandoah Valley at Cedar Creek, where the mortally wounded Confederate general Stephen Ramseur lay dying, while his former West Point classmates—now enemies—held his hand as evening fell. You can drive the country roads west of Petersburg and pause where Grant stopped to read Lee's acceptance of Grant's surrender demand, and recall how Grant later wrote that his migraine headache vanished as if by magic. And you can stand at Appomattox Court House and imagine the last bivouac of the Army of Northern Virginia, the mingled feelings of sadness and relief, the surrender ceremonies, and the slow beginnings of reunion.

You can do all this, with the aid of this guidebook, because thousands of people have worked to preserve these American treasures. The work has just begun. Come join us.

Kathleen S. Kilpatrick
Director, Virginia Department of Historic Resources, and State Historic Preservation Officer

ACKNOWLEDGMENTS

Although writing is regarded as a lonely occupation, no writer of history is ever truly alone as he lurches down the road toward publication. Past historians pave the way; a host of colleagues, friends, and strangers offer directions; and editors, cartographers, and indexers drag him the last few miles to the end of the journey. One of the writer's more pleasant challenges is to acknowledge all this help with a gratitude that mere words cannot express.

Without the support of H. Alexander Wise, Jr., former director, Virginia Department of Historic Resources, this book never would have been written. His confidence in my abilities helped motivate me, his enthusiasm for the project was unflagging, and—most importantly—he granted me the time to write. He has always cheered me on, and his many kind words of encouragement are deeply appreciated.

Likewise, my supervisors over the years have been patient, understanding, and supportive, and I will always be grateful for their assistance. They include (in alphabetical order) Dr. Robert A. Carter, Julie Vosmik Langan, Elizabeth Hoge Lipford, Dr. M. Catherine Slusser, and Marc C. Wagner.

All of my associates at the Virginia Department of Historic Resources have helped me in one way or another. I am indeed fortunate to have such colleagues as friends. They have not only aided me immeasurably with the book, but have made my years at the department among the most enjoyable of my life. Some have read portions of the work, while others have served as sounding boards when I needed someone to listen to my ruminations. Kathleen S. Kilpatrick, director, helped clarify publication strategies. Deborah B. Woodward, public relations specialist, offered valuable editorial suggestions and assistance with publication plans and negotiations. Deborah A. Roddenberry, former director of the Program Services Division, and her talented staff, especially Patricia A. Hurt, budget analyst, Nina K. Pierce, procurement officer, and Reggie L. Williams, fiscal officer, kept this numerically challenged writer on budget. David A. Edwards, director of the department's Winchester Regional Office, provided lodging and boon companionship on my several visits to the Shenandoah Valley.

During the Civil War Sites Advisory Commission study, Jarl K. Jackson, then a student at Virginia Commonwealth University, served as my research assistant. An indefatigable researcher, he gathered countless journal articles and other secondary sources for me and wrote summaries of several Southwest Virginia battles.

When I began writing, I discussed my concept for the book with Sandra Gioia Treadway, then the Library of Virginia's director of the Division of Publications and Cultural Affairs and now the deputy librarian of Virginia, and with Edward D. C. "Kip" Campbell, Jr., director of the Collection Management Services Division. Later, I spoke many times with Gregg D. Kimball, assistant director of publications in the Division of Publications and Educational Services. Each of them gave generously of their time and good advice.

For the past several years, I have served on the board of directors of Virginia Civil War Trails, Inc., representing the Virginia Department of Historic Resources. My interactions with my fellow directors and the members of this consortium, many of whom are Civil War experts, aided me in the writing of the book in many ways. I would especially like to thank John F. "Jack" Berry, chairman of the board of directors; H. Mitchell Bowman, executive director of Virginia Civil War Trails, Inc.; and Don Pierce, of Page One, Inc., and publisher of *Civil War Traveler,* for their support and friendship.

One of the great pleasures of my career has been my close association with the staff of the National Park Service. The service's American Battlefield Protection Program funded the writing of this book. Dr. Marilyn W. Nichols served as chief of the program during the Shenandoah County battlefield survey early in the 1990s, Jan Townsend succeeded her about the time that the Civil War Sites Advisory Commission study began, and H. Bryan Mitchell has directed the program during most of the time that this book was written. I am grateful to all of them for their support.

Edwin C. Bearss, Chief Historian Emeritus, National Park Service, and David W. Lowe, Historian, American Battlefield Protection Program, reviewed every word of the text. Ed, a legend in his own time, is well-known to students of Civil War history throughout the United States; his writings, lectures, and battlefield tours are justly acclaimed. He has always shown me extraordinary kindness and has been most generous in sharing his vast knowledge of the war. David conducted the field work for the Shenandoah Valley study and supervised the field work for the Civil War Sites Advisory Commission survey. A man of many parts—author, songwriter, and Global Positioning System guru—David was my guide on several battlefield treks.

When I called on colleagues at national battlefield parks in Virginia to review my work in light of their specialties, they responded most graciously. Alphabetically by park they include: Fredericksburg and Spotsylvania National Military Park, Donald C. Pfanz; Petersburg National Battlefield, Chris M. Calkins; Richmond National Battlefield Park, Michael J. Andrus, Robert E. L. Krick, and David R. Ruth.

To say that this book has been vastly improved by these experts' careful reviews is an understatement. Any errors that survive are my responsibility, not theirs.

Once the book was written, Dale Evva Gelfand smoothly edited and copyedited the text, cut what needed to be cut, and offered suggestions for seamless transitions. Dale F. and Tracy Harter and Emily J. Salmon spent many long hours carefully compiling the index. Emily also helped proofread many pages of text.

Having some experience myself with the other side of the publishing equation, I especially appreciate the professional talents of the Stackpole Books staff. Leigh Ann Berry, associate editor, oversaw the publication process from start to finish and was a delight to work with. Tracy A. Patterson, vice president of creative services and production, skillfully juggled text, maps, pictures, and captions to design the book. Caroline M. Stover, associate art director, and Wendy A. Reynolds, assistant art director, transformed my scrawls and scribbles into clear, readable, and attractive maps.

Three first-class organizations helped defray the high costs of publication by generously contributing promotional pages to the book, and I want to thank H. Mitchell Bowman, executive director, Virginia Civil War Trails, Inc.; O. James Lighthizer, president, Civil War Preservation Trust; and Robin Edward Reed, executive director, Museum of the Confederacy. I urge every reader of this book to support the Civil War Preservation Trust, tour Virginia Civil War Trails, and visit the Museum of the Confederacy.

I want to thank my parents, Henry S. and Janice Salmon, for a lifetime of encouragement. They introduced me to "heritage tourism" long before the term was invented, as we traveled the West during my childhood and visited one historic place after another.

To my wife, Emily, go my deepest thanks for her unfailing love, support, and assistance. ∎

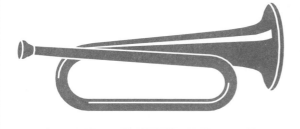

INTRODUCTION

The first Civil War battlefield tourists showed up too early. They found the battlefield easily enough but had barely unpacked their picnic lunches before they had to grab the kids and flee. The date was July 21, 1861, and the place was the northern Virginia countryside near a little hamlet called Manassas Junction. Hundreds of sightseers from Washington, who crowded the hills overlooking Bull Run to witness the first major land battle of the war, soon joined the Union army in a frantic dash for safety as the Confederates swept the field with shot and shell. Civil War tourism suffered a sharp setback.

Today, conditions are much different. No one shoots at tourists, and a first-rate infrastructure of roads, hotels, and restaurants is in place to make visitors feel at home. Virginia's Civil War battlefields, as well as the state's other historic sites, scenic wonders, tourist attractions, and friendly people, offer plenty of reasons to spend time in the commonwealth.

Many books have been published about the Civil War and many guidebooks as well. Interest in the war—spurred by the motion pictures *Glory* (1989) and *Gettysburg* (1993) and especially by Ken Burns's television documentary *The Civil War* (1990)—continues unabated. Reenactments draw huge crowds, visitation to Civil War battlefields and other sites is steady or increasing, and discussions of the war and its causes and effects are periodically provoked by controversies over Confederate symbols in public places. The continuing high level of interest, as well as the Civil War Sites Advisory Commission study of the early 1990s and its consequences, prompted the writing of this book.

Unlike other guidebooks, *The Official Virginia Civil War Battlefield Guide* makes full use of the information gathered for the commission's report, which identified 384 battles out of an estimated 10,500 "armed conflicts" as being most essential to an understanding of the war. Almost a third— 123—are located in Virginia; Tennessee has 38, the next-highest number. The guidebook is arranged by campaign, with a map and overview of each one. Every important battle is also described, and a detailed battlefield driving-tour map accompanies each description, as well as an illustration. A symbol on each map shows the point of view from which each image was photographed or drawn. The troop movements shown on the battlefield driving-tour maps have been simplified, and topographic features and vegetation have been deleted, so that you can read the maps easily. More detailed maps can be found in the books listed in the Bibliography. Troop strength and casualty estimates are taken from the commission's study. The names of battles follow the usual conventions: the victor got to name the battle, and Federal titles generally referred to nearby natural features (Bull Run), while Confederates usually employed the names of manmade landmarks (Manassas Junction).

To make your visit more enjoyable and informative as you explore Virginia's battlefields, check the state's tourism Web site at www.virginia.org. Call or drop by city or county visitor centers for current information on nearby sites and accommodations. If you are near a national park visitor center, stop off for specialized battlefield maps, walking tours, and other information. As you follow the driving tours offered in this book, please remember to keep to public roads. Always respect the privacy of those who live on or near battlefields, and do not trespass.

Two systems of roadside historical markers exist to benefit visitors to Virginia's Civil War battlefields. The first is the state historical marker system originated in 1926, one of the earliest in the nation. Many important Civil War sites are interpreted with these big silver-and-black plaques mounted on poles, and *A Guidebook to Virginia's Historical Markers* can be purchased in most Virginia bookstores.

The second, more recent system is Virginia Civil War Trails, which links sites through five regional networks. Almost 300 sites are interpreted with colorful markers, well over 200 of them at sites previously uninterpreted. The Trails are marked with trailblazing signs—red and blue with a red bugle—that visitors can follow from one stop to another. Each stop can accommodate tour buses and automobiles. The maps in this book show any existing Trails stops on battlefields. The statewide Trails map and individual regional maps are available at most visitor centers, or call 1-888-CIVIL WAR.

The state and Trails markers commemorate the war and the sacrifices of those who served. Even before the war ended, an interest in commemoration had already taken root. President Abraham Lincoln spoke briefly on November 19, 1863, at Gettysburg during the dedication of the Soldiers' National Cemetery there—a few "remarks" soon immortalized as the Gettysburg Address. The first permanent monument in Virginia was erected on the Manassas battlefield in 1865, and before long dozens of others were placed on scores of different sites. Patriotic and memorial associations were formed in the North and in the South, national cemeteries were opened for the Union dead,

Southern ladies gathered Confederate remains into comparable burying grounds, and periodic reunions summoned the dwindling numbers of surviving veterans back to the old battlefields.

As the nineteenth century came to a close, a movement to preserve battlefields gained momentum with the creation of four national military parks in the 1890s: Chickamauga and Chattanooga (1890), Shiloh (1894), Gettysburg (1895), and Vicksburg (1899). In Virginia, national parks were established at Petersburg (1925), Fredericksburg and Spotsylvania County (1927), Appomattox Court House (1935), Richmond (1936), Cumberland Gap (1940), and Manassas (1940). In addition, two state battlefield parks were established in Virginia: Sailor's Creek (1937) and Staunton River Bridge (1957). A variety of other preservation activities have borne fruit, as well. Over the years, local governments have acquired portions of battlefields for parks, such as Fort Clifton in Colonial Heights and Ball's Bluff in Loudoun County. Preservation organizations such as the Association for the Preservation of Civil War Sites and the Civil War Trust (since merged to form the Civil War Preservation Trust) have purchased and protected parts of other battlefields. Most battlefields in Virginia, however, remain in private hands and are therefore at risk.

The pressure of growth and suburban sprawl in northern Virginia in the late 1980s and early 1990s brought the risks to public attention when privately owned battlegrounds at Manassas, Brandy Station, and Bristoe Station faced imminent development. Although the preservation impulse prevailed—at least temporarily—in all three cases there were confrontations with developers and property-rights advocates. All involved agreed that there ought to be a better way to resolve or perhaps even avoid such conflicts.

In 1990 Congress passed two acts with the hope of accomplishing those goals by involving property owners as well as local, state, and federal government officials. The first act authorized a study of Civil War battlefields in the Shenandoah Valley of Virginia in order to locate them, assess their condition, identify short- and long-term threats to their integrity, and provide alternatives for their preservation and interpretation. The second act created the Civil War Sites Advisory Commission to pursue the same aims nationwide. The Shenandoah Valley study resulted in a report completed in 1992; the Civil War Sites Advisory Commission finished its work and reported to Congress in 1993.

The commission's report included the Shenandoah Valley battlefields and identified 384 battles nationwide as being most significant for interpreting the war. The battlefields were ranked according to military significance, degree of integrity, and imminence of threats.

As the staff historian for the Department of Historic Resources, I participated in each study. Important and admirable as both reports were, I knew that they would meet the fate of similar documents and simply be filed away on bookshelves in government offices.

In June 1994 H. Alexander Wise, Jr., was appointed director of the department. He shared my interest in finding a way to put the information behind the reports before the public. We soon agreed that I would use the data as well as secondary sources to write a battlefield guidebook. The department signed a memorandum of agreement with the National Park Service in March 1995, the American Battlefield Protection Program provided funding, and I completed the manuscript about four and a half years later.

The guidebook serves several purposes. The most obvious objective is to inform and direct you to the battlefields, then guide you around each one. Another is to educate visitors and landowners alike about the battlefields, their current integrity, threats to their continued existence, and opportunities for their preservation. Most important, I hope that you will appreciate the fragility of these national treasures and help to preserve them.

Virginia's battlefields, where thousands of Americans struggled and died, need help. By reading this book, and by touring the battlefields themselves, you will learn that some battlefields have disappeared beneath development, while numerous others are threatened with extinction despite the good stewardship of many generations of owners. You will learn that most of Virginia's battlefields are not in or near national parks, and of those that are, only portions are truly protected. Important parts of some of the best-known battlefields—from Chancellorsville and the Wilderness to Richmond and Petersburg—are in danger of obliteration.

Fortunately they are not without friends. On the national level, private groups and government agencies have raised and distributed millions of dollars for battlefield preservation, including the Civil War Preservation Trust and the National Park Service's American Battlefield Protection Program. On the state and local level, the Department of Historic Resources and many organizations such as the Brandy Station Foundation and the Cedar Creek Battlefield Foundation have helped direct efforts toward particular battlefields. And most important of all, private landowners like Harrison Tyler at Fort Pocahontas have labored mightily to preserve those parts of our nation's heritage that are presently in their care.

You can be a friend to Virginia's battlefields, too. Join preservation organizations and national battlefield parks friends' groups; give generously to support their work; start a preservation or friends' group yourself; write and call your national, state, and local representatives; visit the battlefields frequently and be a supportive heritage tourist. And if you are fortunate enough to own a piece of our national heritage, please continue to set an example of good stewardship for others to emulate. We best venerate the memories of the Americans who strove at these important places when we work to preserve them: "honor answering honor."

The organizations listed in the appendix are dedicated to the preservation of Virginia battlefields, either directly (as the Civil War Preservation Trust), indirectly (the American Farmland Trust, by helping farmers keep farming, saves land from development), or as part of a larger conservation mission (the Department of Historic Resources, for instance). Every organization offers some combination of memberships, programs in which you can participate, or funds to which you can contribute.

All royalties from the sale of this book will be directed toward preservation efforts in Virginia. ■

MANASSAS CAMPAIGN, 1861

The United States garrison at Fort Sumter in South Carolina formally surrendered to Confederate forces on April 14, 1861. In Washington the next day, Pres. Abraham Lincoln issued a proclamation calling for 75,000 volunteers to uphold the laws of the United States. The announcement galvanized secession conventions in several Southern states. Seven states—South Carolina, Mississippi, Florida, Alabama, Georgia, Louisiana, and Texas—had left the Union before the fall of Sumter. Virginia seceded on April 17, followed by Arkansas, North Carolina, and Tennessee.

The seceding states joined the Confederate States of America, which had been formed in Montgomery, Alabama, on February 4, 1861. Five days later the Confederate Provisional Congress elected as president Jefferson Davis, who had recently resigned as Mississippi's United States senator. He was inaugurated on February 18. Late in May, seeking to be close to the anticipated theater of war, the Confederate government moved to Richmond, Virginia.

In Washington, Gen. Winfield Scott commanded the United States Army. Born near Petersburg, Virginia, on June 13, 1786, Scott had fought in both the War of 1812 and the Mexican War, becoming a national hero. Junior officers, who referred to him as "Old Fuss and Feathers," thought Scott too old and settled in his ways to organize a huge, modern army. They were right, but Scott was astute enough to formulate the Union grand strategy, popularly known as the Anaconda Plan. Blockade the Southern coast, cut off the West by securing the Mississippi River, and use the border states as a buffer, thereby strangling the Confederacy and avoiding a costly overland war. Although Lincoln did not adopt Scott's plan at first, eventually it became Federal policy—but in conjunction with the bloody war Scott had hoped to evade.

The politicians wanted a quick war, not slow strangulation. The Northern press urged the immediate capture of the Confederate capital with the cry: "On to Richmond!" Both presidents prodded their armies into the field, and many citizens on each side predicted that the war would be settled with one large battle.

On April 19 Lincoln ordered a blockade of Southern ports and harbors from the Rio Grande to the North Carolina–South Carolina border. He then extended the blockade to include the North Carolina and Virginia coasts. In turn, the Confederates in Virginia responded quickly by building artillery batteries on the bluffs overlooking the Potomac River to blockade Washington. By mid-May batteries stood at several points along the Potomac, including Aquia Creek in Stafford County and Cockpit Point in Prince William County. The Union answered with the Potomac Flotilla, a half-dozen steam-powered vessels, but although the Union ships kept the Potomac open to military traffic, as long as Confederate crews manned the batteries, the river was effectively closed to other shipping.

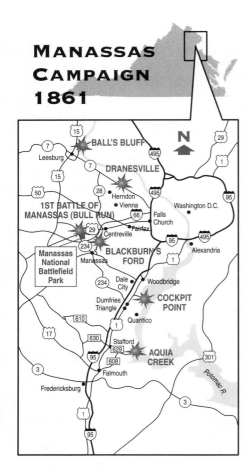

MANASSAS CAMPAIGN 1861

In the meantime, both the Union and Confederate governments strengthened their armies. After the Federals burned the Harpers Ferry armory and abandoned the town on April 18, Confederate troops began to assemble there. The Confederate government commissioned a professor of artillery and natural philosophy at Virginia Military Institute in Lexington, Thomas Jonathan Jackson, a colonel in the Confederate infantry and sent him to train the troops at Harpers Ferry. There he began molding them into an army, drilling them incessantly and drawing their ire for his strict discipline. On May 15 the Confederate War Department ordered Brig. Gen. Joseph E. Johnston, a widely known and

well-respected officer, to assume command of this army. Soon the government promoted Jackson to brigadier general as Johnston's second in command.

The Harpers Ferry pattern was repeated in other parts of Virginia. In Lynchburg, Col. Jubal A. Early raised volunteers and organized them into regiments. Col. Philip St. George Cocke moved from Alexandria to Culpeper Court House, near the center of the state, and established a large training camp. Other Southern states raised their own regiments and sent them to Virginia.

Except for a few regular army units, the Union army also had to be created from scratch. Its thousands of new recruits needed training as desperately as their Confederate counterparts. Brig. Gen. Irvin McDowell undertook the task, using Arlington House, Gen. Robert E. Lee's residence on the Potomac (actually his wife's home), as his headquarters. He did the gentlemanly thing by living in a tent in the front yard and assuring Mrs. Lee by letter that whenever she returned home, she would find nothing out of place. Across the Potomac, Washington became a training camp. Tents covered the Mall, and thousands of Union troops saw their capital for the first time. Outside the city, in western Maryland and southern Pennsylvania, other regiments trained. They became Maj. Gen. Robert Patterson's army when the sixty-nine-year-old Irishman gathered them to recapture Harpers Ferry in June.

Patterson, exhibiting all the caution for which Union generals soon became famous, moved on the arsenal late in May. By the time Patterson approached Harpers Ferry, however, Johnston, who had received ample warning, had salvaged the machinery and tools, burned the key buildings, and marched south through the Shenandoah Valley. He easily eluded Patterson for the next three weeks and camped at Winchester, which he considered a better post than Harpers Ferry, anyway.

Meanwhile, Cocke had received orders from Lee—who commanded all state forces from Richmond—to move from Culpeper northeast to Manassas Junction in Prince William County, about thirty miles outside Washington. There, two vitally important railroads met. The Orange & Alexandria Railroad connected Alexandria with Gordonsville, in Orange County, where the Virginia Central Railroad led to Charlottesville. And the Manassas Gap Railroad extended from the junction through the Manassas Gap near Strasburg in the Shenandoah Valley, less than twenty miles southwest of Winchester, then south to Harrisonburg. If the Confederates held Manassas Junction, they could deny the Federals access to the Shenandoah Valley and central Virginia while protecting the approaches to Richmond and retaining the option to attack Washington via the Valley and western Maryland. Conversely, if the Union army seized the junction, it could more easily protect its capital, march on Richmond, and ride the rails westward.

Lee first sent Brig. Gen. Milledge L. Bonham to command the growing force at the junction, then at the end of May supplanted him with Brig. Gen. Pierre Gustave Toutant Beauregard, who had commanded in Charleston during the bombardment of Fort Sumter. The troop buildup continued, until by mid-July Beauregard had some 22,000 men at the junction.

Responding to Northern pressure, on June 3 Winfield Scott asked McDowell to submit a plan for advancing on Manassas Junction. McDowell complied, hoping that a mere show of force would drive away the Confederates. His plan called for three columns, totaling 39,000 men, to approach the junction by way of the Little River Turnpike (present-day Rte. 236) and the Orange & Alexandria Railroad. Patterson,

with 18,000 troops, was to prevent Johnston's 12,000-man army from leaving the Shenandoah Valley.

By the time McDowell's army began trudging and sweating its way through the hot, humid Virginia countryside on July 16, Beauregard knew his plan. Washington remained at heart, after all, a Southern city, and crawled with Confederate spies. The sheer size of McDowell's force—the largest ever to take the field on American soil—the heat, and the inexperience of his lieutenants all combined to slow its progress to a crawl. By noon the next day McDowell stood at Fairfax Court House, about halfway to his objective. He chose to rest the troops while sending Brig. Gen. Daniel Tyler and a reinforced brigade of about 3,000 men to locate the Confederate eastern flank. Tyler was to avoid an engagement, secure Centreville, scout beyond the village, and report his findings. (Tyler, like his fellow subordinates, did not care for the younger McDowell, whom they regarded as rude and aloof.)

After Tyler entered Centreville on July 18 and found the Confederates had abandoned it, he pushed on toward Mitchell's Ford and Blackburn's Ford on Bull Run. Approaching Blackburn's Ford, he saw only a Confederate battery and a handful of pickets. From his hilltop position, he thought he could see Manassas in the distance. He also thought he could see glory, by capturing the vital rail junction, and a chance to grab the credit from McDowell, if he could press on. He was certain that the Confederates would fall back before his advance, as they had at Centreville. He was wrong.

Tyler began his assault on Blackburn's Ford cautiously, opening with his artillery and gradually committing more and more infantry. On the other side, Brig. Gen. James Longstreet led the brigade that Tyler could not see concealed in the underbrush;

Longstreet fed his troops into the fray at a pace matching Tyler's. McDowell, hearing the uproar, rode to the ford, arriving about 4 P.M. He angrily ordered Tyler to break off the action and return to Centreville, where he established a new headquarters. Tyler and his men felt frustrated, having fought for hours to little effect. McDowell feared that Tyler's disobedience had ruined his plans to capture Manassas Junction. The Confederates, on the other hand, exulted.

McDowell fumed and revised his plans for the next two days. Far away, in the Shenandoah Valley, Patterson inched south and then pulled back while Johnston made military history. Leaving a young cavalryman, Col. James Ewell Brown "Jeb" Stuart, to screen his movement, the Confederate general led his army out of its defenses at Winchester on July 18 and marched twenty miles southeast to Piedmont Station (present-day Delaplane) on the Manassas Gap Railroad. Jackson led the way, driving his men at a furious pace through the villages of Millwood and Paris. On July 19 Johnston's army began boarding a train of freight and cattle cars for the slow ride to Manassas Junction. It took two days to move all the troops, and for the first time in history, a railroad had been used to transport an army to battle.

Once at the junction, however, the army rested. Johnston assumed command and executed Beauregard's scheme to disperse most of their combined force to guard the fords and bridges on Bull Run, northeast of Manassas Junction. At last McDowell, having revised his plan of attack, pressed forward from Centreville on Sunday, July 21, beginning the first battle of Manassas.

His plan called for Tyler to feign an attack on the left of the Confederate line about dawn while McDowell's main force moved upstream to Sudley Springs Ford, then crossed and struck the enemy's left flank. Tyler executed the feint so poorly,

however, that he fooled no one. The Confederate brigades of Col. Nathan G. "Shanks" Evans, Brig. Gen. Bernard Bee, and Col. Francis Bartow detected McDowell's movement to Sudley Springs and countered it at Matthews Hill, south of the ford. Brig. Gen. David Hunter, leading the Union attack, was wounded immediately and succeeded by Brig. Gen. Andrew Porter, who eventually forced the Confederates off Matthews Hill and into retreat toward Henry Hill. Meanwhile, Jackson had led his brigade to the reverse slope of Henry Hill, where it lay hidden from friend and foe alike. Jackson sat on his horse and calmly watched the battle beyond, awaiting orders. When Bee finally saw him, he is said by Virginians to have cried, "There is Jackson standing like a stone wall!" and ordered the remnants of his 4th Alabama Regiment to rally around the former professor. Although some historians believe that anger over Jackson not coming to his aid is what prompted Bee's remark, most agree that he meant it as a compliment. Regardless of his intention, Bee awarded Jackson the nom de guerre by which he would henceforth be called: Stonewall.

For the remainder of the battle, Jackson especially merited the name. His brigade held firm against one Union assault after another. Into the long, hot afternoon the fight raged, until Johnston threw fresh brigades against the Union right and Beauregard ordered a general advance. At 4 P.M. the Federal line crumpled and began a retreat that quickly turned into a rout. The undisciplined Union troops raced for the rear, entangling themselves with the carriages of civilians who, equipped with picnic baskets, had driven out from Washington to watch what they thought would be the only battle of the war. All mixed together, spectators and combatants streamed back to the capital in a panicked mob. The victorious Confederates pursued the Union army toward Centreville but, disorganized and exhausted, soon gave up the chase.

For the Union, First Manassas was a demoralizing defeat. Those who had cautioned against sending a green, undisciplined army into the field shouted, "I told you so!" at the politicians and newspaper editors who had urged them on. President Lincoln, at least, learned from the experience. Six days after the battle he replaced McDowell with Maj. Gen. George B. McClellan, a master of organization who would build and train the army that helped win the war for the Union.

On the Confederate side, sadness over the deaths of many commanders, Bee and Bartow foremost among them, tempered the joy of victory. Jefferson Davis and his lieutenants knew that their army—as raw and ill-trained as the Union force—had been fortunate. The courage of the men and their officers contributed more to the victory than did superb generalship, for the Confederate part of the battle had been improvised from beginning to end.

Over the winter both sides labored to train and supply their armies while keeping an eye on each other. In a futile effort to restore the Union army's tarnished pres-tige, on October 21 Brig. Gen. Charles P. Stone attempted to cross the Potomac at Harrison's Island and capture Leesburg. A timely Confederate counterattack under Col. Nathan Evans drove Stone's force over Ball's Bluff and into the river. The Federals suffered more than 700 captured and some 200 killed, including Col. Edward D. Baker, U.S. senator from Oregon. For days thereafter, Union corpses floated down the river past Washington.

The Northern army did win a technical victory on December 20, however, when Confederate Brig. Gen. J. E. B. Stuart led a brigade-sized force of cavalry, infantry, and artillery to protect a foraging expedition near Dranesville. Union Brig. Gen. Edward O. C. Ord, advancing on the Georgetown Pike, encountered Stuart's cavalry. Both sides deployed as more units arrived on the field, and a sharp firefight developed. Stuart withdrew in midafternoon after dispatching his wagons safely to the rear.

These were the last actions of note fought in northern Virginia in 1861. In the spring of 1862 the seat of war in Virginia shifted to the Shenandoah Valley, where Union and Confederate armies vied for control, and to the southeastern part of the state, where McClellan advanced on Richmond from Hampton. ▪

AQUIA CREEK

During the 1830s and 1840s, the Richmond, Fredericksburg & Potomac Railroad Company built a rail line from Richmond to Aquia Landing in Stafford County, north of Fredericksburg, and finished it in 1846. Passengers covered the distance between Aquia Landing and Washington, D.C., by steamboat. Southbound travelers to Richmond could complete in nine hours a journey that ordinarily took thirty-eight hours by stagecoach.

The war changed everything. A naval blockade of Southern ports disrupted travel south. The Federal government also seized four boats owned by the Potomac Steamboat Company that served the railroad at Aquia Landing, thereby denying the commonwealth of Virginia military use of the boats. Fearing that the Confederates

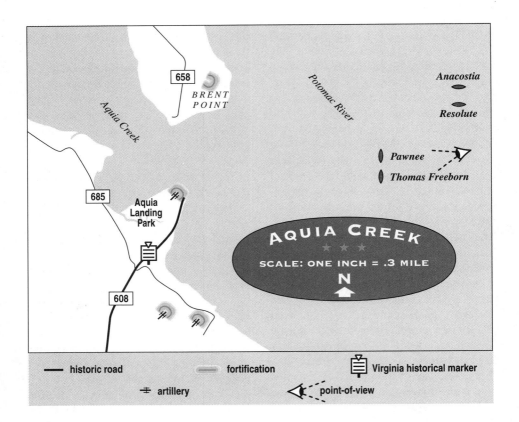

Aquia Creek

SCALE: ONE INCH = .3 MILE

N

historic road	fortification	Virginia historical marker
artillery	point-of-view	

DIRECTIONS: I-95 Exit 140 (Rte. 630, Stafford), e. on Rte. 630 (Courthouse Rd.) about .8 mile through Stafford to U.S. Rte. 1; s. (right) on U.S. Rte. 1 2.2 miles to Rte. 628 (Eskimo Hill Rd.); e. (left) on Rte. 628 2.9 miles to Rte. 608 (Brooke Rd.); e. (left) on Rte. 608 5.5 miles to Aquia Landing Park (Stafford Co. Park & Recreation Dept.), and state historical marker J-92, Aquia Landing, on Rte. 608 in park. The park currently is open only from Memorial Day to Labor Day.

would construct artillery batteries along the Potomac to blockade Washington, the U.S. Navy formed the Potomac Flotilla to patrol the river and keep it cleared for Union shipping.

Worried that the Union army might seize Aquia Landing and use the railroad to attack Fredericksburg, Maj. Thomas H. Williamson, of the Virginia army engineers, began to fortify Aquia Landing on May 8. He placed the battery not atop the bluffs on either side of Aquia Creek but on the shore at the landing itself, to protect the rail terminal. The Aquia battery went undetected by the Potomac Flotilla until USS *Mount Vernon* spotted it on May 14. The ship escaped without an engagement.

On Wednesday, May 29, USS *Thomas Freeborn* fired on the battery to no effect. The next day *Freeborn* and two other boats, *Anacostia* and *Resolute,* exchanged shots for two or three hours with the beach battery plus a new one erected on the bluff south of the creek overlooking the river. Again the action accomplished little.

About 11:30 A.M. on Saturday, June 1, *Thomas Freeborn, Anacostia,* and *Reliance,* accompanied by the sloop-of-war *Pawnee,* opened a bombardment on both batteries that lasted some five hours.

Although more than 500 rounds were fired at them, the Confederates reported only "the death of a chicken, though a stray ball killed a horse." Confederate fire damaged both *Freeborn* and *Pawnee* but neither killed nor seriously wounded any Federals.

Despite occasional small-scale Union attacks, the Confederates strengthened their position at Aquia Landing by building a third battery on the bluff and by constructing a fourth battery on Brent Point, across the creek to the north of the landing. They also completed new batteries up and down the river from Aquia Landing.

On Sunday, July 7, the first use of nautical mines ("torpedoes") in the war occurred at Aquia Landing. The Confederates anchored two off Aquia Creek and *Pawnee* passed within 200 yards of them. Union sailors spotted the mines and dispatched boats from *Resolute* to snag them. One mine sank.

By the end of October 1861, the Confederates had effectively closed the Potomac River with their numerous, strong batteries—for a time Washington communicated with the rest of the Union through Maryland. Then, slowly, the Union navy and merchant fleet discovered the Achilles heel of the batteries: The Confederate gunners could not hit passing vessels. (Part of the gunners' problem, however, appeared to be the quality of gunpowder and other munitions. One battery commander complained that often the first shot from a cannon would strike the Maryland shore, while the second would fall in the middle of the river.) Soon ships ran by the batteries with impunity, especially at night. Civilian shipping did decline, however, when the United States Navy forbade traffic on the river out of concern that the Confederates might score a lucky hit.

The blockade embarrassed Lincoln, who repeatedly ordered the new commander of the Union army, Maj. Gen. George B. McClellan, to destroy the Confederate batteries. McClellan delayed until finally, on March 8, 1862, Lincoln issued General War Order No. 3, which directly ordered the general to attack the batteries. Before the order could be implemented, however, the Confederates burned the gun carriages and huts, spiked the cannon, and abandoned the batteries. Gen. Joseph E. Johnston, anticipating an advance against Richmond by McClellan, had ordered the withdrawal to a line of defense along the south bank of the Rappahannock River.

The Union army recognized the importance of Aquia Landing and built new wharves and a large cluster of storage buildings for supplies. Maj. Gen. Irvin McDowell used it as a supply depot when

USS Freeborn *and* Pawnee *engage Aquia Creek batteries, June 1, 1861.* LIBRARY OF CONGRESS

part of his army guarded Washington while the rest occupied Fredericksburg. Maj. Gen. Ambrose E. Burnside used the depot to supply his army until Lincoln removed him from command in January 1863 following his defeat at Fredericksburg in December 1862. Maj. Gen. Joseph Hooker, Burnside's successor, continued to use the landing. The army burned and abandoned the depot on June 7, 1863, then pursued the Confederate army into Pennsylvania. Grant again used Aquia Landing as a depot in the spring of 1864 as he and the army pushed through the Wilderness to Spotsylvania Court House. After the war, the railroad company reclaimed the landing and extended its line across Aquia Creek and on to Washington in 1872, ending steamboat service.

Today the first Confederate battery, erected on the beach near the depot site, no longer stands. The other three batteries remain on the bluffs, in private hands. Housing developments encroach nearby, but Aquia Landing Park, maintained by the Stafford County Park and Recreation Department, now occupies the site. ■

COCKPIT POINT

Cockpit Point Battery consists of four artillery emplacements connected by earthworks. In addition to the gun pits, the battery contained buildings and "bombproofs" for the protection of ammunition and powder.

Confederate brigadier general Isaac R. Trimble probably built the battery in the fall of 1861. He positioned it on a high bluff—actually Possum Nose, just downriver from Cockpit Point itself—that commanded a significant bend in the Potomac River. With the Freestone Point Battery to the north and Shipping Point Battery to the south, some five miles of the river lay under Confederate guns.

The Confederates sought to close the river to shipping and embarrass the Federals with a blockade of their capital city. The blockade had little effect because the Baltimore & Ohio Railroad provisioned Washington through Maryland, plus the poor marksmanship and munitions of the Confederate artillerymen enabled ships to pass the batteries easily, but it frustrated President Lincoln and angered Northern newspaper editors. The *New York Tribune* called it "one of the most humiliating of

> **DIRECTIONS**: (Cockpit Point Battery, which is listed in the National Register of Historic Places, stands on privately owned land and is not open to the public; these directions are to Freestone Point, a similar site, in nearby Leesylvania State Park.) I-95 Exit 152 (State Rte. 234, Dumfries), e. on Rte. 234 (Dumfries Rd.) about .6 mile to U.S. Rte. 1; n. on U.S. Rte. 1 2.7 miles to Rte. 610 (Neabsco Rd.); e. on Rte. 610 1.5 miles to Leesylvania State Park entrance (admission fee); continue 1.3 miles to observe Cockpit Point to s. (right); continue another 1 mile to Virginia Civil War Trails marker and hiking trail to Freestone Point Battery.

all the national disgraces to which we have been compelled to submit," which damaged the country in the eyes of the world. It cited the Confederates' boast of maintaining constant sway over the Potomac, blockading the Union army's supplies and causing "very great expense and great inconvenience" to the Federal government.

To counter the batteries, Brig. Gen. Joseph Hooker and 8,000 Union soldiers and three field batteries were ordered to Charles County, Maryland. They camped across the river from Cockpit Point and Shipping Point.

One Thursday morning, November 14, 1861, a sailing schooner loaded with fire-

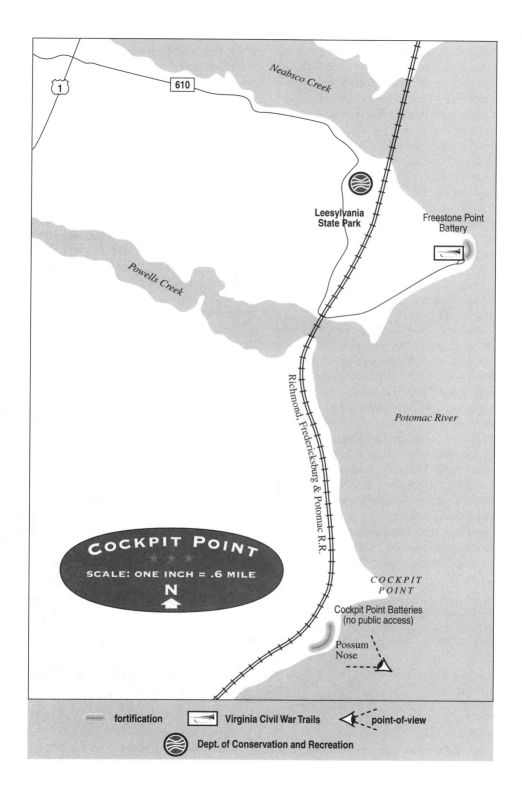

Neabsco Creek

1

610

Leesylvania
State Park

Freestone Point
Battery

Powells Creek

Richmond, Fredericksburg & Potomac R.R.

Potomac River

COCKPIT POINT
★ ★ ★
SCALE: ONE INCH = .6 MILE
N

COCKPIT
POINT

Cockpit Point Batteries
(no public access)

Possum
Nose

fortification   Virginia Civil War Trails   point-of-view

Dept. of Conservation and Recreation

wood tried to slip past Cockpit Point but slowed as the wind died. The batteries opened up, and three rounds found their mark. On board, the sailors panicked, dropping anchor and then abandoning ship to swim for the Maryland shore. A dozen Confederates launched a small boat, rowed to the schooner, and set her afire. As soon as they started for shore, Massachusetts soldiers rowed a small boat from the Maryland side to the burning schooner. Under fire from Cockpit Point, the soldiers boarded the vessel, extinguished the blaze, and towed the ship across the river to safety. Union soldiers cheered as their cannon dueled the Confederate guns to no great effect, except for the loss of a Federal pig and mule.

A series of balloon ascensions across the river from Cockpit Point in November and December 1861 revealed the extent of the Confederate fortifications to Hooker's command. Thaddeus S. C. Lowe, chief of army aeronautics, made his first ascent on November 11, accompanied by William Paulin, his assistant, and Brig. Gen. Daniel E. Sickles. Lowe went up several more times in his balloon, *Constitution,* even at night. On December 8 Col. William F. Small joined him and made a useful drawing of about seven miles of the Virginia shoreline, from Chopawamsic Creek north to the Freestone Point Battery.

Beginning in January 1862, the Cockpit Point Battery fought several engagements with Union gunboats attempting to silence its cannons. The first occurred just after the first of the year and involved USS *Anacostia* and USS *Yankee.* Other engagements involved Hooker's batteries on the Maryland shore.

On Saturday, March 8, 1862, Lincoln ordered McClellan to attack and capture the Confederate batteries, but the next day sailors on *Anacostia* and *Yankee* noticed unusual fires and explosions at Cockpit Point and Shipping Point. Gen. Joseph E. Johnston, suspecting that McClellan soon would march on Richmond, had formed a new line of defense along the south bank of the Rappahannock River and ordered the batteries evacuated and destroyed.

When a Union landing party inspected the Cockpit Point Battery on March 10, it found evidence of a hasty departure: half-baked bread, strewn clothes, and spiked cannons (a railroad spike pounded into the vent atop the barrel to render the weapon unusable). The troops rolled the guns over the cliff to the shore, then loaded them on boats and took them to the Washington Navy Yard. Engraving on one gun read CAPTURED FROM THE YANKEES AT BULL RUN.

Today, Cockpit Point Battery is privately owned and not accessible to the public. Although the battery currently is in excellent condition, its long-term preservation is not assured. ■

Cockpit Point Battery as seen from Budd's Ferry, Maryland. LIBRARY OF CONGRESS

Blackburn's Ford and bridge ruins on Bull Run. LIBRARY OF CONGRESS

On Thursday, July 18, 1861, Brig. Gen. Irvin McDowell sent Brig. Gen. Daniel Tyler with 3,000 men to locate the Confederate left flank. He told Tyler to take Centreville, scout beyond it, and report back to him.

When Tyler found Centreville devoid of Confederates, he marched southeastwardly to Mitchell's Ford and Blackburn's Ford, arriving at the latter about 11 A.M. At first glance the ford appeared lightly defended by artillery positioned on a hill to its south and at Mitchell's Ford, and by a handful of infantry. From the hills above the ford, Tyler looked south across the stream and saw what appeared to be a clear road to Manassas Junction. He failed, however, to see Brig. Gen. James Longstreet's brigade lying concealed in the woods behind the ford, the center of the Confederate defensive line.

Tyler ordered Capt. Romeyn B. Ayres to unlimber his two howitzers nearby and open the attack with an artillery bombardment on the guns of the Alexandria Artillery and the Washington Artillery. Neither barrage wrought any destruction. Suspecting the presence of Southern infantry (which stayed near artillery to defend cannons against capture) and disappointed that they did not reveal themselves, Tyler ordered Col. Israel B. Richardson and part of his infantry brigade forward to the ford.

Hidden from Tyler's view, the 1st, 11th, and 17th Virginia Infantry Regiments fired at the oncoming Federals. The sound of shooting rose in volume; Tyler had found the infantry he sought. He ordered Ayres to move closer with his howitzers accompanied by cavalry and sent the rest of Richardson's brigade toward the ford, where the fight grew hot.

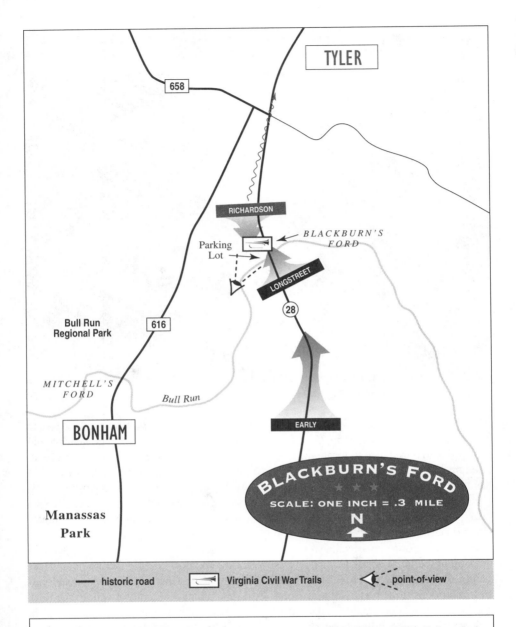

TYLER

658

RICHARDSON

Parking Lot →

BLACKBURN'S FORD

LONGSTREET

28

Bull Run Regional Park

616

MITCHELL'S FORD

Bull Run

BONHAM

EARLY

Manassas Park

BLACKBURN'S FORD

SCALE: ONE INCH = .3 MILE

N

— historic road   ▭ Virginia Civil War Trails   ◁ point-of-view

DIRECTIONS: I-66 Exit 53 (Rte. 28, Centreville Rd.), s. on Rte. 28 about 3 miles to Virginia Civil War Trails marker in Northern Virginia Regional Park Authority parking lot on right at Bull Run.

After about twenty minutes of intense fire, a Federal regiment, the 12th New York, began to retreat. A wave of panic spread through the Union line, and before the officers could regain control, the assault crumpled. Col. Jubal A. Early arrived on the scene with his brigade, having quickly marched two miles northward from Brig.

Gen. Pierre Gustav Toutant Beauregard's headquarters at Wilmer McLean's house, and added to Longstreet's firepower. To Longstreet's rear, the Washington Artillery, reinforced and numbering seven guns, laid an impressive barrage on Richardson's retreating forces.

The Confederates rejoiced at their victory, which had been relatively bloodless. Out of about 7,000 Confederate troops engaged, only some 68 or 70 were killed, wounded, or captured. The Union calculated its losses at 83 of the more than 3,000 that saw combat. On the whole, the Confederate soldiers had performed well in their first action, the artillery especially so. An artilleryman reported that the foot soldiers were so enthusiastic that they threatened to hug the gunners.

Today the site of the battle is astride a four-lane highway (Rte. 28) and is largely built over with residential and commercial development. Part of the bottomland is owned by the Bull Run Regional Park, and the Mitchell's Ford Entrenchments (which did not figure in the battle) are on private land and listed in the National Register of Historic Places and the Virginia Landmarks Register. ■

FIRST BATTLE OF MANASSAS (BULL RUN)

For two days after the engagement at Blackburn's Ford on July 18, the commanders of each army laid their plans for the battle yet to come. Union Brig. Gen. Irvin McDowell abandoned plans for a frontal attack and decided to assault around the Southern left flank (he ruled out an attack against the right because of bad roads) while part of his army demonstrated, or bluffed an attack, against the left of the Confederate front. Confederate Brig. Gen. P. G. T. Beauregard likewise planned an offensive. Brig. Gen. Joseph E. Johnston would lead an attack against the Federal right, and when McDowell wheeled his army to meet it, Beauregard would strike his left flank. First, though, Johnston had to elude Union Maj. Gen. Robert Patterson and move his army from Winchester to Manassas Junction. With Brig. Gen. Thomas J. Jackson leading the way, Johnston's men began their march through Millwood and Paris to Piedmont Station (present-day Delaplane), where they boarded trains and headed east the next day.

When Johnston arrived at Manassas Junction, he agreed with the essential elements of Beauregard's plan, which dispersed his army to guard the river crossings. The combined Confederate armies hovered on the edge of attack, but McDowell acted first.

McDowell's plan was a complicated one for raw recruits to execute (the same could be said of Beauregard's plan), and their inexperience hampered its execution. The marching began nonetheless about 2 A.M., and by 9:30, hours late, Brig. Gen. David Hunter's command arrived at Sudley Springs Ford. Meanwhile, Tyler's demonstration opposite Evans failed to convince the Confederates, but Brig. Gen. James Longstreet, hearing Col. Israel B. Richardson's approach, ordered his men to attack across the stream; Brig. Gen. David R. Jones followed Longstreet's lead.

The grand plans of both sides quickly unraveled. Before Hunter's column waded Bull Run at Sudley Springs Ford, a Confederate signal station to the south spotted it and wigwagged to Col. Nathan "Shanks"

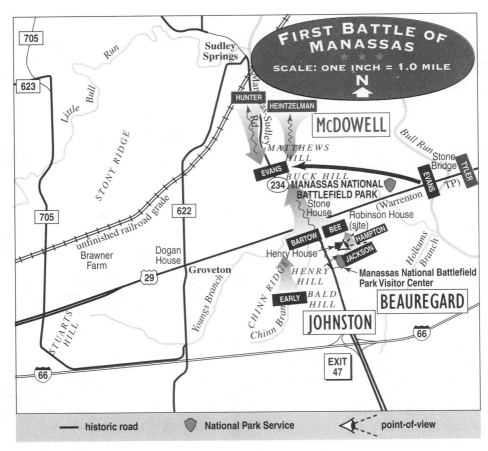

FIRST BATTLE OF MANASSAS

SCALE: ONE INCH = 1.0 MILE

N

705

Sudley Springs

623

HUNTER

HEINTZELMAN

McDOWELL

Little Bull Run

STONY RIDGE

Manassas-Sudley Rd.

MATTHEWS HILL

EVANS

BUCK HILL

234 MANASSAS NATIONAL BATTLEFIELD PARK

Stone House

Bull Run

Stone Bridge

EVANS

TYLER

TP)

(Warrenton

Robinson House (site)

705

622

unfinished railroad grade

BARTOW

BEE

HAMPTON

JACKSON

Henry House

Holkums Branch

Brawner Farm

Dogan House

Groveton

29

HENRY HILL

Manassas National Battlefield Park Visitor Center

CHINN RIDGE

Youngs Branch

EARLY

BALD HILL

Chinn Branch

JOHNSTON

BEAUREGARD

66

STUART'S HILL

66

EXIT 47

— historic road   🛡 National Park Service   ◁ point-of-view

DIRECTIONS: I-66 Exit 47B (Rte. 234 North, Manassas National Battlefield Park), n. on Rte. 234 (Sudley Rd.) about .7 mile to visitor center entrance on right. Manassas National Battlefield Park, located about 26 miles s.w. of Washington, is open daily except Christmas. For advance information, write or call the park for a brochure: Manassas National Battlefield Park, 6511 Sudley Rd., Manassas, VA 22110 (703-754-7107), or visit the National Park Service Web site at nps.gov/parks.html for a virtual tour of this and other national parks.

Evans and Beauregard, "Look out for your left, you are turned." Evans, taking 900 of the 1,100 men guarding the stone bridge on the Warrenton Turnpike (present-day U.S. Rte. 29), hustled west to a position on Buck Hill overlooking the Manassas-Sudley Road (present-day Rte. 234), the

Union route of advance. The Federal force observed his move, and McDowell realized he had lost the element of surprise. Nothing remained but to try to push through Evans's small command.

Even as the rattle of muskets echoed across the Manassas farm fields, help was on its way to Evans. Brig. Gen. Bernard Bee and his brigade, ordered to the stone bridge, marched past it toward the sound of battle, followed by Col. Francis S. Bartow's brigade. Moving four miles at the double-quick, the breathless troops formed up on Henry Hill, just behind Matthews Hill and Evans, on the south side of the Warrenton Turnpike.

After watching the struggle on Matthews Hill, at about 11 A.M. Bee ordered his men to advance. Early in the action, Union general Hunter was wounded, and Brig. Gen. Andrew Porter assumed command. He fed fresh regiments into the line to strengthen and extend it. Bee, reinforced by Bartow, tried to do the same for the Confederates, but it soon became obvious that they would be overwhelmed by numbers. Finally at about 11:30 Porter, reinforced by units from Brig. Gen. Samuel P. Heintzelman's division, launched an assault that sent Bee's command reeling back toward Henry Hill. A Union victory seemed assured.

Where were Johnston and Beauregard? Despite the fight developing on their left, both Confederate commanders remained on a hill overlooking Mitchell's Ford, convinced that the main Union attack would come there and that the affair to the west constituted a feint. Soon the roar of battle convinced them otherwise, and they began to move. Others had already taken the initiative, especially Jackson, who marched his men toward Henry Hill, rounding up artillery on the way.

For perhaps the first time that day, a commander chose his ground brilliantly for maximum tactical advantage. Jackson posted his men on the reverse slope of Henry Hill, thereby keeping them invisible to Union troops and safe from artillery fire. He placed his own artillery atop the hill so that after each piece fired, the recoil carried it slightly backward to the reverse slope, where its crew reloaded it in comparative safety. Jackson's experience as an artillery commander in the Mexican War and his years as an instructor of artillery tactics at Virginia Military Institute repaid him handsomely.

Col. Wade Hampton, a wealthy South Carolinian who had raised and equipped his own mixed command, Hampton's Legion, preceded Jackson to Henry Hill. Witnessing much of Bee's retreat, which

rapidly degenerated into a rout pressed by oncoming Union troops, Hampton led his legion's infantry forward to the lane near the house of James Robinson, a former slave. There the legion stood firm, holding off Union assaults while Bee's and Evans's men sought the safety of Henry Hill.

Col. J. E. B. Stuart, meanwhile, also joined Jackson, and Johnston and Beauregard, seeing Jackson's line holding steady, rallied other Confederate infantry regiments and artillery batteries. Bee reported to Jackson, then rode off to round up his shattered command.

Into the early afternoon the Confederate buildup on Henry Hill continued. The Union forces, likewise, added regiments to their numbers and slowly maneuvered to the west. By 3 P.M. the armies faced each other on an east-west axis.

McDowell pushed his artillery forward, close to the Confederate left flank, and used it to soften the Southern position for an attack by his infantry. Capt. James B. Ricketts and Capt. Charles Griffin posi-

U.S. monument on Henry Hill, dedicated June 11, 1865. VIRGINIA DEPARTMENT OF HISTORIC RESOURCES, JOHN S. SALMON

tioned their batteries on either side of the Henry House, where they could rake the Confederates. Their decision proved a serious tactical mistake, however, for the guns lay well ahead of the Union infantry, open to attack from Southern infantry. Jackson seized the opportunity, and beginning about 3 P.M. the battle for the guns raged back and forth. About 4 P.M., just when it appeared that the Union force would prevail, fresh Confederate units from the brigades of Col. Jubal A. Early, Brig. Gen. Milledge L. Bonham, and Brig. Gen. E. Kirby Smith arrived on the field to reinforce the Southern left flank on Chinn Ridge. The line pressed forward against the Union right flank, which collapsed. Order in the Federal ranks disintegrated, and soldiers streamed back toward the stone bridge.

Beauregard exulted, galloping on his horse up and down the Confederate line, sending his troops in pursuit of the Union army. But so hasty was its retreat and so disorganized were the Confederates in victory that chaos reigned on both sides. Confederate artillery opened up on the Cub Run bridge, where wagons, panic-stricken soldiers, and picnic-basket-toting civilians—who had ridden out from Washington in carriages to watch the Union army whip the rebels—jammed the narrow crossing. Capt. Delaware Kemper unlimbered his guns and sent a few rounds over the mob on the bridge, terrifying horses, capsizing a wagon, and generally creating pandemonium. By sundown the bridge was empty. The Confederates held the field. They gathered around their president, Jefferson Davis, who had arrived as the retreat began, and cheered him long and loudly.

After the battle, Northern morale plummeted, and the search for scapegoats began. Lincoln removed McDowell from command and appointed Maj. Gen. George B. McClellan in his place. Why did the Federal army lose? Union mistakes and Confederate opportunism produced defeat.

For the Southern army, the victory carried a high cost: Bartow and Bee killed and many field officers dead or wounded. The high casualty rate among officers probably resulted from their efforts to prove themselves to their men.

Each side learned from its experience that the war would be long and costly. The horror of it all stunned the survivors, who filled their letters home with descriptions of mangled men and horses, of brothers and friends blown to bits. Yet compared to Civil War battles still to come, First Manassas was not an unusually bloody affair. Of the 60,680 men engaged altogether, some 4,700—about 8 percent—became casualties (killed, wounded, captured, or missing). The Union, with about 28,450 on the field, lost an estimated 2,950, and the Confederates, who numbered around 32,230, lost about 1,750. The next time the two armies met there, they would be much more skillful at killing, and the casualty rate would be more than 18 percent.

Today most of the First Manassas battlefield is within the boundaries of the Manassas National Battlefield Park. Roughly 15 percent of the battlefield is privately owned. U.S. Rte. 29 bisects the park, and Interstate 66 runs along its southern border. Heavy traffic and surrounding development continues to impinge on the park's setting. ■

BALL'S BLUFF

In October 1861 Pres. Abraham Lincoln's administration and the Union army faced a potential threat some thirty-five miles upriver from Washington. The Confederate command of Brig. Gen. Nathan "Shanks" Evans, stationed in and around Leesburg, Virginia, guarded the ferry crossings that led to the Maryland side. The ferries included Conrad's, about four miles northeast of Leesburg, and Edwards Ferry, an equal distance to the east; Harrison's Island occupied the middle of the river beneath Ball's Bluff, just downriver from Conrad's ferry. The Union division of Brig. Gen. Charles P. Stone watched Evans's pickets from the far shore.

In Washington, Maj. Gen. George B. McClellan, newly appointed commander of the Union army, faced increasing pressure. Prodded by the public and by Lincoln to make a noise, McClellan finally acted in October. He ordered Brig. Gen. George A. McCall to lead his division from Camp Pierpoint to Dranesville, about

DIRECTIONS: I-66 Exit 40 (U.S. Rte. 15 North, Leesburg), n. on U.S. Rte. 15 about 21.2 miles to State Rte. 7/U.S. Rte. 15 Bypass; n.e. on Bypass 3.2 miles to Battlefield Pkwy.; e. on Battlefield Pkwy. .2 mile to Ball's Bluff Rd.; n. (left) on Ball's Bluff Rd. .4 mile to Ball's Bluff Regional Park (Battlefield and National Cemetery).

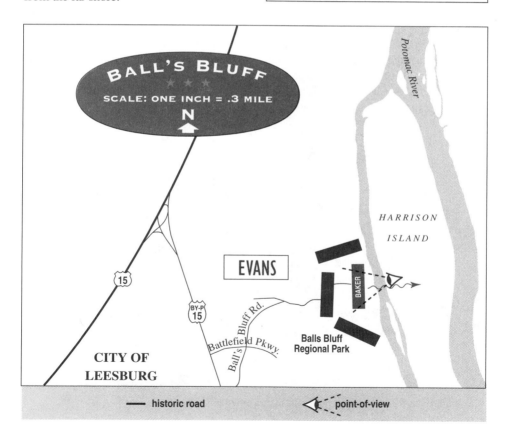

historic road

point-of-view

fifteen miles southeast of Leesburg, and then to make a strong reconnaissance in Evans's direction.

On the afternoon of October 20, Stone sent a small force across the river at Edwards Ferry, then brought it quickly back again. He ordered a night reconnaissance, and the scout reported seeing just a small Confederate camp near Leesburg. Stone placed Col. Edward D. Baker, a senator from Oregon and a friend of Lincoln, in charge of capturing the town.

The detachments began crossing the Potomac at Harrison's Island at dawn on Monday, October 21. Ominously, the shortage of boats delayed the main force for hours. When the first elements ascended Ball's Bluff and pushed inland, Confederate pickets immediately fired on them. The battle developed slowly over the course of the day as additional Union troops arrived. Evans at first countered with only enough force to confine the attackers near the bluff until he discerned their intentions.

Senator Baker—a handsome man, a noted orator, and a veteran of a few months' service in the Mexican War—was undone by the challenges he faced. Arriving on the field shortly after 2 P.M., he strutted about and struck poses with his drawn sword, issued vague orders, recited Sir Walter Scott's "Lady of the Lake," and seemed unaware that the enemy surrounded his command on three sides, ready to obliterate it. About 5 P.M. a small group of Confederates burst from the woods, and one of them emptied his revolver at Baker, killing him instantly. The sight of Baker's body being carried to the rear, coupled with a Confederate charge at sunset, demoralized the Union troops, who stampeded over the bluff.

In the gathering dark, uninjured men fought the wounded for space in the few, hopelessly overcrowded, boats. Others tried to swim the swollen river while Confederates shot at them from the bluff, the hail of bullets churning the water white. Scores drowned in the strong current,

U.S. soldiers attempt to swim the Potomac to Harrison's Island at Ball's Bluff.
ILLUSTRATED LONDON NEWS

which bore their bodies downstream to Washington. Of the 3,600 troops engaged (about 2,000 Federal and 1,600 Confederate), the North suffered some 921 casualties (more than 700 captured and confined in Richmond warehouses) and the South, 149. The South boasted of another victory, while morale dropped in the North again.

The defeat devastated the capital. Lincoln wandered the White House grounds, hands over his face, weeping for his dead friend. Anger and the search for a scapegoat followed on the heels of shock. Federal authorities arrested Stone at midnight on February 8, 1862, alleging that he had secret Southern sympathies, imprisoned him without trial for 189 days, then released him. He resumed his military service but eventually resigned his commission in 1864.

The political effects of the battle of Ball's Bluff far outweighed its military significance. The Congressional Joint Committee on the Conduct of the War, established in December 1861, was created to investigate the defeats at Manassas and Ball's Bluff. The committee survived until July 1865 and harassed the Union generals it considered "soft" on slavery and lacking in a properly vengeful attitude toward the South. It helped lay the groundwork for the Radical Republican approach to Reconstruction that followed the war.

Today at Ball's Bluff stands the smallest national cemetery in the United States, established in December 1865. Within low brick walls are buried fifty-four Union soldiers (one known—James Allen—and fifty-three unknown) killed in the battle. The grave sites are arranged in a circle around an empty flagstaff platform. Because of repeated acts of vandalism, Ball's Bluff is the only national cemetery at which the Stars and Stripes are not flown.

A hundred feet west of the cemetery, a granite marker indicates the grave of a Confederate soldier, Clinton Hatcher, killed in the battle. The spot where Edward Baker fell is identified by a marker erected by Congress in the early 1890s. It stands a few feet east of the cemetery, near a path leading down the bluff toward Harrison's Island, where so many men drowned.

In 1984 the Secretary of the Interior designated seventy-six acres of the battlefield, including the cemetery, a National Historic Landmark; it is also listed in the National Register of Historic Places and the Virginia Landmarks Register. Of the core area of the battlefield as defined by the Civil War Sites Advisory Commission (some 850 acres), about 170 acres are owned by the United States or the Northern Virginia Parks Authority. The remainder is privately owned, and residential development has occurred not far from the cemetery. ▪

DRANESVILLE

Following the Union debacle at Ball's Bluff, both armies settled into camps to wait out the winter. Generally the campaign season lasted from April to October, when warmer, drier weather allowed the movement of men and equipment over unimproved roads. During the colder, wetter winter months the armies were resupplied and drilled. Limited combat continued, however, as patrols probed each other's lines and foraged for hay and feed for thousands of horses. Few casualties resulted from these small-scale hostile encounters.

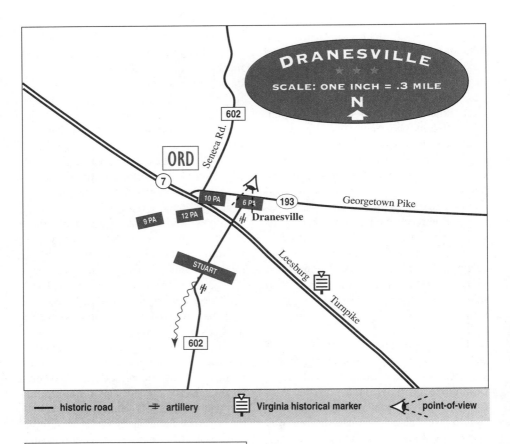

| historic road | ⚓ artillery | 🏛 Virginia historical marker | ◁ point-of-view |

DIRECTIONS: I-495 Exit 47A (State Rte. 7 West, Leesburg Pike), w. on State Rte. 7 about 8.9 miles to state historical marker T-36, Action at Dranesville; continue .5 mile farther to State Rte. 193 (Georgetown Pike).

On a chilly Friday morning, December 20, 1861, two hostile teams of foragers marched through the Virginia countryside south and east of Leesburg. One, led by Confederate Brig. Gen. J. E. B. Stuart, consisted of a brigade-sized mixed force of cavalry, infantry, and artillery as well as almost every wagon in Gen. Joseph E. Johnston's army. Stuart had set out at dawn some sixteen miles south of Dranesville, in northern Fairfax County. Union brigadier general Edward O. C. Ord commanded a detachment that included a reinforced in-

fantry brigade, two cavalry squadrons, and a four-gun artillery battery. Ord approached Dranesville from the southeast, having begun his march about twelve miles away.

Around noon the advance elements of Ord's force arrived at Dranesville by way of the Georgetown Pike (present-day Rte. 193) and drove off a handful of Confederate cavalry pickets, then passed northeastwardly through the village on present-day Rte. 7. Shortly before 1 P.M. Stuart's cavalry emerged from the woods south of Dranesville, observed by the rear of the Union force. Ord wheeled his detachment about; his artillerymen took the high ground and unlimbered their four cannons.

Stuart reacted to the Union show of strength by positioning his artillery about 300 yards south of Ord's, then ordering his

U.S. artillery going into action at Dranesville. VIRGINIA HISTORICAL SOCIETY, RICHMOND, VA.

infantry forward. The Confederate gunners overshot their targets while the Union artillerymen hit theirs and quickly knocked most of the Southern guns out of action. Ord deployed a skirmish line, then committed most of his infantry regiments. Stuart responded in kind, and the ensuing battle took place mostly between the two battery positions on either side of present-day Rte. 602. The Union infantry fought well, inflicting more damage on their opponents than they received. Stuart became convinced that he faced a much larger force and two artillery batteries. About 3 P.M., certain that his wagons had avoided capture and left the area, he ordered a withdrawal. Ord pursued him for half a mile, then stopped.

The affair, though small, constituted the first Union victory in the field in Virginia. The Confederates suffered more casualties (230 to the Union's 71) and left the battleground to their opponents. Washington and the Northern press rejoiced. Some may have grasped the irony that earlier, supposedly well-planned attacks had left the Union forces defeated. But in this impromptu encounter, the artillery used the terrain properly, the commanders made excellent decisions, and the infantry fought well and successfully.

Development has altered much of the Dranesville battlefield site. For example, commercial buildings stand on the now-flattened hill seized by Ord's infantry, and a parking lot covers the Union artillery position. The prospect of development threatens the remainder of the battlefield. ∎

SHENANDOAH VALLEY CAMPAIGN, 1862

The present-day preeminence of Robert E. Lee in the Southern—as well as the national—pantheon of Confederate military heroes obscures the fact that for the first two years of the war, Thomas J. Jackson, not Lee, was the idol of the Confederacy. At Manassas, Jackson earned his nom de guerre and a reputation for dependability. In the spring of 1862, in the Shenandoah Valley, Stonewall led his men in a campaign that brought him and them international renown and a kind of immortality. Among his colleagues in the service, Lee was well known and highly regarded; but he was little known to the public. By June 1862, in contrast, Stonewall Jackson's name was on everyone's lips, military and civilian, Northerner and Southerner and European alike.

Time has not dimmed the luster of Jackson's Shenandoah Valley campaign, especially among military historians. However, today the Valley is sometimes erroneously considered a sideshow to the "real war" in eastern Virginia, and our national understanding of the military significance of the Shenandoah Valley to the war in Virginia—to both Union and Confederate commanders, who contested hotly for control of the region—has faded.

Topography and transportation made the region strategically important. The Valley extends from the headwaters of the Shenandoah River near Lexington, Virginia, to its confluence with the Potomac River at Harpers Ferry, West Virginia, about 150 miles northeast, and averages about twenty-five miles in width. Because the Shenandoah drains from south to north (that is, the altitude in the south near Lexington is higher than at Harpers Ferry in the north), one goes "down" the Valley heading north and "up" the Valley traveling south. The Shenandoah Valley itself angles from southwest to northeast and is bounded on the east by the Blue Ridge Mountains and on the west by the Appalachian Mountains, and from Harrisonburg northeast to Strasburg the Valley is bisected by Massanutten Mountain.

The Blue Ridge Mountains are pierced by a series of gaps; at the time of the Civil War, turnpikes or railroads passed through most of the gaps from the east to major towns in the Valley. Several turnpikes and roads also ran up and down the Shenandoah Valley, joining most of the turnpikes from the east. The way the Valley slants through western Virginia made it an ideal route of invasion for the Confederate army. Movements up or down could be protected from Union attack from the east by guarding the Blue Ridge gaps. The lower, or northern, end of the Valley is only some fifty-five miles from Washington and leads into western Maryland and Pennsylvania. Lee used this route in 1862 and 1863 before and after the battles of Antietam and Gettysburg, while Lt. Gen. Jubal A. Early employed it in 1864 to occupy Hagerstown and Frederick, Maryland, and to threaten the defenses of Washington.

From the Union perspective, securing the Valley was essential to protecting the

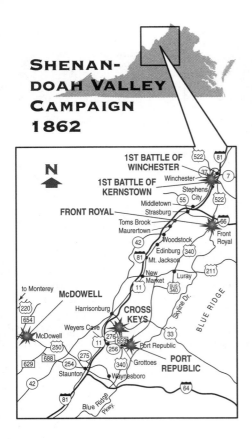

SHENANDOAH VALLEY CAMPAIGN 1862

N

1ST BATTLE OF WINCHESTER
1ST BATTLE OF KERNSTOWN
FRONT ROYAL
Winchester
Stephens City
Middletown
Strasburg
Toms Brook
Maurertown
Woodstock
Edinburg
Mt. Jackson
New Market
Luray
to Monterey
McDOWELL
Harrisonburg
CROSS KEYS
Weyers Cave
McDowell
Port Republic
Staunton
Grottoes
Waynesboro
PORT REPUBLIC
BLUE RIDGE
Skyline Dr.
Blue Ridge Pkwy.

national capital and avoiding the embarrassment of fighting Southern troops on Northern soil. It also provided a "back door" to Richmond and access to the rear of Lee's army, which Maj. Gen. David Hunter threatened in 1864 until Early drove him into West Virginia.

By March 1862 the string of Confederate victories that began with the first battle of Manassas had been broken. Union victories in North Carolina, Kentucky, Tennessee, Arkansas, and Missouri had eroded Confederate morale and boosted that of the Union. In and around Washington, Maj. Gen. George B. McClellan, who had reawakened Northern hopes for a great Union victory and a quick end to the war, molded some 150,000 fresh volunteers into a well-equipped and -trained army.

Meanwhile, Gen. Joseph E. Johnston's Confederates abandoned Manassas Junction to defend Richmond, leaving behind "Quaker guns" (logs painted black to resemble cannons) for the enemy and burning a million pounds of beef, rations that they could not carry away with them. His army marched away ill-supplied and hungry as the scent of steak tinged the winter air—a fitting symbol of the past year's successes and that year's failures. Southerners were as starved for victories as the troops were for victuals.

McClellan decided against a direct overland campaign from Washington to Richmond, choosing instead an amphibious landing at Fort Monroe and Newport News, followed by a march up the Peninsula past Yorktown and Williamsburg to the Confederate capital. Lincoln, anxious for the security of Washington, got a promise from McClellan to protect the city. In February 1862 McClellan detailed the duty to Maj. Gen. Nathaniel P. Banks and his corps—then located in western Maryland—but ordered him first to clear the lower Shenandoah Valley of Confederates by driving them from Winchester. Thereafter, Banks was to post a small force in the town to protect the region's railroads and turnpikes, then proceed with most of his troops to Manassas Junction to guard the approaches to the national capital. By February 24 Banks had occupied Harpers Ferry with his 28,000 men and less than two weeks later had marched south to within twelve miles of Winchester. Maj. Gen. Thomas J. "Stonewall" Jackson and his 4,600-man Valley Army defended the town.

To the east, Joseph E. Johnston, the commander of Confederate troops in Virginia, expecting McClellan to march overland toward Richmond from Washington, disposed his army to defend the Confederate capital. In early March he ordered

Jackson to protect the main army's left flank by guarding the Blue Ridge gaps and advancing or retreating in concert with Johnston's forces near Richmond. Jackson, however, had no intention of retreating and instead requested reinforcements so that he could defeat Banks's army—or at least strike the enemy and keep him off balance. Johnston did not reply, and Jackson soon found his army further outnumbered when Union brigadier general James Shields arrived from western Virginia to join his 12,000-man division with Banks's.

Despite the numerical odds against him, Jackson possessed a knowledge of the Valley and, soon, excellent maps—both important advantages. On March 26, 1862, just three days after his defeat at Kernstown, Jackson told Jedediah Hotchkiss, a talented young amateur cartographer who had recently joined his command: "I want you to make me a map of the Valley, from Harper's Ferry to Lexington, showing all the points of offence and defence in those places." Hotchkiss set to work at once, drawing maps that remain remarkable for their clarity, beauty, and accuracy. The maps became Jackson's secret weapon. In contrast, his Union counterparts marched up and down the Valley with out-of-date, sketchy, and inaccurate maps—when they had maps at all.

What kind of man was this Jackson? To answer the question, one must separate Jackson the legend from Jackson the man. Fortunately, the noted Virginia historian James I. Robertson, Jr., accomplished that task in his outstanding 1997 biography, *Stonewall Jackson: The Man, the Soldier, the Legend.* Jackson the legend was "Old Tom Fool," as his young students called him, an eccentric and ineffectual college professor, even insane, according to some. Jackson the legend could fall asleep instantly anywhere, anytime. He preferred standing to sitting—to align his internal organs for improved digestion—and constantly sucked lemons, even in combat. He was a religious fanatic who often refused to converse, and his subordinates found him extraordinarily secretive. Yet this supposedly crazy man conducted a perfect military campaign against overwhelming odds and outsmarted his opponents at every turn, according to the legend.

Jackson the man is far more interesting. The real Jackson was a painfully shy orphan born in present-day West Virginia. A consuming ambition to improve his lot and find social acceptance impelled him to the military academy at West Point, where he overcame his woefully inadequate elementary education through sheer determination and hard work. After a heroic stint as an artillery officer in the Mexican War, Jackson served unhappily as second in command to a martinet in Florida and resigned his commission. He joined the faculty at Virginia Military Institute in Lexington, where the same students who had mocked him during their freshman year admired him greatly by their senior year. Although stiff and awkward in society, Jackson slowly made friends who discovered the kind and generous heart behind his wall of reserve. In the Valley town he at last found a home, something he had longed for all his life. He found love and family there, too, and joy mixed with tragedy: His beloved first wife died in childbirth, and the baby was stillborn; less than three years later he remarried, but his first child died four weeks after her birth. Jackson's own life underwent renewal when he joined the Presbyterian Church. His religious faith sustained him in adversity and became as natural a part of him as his skin. His health, particularly as it related to his digestive system, remained delicate, and he based many of his seemingly hypochondriacal remedies on current medical advice, or at least his own logic.

Jackson often had difficulty sleeping when on campaign, and his famous impromptu naps could be credited to exhaustion. He rarely ate lemons, but he consumed any fruit he could put his hands on, liking peaches best. He had no discernible sense of humor and never understood a joke, but he adored children and loved to frolic with them. His secretiveness arose naturally from his shyness—and also from a desire to confuse the enemy. His Valley campaign, while a work of genius in its entirety, was far from perfect in its parts. Jackon improvised in the field, often brilliantly, but often to compensate for his own errors of judgment as well as to take advantage of his opponents' lapses. He learned quickly from experience but was not infallible; Jackson in June 1862 was a far more skillful commander than he had been in February, but still he got caught napping at Port Republic.

What made Stonewall Jackson a great general? Strategic and tactical brilliance, to be sure, and an unwavering faith that God would not permit the failure of what Jackson viewed as a just cause, but even more importantly a grim determination to defeat his enemies—the same unyielding will that saw him through four demanding years at West Point. At a time when many men viewed war as a romantic adventure, Jackson was as utterly unromantic in his attitude as William Tecumseh Sherman. Stonewall believed that "war is the greatest of evils," but once under way the commander should inflict "all possible damage in the shortest possible time" on the enemy, to the point of taking no prisoners. When one of his subordinates expressed regret at the deaths of three Union cavalrymen who bravely charged his position, Jackson responded: "No, Colonel, shoot them all. I don't want them to be brave." Jackson's seeming ruthlessness concealed an intense desire for peace, a physical ache

to be at home with his family. "To move swiftly, strike vigorously, and secure all the fruits of victory, is the secret of successful war," he told a minister. His Valley campaign succeeded because he followed his favorite maxim: "Never take counsel of your fears." And it succeeded because he inspired his soldiers to victory.

His men cursed this tough disciplinarian who refused to grant furloughs, even to himself, who marched them bloody footed, who urged them ever forward (with a curt, "Press on, press on"), who rarely praised, who was quick to punish, and who was slow to forgive. But he gave them victories, and the men of his beloved Stonewall Brigade relished their reputations as his "foot cavalry." Many soldiers wrote home that it was far more pleasant to read about Jackson's exploits in the newspapers than to take part in them, but they all admitted they would follow him anywhere.

At this moment in March 1862, however, Jackson commanded largely untested soldiers as eager for combat as he was, despite odds of nine-to-one against them. After preliminary skirmishes in which Col. Turner Ashby and his cavalry held Banks at bay, on the afternoon of March 11 the Union army began to advance in earnest against Winchester. Jackson ordered his wagons south of town, then directed the infantry to join them, cook rations, and await orders. That night Jackson called his first council of war with his lieutenants.

He presented them with an audacious plan: March his men back through Winchester, and strike Banks in a predawn attack. The shock of the assault, he reasoned, should unnerve the even less experienced Federals and stampede them. After a brief silence, it probably fell to Brig. Gen. Richard Garnett, the senior subordinate present, to inform Jackson that his plan could not be executed. His army was farther away than Jackson realized because the wagons had gone some six miles south of town before stopping. The men would have to march about eight miles in the dark before they would be in position to attack. The army would be exhausted and incapable of holding its own against a force so many times its size. It could not be done.

After futile arguing, Jackson conceded and ordered a retreat. As he and his headquarters staff withdrew, however, a perfect fury of frustration seized him. Ignoring the fact that his subordinates had probably saved his army from disaster, he vowed never again to convene a council of war. His first had been his last.

Thus one of the most illustrious campaigns in the history of American warfare began with a retreat on the part of the eventual victor. For ten days, between March 12 and 21, Jackson and Banks kept their armies apart; Jackson encamped his army around Mount Jackson, while Banks stopped his cautious pursuit at Strasburg, roughly twenty-three miles northeast of Mount Jackson and about seventeen miles southwest of Winchester. On March 21 one of Ashby's troopers informed Jackson that Banks was moving back toward Winchester. Jackson followed, sending Ashby ahead to harry the Union rear. Two days later, just south of Winchester at the first battle of Kernstown, the Federal force—at first under Brig. Gen. James Shields and then under Col. Nathan Kimball after Shields fell wounded—turned to fight. Jackson deployed Col. Samuel Fulkerson's brigade to the left and, after some confusion of orders, Garnett joined the line on Fulkerson's right.

Jackson suffered his first and only defeat at Kernstown, late in the afternoon of March 23, when the Union right began to overwhelm the Confederate center as Garnett's men ran out of ammunition. Without orders, Garnett retreated with his command, leaving Fulkerson dangling and

causing a general collapse of Jackson's line and a near rout. Garnett's decision earned him Jackson's never-ending enmity and an abbreviated court-martial—a stain on his record that he finally erased with his gallant death at Gettysburg two years later in "Pickett's Charge" (actually the Pickett-Pettigrew-Trimble Charge, or Longstreet's Attack).

Jackson retreated once more. Strategically, however, he gained more than he lost. The savagery of the Kernstown battle convinced Banks—who had been in the act of leaving the Valley for Manassas Junction—that the little Confederate army indeed presented a threat. He decided to remain west of the Blue Ridge until either he pinned it down and destroyed it or it fled the Valley. For the next several weeks, the armies teased each other with cavalry and artillery engagements as Jackson withdrew to Swift Run Gap.

Early in April the Union strategy in eastern Virginia became clear as McClellan began his slow march up the Peninsula toward Richmond. The Confederates feared a second advance against Richmond as Maj. Gen. Irvin McDowell assembled a Union force north of Fredericksburg that in reality was intended to protect Washington. In western Virginia Brig. Gen. Louis Blenker's 10,000-man division augmented Maj. Gen. John C. Frémont's Mountain Department army, on its march eastward toward the Valley. Returning to Winchester, Banks once more moved south, up the Valley. On the Confederate side, Gen. Robert E. Lee, in his capacity as military adviser to President Jefferson Davis, changed Jackson's orders: Abandon the defensive and take the offensive.

Jackson quickly formulated a plan of action, sent it to Lee on April 29, and put his army in motion without waiting for a reply. With the number of his men increased to 14,500 by the addition of

Maj. Gen. Richard S. Ewell's division, Jackson marched from Port Republic eastward through Brown's Gap and out of the Valley, fueling rumors that he was taking his army to Richmond. At Mechum's River Station on the Virginia Central Railroad, he and his men boarded railroad cars and rode west through Rockfish Gap back into the Valley to Staunton. Soon the army marched west toward Highland County and Frémont. On May 8, at Sitlington's Hill just east of the village of McDowell, Jackson defeated Frémont's advance force, commanded by Brig. Gen. Robert C. Schenck and Brig. Gen. Robert H. Milroy. After pursuing Frémont for a few days, Jackson returned to the Valley and headed north against Banks.

Jackson used the Luray Valley to conceal his movements and then, with Ewell, overran the Federal garrison at Front Royal on May 23, exposing Banks's right flank and causing him to retreat north. Two days later, in the first battle of Winchester, Jackson enveloped Banks's right flank, pursuing Bank's defeated army until it fled across the Potomac River into Maryland.

Lincoln, ever mindful of the Confederate threat against Washington, sent McDowell's divisions at Fredericksburg, recently reinforced by Shields's division, into the Shenandoah Valley under Shields's command. Marching through Manassas Gap, Shields recaptured Front Royal and planned to join Frémont in Strasburg, thereby stranding Jackson between three Union forces. Jackson, however, abandoned his positions above Winchester on May 31 and slipped south, up the Valley Turnpike. Two Union forces—Frémont's on the Valley Turnpike and the advance of Shields's on the Luray and Front Royal Turnpike—pursued Jackson down muddy roads through a week of heavy rain.

At Cross Keys on June 8, Shields caught Jackson napping, but when Frémont attacked from the northwest, Ewell battled him to a standstill. The next day Jackson stalled Frémont with a rearguard action and then burned the bridge over the Shenandoah River at Port Republic to isolate him on the west side of the rain-swollen South Fork. Meanwhile, he attacked Shields's vanguard under Brig. Gen. Erastus B. Tyler and drove it from the field. Shields and Frémont withdrew northward the next day with Massanutten Mountain between them, leaving Jackson in control of the southern end of the Valley.

Jackson's Shenandoah Valley campaign was a spectacular strategic success. During a five-week period, with no more than 17,000 troops, he marched more than 650 miles and defeated three Federal armies numbering 52,000 men by attacking them separately when his own force was numerically superior to his opponent's. He inflicted some 7,000 Union casualties while losing about 2,500 of his own men. He made his name famous throughout and even beyond the country, worried Lincoln endlessly, and, most importantly, caused the diversion of thousands of Union troops toward the defense of Washington and away from McClellan's campaign. McClellan later claimed that the additional troops would have enabled him to capture Richmond. Now, in mid-June 1862, it was Jackson and his army, not Banks's or McDowell's, who were marching toward Richmond. ∎

Maj. Gen. Thomas J. "Stonewall" Jackson and his army retreated south from Winchester on the night of March 11–12, 1862. Except for occasional skirmishes, the opposing armies avoided each other for the next week and a half.

On March 21, word came that Maj. Gen. Nathaniel P. Banks's corps was falling back from Strasburg toward Winchester. Jackson ordered his cavalry chief, Col. Turner Ashby, to shadow the Union withdrawal. In two days Jackson's men advanced some forty miles to Kernstown, in one of the more grueling forced marches of the war.

Ashby harassed the Federal rear with cavalry and artillery, reporting back to Jackson that Banks had virtually abandoned Winchester and that in his view the opposition appeared weak. His estimations of Union strength and dispositions proved erroneous, however. Jackson's 3,800 men faced a Union force of about 8,500, not the 3,000 that Ashby reported, and although Banks had begun to move his army out of Winchester toward Manassas, most of it remained near the Valley town.

Banks himself made plans to leave for Manassas on March 23. He and his second in command, Brig. Gen. James Shields, knew that their army greatly outnumbered Jackson's. Furthermore, they considered only Ashby an immediate threat. Indeed, Ashby skirmished vigorously with the Federals on March 22, and the encounters claimed Shields as a casualty in the afternoon when a shell fragment broke his arm, forcing him to turn over his division to Col. Nathan Kimball. At dawn on March 23, Kimball moved to block Ashby on the Valley Turnpike, posting part of his command astride the road just north of Kernstown and ordering his artillery to Pritchard's Hill to counter Ashby's batteries near Opequon Presbyterian Church.

By 11 A.M. Jackson arrived south of

U.S. charge on the stone wall, Kernstown. LIBRARY OF CONGRESS

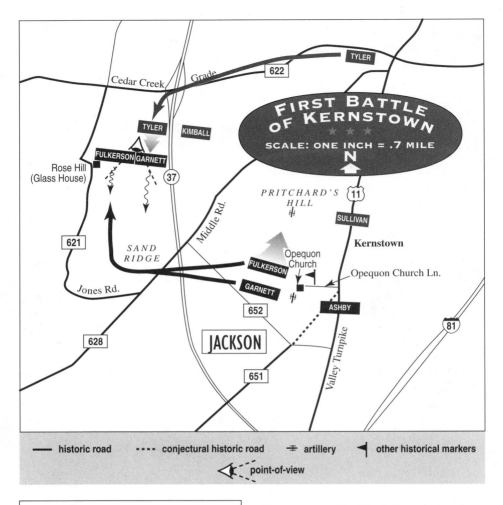

First Battle of Kernstown

SCALE: ONE INCH = .7 MILE

- historic road
- ---- conjectural historic road
- ⚔ artillery
- ◀ other historical markers
- ◀ point-of-view

DIRECTIONS: I-81 Exit 310 (Rte. 37 West) about .2 mile to U.S. Rte. 11; n. (right) on U.S. Rte. 11 .7 mile to Rte. 652 (Apple Valley Rd.); w. (left) on Rte. 652 1.3 miles to Rte. 628 (Middle Rd.); s. (left) on Rte. 628 .4 mile to Rte. 621 (Jones Rd.); w. (right) on Rte. 621 1.4 miles to Glass House (area of Garnett's position), then .6 mile farther to Rte. 622 (Cedar Creek Grade); e. (right) on Rte. 622 1.9 miles to U.S. Rte. 11; s. (right) on U.S. Rte. 11 1.6 miles to Opequon Church Lane; w. (right) on Opequon Church Lane .2 mile to church, cemetery, and Winchester–Frederick County Historical Society interpretive marker; return to U.S. Rte. 11, s. (right) on U.S. Rte. 11 1.5 miles to Rte. 37; e. (left) on Rte. 37 .2 mile to I-81.

Kernstown with his infantry. At about 2 P.M. he feinted toward Kimball's position on the Valley Turnpike while marching his main force—two brigades under Col. Samuel Fulkerson and Brig. Gen. Richard B. Garnett—to attack the Union artillery on Pritchard's Hill. Fulkerson took the lead and was repulsed. Jackson then sought to flank the Union right. Kimball, recognizing Jackson's maneuver, ordered Col. Erastus B. Tyler and his brigade westward to counter it. Tyler deployed his men on the Union right flank about 4 P.M., and soon Kimball and his brigade joined him to bolster the center. Garnett's brigade, in the center of the Confederate line behind a stone wall east of the Glass House, soon bore the brunt of the heaviest Federal attacks.

The roar of battle told Jackson that he had misjudged the strength of his opponent. When an aide returned from reconnoitering the front and confirmed Jackson's fears, Stonewall ordered reinforcements forward. But before they arrived, Garnett, whose men were running out of ammunition, pulled his brigade back, leaving Fulkerson's right flank exposed. Soon the Confederate left flank followed in a general retreat.

An enraged Jackson tried to stop the near rout. He ordered men who were out of bullets to turn and give the enemy the bayonet; he commanded a drummer boy to beat the rally; he bellowed at Garnett to "Halt and rally!" Nothing worked, and soon Jackson followed his army up the Valley Turnpike. Vicious rearguard actions kept Kimball at bay until darkness ended the fighting. The Federals suffered some 590 casualties, the Confederates 718.

A week later Jackson had Garnett arrested and charged with several counts that added up to neglect of duty. Early in August a court-martial convened, but the next campaign cut it short when the hearing was not going well for Jackson, and Garnett returned to the field, though not with the Stonewall Brigade. Jackson's old unit never quite forgave him for his treatment of Garnett, whom the men credited with saving the army from annihilation by his timely, if unauthorized, retreat.

Jackson suffered a tactical loss at Kernstown but he won a strategic victory when Lincoln and Banks, alarmed by Stonewall's audacity, agreed that the Valley had to be cleared of this threat before McClellan could be reinforced. McClellan later claimed that the additional troops would have enabled him to capture Richmond. Banks returned to lead his army against Jackson's in what became one of the great campaigns in military history. Its outcome—defeat for Banks—would entitle Col. Nathan Kimball to boast for the rest of his life that he was the only Union field commander to defeat Stonewall Jackson.

Today the First Kernstown battlefield retains its integrity in about half of its overall area and more than two-thirds of its core, or most important part. Pritchard's Hill, as well as the Glass House, stone wall, and farm, remain much as they were when the battle took place. ■

McDOWELL

After his defeat at Kernstown on March 23, 1862, Maj. Gen. Thomas J. "Stonewall" Jackson remained on the defensive for more than a month in obedience to Gen. Joseph E. Johnston's orders. The two Valley armies sparred with artillery and cavalry but avoided a general engagement, and Jackson eventually encamped at Conrad's Store (present-day Elkton) near Swift Run Gap, east of Harrisonburg. Maj. Gen. Richard S. Ewell and his division, posted east of the Valley in Orange County, stood ready to assist Jackson if called on. Meanwhile, in eastern Virginia, as Maj. Gen. George B. McClellan advanced on Richmond by slow degrees, Maj. Gen. Irvin McDowell assembled a Union force north of Fredericksburg, and in western Virginia, Brig. Gen. Louis Blenker and his 10,000-man division joined Maj. Gen. John C. Frémont's Mountain Department army, doubling its numbers.

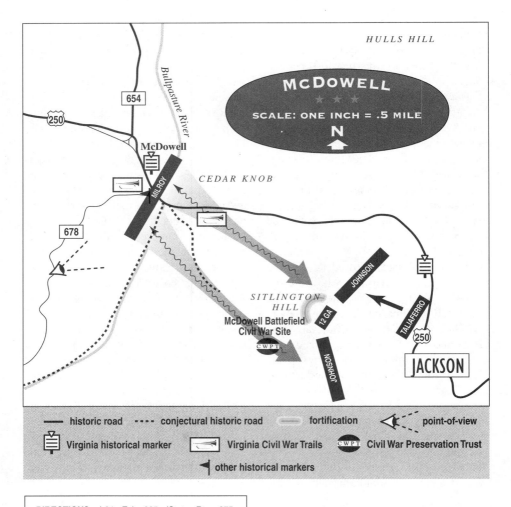

MCDOWELL
★ ★ ★
SCALE: ONE INCH = .5 MILE
N

HULLS HILL

Bullpasture River

654

250

McDowell

MILROY

CEDAR KNOB

678

SITLINGTON HILL

McDowell Battlefield
Civil War Site

CWPT

JOHNSON

12 GA

JOHNSON

TALIAFERRO

250

JACKSON

— historic road   ···· conjectural historic road   ⬭ fortification   ◁--- point-of-view

Virginia historical marker   Virginia Civil War Trails   CWPT Civil War Preservation Trust

◀ other historical markers

DIRECTIONS: I-81 Exit 225 (State Rte. 275, Woodrow Wilson Parkway), w. on State Rte. 275 about 5.2 miles to U.S. Rte. 250; w. on U.S. Rte. 250 31.1 miles to Rte. 678 and Virginia Civil War Trails and United Daughters of the Confederacy markers at McDowell Presbyterian Church. Return .3 mile to parking lot on right at foot of Sitlington Hill (Virginia Civil War Trails marker and hiking trail up Sitlington Hill to Confederate position).

NOTE: Hiking trail is steep and about a mile long; no handicapped access.

In Richmond, Gen. Robert E. Lee assessed the situation. Should Frémont unite his force with Banks, Jackson would face a larger army than the one that defeated him at Kernstown. And McDow-ell's intentions were unclear to Lee. Hoping that McDowell could be lured away from Fredericksburg and Richmond to assist Banks and Frémont, on April 21 Lee suggested to Jackson that he abandon the defensive and attack—a suggestion the Valley commander eagerly accepted. Jackson replied to Lee on April 29 with a plan that called for Maj. Gen. Richard S. Ewell and his division to take up Jackson's position and watch Banks while Jackson left to attack and defeat Frémont, then reunite with Ewell and attack Banks. Success depended on rapid, secret marches and sudden strikes against the enemy.

View from McDowell east to Sitlington Hill (right). VIRGINIA DEPARTMENT OF HISTORIC RESOURCES, JOHN S. SALMON

Jackson marched and countermarched his army to confuse Banks. Ewell, on Jackson's orders, likewise moved his division about. Jackson's changing orders confused everyone—Banks, Ewell, the soldiers of both armies—everyone, that is, except Jackson.

On May 3 Jackson stopped his army at Mechum's River Station east of the Valley on the Virginia Central Railroad, which linked Richmond and Staunton. The next day, Sunday, part of the army boarded the trains that chugged west. They were returning to the Valley.

Jackson's trains arrived in Staunton late in the afternoon (the rest of the army followed on foot). There Jackson met with Brig. Gen. Edward "Allegheny" Johnson, a tough, profane old soldier whose own men as well as Jackson regarded him highly. The head of Frémont's army, commanded by Brig. Gen. Robert H. Milroy, was twenty rugged miles northwest of Staunton in Highland County, a place of high hills and deep valleys. Jackson sent Johnson ahead and then followed with most of his army at dawn on May 7, marching west on the Staunton and Parkersburg Turnpike (present-day Rtes. 254, 688, 629, and U.S. Rte. 250) toward the Allegheny Mountains.

On the afternoon of May 8, Johnson took up a position on Sitlington Hill, a spur of Bullpasture Mountain overlooking

the village of McDowell. From his vantage point, Johnson easily observed Milroy's force; Milroy saw Johnson, too, and deployed skirmishers to engage his troops as Johnson deployed them. In the midst of this activity, Jackson arrived. Ignoring the occasional bullet ricocheting off the boulders, the two generals reconnoitered. Jackson decided against a frontal assault on the Union force; his guns and the infantry to protect them still were struggling up the turnpike. He sent his cartographer, Jedediah Hotchkiss, to determine a route by which he might outflank Milroy and attack him in the morning. Leaving Johnson in command on Sitlington Hill, Jackson ordered Brig. Gen. William B. Taliaferro's brigade forward to Johnson's aid. Down in McDowell, meanwhile, Milroy decided to assault Sitlington Hill.

Despite its height, the hill was vulnerable. Deep ravines and heavy woods covered its western slope, offering protection to the Federals as they climbed. Johnson arranged his regiments in the shape of a U in a clearing atop the hill, with his right flank on the turnpike and his left at the edge of a steep ravine on the south slope. At the apex of his position, Johnson posted his old regiment, the 12th Georgia. When the attack came, about 4:30 in the afternoon, the Georgians bore the brunt.

Johnson's defenders outnumbered Milroy's attackers slightly, 2,800 to 2,300, but they were too inexperienced to realize that they were silhouetted against the sky, making them easy targets. The Georgians fell back after desperate fighting, and Johnson took a bullet in the ankle (Taliaferro assumed command) and was carried in a wagon to the rear, where he encountered Jackson. Stonewall ordered his namesake brigade into the fray and led it forward himself. By the time he arrived at the top of the hill, however, it was 9 P.M., darkness had fallen, the Federals had withdrawn to McDowell, and the battle had ended.

The next day, Jackson began his pursuit of Milroy, first telegraphing Richmond, "God blessed our arms with victory at McDowell yesterday." Then, at about noon, he put the army in motion. He pursued Schenck and Milroy for three days through present-day West Virginia as the Union generals led the remnants of their commands to the protection of Frémont's main force near Franklin. Jackson stopped the pursuit, reversed course, and marched back to McDowell and then to Staunton. Frémont abandoned the idea of joining Banks and remained near Franklin for the next two weeks.

Jackson's (or rather, Johnson's and Taliaferro's) victory came at a high cost. Milroy lost 34 killed, 220 wounded, and 5 missing, while Jackson's casualties were 116 killed, 300 wounded, and 4 missing. Tactically, the battle was messy and confused. Strategically, however, the fight accomplished one of Jackson's goals: Check Frémont's advance to prevent his union with Banks.

Difficult to reach, the heart of the McDowell battlefield on Sitlington Hill is among the best preserved of the Valley sites associated with Jackson. The Civil War Preservation Trust owns most of the hilltop. In the village of McDowell, the Felix Hull House (Jackson's headquarters after the battle) still stands, and the Union artillery position to the south remains visible. ■

FRONT ROYAL

B y the time word of Maj. Gen. Thomas J. Jackson's victory at McDowell on May 9, 1862, reached Maj. Gen. Richard S. Ewell at Conrad's Store soon thereafter, the subordinate had exploded in anger at his chief. He knew that a large part of Banks's army, Brig. Gen. James Shields's division, was marching out of the Luray Valley by way of Thornton's Gap to join Maj. Gen. Irvin McDowell at Fredericksburg. But he had lost contact with Stonewall, who had ordered him to stay put and keep an eye on Maj. Gen. Nathaniel P. Banks, and was seething with frustration that he could not stop Shields.

DIRECTIONS: I-66 Exit 6 (U.S. Rte. 340/522, Front Royal), s. on U.S. Rte. 340/522 about 1 mile to State Rte. 55; e. (left) to Virginia Civil War Commission (Circle Tour) interpretive markers at s.e. corner of intersection; return to intersection, turn left, and proceed s. on U.S. Rte. 340/522 and U.S. Rte. 340 2.5 miles to Downtown Visitors Center and two Virginia Civil War Trails markers, following directional signs; return .2 mile from Downtown Visitors Center to Royal Ave. (U.S. Rte. 340); s. (left) on Royal Ave. .3 mile to Prospect St.; w. (right) on Prospect St. .1 mile to Prospect Hill Cemetery; follow road to Confederate section at top of hill for views of Front Royal. To visit Cedarville section of battlefield (surrender ground): I-66 Exit 6 (U.S. Rte. 340/522, Front Royal), n. on U.S. Rte. 340/522 2.7 miles to battlefield at stone house on e. side of road, .3 mile s. of Rte. 675 (Success Rd.).

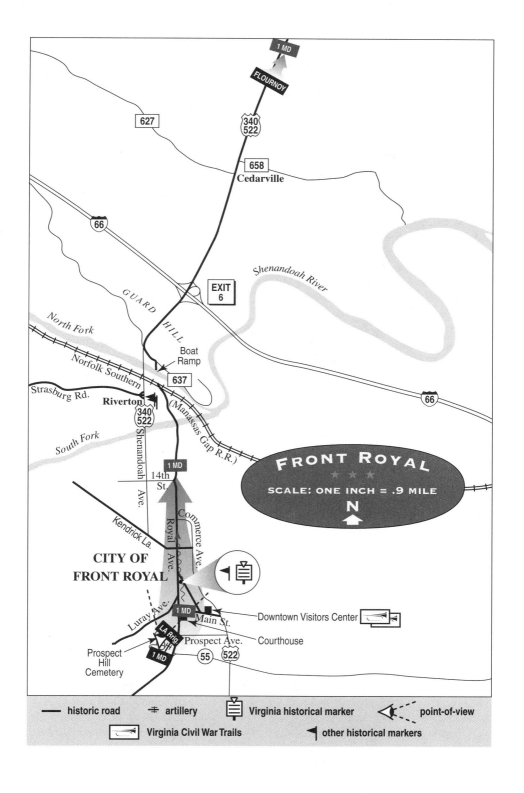

1 MD

FLOURNOY

627

340
522

658
Cedarville

66

Shenandoah River

GUARD HILL

EXIT 6

North Fork

Boat Ramp

Norfolk Southern

637

Strasburg Rd.

Riverton

340
522

Shenandoah Ave.

(Manassas Gap R.R.)

66

South Fork

1 MD

14th St.

FRONT ROYAL
★ ★ ★
SCALE: ONE INCH = .9 MILE
N

Kendrick La.

Royal Ave.

Commerce Ave.

CITY OF
FRONT ROYAL

Luray Ave.

1 MD

Main St.

Downtown Visitors Center

Courthouse

LA Bde.

Prospect Ave.

55 522

Prospect Hill Cemetery

1 MD

—— historic road   ╪ artillery   Virginia historical marker   ◁--- point-of-view

Virginia Civil War Trails   ◀ other historical markers

Meanwhile, Lee telegraphed Jackson, urging him to resume the offensive and keep Banks (and Shields) in the Valley. Jackson sent word to Ewell to prepare for an attack; simultaneously, Jackson and Ewell received orders from Gen. Joseph Johnston to prepare instead to join him before Richmond. The Valley campaign lurched to a halt. Ewell rode through the night of May 17 to confer with Jackson at Mount Solon in Augusta County. By the time he arrived the next morning, Jackson had written Johnston, asking him to reconsider his orders. Jackson and Ewell, knowing that Lee supported them and Johnston did not understand the situation in the Valley, decided to proceed against Banks until Jackson received a reply from Johnston. Each general would lead his command to Luray, join forces, and attack Banks at Strasburg, where he was entrenching. That would draw Shields back into the Valley, they concluded.

The armies raced down the Valley. Suddenly, on May 20, Jackson received his reply from Johnston: Ewell must march for Richmond at once, leaving Jackson to monitor Banks. In an outright act of insubordination, Jackson telegraphed Lee to seek his intercession and ordered Ewell not to leave until Lee responded. Jackson's indiscretion was unnecessary, as it turned out. Because of telegraph delays, his and Johnston's earlier messages had crossed. Johnston, when he finally understood the circumstances in the Valley, telegraphed a clear order to Ewell that if he and Jackson were not too late to attack Banks, "then attack." Lee likewise sent a message of approval.

At last! Jackson and Ewell pressed on. On May 21 they joined forces near Luray, and by the next evening they bivouacked at Bentonville in the Luray Valley. They were just ten miles south of Front Royal, which Banks had garrisoned with 1,000 infantry and two cannons under the command of Col. John R. Kenly to guard his left flank, while he and his army entrenched at Strasburg, some twelve miles west. If Jackson could capture Front Royal, he would turn Banks's flank. A young woman named Belle Boyd walked south from town to find Jackson and inform him of the garrison's numbers and dispositions.

Jackson ordered Col. Turner Ashby and his cavalry to cover the Strasburg Road west of Front Royal. He sent Ewell, whose division occupied the head of his column, up the Gooney Manor Road to attack the town itself. Ewell assigned the task to Col. Bradley T. Johnson, commander of the 1st Maryland Regiment, who sped ahead of the rest of the army. Ironically, the regiment's principal opponent in Front Royal was the 1st Maryland Regiment (Federal). Supposedly Jackson chose Johnson's regiment deliberately to smite the invading infidels from their homeland.

Louisianans joined Johnson's Marylanders just south of town on a hill, the site of present-day Prospect Hill Cemetery, and along the ridge to the east. Commanded by the aristocratic Brig. Gen. Richard Taylor, son of former president Zachary Taylor, the Louisiana Brigade included one of the most colorful units in the army, Wheat's Louisiana Tigers. It allegedly consisted of the roughest, meanest, most intractable barflies and wharf rats in New Orleans, under the command of 240-pound, six-foot-four Maj. Roberdeau Wheat. At 2 P.M. on the afternoon of May 23, the Tigers stood in a long line on the hillside in front of the Confederate Marylanders and awaited the word from Jackson. He gave it, and the line sprang forward.

The attack stunned the Federal garrison, which fled northward through the town, taking cover in and behind buildings momentarily, then scurrying away. Union soldiers and Confederates rushed to the South Fork railroad and wagon bridges. Kenly organized a defensive line on Camp Hill, between the town and the river, and stalled the Confederate assault momentarily with artillery fire while soldiers torched the bridges; Jackson's men pushed forward and extinguished the fires, but Kenly hurried to the Pike Bridge over the North Fork, repeated his tactic, and then fled north. Jackson, eager to capture the Union command, ordered Maj. Thomas S. Flournoy and his cavalry to ford the North Fork. Flournoy led the way and Jackson followed.

Two and a half miles north of the bridge, at a community called Cedarville, Kenly turned to fight. Flournoy formed his men for a charge as Jackson watched. Whooping and yelling, slashing with sabers and firing pistols, the cavalry broke through the Federal lines, reformed, and charged again. In a few minutes the fight ended as Kenly's men threw down their weapons.

Jackson was elated. Some 900 out of 1,000 Union officers and soldiers were dead or captured, against fewer than 100 of his own force. In addition, he now possessed two rifled Parrott guns, a long train of wagons, two locomotives, and a huge cache of supplies that had belonged to the Federals. Most importantly, Banks's flank was turned, and the road to Winchester was clear.

The town of Front Royal has spread out in every direction since the battle, obscuring much but not all of the ground. Residential neighborhoods cover the Confederate positions on the southern ridges,

C.S.A. artillery position, now Prospect Hill Cemetery, looking north to Front Royal.

but clear ground exists at Prospect Hill Cemetery, affording a good view of the town and most areas of the battlefield. The center of the old town stood around the courthouse, where the early street network still survives. To the north, dwellings cloak Camp Hill, but several landmarks stand at Cedarville, and much of the ground remains open farmland. Guard Hill, although partially chewed away by road-widening activities, is still a prominent landmark. ∎

FIRST BATTLE OF WINCHESTER

In Strasburg on the night of May 23, 1862, Maj. Gen. Nathaniel P. Banks met with his officers, who urged retreat. At first he angrily refused, but finally his lieutenants persuaded him, and at sunrise, he ordered his army to withdraw to Winchester.

Maj. Gen. Thomas J. "Stonewall" Jackson, too, put his army in motion at dawn, but he halted Maj. Gen. Richard S. Ewell's division three miles north at Ninevah. Jackson had received no reports from his cavalry, which he earlier had ordered to cover the Valley Turnpike north of Strasburg. What was Banks doing? A courier suddenly arrived from Brig. Gen. George H. "Maryland" Steuart, whose cavalry Jackson had directed to Newtown, a few miles south of Winchester. Steuart's men had found a long line of Federal wagons moving north at Newtown and attacked them. Jackson's question was answered: Banks was headed for Winchester.

Cut off his retreat in the open, Jackson decided. Ewell pressed on with his division toward Winchester on the Front Royal Turnpike (present-day Rte. 522), the Stonewall Brigade having crossed the North Fork of the Shenandoah River, while Jackson then marched west from Cedarville through occasional rain showers the seven miles to Middletown. There Jackson encountered the rear of Banks's supply train and ordered the artillery into action, wreaking havoc. The survivors raced north on the Valley Turnpike with Jackson in pursuit. At Middletown, Jackson found Brig. Gen. Turner Ashby's cavalry plundering abandoned Union supply wagons; he was furious that the cavalry had failed in its duty.

All through the night, Jackson urged his infantry on. Most of the soldiers were exhausted; some fell asleep while marching; all kept moving. Finally, at about 2 A.M. on Sunday, May 25, Jackson ordered the army to halt for two hours' rest. Before 4 A.M. he ordered the march resumed. Banks had escaped into Winchester, and he had to be flushed out.

The Federal commander enjoyed several advantages over Jackson at Winchester. Union forces had occupied the town long enough to become familiar with the terrain as well as construct substantial fortifications. South of Winchester, a series of hills extended from west to east. Banks positioned his men there, about 1,000 to the west of the turnpike and some 4,000 to the east, giving the Federals an enfilading line of fire over the low ground the Confederates had to cross to attack.

Jackson arrived in Banks's front at about 6 A.M. and deployed his force. Ewell already pressured the Union left with the Stonewall Brigade, led by Brig. Gen. Charles Sydney Winder, a tough disciplinarian who had replaced the popular Richard Garnett after the latter's failure at the first battle of Kernstown. Jackson brought up his artillery, taking but also delivering a terrible battering in the ensuing hour-long duel with Federal cannons. The Union guns held their ground, and Winder pressed forward alongside Col. John Campbell's brigade to attack the Federal left flank, but Banks quickly shifted troops to protect it. His attack stalled, Jackson summoned Richard Taylor and his Louisiana Brigade to Winder's aid and followed them toward the front. From Taylor's objective, steep Bowers Hill with its stone wall, the Federals rained down a storm of shot and shell, causing Taylor's men to flinch. Bellowing at them to stop dodging, Taylor led his men forward.

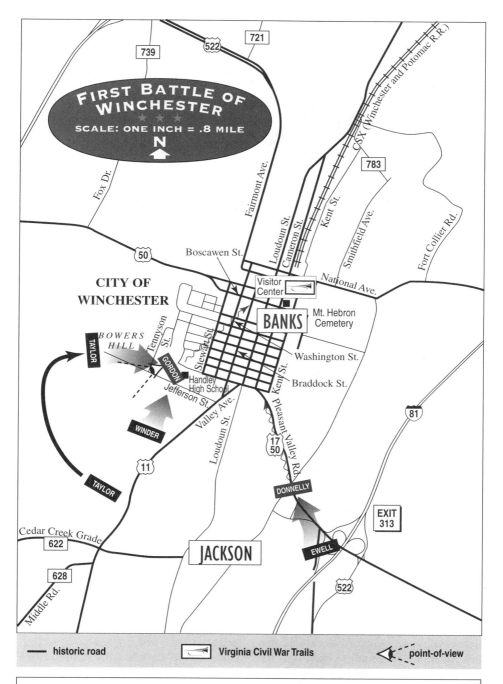

FIRST BATTLE OF WINCHESTER
★ ★ ★
SCALE: ONE INCH = .8 MILE
N

721

739

522

CSX (Winchester and Potomac R.R.)

783

Fox Dr.

Fairmont Ave.

50

Boscawen St.

Loudoun St.

Cameron St.

Kent St.

Smithfield Ave.

Fort Collier Rd.

CITY OF WINCHESTER

Visitor Center

National Ave.

BANKS

Mt. Hebron Cemetery

BOWERS HILL

TAYLOR

Tennyson St.

Stewart St.

GORDON

Handley High School

Jefferson St.

Washington St.

Kent St.

Braddock St.

WINDER

Valley Ave.

Loudoun St.

Pleasant Valley Rd.

17 50

81

TAYLOR

11

DONNELLY

EXIT 313

Cedar Creek Grade

622

JACKSON

EWELL

628

Middle Rd.

522

—— historic road   Virginia Civil War Trails   point-of-view

DIRECTIONS: I-81 Exit 313 (U.S. Rtes. 17/50/522, Millwood Pike, Winchester), w. into Winchester on Millwood Pike (Rte. 17/50); remain in center lane and follow U.S. Rte. 522 signs n.w. about 1 mile to Braddock St. (U.S. Rte. 11, also called Valley Ave.); s. (left) on U.S. Rte. 11 past John Handley High School campus on right; w. (right) on Jefferson St. on s. side of campus; up Bowers Hill .4 mile to Tennyson St., behind (w. of) Handley High School; n. (right) on Tennyson St. and park at curb; walk up slope to e. (right) to flat area (former site of radio tower).

View northwest from Bowers Hill to direction of Taylor's flank attack. VIRGINIA DEPARTMENT OF HISTORIC RESOURCES, JOHN S. SALMON

Halfway up the hill, he ordered a charge, and the brigade rushed up and over the Union position. Simultaneously, Ewell's division launched an all-out assault on the Federal left, and suddenly both flanks collapsed. The hills rang with the Rebel Yell as the Union soldiers fled through Winchester in growing panic, the Confederates in hot pursuit. It was 8:30 A.M.

As often occurred in such situations, the victors soon found themselves in as much disarray as the defeated. Banks sought to get his army through the town and across the Potomac River; Jackson determined to stop him. An orderly retreat turned into pandemonium when Ewell's division reappeared on the Union left flank. The soldiers stampeded, and men got tangled with horses and wagons and civilians who rushed from buildings to hurl objects at the departing Federals and hug the arriving Confederates. About 10 A.M. Jackson arrived at the north end of town, where he beheld the plain before him filled with fleeing soldiers ripe for attack by cavalry. But where was Ashby? No one knew, and Jackson paced in frustration.

Jackson urged his infantry forward, but they were spent. He even ordered artillerymen to unhitch their horses and ride them

after the fleeing enemy; it was no use, for the horses were as exhausted as the men. Finally, Jackson gave up and returned to Winchester, but not before blistering Ashby when he finally arrived on the field.

Although Banks had made good his escape, Jackson had accomplished the task of driving him from the Valley, at a cost of about 400 casualties to Banks's 2,000. In barely two weeks Jackson's army had vanquished two Union forces, Frémont's vanguard and Banks's army, thereby clearing the Shenandoah Valley of Federals. The news of Jackson's victory and Banks's defeat shocked Washington. Lincoln ordered additional troops to protect the capital, recalled McDowell away from Richmond to Fredericksburg, and directed him to send 30,000 soldiers to the Valley.

Today little is left of the First Winchester battlefield. The hills remain, of course, although they are covered with houses. John Handley High School, a residential neighborhood, and a water tower occupy Bowers Hill, the site of the pivotal attack by the Louisiana Brigade. Behind the school to the west, from a grassy field, one still finds a magnificent view of the city and the Blue Ridge Mountains to the east. ■

Fresh from their victory at Winchester, Maj. Gen. Thomas J. Jackson and his army took to the road again on May 28, 1862, marching northeast toward Charlestown. Stonewall's strategy, developed with the encouragement of the Confederate War Department, caused Abraham Lincoln to wonder whether he intended to attack Harpers Ferry or Washington or to invade Maryland. Lincoln reacted with a plan of his own.

Maj. Gen. John C. Frémont, already returning to the Shenandoah Valley from present-day West Virginia, was to march to Strasburg, there to be joined by Brig. Gen. James Shields and two divisions released from McDowell's army at Fredericksburg. Meanwhile, a reinforced Maj. Gen. Nathaniel P. Banks would drive up the Valley from the vicinity of Harpers Ferry. The Union pincers movement would confine Jackson to the lower Valley, and then the combined forces of three armies would crush him.

Jackson learned of the Federal strategy on May 30. He quickly acted to block Frémont's and Shields's routes into the Valley and secure his own route of withdrawal south. Brig. Gen. Turner Ashby and his cavalry galloped southwest to guard the road over North Mountain that led east to Strasburg from West Virginia. The 12th Georgia Regiment already was in Front Royal to confront any force that approached from the east through Manassas Gap.

As Jackson and his army moved south toward Winchester, a courier delivered catastrophic news: The Georgians at Front Royal had been routed by the advance of Shields's force. Now only Ashby could prevent the juncture of Frémont and Shields.

The next day, May 31, Jackson and his army marched south on the Valley Turnpike in a fifteen-mile-long column—seven miles of soldiers, eight of wagons. By the time the head of the column passed Strasburg, the tail left Winchester. And yet no Union army appeared to attack this inviting target. Why? Jackson wondered.

Both Federal commanders stayed put. Frémont, with a caution that made McClellan look reckless by comparison, first marched more than a hundred miles out of his way to the Valley when he found several mountain gaps blocked, then made progress at a rate that varied between zero and ten miles a day. On May 31, as Jackson passed by, Frémont halted his army four miles west of Strasburg and the turnpike and rested peacefully; the next day he was overawed by troops of Maj. Gen. Richard S. Ewell's division. Shields, meanwhile, after recapturing Front Royal, waited for his trailing division to join him. Ashby made a demonstration against Shield's skirmish line north of the town, reinforcing Shields's conviction that Jackson's force greatly outnumbered his. Jackson, who had been prepared to fight at Strasburg, passed through the town unscathed and continued south through weeklong heavy rain.

Frémont and Shields pursued, but their armies failed to rendezvous. Frémont followed in the main valley, with cavalry attacks that Ashby easily repulsed. Shields remained in the Luray (Page) Valley, separated by Massanutten Mountain from Frémont. Both Union forces bogged down, Frémont from a lack of initiative (and Ashby's defense), and Shields because of muddy roads, swollen rivers, and burned bridges. Jackson, meanwhile, moved quickly up the Valley Turnpike.

The march up the Valley became a nightmare for all involved. Although the weather helped Confederates keep ahead of the Federal forces, the incessant rain made them just as miserable as their pursuers.

At New Market on June 4, Jackson decided to make for Port Republic (called Port by its inhabitants), southeast of Harrisonburg. He based his strategy on the Valley's topography. The south end of Massanutten Mountain, half a dozen miles north of Port, stood an equal distance west of Conrad's Store (present-day Elkton), where Jackson and his army had camped just a few weeks earlier. There Shields could emerge from the Luray Valley, cross the rain-swollen South Fork of the Shenandoah River over the Conrad's Store bridge, march west around the mountain barrier, and join Frémont. If the bridge was burned, however, Shields would have to march to Port Republic and cross the North River over the bridge there to link up with Frémont. If Jackson occupied Port, then he would control the bridge and be able to move his army to one side or the other of the North River.

Jackson dispatched Ashby to burn the bridge at Conrad's Store and marched his weary army toward Port Republic. They began to arrive on June 6, the first day in a week without rain. Jackson and his men were too exhausted to do anything but settle into defensive positions and dry themselves. Stonewall had written to Richmond, requesting reinforcements so he could drive north, possibly even invade Maryland. At his new headquarters just west of the village at Madison Hall, he received a reply to his request: no reinforcements. Jackson assumed that the Valley campaign was over.

His cavalry, led by Ashby, remained at Harrisonburg to keep an eye on Frémont. At about 2 P.M. on June 6, Federal cavalry galloped through the town and into a Confederate ambush southeast of Harrison-

DIRECTIONS: I-81 Exit 235 (State Rte. 256, Weyer's Cave–Grottoes); e. on State Rte. 256 about 1.1 miles to State Rte. 276 (Cross Keys Rd.); n. (left) on State Rte. 276 6.5 miles to Rte. 679; s. (right) on Rte. 679 at Cross Keys .1 mile to Ruritan meeting hall (former Union Church) and Virginia Civil War Trails marker on right, and cemetery on left; return to State Rte. 276; n. (right) on State Rte. 276 .3 mile to Virginia Civil War Commission (Circle Tour) interpretive markers on s. side of road; continue on State Rte. 276 .5 mile to Rte. 659 (Port Republic Rd.); s.e. (right) on Rte. 659 .3 mile to Rte. 708; e. (left) on Rte. 708 1.6 miles to location of Trimble's attack on 8th New York Infantry, then continue .4 mile farther to Rte. 676; w. (right) on Rte. 676 and follow its meanders to right, along reverse of Trimble's route, to Rte. 659; n.w. (right) on Rte. 659 .2 mile to Rte. 848; w. (left) on Rte. 864 1.5 miles to Rte. 671; w. (left) on Rte. 671 .2 mile to State Rte. 276; n.e. (right) on State Rte. 276 1.3 miles to Rte. 679; s. (right) on Rte. 679 1.3 miles to Rte. 659; n. (left) on Rte. 659 1.3 miles to junction with Rte. 708 and bear left on Rte. 659 .3 mile to State Rte. 276; s.w. (left) on State Rte. 276 and return 7.3 miles to State Rte. 256; w. (right) on State Rte. 256 about 1.1 miles to I-81. To proceed directly to Port Republic battlefield, proceed s. on Rte. 659 (Port Republic Rd.) and drive about 3.8 miles (from State Rte. 276) to Port Republic.

burg. In the ensuing cavalry engagement, Ashby's horse was killed. On foot, leading a charge across Chestnut Hill, Ashby was shot through the heart and fell dead. The Union force was beaten back, and that afternoon grieving Confederate cavalrymen brought Ashby's body to Port and laid him out in Frank Kemper's parlor. Jackson genuinely mourned Ashby's death. Although the two men had feuded publicly and frequently over Ashby's lack of discipline, Jackson had liked him personally and greatly admired his courage and audacity in battle. Now, when Jackson needed him most, he was gone.

Throughout June 7, Jackson considered the terrain around Port, which dictated the disposition of his army in case Frémont or Shields approached. Jackson knew Frémont was at Harrisonburg; he assumed Shields still slogged through the mud in the Luray Valley, as he had heard nothing to the con-

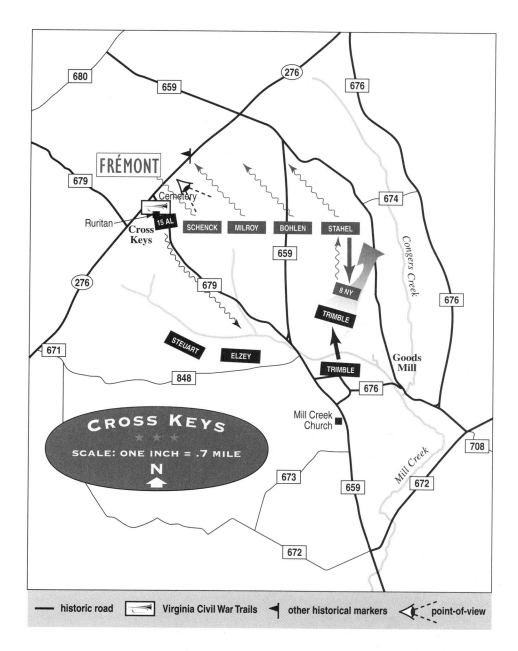

680 659 276 676

FRÉMONT

Cemetery

679

Ruritan

Cross Keys

15 AL

SCHENCK MILROY BOHLEN STAHEL

674

Congers Creek

276

679

659

8 NY

676

TRIMBLE

STEUART

ELZEY

671

TRIMBLE

Goods Mill

848

676

Mill Creek Church

CROSS KEYS

★ ★ ★

SCALE: ONE INCH = .7 MILE

N

673

659

Mill Creek

672

708

672

— historic road | Virginia Civil War Trails | ◀ other historical markers | ◀ point-of-view

trary from his scouts. Ewell encamped in and around a hamlet named Cross Keys for a local tavern, and Brig. Gen. Charles S. Winder bivouacked three miles south, just short of the North River, while Jackson and his staff set up headquarters on the opposite side of the river in Port.

Although the terrain favored the defense, it also presented difficulties to Jackson. Port stood between the North and South Rivers, which joined just east of the village to form the South Fork of the Shenandoah River. The only access to the west side of the South Fork was the bridge over the North River at Port; high water reduced the usefulness of the two fords near either end of the village. The shallower South River could be forded to gain access to the bottomland to the east of Port.

Jackson's dilemma was this: If he attacked Frémont near Harrisonburg, Shields could slip into Port behind him. If he put his army on the east side of the South Fork to confront Shields (presumably marching south from the Luray Valley), Frémont could occupy the bluffs on the west side and blast him with artillery. Furthermore, Jackson would have to destroy the North River bridge to protect his rear while fighting Shields, which would prevent him from recrossing the river to fight Frémont. Jackson, weary and unable to solve his dilemma for the present, quit trying and went to bed at Madison Hall, leaving his army encamped across the North River just north of Port, with the bridge and high water between them. Small detachments of cavalry guarded the fords, while the huge Confederate supply train stood parked on the road to Staunton

behind Jackson's headquarters. No pickets stood guard over either the train or headquarters. While Jackson slept through the night, Shields's vanguard marched out of the Luray Valley toward Port.

On Sunday, June 8, Jackson looked forward to a quiet day of reflection and religious services. Suddenly, a cavalry captain reined in his mount at headquarters and shouted that Federal cavalry had been spotted on the road leading to Conrad's Store. Two cannons abruptly boomed; a cavalryman galloped up to announce that Union troopers were in the village. Jackson and his officers—in danger of being cut off from the army, even captured—swung into their saddles and dashed for the North River bridge as Federal cavalry at the other end of town headed for the same place.

Jackson won the race, emerging from the north end of the covered bridge just as the Union cavalry arrived at the south end. Back at headquarters, Confederate artillery opened up on the cavalry, halting it in the village. Meanwhile, across the North

Battle of Cross Keys as sketched by Edmund Forbes. LIBRARY OF CONGRESS

River, Jackson prepared a counterattack. When Union artillery unlimbered on the south bank, the Confederate gunners shelled them, and Col. Samuel V. Fulkerson charged across the bridge with the 37th Virginia Infantry. The Federal cavalry fled the way it had come, and Winder's division took up positions on the bluffs overlooking the South Fork. Soon artillerymen spotted a Union infantry column to the northeast marching in support of the cavalry; the gunners raked it with cannon fire, and the Federals retreated three miles north.

At about 10 A.M. the rumble of artillery rolled in from the northwest. It was Frémont at last, attacking Ewell's division near Cross Keys.

As usual, Frémont proceeded with extreme caution, assuming that he faced a force that outnumbered him; in reality, he outnumbered the Confederates two-to-one, 11,500 versus 5,800. After driving off the first opponent he encountered, the 15th Alabama Infantry Regiment, which had bivouacked near Union Church and cemetery, Frémont laid down the ineffective artillery barrage that alerted Jackson and his lieutenants.

Frémont deployed his army from northeast to southwest, parallel to the Keezletown Road. The battle line turned south as it marched toward Ewell's division, which had moved to good defensive positions on ridges closer to Cross Keys and overlooking Mill Creek, roughly a mile south of Frémont. The Confederate line, about a mile in length, consisted of the brigades of brigadier generals George H. Steuart, Arnold Elzey, and Isaac R. Trimble.

The Union attack developed slowly. At about noon, one Federal brigade encountered North Carolina skirmishers in the woods who fell back across a clearing and up a hill. The 500 men of the 8th New York Infantry Regiment set off in pursuit, but near a fence at the crest of the hill, a wave of musket fire hit them, and the New Yorkers suffered nearly 50 percent casualties.

Meanwhile, the left and center of the Confederate line remained in position on the ridge and engaged Frémont's center and right with artillery and musket fire. After word of the defeat on the Union left reached Frémont, the commander realigned his army on the Keezletown road, and Ewell moved his forward to occupy the Federal battle positions. By the time darkness fell, Frémont was back where he had begun.

The casualties were relatively light on both sides, with 664 Federals killed, wounded, missing, and captured, and 287 for the Confederates. As battles go, Cross Keys was more of a skirmish, considering the numbers of troops engaged, but it resulted in the further fraying of Frémont's already weak nerves.

The Cross Keys battlefield retains excellent integrity today and, with the Port Republic ground, constitutes one of the most beautiful parts of the Shenandoah Valley. Large, prosperous farms roll away in every direction, several antebellum dwellings stand, and the terrain allows the visitor a clear understanding of the battle events, tactics, and strategies. In Port Republic the Frank Kemper house is now the Turner Ashby House museum. The Lee-Jackson Foundation owns seventy acres of the Cross Keys battlefield, the Civil War Preservation Trust is co-owner of another tract, and yet another part is under a preservation easement; the future looks bright for the protection and improved interpretation of this landmark. ∎

After darkness settled over the Cross Keys battlefield on June 8, 1862, Maj. Gen. Thomas J. "Stonewall" Jackson spent the night disposing his army for the action he anticipated the next day. He concluded that after defeating Maj. Gen. John C. Frémont so handily, he could hold the nervous Union general at bay with only a token force. Jackson met with Maj. Gen. Richard S. Ewell and Col. Thomas T. Munford, his chief cavalry commander, at Cherry Grove (which still stands on the south side of South River). He ordered Ewell to withdraw most of his division from Frémont's front under cover of darkness and prepare to engage Maj. Gen. James Shields, while Munford was to ascertain whether the route to Brown's Gap was open—as an escape route if needed.

Jackson chose to attack Shields rather than Frémont for several reasons. He and his army were closer to Shields, his force outnumbered Shields's, he remained closer to his base of supply by attacking Shields, if necessary the Confederates could retreat more easily from Port Republic than from north of the North River, and Frémont's main avenue of retreat—the road to Harrisonburg—was open whereas Shields's retreat route consisted of bad roads, enabling Jackson to pursue and destroy him.

View south along U.S. line of battle to The Coaling. VIRGINIA DEPARTMENT OF HISTORIC RESOURCES, JOHN S. SALMON

Before the fight began, however, Jackson had one bridge to destroy, another to build. In the middle of the night of June 9 Capt. Claiborne R. Mason, a sixty-two-year-old engineer, and his black workmen (called the African Pioneers) erected a flimsy bridge over the South River—actually, several wagons dragged into the water and overlaid with loose planks—and about dawn Jackson's army crossed the stream and marched northeast toward the flat bottomland on the eastern bank of the North Fork. Near Cross Keys, most of Ewell's men slipped away from Frémont's front just before daybreak and crossed the North River bridge, which was then burned to prevent Frémont from crossing.

Frémont could have affected the outcome of the battle even without crossing the North River. From the bluffs overlooking the North Fork and the plain to the east, his artillery could have shelled Jackson's army into oblivion as it attacked Shields. Instead, Frémont first put his force in battle formation, even though he knew Ewell had withdrawn and was hastening to join Jackson. When the long front finally moved forward, it disintegrated at each natural obstacle and had to halt to reform. At that jerky pace it took most of the morning to reach the bluffs.

In contrast, Brig. Gen. Erastus B. Tyler, who commanded the 3,500-man vanguard of Shields's division, took advantage of the terrain. He concealed his main force in woods and threw out his skirmish line about a mile to his front, just southwest of Little Deep Run. On one of the knobs that bordered the gently undulating bottomland east of the South Fork, about a mile and a half northeast of Port Republic at the southeast end of Lewiston Lane (present-day Rte. 708), called The Coaling, Tyler placed six guns from three batteries.

Jackson's forces, the Stonewall Brigade in the lead, made their way gingerly over the makeshift South River bridge and marched down present-day Rte. 955 toward the Conrad's Store road (Rte. 340). The 2nd and 4th Virginia, accompanied by Capt. Joseph Carpenter's Allegheny Artillery, headed the column. About a mile from the village, Confederate skirmishers were told that a Federal skirmish line lay concealed just ahead. Two guns unlimbered and joined the infantry in firing a volley. A few bullets buzzed overhead in return as the Union line melted away. It was 7 A.M.

The Confederates moved forward into the South Fork bottomland, not knowing exactly where the Union positions were located. Suddenly one cannon, then another, roared half a mile ahead and to the right, at The Coaling. Jackson's army was in serious trouble.

As catastrophe threatened the Confederate front, disaster menaced its rear. The wagon-and-plank bridge began disintegrating from all the troops, horses, and cannons of Winder's Stonewall Brigade passing over it. By the time Brig. Gen. Richard Taylor and his Louisiana Brigade reached the bridge, the men were compelled to cross the shaky structure in single file. A wide gap opened between the two brigades, so at first only half of Jackson's force did battle on a field swept by Federal artillery.

Jackson decided to send two infantry regiments, the 2nd and 4th Virginia, with Carpenter's battery, toward The Coaling in hopes that they could capture the high ground. Meanwhile, he deployed the 5th and 27th Virginia Regiments together with Capt. William T. Poague's Rockbridge Artillery to engage the Federals in the bottomland. The ensuing artillery engagement favored the Union guns, which had an unobstructed field of fire to the Confederates below. The Rockbridge artillerists

were forced to elevate their guns because of the height of The Coaling, so most of their rounds passed harmlessly over their opponents. Union shells, though, fell among them with devastating effect.

As the two-hour-long artillery duel raged, Tyler deployed his infantry about three-quarters of a mile north of Jackson's on a rise of ground in front of Lewiston Lane. One regiment anchored the Union right near the South Fork, with artillery to its left. Four other regiments held the Federal left at the foot of The Coaling. Two regiments were held in reserve, and the 66th Ohio, in two separate formations, guarded the guns on The Coaling.

Meanwhile, Jackson's flanking movement crawled along. The woods were impassable for artillery—Carpenter gave up and rejoined Poague—and the two Virginia infantry regiments struggled to maintain cohesion through thick undergrowth. Finally they emerged on a ridge across from The Coaling and opened fire, surprising the Federals. However, the Union gunners shifted their fire to this new threat and soon drove the Virginians back.

Down on the bottomland, the 5th and 27th Virginia Regiments of the Stonewall Brigade recoiled when the guns on The Coaling, joined by fire from Tyler's line, shifted their attention back to the river plain. Soon thereafter, Taylor's Louisianans arrived on the field. Jackson then directed Taylor to leave one regiment—the 7th Louisiana—then assault The Coaling with the rest of his brigade and capture the Federal guns. With Jedediah Hotchkiss leading the way down a newly discovered path through the woods and thickets, Taylor set off at once.

As Taylor proceeded, the Stonewall Brigade, strengthened by the addition of the 7th Louisiana Regiment, led by Col. Harry T. Hayes, reformed for an assault on Tyler's line. Fire from The Coaling raked the Confederate right, while musket fire

DIRECTIONS: I-81 Exit 235 (State Rte. 256, Weyer's Cave–Grottoes); e. on State Rte. 256 about 4.7 miles to Rte. 605 (Lee Roy Rd.); n (left) on Rte. 605 2.7 miles to T intersection at Madison Hall, site of Jackson's headquarters, on right; turn right, then left onto Main Street (Rte. 605) and continue .6 mile to Rte. 659; cross Rte. 659 onto Rte. 1605 .1 mile (1 block) to site of North River bridge and continue to right .2 mile to Frank Kemper (Turner Ashby) House on right on corner of Rte. 659; n. (right) on Rte. 659 half a block to Virginia Civil War Commission (Circle Tour) interpretive marker; s. (left) on Rte. 659 .25 mile to Rte. 955; e. (left) on Rte. 955 1.9 miles to U.S. Rte. 340; n. (left) on U.S. Rte. 340 .7 mile to Rte. 708; e. (right) on Rte. 708 and stop at Port Republic Battlefield Park for self-guided walking tour of The Coaling; return to U.S. Rte. 340 and cross on Rte. 708 1.5 miles to Rte. 655 (note main combat area on left and Lynnwood house on right just before bridge over South Fork); w. (left) on Rte. 655 along ridge from which Frémont shelled the field 4.5 miles to Rte. 659; s. (left) on Rte. 659 .3 mile to Rte. 605 (Main Street); retrace route to State Rte. 256 and I-81.

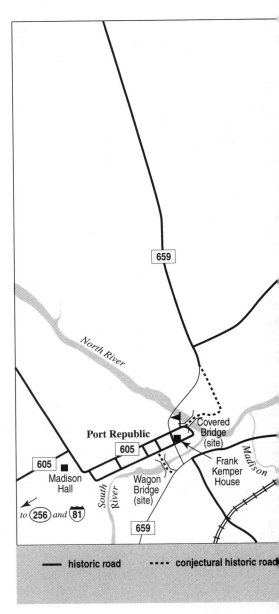

from the Union line struck the left. Tyler ordered his reserves into the action, as well as the regiment that had been guarding The Coaling. The Confederates arrived at a fence just in front of the Federal line, where the attackers stood and delivered a heavy return fire for half an hour until they ran out of ammunition. Finally there was nothing left to do but fall back. The Federal line surged forward in pursuit. Suddenly, though, the course of the battle changed dramatically.

Jackson had understood from the opening moments of the engagement that The Coaling held the key to success or failure. The only way to dislodge Tyler's infantry was to capture The Coaling and the Federal guns there. Hays's assault ultimately succeeded because it had caused Tyler to shift three infantry regiments away from The Coaling, leaving only a handful of skirmishers to protect the guns. As soon as the 7th Louisiana's attack failed, Tyler ordered the Ohioans back, but they were still en route when Taylor struck The Coaling.

Taylor had just placed his brigade in battle formation when a cheer arose from the Federal lines to his left as the Stonewall Brigade broke for the rear. The Louisiana Brigade charged up the slope of The Coaling, screaming the Rebel Yell all the way. On the hillside, the Federal guns fell quiet as their crews struggled to turn

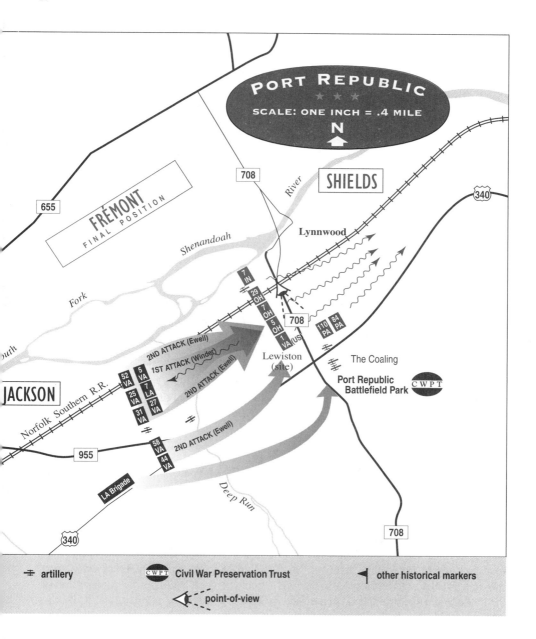

PORT REPUBLIC
★ ★ ★
SCALE: ONE INCH = .4 MILE
N

655

708

SHIELDS

340

FRÉMONT
FINAL POSITION

Shenandoah

River

Lynnwood

Fork

South

7 IN

29 OH

7 OH

5 OH

1 VA (US)

708

110 PA   84 PA

JACKSON

Norfolk Southern R.R.

2ND ATTACK (Ewell)

1ST ATTACK (Winder)

2ND ATTACK (Ewell)

52 VA   5 VA

25 VA   7 LA

31 VA   27 VA

58 VA

44 VA

Lewiston (site)

The Coaling

Port Republic
Battlefield Park   CWPT

955

2ND ATTACK (Ewell)

LA Brigade

Deep Run

340

708

⚊ artillery   CWPT Civil War Preservation Trust   ◀ other historical markers

◀--- point-of-view

them against the Confederates while the Union pickets fired and reloaded frantically. Then the shooting died away as the clubbed muskets, ramrods, bayonets, knives, and swords came into play—the blood and gore later appalled survivors on both sides of the fray. Confederates and Federals alike shot or slit the throats of

dozens of artillery horses to prevent the other side from riding off with the guns, adding to the horror of the site. Within minutes the fight was over, and a cheer arose from the Confederates watching from the plain.

Tyler at once ordered a counterattack, and possession of The Coaling soon changed sides several times. When the 66th Ohio recaptured the position, the Louisiana Brigade formed reluctantly for yet another assault. Then Ewell and reinforcements arrived on the scene, spurring Taylor's men onward. This time they held the hill as the exhausted and outnumbered Ohioans fell back.

Now that Tyler's left flank was turned, his line slowly collapsed. An orderly withdrawal turned into a rout as regiments on the Union right, farthest from The Coaling, raced toward the Conrad's Store road, the only available path of retreat. Taylor's and Ewell's men pursued the increasingly disorganized Federal forces in a chase that would go on for five to eight miles. And then Frémont arrived at about 10:30 A.M., just after the Union line collapsed. He was too late to take part in the battle, but not too late to perform an act that angered friend and foe alike.

When Jackson had begun his march in the morning, he left Brig. Gen. Isaac R. Trimble on the west side of the South Fork to hold back Frémont with a small rear guard. Fortunately, Frémont was moving slowly and with extreme caution toward the rising sound of battle to the east. Trimble and his men marched over the North River bridge, burned it, then hastened to join the battle still raging on the bottomland, but they were too late.

Frémont arrived on the bluff overlooking the South Fork and deployed his infantry, cavalry, and artillery. A house on the battlefield, Lynnwood, had been turned into a hospital for both Confederate and Federal wounded and was conspicuously marked with a yellow flag. Suddenly, artillery shells burst on the field and around the house as Frémont's artillery opened up. Those ministering to the injured were incredulous, then outraged. They abandoned their Union charges and hustled the Confederate wounded out of range. During a later exchange of letters with Shields, Jackson referred to "the unsoldierly conduct of General Frémont's command," code words for cowardice.

The next day, Jackson prepared to resume the fight if needed, but Frémont withdrew past Harrisonburg to Mount Jackson, and Shields retreated down the Luray Valley, leaving Jackson in control. The Shenandoah Valley campaign was over. The Confederates suffered about 800 casualties out of 6,000 men, the Federals more than 1,000 out of about 3,500, at Port Republic.

The Union soldiers who had fought in the battle were disgusted with their commanders, particularly Shields and Frémont; the Lincoln government agreed. Shields faded from view, resigning from the army in 1863, and Frémont resigned just weeks after Port Republic when Maj. Gen. John Pope, who was junior in date of rank, was promoted over him. Jackson, in contrast, managed to tie up thousands of Union troops—keeping them from reinforcing McDowell or McClellan—defeat three Federal armies, and make his foot cavalry and his own name immortal.

Port Republic, like Cross Keys, remains virtually as Jackson saw it. Historic roads, houses, farms, and views abound. The Civil War Preservation Trust owns nine acres of The Coaling at the intersection of Rtes. 340 and 708 (Port Republic Battlefield Park), where brochures and a short walking trail to key viewing points are available. Unfortunately, due to the steepness of the trail, The Coaling is not accessible by wheelchair. ∎

PENINSULA AND SEVEN DAYS' CAMPAIGNS, 1862

The Peninsula and Seven Days' campaigns constitute one of the oddest episodes in the course of the Civil War in Virginia. Both commanders made costly errors of judgment; the wizard of the Shenandoah Valley campaign, Stonewall Jackson, often was present on the battlefield physically but not mentally; and the Confederate army, which lost or fought to a draw almost every battle, emerged the victor.

Maj. Gen. George B. McClellan, the thirty-five-year-old commander of the Army of the Potomac, seemed destined for success in the spring of 1862. Born in Philadelphia, the scion of a distinguished family, McClellan entered West Point in 1842 after attending the University of Pennsylvania. He graduated second in his academy class in 1846 and while serving in the Mexican War earned two brevet promotions. During his eleven-year military career, he rose to the rank of captain, built forts, taught at the U.S. Military Academy, and designed a saddle that the army adopted as its standard. He was sent to Europe during the Crimean War as an official observer and was present at the siege of Sebastopol. After resigning his commission in 1857, he pursued a new career in railroading, becoming president of the Ohio and Mississippi Railroad in 1860.

When the war began, Ohio governor William Dennison appointed McClellan major general in the Ohio volunteers. In July 1861, just before the first battle of Manassas, McClellan won victories at Rich Mountain and Corrick's Ford in western Virginia, helping secure for the Union what would become West Virginia and gaining instant fame. Following the Federal defeat at First Manassas on July 21, 1861, President Abraham Lincoln removed Brig. Gen. Irvin McDowell as commander of the principal Union force and appointed McClellan in his place. On November 1, 1861, McClellan replaced Bvt. Lt. Gen. Winfield Scott as general in chief of the United States Army.

McClellan took command of a demoralized, poorly trained army and over the next few months transformed what had been essentially an armed mob of 100,000 men into a professional, well-supplied, thoroughly drilled, massive war machine. The soldiers adored McClellan, who had restored their pride and confidence. They were ready to fight.

Their general, however, demonstrated an intense reluctance to do so. Politically ambitious, he more than anything wanted to become president. If he took his great army into battle and lost, he believed, his hoped-for political career would be stillborn. If, however, he delayed his campaign until he had an overwhelming superiority in men and supplies and fought only when victory was assured, his political success, too, would be assured. Also, he did not wish to shame the South by crushing its army if he could help achieve a negotiated settlement. Additionally, convincing the public that Lincoln and his Republican administration were not giving him the men he needed to save the Union meant the responsibility for any military defeat could shift from his shoulders to theirs.

PENINSULA & SEVEN DAYS' CAMPAIGNS

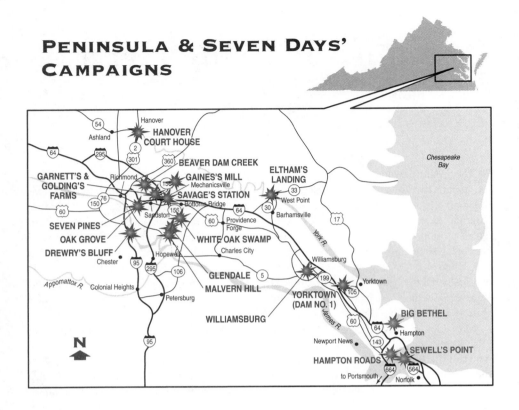

McClellan adopted a strategy of delay while constantly soliciting reinforcements from Lincoln. Once in the field, McClellan moved with caution, frustrating not only Lincoln but his own subordinates. McClellan's motives and behavior, his ambitions and his hesitations, have been much debated by historians. It is fair to say, however, that his military strategy, as executed, was not so much to fight to win as to fight not to lose.

Two Confederate generals, Joseph E. Johnston and Robert E. Lee, stood ready to oppose McClellan and his Army of the Potomac. Johnston, a native of Prince Edward County, Virginia, graduated from West Point in 1829 (thirteenth in his class, which included Robert E. Lee) and served for eight years as an artillery officer, then resigned to pursue a civil engineering career. In 1838, on an expedition to Flor-

ida, Johnston skillfully defended his party against an Indian attack, thereby earning a first lieutenant's commission in the Topographical Engineers. Having served with distinction in the Mexican War, he eventually rose to quartermaster general with the rank of brigadier general. He resigned from the U.S. Army on April 22, 1861, and joined the Confederate army, assuming command at Harpers Ferry from Thomas J. Jackson in May 1861. Johnston led his army to Manassas Junction in July 1861, where on July 21 he combined forces with Brig. Gen. P. G. T. Beauregard to turn the tide of battle for the Confederacy. President Jefferson Davis promoted him to full general. He reported to Richmond and organized its defenses, a task at which he was an acknowledged master. When McClellan began his march up the Peninsula toward Richmond, Johnston crafted a strategic withdrawal of his army to the strong defensive works protecting the Confederate capital. Wounded early in the fighting there, Johnston was replaced by Robert E. Lee.

Lee, like McClellan, was descended from an illustrious family, although one that had fallen on hard times. Born in 1807 at the ancestral home, Stratford Hall, in Westmoreland County, Virginia, Lee was the son of Henry "Light Horse Harry" Lee, a Revolutionary War cavalry hero who first was jailed for debt, then abandoned his family when Robert was six. Young Lee attended Alexandria Academy and, as a dutiful son, helped his mother rear his younger siblings. The family lived somewhat above the "genteel poverty" line, but money always was a concern, and Lee's elder half-brother sold Stratford Hall in 1822.

Lee entered West Point in 1825 and graduated second in his class in 1829 without receiving a single demerit. He entered the Corps of Engineers as a brevet second lieutenant, beginning a military career that would last some thirty-two years for the United States and four years for the Confederate States. During his long tenure in the U.S. Army, Lee built forts (including part of Fort Monroe, in Virginia) and other engineering projects, served with distinction in the Mexican War, superintended the academy at West Point, and rose to the rank of colonel. In October 1859 he led the contingent of U.S. Marines that captured the abolitionist John Brown at Harpers Ferry. Lee's fellow officers esteemed him highly, yet Lee often felt frustrated by military politics, and his desire to care for his family and tend his wife's estate (Arlington) led him to consider resignation more than once.

Lee, like Stonewall Jackson, tended toward shyness when in the presence of strangers, but was highly sociable with friends and flirtatious with women. Physically, Lee was considered the handsomest man in the army—five foot eleven, black hair and brown eyes, graceful and athletic, of military bearing but never stiff. He possessed a wry wit, occasionally risqué but not vulgar, and had a temper that he controlled with his iron will, sometimes with difficulty. The most important words in his life were duty, service, and honor, and his religious faith was quiet and pietistic. However, Lee was a human being with ambitions and self-doubts, overbearing though loving as a father, and sometimes unclear in his orders as a military leader. As with Jackson, Lee the mortal man is much more interesting than Lee the myth, the perfect "Marble Man."

Early in his career as a Confederate general, the Marble Man showed feet of clay. Following his resignation from the U.S. Army on April 20, 1861 (he had been offered field command of the Union army two days earlier but declined), Lee was given the rank of major general and placed in charge of Virginia's defenses by Gov. John Letcher. In August 1861, promoted to full general to rank from mid-June, he led an unsuccessful campaign in western Virginia. Lee's reluctance to attack an entrenched Union force with his own poorly organized troops led to his being called "Granny Lee" by armchair generals and newspaper editors.

Lee next saw service in South Carolina, where Davis sent him in November to organize the coastal defenses and where he purchased Traveller, his dappled gray gelding (whose gait, which most riders found bone-jarring, suited Lee). Lee's plans ran counter to the desires of certain politicians and wealthy planters, however, making him increasingly unpopular there. By March 1862 Davis ordered him back to Richmond to serve as the president's military adviser. Lee hit his stride, gaining invaluable knowledge of the Confederate command structure, acquiring supporters among Confederate politicians, and beginning (by mail and telegraph) a relationship with the man who would be his most important lieutenant in campaigns to come, Maj. Gen. Thomas J. Jackson. But when Lee assumed command of the Army of Northern Virginia on June 1, after Johnston fell wounded, he set the men to digging and strengthening Richmond's defenses. This caused some to dub Lee the "King of Spades" and voice fears that Granny Lee would never attack McClellan. Lee's critics were as mistaken in their judgments of him as McClellan's supporters were in their assessments of the Union commander.

President Lincoln, certain that he had appointed the right man to lead the Army of the Potomac, waited for McClellan to take it into the field—and waited and waited some more. Finally, Lincoln ordered McClellan into battle, to no avail. The general offered reason after reason for not crossing the Potomac ("All quiet along the Potomac," a popular phrase, began to sound ironic) and offering battle to the Confederates, who until late in September were entrenched within sight of Washington. To be fair, McClellan did have a plan of attack, the so-called Urbanna Plan, which involved a flanking maneuver around Johnston's right near the Middlesex County village for which it was named, but he kept it secret even from Lincoln. When he finally disclosed it to the president, its complexity and the consequences of certain Confederate strategic decisions soon rendered it obsolete.

South of the Potomac, Davis ordered Johnston to withdraw his outnumbered army from northern Virginia and set up a new defensive line closer to Richmond to protect the capital against the attack that McClellan was certain to launch. Concerned that such a move would expose his left flank to attack from the Shenandoah Valley, where a Union army led by Maj. Gen. Nathaniel P. Banks lurked among the hills, Johnston ordered Stonewall Jackson to adopt a defensive mode (Lee later changed these orders to enable Jackson to begin his Valley campaign), then carried out the withdrawal as ordered, evacuating his army from Centreville and Manassas Junction on March 8–9, 1862. The troops burned all the stores and baggage that they could not carry as well as mountains of supplies stockpiled in Confederate magazines. The odor of burning beef and bacon followed the retreating Confederates for twenty miles, adding to their ill humor at turning their backs on their foes.

After several evolutions, McClellan developed a final plan: Transport his mighty force to Newport News and Fort Monroe, which remained in Federal hands. The army would then disembark and march up the Peninsula, between the York and James Rivers, to Richmond. There McClellan, as his supporters believed, would save the Union with one great battle.

The Peninsula was a flat land of large plantations and smaller farms worn out by repeated crops of tobacco. Located between the Chesapeake Bay and Richmond, the Peninsula is part of Tidewater Virginia, where the terrain is cut by slow-flowing rivers and swamps. Historically, it is one of the most significant places in Virginia. The list of historic sites was well-known to McClellan: Jamestown, where the colonists established their first permanent settlement; Old Point Comfort at Fort Monroe, the new colony's window on the Chesapeake to guard against Spanish marauders; Williamsburg, the second colonial capital; Yorktown, where Washington captured Cornwallis and his army, effectively ensuring the survival of the fledgling United States. Grand plantations associated with old Virginia names—Harrison,

Carter, Tyler, Byrd—lined the banks of the James River. McClellan must have felt that the forces of history summoned him to reclaim the land where the United States was born.

In March 1862 the Army of the Potomac moved at last. First, though, McClellan acceded to Lincoln's urging to capture the Confederate batteries at Freestone and Cockpit Points and elsewhere to end the embarrassing Potomac River blockade of Washington. He found the batteries empty, however, as the men and guns had withdrawn with the rest of Johnston's army. McClellan also marched his army out to Centreville and Manassas Junction and back again, finding the Confederates gone and "Quaker guns" (logs painted black to resemble cannons) guarding the empty earthworks. Although McClellan had known of the faux artillery for several weeks, Washington's newspaper reporters had not. Their claims that painted logs had fooled him into not attacking Johnston made the Union general look silly.

Beginning on March 17 and continuing for the next three weeks into early April, McClellan's army steamed down the Potomac River from Alexandria, bound for Fort Monroe and the Peninsula. The logistics of moving so many men, horses, cannons, and supplies were daunting. Some 389 vessels (ranging from Long Island steamers to Philadelphia ferryboats) transported 121,500 men, 14,592 animals, 1,224 ambulances and wagons, 44 artillery batteries, and countless tons of equipment and supplies. Accompanied by bands and flags, the Army of the Potomac turned its short voyage into a grand procession.

The army's destination already had experienced warfare both on land and on the water—combat that had secured the lower Peninsula for the Union. Almost a year earlier, on May 18–19, 1861, two

United States gunboats dueled with Confederate batteries at Sewell's Point near Norfolk as they attempted to enforce the Union blockade of Hampton Roads, the main shipping lane between the James River and Chesapeake Bay. Capt. Henry Eagle, U.S.N., of USS *Monticello,* with support from USS *Thomas Freeborn,* fired on the batteries, commanded by Capt. Peyton H. Colquitt, on May 18, then alone the next day, until the gunboat exhausted its ammunition. Neither side suffered serious damage.

The next month, on June 10, 1861, the first land battle in present-day Virginia took place on the western edge of Hampton in York County at a community called Big Bethel (an engagement at Philippi, in what is now West Virginia, had occurred on June 3). Maj. Gen. Benjamin F. Butler, commanding at Fort Monroe, sent converging columns from Hampton and Newport News against advanced Confederate outposts at Little and Big Bethel. The 1,500 Confederates, led by colonels John B. Magruder and D. H. Hill, abandoned Little Bethel and fell back to their entrenchments behind Brick Kiln Creek, near Big Bethel Church. The 3,500 Federals, under the immediate command of Brig. Gen. Ebenezer W. Pierce, pursued, attacked frontally along the road, and were repulsed. Crossing downstream, the 5th New York Zouaves attempted to turn the Confederate left flank but were likewise repulsed. The Union forces soon retired to Hampton and Newport News. The Confederates lost 8 men killed and wounded, while Union casualties numbered 79, some from "friendly fire," in this embarrassing Federal debacle that left their opponents in control of the Peninsula.

More to the point for McClellan and his men were the recent naval actions at Hampton Roads on March 8–9, 1862, the very days that Johnston withdrew from

Centreville and Manassas Junction and McClellan found the Potomac River batteries abandoned. In June 1861 the Confederate secretary of the navy, Stephen R. Mallory, began an ambitious project to build an ironclad navy that would overpower its wooden Federal counterpart and break the Union blockade of the Southern coast. The first such vessel, the former USS *Merrimack,* was clad in iron plates forged at the Tredegar Iron Works in Richmond and renamed CSS *Virginia.* Ostensibly taking the ship on a shakedown cruise near Hampton Roads on March 8, its commander, Capt. Franklin Buchanan, instead engaged the Union blockaders there. *Virginia* rammed and sank USS *Cumberland,* then turned on USS *Congress*—which ran aground in its futile effort to escape—and set it afire. Wounded in the latter action, Buchanan was replaced by Lt. Cmdr. Catesby ap R. Jones, who brought *Virginia* out again the next day. This time Lt. John L. Worden's USS *Monitor,* the Union ironclad, came out to meet it. Neither vessel seriously damaged the other in the ensuing "Battle of the Ironclads," although the sailors must have suffered headaches from the din of iron projectiles clanging off the metal hulls. *Virginia* withdrew first, but neither side could claim a victory. Although *Virginia* retained control of the James River, Worden's sturdy defense preserved the Union blockade and made the Hampton Roads anchorage safe for McClellan's convoy.

Soon the area around Fort Monroe and Newport News turned into a great tent city as McClellan's army encamped. The army had scarcely settled in, however, before the general called it out. On April 4 McClellan, with close to 70,000 men and nineteen artillery batteries in the vanguard of his army, set forth on the march to Richmond. All that stood in his way, he estimated—accurately, for the only time in the campaign—was Colonel Magruder with about 14,000 Confederate troops. Magruder had built three lines of earthworks and fortifications that stretched southward across the Peninsula: the first, mostly for show, about a dozen miles west of Fort Monroe; the second and strongest from Yorktown to Warwick River, a tributary of the James, down the Warwick to Lee's Mill, then westward to Skiffe's Creek, which fed into the James River; and the third around a key road junction located just east of Williamsburg between College Creek and Queen's Creek.

If the conflict could have been reduced to a battle of egos only, McClellan would have met his match in "Prince John" Magruder. Born in Port Royal, Virginia, in Caroline County, in 1807, Magruder graduated from West Point in 1830, the year after Robert E. Lee. An artillerist, he served well in the Second Seminole War in Florida and also in the Mexican War. He remained on active duty until Virginia seceded, then resigned his commission in the U.S. Army and accepted one as a colonel in the Confederate infantry.

His reputation for flamboyance preceded him to the Peninsula. Early in his career, the low-paid lieutenant invited several distinguished British officers to an elaborate supper and dazzled them with the fine crystal and silver that he had secretly begged and borrowed for the occasion. Posted in Rhode Island in 1857, Bvt. Lt. Col. Magruder made himself the hit of the social season in Newport.

For all his theatrics, Magruder was an artillerist of some skill. Across the Peninsula he built two lines of earthworks, both bristling with guns (some of them "Quaker cannon," or logs painted black). The first line, a few miles west of Fort Monroe, served principally to delay the Federals; the second, extending south from Yorktown, constituted his principal defensive position.

He built strong batteries at Yorktown and Gloucester Point, across the York River in Gloucester County. Around the site of Cornwallis's defeat, Magruder's men reworked and strengthened the lines created by the British some eighty years earlier (most of the earthworks seen today by tourists at Colonial National Military Park date from the Civil War, not the Revolution, thanks to Magruder). They extended the line south to the Warwick River, a sluggish, boggy stream that flowed east and south to empty into the James River at Mulberry Island. Magruder used the Warwick as part of his defensive work, damming the river to create three additional ponds besides those already at Lee's Mill and Wynn's Mill. The Yorktown line contained some 140 artillery pieces, but only a relative handful of troops were available to man the fourteen-mile-long stretch of batteries, earthworks, and rifle pits.

Magruder's strategy of "defense in depth"—building two lines across the Peninsula—helped confuse McClellan. The Union commander, although apparently brimming with overconfidence in his own skills, readily accepted as true any piece of information, no matter how dubious, that would cast himself in the role of underdog. Before he landed at Fort Monroe, McClellan learned from two of his generals that the Confederates opposing him numbered between 15,000 and 20,000, not far from the actual 14,000.

When the Union commander encountered Magruder's Yorktown defenses on April 5, however, his instinct for caution rose to the surface. Within hours McClellan had convinced himself—based on the inflated claims of a few Confederate prisoners—that he faced a 100,000-man army and that the Yorktown line required a full-scale siege. On the Confederate side, in contrast, Magruder concluded that an attack was imminent and that Johnston, who was coming from Richmond with reinforcements, would be too late. McClellan sent word to his lieutenants to prepare for a siege; the resulting delay afforded Johnston plenty of time to reinforce Magruder.

Even with more troops, however, the Confederates numbered only about 50,000, roughly half the size of McClellan's army, and several weak spots existed in the Yorktown–Warwick River line. On April 16, the only battle near Yorktown occurred when McClellan probed the line at Dam No. 1, or Burnt Chimneys, but failed to follow up on early success and was beaten back. McClellan delayed for two more weeks while he tried unsuccessfully to convince the navy to maneuver past the big Confederate guns at Yorktown and Gloucester Point and ascend the York River to West Point, thereby outflanking the Yorktown–Warwick River line. When the Union commander finally launched his attack on Yorktown on May 4, he found the works empty. After a delay of some twelve hours, he pursued Johnston's rear guard vigorously and caught up to it at Williamsburg the next day.

The clash at Williamsburg was the first major battle of the Peninsula campaign. McClellan's vanguard, consisting of almost 41,000 troops, including two divisions led by Brig. Gen. Joseph Hooker and Brig. Gen. William F. Smith, encountered Johnston's rear guard, some 32,000 men commanded by Maj. Gen. James Longstreet, about two miles southeast of the former colonial capital. A four-mile-long set of earthworks prepared by Magruder two months earlier, with Fort Magruder in their center, protected the Confederates. Smith and Hooker attacked, with the latter striking Fort Magruder, while a brigade led by Brig. Gen. Winfield Scott Hancock marched around Longstreet's left flank and assaulted from the northeast and rear, occupying two redoubts. Longstreet counterattacked and threatened to overwhelm Hooker until Brig. Gen. Philip Kearny's division arrived to stabilize the line. A counterattack against Hancock, led by Brig. Gen. Jubal A. Early, failed because it was hastily prepared and executed piecemeal. Early fell seriously wounded, while Hooker, because of his vigorous though unsuccessful assault on Fort Magruder, earned the nom de guerre "Fighting Joe." During the night, the Confederates slipped away from the field and continued their withdrawal. Federal casualties totaled 2,283, while those of the Confederates amounted to about 1,560.

Johnston posted Maj. Gen. Gustavus W. Smith and his division at Barhamsville, in New Kent County, to guard the Confederate wagon train. On May 6, Brig. Gen. William B. Franklin's division disembarked from Federal troop transports at Eltham's Landing, on the south side of the York River across from West Point, and entrenched about a mile inland. Smith, waiting to see whether Franklin could be lured into the open, sent for reinforcements from Johnston. The next day, with the entire Confederate army nearby, Smith ordered Brig. Gen. W. H. Chase Whiting to lead his division against the Federals. When he learned that the Confederate artillery could not reach the Union gunboats in the York River, and therefore could not protect Whiting's men from Federal bombardment, Smith broke off the advance. Confederate losses amounted to 48, and Union casualties totaled 194. Johnston continued to withdraw, his wagon train secure, and McClellan followed.

When Johnston pulled his army out of Yorktown, he left behind Maj. Gen. Benjamin Huger, commander of the Department of Norfolk, to protect Confederate interests on the south side of the James River. Huger abandoned Norfolk and marched to join Johnston on May 10 when pressed by Federal troops under the command of Maj. Gen. John E. Wool. Now exposed to mass attack by Union artillery and gunboats, Flag Officer Josiah Tattnall, commander of the ironclad CSS *Virginia,* blew up his vessel when he found he could not lighten it enough to escape up the James. His action left the river open to the Union fleet, and a few days later several gunboats steamed toward Richmond to test its defenses.

The Union ironclads *Monitor, Galena,* and *Stevens Battery (Naugatuck)* led the way under Cdr. John Rodgers, accompanied by two wooden warships, *Aroostook* and *Port Royal.* At Drewry's Bluff, located on the south side of the James River in Chesterfield County a few miles below Richmond, heavy guns commanded a sharp turn in the river. The Union flotilla approached the bluff on May 15 to find obstructions, including weighted vessels, sunk in the river, blocking its way. The guns above then opened fire, damaging *Galena,* while some of the Union ships could not elevate their cannons enough to hit the fort. The Federal fleet broke off the attack and retired, leaving Richmond's defenses intact.

Meanwhile, McClellan continued his pursuit of Johnston up the Peninsula. The Confederate commander hastened toward the Chickahominy River, which flowed sluggishly, through swamps and floodplains, southeastwardly to the James. In the dry season the Chickahominy did not look like much, but when the spring rains struck, it flooded easily, becoming a substantial barrier. Johnston wanted the now-swollen river between his army and McClellan's. McClellan, moving slowly, advanced up the parallel Pamunkey River, which joins with the Mattaponi River on the north at West Point to form the York River. By May 15 he was at White House, the home of one of Robert E. Lee's sons, Col. William H. F. "Rooney" Lee, where he established an enormous supply depot. The army then slogged slowly on through rain and mud, or heat and dust, along the Richmond and York River Railroad toward Richmond.

Johnston achieved his goal, crossing most of his army over the Chickahominy and into strong defensive works north and east of Richmond, to counter McClellan. Toward the end of May the Union army trudged into position some six miles east of Richmond. The weary soldiers could see the church spires of the city, and to them as well as to McClellan, victory seemed near at hand.

McClellan crossed his army over the Chickahominy River corps by corps, carefully rebuilding bridges destroyed or damaged by the retreating Confederates. Hearing reports of enemy troops advancing on Hanover Court House, to McClellan's right rear, the Union general dispatched Brig. Gen. Fitz John Porter, a close friend, and one of his two divisions to eliminate the threat. On May 27, at a crossroads two miles south of the courthouse village, Porter encountered Brig. Gen. Lawrence O'B. Branch's brigade and defeated it in a confused, bloody fight. The Federals lost 397 men, the Confederates 930, most of the latter as prisoners.

By May 30 McClellan had crossed two corps, his left wing, over to the south bank of the Chickahominy, while three—his right—remained on the north side. Johnston decided to strike McClellan's left flank before the other corps could cross. Nature aided him in the form of a violent thunderstorm that evening; it washed away two bridges and raised the water level, effectively isolating roughly half of the Union army on the south side of the river. On May 31 Johnston attacked at Seven Pines (Fair Oaks) in three columns. Along

Nine Mile Road to the north, Maj. Gen. James Longstreet was to lead his corps, reinforced by Brig. Gen. W. H. Chase Whiting's division. On Longstreet's right, approaching on Williamsburg Road, would be Maj. Gen. Daniel H. Hill's division, and to Hill's right, Maj. Gen. Benjamin Huger, on Charles City Road. Johnston's plan fell apart, however, as he had issued orders to Longstreet verbally instead of in writing. Longstreet marched down Hill's and Huger's roads instead of his own, entangling his command with Huger's. By the time the units sorted themselves out, the attack was hours late, and the various divisions entered the battle piecemeal rather than in concert. That evening, Johnston rode along his lines as the battle died away; suddenly, a bullet struck him in the right shoulder, followed immediately by a shell fragment in the chest. Command devolved on Maj. Gen. Gustavus W. Smith.

The next day the Confederates mounted a half-hearted attack, but it ended when Longstreet was repulsed. Smith's role as commander of the Army of Northern Virginia ended, too, as President Davis replaced him with Davis's military adviser, Gen. Robert E. Lee. Lee ordered an immediate withdrawal to the previous morning's lines so that his army might recover and reorganize. By the night of June 1, both armies were in their original positions. Each had thrown about 40,000 men into the fight, but the Federals had suffered fewer casualties, about 5,700 to the Confederates' 6,100. McClellan lost no ground, but the sight of all the mangled dead shocked him and, coupled with his vast overinflation of his opponents' numbers, reduced his will to fight.

McClellan harangued the Lincoln administration for more men and began to believe that he was the victim of a Republican plot to undermine his campaign. He also claimed to be heavily outnumbered by the Confederates. Whether in fact he believed this or inflated the numbers to win sympathy and gain reinforcements is subject to debate.

For the next two weeks, while McClellan heated up the telegraph wires to Washington, Lee had his army dig in and improve the trenches protecting Richmond, reinforcing his reputation as the King of Spades. Lee also reconnoitered McClellan's lines, sending Brig. Gen. J. E. B. Stuart on his famous "Ride Around McClellan" on June 12. Stuart's achievement bolstered Confederate spirits and gave Lee the valuable information that McClellan's right flank was not secured by any natural or man-made obstacle.

On June 25 Lee prepared to take the offensive, beginning what would be called the Seven Days' campaign. He had never intended to remain in his earthworks, of course, but instead strengthened them so that Richmond could be defended by a smaller force, leaving most of his army free to attack the Federals in the open. He planned to advance against McClellan's right, consisting of Porter's reinforced corps (about 30,000 men), with some 60,000, including the army of Stonewall Jackson just arrived from its successful Shenandoah Valley campaign. The attack was scheduled for June 26, but the day before it began, McClellan sent a reconnaissance in force westward to probe the Confederate lines and bring Richmond within range of his siege guns. He struck Lee's army at Oak Grove, with Maj. Gen. Samuel P. Heintzelman's corps confronting Huger's four brigades. Most of the fighting took place forward of the Confederate lines; at the end of the day Huger's men were back in their earthworks, having halted the Federal advance.

The unexpected attack did not derail Lee's own plans for the next morning. The Confederates crossed the Chickahominy River and confronted Porter's corps east of Mechanicsville. The attack soon stalled as the Confederate divisions of major generals James Longstreet, A. P. Hill, and Daniel H. Hill awaited the arrival of Jackson, who was to strike Porter from the north, flanking him. Jackson—mentally and physically exhausted from the Valley campaign and confused by Lee's orders—never arrived on the field but stopped just short of his objective. In midafternoon an exasperated A. P. Hill launched his own attack across Beaver Dam Creek near Ellerson's Mill, just east of Mechanicsville. The assault, over swampy ground and against dug-in Federals on a hillside, was repulsed with heavy losses as Porter's men threw back successive Confederate waves: some 1,450 Southern casualties to 360 Federal. Finally the attacks ceased with the darkness. During the night, aware of Jackson's nearness on his right, Porter withdrew on McClellan's orders a few miles south and east to a strong position behind Boatswain's Swamp.

There, at Gaines's Mill, Lee struck again on June 27. Porter arranged his corps in a semicircle on a bluff, and in midafternoon A. P. Hill attacked again and again across the soggy, uneven ground. Longstreet came to Hill's support, on his right, and Jackson and D. H. Hill, late, on Hill's left. Finally, under concerted Confederate attacks in the evening, Porter's line caved in. The Federals withdrew, joining the rest of McClellan's army in its retreat toward the James River. The carnage, however, was dreadful: about 6,800 Union casualties and 8,700 Confederate.

While the battle of Gaines's Mill raged north of the Chickahominy River, to the south occurred the opening phase of the battles of Garnett's and Golding's Farms. Magruder demonstrated against the Union line south of the river at Garnett's Farm. To escape an artillery crossfire, the Federal defenders from Heintzelman's corps pulled back their line along the river. The Confederates attacked again the next morning a short distance away near Golding's (Gouldin's) Farm but were easily repulsed. These sharp probes heightened McClellan's fear that an all-out assault was under way both north and south of the river, and he decided to withdraw, or "change his base," to the James River (ultimately, Harrison's Landing at Berkeley plantation). McClellan justified the move as a strategic withdrawal, but his critics, including his own men, called it the "great skedaddle." By whatever name, it was a retreat, with Lee in hot pursuit.

The aggressive Lee was superbly suited to command an aggressive army, and he cultivated first-rate lieutenants to compensate for any gaps in his knowledge. As an engineer, he was expert in fortification design and also understood the weaknesses of fixed positions; his last assignment in the United States Army had been in the cavalry, so he well knew the use of that arm and now had Jeb Stuart besides; he could rely on the judgment of his other subordinates who were accomplished in the use of infantry and artillery; and he had an instinct for the jugular of his opponent.

Lee's audacious nature contained potential flaws, however, that could lead to disaster in the wrong circumstances. He commanded through discretionary orders, trusting his field officers to adjust to the particular circumstances they faced at the scene yet still achieve tactical success. This style of command suited the independent-minded Stonewall Jackson perfectly, later resulting in one of history's great military partnerships, but other generals needed closer direction, which Lee did not always provide. And when Lee's "blood was up," as some observers put it, his aggressive nature could blind him to weaknesses in his plan of attack, as soon occurred east of Richmond and as later happened at Gettysburg.

On June 29, as McClellan changed his base of operations, Magruder struck the retreating Federals at Savage's Station on the Richmond and York River Railroad north of Williamsburg Road. Lee had hoped for a more vigorous attack to pin the Union army against White Oak Swamp to the south, but Magruder assaulted McClellan's rear guard, commanded by Maj. Gen. Edwin V. Sumner, with only part of his force. Jackson, occupied with operations along the north side of the Chickahominy, did not support Magruder's left, and Huger, moving slowly down Charles City Road, failed to support his right. Sumner held off the Confederate attack, enabling the rest of McClellan's army to escape through the swamp. Confederate casualties amounted to some 400 versus about 900 for the Federals, but when the Southerners swept through Savage's Station the next day, they captured 2,500 wounded or sick Union soldiers left behind at the field hospital in and around the Savage house.

Lee caught up with McClellan at Glendale and White Oak Swamp on June 30, sending Huger's, Longstreet's, and A. P. Hill's divisions against the retreating Union army at Frayser's farm near present-day Glendale, a crossroads in eastern Henrico County. Longstreet's and Hill's attacks penetrated the Union defense near Willis Church, routing Brig. Gen. George A. McCall's division in McClellan's center and capturing McCall. Union counterattacks by Hooker's and Kearny's divisions sealed the break, however, and saved their line of retreat along the Willis Church Road, while felled trees on the Charles City Road stopped Huger's advance and protected the Union center. Jackson, directed to attack the Union right from the north, was delayed by the II Corps and VI Corps divisions at White Oak Swamp.

Confederate Maj. Gen. Theophilus H. Holmes made a feeble attempt to turn the Union left flank at Turkey Bridge but was driven back by Union artillery on Malvern Hill and by Federal gunboats in the James River. Thus, Lee lost his best opportunity to cut off and destroy the Union army piecemeal during its retreat to the James River at a cost of 3,600 casualties to his opponent's 2,800. That night, McClellan established a strong position on Malvern Hill, three miles south of the Frayser's farm battlefield.

The battle of Malvern Hill brought the Seven Days' campaign to a bloody close on July 1. Brig. Gen. Fitz John Porter had prepared a strong defensive position there even as the previous day's battles had raged. Some forty Union cannons lined the crest of the hill, facing north and west, with another 150 in reserve and on the flanks. The rest of McClellan's army moved onto ridges to the east of Malvern Hill to await the Confederate attack. Lee ordered Jackson's divisions into position on the Southern left, with Magruder in the center and Huger on the right. His plans were foiled, though, when Magruder went astray and spent three hours marching and countermarching to the front. Other units arrived on the field piecemeal, and Lee ordered his artillery to engage Porter's; the resulting duel ended in the silencing of the Confederate guns. Lee then fed his infantry into the grinder in one futile frontal assault after another, and the Union artillery chewed them up. Lee suffered more than 5,300 casualties, while McClellan lost some 3,200 men. D. H. Hill summed up the scope of the disaster when he later observed, "It was not war—it was murder."

Against the wishes of McClellan's generals, who hoped to counterattack after their initial success, he ordered the retreat to continue. A member of the Union picket line left behind on Malvern Hill to observe Confederate activities noted, as he gazed down on the field of battle over the bodies of fallen Southerners, that "enough were alive and moving to give the field a singular crawling effect."

During the Seven Days' campaign, the Army of Northern Virginia sustained some 20,000 casualties, and the Union army lost about 16,000. The fighting around Richmond (including Seven Pines) resulted in 20 percent casualties for McClellan and a staggering 30 percent for Lee. Lee's savage attacks, despite their high cost, drove McClellan from the outskirts of Richmond, and Southerners hailed the Confederate general as the city's savior.

It was McClellan, not Lee, who emerged from the 1862 contest with his reputation in tatters. With the largest army then on the planet, he had failed to defeat a smaller force. McClellan's overestimations of his opponent's strength, coupled with his lack of aggressiveness, caused him to lose the campaign although he won most of the battles.

Conversely, Lee won the campaign but lost most of the battles because of poor Confederate coordination, confusing orders, and battle plans that were too complicated for the terrain. Too often, his forces were stalled—as were McClellan's—by swollen rivers, murky swamps, thick undergrowth, and abysmal roads. But Lee and his generals learned much about each other during the Seven Days and, once on better ground, Lee's tactical style would come into its own. More importantly, the new partnership between Lee and Jackson soon would produce an almost unbroken yearlong string of the Confederate commander's greatest offensive victories. ■

In the weeks following Virginia's secession from the Union on April 17, 1861, Confederate authorities sought to challenge Federal control of Hampton Roads, the vital shipping lane between Norfolk and Hampton. The United States Navy was enforcing a blockade to keep Confederate vessels from entering or leaving. Although the Union position at Fort Monroe was impregnable to the Confederate military forces, other points nearby could be fortified to protect Southern ships and bombard Northern vessels. Sewell's Point was one such place.

By mid-May, the Confederates were well along in the construction of a fortification for an artillery battery at Sewell's Point. Before it could be completed, armed with cannons, and fully manned, however, the Union navy attacked the works on May 18–19, 1861.

Capt. Henry Eagle, commanding USS *Monticello,* was patrolling Hampton Roads on Saturday, May 18, when he observed work going on in the unfinished battery at Sewell's Point late in the afternoon. He began firing at the battery but received no fire in return, as the Confederates had not yet mounted cannons in the fort. Soon the steamer USS *Thomas Freeborn,* a converted side-wheel excursion boat, joined the action. *Freeborn* fired twelve to fourteen rounds from its forward gun, a 32-pounder, while *Monticello* probably fired a

DIRECTIONS: I-64 Exit 276B (I-564, Naval Base), about 3.3 miles on I-564, which becomes Admiral Taussig Blvd., to Hampton Blvd. (Rte. 337); n. (right) on Hampton Blvd. through Gate 2 onto Maryland Ave. and continue .8 mile to Massey Hughes Dr.; e. (right) on Massey Hughes Dr. .3 mile to Hampton Roads overlook in parking lot to left.

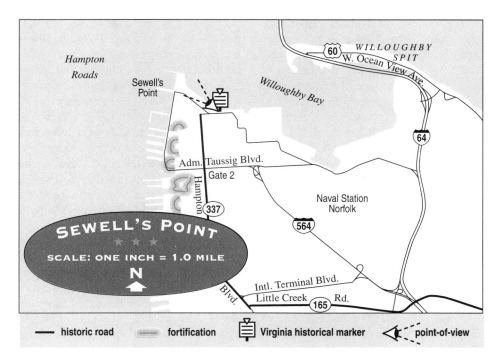

Sewell's Point, now U.S. Naval Station Norfolk, looking west. VIRGINIA DEPARTMENT OF HISTORIC RESOURCES, JOHN S. SALMON

similar number. After causing some slight damage to the works, the two ships retired.

That night, while Eagle remained on patrol, he heard noises coming from the general direction of the battery but could not pinpoint them. He opened fire and the Confederates returned fire.

The sounds Eagle had heard during the night were indeed those of the battery being reinforced and cannons emplaced. Maj. Gen. Walter Gwynn, commander of the Confederate forces guarding the harbor at Norfolk, had ordered the battery garrisoned by the City Light Guards of Columbus, Georgia, Wood's Rifles of Norfolk, a detachment of the Norfolk Juniors, and a detachment of Light Artillery Blues. Capt. Peyton H. Colquitt, of Georgia, commanded the garrison, which succeeded in mounting three 32-pounder cannons and two small rifled guns just before *Monticello* opened fire.

On board *Monticello* Eagle had a more formidable arsenal, including a 10-inch Dahlgren naval gun (only a few ever saw service) as well as two 32-pounder cannons. He also had an impressive array of ammunition, which he unleashed on the

Sewell's Point battery for the next hour and a quarter until at last he ran out. Colquitt reported to Gwynn after the engagement that *Monticello* had fired with great precision, hitting one 32-pounder in the battery. Two courageous members of the City Light Guards, Colquitt and Gwynn later wrote, went outside the battery during the height of the engagement and cleared obstructing sand away from the muzzle of one of Colquitt's guns while shells and shot struck all around them.

Colquitt did not report the exact number of shots fired from the fort, except to say that the stock of ammunition was small and by the end of the engagement only two rounds remained. Five of his rifled cannon shots did strike *Monticello,* however, which was estimated to be half a mile away, as did a few minié bullets. They did no serious damage.

The fragments of a rifled shell that lodged in the hull were sent to Washington, where John A. B. Dahlgren, inventor of the Dahlgren gun and commandant of the navy yard there, analyzed them to determine Confederate artillery capabilities as well as to critique the performance of Federal guns. On May 30 he reported his findings to Gideon Welles, secretary of the navy.

There were only a handful of injuries on both sides as a result of these brief engagements. The battery remained intact, and later, during the first phase of what became known as the "Battle of the Ironclads" in Hampton Roads, it joined in shelling the Union fleet on March 8, 1862, while the CSS *Virginia* (formerly *Merrimack*) wreaked its havoc. Sewell's Point battery was the subject of another Union naval bombardment on May 9, the day before Confederate forces abandoned Norfolk. When the Union army took control the next morning, the Sewell's Point battery was deserted.

No sign of the battery now remains, as the area has been developed by the United States Naval Base there. ■

BIG BETHEL

The first land battle of the Civil War in present-day Virginia took place at a community called Big Bethel on Monday, June 10, 1861.

Union forces in and around Fort Monroe, located at Old Point Comfort and overlooking Hampton Roads, were commanded by Maj. Gen. Benjamin F. Butler, a Massachusetts criminal lawyer and Democrat politician. He was one of Abraham Lincoln's many "political generals"—politicians with little or no military experience who received commissions because of their strong support for the Union and their ability to attract recruits.

Butler first came to Lincoln's attention when, as a brigadier general, he led the 6th Massachusetts Infantry back into Baltimore, a city with strong Southern sympathies whose citizens had rioted the first time the regiment passed through on its way to Washington, D.C. The riot, which occurred on April 19, 1861, resulted in casualties on both sides. Butler returned to the city with his unit on May 13 and dug in on Federal Hill overlooking the harbor. From then on Baltimore was a Federally occupied city, and Union troops moved through it unimpeded. Lincoln rewarded Butler with a promotion to major general and the command of Fort Monroe.

In the spring of 1861, Butler had to ensure that the Confederates on the Peninsula could not impede the free movement of the Union army by building and defending fortifications too close to his own. The Confederates, in fact, were doing just that. On June 6 several regiments marched from Yorktown some fifteen miles southeast and encamped around Big Bethel Church, which was located on the western edge of Hampton in York County, as well as at nearby Little Bethel, about four miles south. At Big Bethel, on the north side of a creek of the same name, they reworked some old fortifications thought to date from the Revolutionary War. Confederate and Union scouting parties confronted each other nearby several times over the next few days, and word of the new works reached Butler, who decided to act.

Butler placed Brig. Gen. Ebenezer W. Pierce in overall command of an expedition to drive the Confederates out of the Big Bethel fortifications. Pierce led some 3,500 men in seven infantry regiments (4th Massachusetts, 1st Vermont, and 1st, 2nd, 3rd, 5th, and 7th New York), as well as several guns from the 2nd U.S. Artillery in a night march that began about 10 P.M. on Sunday, June 9. Col. Abram Duryée, commanding the colorful 5th New York

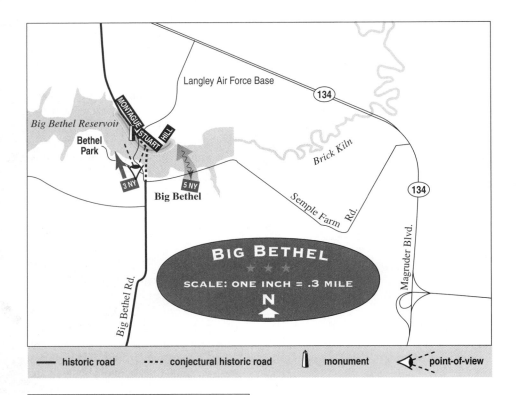

BIG BETHEL
★ ★ ★
SCALE: ONE INCH = .3 MILE
N

—— historic road   ···· conjectural historic road   ⬤ monument   ◁ point-of-view

DIRECTIONS: I-64 Exit 263A (U.S. Rte. 258 South, Mercury Blvd., James River Bridge), s. on U.S. Rte. 258 about 1.4 miles to Big Bethel Rd.; n. (right) on Big Bethel Rd. ("friendly fire" incident occurred just south of intersection) 4.5 miles to Bethel Park on left; w. (left) into Bethel Park if open and continue .3 mile to parking area to observe Confederate position across Big Bethel Reservoir on north shore (now part of Langley Air Force Base and not accessible). Return to park entrance; turn left onto Big Bethel Rd. and continue .2 mile to fenced Confederate cemetery on left (note "Bethel Monument 1905" in cemetery, which is part of Langley Air Force Base and not accessible); turn around at first street on right after cemetery and proceed s. (left) on Big Bethel Rd. .4 mile to Semple Farm Rd.; e. (left) on Semple Farm Rd. 1.75 miles to Rte. 134 (Magruder Blvd.); s. (right) on Magruder Blvd. 3 miles to I-64.

Zouaves, led the march from Hampton, followed by the 3rd New York, which Pierce accompanied. This column proceeded northwest up Big Bethel Road. The remainder of the expedition, commanded by Col. John E. Bendix, was to join Pierce at a road junction, and then the combined force would press on to attack the Confederates at dawn.

The Hampton column had just passed over the New Market Creek bridge at about 12:30 A.M. when a large force suddenly loomed up from the darkness on its left, unlimbered an artillery piece, and opened fire on the 3rd New York. Shouting the assigned password "Boston," but hearing no countersign, the New Yorkers counterattacked. The melee resulted in twenty-one casualties before Pierce discovered that it was the 7th New York that had opened fire in the dark. Apparently Bendix had never received the password and countersign, the men of the 7th were clad in gray uniforms, and they were not wearing the requisite white patches on their jacket sleeves to aid in identification—any of which could have stopped the

Big Bethel battlefield and C.S.A. earthworks, Apr. 4, 1862. VIRGINIA HISTORICAL SOCIETY, RICHMOND, VA.

shooting. About the same time, an advance party of the 5th New York on Big Bethel Road encountered the Confederate picket line, and after a brief exchange of fire, the 5th took several prisoners. All this activity eliminated the element of surprise, and several of Pierce's subordinates advised him to retire to Hampton. He refused, and the expedition ground ahead.

Four miles up the road, at Big Bethel, the Confederates prepared for the attack they knew was coming. Col. John B. Magruder commanded the garrison, which consisted of Col. Daniel H. Hill's 1st North Carolina Infantry, Lt. Col. William D. Stuart's 3rd Virginia Infantry, Maj. Edwin B. Montague's Virginia Battalion, and Maj. George W. Randolph's howitzer company. The Confederates numbered about 1,500 against Pierce's 3,500.

At about 8 A.M. on Monday, June 10, the advance guard of the 5th New York attacked pickets south of the principal Confederate works at Big Bethel. Pierce deployed the rest of the 5th to the right of the road, about 800 yards from the works. The attack got under way at about 9:30 but soon stalled under heavy fire from Confederate artillery and muskets. Pierce ordered the 3rd New York to the left, to press the Confederate right, but one company of the regiment got separated from the rest by a ditch covered with overgrowth. When the company began to reemerge from the tangle, bayonets gleaming in the morning sunlight, their comrades mistook it for Confederate reinforcements and retreated. By then Pierce had decided that the fortifications were too strong and ordered a withdrawal.

The Union attack failed largely because of the incompetence of its leaders. Regiments attacked piecemeal, first against one Confederate flank and then the other, and the defenders easily repulsed the assaults. Butler tried feebly to put a good face on the debacle in his report by pointing out mistakes and what could be learned from them.

On the Confederate side, Magruder became the hero of the hour (although Hill had actually done most of the work). In Magruder's own eyes and those of his admirers, he had dealt the enemy a significant blow—unaware that the Federals had dealt themselves the first fatal blow back at the New Market Creek bridge in the middle of the previous night.

The casualties in this sorry affair were light: 8 Confederates dead and wounded to 79 Federals (21 from their own fire).

Most of the Big Bethel battlefield, as well as the Little Bethel site and the scene of the unfortunate engagement at New Market Creek, has vanished beneath residential and commercial development. Fragments of the battlefield remain but are not readily identifiable. ■

HAMPTON ROADS

At the beginning of the Civil War both sides sought to protect their own navies and dominate their opponent's by constructing vessels clad in iron. The Confederates and Federals each raced to complete the first ironclad, a race the Southerners won.

When the Union navy abandoned Norfolk on April 20, 1861, it burned the nation's principal shipyard, the Gosport Navy Yard, including buildings, wharves, and vessels. One of the latter, *Merrimack,* did not burn completely; its hull and engines were salvaged to build the first Confederate ironclad. The Tredegar Iron Works in Richmond cast the two-inch-thick plates for the vessel, renamed *Virginia.* The new ship's hull was topped by a casemate, with its sides at a forty-degree angle to deflect shot and ten heavy guns poking through openings in the casemate's walls. The prow of the ship was clad in iron and sharply pointed to serve as a ram, while much of the rest of the hull was invisible below the waterline. When it was launched on February 17, 1862, *Virginia* crawled ominously through the water and resembled nothing any sailor had ever seen before, looking like "a huge half-submerged crocodile." Capt. Franklin Buchanan, a forty-six-year U.S. Navy veteran,

commanded *Virginia.*

Virginia's construction prompted a wave of hysteria in the North, where attacks by the vessel were expected every day. To counter the threat, the U.S. Navy built USS *Monitor,* launched on January 30, 1862. It was even more peculiar looking than *Virginia* and was described as resembling "a cheesebox on a raft." Its hull indeed resembled a streamlined raft, 172 feet long by $41\frac{1}{2}$ feet wide. The "cheesebox"—an armored turret—contained two 11-inch smoothbore Dahlgren guns. Lt. John L. Worden commanded *Monitor* with ten officers and a crew of forty-seven. *Monitor* left New York for Hampton Roads on March 6.

The next day, in Norfolk, *Virginia* took on munitions, including all the powder its commander could get. On March 8, a Saturday, Buchanan steamed down the Elizabeth River at 11 A.M., ostensibly to test *Virginia* in open waters. Buchanan had another idea for a shakedown cruise, however. As he steamed into Hampton Roads, he could turn east and confront several Union ships at Fort Monroe, including *Roanoke, Minnesota,* and *St. Lawrence,* or he could head up the James River toward Newport News, where the fifty-gun *Congress* and the thirty-gun *Cumberland* were anchored some seven miles above Fort Monroe. He decided to turn upriver. At the first sight of *Virginia,* all three of the large Union warships at Fort Monroe ran aground in their frantic efforts to get under way without the assistance of tugs. In contrast, the Federal captains and their crews in Newport News seemed strangely oblivious to the odd vessel churning its way upriver toward them. After an hour and a half, *Virginia* finally reached the anchorage.

Buchanan made *Cumberland* his first target. The opening shots were fired by a small picket boat and Union shore batteries as *Virginia* made a wide, slow turn in the river to head toward its objective. It scored a direct hit on *Cumberland* with its first shot, then exchanged broadsides with *Congress* as it steamed past, knocking out several of the Federal ship's guns and killing entire gun crews. The Union gunners' shot just bounced off *Virginia*'s heavily greased iron plates, which sizzled

under the barrage. Implacably, *Virginia* rammed its iron beak into *Cumberland,* reversing its engines even as it attacked. When it pulled its prow out and backed away, *Virginia* left its iron ram stuck in its victim's side. *Cumberland* soon settled to the bottom of the shallow riverbed, its guns blazing and its ensign flying.

To attack *Congress,* Buchanan first had to steam some distance upriver and turn *Virginia* around. Meanwhile, three wooden ships of the Confederate James River Squadron joined in the attack, and they and *Virginia* blasted the Union vessel with deadly fire. Attempting to get away, *Congress* ran aground in a manner that prevented its crew from firing broadsides in return, and soon its ensign came down in surrender. When two ships of the James River Squadron pulled alongside the *Congress* to remove prisoners and wounded, however, Union infantry and artillery on shore fired on them, wounding several

Battle of the ironclads Monitor *(foreground) and* Virginia, *Mar. 9, 1862.* PAINTING BY XANTHUS SMITH. VIRGINIA WAR MUSEUM, NEWPORT NEWS, VA.

DIRECTIONS: I-664 Exit 5 (35th St.), w. about .3 mile on 35th St. to West Ave.; s. (left) on West Ave. .3 mile to Christopher Newport Park between 27th and 26th Sts. Park and walk to Virginia Civil War Trails marker (*Congress* and *Cumberland* Overlook). Return to 28th St.; e. (right) on 28th St. 1.7 miles to Oak Ave.; s. (right) on Oak Ave. .7 mile to 16th St.; e. (left) on 16th St. .3 mile across bridge to Newport News historical marker (*Monitor-Merrimack*) at *Monitor-Merrimack* Overlook Park; turn right into parking lot and Virginia Civil War Trails marker; return w. (left) on 16th St. to Oak St.; turn n. (right) .6 mile to 27th St.; e. (right) onto 27th and then w. (left) onto Parish Ave. and enter Greenlawn Memorial Park; follow Civil War Tour signs straight ahead n. and then w. (left) and s. to Virginia Civil War Trails marker for Newport News P.O.W. Camp; return s. to cemetery park entrance (driving toward U.S. flag); w. (right) out of cemetery onto 28th St. 1.3 miles to Jefferson Ave.; s. (left) on Jefferson Ave. two blocks to 26th St.; w. (right) on 26th St. to I-664.

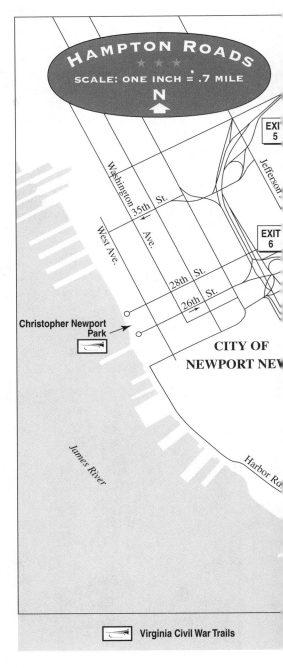

Virginia Civil War Trails

sailors and driving the Confederate vessels off. This breach of naval etiquette so angered Buchanan, who was wounded himself, that he ordered *Congress* set afire with red-hot shot and destroyed.

By this time it was 5 P.M., an hour from sunset. Lt. Catesby ap R. Jones relieved Buchanan and steamed *Virginia* back downriver to Norfolk. Not long after, *Monitor* arrived at Fort Monroe, where Worden learned of the day's events. He decided to stand by *Minnesota* and defend it from further attack by *Virginia*.

The next morning, March 9, *Virginia* got under way just after dawn and steamed directly toward the Union fleet at Fort Monroe. As soon as it was sighted, *Monitor* brought its steam up and prepared for combat. Shortly after 8 A.M., the first shot from *Virginia* whistled by on its way to *Minnesota*. *Monitor* steamed out, cut its engines next to *Virginia*, rotated the turret, and opened fire. The "Battle of the Ironclads" was under way.

For the next four hours, the two vessels conducted a slow, lumbering dance: circling away, coming close enough almost to touch, blasting at each other's armor,

and then circling away again for another try. In addition to the constant shelling, each ship tried to ram the other. Eventually the strain began to tell on *Virginia*, which began leaking. In addition, a few of its iron

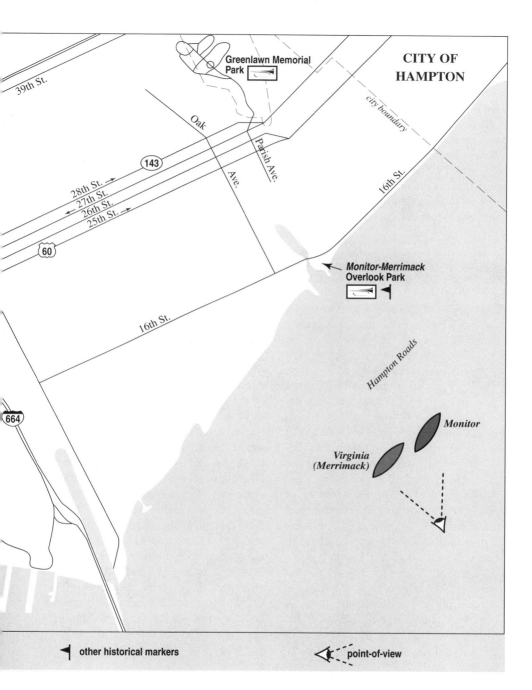

39th St.

Greenlawn Memorial Park

CITY OF HAMPTON

city boundary

Oak

Parish Ave.

143

Ave.

28th St.
27th St.
26th St.
25th St.

16th St.

60

Monitor-Merrimack Overlook Park

16th St.

664

Hampton Roads

Monitor

Virginia (Merrimack)

◀ other historical markers

◀┄┄ point-of-view

plates began to separate from their wooden backing. Finally, shortly after noon, *Virginia* fired at *Monitor*'s turret just as Worden looked through the observation slit. Shell fragments flew through the opening, wounding Worden in the face and temporarily blinding him. As crew members tended to him, *Monitor,* which had been steaming toward Fort Monroe at that point in the engagement, continued for some distance before it could be turned around. By then Jones, thinking *Monitor* had broken off the action, kept *Virginia* on its course for Norfolk. Officially, the engagement ended in a draw.

It has been written that the battle demonstrated the obsolescence of the old wooden navy. Actually, the one-sided engagement of the day before offered a better illustration of that fact. The battle between *Virginia* and *Monitor* did prove, however, the necessity of developing a new set of tactics appropriate to combat involving opposing ironclads.

The two days of naval action off Newport News and Hampton cost the United States 409 killed, wounded, and captured, and 24 casualties for the Confederates.

Viewing points on shore enable the visitor to see the sites of the two actions. Hampton Roads remains a busy shipping channel, while Newport News continues to be one of the country's busiest shipbuilding facilities. ■

YORKTOWN (DAM No. 1)

On April 4, 1862, Maj. Gen. George B. McClellan moved his army easily through Col. John B. Magruder's first line of defense toward Yorktown. The next day, however, he confronted Magruder's Yorktown–Warwick River line and believed the claim of captured Confederates that the line was manned by some 40,000 troops and that Gen. Joseph E. Johnston's arrival with 60,000 more was imminent. McClellan instantly accepted these unsubstantiated figures (Magruder's line prevented close observation by the Federals to verify or refute this assessment) and despite urgent orders from Pres. Abraham Lincoln and to the dismay of his army—and to the astonishment of Magruder, Gen. Joseph E. Johnston, and Gen. Robert E. Lee—McClellan ordered the Army of the Potomac to entrench, dig works paralleling those of Magruder's, and besiege Yorktown.

For the next ten days, McClellan's soldiers wielded shovels instead of muskets. The delay enabled Johnston's reinforcements to arrive in numbers sufficient to swell Magruder's army to some 35,000 by mid-month—though even that was barely adequate to cover the Yorktown–Warwick River line.

Finally, on April 16 McClellan probed Magruder's lines with an attack on one of his newly created strong points on the Warwick River at Dam No. 1, near Lee's Mill. The Confederates were steadily improving their position on the west bank of the river overlooking the earthen dam and the shallow pond behind it. Brig. Gen. Howell Cobb, with three regiments, protected the dam, with Col. Thomas R. R. Cobb (General Cobb's brother) and his Georgia Legion plus six other regiments close by. McClellan issued confusing orders to Brig. Gen. William F. "Baldy" Smith: Hamper the enemy in completing the works, but do not bring on a general engagement. Smith moved Capt. Romeyn B. Ayres's battery into abandoned Confederate earthworks near the ruins of the Garrows house on the east side of the river and then, because he was uncertain of his opponent's strength, ordered three infantry brigades into position to protect his artillery.

On the morning of Wednesday, April 16, Capt. Thaddeus Mott's battery moved closer to the river on the Union side from its rearward position. At about 8 A.M. he shelled the Confederates, who scurried for

Dam No. 1, photographed from U.S. position soon after battle; C.S.A. works in background have been preserved. VERMONT HISTORICAL SOCIETY, MONTPELIER, VT.

shelter. Brig. Gen. William T. H. Brooks, commanding the Vermont Brigade, sent skirmishers forward near the riverbank to bring musket fire to bear on the Confederates. By afternoon it appeared that the defenders were withdrawing. McClellan arrived on the scene for a quick visit and told Smith to gain a foothold across the river if in fact they departed.

By 3 P.M., four companies of the 3rd Vermont Regiment under Capt. Fernando C. Harrington, picked their way across the dam, routed the remaining defenders, and entered the abandoned Confederate works nearest the river while Union artillery boomed in support. Behind the Confederate lines, unseen by Brooks or Harrington, Brig. Gen. Howell Cobb organized a defense. Forming a battle line with the four regiments and Col. Thomas Cobb's Georgia Legion from left to right, he attacked the Vermonters, who stubbornly held their position in the Confederate rifle pits for about an hour.

Frantically, Harrington signaled Col. Breed Hyde, commander of the 3rd Vermont, for the reinforcements that Brooks had promised if the captain became engaged. Hyde sent word to Brooks, but received no response—and no reinforcements. Harrington slowly withdrew across the dam, suffering additional casualties as the men retreated. Baldy Smith then ordered the 6th Vermont, with artillery support, to attack Confederate positions downstream from the dam while the 4th Vermont feinted an assault on the dam itself. The ruse, which got under way at about 5 P.M., failed as the 6th Vermont came under heavy Confederate fire and retired. Some wounded men fell and drowned as they attempted to wade back across to the east side of the shallow pond.

The battle of Dam No. 1 cost the Federals 35 dead and 121 wounded, while the Confederates suffered between 60 and 75 casualties. The entire episode was, from the Union perspective, pointless. On the other

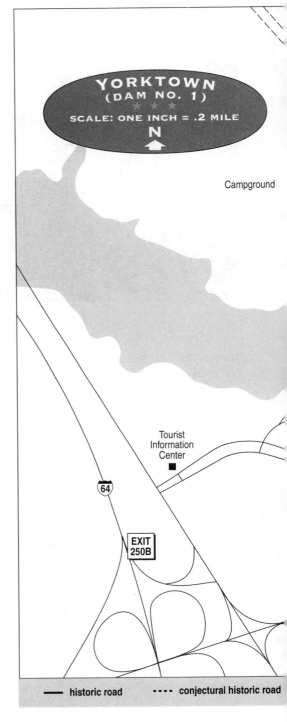

side, the Confederate defenders had the satisfaction of repelling two separate attacks on their works by the man who had proclaimed himself the Savior of the Union.

As April wound down and the Federal siege lines neared completion, Johnston prepared to withdraw his 57,000 men from the Yorktown–Warwick River line and fall back toward Richmond. He established the final withdrawal deadline as the night of Saturday, May 3, and started the Confederate wagon trains northwestward. When escaped slaves reported the movement to McClellan's headquarters, the Union commander refused to believe them. His personal detective, Allan Pinkerton, reconfirmed McClellan's illusions that not only would Johnston stand and fight, but he would do so with an army conservatively numbered between 100,000 and 120,000.

McClellan set May 5 as the date he would flatten the Yorktown–Warwick River line with a colossal artillery bombardment, followed by an almost bloodless storming of the works at Yorktown. After dark on May 3, however, the Confederates let loose a bombardment of their own. Suddenly the guns fell silent and remained quiet for the rest of the night. At first light, Brig. Gen. Samuel P. Heintzelman went up in an observation balloon to find the Confederate earthworks empty.

Some of the remaining trench lines built by Magruder and McClellan still stand in Colonial National Military Park at

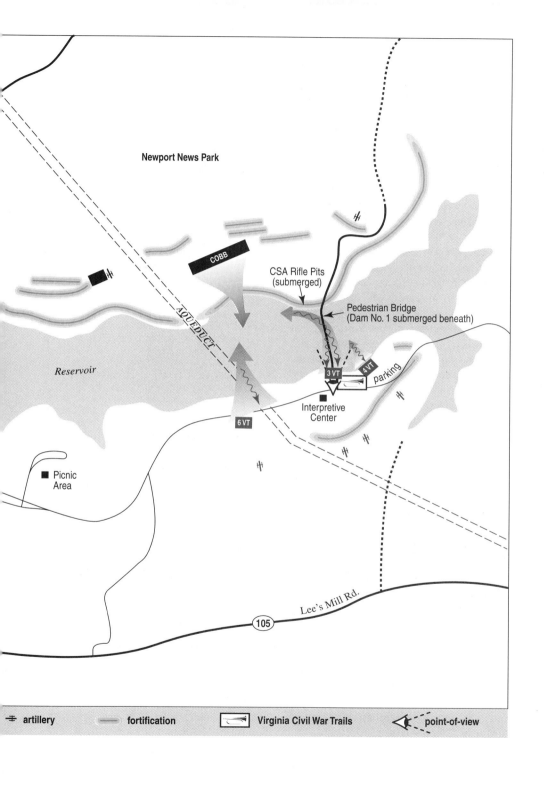

Newport News Park

CSA Rifle Pits
(submerged)

Pedestrian Bridge
(Dam No. 1 submerged beneath)

COBB

AQUEDUCT

Reservoir

3 VT

4 VT

parking

6 VT

Interpretive
Center

Picnic
Area

Lee's Mill Rd.

105

⊹ artillery   fortification   Virginia Civil War Trails   point-of-view

Yorktown. Others are on private property south of the town. Most of the site of the battle of Dam No. 1, as well as several miles of well-preserved earthworks, survives in Newport News Park. The dam itself, along with the Confederate rifle pits occupied during the battle by the companies of the 3rd Vermont Regiment, is submerged under the waters of the Newport News Reservoir. ∎

WILLIAMSBURG

Gen. Joseph E. Johnston's sudden evacuation of the Yorktown–Warwick River line on the night of May 3, 1862, so stunned Maj. Gen. George B. McClellan that it caught him unprepared to mount a pursuit. Hastily his troops threw their gear together and marched off to begin the chase, but Johnston had a twelve-hour start.

McClellan himself was overjoyed that Yorktown had fallen with no bloodshed, but others thought that the capture of the little town was far from a great victory. McClellan's huge army, after laying formal siege for a month, had taken an antique village while Johnston and his force had escaped.

On May 4 McClellan sent Brig. Gen. George Stoneman and his cavalry in pursuit of Johnston's rear guard, followed by several infantry divisions, about half of his army. He also ordered Brig. Gen. William B. Franklin and his 11,300-man division, which had just disembarked from transport vessels at Yorktown, to re-embark and sail up the York River, then land and cut off Johnston's retreat. It took two days just to get all the men and equipment back on board.

Stoneman, meanwhile, nipped at Johnston's heels. Johnston's army marched in columns up two roads leading to Williamsburg; Brig. Gen. J. E. B. Stuart and his cavalry formed the rear guard. Periodically, Stoneman caught up with Stuart, skirmished, then fell back.

The rainy morning of Monday, May 5 found Johnston's progress, already slow

DIRECTIONS: I-64 Exit 242A (Rte. 199 West, Williamsburg, Busch Gardens), w. on Rte. 199 about .7 mile to U.S. Rte. 60 West/Williamsburg exit; turn right onto exit to Rte. 60; w. (left) on U.S. Rte. 60 West .4 mile to Virginia Civil War Trails marker on left; continue .4 mile farther to state historical markers W-43 (Battle of Williamsburg) and W-44 (Magruder's Defenses); continue another .3 mile to Fort Magruder Inn and Conference Center on left; park and walk through lobby to earthwork remnant behind building; leave Center, w. (left) on U.S. Rte. 60 West .2 mile to Quarterpath Rd.; left on Quarterpath Rd. (Quarterpath Park on the right followed by state historical markers W-37, Peninsula Compaign, and W-42, Quarterpath Road, on right), and continue .3 mile to last entrance to park; turn right into parking lot and right again to three markers: Virginia Civil War Trails markers for Williamsburg line and Quarterpath Road and City of Williamsburg / Williamsburg Civil War Round Table marker for the Battle of Williamsburg; return to U.S. Rte. 60 West and continue w. on U.S. Rte. 60 .5 mile to Page St.; n. (right) on Page St. .3 mile to Second St.; e. (right) on Second St. .5 mile to Rte. 143; e. (bear right) on Rte. 143 .5 mile to Rte. 641 (Penniman Rd.); e. (left) on Rte. 641 .1 mile to Hubbard Lane; n. (left) on Hubbard Lane through a residential area 1 mile to Lakeshead Dr.; e. (right) on Lakeshead Dr. and pass a sign for New Quarter Park; continue 1.4 miles to Virginia Civil War Trails marker for Redoubt #12 on right just before park entrance; return to Hubbard Lane and Rte. 641 (Penniman Rd.); left on Rte. 641 .4 mile to juncture of Queens Creek Rd. (Rte. 642) and Rte. 641 (on right a Virginia Civil War Trails Fort Magruder marker); continue .2 mile and veer right onto Rte. 642 (Oak Drive); continue .3 mile to Rte. 677 (Government Rd.); right on Rte. 677 .5 mile to Rte. 143 (Merrimac Trail); left on Rte. 143 .2 mile to Rte. 199 and return to I-64.

because of muddy roads, reduced to a crawl. To buy time for the rest of his army, Johnston decided to detach part of it to make a stand at Magruder's third line of defense east of Williamsburg.

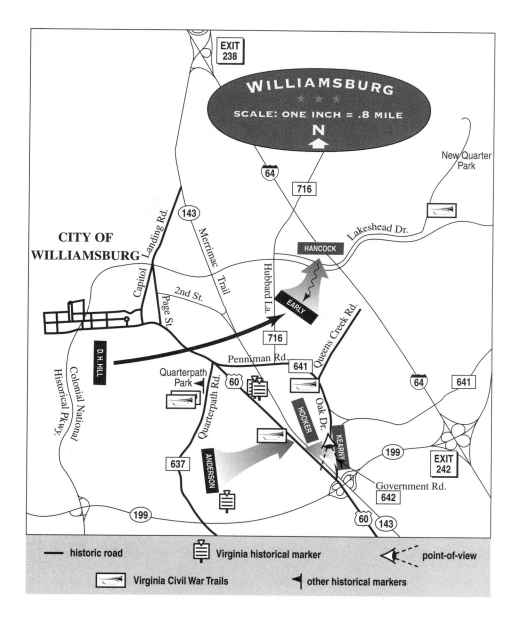

EXIT
238

WILLIAMSBURG
★ ★ ★
SCALE: ONE INCH = .8 MILE
N

New Quarter
Park

64

716

143

Lakeshead Dr.

CITY OF
WILLIAMSBURG

Landing Rd.

Merrimac Trail

Hubbard La.

HANCOCK

Capitol

2nd St.

Page St.

EARLY

Queens Creek Rd.

716

Penniman Rd.

641

D. H. HILL

Quarterpath
Park

Quarterpath Rd.

60

64

641

Oak Dr.

HOOKER

Colonial National Historical Pkwy.

637

ANDERSON

KEARNY

199

EXIT
242

Government Rd.

642

199

60   143

— historic road

Virginia historical marker

point-of-view

Virginia Civil War Trails

other historical markers

Maj. Gen. James Longstreet and his division marched into the Williamsburg line while the remainder of the army moved through the old colonial capital. Col. John B. Magruder's defenses consisted of a large earthen fortification—Fort Magruder—located near the intersection of the Lee's Mill and Yorktown roads, as well as a series of earthworks and redoubts stretching west and south to the branches of College Creek, and north and east to the tributaries of Queen's Creek. Longstreet concentrated his force around Fort Magruder, knowing that McClellan's army was advancing up the Lee's Mill and Yorktown roads.

Brig. Gen. Edwin V. Sumner, a sixty-five-year-old cavalryman thought to have

Kearny leading his division to Hooker's aid through the rain at Williamsburg. LIBRARY OF CONGRESS

risen well above his competence level, commanded the half of the Army of the Potomac that pursued Johnston. Two corps commanders, Maj. Gen. Erasmus Keyes and Maj. Gen. Samuel P. Heintzelman, served under Sumner with parts of their corps. Keyes had Brig. Gen. William F. "Baldy" Smith's division, while Heintzelman's command consisted of Brig. Gen. Joseph Hooker's division with Brig. Gen. Philip Kearny's division trailing in the mud.

"Fighting Joe" Hooker's skirmishers and artillery opened the battle at about 7 A.M., but the artillery soon fell back as Longstreet's batteries responded with a heavy fire from Fort Magruder and nearby redoubts. Hooker then increased his volume of fire with a second battery and waited for Smith's division, approaching along the Yorktown road to the north, to follow the sound of battle and support Hooker's right. Smith never arrived. Sumner, convinced that the Confederates would leave their fortifications and attack him on the Yorktown road, halted Smith

more than a mile from the beleaguered Hooker.

Longstreet did in fact leave his works and attack, but he sent Brig. Gen. Cadmus M. Wilcox and his brigade against Hooker, not Sumner and Smith. Hooker's line threatened to collapse under pressure from Wilcox's reinforced command. Heintzelman ordered several regimental bands, about to be trampled by their retreating comrades, to play "Yankee Doodle" to rally the troops. The bands played, the retreat slowed, and suddenly Kearny and his division arrived to turn the tide, pushing Wilcox back toward Fort Magruder.

To the north, Hancock opened fire on Longstreet's flank at long range. Maj. Gen. D. H. Hill detached Brig. Gen. Jubal A. Early's brigade and posted it on the green at the College of William and Mary. Now, accompanied by Hill, Early hustled northeast toward the sound of Hancock's cannon.

Early divided his force, leading two Virginia and two North Carolina regiments through thick, dripping woods toward Hancock while Hill accompanied one of Early's North Carolina regiments on the right. However, instead of reconnoitering to pinpoint his opponent's position, Early simply moved toward the sound of cannon fire, emerged from the woods, and found to his dismay that he had not flanked Hancock but had landed squarely in front of his guns. Rather than pull back, however, Early sent one regiment after another ahead in bloody, fruitless charges.

It was almost 5 P.M. when Early began his assault, leading his old regiment, the 24th Virginia, in person. Soon he fell wounded with a bullet through the shoulder. Hill came out of the woods with the 5th North Carolina and ordered a charge. Fortunately it dawned on him that his 1,200 men were facing some 3,400 Union soldiers and 8 cannons in a strong position. He called off the assault. But the Union commander also ordered a charge, and the Confederates took heavy casualties, almost 70 percent, as they fell back.

As Hancock swept Early's brigade before him and Kearny pushed Wilcox's reinforced command into the Confederate defenses, McClellan arrived at Sumner's headquarters. The firing soon quieted, and McClellan never saw any of the actual fighting—although his generals had sent messengers to him in Yorktown throughout the day with urgent requests for him to come to the front.

The Union army engaged some 41,000 men to the Confederates' 32,000 and suffered more casualties: about 2,300 versus 1,600. Longstreet slipped away in the night and continued with Johnston on his march toward Richmond. The next morning, Union soldiers resumed their pursuit of Johnston while Franklin's flotilla at last got under way on the York River.

Most of the Williamsburg battlefield has been buried under urban sprawl as the town expanded to serve the needs of tourists. A section of Fort Magruder has been preserved and protected in a parklike setting by the local chapter of the United Daughters of the Confederacy. Large portions of the core areas of the battlefield—Hancock's position, including Redoubts 11, 12, and 13—remain largely intact though inaccessible. ▧

ELTHAM'S LANDING

Early in the morning of May 6, 1862, a Tuesday, Brig. Gen. William B. Franklin and his division, about 11,300 men, pulled away from the docks at Yorktown and steamed twenty miles up York River in a belated attempt to intercept Johnston's line of retreat.

Franklin's destination was Eltham's Landing on the south bank of the Pamunkey River across from West Point, the small-town terminus of the Richmond and York River Railroad. The town stood on a spit of land flanked by the Mattaponi River to the east and the Pamunkey to the west; there the two streams joined to form the York.

A road led south from the landing, up over a bluff and through woods to other ridges beyond, to the settlement of Barhamsville some half a dozen miles south of the river. The road to New Kent Court House intersected the landing road, where most of Johnston's army passed by on the afternoon of May 6 as Franklin disembarked. Confederate pickets stationed on the heights overlooking the landing

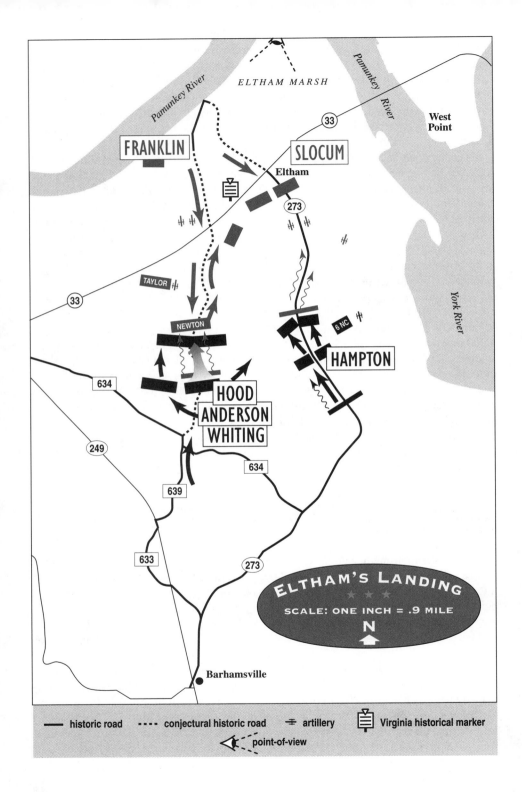

FRANKLIN

SLOCUM

West Point

Eltham

TAYLOR

NEWTON

6 NC

HAMPTON

HOOD
ANDERSON
WHITING

ELTHAM MARSH

Pamunkey River

Pamunkey River

York River

33

273

33

634

249

639

634

633

273

Barhamsville

ELTHAM'S LANDING
★ ★ ★
SCALE: ONE INCH = .9 MILE

N

—— historic road   ---- conjectural historic road   ╪ artillery   Virginia historical marker

◁--- point-of-view

DIRECTIONS: I-64 Exit 227 (State Rte. 30, West Point, Toano), n. on State Rte. 30 about 2.3 miles to Barhamsville and Rte. 633; n. (right) on Rte. 633 .5 mile to Rte. 273 (Farmer's Dr.); n.e. (right) on Rte. 273 5.2 miles to State Rte. 30/33 at Eltham; w. (left) .4 mile to state historical marker WO-31, Peninsular Campaign, on right; return e. on State Rte. 30/33 to Rte. 273; return 3.7 miles to Rte. 634 (Polish Town Rd.); w. (right) on Rte. 634 1.4 miles to Rte. 639/634 (Broad/Mt. Nebo Rd.); n.w. (right) on Rte. 639 3 miles through Hood's position to right-angle left turn at Henrico Co. Regional Jail Farm; return on Rte. 639 .8 mile to State Rte. 30; left on State Rte. 30 1.5 miles to Barhamsville and Rte. 633/30; continue 2.3 miles to I-64. Alternative route: I-64 Exit 220 (State Rte. 33 East, West Point), n.e. on State Rte. 33 2.6 miles to State Rte. 30; continue n.e. on State Rte. 30/33 2.6 miles to state historical marker WO-31, Peninsular Campaign, on left; continue .4 mile to Rte. 273; s. on Rte. 273 3.7 miles to Rte. 634 (Polish Town Rd.) and continue as above. ·

Eltham Marsh and Eltham's Landing site viewed from north bank of York River. VIRGINIA DEPARTMENT OF HISTORIC RESOURCES, JOHN S. SALMON

fired random shots, but Franklin continued unloading his division and its supplies on a specially constructed, 400-foot-long pontoon wharf, finishing the task by torchlight late in the evening. Light skirmishing continued in the woods until 10 P.M.

Johnston assigned Maj. Gen. Gustavus W. Smith to block Franklin's advance to Barhamsville. Smith accordingly posted Brig. Gen. W. H. Chase Whiting's division and Col. Wade Hampton's Legion on the Eltham's Landing road. On the morning of May 7 Franklin placed one brigade on both sides of the road in the woods, with parts of two other brigades, as well. Brig. Gen. John Bell Hood and his Texas Brigade, supported by Hampton with two regiments on Hood's right, pushed forward on the landing road into the woods, driving the skirmish line back toward the river. Another brigade followed Hood on his left, and soon the Union line had retreated down onto the plain, under cover of Federal gunboats.

Whiting attempted to shell the gunboats, but as they were out of his range while he was within theirs, he wisely abandoned the effort and disengaged from Franklin at about 2 P.M. The Federals moved back into the woods after the Confederates retired, but neither side made further efforts to renew the engagement. This small skirmish protected Johnston's trains and enabled him to continue his retreat unmolested. Franklin suffered 194 casualties and Whiting 48.

Although residential development covers some of the engagement area, the majority of the battlefield retains a high degree of integrity. Woodlands, farms, and historic road traces remain as landmarks. ■

DREWRY'S BLUFF

Gen. Joseph E. Johnston's evacuation of the Yorktown–Warwick River line on May 3, 1862, exposed the lower James River and Norfolk to Federal occupation. Only the Confederate ironclad *Virginia* stood in the way, but its great weight prevented its commander, Flag Officer Josiah Tattnall, from escaping up the river toward Richmond. When Maj. Gen. Benjamin Huger and his garrison were forced to evacuate Norfolk on May 10, 1862, Tattnall decided to scuttle the ship. He ran it aground near the mouth of the Elizabeth River and set it afire. Just before dawn on May 11, the flames reached the ship's magazines, and *Virginia* exploded with a roar. Now no Confederate vessel could prevent the Union fleet from sailing all the way to Richmond.

DIRECTIONS: Recommend first visiting the Richmond National Battlefield Park Visitor Center (open 9–5 daily) at Tredegar Iron Works in downtown Richmond: I-95 Exit 74C (U.S. Rte. 33 West/U.S. Rte. 250 West, Broad St.) and follow blue-and-green signs to visitor center, Brown's Island, and Belle Isle, w. on Broad St. about .4 mile (5 blocks) to 8th St.; s. (left) on 8th St. 5 blocks to Canal St.; w. (right) on Canal St. 3 blocks to 5th St.; s. (left) on 5th St. 2 blocks to Tredegar St.; w. (right) on Tredegar Street .1 mile to visitor center and parking lot. Visit the National Park Service Web site at nps.gov/parks.html for a virtual tour of this and other national parks. To visit the battlefield directly: I-95 Exit 64 (Willis Rd., Rte. 613), follow brown National Park Service signs for Drewry's Bluff/Fort Darling Unit w. on Rte. 613 (Willis Rd.) about .4 mile to U.S. Rte. 1/301; n. (right) on U.S. Rte. 1/301 .4 mile to state historical marker S-8, Battle of Drewry's Bluff, then continue .2 mile to Rte. 656 (Bellwood Rd.); e. (right) on Rte. 656 .6 mile under I-95 to Rte. 1435 (Fort Darling Rd.); n. (left) on Rte. 1435 .35 mile to Richmond National Battlefield Park Drewry's Bluff / Fort Darling Unit entrance on right.

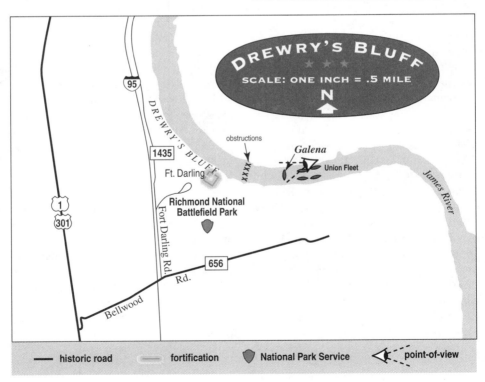

Battle of Drewry's Bluff as drawn by a U.S. sailor, showing (left to right) Galena, Monitor, Aroostook, Port Royal, *and* Naugatuck. U.S. NAVAL HISTORICAL CENTER

Led by Cdr. John Rodgers, the Union ironclads *Monitor, Galena,* and *Stevens Battery (Naugatuck),* accompanied by two wooden warships, *Aroostook* and *Port Royal,* soon steamed upriver and bombarded Confederate fortifications. At 6:30 A.M. on Thursday, May 15, the squadron came within sight of the principal Confederate stronghold on the river, just seven miles below Richmond: Drewry's Bluff.

Known to the Federals as Fort Darling, the works commanded mile-long reaches of the James River both up- and downstream. Eight cannons were posted in the works, including a battery and five naval guns, some from CSS *Virginia.* The gunboat CSS *Patrick Henry,* just upriver, added its gun to those in the fort, while sharpshooters gathered on the riverbanks. Below the bluff and a short distance downstream, sunken hulks, submerged pilings, and other debris obstructed the channel and prevented the passage of warships.

At 7:45 A.M., Rodgers approached in *Galena* to within 600 yards of the fort to open fire, but before he got into position, two rounds were put through the lightly armored Union vessel. For the next three and a half hours the battle raged; *Galena* took forty-five hits.

Confederate gunners blazed away at the thickly plated *Monitor* to little effect, but the ironclad could not elevate its guns enough to strike the Drewry's Bluff emplacements, and *Naugatuck* soon passed from action when its Parrott rifle exploded. The two wooden warships wisely remained out of range and contributed little to the action. Shortly after 11 A.M., the Union flotilla withdrew to City Point. The Union goal of shelling Richmond into submission from the river had failed.

Drewry's Bluff, a unit of the Richmond National Battlefield Park, is threatened by erosion rather than by development. The National Park Service is taking steps to counter the threat. Drewry's Bluff is open to the public year-round and affords spectacular views of the James River. ■

It took Gen. Joseph E. Johnston the first part of May 1862 to march his army from Yorktown to the eastern outskirts of Richmond. The Union army commanded by Maj. Gen. George B. McClellan fared no better.

As the two armies trudged northwestward up the Peninsula, word arrived of the Confederate victory at Drewry's Bluff (Fort Darling) on May 15. Johnston decided that he would anchor his right flank on the James River opposite the guns of Drewry's Bluff. His center and left would lie behind the Chickahominy River, a sluggish stream that arose northwest of Richmond and flowed southeast to the James River. The Chickahominy meandered through swamps and broad plains, and when its water level rose, as it had in May 1862 with the spring rain, the swamps expanded in size, and the plains turned to muck. Johnston wanted this natural barrier between his army and McClellan's.

North of the Chickahominy, the Pamunkey River followed a parallel course to the James. McClellan advanced up this tributary toward Richmond, hoping to get around Johnston's left flank. By May 15, McClellan had reached a farm called White House, the home of one of Gen. Robert E. Lee's sons. McClellan posted a guard over the house and established the army's "base," or main supply depot, on the property.

Near Richmond, meanwhile, Johnston crossed his army over the Chickahominy—burning most of the bridges behind it—and into strong defensive works north and east of the city. Meanwhile, McClellan slowly advanced on the capital from the Pamunkey along the Richmond and York River Railroad, which enabled him to bring his big guns to Richmond on rail

DIRECTIONS: Recommend first visiting the Richmond National Battlefield Park Visitor Center (open 9–5 daily) at Tredegar Iron Works in downtown Richmond: I-95 Exit 74C (U.S. Rte. 33 West/U.S. Rte. 250 West, Broad St.) and follow blue-and-green signs to visitor center, Brown's Island, and Belle Isle, w. on Broad St. about .4 mile (5 blocks) to 8th St.; s. (left) on 8th St. 5 blocks to Canal St.; w. (right) on Canal St. 3 blocks to 5th St.; s. (left) on 5th St. 2 blocks to Tredegar St.; w. (right) on Tredegar Street .1 mile to visitor center and parking lot. Visit the National Park Service Web site at nps.gov/parks.html for a virtual tour of this and other national parks. To visit the battlefield directly: I-95 Exit 92A (State Rte. 54 East, Hanover), State Rte. 54 East about 5.4 miles to Hanover and U.S. Rte 301/Rte. 2 South; s. (right) on U.S. Rte 301/Rte. 2 South .4 mile to Virginia Civil War Trails marker in parking lot of Hanover Tavern on right; continue 2.6 miles to Rte. 657 (Peaks Rd.) at Crosses Corner; w. (right) on Rte. 657 1 mile to Rte. 695 (Cadys Mill Rd.); continue on Rte. 657 .4 mile to Peaks depot site; continue 3.2 miles to Rte. 802 (Lewistown Rd.); w. (left) on Rte. 802 .4 mile to I-95 Exit 89 (Rte. 802, Lewistown Rd.).

cars. By mid-May McClellan had decided to besiege the place and bombard it into submission.

On May 20 the head of McClellan's army began fording the Chickahominy when Brig. Gen. Silas Casey and his division of Brig. Gen. Erasmus D. Keyes's corps crossed at Bottom's Bridge on Williamsburg Road, thereby establishing the army's left flank on the south bank of the river. Encountering no Confederate opposition, McClellan ordered part of Keyes's corps westward to Seven Pines near the Richmond and York River Railroad station at Fair Oaks. Four days later, the vanguard of Brig. Gen. William F. "Baldy" Smith's division of Brig. Gen. William B. Franklin's corps occupied Mechanicsville on the north side of the Chickahominy, about six miles northeast of Richmond, thus creating McClellan's

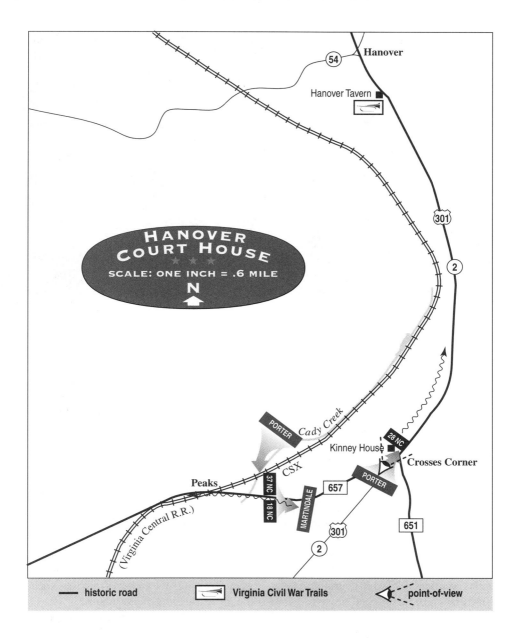

Hanover

54

Hanover Tavern

301

2

HANOVER
COURT HOUSE
★ ★ ★
SCALE: ONE INCH = .6 MILE
N

PORTER

Cady Creek

28 NC

Kinney House

Crosses Corner

CSX

PORTER

Peaks

37 NC

18 NC

657

MARTINDALE

301

2

651

(Virginia Central R.R.)

— historic road   Virginia Civil War Trails   point-of-view

right flank. Now McClellan had to get the rest of his army across the river.

Over the next few days the army's attention turned to bridge building. Men from Brig. Gen. Edwin V. Sumner's corps constructed two bridges over the river to replace those the Confederates had destroyed; the more famous of the two was Grapevine Bridge. Because of the marshy land along the riverbank, both bridges were a quarter-mile long. Both were completed by May 29, and Brig. Gen. Samuel P. Heintzelman crossed his corps over quickly, thus placing about a

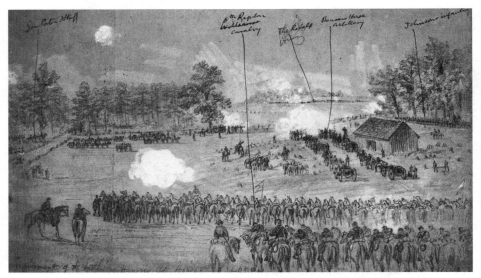

Porter's artillery in action. LIBRARY OF CONGRESS

third of McClellan's army on the south side of the river, and two-thirds north of it.

McClellan got disturbing news, however, amid the success of the crossing. A rumor reached him that 17,000 Confederates were marching on Hanover Court House, north of Mechanicsville, thereby threatening his right flank. Although a subsequent cavalry reconnaissance reduced the number to 6,000, McClellan ordered Brig. Gen. Fitz John Porter, a close personal friend and the commander of a newly created corps, to eliminate the threat.

The Confederates at Hanover Court House (actually at Peake's Crossing, four miles southwest of the courthouse near Slash Church), positioned there to guard the Virginia Central Railroad, which connected Richmond with Gordonsville near the Shenandoah Valley, consisted of some 4,000 men. Another brigade took post at Hanover Junction, where the Virginia Central Railroad intersected the Richmond, Fredericksburg & Potomac Railroad, about ten miles north of Peake's Crossing.

Porter's command, which included an infantry division and a cavalry brigade and numbering about 12,000, marched out of camp about 4 A.M. on Tuesday, May 27, in a driving rain. The rain stopped around midmorning, but mud remained to hamper Porter's advance. His vanguard, the 25th New York Infantry Regiment, approached a farm owned by Dr. Thomas H. Kinney from the southwest along New Bridge Road (approximately present-day U.S. Rte. 301) at the same time that the 28th North Carolina returned to the same spot from a reconnaissance to the south on Taliaferro's Mill Road (Rte. 651). The two collided at Kinney's house in a sharp engagement about noon, with the North Carolinians scouring the New Yorkers from the wheat fields surrounding the farmhouse.

Soon Union reinforcements arrived on the scene, however, and Col. James H. Lane, commander of the 28th North Carolina, found himself outnumbered. Pressed by four regiments as well as four cannons to his two, Lane's line disintegrated, ending the first phase of the battle. The victorious regiments set off in pursuit of the remnants of Lane's command toward Hanover Court

House, thereby exposing the rear of Porter's corps to attack by the rest of the Confederate force at Peake's Crossing, a mile west of Dr. Kinney's house.

Porter left Brig. Gen. John H. Martindale with three regiments along with two cannons to guard the New Bridge and Hanover Court House Roads intersection just west of the Kinney farm. From Peake's Crossing, Col. Charles C. Lee led his own regiment, the 37th North Carolina, along with the 18th North Carolina and a two-gun section from Latham's Battery, to attack the Federals.

Lee's assault developed slowly, resulting in the 18th North Carolina charging Martindale's line. The attack failed, and the 18th fell back to rejoin the 37th North Carolina. A stand-up fight ensued, with the heavy fire of the two Confederate regiments nearly shattering Martindale's force.

When word of the fight reached Porter, he immediately ordered the 9th Massachu-setts and 62nd Pennsylvania Regiments back to the Kinney farm. The Confederate line dissolved, retreating through Peake's Corner and Ashland. Porter held the battlefield and could therefore claim victory in this sloppy, disorganized fight.

Porter had assumed that the main Confederate force held Hanover Court House and failed to scout to the west of the Kinney farm, where he would have encountered Branch. The Confederate commander, for his part, acted without understanding that his opponent outnumbered him three to one. Porter lost 397 men in the battle and Branch 930, most as prisoners. Technically, McClellan's right flank remained secure, although in reality Branch had never threatened it.

Today, the Hanover Court House battlefield retains very good integrity despite the intrusion of U.S. Rte. 301. The two-story frame Kinney house still stands. ■

SEVEN PINES

When Maj. Gen. George B. McClellan crossed a third of his army to the south side of the Chickahominy River, leaving two-thirds on the north side, Gen. Joseph E. Johnston decided the time to strike had arrived. Thinking that Maj. Gen. Irvin McDowell's army was marching south from Fredericksburg to reinforce McClellan's right flank, Johnston intended to attack the right before McDowell got there. On Tuesday, May 27, 1862, however, the same day as the battle of Hanover Court House occurred, Johnston learned that McDowell had turned back, presumably to head for the Shenandoah Valley.

Johnston altered his plans. Rather than attack across his own natural defensive line—the Chickahominy River—he would strike McClellan's troops that already had crossed to Johnston's side of the line, near Seven Pines. For two days Maj. Gen. D. H. Hill reconnoitered McClellan's flank, reporting to Johnston that he would face Maj. Gen. Erasmus D. Keyes's entire corps. Brig. Gen. Samuel P. Heintzelman and his corps also had crossed to the south side of the river, to the rear of Keyes, but Johnston planned to throw enough of his army into the fray to defeat two Union corps. He set the attack for May 31.

Johnston's plan seemed simple enough: one corps would approach along Nine Mile Road, a division would approach on Williamsburg Road, and three brigades would march to battle on Charles City Road. Most of the force, which totaled

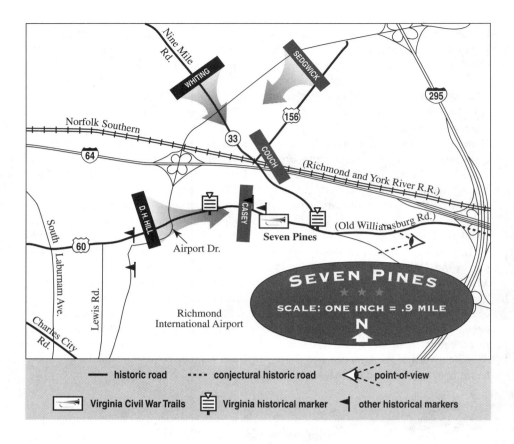

── historic road	---- conjectural historic road	◁⋯ point-of-view
[icon] Virginia Civil War Trails	[icon] Virginia historical marker	◀ other historical markers

more than 50,000 counting brigades from Brig. Gen. John B. Magruder's reserve, would attack Seven Pines directly, where about 33,000 Federals waited in isolation from the rest of McClellan's command.

Johnston erred, however, in how he announced his plan to his generals. One, Maj. Gen. Benjamin Huger, found his written orders vague. Other generals found his orders contradictory. Johnston issued nothing in writing to Maj. Gen. James Longstreet, on whom the battle hinged, instructing him verbally instead in a long, rambling face-to-face meeting. In addition, although the plan looked feasible on Johnston's map, in reality the three attacking forces would be out of each other's sight on three separate roads, which meant that their timing had to be impeccable to strike

the Federal line simultaneously.

On the night of May 30, though, an awesome thunderstorm pelted the area with sheets of rain and deadly lightning that killed men in both armies. The rain fell for hours, and the Chickahominy rose out of its banks, sweeping away several bridges and separating the two parts of McClellan's army.

The next morning Johnston launched his attack and waited at his headquarters on Nine Mile Road with his second in command, Maj. Gen. Gustavus W. Smith, for word of its progress. The word came soon enough, but it was not what Johnston wanted to hear: The attack was falling apart before it had fairly begun. Longstreet had marched across Nine Mile Road instead of down it and disappeared.

DIRECTIONS: Recommend first visiting the Richmond National Battlefield Park Visitor Center (open 9–5 daily) at Tredegar Iron Works in downtown Richmond: I-95 Exit 74C (U.S. Rte. 33 West/U.S. Rte. 250 West, Broad St.) and follow blue-and-green signs to visitor center, Brown's Island, and Belle Isle, w. on Broad St. about .4 mile (5 blocks) to 8th St.; s. (left) on 8th St. 5 blocks to Canal St.; w. (right) on Canal St. 3 blocks to 5th St.; s. (left) on 5th St. 2 blocks to Tredegar St.; w. (right) on Tredegar Street .1 mile to visitor center and parking lot. Visit the National Park Service Web site at nps.gov/parks.html for a virtual tour of this and other national parks. To visit the battlefield directly: I-295 Exit 28 (I-64, U.S. 360, Norfolk, Richmond; then U.S. Rte. 60 West, Seven Pines), or I-64 Exit 200 (I-295, U.S. Rte. 60, Rocky Mount, N.C., Washington; then Rocky Mount, N.C., exit; then U.S. Rte. 60 West, Seven Pines, exit), w. on U.S. Rte. 60 West (Williamsburg Rd.) about 1.7 miles to Seven Pines National Cemetery at State Rte. 33 West intersection and state historical marker W-9, McClellan's Second Line; continue w. on U.S. Rte. 60 West .6 mile to Richmond Battlefield Markers Association marker (Seven Pines) and 1.5 miles total to Airport Dr.; s. (left) on Airport Dr. .8 mile to second crossover past the Virginia Aviation Museum; make U turn and return on Airport Dr. .1 mile to Richmond Civil War Artillery marker on right and note gun battery (also represents Oak Grove); continue .7 mile on Airport Dr. to U.S. Rte. 60; w. (left) on U.S. Rte. 60 .7 mile to Lewis Rd. and make U turn at traffic light; return e. .3 mile to Richmond Battlefield Markers Association marker (Richmond Defences); continue past Airport Dr. .4 mile to state historical marker W-4, McClellan's Picket Line, on right; continue .55 mile to Virginia Civil War Trails marker and Richmond Battlefield Markers Association marker (Battlefield of Seven Pines) at library on right; continue .5 mile to Seven Pines National Cemetery on left; return to I-64.

Just east of Richmond, meanwhile, Huger and his staff were still asleep, for instead of specifying a time for marching, Johnston's orders said only that Huger should move as early as possible. When Huger was awakened by the noise made as a division marched by, the South Carolina general learned for the first time that there was to be a battle that day. Soon the opening of the battle was four hours behind schedule.

Meanwhile, Maj. Gen. Daniel H. Hill, who was on Williamsburg Road close to the front, was about to explode with impatience. He had been ready to attack since dawn and he wondered why Huger had not arrived at his assigned position hours earlier. Finally Hill ordered his men forward. It was 1 P.M., fully five hours after the attack was to have begun.

Hill's column struck the Federal line at one of its most vulnerable points and overwhelmed the raw recruits forward of the Union entrenchments. The fighting for possession of the earthworks was savage, with heavy casualties on both sides. Finally, the Confederates broke through, capturing a Federal redoubt, and charged on to the second line of works at Seven Pines.

The Union chain of command was far removed from the scene of action. McClellan rested in his tent headquarters near New Bridge, weak with malaria, and received only periodic reports that minimized the battle. As late as 2:30 P.M., Heintzelman, at his headquarters at Savage's Station, reported to McClellan that he had received no word from Keyes. A few minutes later, however, messengers arrived to tell Heintzelman that Keyes's front was being driven in.

On the Confederate side, Joseph Johnston did not even know the battle had begun. Around noon he had moved his headquarters closer to the front, only two and a half miles from the scene of action. The sounds of cannons and musketry were clearly audible for miles around the battlefield, but Johnston's headquarters lay in an "acoustical shadow," a natural phenomenon caused by atmospheric conditions, and it was 4 P.M. before he and his staff knew the fight was on.

South of the battle on the Williamsburg Road, Longstreet divided his force into two parts with three brigades each, marched them toward the fight, and then halted. Only one of his brigades got into the action that day. Without help on Hill's flanks, his

Bayonet charge by 2nd Regiment, Excelsior Brigade (New York) at Seven Pines. LIBRARY OF CONGRESS

attack stalled at the second Union line. To continue his assault, Hill organized a flanking movement of his own, sending first three, then four regiments under Col. Micah Jenkins of Longstreet's command around his left flank to attack Keyes's right. Jenkins drove five separate Union lines before him and collapsed the Federal line right back to Williamsburg Road a mile and a half beyond Seven Pines. About 6 P.M. the fighting died down, and it had largely stopped by 7:30.

At the height of the late afternoon's combat, a second battle developed to Hill's left. Just north of Seven Pines, near Fair Oaks Station on the Richmond and York River Railroad, Brig. Gen. W. H. Chase Whiting led his division forward to attack the Union right flank. Johnston rode with him. Just north of Fair Oaks, Whiting ran into stiff resistance from artillery and infantry. About 5:30 P.M., Brig. Gen. John Sedgwick arrived in support. Whiting fed more brigades into the attack as Sedgwick's men kept coming, but the Union line held. Finally, darkness ended the engagement.

At dusk, Johnston watched the last of the battle from a knoll 200 yards north of Fair Oaks Station, on Nine Mile Road. Bullets and the occasional shell sailed by, and Johnston was chuckling at a colonel's ducking and dodging when a bullet hit him in the shoulder; a few seconds later a shell exploded in front of his horse, striking Johnston's chest with a large fragment. Johnston would be out of action for the next six months.

With Johnston's wounding, the leadership of the Army of Northern Virginia passed to his second in command, Maj. Gen. Gustavus W. Smith. Unfortunately, Smith was unequal to the task. He had no idea what to do next, and he made his indecisiveness clear in conversations with Pres. Jefferson Davis and Gen. Robert E. Lee when they met with him to discuss his plans for the next day's battle.

During the night, Smith finally made up his mind to attack at dawn on June 1. He told Longstreet to press north toward the railroad from Williamsburg Road rather than east, and he would reinforce him with Whiting's division on Nine Mile

Road once he was fully engaged. On the Union side of the battlefield, the Federals anticipated Smith's plan and positioned themselves to counter it. Sedgwick's division faced east on Nine Mile Road, toward Whiting, while that of Brig. Gen. Israel B. Richardson faced south along the Richmond and York River Railroad track, toward Longstreet.

The attack started on time, but it soon slowed as Longstreet encountered stiff resistance and thick woods. Hill's and Huger's commands bore the brunt of the assault and took the heaviest casualties. Huger's inexperienced troops broke under Union counterattacks and ran for the rear. By 11:30 A.M. the firing died away as each side realized it was making no progress. Smith, like Johnston before him, remained at headquarters and relied on the sound of battle to tell him what was happening. Although by early morning the roar of the muskets and artillery had reached a crescendo, Smith's nerve failed him, and he never ordered Whiting forward. The battle ended before noon with each army in the same position it had occupied at dawn. During two days of fighting to a draw, the Confederates suffered 7,997 casualties and the Federals 5,739.

McClellan finally came to the front after the fighting stopped. His presence inspired the troops, but when he beheld the dead and wounded lying mangled on the battlefield, it hardened his resolve to take Richmond by siege, not by combat.

President Davis likewise rode forward for a short visit to Smith's headquarters, then departed. About 2 P.M., a man on a dappled gray horse appeared there. Robert E. Lee had taken command of the Army of Northern Virginia.

The Seven Pines battlefield no longer exists, having long ago succumbed to development. Only tiny fragments survive: a few earthwork remnants at Richmond International Airport, a small piece of the battlefield at U.S. Rte. 60 and Rte. 33 occupied by the Seven Pines National Cemetery, and a parcel of land north of Fair Oaks Station at the Adams House. One can no longer make much sense of the action of May 31–June 1, 1862. ◾

OAK GROVE

After the battle of Seven Pines fizzled to an end on June 1, 1862, Gen. Robert E. Lee ordered the army out of its forward positions, which the Federals quickly occupied, and back into its trenches closer to the city. The morale of many of his soldiers dropped as they wielded shovels instead of weapons, for they were convinced that they had almost broken McClellan's line in the earlier fighting and with adequate generalship they could still do it.

In the Army of the Potomac, McClellan's soldiers had gained confidence from their recent battles and had advanced within sight of Richmond's church steeples. McClellan had promised to lead them into the city, and they were certain he would keep his word. His big guns, with which he intended to pound the capital into submission, were on their way to the front.

Lee knew that the city and the army could not withstand a siege. He hastened to strengthen the defensive works and thereby free more of the Army of Northern Virginia for duty in the field. He strengthened his own position as well, by keeping Jefferson Davis informed and soliciting his

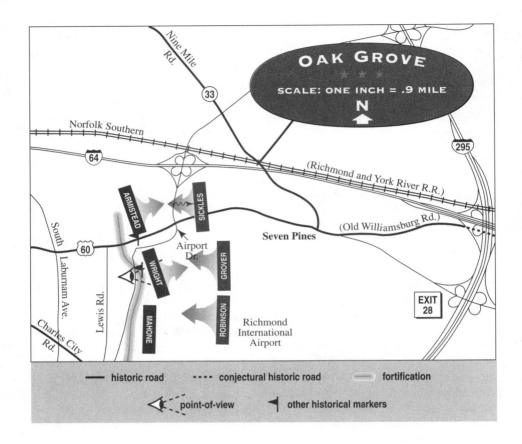

OAK GROVE
★ ★ ★
SCALE: ONE INCH = .9 MILE
N

historic road — conjectural historic road — fortification

point-of-view — other historical markers

advice, thereby gaining the president's trust and support for his plans.

Lee also wanted Maj. Gen. Thomas J. "Stonewall" Jackson and his Valley army to join him and increase the odds in his favor. He dispatched three brigades to Jackson to confound the Federals. In the meantime, Lee reorganized the Army of Northern Virginia, added and trained new recruits, and met with his generals so they could all get to know each other. By the time Jackson arrived with his army, Lee would command some 92,000 men—as close to parity with his opponents as he would ever come.

Lee sought to learn all he could about the Union army's position. His battle plans called for sending Jackson around McClellan's right flank, thought to be in the vicin-

ity of the South Anna River in Hanover County. One of Brig. Gen. J. E. B. Stuart's cavalry scouts, a skinny young lieutenant named John Singleton Mosby, discovered that the roads that Jackson would have to use appeared to be open. Lee ordered Stuart to make a reconnaissance in force to be certain. At 2 A.M. on the morning of June 12, a Thursday, what would become Stuart's famous "Ride around McClellan" was under way.

With some 1,200 horsemen and a two-gun section of horse artillery, Stuart led his force north out of Richmond to the South Anna River above Ashland, southeast along the Pamunkey River to Tunstall's Station a few miles southwest of White House (cutting across McClellan's supply line), south to Charles City Court House,

the painting shortly became one of the most cherished Southern icons of the war.

At about 3 P.M. on Monday, June 23, a dusty figure on a small sorrel horse dismounted at Lee's headquarters. It was Stonewall Jackson, whom everyone, Confederate and Federal alike, thought was still in the Shenandoah Valley. But after defeating Frémont and Shields at Cross Keys and Port Republic on June 8–9, Jackson's army had slipped away and, moving by train and on foot, was about halfway between the Blue Ridge and Richmond. Soon thereafter, Maj. Gens. D. H. Hill, A. P. Hill, and James Longstreet joined him.

Lee's plan called for Jackson to strike McClellan's right flank from the north and rear of the Union line while A. P. Hill, after crossing the Chickahominy upstream, would march down the north bank, uncovering bridges near Mechanicsville for Longstreet and D. H. Hill to cross and join in the battle. The attack would begin at 3 A.M. on June 26.

McClellan, meanwhile, learned from Confederate deserters and Allan Pinkerton's spies that Jackson was in the area and Lee was preparing to move. McClellan increased his cavalry patrols along the northern roads and organized an attack of his own. He wanted to take the high ground on Nine Mile Road around Old Tavern, thereby advancing his line a mile and a half closer to Richmond and obtaining a good position for his siege guns. However, he needed to capture a key position south of Old Tavern called Oak Grove so that he could attack his objective from its right flank as well as from the front. Oak Grove, just south of the Richmond and York River Railroad, was the position from which D. H. Hill had assaulted the Union line on May 31. First, McClellan decided, he would take Oak Grove on June 25, and then he would capture Old Tavern the next day or the day after.

and then west to Richmond on the River Road. Stuart and his men learned that McClellan's right flank was not anchored on the South Anna River and that the roads in that vicinity were indeed unguarded. The troopers burned Union supplies at Tunstall's Station, fought several skirmishes with Federal cavalry, and generally caused a commotion in McClellan's army. Stuart lost only one man; Capt. William Latané was slain in an engagement near Linney's Corners west of Old Church in Hanover County. Taken to a nearby farm called Summer Hill, Latané's body was interred in the family graveyard there, and the women of the house conducted the burial ceremony. Soon a poem describing the burial was published, and then a painting of the imagined scene; engravings made from

The Union attack began at 8:30 A.M. on June 25, a Wednesday. Brig. Gen. Cuvier Grover's brigade in the center and Brig. Gen. John C. Robinson's brigade on the left made good progress, but Brig. Gen. Daniel E. Sickles's brigade on the right, which had only a light skirmish line to clear the way in front of it, encountered stiff Confederate resistance. This, coupled with difficulties in moving through the upper reaches of White Oak Swamp, slowed the advance of the Union left. Taking advantage of the raggedness of the Federal assault, Maj. Gen. Benjamin Huger counterattacked with Brig. Gen. Ambrose R. "Rans" Wright's brigade against Grover's. The rising battle raged back and forth across fields and woods. At a crucial moment Wright ordered the 25th North Carolina Regiment, just arrived from Richmond, onto the field. The regiment delivered a careful massed fire against Sickles's brigade that broke up its tardy attack and sent a large part of it racing for the rear.

McClellan himself was in the rear, three miles from the front, attempting to manage the battle by telegraph. Hearing of Sickles's collapse, at 10:30 McClellan ordered Hooker to break off the attack and retire to his lines. McClellan then rode forward to the field to see for himself, arriving at about 1 P.M. Finding the situation not nearly as bad as he had feared, he ordered the attack resumed, compelling his troops to recover the ground they had taken and then yielded. Only now the ground was covered with their dead and wounded. When darkness at last ended the battle, the Federals had advanced their line about 600 yards. The Union army suffered 516 casualties, the Confederates 316.

On the Confederate side, Lee also rode to the front in the afternoon. He assessed the situation and concluded that he did not need to alter his plans for the next day's offensive.

While Lee completed his plans for the morning's attack, McClellan already was organizing a retreat. During the afternoon's engagement, a fugitive slave had crossed into Porter's line near Mechanicsville with the news that not only had Jackson arrived, but Gen. Pierre G. T. Beauregard as well, with enough reinforcements to swell Lee's army to 200,000. McClellan bought the fiction wholesale, telegraphed Washington begging for more troops, resolved to die fighting along with his magnificent army if overwhelmed by the two-to-one odds he now imagined against him, and laid plans for a retreat to the James River. And not a shot had been fired in Lee's offensive.

The Oak Grove battlefield, which covered part of the Seven Pines field, has likewise disappeared under development. Much of the ground is now occupied by Richmond International Airport. ∎

A few C.S.A. earthworks survive at Richmond International Airport. VIRGINIA DEPARTMENT OF HISTORIC RESOURCES, JOHN S. SALMON

BEAVER DAM CREEK

The success of Gen. Robert E. Lee's attack against Maj. Gen. George B. McClellan's army on Thursday, June 26, 1862, depended on Maj. Gen. Thomas J. "Stonewall" Jackson. During the night of June 25, Jackson struggled to move his army to its assigned position for the morning's battle. Two days before, his force had been strung out along the roads and rail line for more than twenty miles. When he rode into Beaver Dam Station in western Hanover County on the morning of June 24, Jackson expected to find his army assembled there, ready to march to its jumping-off point for his attack on the Union army's right flank, Slash Church on the Hanover Court House battlefield. Instead, he found only the vanguard of his force at the station; the rest of the army still was poking along miles to the west. The constant shifting from muddy roads to trains and back to roads again had gotten the better of his vaunted foot cavalry. The front of the army had barely reached Ashland before dark on June 25, five miles away from Slash Church.

Jackson sent a courier to Lee to inform him of the army's problems and promised to start it early toward the point of attack, beginning his march at 2:30 instead of 3 A.M. on June 26. He failed to meet that deadline by two and a half hours, not getting under way until 5 A.M. Lee and the rest of the army, which had marched to its assigned positions on time, expected to hear the sound of battle to the north between 8 and 9 A.M., but the hours came and went in silence. It was about this time that Jackson's courier arrived with his message of delay. Lee rode northward from the Dabb house to a bluff overlooking the Chickahominy River and Mechanicsville, to watch and listen for Jackson.

Ellerson's Mill on Beaver Dam Creek, photographed in 1865 after the war by John Reekie. LIBRARY OF CONGRESS

Meanwhile, Jackson marched his army through Hanover County in fits and starts. Federal cavalry had felled trees to obstruct the roads leading to his flank, and Jackson halted to reconnoiter and clear each blockade he encountered. His march from Ashland eastward took him through heavily wooded, unfamiliar terrain. Jackson had slept little in the past couple of weeks, particularly during the last few days, and exhaustion and uncertainty made him lethargic. By 9 A.M., when he at last reached Slash Church, he was six hours behind schedule. On this day he never would reach the battlefield.

Like Jackson, Maj. Gen. George B. McClellan and Brig. Gen. Fitz John Porter moved in a fog of uncertainty, at least in regard to the enemy situation. Cavalry pickets reported to Porter that they saw opposing columns marching here, there, and everywhere, but gave him nothing on which to base his defensive tactics. McClellan thought the quiet at the front unnatural and wondered what Lee was up to.

From his observation post overlooking the Chickahominy, Lee waited, maintaining an outwardly calm appearance. At

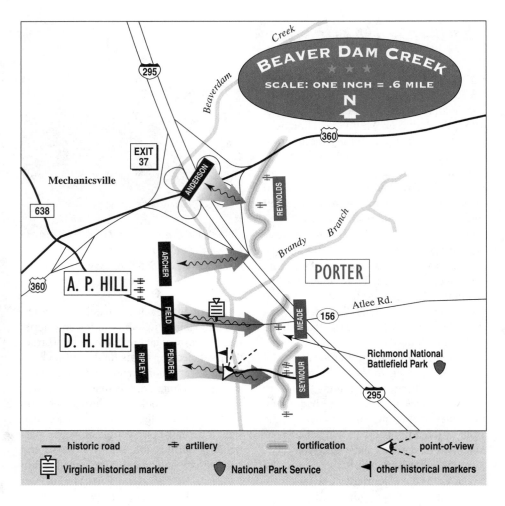

BEAVER DAM CREEK
★ ★ ★
SCALE: ONE INCH = .6 MILE
N

—— historic road	⚏ artillery	⚏⚏ fortification	◁⋯ point-of-view
🏛 Virginia historical marker	🛡 National Park Service	◀ other historical markers

about 4 P.M., he saw troops in motion near Mechanicsville, as blue and gray soldiers contended near an orchard. At last, Jackson was attacking. Lee ordered Maj. Gen. D. H. Hill and Maj. Gen. James Longstreet, who was waiting with him, across the river. However, it was not Jackson who had launched his assault. The impatient Maj. Gen. A. P. Hill had finally had enough of waiting for Jackson and attacked Porter's advance guard on his own.

Porter had posted an infantry regiment at Mechanicsville and six companies of Pennsylvanians farther west at Meadow Bridges. Hill's attack sent the Federals

scrambling back across Beaver Dam Creek to the main defensive line. Sixty-foot-high bluffs rise on each side of the creek, and Porter's men were dug in on the eastern bank. About half a mile north of the creek's mouth stood Ellerson's Mill, which marked one of the strongest points on Porter's line and became the focus of the late-afternoon Confederate assaults.

Lee rode across the river to Mechanicsville to confer with A. P. Hill and learned that Hill had no idea of Jackson's whereabouts and had acted on his own. Lee decided to continue the attack, for if he were to break it off, McClellan surely

DIRECTIONS: Recommend first visiting the Richmond National Battlefield Park Visitor Center (open 9–5 daily) at Tredegar Iron Works in downtown Richmond: I-95 Exit 74C (U.S. Rte. 33 West/U.S. Rte. 250 West, Broad St.) and follow blue-and-green signs to visitor center, Brown's Island, and Belle Isle, w. on Broad St. about .4 mile (5 blocks) to 8th St.; s. (left) on 8th St. 5 blocks to Canal St.; w. (right) on Canal St. 3 blocks to 5th St.; s. (left) on 5th St. 2 blocks to Tredegar St.; w. (right) on Tredegar Street .1 mile to visitor center and parking lot. Visit the National Park Service Web site at nps.gov/parks.html for a virtual tour of this and other national parks. To visit the battlefield directly: I-295 Exit 37B (Mechanicsville, U.S. Rte. 360 West), U.S. 360 w. about 1.1 miles to State Rte. 156 South/U.S. Rte. 360 Bus., then .3 mile to State Rte. 156 (Cold Harbor Rd.); continue 1.6 miles to Chickahominy Bluffs Richmond National Battlefield Park unit on e. (left) and state historical marker O-5, Outer Fortifications; return 1.6 miles to State Rte. 156 (Cold Harbor Rd.); s. (right) on State Rte. 156 .8 mile to Beaver Dam Creek Richmond National Battlefield Park unit entrance and state historical marker PA-4, Seven Days' Battles, Mechanicsville; s. (right) into park unit, .2 mile to parking lot and Richmond Battlefield Markers Association marker (Beaver Dam Creek); return to State Rte. 156; e. (left) on State Rte. 156 .5 mile to U.S. Rte. 360 East; e. (right) on U.S. Rte. 360 East .3 mile to I-295.

would counterattack there or press on through the Confederate lines to the south and into Richmond. Lee then rode back toward the Chickahominy to a knoll south of Mechanicsville where he could observe the action at Beaver Dam Creek, half a mile east. Soon Jefferson Davis joined him, but as they were within range of Federal artillery, Lee sent Davis and his entourage to the rear. Davis stopped as soon as he got out of Lee's sight.

Brig. Gen. George A. McCall and his 9,500-man division anchored the Union defenses at Beaver Dam Creek. Hill attacked the far right of McCall's line, north of Old Church Road. The Pennsylvanians, firing from the safety of their log-and-earth fortifications, easily repulsed this and subsequent assaults.

Downstream, around Ellerson's Mill, the brigade of Brig. Gen. W. Dorsey Pender tried to attack across the creek against the Federal earthworks but were caught in a crossfire of muskets and artillery and nearly cut to pieces. Hill reinforced the attack with Brig. Gen. Roswell S. Ripley's brigade from D. H. Hill's division, and tried again. As darkness fell, Ripley's men likewise failed to cross the creek, and the battle ended.

Lee had intended to throw almost 56,000 men against Porter's line, but because of Jackson's disappearance and the piecemeal manner in which the battle developed, he fielded some 14,000 against Porter's entrenched 15,000. The Confederates suffered about 1,450 casualties and the Federals only 360.

The campaign of Beaver Dam Creek did not achieve Lee's tactical goal—crushing McClellan's right flank and rolling up his line. Despite Lee's tactical failure, however, he achieved a bloody strategic success. Within a few hours of darkness, McClellan directed Porter to pull back preparatory to crossing to the south side of the Chickahominy. Lee owned the initiative.

Most of the battlefield has disappeared beneath housing subdivisions, shopping centers, and an interstate highway interchange. The National Park Service maintains a unit on Beaver Dam Creek around the site of Ellerson's Mill, the location of the early evening attacks by Pender and Ripley. The Union position on the eastern bluff overlooking the creek has been obliterated by a housing development, and other construction projects surround the park unit and threaten to encroach on it further. ∎

Although the defeat at Drewry's Bluff on May 15, 1862, prevented the Union gunboat squadron from approaching any closer to Richmond by way of James River, it left the downstream portion of the river firmly in Federal control. Roughly fifteen miles away from the Union defensive line, almost due south at Berkeley plantation, was Harrison's Landing, named for the family that had owned the land there for generations. The terrain around the landing was broad and level enough to support a Union supply depot, and the river was wide and deep enough to float the many vessels needed to transport an army to Hampton Roads.

In the middle of the night, after the battle of Beaver Dam Creek on June 26, Maj. Gen. George B. McClellan resolved privately to change his base from the White House depot on the Pamunkey River to the James River, in order to protect his army from the overwhelming odds that he imagined it faced. By any name, this maneuver constituted a retreat. After the movement was under way, McClellan fixed on Harrison's Landing as his destination.

McClellan spent the first part of the night at the headquarters of Brig. Gen. Fitz John Porter, whose corps had repulsed Gen. Robert E. Lee's attacks on the Union right flank. McClellan first ordered Porter to hold his position, then sent word to fall back to the north bank of the Chickahominy River and hold the bridges. McClellan feared that Stonewall Jackson would roll up his flank unless Porter changed his front to face this new threat.

Porter received McClellan's orders about 3 A.M. on June 27, a Friday, and began at once to extract his brigades from their fortifications on Beaver Dam Creek, leaving a small rear guard to impede any

Confederate advance. A new position for Porter's corps had been scouted atop a broad plateau just north of the Chickahominy, from which Porter could guard four key bridges over the river. Boatswain's Swamp bordered the northern and western edges of the plateau; a half-mile to the west lay Powhite Creek and Dr. William F. Gaines's mill.

By dawn on June 27, Porter's men were on the road, and Maj. Gen. A. P. Hill was pushing his division across Beaver Dam Creek and into the abandoned Federal earthworks, then along Old Cold Harbor Road. To the north, Maj. Gen. D. H. Hill took the Old Church Road to Bethesda Church, then turned south on the road to Old Cold Harbor. Farther south, McClellan was in a dither of indecision. Convinced that he was outnumbered two to one, the Union commander was confronted by reports of Confederate activity to his left as well as to his right. As was the case the day before, enemy troops were marching everywhere at once, it seemed. In reality, Brig. Gen. John B. Magruder was shifting his regiments from one spot to another and back again, even utilizing "regiments" of drum-beating slaves, to give the illusion of impending attacks south of the Chickahominy. The ruse worked. McClellan grew increasingly concerned about how he might salvage his army from the imagined overwhelming numbers and gave little thought to strengthening Porter so that he could counterattack and defeat the Confederates.

Lee had not imagined McClellan would give up so easily, and his plans for the day's battle essentially repeated his tactical outline of the day before. By midmorning Jackson had pressed south to Walnut Grove Church on Old Cold Harbor Road, but not before Porter's corps had crossed his front in its retreat, pursued (unknown to Jackson and Lee) by D. H. Hill's division on Old Church Road and Walnut Grove Church Road. Lee thought that Porter's new defensive line would be along Powhite Creek near Gaines's Mill, and he laid his plans accordingly when he met with Jackson and Maj. Gen. A. P. Hill at Walnut Grove Church. Hill would continue his march down Old Cold Harbor Road to assail the Federal line near the mill, while Maj. Gen. James Longstreet's division would support Hill on his right. Jackson, meanwhile, would press south to assault the Federal rear in concert with D. H. Hill. Lee and Jackson parted about 11 A.M. to set the scheme in motion.

Unknown to Lee and Jackson, however, D. H. Hill soon was occupied in a raging fight. Hill marched south through Old Cold Harbor without pausing for Jackson and at about 2 P.M. encountered Union skirmishers, then Federal artillery, to his front. Hill returned fire with his guns and settled down to wait for Jackson. Because of acoustical shadows, however, Lee, headquartered just a few miles west, heard no sound of this first engagement with Porter's corps.

About the same time, A. P. Hill's vanguard, Brig. Gen. Maxcy Gregg's South Carolina brigade, reached Gaines's Mill on Powhite Creek, where Lee had expected to find Porter's main line. Instead, light Federal resistance enabled Gregg to push across the creek easily, and he and his men turned south. As they approached Boatswain's Swamp, a sudden fire of muskets and cannons erupted from a hill rising to the south. Gregg had found Porter's true position.

Porter had arranged his defense in a semicircle along the edge of the plateau above the swamp. On the southwest, his left flank, was one division, with another division on the right and two other divisions in reserve behind the line. Porter's artillery, stationed between the brigades of each division, added significantly to his firepower.

A. P. Hill deployed his division on the west and north sides of Boatswain's Swamp in a three-quarter-mile-long semicircle corresponding to Porter's left flank and center on the heights. At about 2:30 P.M., with Lee beside him watching through field glasses, Hill launched his assault. Over the next two hours, one brigade after another, beginning with

Confederates attack Porter's line at Gaines's Mill. LIBRARY OF CONGRESS

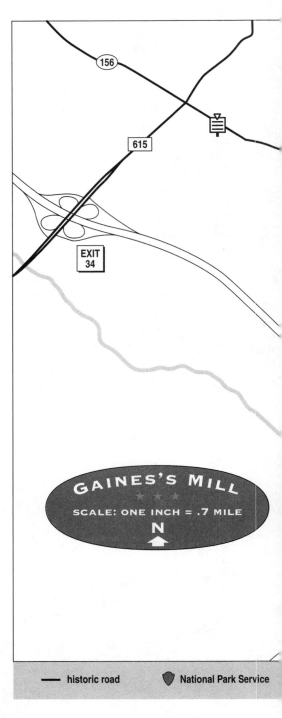

DIRECTIONS: Recommend first visiting the Richmond National Battlefield Park Visitor Center (open 9–5 daily) at Tredegar Iron Works in downtown Richmond: I-95 Exit 74C (U.S. Rte. 33 West/U.S. Rte. 250 West, Broad St.) and follow blue-and-green signs to visitor center, Brown's Island, and Belle Isle, w. on Broad St. about .4 mile (5 blocks) to 8th St.; s. (left) on 8th St. 5 blocks to Canal St.; w. (right) on Canal St. 3 blocks to 5th St.; s. (left) on 5th St. 2 blocks to Tredegar St.; w. (right) on Tredegar Street .1 mile to visitor center and parking lot. Visit the National Park Service Web site at nps.gov/parks.html for a virtual tour of this and other national parks. To visit the battlefield directly: I-295 Exit 34A (Rte. 615 East, Creighton Rd.), e. on Rte. 615 about .8 mile to State Rte. 156 (Cold Harbor Rd.); e. (right) on State Rte. 156 about .25 mile to state historical marker PA-20, Seven Days' Battles—Gaines's Mill; continue 1.4 miles to Rte. 718 (Watt House Rd.); s. (right) on Rte. 718 .7 mile to Gaines's Mill Richmond National Battlefield Park unit and state historical marker PA-25, Seven Days' Battles—Gaines's Mill; return to State Rte. 156; e. (right) on State Rte. 156 1.2 miles to state historical marker PA-80, Seven Days' Battles—Gaines's Mill, then .1 mile to Old Cold Harbor intersection with Rtes. 619 and 633 and state historical markers PA-23 and PA-60, Seven Days' Battles—Gaines's Mill; s. (right) on State Rte. 156 (Battlefield Park Rd.) 2.7 miles to Rte. 630 (Market Rd.); w. (right) on State Rte. 156 .75 mile to state historical marker PA-105, Seven Days' Battles—Grape Vine Bridge, and Richmond Battlefield Markers Association marker (Grapevine Bridge); continue on State Rte. 156 .5 mile to I-295 Exit 31A (State Rte. 156 North, Cold Harbor).

Gregg's, fought their way through the swamp, only to be thrown back with heavy casualties on reaching the Federal lines.

As the battle raged, the previous day's question was raised again: Where was Jackson? After marching his men for two miles down Walnut Grove Church Road in the care of a guide who was leading them as Jackson had instructed to Old Cold Harbor, Jackson suddenly said that his orders were to go around Old Cold Harbor so as to swing his army east of the community. The guide snapped back that if Jackson had told him that in the first place, he would have taken him by that route instead of this one. Now there was nothing to do

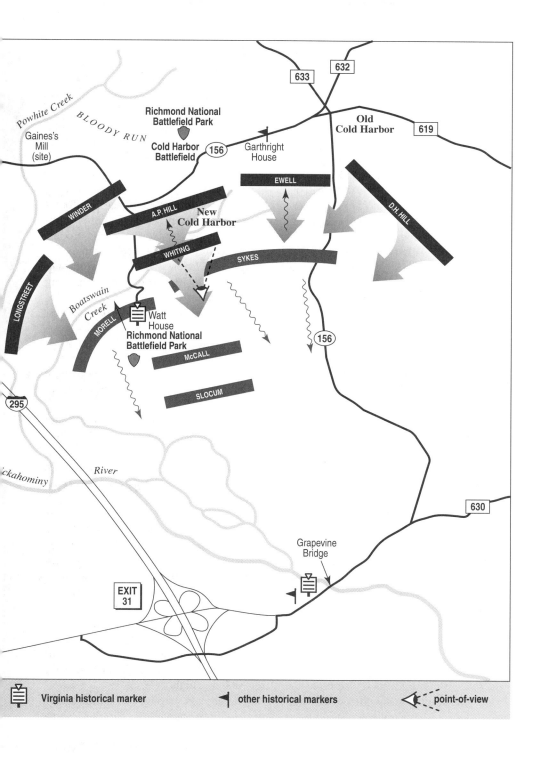

Powhite Creek

BLOODY RUN

Gaines's
Mill
(site)

Richmond National
Battlefield Park

Cold Harbor
Battlefield

156

Garthright
House

Old
Cold Harbor

619

633

632

EWELL

WINDER

A.P. HILL

New
Cold Harbor

WHITING

SYKES

D.H. HILL

LONGSTREET

Boatswain
Creek

MORELL

Watt
House

Richmond National
Battlefield Park

McCALL

SLOCUM

295

ickahominy

River

630

Grapevine
Bridge

EXIT
31

156

Virginia historical marker

other historical markers

point-of-view

but turn the column around, march back to a fork in the road, take the other road, and march around the other side of Old Cold Harbor. This countermarch would consume three hours and take the column some six miles out of its way.

It was approaching 3:30 P.M. when the head of Jackson's column, led by Maj. Gen. Richard S. Ewell, reached Lee. The commanding general told Ewell to lead his three brigades against the Union center. Ewell did not hesitate, but sent in his lead brigade, the Louisiana Brigade, before the other two arrived. Maj. Roberdeau Wheat and his Tigers led the way, and Wheat was killed instantly by a bullet through his brain. On the heels of the Louisianans came part of Brig. Gen. Isaac R. Trimble's brigade, but it likewise was repulsed. About the same time, Longstreet sent his division against the Union left flank at Lee's direction, as a diversion, but without success.

Jackson ordered two of his divisions, commanded by Brig. Gen. W. H. Chase Whiting and Brig. Gen. Charles S. Winder, to move by echelons to their right and support Ewell. Unfortunately, he sent his orders verbally by Maj. John A. Harmon, his quartermaster, who had a limited understanding of tactical directions. By the time he found Whiting and Winder, Harmon had gotten his instructions hopelessly garbled. Eventually the orders got corrected and the divisions moved forward, but by then it was early evening.

Lee finally found Jackson on the battlefield and told the Valley general that he had decided to launch an all-out attack against the entire Union position rather than continue the piecemeal assaults. Jackson rode off to urge his divisions to the front. The terrain and undergrowth hindered their advance, and by the time the final assault began, the time was 7 P.M. and the sun was about to set.

McClellan, meanwhile, was packing up his headquarters two miles to Porter's rear. All day long the Union commander had attempted to keep track of events and rumors by telegraph wire. Porter had obliged with a stream of messages: Hill's attack had failed; Hill again threatened his position; Porter needed reinforcements; Hill had been repulsed; the day was won; the day was lost. Finally, after much vacillation, McClellan promised reinforcements, then asked his other corps commanders if they could spare any troops. When their answers ranged from no to maybe, McClellan stood around worrying, holding a telegram from Porter reporting that he was about to be driven from his position. Finally, McClellan ordered forward just two brigades from Sumner's corps—about a tenth of the forces at his disposal. They arrived on the field just as Porter's line collapsed under Lee's assault, and helped hold back the victorious Confederates as Porter's men fled.

Although many Confederate units later claimed to have been the first to have broken Porter's line, the breakthroughs occurred at several points simultaneously. Porter's defense had been gallant—and not without cost.

The Confederates swept over the crest of the plateau screaming the Rebel Yell. Porter's men fell back fighting through the heavy undergrowth; many were surrounded and taken prisoner. The rest were saved by the rapidly descending darkness, the disintegration of the assaulting Confederate line amid the gloom and thickets, and the timely arrival of Sumner's brigades. Porter and his men joined the rest of McClellan's army in its continuing retreat in the night.

The carnage wrought at Gaines's Mill was without parallel in Virginia: about 6,800 Union casualties and 8,700 Confederate, out of about 40,000 and 57,000 men engaged respectively. Lee had dealt McClellan his only true defeat of the Peninsula and Seven Days' campaigns.

Although Lee was pleased with the results of the day's action, he was far from satisfied with Jackson's performance. Had Jackson not wandered miles and hours out of his way, thereby missing his appointed deadlines, Lee could have massed his entire army for an attack that may have sent the Federal army into a panicked flight. As it was, McClellan's Army of the Potomac remained intact and withdrew in good order, and Lee's Army of Northern Virginia faced stiff fighting ahead.

The Gaines's Mill battlefield has suffered from recent development and highway construction, yet large portions of it remain intact and are still used as farmland. Richmond National Battlefield Park owns more than sixty acres around the Watt House at the center of Porter's line and two acres at the Garthright House. Hanover County owns a tract of about fifty acres around the Garthright House that includes significant Federal earthworks dating from the battle of Cold Harbor in 1864. Several key farms in the area have been held by the same families for generations; if they are subdivided, some of the most important parts of the battlefield will be lost. ■

GARNETT'S AND GOLDING'S FARMS

Both armies spent most of Saturday, June 28, 1862, marching and reconnoitering and recovering from the bloody exertions of the day before. Maj. Gen. George B. McClellan's Army of the Potomac retreated southeastward to White Oak Swamp in Henrico County, looking for north-south roads to take it to Harrison's Landing on the James River, some fifteen miles south of the Chickahominy. In the swamp, engineers rebuilt bridges so that the army could cross, but progress was slow as men and matériel jammed the narrow, gloomy paths.

To the north, Gen. Robert E. Lee strove to learn McClellan's intentions. Because Federal artillery and rear guard commanded the Chickahominy River crossings, Lee could not reconnoiter to the south but instead could only watch for dust clouds beyond the stream to tell him which way McClellan was moving. He also sent cavalry to the east, north of the Chickahominy, to check the Richmond and York River Railroad and White House

Behind Smith's line at Garnett's and Golding's farms. VIRGINIA DEPARTMENT OF HISTORIC RESOURCES, JOHN S. SALMON

to see if they were being strongly defended. Soon the report came back: the railroad was abandoned and the White House depot evacuated, with massive piles of supplies still afire. That news, coupled with a dust cloud Lee observed to the southeast, convinced him that McClellan was heading for the James River.

To the south of the Chickahominy, east of Richmond, Confederate generals suspected that McClellan's army was on the move and decided to find out with a recon-

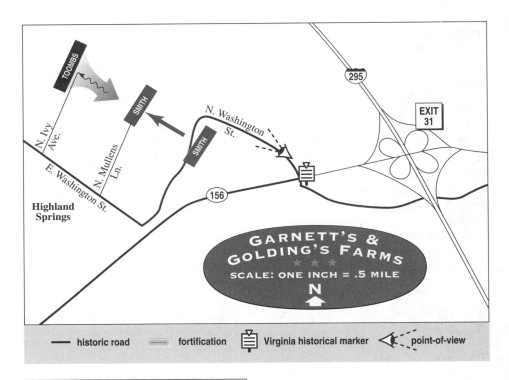

GARNETT'S &
GOLDING'S FARMS
★ ★ ★
SCALE: ONE INCH = .5 MILE
N

Highland
Springs

— historic road ═══ fortification [symbol] Virginia historical marker ◄--- point-of-view

DIRECTIONS: Recommend first visiting the Richmond National Battlefield Park Visitor Center (open 9–5 daily) at Tredegar Iron Works in downtown Richmond: I-95 Exit 74C (U.S. Rte. 33 West/U.S. Rte. 250 West, Broad St.) and follow blue-and-green signs to visitor center, Brown's Island, and Belle Isle, w. on Broad St. about .4 mile (5 blocks) to 8th St.; s. (left) on 8th St. 5 blocks to Canal St.; w. (right) on Canal St. 3 blocks to 5th St.; s. (left) on 5th St. 2 blocks to Tredegar St.; w. (right) on Tredegar Street .1 mile to visitor center and parking lot. Visit the National Park Service Web site at nps.gov/parks.html for a virtual tour of this and other national parks. To visit the battlefield directly: I-295 Exit 31B (State Rte. 156 South, Highland Springs), e. on State Rte. 156 (Airport Dr.) about .3 mile to N. Washington St., state historical marker PA-125, Seven Days' Battles—Golding's Farm, on s. side of State Rte. 156; n. (right) on N. Washington St. 1.2 miles to E. Washington St., following trace of Federal earthworks; w. (right) on E. Washington St. .3 mile to N. Mullens Lane; n. (right) on N. Mullens Lane .5 mile to Smith position; return to E. Washington St.; w. (right) on E. Washington St. .35 mile to N. Ivy Ave.; (n.) on N. Ivy Ave. .4 mile to Toombs position; return to E. Washington St.; e. (left) on E. Washington St. .7 mile to State Rte. 156; n. (left) on State Rte. 156 about 1.3 miles to I-295.

naissance in force. During the height of the battle of Gaines's Mill, Brig. Gen. John B. Magruder ordered an attack on McClellan's southern front, against Brig. Gen. William F. "Baldy" Smith's division, near Old Tavern at James M. Garnett's and Simon Gouldin's (a.k.a. Golding) farms. A sharp firefight developed, and Brig. Gen. Robert A. Toombs's brigade of Georgians suffered 271 casualties before he withdrew. It was the only significant threat to McClellan's force south of the Chickahominy all day.

Now, on June 28, Toombs pressed forward again over the same ground. This time Brig. Gen. George T. "Tige"Anderson and his brigade accompanied Toombs, who decided to attack Smith again rather than merely reconnoiter as ordered. Anderson's 7th and 8th Georgia Regiments, which Toombs posted in front of his own, bore the brunt of a vigorous Federal counterattack by the 44th Pennsylvania and

33rd New York Regiments. Anderson lost some 156 men in the futile adventure, bringing the Confederate total for the two days to 438, as opposed to 189 Union troops. The actions at Garnett's and Golding's farms accomplished little beyond fixing the idea of imminent Confederate attacks from the west in McClellan's mind.

Although much of the battlefield is covered with housing subdivisions, enough of the original contours remain to tell part of the story of the engagement. The Golding house, and a trace of Union fortifications, may survive. ■

SAVAGE'S STATION

On Sunday, June 29, 1862, Gen. Robert E. Lee pursued the retreating Army of the Potomac with the intention of catching and destroying it. The day before, convinced that Maj. Gen. George B. McClellan's objective was the James River, Lee ordered Brig. Gen. John B. Magruder to lead the pursuit with his three divisions, moving directly east along the Williamsburg Road and the Richmond and York River Railroad. Magruder was to press the Union rear guard. Maj. Gen. Benjamin Huger would march southeast down the Charles City Road and cross White Oak Swamp on his left. Huger would intercept McClellan's line of retreat at Glendale, where the Charles City Road intersected the Long Bridge and Willis Church Roads, down the latter of which McClellan intended to take his army to the river. Maj. Gen. Richard S. Ewell's division, along with Brig. Gen. J. E. B. Stuart's cavalry, would remain north of the Chickahominy River in the vicinity of Bottom's Bridge, on the unlikely chance that McClellan was bluffing a move south and

Battle of Savage's Station, sketched during the engagement. VIRGINIA HISTORICAL SOCIETY, RICHMOND, VA.

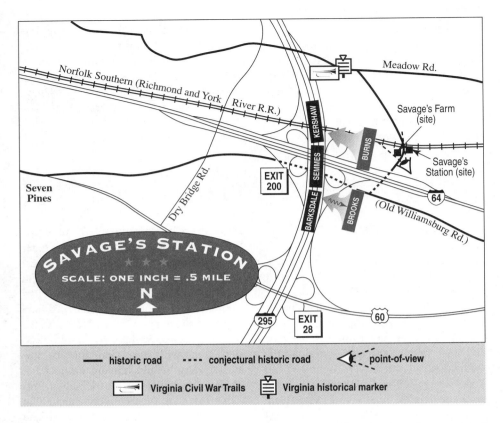

Norfolk Southern (Richmond and York River R.R.)

Meadow Rd.

Savage's Farm (site)

Savage's Station (site)

KERSHAW
SEMMES
BARKSDALE
BROOKS
BURNS

EXIT 200

64

Seven Pines

Dry Bridge Rd.

(Old Williamsburg Rd.)

SAVAGE'S STATION
★ ★ ★
SCALE: ONE INCH = .5 MILE

N

295

EXIT 28

60

— historic road   ···· conjectural historic road   ◄ point-of-view

Virginia Civil War Trails   Virginia historical marker

intended to march down the Peninsula.

Maj. Gen. James Longstreet and Maj. Gen. A. P. Hill, still encamped on the Gaines's Mill battlefield, were to make a long march west to the New Bridge, cross the Chickahominy, march down Nine Mile Road, head to Darbytown Road, take that to Long Bridge Road, and then follow it to Glendale. Maj. Gen. Theophilus H. Holmes would march his division down the River Road (present-day Rte. 5) to get farther below McClellan at Malvern Hill, just north of the James River. Maj. Gen. Thomas J. "Stonewall" Jackson, commanding his own division plus Maj. Gen. D. H. Hill's and Brig. Gen. W. H. Chase Whiting's, would march due south from his position near Gaines's Mill, head over the Chickahominy River, and press on to Savage's Station on the Richmond and

York River Railroad, where Lee expected Magruder to catch up with McClellan. Together the six divisions would smash the Union army's rear guard and roll over the rest of the retreating column. Once the fighting started, the other divisions would join in what Lee believed would be the certain destruction of the Army of the Potomac.

Lee anticipated a two-day battle, with Longstreet, Hill, and Holmes not fully involved until Jackson, Magruder, and Huger had completely engaged the Federals. Timing was essential to assemble enough firepower on McClellan's rear to bring him to bay.

Lee earnestly tried to make his directions clear to his commanders. Early in the morning, he crossed New Bridge and found Magruder on Nine Mile Road. The two generals rode together to Fair Oaks Station, with Lee explaining Magruder's and the other commanders' responsibilities in detail. At the station they parted, with Lee riding south to find Huger and talk with him, as well. Unfortunately, Magruder, who suffered from indigestion, had been drugged with morphine by his physician and did not truly comprehend everything Lee told him. Magruder especially failed to absorb the instruction that the entire operation depended on his close and aggressive pursuit of McClellan.

McClellan's army, meanwhile, had abandoned its remaining works in the night and was marching toward the James as fast as it could. To lighten their load, the troops destroyed everything that they could not carry with them. Huge fires raged along the route of march as supplies and even railroad cars burned, and towering columns of black smoke further betrayed McClellan's intentions to Lee. Union morale sharply declined, especially among the thousands of wounded at Savage's Station who had been expecting evacuation. Instead, wagons and ambulances left empty (in anticipation of the next battle), and the soldiers realized they were being abandoned unless they were well enough to walk.

McClellan's rear guard consisted of Brig. Gen. Edwin V. Sumner's corps, with two divisions, Brig. Gen. Samuel P. Heintzelman's corps, also with two, and Brig. Gen. William B. Franklin, with one. McClellan regarded Sumner, the senior corps commander, as incompetent, so rather than appoint him commander of the guard, he appointed no one.

Magruder's close pursuit got under way before 9 A.M., when Confederate cavalry collided with Union pickets. Magruder's advance infantry struck the rear of the column about the same time two miles west of Savage's Station, on the farm and in the orchard owned by a Mr. Allen. The engagement at Allen's Farm opened the battle of Savage's Station as two Georgia regiments from Brig. Gen. George T. Anderson's brigade fought two Pennsylvania regiments from Sumner's corps for some two hours. Finally, the engagement broke off, and the opposing units backed away from each other.

After the Allen's Farm engagement, Magruder should have pressed on at once, but addled by morphine, he became convinced instead that he was about to be attacked and overwhelmed by a superior force. He sent a frantic message to Lee, who was with Huger, begging for reinforcements. Lee ordered two brigades from Huger to Magruder, instructing that they return if they were not engaged by 2 P.M. Lee did not want the chance for a decisive action to slip away as at Gaines's Mill.

Jackson's advance, meanwhile, had stalled at the Grapevine and Alexander bridge sites, in part because both of the narrow bridges had to be rebuilt for his large force to pass over them efficiently. The other reason for Jackson's coming to a dead halt in his march was Lee's contingency directive: If McClellan tried to send all or part of his army down the Peninsula near the Chickahominy, instead of continuing to the James River, Stuart and Jackson should prevent that movement until Lee could send reinforcements. Unfortunately, Lee's chief of staff garbled the order, which convinced Jackson that he was now supposed to stay on the north side of the Chickahominy to guard the river crossings instead of passing over to the south bank as planned to join Magruder. Between bridge problems and confusion over Lee's discretionary order, Jackson stayed put.

Just as Confederate plans fell apart, the Union rear guard began to disintegrate. Heintzelman, whose corps was to the south of Sumner's and Franklin's corps, decided on his own that the other units were more than sufficient to defend Savage's Station. He decided to follow the rest of the army but neglected to tell his fellow generals. They did not see him leave, as a wood separated his corps from their commands.

At 2 P.M. Huger arrived at Magruder's headquarters to reclaim his two brigades. Soon thereafter, Jackson sent word to Magruder that he would not be joining him because of the (misunderstood) orders from Lee. It now was up to Magruder to attack Sumner's 26,600 men with his own 14,000.

Finally, after more hesitation, at 5 P.M. Magruder acted, sending two and a half brigades forward. When the force deployed, Brig. Gen. Joseph B. Kershaw took the left flank, Brig. Gen. Paul J. Semmes took the center, and Brig. Gen. Richard Griffith was on the right.

On the Union side, Brig. Gen. William B. Franklin and Brig. Gen. John Sedgwick were reconnoitering to the west of Savage's Station when they saw Kershaw's brigade approaching. They galloped back to the station and ordered skirmishers forward, followed by Brig. Gen. William W. Burns's Philadelphia brigade, to engage the Confederates. Sumner reinforced Burns with regiments from one brigade and then another, until both sides had more or less equal numbers on the field. Brig. Gen. William T. H. Brooks's brigade held the Union left flank. The Confederates, ensconced in the woods, held the tactical advantage against the Federals, who had to cross open fields to attack them. The battle went on until darkness ended it.

By the end of the day, counting the opening engagement at the Allen Farm, the battle of Savage's Station had resulted in the loss of some 1,038 Federals (not counting 2,500 wounded or sick Union soldiers abandoned by the retreating army at the field hospital in and around the Savage house) and 473 Confederates. Lee, disappointed that his opportunity to crush McClellan seemed to be slipping away, reprimanded Magruder for making so little progress against the enemy. True, Magruder had wasted most of the day, but by the time he did attack he was vastly outnumbered. Once more sloppy staff work at Lee's headquarters and Jackson's confusion had combined to deny the Confederate commander a clear victory.

Two interstate highways—I-64 and I-295—intersect on top of the Confederate position at the Savage's Station battlefield. The interchange there obliterates all but Griffith's ground to the southwest and most of the Union position, as well. At the station site itself, a later house and a few outbuildings (one of which may be antebellum) remain in derelict condition; the station is long gone. The remainder of the battlefield is targeted for development. ◾

During the night of June 29–30, 1862, the Union retreat continued. For the army, the night was a nightmare of marching, halting, countermarching, halting, marching some more, and halting again. Furthermore, the deep woods were so black, whole brigades got lost. Besides exhaustion, heat and dust added to the army's miseries.

At Savage's Station, the Union rear guard joined in the retreat, except for the corps of Brig. Gen. Edwin V. Sumner, who was convinced he could defeat the Confederates in the morning. Maj. Gen. George B. McClellan, commander of the Army of the Potomac, finally got Sumner to move south by threatening to arrest him.

The last unit to leave the battlefield was the 4th United States Artillery. The artillerists hurried after the rest of the army at first light and burned the White Oak Swamp bridge after they crossed. Behind them, some 2,500 wounded Union soldiers abandoned in the field hospital at Savage's Station awaited capture and imprisonment.

By Monday, June 30, two-thirds of the Federal army was still marching between White Oak Swamp and Glendale while one-third had reached the James River. After inspecting the line of march in the morning, McClellan rode southwest to Haxall's Landing just upriver from Malvern Hill and boarded the ironclad *Galena*. That night McClellan would enjoy a good meal and wine served on white linen tablecloths.

Gen. Robert E. Lee revised his plans for the day's activities. Stonewall Jackson finally met with Lee, who instructed him on what to do next. Jackson was to press the Union rear guard at the White Oak Swamp crossing. Meanwhile, the largest part of Lee's army, some 45,000 men, would attack McClellan's column at Glendale, just over two miles southwest, splitting the Union force in two. Maj. Gen.

Headquarters of Maj. Gen. Samuel P. Heintzelman, sketched during the battle of Glendale.
VIRGINIA HISTORICAL SOCIETY, RICHMOND, VA.

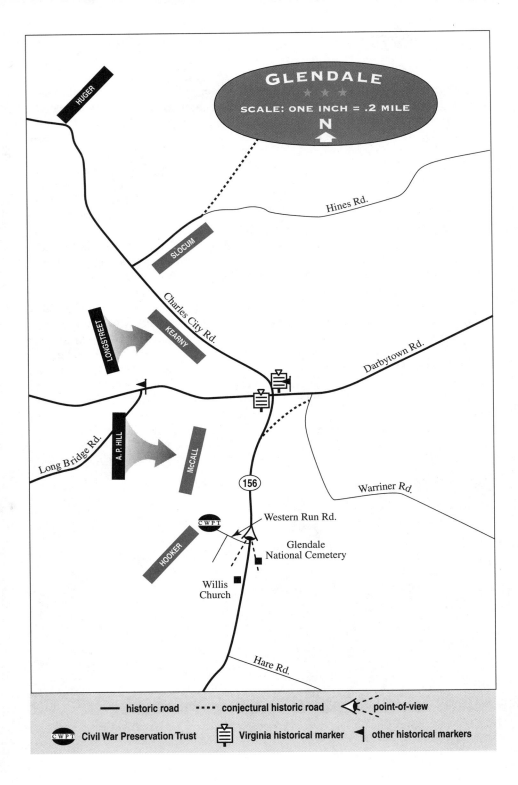

DIRECTIONS: Recommend first visiting the Richmond National Battlefield Park Visitor Center (open 9–5 daily) at Tredegar Iron Works in downtown Richmond: I-95 Exit 74C (U.S. Rte. 33 West/U.S. Rte. 250 West, Broad St.) and follow blue-and-green signs to visitor center, Brown's Island, and Belle Isle, w. on Broad St. about .4 mile (5 blocks) to 8th St.; s. (left) on 8th St. 5 blocks to Canal St.; w. (right) on Canal St. 3 blocks to 5th St.; s. (left) on 5th St. 2 blocks to Tredegar St.; w. (right) on Tredegar Street .1 mile to visitor center and parking lot. Visit the National Park Service Web site at nps.gov/parks.html for a virtual tour of this and other national parks. To visit the battlefield directly: I-295 Exit 22A (State Rte. 5 East, Charles City), e. on State Rte. 5 (New Market Rd.) about 1.8 mile to Long Bridge Rd.; n. (left) on Long Bridge Rd. 1.2 miles to Darbytown Rd. and Richmond Battlefield Markers Association marker, Frayser's Farm; e. (right) on Darbytown Rd. .5 mile to State Rte. 156 (Willis Church Rd.) and state historical marker PA-159, Seven Days' Battles—Glendale (Frayser's Farm) and Richmond Battlefield Markers Association marker, Riddell's Shop; s. (right) on State Rte. 156 and state historical marker PA-175, Seven Days' Battles—Glendale (Frayser's Farm), then continue .6 mile to Western Run Rd. at n. end of Glendale National Cemetery and proceed 2 blocks to Civil War Preservation Trust Glendale battlefield site at end of cul-de-sac; return to State Rte. 156; s. (right) on State Rte. 156 3.1 miles to State Rte. 5 (New Market Rd.); w. (right) on State Rte. 5 4.5 miles to I-295.

Benjamin Huger, approaching from the northwest on Charles City Road, would strike first with his division, then be supported by those of Maj. Gen. James Longstreet and Maj. Gen. A. P. Hill. Huger had only three miles to march, while Longstreet and Hill were about seven miles west. Far to the south, Maj. Gen. Theophilus H. Holmes marched his division eastward on River Road.

The Union commanders left behind by McClellan did the best they could to guard the long train of supply wagons and artillery. A VI Corps division and a II Corps division stood at the northern end of the column to contest the White Oak Swamp crossing. To the west, Brig. Gen.

Henry W. Slocum's division blocked Huger's approach. Two divisions from Heintzelman's corps, commanded by Brig. Gen. Philip Kearny and Brig. Gen. Joseph Hooker, extended the Union line two miles south of Slocum but with a gap between them that was filled with a division from Brig. Gen. Fitz John Porter's corps (the rest of the corps was already at Malvern Hill), while a division of Brig. Gen. Edwin V. Sumner's corps was posted behind and to the left of McCall. It was a jagged, discontinuous defensive line, resulting from the lack of command coherence.

Huger, as cautious as Magruder had been the day before, edged his way southeastward through the woods on Charles City Road. Ahead of him, pioneers from Slocum's division felled trees across the road to slow his advance. Huger cooperated with Slocum's tactic by halting his division and ordering his axmen to cut a new road through the thick woods. Several miles to the southwest, Lee waited with Longstreet, listening in vain for the sound of Huger engaging the Federals.

Longstreet and Hill arrived at the Long Bridge Road intersection with the Darbytown Road before noon, accompanied by Lee. At 2 P.M. the sound of gunfire arose to Lee's left, but too far away to be Huger (it was Jackson, at White Oak Swamp). At the same time, Pres. Jefferson Davis arrived at the front with an entourage, joining Lee as he attempted to find out what was happening. Soon Hill's picket line, advancing down the Long Bridge Road, ran into their Federal counterparts, and a sharp fight ensued. Artillery shells began landing near Lee and Davis, prompting Hill to summarily order both men to the rear of his sector.

Lee finally learned that a third of McClellan's army had already reached the James River behind Malvern Hill, while the remainder was at White Oak Swamp and Glendale. When the situation before him had not changed by 4 P.M., Lee decided to attack both ends of McClellan's army simultaneously and salvage the day. He ordered Brig. Gen. John B. Magruder's divisions, which were in reserve, to join Holmes on the River Road and attack Malvern Hill, while Longstreet and Hill would press on against Glendale. Meanwhile, he expected Huger to join in soon there and Jackson to strike at White Oak Swamp. Neither expectation would be met.

Nor would his expectations for Holmes, an old, deaf soldier far past his prime. Unaware that the larger part of the Union artillery reserve was on Malvern Hill, or that Porter had most of two infantry divisions nearby, or that the Union gunboats *Galena* and *Aroostook* were on the James River, Holmes opened up on Malvern Hill shortly after 4 P.M., and the Federal response was overwhelming and devastating. Magruder's infantry arrived at Holmes's headquarters, but the befuddled commander had no idea what to do with them. Magruder later was recalled to the Glendale front. Lee's southern thrust ended in a debacle.

At Glendale, Hill's and Longstreet's divisions engaged McCall's just west of the farm owned by R. H. Nelson. The attacking line was composed of one brigade on the right, one in the center, and one on the left. Charging through thick woods, the right flank of the line emerged in front of five batteries of McCall's artillery. The brigade, which had not yet seen combat during the Seven Days, lost all order in their enthusiasm, but their momentum carried them through the guns and into McCall's main line, which broke under the impact. Soon the other two brigades joined in, each meeting stiff resistance. Opposing the Confederates were the brigades of Brig. Gen. George G. Meade on the right and Brig. Gen. Truman Seymour on the left.

In places the fighting was hand-to-hand, with clubbed muskets, knives, ramrods, and even fists being used. (One Union captain in the thick of the melee rallied his troops only to find that he was trying to command Confederates. He managed to avoid being captured or killed after he discovered his mistake.) The ground changed hands time and again, but eventually McCall's line broke, and some of his artillery fell into Confederate hands.

On McCall's flanks, Kearny to the north and Hooker to the south held the line against repeated Confederate attacks. Before the battle ended after sunset, Longstreet and Hill had committed virtually every brigade at their disposal to the fray, while on the Union side Sumner had fed reinforcements piecemeal into the line to contain the breakthrough. Sedgwick's division, some from the reserve position and others from White Oak Swamp, rushed forward and plugged the gap after a brutal counterattack. When darkness fell soon after 8:30 P.M., the Union line held.

The battle of Glendale, which included some of the fiercest fighting many of the troops had seen until then, thus ended with nightfall. The Union army incurred some 2,800 casualties, the Confederates 3,600. Lee's best opportunity to trap and destroy the Army of the Potomac had been lost.

The Glendale battlefield remains largely agricultural or forested, with some light development along the roads. Woodlots make visual observation of the battlefield difficult in places. The Civil War Preservation Trust has acquired part of the site. ∎

WHITE OAK SWAMP

Gen. Robert E. Lee's orders to Maj. Gen. Thomas J. "Stonewall" Jackson before the battle of Glendale remain a mystery. The two men met privately early in the morning of Monday, June 30, 1862, and apparently Lee's orders were for Jackson to march to White Oak Swamp and engage the Union force there with sufficient vigor to prevent its reinforcing the remainder of the rear guard at Glendale. Jackson was partially successful.

Commanded by Brig. Gen. William B. Franklin, Brig. Gen. William F. "Baldy" Smith's and Brig. Gen. Israel B. Richardson's divisions contested the White Oak Swamp crossing at the northern end of the Federal column. Jackson approached the swamp from the north, marching down White Oak Road with his artillery chief, Col. Stapleton Crutchfield, at the head of the column.

Crutchfield observed Federal artillery and infantry beyond the swamp on the east side of the road and looked for high ground on which to place his guns. He found a position near White Oak Road, paralleling the stream and allowing him a field of fire diagonally across the swamp to the Union batteries.

Jackson arrived at noon and approved Crutchfield's arrangements. Seven batteries, thirty-one guns, faced the Federals. At 2 P.M., the Confederate cannons opened up on the Union line, sending teamsters flying southward and disabling several cannons.

Jackson and Maj. Gen. D. H. Hill led a reconnaissance with Col. Thomas T. Munford's 2nd Virginia Cavalry Regiment across White Oak Swamp near the ruined bridge. Suddenly they came under artillery fire themselves from Union guns that had been screened from Crutchfield's view by trees. Jackson and Hill withdrew to the north side of the swamp while Munford led his men eastward and found a ford a quarter-mile downstream. He reported his discovery to Jackson, saying that he thought infantry could cross there easily and come in behind the Federals.

Brig. Gen. Wade Hampton, meanwhile, had been conducting his own reconnaissance and found another, even closer crossing point. He reported to Jackson that

Confederate artillery bombarding Franklin's rear guard at White Oak Swamp. LIBRARY OF CONGRESS

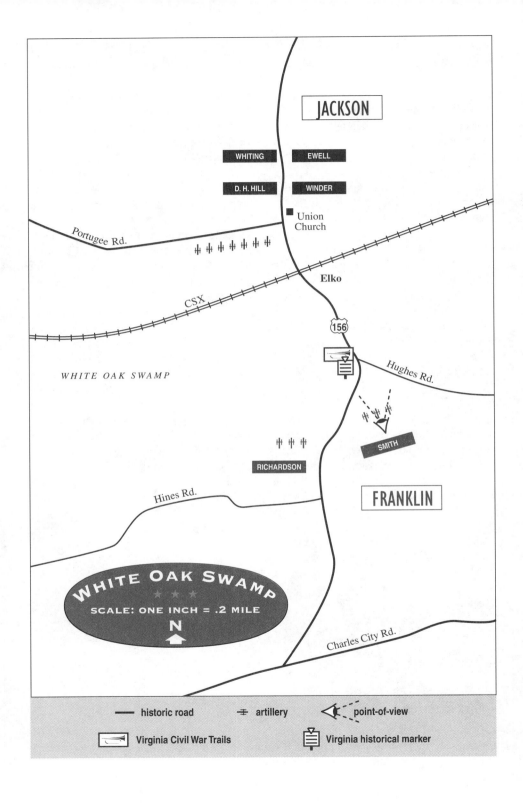

JACKSON

WHITING   EWELL

D. H. HILL   WINDER

Union
Church

Portugee Rd.

Elko

CSX

156

Hughes Rd.

WHITE OAK SWAMP

SMITH

RICHARDSON

Hines Rd.

FRANKLIN

WHITE OAK SWAMP
★ ★ ★
SCALE: ONE INCH = .2 MILE
N

Charles City Rd.

—— historic road   ╪ artillery   ◁⋯ point-of-view

Virginia Civil War Trails   Virginia historical marker

Jackson had decided that Franklin's command was too strong for him to attack without the artillery essential to countering the Federal guns, so he and his four divisions proceeded no farther. As a result of his inaction, regiments were detached from Franklin's command in the late afternoon to help reverse the Confederate tide at Glendale.

Jackson never informed Lee of his predicament, and Lee did not send anyone to find Jackson until it was too late. For that matter, Lee did not intervene to push Maj. Gen. Benjamin Huger along when the South Carolina aristocrat allowed felled trees on the Charles City Road to prevent his crucial attack on the Union center.

The casualties on both sides were low at White Oak Swamp: three Confederate artillerymen killed and a dozen wounded, plus an indeterminate number of Federals.

The White Oak Swamp battlefield is largely intact except for Jackson's artillery position, which is covered by a housing subdivision. There has otherwise been little development in the area, and the swamp is a natural wetland not subject to development. ■

it could be bridged but only for infantry and was told to build his bridge. However, when Hampton carried out the order and returned to inform Jackson, he was met only with silence.

MALVERN HILL

During the Peninsula and Seven Days' campaigns, the Army of the Potomac never saw a better defensive position than Malvern Hill in Henrico County. The hill, actually a broad plateau, is located about a mile north of the James River. It stands some 120 feet higher than the river, is about three-quarters of a mile wide and just over a mile deep. In 1862 it provided clear views across farms to the west and north.

The army had spent the last week in June retreating to Malvern Hill to gain the shelter of the gunboats on James River and to regroup for the short march southeast to its new supply and future embarkation point, Harrison's Landing at Berkeley plantation. In the early morning hours of Tuesday, July 1, as the sun rose promising another hot day, most of the Union soldiers felt certain they would see combat again before the light faded.

The previous evening, as the sun set and the bloody fight at Glendale dwindled away, Maj. Gen. George B. McClellan

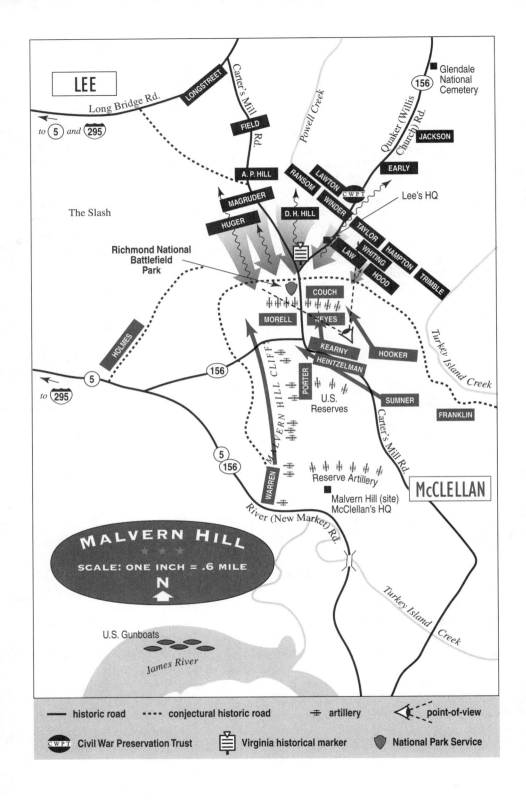

LEE

Long Bridge Rd.

LONGSTREET

Carter's Mill Rd.

to (5) and (295)

FIELD

Powell Creek

Glendale National Cemetery

156

Quaker (Willis) Church Rd.

JACKSON

EARLY

A. P. HILL

RANSOM

LAWTON

WINDER

CWPT

Lee's HQ

MAGRUDER

The Slash

HUGER

D. H. HILL

TAYLOR

HAMPTON

Richmond National Battlefield Park

LAW

WHITING

TRIMBLE

HOOD

COUCH

HOLMES

MORELL

KEYES

Turkey Island Creek

(5)

to (295)

156

MALVERN HILL CLIFF

KEARNY

HEINTZELMAN

PORTER

U.S. Reserves

HOOKER

SUMNER

FRANKLIN

Carter's Mill Rd.

5
156

WARREN

Reserve Artillery

McCLELLAN

Malvern Hill (site)
McClellan's HQ

River (New Market) Rd.

MALVERN HILL
★ ★ ★
SCALE: ONE INCH = .6 MILE
N

Turkey Island Creek

U.S. Gunboats

James River

─── historic road   ---- conjectural historic road   ‡ artillery   ◁ point-of-view

CWPT Civil War Preservation Trust   Virginia historical marker   National Park Service

DIRECTIONS: Recommend first visiting the Richmond National Battlefield Park Visitor Center (open 9–5 daily) at Tredegar Iron Works in downtown Richmond: I-95 Exit 74C (U.S. Rte. 33 West/U.S. Rte. 250 West, Broad St.) and follow blue-and-green signs to visitor center, Brown's Island, and Belle Isle, w. on Broad St. about .4 mile (5 blocks) to 8th St.; s. (left) on 8th St. 5 blocks to Canal St.; w. (right) on Canal St. 3 blocks to 5th St.; s. (left) on 5th St. 2 blocks to Tredegar St.; w. (right) on Tredegar Street .1 mile to visitor center and parking lot. Visit the National Park Service Web site at nps.gov/parks.html for a virtual tour of this and other national parks. To visit the battlefield directly: I-295 Exit 22A (State Rte. 5 East, Charles City), e. on State Rte. 5 (New Market Rd.) about 4.3 miles to state historical marker PA-240, Engagement at Malvern Cliffs; continue on State Rte. 5 .2 mile to State Rte. 156 North; n. (left) on State Rte. 156 2.2 miles to Malvern Hill Unit, Richmond National Battlefield Park, and state historical marker PA-235, Seven Days' Battles—Malvern Hill, and Richmond Battlefield Markers Association marker, Battlefield of Malvern Hill; return to State Rte. 156 and turn n. (left) .1 mile to state historical marker PA-230, Seven Days' Battles—Malvern Hill, then .1 mile to state historical marker PA-220, Seven Days' Battles—Malvern Hill, then .2 mile to Civil War Preservation Trust site at Methodist Parsonage; return s. .1 mile to Carter's Mill Rd.; w. (right) on Carter's Mill Rd. 1.4 miles to Long Bridge Rd.; left on Long Bridge Rd. 2.6 miles to State Rte. 5; w. (right) on State Rte. 5 1.8 miles to I-295.

disembarked from the ironclad *Galena* at Haxall's Landing and rode the few miles east to Malvern Hill. About forty-five minutes later he reboarded the vessel, satisfied at the defensive dispositions his staff had made, and steamed away downstream to Harrison's Landing. Once again his army was without its commanding general, although McClellan would later rejoin his army on its extreme right flank, far away from the action.

As the first corps commander to reach Malvern Hill, arriving the morning of June 30, Brig. Gen. Fitz John Porter assumed responsibility for its defense. He posted the artillery reserve overlooking the River Road, where it wreaked havoc on Maj. Gen. Theophilus H. Holmes of the Army of Northern Virginia. Now, on the morning of July 1, Porter extended his line north and east, adding artillery and infantry as they marched up the hillside.

Brig. Gen. George Sykes's division formed the Union left above the River Road, with the divisions of Brig. Gen. Darius N. Couch of Brig. Gen. Erasmus D. Keyes's corps, and of Brig. Gen. George W. Morell to Sykes's right on the northern end of Malvern Hill. The Union right flank extended some two and a half miles to the east and south from Couch's position. The remainder of Keyes's corps guarded Haxall's Landing.

A few miles to Porter's north, Gen. Robert E. Lee met at first light on the Long Bridge Road with Brig. Gen. John B. Magruder and Maj. Gens. James Longstreet, A. P. Hill, and Stonewall Jackson. Lee decided to place the divisions of Jackson, Magruder, and Maj. Gen. Benjamin Huger—still struggling through the woods near the blocked Charles City Road—in the forefront, as they had not been engaged the day before. Longstreet and Hill would form the reserve.

All the generals were eager to renew the offensive, despite the Union army's strong position atop Malvern Hill. Lee directed Jackson to march down Willis Church or Quaker Road, with Magruder following while Huger made his way along a farm lane leading from Long Bridge Road south. Longstreet's and Hill's division would form on the Carter farm to the west of Malvern Hill. Feeling unwell, Lee asked Longstreet to turn his command over to Brig. Gen. Richard H. Anderson and ride beside him so that he could take over if the need arose.

The march got off to a poor start when a local guide led Magruder and his men down the wrong Quaker Road. Apparently the local folk also called other lanes by that name, and Magruder was led away from the battlefield on an alternate Quaker Road. Longstreet rode after Magruder and got him turned around, but the mess took three hours to untangle.

Jackson, for the only time since he left the Shenandoah Valley, arrived on the battlefield first. He took his position on the Confederate left flank, to the east of Willis Church Road, with three other divisions, and placed his artillery there, as well. Maj. Gen. D. H. Hill posted his five brigades to Jackson's right, their left anchored on the road. Two brigades from Huger's division, Brig. Gen. Lewis A. Armistead's and Brig. Gen. Ambrose R. Wright's, went into the Confederate line to Hill's right, which Lee had intended for Magruder. The rest of Huger's division and all of Magruder's were nowhere to be seen.

Lee and Longstreet scouted the Union position and sought good sites for the Confederate artillery. Each found a high hill with clear fields of fire. Lee quickly formulated his plan. Two "grand batteries" would pound the Union guns into submission, then the infantry would attack, marching up the long, gentle northern slope of Malvern Hill.

Immediately, things started going wrong. Instead of two massed batteries hammering the Union front, only sixteen guns were assembled to form the left grand battery, and as soon as they opened up, the thirty-seven Federal cannons on the north slope of Malvern Hill responded with a devastating fire. The right grand battery fared as poorly. Of thirty-six guns in the vicinity, only six got into the fight, and they soon were blasted out of action. Union warships in the James River joined in, but a number of their rounds fell short and inflicted several casualties on the hill until their fire was stopped. The unequal artillery duel died away about 4 P.M.

Lee compounded the problem by issuing two confusing orders. The first was written for him by chief of staff Col. Robert H. Chilton, who had previously badly mangled Lee's instructions. Now Chilton struck again, wording the order so as to leave the decision to attack with the infantry up to Armistead alone and neglecting to write the time of the order down. Copies were widely distributed, specifying that Armistead would signal his attack to the rest of the army with the Rebel Yell.

Lee's second, verbal order was to Magruder, who finally arrived on the field in time to see Armistead advance three regiments against Union sharpshooters, then take cover from Union guns in a ravine near Malvern Hill. Magruder interpreted this as a successful operation and sent a courier to find Lee and report it. Earlier, during the artillery duel, some Confederate shells landed among Sumner's corps on Malvern Hill, and many of the men ran to the rear for cover. Brig. Gen. W. H. Chase Whiting, misinterpreting this movement as a general flight by McClellan's army, reported it to Lee, who received both reports as he was reconnoitering on his left, out of sight of the front. Lee in turn sent word to Magruder to follow up on Armistead's "success" with an attack of his own. Magruder, still smarting from Lee's rebuke for his lack of initiative at Savage's Station, hastened to comply and looked for troops to command.

Four of Huger's brigades—those of Armistead, Wright, Brig. Gen. Robert Ransom, Jr., and Brig. Gen. William Mahone—were at the front near Magruder, who sent an aide to the rear to find Huger. The South Carolinian firmly declined either to come forward with the rest of his command or to release any of his brigades at the front to Magruder's authority. Armistead, of course, already had committed half his force, and Wright and Mahone volunteered despite Huger's orders, while

Union artillery on Malvern Hill fires over Porter's infantry at advancing Confederates. LIBRARY OF CONGRESS

Ransom declined. Magruder assembled his makeshift command in a rough line of battle.

The Union artillery quickly found the range as the Confederates emerged from the woods. Magruder's line fell apart, with Wright driving ahead of Mahone in the center, scattering the 14th New York and gaining a toehold at the top of the steep northwest slope, while Armistead's men were pinned down on the left. Federal marksmen known as Berdan's Sharpshooters (officially, the 1st U.S. Sharpshooters Regiment) found the pickings easy. As the Confederate charge approached, the sharpshooters fell back to Morell's main line, where they joined with the artillery to stop Wright's men some 300 yards short of their objective. Mahone, following behind Wright, also was driven back.

To the rear of the Confederate line, D. H. Hill had started preparing a bivouac for the night when he heard the Rebel Yell resounding from the front, about where he knew Armistead to be. Quickly, he ordered his division into the fray. One brigade after another struggled through the woods and into an open field toward the sound of battle and, one at a time, all five charged up Malvern Hill in a futile, uncoordinated assault. All were beaten back, with enormous losses, by massed artillery and rifle fire. Atop the hill, Porter shifted his infantry effectively to meet the successive Confederate attacks.

Lee, meanwhile, sought to salvage the day by committing the rest of his army in a coordinated attack as he had at Gaines's Mill. Unlike that success, however, Lee would be stymied by the chaotic situation at his front and rear. Magruder rode frantically all over the field, throwing in each regiment as it arrived. Jackson's division, attempting to move forward to Hill's support, found itself in a sea of stragglers and walking wounded that blocked the narrow roads.

The final assault, which came as darkness descended on the battlefield, was directed by Maj. Gen. Lafayette McLaws, who sent in two of his own brigades and picked up the remnants of Armistead's and

Wright's in what looked to Union defenders like an attack by an armed mob. For a while after dark, the Federal cannons kept firing, giving the battlefield an appropriately red, hellish glow. The Army of Northern Virginia suffered 5,300 casualties, the Army of the Potomac about 3,200. The Seven Days' campaign was over.

The next morning, the Confederates found the Union army gone, except for some pickets watching them from Malvern Hill. Porter had spent half the night trying to convince McClellan to counterattack, but the Union commander continued the withdrawal to Harrison's Landing. Most of Lee's generals were amazed that they were not under attack by dawn. Lee sent Jeb Stuart to find the Federals, and he located them downriver in a strong defensive position near Harrison's Landing. Lee's army marched in pursuit on Wednesday, July 3, but was slowed by a heavy downpour and muddy roads. On July 4 Lee carefully reconnoitered the ground. After noting the strength of the Union defenses and the gunboats in the river, he decided not to attack. McClellan had escaped.

Malvern Hill is the best preserved of the Seven Days' battlefields. Richmond National Battlefield Park owns a unit there, more than 500 acres that includes the heart of Porter's artillery position and the area on the Union left and front across which Huger's and Magruder's Confederates repeatedly attacked and recoiled. Some of the battlefield remains privately owned, however, and is subject to development or other uses. A few years ago it appeared likely that part of the Federal position would be chewed away by a gravel-mining operation. That land recently was saved. ■

NORTHERN VIRGINIA CAMPAIGN, 1862

Gen. Robert E. Lee kept a wary eye on Maj. Gen. George B. McClellan and the Army of the Potomac for several days following the end of the Seven Days' campaign on July 1, 1862. The Union army had successfully evaded Lee's attempts to crush it and still presented a formidable front behind its strong fortifications at Harrison's Landing on the James River. Lee mustered about 72,000 men of his Army of Northern Virginia to face McClellan's 90,000.

In addition to McClellan's force in Charles City County, Lee faced threats in two other parts of the state. Maj. Gen. Ambrose E. Burnside, freshly arrived at Fort Monroe with 7,000 men from his successful expedition against Confederate strong points on the North Carolina sounds, stood poised to march to McClellan's aid from the eastern end of the Peninsula. To the north, Maj. Gen. John Pope, in command of three armies dubbed the Army of Virginia, had a combined force of some 40,000 men.

McClellan claimed to Maj. Gen. Henry W. Halleck, the newly appointed general-in-chief of the United States Army, that he could defeat Lee's force, which he overestimated at 200,000 men, if only he had Pope's and Burnside's armies with him and some 20,000 soldiers from the western armies, as well. He had also spelled out his plans to Abraham Lincoln when the president made a visit to Harrison's Landing on July 8. Both of McClellan's superiors were cool to his ideas, however, and on August 3 Halleck wired him to evacuate his army from the Richmond front and join forces with Pope. McClellan had been replaced as commander of an active Union army in the field.

At the same time, Lee learned from Lt. John S. Mosby—who had been captured by the Federals and then released at Fort Monroe—that Burnside had been ordered north. Seeing McClellan's army embarking on its steamers, Lee knew that the campaign against Richmond from the Peninsula was over, and the next theater of war would open in northern Virginia. If he moved quickly enough, his principal opponent would be Pope, not McClellan.

John Pope was a difficult man to like. If possible, Pope was even more full of himself than McClellan—pompous, impetuous, abrasive, loud-mouthed, and a braggart. Given to windy proclamations, he allegedly datelined his pronouncements "headquarters in the saddle." Both Union and Confederate wags quickly joked that his headquarters were where his hindquarters ought to be, and he didn't know the one from the other.

Even Pope's detractors, however, usually would admit that the man was highly intelligent and personally courageous as a field commander. His recent promotion had come on the heels of his successful campaign against several Confederate positions along the Mississippi River. Pope's tendency to hog the credit for success while delegating the blame for failure to every subordinate from general to private

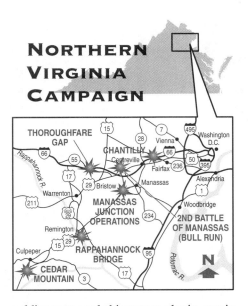

NORTHERN VIRGINIA CAMPAIGN

ginia from Sperryville, at the eastern base of the Blue Ridge Mountains, to Falmouth, just above Fredericksburg. Maj. Gen. Franz Sigel, a veteran German officer, led Pope's right flank at Sperryville, replacing Maj. Gen. John C. Frémont, who had resigned. Maj. Gen. Irvin McDowell, the loser at the first battle of Manassas and subsequently commander of the defenses of Washington, held the left flank at Falmouth, with one of his divisions separated and stationed at Waterloo Bridge a few miles west of Warrenton. Maj. Gen. Nathaniel P. Banks led the third corps, which was positioned in the center of Pope's line at Washington (usually called Little Washington), in Rappahannock County. Brig. Gen. Samuel W. Crawford's brigade was detached from Banks's command and stationed some twenty miles in advance of the main line at Culpeper Court House, accompanied by Brig. Gen. John P. Hatch's cavalry.

After Lee learned that Crawford was in Culpeper, he countered the threat to his rear even before he was certain of McClellan's intentions. He divided his army and on Sunday, July 13, ordered Jackson to march toward Pope to watch the enemy's movements and take any opportunity to attack. While Jackson ultimately would have about 24,000 men with which to confront Pope's growing army (its numbers had risen to almost 50,000), Lee retained most of the Army of Northern Virginia near Richmond while McClellan threatened the capital. Lee entrusted Jackson with semi-independent command, and Stonewall soon demonstrated that Lee's confidence was not misplaced.

By July 19 Jackson had reached Gordonsville, a key railroad junction thought to be Pope's objective, where the Virginia Central Railroad touched the southern terminus of the Orange and Alexandria Railroad. Gordonsville became Jackson's

soldier soon made him unpopular in certain quarters of his new command. Officers especially were incensed by a patronizing proclamation in which he implied he had arrived from the West to turn cowards into heroes.

Pope also angered Virginia civilians by threatening to wage war on them as well as on the Southern armies. In Missouri, where Pope had served, a guerrilla war was raging within the state in addition to the larger conflict. Perhaps anticipating similar tactics by supposedly "noncombatant" Virginians, Pope threatened to hold them responsible for actions by Confederates against Union forces in their counties, even to the point of summary execution. He also ordered his army to commandeer supplies from civilians without recompense. At a period of the war when some semblance of chivalry still existed in both eastern armies, such orders appalled many military men on both sides as well as their intended victims. Some of Pope's officers were in a state of near mutiny as the campaign opened.

Pope's army consisted of three corps spread in an arc across north-central Vir-

headquarters, his army's supply depot, and his base for operations against Pope.

In early August Jackson got word that part of Pope's army was moving south from Culpeper Court House. Unknown to Jackson, Pope's plan was to march to the Rapidan River, an east-west tributary of the Rappahannock that separated Culpeper County from Orange County to the south, where he planned a southwestward feint toward Charlottesville to compel Jackson either to fall back in that direction, split his force, or head north to offer combat. Jackson chose the last-named course, intending to meet and defeat the vanguard of Pope's army before the rest could arrive in support. His army marched out of Gordonsville on the afternoon of Thursday, August 7.

August in Virginia means summer at its hottest and most humid, and both Jackson's and Pope's armies suffered dreadfully as they marched toward each other on the Culpeper-Orange Road. The dust rose in clouds, choking men and horses, and soldiers straggled and fell by the roadside, prostrated by the intense heat.

The two armies collided on Saturday, August 9, at Cedar Mountain in southwestern Culpeper County, about four miles north of the Rapidan River. Maj. Gen. Richard S. Ewell and his division led Jackson's column, followed by Brig. Gen. Charles S. Winder's division, with Maj. Gen. A. P. Hill and his division in the distance bringing up the rear. Late in the afternoon, Jackson deployed his army across the Culpeper-Orange Road (today in some parts U.S. Rte. 15) with his right, under Ewell, anchored on the northern base of Cedar Mountain and his left, commanded by Winder, in a wood to the west of the road. Banks threw a division into the fight. Jackson's left crumpled, and Winder fell mortally wounded. Just as the Union attack ran out of steam, Hill arrived

to renew the Confederate assault. Jackson's men pursued Banks's even after darkness fell, overrunning Pope's headquarters before breaking off the engagement. The battle, not well managed by Jackson, was nonetheless a clear Confederate victory. Jackson had more than 18,000 men engaged and suffered some 1,300 casualties, while Banks committed about 8,000 and lost around 2,400.

Once Jackson had accomplished his goal of stopping Pope's advance at Cedar Mountain, he retired with his army to Gordonsville and sent cavalry probes northward to search out other avenues for attack. Lee arrived by train to confer with him on the afternoon of August 14. Pope, Jackson informed Lee, had encamped most of his army (now some 70,000 men) on the "peninsula" formed by the confluence of the Rapidan and Rappahannock Rivers in the southeastern corner of Culpeper County. Pope's best route of withdrawal, should the need arise, was the Rappahannock River railroad bridge (at present-day Remington). If the Confederates could seize the bridge, Pope would be trapped between the two rivers.

Lee grasped the opportunity but waited until his cavalry and the supply train arrived. He sent Jackson stealthily forward to the Rapidan River, but on August 18, just before Lee's planned advance, fugitive slaves revealed his scheme to Pope, and the Union army began to withdraw across the Rappahannock. Lee then resorted to probes along the Federal front, with the idea of swinging Jackson's Valley army—now the left wing of the Army of Northern Virginia—around Pope's right flank for an assault on the Union flank and rear.

At Rappahannock Bridge, McDowell's corps still clung to the south bank of the river. Concerned that Pope could use the bridgehead to launch an assault against his army's rear as it moved around the Union right, Lee ordered Longstreet to attack McDowell and capture the bridge. At the same time, Pope ordered McDowell to withdraw across the bridge and then destroy it, securing his right flank and rear from direct assault. Both orders were executed more or less simultaneously on Saturday, August 23, with Longstreet attacking the bridgehead as McDowell's rear guard defended his departure with artillery fire from both banks of the Rappahannock River. The Federals then burned the bridge—inadvertently also accomplishing Lee's goals.

The next day Lee informed his generals that McClellan was moving his army to Aquia Creek on the Potomac River. If he joined Pope, the combined armies might number 130,000 against Lee's 55,000. Lee had to act before that happened.

He proposed sending Jackson on a broader sweep around Pope's right flank toward Manassas Junction where the Manassas Gap Railroad joined the Orange & Alexandria Railroad. Such a turning movement would disrupt Pope's supply line and put part of the Confederate army on a course toward the defenses of Washington. Surely Pope would react to such threats, and if he moved against Jackson, Lee's and Longstreet's two wings of the Confederate army would crush Pope between them.

At the appointed time—about 3 A.M. on Monday, August 25—Jackson marched his men northwest toward Salem (present-day Marshall) on the Manassas Gap Railroad. Pope, to whom the move was reported, thought Jackson was returning to the Shenandoah Valley and was unconcerned. Jackson drove his men hard all day, forcing them to eat while walking, and by dark the army had covered the twenty-six miles to Salem.

At dawn on Tuesday, August 26, Jackson trekked eastward toward Manassas

Junction by way of unguarded Thoroughfare Gap in the Bull Run Mountains. When the army reached Gainesville, Jackson swung his army on the right fork, southeastward toward Bristoe Station on the Orange & Alexandria Railroad. An hour before sunset his vanguard swept away a small Union force but failed to derail a passing train bound for Manassas Junction. The Confederates soon had better luck when they threw a switch and derailed a second northbound train, then watched as a third plowed into its rear. The engineer in a fourth train spotted the wreckage ahead in time to reverse to Warrenton Junction; soon both Washington and Pope would know that Confederates were approaching Manassas Junction. Jackson ordered an unusual night attack on the junction; it succeeded, and he now controlled two key railroad depots. Jackson posted much of his army in a strong defensive position near the junction, leaving most of Ewell's division at Bristoe Station as a rear guard.

The Union commanders thought at first that Maj. Gen. J. E. B. Stuart was on another of his famous raids, and a Union brigade under Brig. Gen. George W. Taylor headed to Manassas Junction on August 27 to drive the intruders away. When Taylor approached Manassas, the Confederates almost obliterated the Federal expedition. Now Pope knew for sure that this was no cavalry raid.

Jackson, aware that Lee and Longstreet would arrive by way of Thoroughfare Gap, withdrew his force northwest to Groveton, first destroying all the supplies that could not be eaten or carried off. His army occupied a ridge just north of and out of sight of the main east-west road there, the Warrenton Turnpike, with its left flank on Dogan's Branch and his right near the farmhouse of John Brawner. On Thursday, August 28, Pope sent the vanguard of his army northeast through Manassas Junction, then west on the turnpike toward Jackson, who was notified of the move early in the afternoon. Neither commander was certain of the other's intentions: Jackson thought Pope would rendezvous with McClellan, while Pope suspected Jackson was retreating.

About that time, the head of Longstreet's 28,000-man column reached Thoroughfare Gap and fought a brief engagement with the division commanded by Brig. Gen. James B. Ricketts. Ricketts had marched his men from their camp at New Baltimore along the east side of the Bull Run Mountains to the gap. They arrived at the gap from one side about the same time—3 P.M.—as Longstreet's vanguard, composed of Georgia regiments, approached from the other. After a sharp firefight Ricketts gave way, and Longstreet began his march through the gap, with the Texas Brigade in the lead.

Located some nine miles east at the Brawner farm, Jackson could not hear the fight at the gap. At about 5 P.M. Brig. Gen. Rufus King's division, one of three in McDowell's corps, swung into Jackson's line of view. At 6:30 Jackson attacked, beginning the second battle of Manassas.

The Brawner farm engagement lasted for some two and a half hours. As night fell the fighting died away, with the evening given over to the cries of the wounded. Jackson rode a mile west of his lines toward Thoroughfare Gap, hoping that Lee had arrived with Longstreet's half of the army, but he found the road empty. He rode back to his lines with some apprehension because he knew that Pope was now certain of his location, and in the morning he would face the entire Federal force.

When the dawn came, some 25,000 of Pope's men were to the east deploying against Jackson's own 20,000. Pope hoped to position another 25,000 to the west of Jackson and crush the Confederates between the two forces. Jackson responded by drawing his army back to an unfinished railroad grade that formed a strong defensive position just behind the Brawner farm. Here Jackson awaited Pope's attack and Lee's arrival.

Pope opened the day's combat at about 6:30 A.M. on Friday, August 29, with probes all along Jackson's line. Shortly before noon the Union general prepared to launch a massive assault against the Confederate left. To the west, a gray column appeared on the Thoroughfare Gap road, and a courier rode forward to inform Jackson that Brig. Gen. John B. Hood's division, which included the Texas Brigade, had arrived. Longstreet was entering the field. Jackson assigned the Texans to reinforce his right flank, then braced for the attack. It began at about 2 P.M., when Pope's men attacked six or seven times in successive waves. At one point, temporarily out of ammunition but unwilling to retreat a single step, some of the Confederates at the railroad cut grabbed stones and hurled them at the Federals. Finally, as on the day before, darkness ended the fighting, which had been unusually brutal.

Late in the afternoon Lee set up his headquarters on Stuart's Hill, a partly wooded knoll that afforded a good view of the action. Longstreet's forces arrived behind Lee, who kept them out of sight in the woods at the hill's eastern base. After the fighting ended, Jackson reported to Lee, but the commander was away on a reconnaissance. Jackson laid down in another tent and promptly fell asleep.

The next morning, Saturday, August 30, the battle resumed at about 8 A.M. with some desultory shelling of Jackson's line by the Federals. Then an ominous silence settled over the battlefield. Jackson reviewed his lines, then returned to Stuart's Hill, where he joined Lee, Longstreet, and

J. E. B. Stuart. The silence stretched into the afternoon.

For some reason Pope ignored reports of Longstreet's arrival on the field. He had convinced himself that Jackson would retreat rather than face his army without support. Pope waited until about 3 P.M., then unleashed his "pursuit." The attacking Federals marched directly into massed cannon and musketry, and the effect was devastating. Attack followed attack. Suddenly, as the third rank of Union soldiers began to crumple, Longstreet's 25,000 men swept onto the field, rolling over the long blue line from the Union left like an irresistible wave. The Federals fled to the safety of Henry Hill, where ironically, Jackson had stood like a stone wall little more than a year before. As darkness fell, the Union line reformed and fended off the last Confederate assaults.

All night long rain poured down on the living, the wounded, and the dead. Lee and Jackson conferred on the gray morning of Sunday, August 31. Lee's "blood was up," as those who knew him put it. He proposed to send Jackson on a flanking march to the north of Pope and into his rear, pin down the Union army, and then follow up with Longstreet and destroy it. As Lee and Jackson and Longstreet now functioned as a team, there would be no more misunderstood orders, uncoordinated attacks, or lost divisions.

Jackson set off in pursuit that afternoon. By dark his corps had marched ten miles north and encamped in rain and mud at Pleasant Valley Church after turning southeastward on the Little River Turnpike (present-day U.S. Rte. 50). The rain finally stopped at about 8 A.M. on Monday, September 1, but the sky remained darkly overcast. Jackson resumed his march down the turnpike toward Fairfax Court House. Stuart arrived to report Union soldiers around a plantation named Chantilly,

near a low ridge called Ox Hill. Pope may have been a blustering blowhard, but he was no fool; his cavalry had detected Jackson's move, and the Union commander was ready for it.

At about noon Jackson halted his column to give Longstreet time to catch up. When he learned that the other corps was now only a couple of miles behind him, Jackson resumed the march. At Chantilly he found the Union line strongly posted and settled down to wait for Longstreet, as Lee had ordered.

Pope did not wait. At about 4 P.M., he launched an assault against Jackson's line. Jackson responded with a strong counterattack just as a massive rainstorm burst over the battlefield. For some two and a half hours, both sides fought viciously while the drenching rain soaked gunpowder, reduced visibility, and so muffled the sounds of combat that commanders could hardly see or hear the enemy. The Union force disengaged first, after Maj. Gen. Philip Kearny, one of the best and most experienced field officers in the Federal army, rode into Jackson's lines in the confusion and was shot down. Jackson remained in place, Longstreet arrived, and darkness fell.

The next morning found Pope successfully withdrawing past Fairfax Court House to the defenses of Washington, with the Army of Virginia seriously damaged after some of the bloodiest fighting of the war. The Union army suffered some 17,000 casualties during the campaign, the Confederates about 11,000. John Pope was the final casualty: on September 2 Lincoln replaced him with McClellan.

The initiative remained with Lee, who decided for several reasons to move north. If he remained in northern Virginia to await a renewed Union attack, his army would starve because the countryside had been picked clean, and the Federal depots at Manassas Junction and other stations had long since been consumed or destroyed. Plus Lee wanted to carry the war into the North and give his adversaries a taste of what Virginia had suffered. In addition, Maryland, just across the Potomac River from Virginia, was considered by many on both sides to be a Southern state held in the Union by military occupation alone, and Lee hoped that sympathetic residents would respond favorably to the arrival of his army by feeding and joining it. Finally, if Lee could operate successfully on Northern soil, both he and President Jefferson Davis believed that one or more European countries might support the Confederacy—at least with diplomatic recognition and perhaps with matériel and military assistance.

Lee's first invasion of the North, later called the Antietam campaign, began when the vanguard of the Army of Northern Virginia crossed the Potomac River on September 4 at White's Ford northwest of Leesburg, near the Ball's Bluff battlefield. To protect his rear and secure his supply line, Lee divided his army again, sending Jackson west to capture Harpers Ferry and then rejoin the main force. A lost copy of Lee's order detailing his strategy was found by a Union soldier and carried to McClellan, who had sallied forth from Washington with the Army of the Potomac in pursuit. Boasting that he could beat the separate elements of the Confederate army, McClellan nonetheless dallied, enabling Jackson to reunite his corps with Longstreet's at Antietam Creek, just east of the town of Sharpsburg. On Wednesday, September 17, the approximately 75,000 soldiers in McClellan's command engaged close to 50,000 in Lee's in what was the bloodiest single day of the war. The battle lasted twelve hours, and at its conclusion 12,469 Federals and 10,318 Confederates

were dead, wounded, or missing. Neither army drove the other from the field despite a day of desperate charges and countercharges. The next day they simply faced each other, seemingly too stunned by the carnage to resume the fight. During the night of September 18–19, Lee and the Army of Northern Virginia withdrew across the Potomac while McClellan pursued cautiously.

Lee's invasion of the North ended in failure. The western Maryland civilians, wary of his army, contributed or sold food grudgingly and hardly flocked to enlist. Desertions, in fact, increased in frequency, perhaps because some Confederates could not bring themselves to do what they accused the Federals of doing: invade another's country. Far from encouraging European recognition of the Confederacy, Lee's invasion and repulse became instead a propaganda coup for Lincoln, who issued a preliminary emancipation proclamation on September 22 freeing slaves in unoccupied Confederate states.

Jackson's corps occupied the northern end of the Shenandoah Valley around Winchester while Longstreet's encamped at Culpeper Court House. McClellan only inched toward Lee until an exasperated Lincoln relieved him for the second time on November 7. In his place Lincoln put Maj. Gen. Ambrose E. Burnside, an amiable man (whose impressive side whiskers inspired the term "sideburns") who already had declined the appointment twice, expressing doubts in his own abilities. While Lee's army reorganized and refitted, Burnside seized the initiative by marching on Richmond by way of Fredericksburg, around Lee's right flank. Lee countered by moving Jackson from the Shenandoah Valley to reunite the army in the proximity of Fredericksburg. ▨

On August 6, 1862, Maj. Gen John Pope instructed his army to concentrate at Culpeper Court House. On orders from Gen. Robert E. Lee, Maj. Gen. Thomas J. "Stonewall" Jackson marched his corps from Gordonsville into Culpeper County to counter Pope.

Saturday, August 9, dawned with the promise of a scorching day. By midmorning, Maj. Gen. Richard S. Ewell's division had crossed the Rapidan River and marched to its assigned position in front of Brig. Gen. Charles S. Winder's division. In the rear of Jackson's corps, Maj. Gen. A. P. Hill's men trudged north toward the Rapidan, eating the army's dust. Soon, the lead element of Ewell's column approached Cedar Mountain, a few miles south of Culpeper Court House.

Brig. Gen. Jubal A. Early commanded the lead brigade, having just returned to duty after recovering from a serious wound suffered at the battle of Williamsburg on May 5. Sarcastic and foul-mouthed, Early may have been the most disliked commander in the Army of Northern Virginia. However, Early was an effective field officer, courageous to the point of recklessness and always spoiling for a fight.

Now Early came to a fork in the road; the left led to Madison County, the right to Culpeper Court House. Just beyond the fork, the Culpeper road turned sharply to the east and paralleled Cedar Mountain. A ridge rose gently from the road to the mountain's north face, where the house of the Rev. Philip Slaughter stood. A farm lane ran from a gate on the road along the ridge for about a mile to the dwelling of Mrs. Catherine Crittenden. Cedar Run, which flowed just below Mrs. Crittenden's house, branched to the north of Cedar Mountain. The north fork extended across

the Culpeper road; behind the fork to the east, a long ridge ran roughly parallel to the Crittenden farm lane ridge. Atop the Cedar Run ridge, as Early marched up the Culpeper road, stood Federal cannons. Some Union cavalrymen in the road at the Crittenden gate withdrew to the ridge as Early unlimbered his own guns and opened fire.

The battle of Cedar Mountain began at about 2 P.M. The temperature probably was above 98° in Culpeper County. To the north and to the south, the opposing commanders urged their men to greater speed despite the dreadful heat.

As the smoke and noise of the artillery fight increased, Ewell's division arrived to form the Confederate right flank while Winder's took the left. Six of Ewell's guns were rushed to a low spur on the northern end of Cedar Mountain; his infantry stretched from just north of the Crittenden house up the lane and almost to the gate, with Early's brigade closest to the house. Brig. Gen. William B. Taliaferro, of Winder's division, took his position on the farm lane to Early's left. Most of Jackson's artillery filled in the gap between Taliaferro and the gate. Across the road, on the edge of woods and wheat field, Col. Thomas S. Garnett's brigade, also of Winder's division, took cover from Union artillery shells; Col. Charles A. Ronald's Stonewall Brigade formed the far left of Jackson's line. Shortly after 5 P.M., as the gunners on both sides slackened their fire, Hill's division began to arrive and its brigades were deployed. Col. Edward L. Thomas and his men were sent to Early's right to lengthen the infantry line almost to Cedar Mountain and to protect the artillery there and in front of the Crittenden house.

The Union line on the Cedar Run ridge

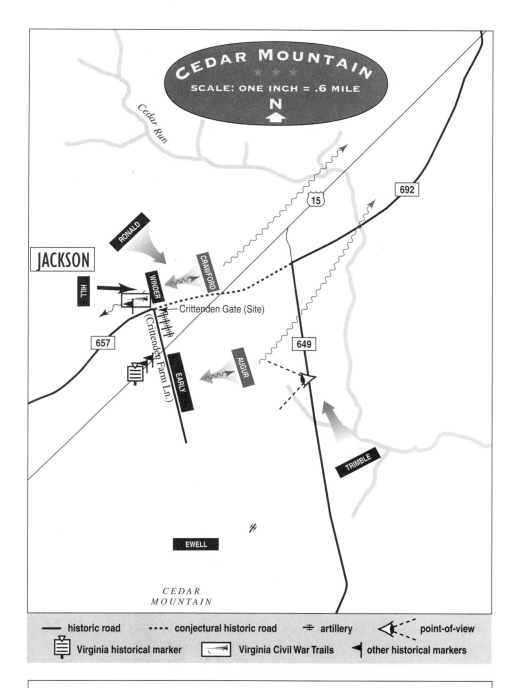

CEDAR MOUNTAIN
★ ★ ★
SCALE: ONE INCH = .6 MILE
N

692

15

RONALD

JACKSON

CRAWFORD

WINDER

HILL

Crittenden Gate (Site)

(Crittenden Farm Ln.)

657

649

AUGUR

EARLY

TRIMBLE

EWELL

CEDAR
MOUNTAIN

Cedar Run

—— historic road   •••• conjectural historic road   ‡ artillery   ◀ point-of-view

Virginia historical marker   Virginia Civil War Trails   ◀ other historical markers

DIRECTIONS: U.S. Rte. 15 s. from U.S. Rte. 15/29 about 4.4 miles to Rte. 657 (General Winder Rd.); state historical marker F-20, Battle of Cedar Mountain, and two markers erected by the Culpeper Cavalry Museum (The Battle of Cedar Mountain and Hand-to-Hand Fighting) on e. (left) side of U.S. Rte. 15; w. (right) on Rte. 657 .2 mile to Virginia Civil War Trails marker and United Daughters of the Confederacy marker; return to U.S. Rte. 15.

Battle of Cedar Mountain looking south from behind U.S. lines. LIBRARY OF CONGRESS

consisted of Brig. Gen. Samuel W. Crawford's brigade on the right, across the wheat field from Garnett's Confederates, while Brig. Gen. Christopher C. Augur commanded a three-brigade division south of the Culpeper road on the Union left. Brig. Gen. John W. Geary's brigade was closest to the road, opposite Taliaferro, and Brig. Gen. Henry Prince's brigade faced Early on the Union far left. To Prince's rear, a small brigade under Brig. Gen. George S. Greene waited in reserve.

Shortly after 5:30 Geary and Prince attacked the Confederate line, sweeping down from their ridge and across the broad cornfield that separated them from Taliaferro and Early. At the time, Early was near Cedar Mountain posting Thomas's brigade. He galloped back to find his own brigade threatening to dissolve under the Federal onslaught. Meanwhile, Crawford hammered Garnett's brigade, causing Jackson's left to collapse. Winder fell, mangled and mortally wounded by a shell fragment. By 6:30 the Confederates seemed close to defeat.

Into the fray at the Crittenden gate galloped Jackson. He tried to draw his sword but found it rusted in the scabbard, so he unbuckled it and waved it over his head, scabbard and all, then grabbed a battle flag from a fleeing standard bearer and bellowed at the troops to stop and rally. The panicky Confederates, spellbound by the

sight, obeyed, even as bullets whizzed past and shells burst nearby.

What in fact saved the day for Jackson, however, was the timely arrival of Confederate reinforcements who immediately counterattacked, the intense artillery fire directed at the Federals by Jackson's gunners, and the ebbing of Union energy in the hot weather. On the Confederate left, Ronald's Stonewall Brigade charged across a brushy field at the north end of the wheat field to strike Crawford's right flank as two of Hill's brigades rushed through the woods to take the places in the line vacated by Winder's. As the Confederate left steadied and held firm, the Union right flank collapsed. The sight of fleeing Federals on the right in turn contributed to the failure of Geary's and Prince's assault of the Confederate center and right. Fresh regiments—one from Brig. Gen. Isaac R. Trimble's brigade—made a sweeping assault from Cedar Mountain on the Union left flank. By 7 P.M. the tide of battle had turned, and the Confederates, not the Federals, were on the attack.

The pursuit of the fleeing Union force continued until well after dark. Both Banks and Pope had ridden to the front at times during the day and had established their headquarters at the Nalle house about a mile behind the Federal line. Brig. Gen. William E. "Grumble" Jones, leading a large portion of the 7th Virginia Cavalry, charged into the Nalle farmyard in the dark, sending Banks and Pope scrambling for their horses. About 10 P.M. all action ceased except for some artillery fire.

The next afternoon, as a wall of thunderstorms swept over the battlefield to break the heat wave briefly, Jackson gathered his wounded and waited for an attack by Pope that never came. On August 11 the Confederate force began falling back south of the Rapidan River. Jackson had accomplished the goal set for him by Lee. Now he would wait for Lee and the rest of the Army of Northern Virginia. Within a few days Pope would abandon his planned advance to the Rapidan and retreat almost to the Rappahannock.

Jackson would regard the battle as one of his finest achievements, but in fact he had mismanaged it, and only the sturdy defense mounted by Early and Hill had saved the day for him. Otherwise, Banks's much smaller force of 8,000 may well have defeated his own 18,000. The Confederates lost about 1,300 while the Federals lost about 2,400 in dead, wounded, and missing.

The Cedar Mountain battlefield, located in southern Culpeper County, retains excellent integrity except for the intrusion of U.S. Rte. 15, which cuts through the heart of the field and obliterates portions of the Culpeper road. Ignoring the modern highway, however, one can easily follow the movements of the competing armies. Most of the terrain still is open, and the sites of the wheat field and cornfield can be observed from public roads. The Civil War Preservation Trust owns an interest in a small part of the battlefield. ▪

RAPPAHANNOCK BRIDGE

Late in the afternoon of August 14, 1862, Gen. Robert E. Lee stepped out of a passenger car at the Gordonsville train station. He already had started Maj. Gen. James Longstreet's wing toward Gordonsville to join that of Maj. Gen. Thomas J. "Stonewall" Jackson, thereby reuniting the Army of Northern Virginia. Now he had arrived to confer with his commanders, to analyze the military situation regarding Maj. Gen. John Pope's Army of Virginia, and to plan the next Confederate move.

After his defeat at Cedar Mountain, Pope had marched most of his 50,000-man army southeast to a neck of land formed by the juncture of the Rapidan to the south and the Rappahannock River to the north. If compelled to do so, he would retreat by way of the Rappahannock Bridge crossing of that river. Lee, Jackson, and Longstreet immediately recognized the strategic importance of the bridge, as well as several nearby fords. If Rappahannock Bridge fell into Confederate hands, Pope would be "bottled up" on the Rappahannock-Rapidan "peninsula."

Lee postponed Jackson's proposed date of attack from August 16 until the next day to allow Longstreet's corps to replenish its supplies. Jackson then marched his corps five miles northeast of Orange Court House along the road leading to Somerville Ford on the Rapidan and bivouacked. One delay soon followed another. Pope, meanwhile, learned of the movements and marched his army northeastward, out of the "peninsula" trap, and began crossing to the north side of the Rappahannock River in Fauquier County.

Brig. Gen. Jesse L. Reno and the twelve regiments under his command

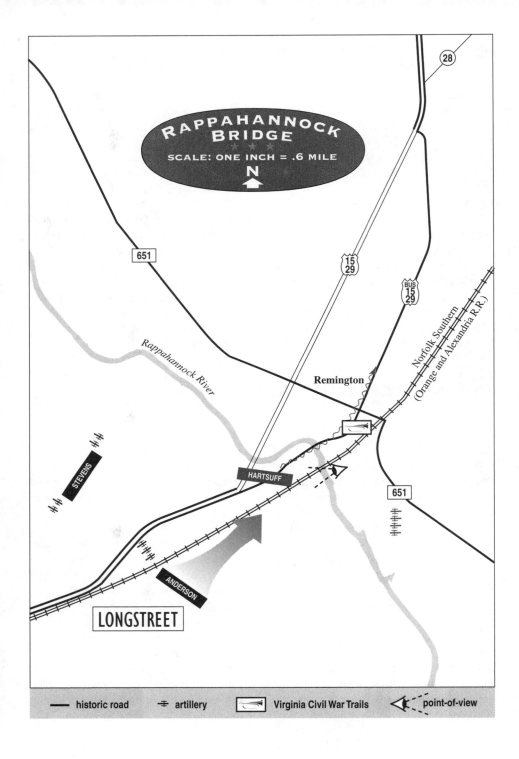

DIRECTIONS: I-95 Exit 133 (U.S. Rte. 17 North, Warrenton), n. on U.S. Rte. 17 about 23.8 miles to Rte. 28; w. (left) on Rte. 28 2 miles to U.S. Rte. 15/29 South; s.w. (left) on U.S. Rte. 15/29 South 2 miles to Rte. 651 (Freemans Ford Rd.); e. (left) on Rte. 651 .6 mile to U.S. Rte. 15/29 Bus. (Remington Rd.); s. (right) on Remington Rd. .1 mile to Virginia Civil War Trails marker on left; continue s. on Remington Rd. .8 mile over Rappahannock Bridge to U.S. Rte. 15/29.

anchored the left of the nine-mile-long Union line at Kelly's Ford, between Culpeper and Fauquier Counties. Maj. Gen. Irvin McDowell and his divisions were posted in the Union center, from Norman's Ford upriver to Rappahannock Station and the railroad bridge. Given the crucial importance of the bridge, McDowell sent a brigade of infantry under Brig. Gen. George L. Hartsuff to the Culpeper County side, to form a first line of defense there. Back on the Fauquier County side, Maj. Gen. Franz Sigel's corps constituted the Federal right flank, centered around Beverly's Ford.

On Friday, August 22, Lee sent Maj. Gen. J. E. B. Stuart up the south side of the Rappahannock to find a crossing around Pope's right flank. Jackson followed Stuart, prepared to back up the cavalry with infantry should an opportunity arise. The Army of Virginia was well and strongly positioned, however, and after a brief artillery clash at Freeman's Ford, Lee changed his mind. He ordered Stuart to swing far around Pope's right and strike the Orange & Alexandria Railroad in the Union rear, tearing up tracks, burning a bridge, and otherwise disrupting Pope's supply line. The result was the next day's Catlett Station Raid, which did little damage but resulted in Stuart's capture of Pope's order book and gaudy dress-uniform coat.

Jackson, meanwhile, marched upriver to the crossing at Fauquier White Sulphur Springs, arriving there at about 4 P.M. The Union army had destroyed the bridge at the springs; Jackson ordered Ewell to send Brig. Gen. Alexander R. Lawton's brigade and two batteries across to occupy the abandoned resort. Brig. Gen. Jubal A. Early likewise would cross over just downstream with his brigade. Meanwhile, rain began to fall. At about 5 P.M. on August 22, the rain slowed to a drizzle, and the crossings began. Part of Lawton's brigade and all of Early's got to the east side of the river before darkness descended and the rain poured down again.

By 9 P.M. Pope had learned of Early's and Stuart's crossings. After considering his alternatives, he decided to attack across the Rappahannock Bridge the next day. As the night wore on and the rain continued to fall, however, he changed his mind and called off the attack. At dawn on Saturday, August 23, Pope reassessed the situation. The rising river had negated his need to cover the fords, and the only open crossings were at Rappahannock Bridge and Waterloo Bridge. Meanwhile, in and around the sulphur springs resort, Early's and Lawton's men were isolated, ready to be crushed by a forceful assault. Pope ordered Sigel to march to the springs with all haste, and attack.

Rappahannock Bridge, with U.S. troops and horses crossing to west bank, Aug. 1862.
LIBRARY OF CONGRESS

Upriver on the west bank, Jackson frantically struggled to extract Lawton and Early. Given the high water, the only chance lay in cobbling together a new bridge on the old abutments and piers near the springs. Jackson hovered nearby as the engineers labored all day to repair his tactical error.

Lee, meanwhile, needed to block any potential Federal move against his army by way of the Rappahannock Bridge, where Hartsuff already had a foothold on Lee's side of the river. If Pope could expand the bridgehead, he could punch through Lee's line and attack the Confederates. Lee decided to launch a preemptive strike against Hartsuff and drive him across the river. He ordered Longstreet to make the attack.

Longstreet tried first to reduce the Federal lodgment with artillery fire; the Union artillery responded in kind, producing a gunners' duel that inflicted little damage on either side. Frustrated, Longstreet launched an infantry attack, sending the 11th Georgia Regiment and Holcombe's Legion in the vanguard, followed by the remainder of the brigades. The advance regiments captured an artillery position, but the gunners had fled with their cannons across the bridge.

McDowell was, in fact, as eager to abandon the bridge as the Confederate generals were to drive him away. Pope had ordered McDowell to withdraw to Warrenton, and Hartsuff and the rest of McDowell's corps already were across the bridge and on their way north. Longstreet was encountering McDowell's rear guard, a brigade commanded by Brig. Gen. Zealous B. Tower, as well as most of McDowell's artillery. Tower tried unsuccessfully to destroy the bridge with artillery shot, then managed to burn it. Now neither combatant could cross and attack the rear of the other.

Upriver, meanwhile, Sigel crawled toward Early and the sulphur springs. The Federal general and his corps moved so slowly that it was nearly dark before they were in a position to attack. Early struck back with a strong skirmish line and artillery fire, concealing most of his brigade from view, and brought Sigel's assault to a standstill. Down on the river, Jackson's engineers completed the bridge as darkness fell. Lawton and Early crossed the river to safety before dawn on August 24.

The Rappahannock Bridge engagement, together with all the other actions along the river during the two-day chess match between Lee and Pope, cost both sides some 225 casualties. More importantly, Lee's unsuccessful attempts to outflank Pope, and Pope's successful countermoves, had shifted both armies northward from Rappahannock Bridge. Now Lee would be compelled to swing much farther north and march a greater distance than he had intended in order to flank Pope.

Today the scene of the Rappahannock Bridge fight has been altered by the growth of the town of Remington in Fauquier County, and by the construction of U.S. Rte. 29/15. The highway consists of four lanes, a modern bridge, and a modern alternate route into Remington that has obliterated part of the battlefield. Many of the other engagement sites, however, such as Beverly's Ford, Freeman's Ford, the springs crossing, and Waterloo Bridge, remain virtually unaltered. ■

MANASSAS JUNCTION OPERATIONS

As the days of August 1862 dwindled, the Confederate and Union armies maneuvered northward along the Rappahannock River. On Sunday afternoon, August 24, Gen. Robert E. Lee conferred with his corps commanders, Maj. Gen. Thomas J. "Stonewall" Jackson and Maj. Gen. James Longstreet, and his cavalry chief, Maj. Gen. J. E. B. Stuart, at his headquarters about two miles west of Fauquier White Sulphur Springs. There Lee revealed his new plans.

Units from Maj. Gen. George B. McClellan's Army of the Potomac were disembarking at Aquia Creek, a terminus of the Richmond, Fredericksburg & Potomac Railroad. From the landing, McClellan had a short march to Fredericksburg, then up the Rappahannock River to join Maj. Gen. John Pope's Army of Virginia around Warrenton.

To draw Pope away, Lee proposed dividing the Army of Northern Virginia and sending Jackson on a wide sweep around Pope, first marching north and west, then turning east and striking the Orange & Alexandria Railroad, Pope's supply line. The objective would be Manassas Junction,

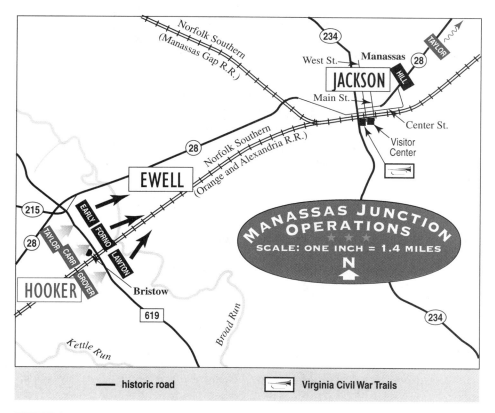

DIRECTIONS: I-66 Exit 53 (Rte. 28, Centreville Rd.), s. on Rte. 28 about 7.2 miles to West St. in Manassas; left on West St. 2 blocks to visitor center at old train depot (parking and Virginia Civil War Trails marker on right).

the Union supply depot. Pope, to defend his rear and counter the implied Confederate threat to Washington, would be compelled to hurry north from Warrenton, leaving the slow-moving McClellan trailing. Longstreet, meanwhile, first would move his corps into Jackson's position on the Rappahannock, then follow him, slip in behind Pope, and join Jackson in crushing the Army of Virginia between the two Confederate corps.

Jackson ordered his men to cook three days' rations, issued directives to his three division commanders for the order of march—Maj. Gen. Richard S. Ewell, followed by Maj. Gen. A. P. Hill, with Brig. Gen. William B. Taliaferro in the rear—and prepared his topographical engineer, Lt. James Keith Boswell, for a scouting mission to find a well-concealed route for the march toward the Blue Ridge Mountains. On August 25 the corps got under way at Jackson's favorite starting time, about 3 A.M.

Only two men out of about 24,000 knew Jackson's proposed route of march: Jackson and Boswell. Despite Jackson's attempt at secrecy, Pope learned of his movement soon after it started but misinterpreted it. The Union general believed Jackson was returning to the Shenandoah Valley, with the rest of the Army of Northern Virginia following. For the next two days, Pope made desultory probes along the Rappahannock in a feeble attempt to understand the situation to his front, thereby allowing Jackson a significant head start.

While Pope dithered, Jackson marched. Moving like the "foot cavalry" of old, his corps tramped northwest to Amissville, north to Orleans, then northeast to Salem (present-day Marshall) on the Manassas Gap Railroad, a total of twenty-six miles.

Back on the Rappahannock, Lee and Longstreet watched Pope and contemplated whether to force a crossing at Fauquier White Sulphur Springs. News of Jackson's rapid progress, however, persuaded them that the more prudent move would be to follow in his footsteps. Late on the afternoon of August 26, while Jackson was marching east along the Manassas Gap Railroad toward Gainesville, Longstreet started his corps along Jackson's route.

Meanwhile, to the north, Stuart joined Jackson to protect his right flank as he approached Gainesville in midafternoon. The road forked at the village, with the left fork leading to Manassas Junction, where the Manassas Gap Railroad joined the Orange & Alexandria Railroad, and the right to Bristoe Station, also on the Orange & Alexandria Railroad but four miles southeast of Gainesville and an equal distance southwest of Manassas Junction. Jackson knew that Manassas Junction, a major Union depot, would be more heavily defended than Bristoe Station, and that striking Bristoe first would fulfill his orders to disrupt Pope's supply route. He ordered the corps directed to Bristoe. The day's hike for his force would be twenty miles, a two-day total of forty-six.

An hour before sunset, the Confederates struck. Cavalrymen and infantry stormed into Bristoe Station, scattering the small Federal garrison. A train had already passed, but almost immediately another was heard approaching from the southwest. Quickly the troops piled wooden ties on the tracks. The train hit the ties at full throttle, sending them flying in every direction. Another train approached from the same direction; this time the soldiers threw a switch, waited until the train entered the village, and opened fire. The engine and cars derailed, and the Confederates started rummaging through the wreckage. Suddenly, another train, also from the southwest, came into view; as the soldiers watched, it plowed into the rear of the derailed cars. Yet another train approached, but its engineer spotted the debris ahead in time to stop and reverse his engine. Soon news of the Bristoe attack would be sent out over the telegraph wires from Manassas Junction and points south.

Knowing of the huge Union depot just four miles up the line at Manassas Junction, Jackson decided on a night attack in order to secure this strategic objective before it could be reinforced. Brig. Gen. Isaac R. Trimble volunteered to lead his 21st Georgia and 21st North Carolina Regiments to the depot. Jackson sent him on his way at about 9 P.M., then dispatched Stuart after him to provide cavalry support. The surprise attack succeeded brilliantly; Trimble and Stuart routed the Federal picket line, charged into the depot, and with 500 Confederates captured some 300 Union soldiers. They also took eight cannons, a large number of horses, and all the rolling stock.

John Pope had blundered badly in failing to protect his army's rear and flank. Now Pope faced two choices: Retreat to Fredericksburg and link his army with McClellan's or march against Lee. Pope chose the second course, in part because he realized that Lee had presented him with an opportunity. Either Lee had divided his army, or else it was spread out over a sixty-mile-long line of march; therefore, if Pope could strike swiftly enough, he could defeat the enemy's vanguard, then attack the rest of it, thereby turning disaster into victory.

By dawn on Wednesday, August 27, Pope's army was marching northeast up the Orange & Alexandria Railroad toward Manassas. From Washington, an infantry brigade plus two Ohio regiments, all under command of Brig. Gen. George W. Taylor, rode a train southwest down the same track, heading toward Manassas Junction to drive away what were thought to be

U.S. soldiers with remains of Orange & Alexandria R.R. rolling stock, allegedly soon after Jackson's raid, Aug. 1862. Exact site unknown. LIBRARY OF CONGRESS

Confederate cavalry raiders. At the junction, Jackson deployed Hill's and Taliaferro's divisions (he had left Ewell at Bristoe Station to guard his rear) in the Confederate earthworks built the year before. When Taylor detrained his command and marched toward Manassas Junction at about 7 A.M., he walked into an ambush. Volley after volley of Confederate gunfire slammed into the Federals; Taylor received a leg wound that soon killed him. Only a stiff rearguard action by the Ohioans prevented the obliteration or capture of the entire force.

Once Taylor's brigade had been driven off, Hill's and Taliaferro's men turned their attention to the huge quantities of Union supplies at Manassas Junction. The foodstuffs received their special devotion, though Jackson ordered the stores of liquor destroyed, knowing he had hard fighting ahead. While two of Jackson's divisions feasted, the third suddenly found itself under attack near Bristoe Station, where Ewell had deployed Brig. Gen. Alexander R. Lawton's brigade to the south of the railroad and Col. Henry Forno's Louisiana brigade to the north of it. Brig. Gen. Jubal A. Early's brigade formed to the right of Forno's.

Pope's army marched up the railroad, led by Brig. Gen. Joseph "Fighting Joe" Hooker. His point regiment, the 72nd New York Infantry, encountered Ewell's skirmish line in the afternoon. Hooker immediately attacked, sending three regiments against Forno. Hooker personally led two regiments on a swing to the north, in hopes of flanking the Confederate right. Thus pressed, and realizing that the remainder of Pope's army probably was behind Hooker, Ewell planned to retreat but hesitated, fearing Jackson's wrath. Fortunately, soon after 4 P.M., Ewell received orders from his chief to fall back fighting to Manassas Junction. Ewell handled the disengagement and withdrawal superbly, protected by Early's strong rearguard action, and the division rejoined Jackson at the junction.

As darkness descended, Jackson decided the time had come to withdraw to a more easily defensible position and wait for Longstreet. He directed his corps to march half a dozen miles northwest of the junction, near a community called Groveton. He also ordered the burning of all the captured supplies that could not be carried off, and the flames from that conflagration were visible to John Pope when he entered Bristoe Station.

The Manassas Junction operations resulted in about 1,100 casualties, mostly on the Union side, with about half of them prisoners. The Confederate figures are not known but probably were relatively light.

The Bristoe Station battlefield retains good integrity but is threatened by development due to the great demand for housing in Prince William County, which is steadily becoming a Washington bedroom suburb. The scene of the actions at Manassas Junction have long since been obliterated by the growth of the city of Manassas. ■

THOROUGHFARE GAP

Three peaks comprise the range known as the Bull Run Mountains: Mother Leathercoat, Pond, and Baldwin Ridge; Thoroughfare Gap divides the southern end of Mother Leathercoat from Pond and Baldwin. Broad Run, a public road, and the Manassas Gap Railroad all pass through Thoroughfare Gap some fourteen miles west of Manassas Junction, making the narrow defile a place of strategic military importance.

Maj. Gen. Thomas J. "Stonewall" Jackson and his forces marched through the undefended gap on August 26, 1862, on their way to attack the supply line of the Union Army of Virginia on the Orange & Alexandria Railroad. Maj. Gen. James Longstreet's corps, the other half of Gen. Robert E. Lee's Army of Northern Virginia, approached the gap from the west one day later.

Brig. Gen. James B. Ricketts's division of Maj. Gen. Irvin McDowell's corps had been marching with the rest of Maj. Gen. John Pope's army from Warrenton toward Manassas Junction in response to Jackson's attacks there. On August 27 McDowell, concerned about the possibility of attack on the Union left flank from the direction of Thoroughfare Gap, left Ricketts six miles east of it in Gainesville to keep an eye on the gap and move quickly to counter any threat there. The 1st New Jersey Cavalry, commanded by Sir Percy Wyndham, a British adventurer, occupied the gap to give Ricketts early warning.

At 9:30 A.M. on Thursday, August 28, some of Wyndham's cavalrymen were

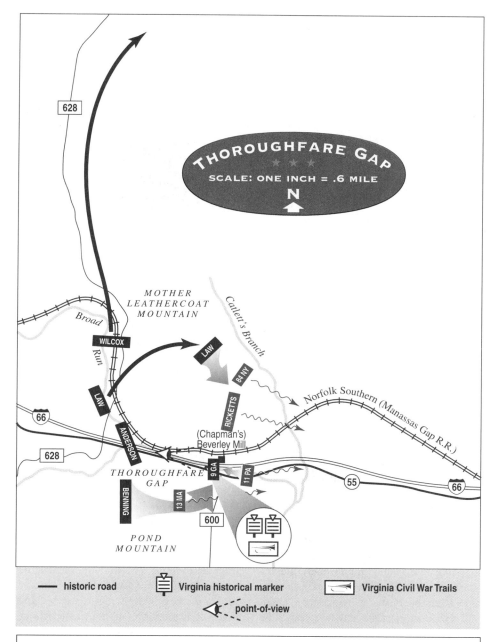

THOROUGHFARE GAP

SCALE: ONE INCH = .6 MILE

N

628

MOTHER
LEATHERCOAT
MOUNTAIN

Catlett's Branch

Broad

WILCOX

LAW

84 NY

Run

LAW

RICKETTS

Norfolk Southern (Manassas Gap R.R.)

66

ANDERSON

(Chapman's)
Beverley Mill

628

9 GA

11 PA

55

66

THOROUGHFARE
GAP

BENNING

13 MA

600

POND
MOUNTAIN

—— historic road   🗋 Virginia historical marker   Virginia Civil War Trails

point-of-view

DIRECTIONS: I-66 Exit 40 (U.S. Rte. 15 South, Haymarket), s. on U.S. Rte. 15 about .2 mile to State Rte. 55; w. (right) on State Rte. 55 .8 mile to Rte. 681 (Antioch Rd.); n. (right) on Rte. 681 across I-66 .2 mile to view of Thoroughfare Gap to west; return to State Rte. 55; right on State Rte. 55 3 miles to state historical markers (C-50, Thoroughfare Gap, and FA-1, Campaign of Second Manassas) and Virginia Civil War Trails marker; continue on State Rte. 55 .6 mile to Rte. 628 (Bust Head Rd.), the route of Longstreet's approach; n. (right) on Rte. 628 .3 mile to railroad track; return to State Rte. 55 and retrace route to I-66.

Thoroughfare Gap in 1863. VIRGINIA HISTORICAL SOCIETY, RICHMOND, VA.

wielding axes to obstruct the road through the gap when one of his patrols encountered Longstreet's vanguard. Wyndham immediately notified McDowell and Ricketts, and the latter sent his division marching westward. However, the men were hot and tired, and Ricketts did not arrive at Haymarket, some three miles east of the gap, until about 2 P.M. By then Wyndham had ordered a retreat, as Longstreet's advance force was far too large to resist. Ricketts was therefore faced with driving Longstreet from the gap to recapture it.

Wyndham's tree felling would have been more helpful to the Union advance on the western side of the gap rather than on its eastern end. Col. Richard Coulter, commanding the 11th Pennsylvania Infantry from Col. Robert Stiles's brigade, struggled over the obstacles. Suddenly, about half a mile short of the gap, he ran into the head of Longstreet's column, the 9th Georgia Infantry led by Col. Benjamin Beck, from Col. George T. "Tige" Anderson's brigade. Under heavy pressure from Coulter, and with the rest of Stiles's brigade in view, the Georgians fell back to the gap.

Whoever controlled Mother Leather-

coat and Pond Mountains would hold the gap. To the east low ridges furnished the Federals with strong positions from which to launch an attack or defend the highway and railroad even if they could not seize the gap itself. The Confederate solution was to capture the gap and also flank the Union line on the eastern ridges. First, however, both sides contended for Thoroughfare Gap.

Anderson arrived and reorganized the retreating 9th Georgia, posting it at the eastern end of the gap with the regiment's left anchored on Chapman's Mill, a massive stone structure. The unit repulsed an attack there by the 11th Pennsylvania Infantry. Anderson ordered the rest of his brigade to climb to the top of Mother Leathercoat, while Col. Henry Benning sent two other Georgia regiments, the 2nd and 20th, scrambling up the western slope of Pond Mountain. Benning's men reached the summit just before the 13th Massachusetts Infantry completed the climb from the other side and drove the Federals back. With Anderson holding firm on the Confederate left, Lee and Longstreet directed Brig. Gen. John Bell Hood to send Col. Evander M. Law's brigade over Mother Leathercoat Mountain and down the other side to strike Ricketts's right flank and drive him from the eastern ridges. Lee also ordered Brig. Gen. Cadmus M. Wilcox to lead his three-brigade division some six miles north and encircle Ricketts to strike the rear of his force. Lee understood that Wilcox probably would not accomplish this task until the next morning; with luck, Ricketts would have fled by then.

When Law and his men got over the mountain and attacked Ricketts, the Union commander responded by ordering the 84th New York Infantry forward in support of his right flank, hoping to hold the line until nightfall. The ploy stalled Law's advance, but Ricketts discovered that the 2nd and 20th Georgia Infantry, having driven the 13th Massachusetts down the eastern slope of Pond Mountain, now pressed Ricketts's left flank. The Union general decided to march his division back toward Gainesville, leaving Thoroughfare

Gap to Lee and Longstreet. Ricketts's force, some 5,000 men, was insufficient to defend his position against Longstreet's 28,000, particularly when subject to attack from several different mountain passes along a six-mile front.

The Thoroughfare Gap battle resulted in only about a hundred casualties altogether, although the engagement was enormous in its consequences. Longstreet and Lee could continue to the battlefield near Manassas Junction unimpeded to reinforce Jackson and complete Lee's planned envelopment of Pope.

Little has changed at Thoroughfare Gap since the battle, except for the addition of an interstate highway, I-66, along the same route as the historic road and railroad bed; the gap has been widened as a result. Chapman's Mill burned in 1998, but reconstruction is planned, and most of the battleground remains either in open farmland or woods. The battlefield is listed on the National Register of Historic Places. ■

SECOND BATTLE of MANASSAS (BULL RUN)

It was almost midnight on Wednesday, August 27, 1862, when Maj. Gen. Thomas J. "Stonewall" Jackson and his army abandoned Manassas Junction and marched north. The Confederate commander knew that Maj. Gen. John Pope and his Army of Virginia were on the way to confront him, and he wanted to withdraw to a more defensible position near Groveton, approximately six miles northwest of the junction.

Secrecy was Jackson's obsession, but it frequently confused his own subordinates as well as the enemy. That night was no exception: The only division that arrived at the new position on time was Brig. Gen.

William B. Taliaferro's—mainly because Jackson accompanied it. The other two, commanded by Maj. Gen. A. P. Hill and Maj. Gen. Richard S. Ewell, wandered around for hours in the dark as they missed their guides or got entangled with each other.

Groveton, a cluster of buildings, lay at the intersection of the Warrenton Turnpike (present-day U.S. Rte. 29) and the Sudley Springs road (Rte. 622, called Featherbed Road north of U.S. Rte. 29). The turnpike ran approximately east-west, while the Sudley Springs road meandered northward to a ford on Bull Run. Along a low ridge line lay the grade of an unfinished railroad

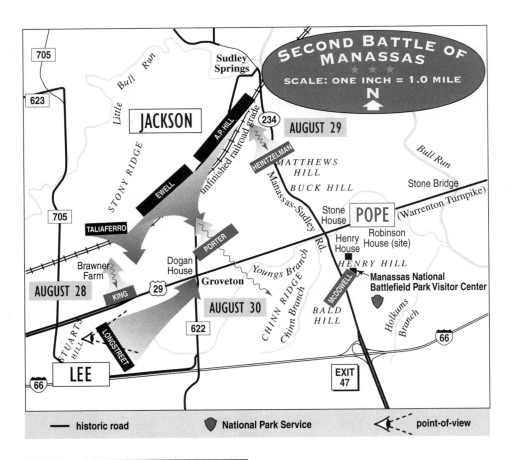

SECOND BATTLE OF MANASSAS

SCALE: ONE INCH = 1.0 MILE

N

historic road • National Park Service • point-of-view

DIRECTIONS: I-66 Exit 47B (Rte. 234 North, Manassas National Battlefield Park), n. on Rte. 234 (Sudley Rd.) about .7 mile to visitor center entrance on right. Manassas National Battlefield Park, located about 26 miles s.w. of Washington, is open daily except Christmas. For advance information, write or call the park for a brochure: Manassas National Battlefield Park, 6511 Sudley Rd., Manassas, VA 22110 (703-754-7107). Visit the National Park Service Web site at nps.gov/parks.html for a virtual tour of this and other national parks.

that paralleled the turnpike just north along Stony Ridge to the west of the Sudley Springs road, crossed the road, and then veered slightly north and paralleled it to and beyond Bull Run. Half a mile east of Stony Ridge and also north of the turnpike stood Dogan Ridge, while south, below

each ridge respectively, stood Stuart's Hill and Chinn Ridge. Half a mile west of Groveton, just north of the turnpike, was the farm of John Brawner. Most of Jackson's corps occupied the unfinished railroad north of the Brawner farm, with Taliaferro on the right, Ewell in the center, and Hill on the left.

Thursday, August 28, dawned warm and cloudy. Pope's army marched up the Warrenton Turnpike from Gainesville, roughly five miles west of Jackson's position. The Confederate marches and countermarches of the night before had confused Pope as badly as Jackson's lieutenants. Where was Jackson? Was he retreating? For his part, Jackson was almost as uncertain of Pope's location and intentions. Each commander searched for the other, until, late in the afternoon, Pope's army stumbled across Jackson's.

At about 5 P.M., a long blue column marched up the turnpike below the Brawner farm, headed for Groveton. A solitary figure on a sorrell horse emerged from the woods behind John Brawner's house and watched the soldiers march by. Then he reentered the tree line and gave the orders that began the second battle of Manassas.

The blue column on the road belonged to Brig. Gen. Rufus King. Brig. Gen. John P. Hatch's brigade led the column, with Brig. Gen. John Gibbon's brigade next, then Brig. Gen. Abner Doubleday's, and finally Brig. Gen. Marsena R. Patrick's. A few minutes later, at about 6:30 P.M., Confederate artillery shells rained down on the column.

John Pope had concluded earlier that day that Jackson had retired to Centreville, about seven miles east of Groveton, so Gibbon decided that the guns firing at him must therefore be from Maj. Gen. J. E. B. Stuart's cavalry and deployed the 2nd Wisconsin Infantry Regiment, commanded by Col. Edgar O'Conner, to capture them or drive them away. O'Conner moved to attack, but before he reached the cannons the gunners rode away with them. In their place, out of the woods, came a brigade of Confederates in battle array. Now O'Conner, then Gibbon, and finally Pope would know for certain where Jackson was.

Following Jackson's orders, Taliaferro sent the Stonewall Brigade onto the field against the 2nd Wisconsin. For twenty minutes a stiff fight ensued while each commanding general ordered more regiments and brigades into the fray. Soon Brig. Gen. Alexander R. Lawton's brigade lengthened Taliaferro's line to his right; on the Union side, Gibbon hurried his remaining regiments to the support of the 2nd Wisconsin. Two of Doubleday's regiments joined the Federal line, extending its length to about half a mile.

Jackson became increasingly frustrated as his attempts to overwhelm Gibbon failed, and the tough Federal defense succeeded in holding his commanders and their units at arm's length. Soldiers on both sides took whatever cover they could find: trees, fences, outbuildings. At the battle's height, Ewell crouched under a pine tree to get a better look at the field while Lawton marched forward. A bullet struck Ewell's left kneecap, shattering his leg. The amputation that followed would sideline him for eight months; Lawton took his place. Jackson lost his second division commander, Taliaferro, to a battle wound; Brig. Gen. William E. Starke replaced him. Late in the evening, as the sun slid toward the horizon, the brigade of Brig. Gen. Alexander G. Taliaferro (the other Taliaferro's uncle) struck the Union left flank just as a ragged Confederate charge began against the right and rippled across the front. Capt. John Pelham's horse artillery unlimbered on Taliaferro's right and blasted the Union line from less than a hundred yards away. Still, little ground was lost or gained by either side; exhaustion and darkness finally caused the steady roll of musketry to die away.

Nine miles west, at Thoroughfare Gap, Maj. Gen. James Longstreet had that afternoon won a victory that would enable him to join Jackson by overcoming the brief resistance offered by Brig. Gen. James B. Ricketts. Accompanied by Gen. Robert E. Lee, Longstreet prepared to march through the gap the next morning and unite his corps with Jackson's.

Dawn on Friday, August 29, found Pope's Army of Virginia stumbling onto the field to occupy Dogan Ridge. Pope believed that Jackson was retreating and that Longstreet remained encamped along the Rappahannock River line. In his mind the Army of Virginia was positioned between the two corps of a divided Army of Northern Virginia. Jackson, meanwhile, had replaced the wounded Ewell with Lawton and was busily pulling back his lines from the Brawner farm to positions just behind the unfinished railroad. He understood that before the day was over he probably would face the entire Union army with his dwindling corps, and unless Longstreet arrived soon, his situation would become desperate. But Stonewall would not retreat.

Jackson's wing consisted of 20,000 men; Pope had divided his army into two roughly equal 25,000-man parts. Imagining Jackson to be retreating westward and open to attack, Pope positioned half his force along Dogan Ridge commanded by Maj. Gen. Samuel P. Heintzelman (of McClellan's Army of the Potomac), and the other half along the Sudley Springs road both north and south of the Warrenton Turnpike. Maj. Gen. Irvin B. McDowell's corps and Maj. Gen. Fitz John Porter's (of the Army of the Potomac) were on the march from Gainesville.

Behind the railroad grade, Jackson posted Starke's division on the right, from Stony Ridge almost to the Sudley Springs road, Lawton's in the middle (less two brigades guarding the road from Thoroughfare Gap), and Hill's on the left, extending almost to Catharpin Run, a branch of Bull Run. Stuart's cavalry guarded the flanks, and Jackson's artillery dotted the high ground behind the infantry. Between Starke's and Lawton's divisions was the Dump, a hundred-yard gap in the railroad grade where construction workers had dumped stones. Because the area offered little protection and Jackson did not want to waste good troops in its seemingly hopeless but necessary defense, he positioned stragglers and skulkers and other miscreants of his corps there.

At about 10 A.M., the Union artillery opened fire; the Confederate guns responded, and a hot duel raged. Under cover of the Union barrage, some of Heintzelman's infantry shifted north to attack Hill on Jackson's left. Hill's position was one of the weakest in an otherwise strong line, being heavily wooded, allowing no supporting artillery fire, and with a sizeable gap between Brig. Gen. Maxcy Gregg's brigade on the extreme left and Brig. Gen. Edward L. Thomas's brigade on Gregg's right. After repeated assaults, at about 2 P.M. the Federals under Maj. Gen. Joseph Hooker broke through the gap but were driven back when Thomas's reserve counterattacked.

During the battle, good news arrived for Jackson: Longstreet had marched through Thoroughfare Gap and was approaching the battlefield. The Texas Brigade of Brig. Gen. John Bell Hood's division formed the vanguard; Jackson ordered Hood to reinforce his right flank on the turnpike. As the rest of Longstreet's corps filed in, it deployed to Hood's right. By the end of the day the Confederate front would be some three miles long, with Jackson's corps stretching northeast from the turnpike and Longstreet's almost due south, thereby resembling the jaws of a vise. Lee encouraged Longstreet to attack at once but he preferred to wait until Pope's army ventured into the trap; most of it was too far east.

At about 4 P.M., Col. James Nagle led his Union brigade in a futile attack against the Confederate center. An hour later Maj. Gen. Philip Kearny led his division against Hill on Jackson's left and was repulsed with a countercharge. As darkness approached, the sounds of battle dwindled; Jackson's men were through for the day.

To the south, however, a significant encounter occurred at about 7 P.M. Pope had visited the front at sunset and, observing Confederate wagons moving westward on the Warrenton Turnpike, concluded that Kearny's attack had succeeded after all. Obviously Jackson was in full retreat and should be attacked at once. George Ruggles, Pope's chief of staff, ventured that the wagons looked like ambulances bearing the Confederate wounded to the rear, but Pope ordered Maj. Gen. Irvin McDowell to mount a swift pursuit of the fleeing enemy. McDowell chose Hatch and his brigade; when Hatch advanced on the turnpike, he encountered Hood's division, which gave him a sharp response. A nasty firefight erupted in the gathering darkness. Most of the fighting was in woods, and soon one could not tell friend from foe (Maj. Charles Livingston, of the 76th New York Regiment, was made prisoner by an officer of the 2nd Mississippi when he mistakenly attempted to rally and redirect the Mississippians). By 8 P.M. the fighting ceased and Hatch retreated; now it was obvious even to Pope that Longstreet had arrived. Pope concluded, however, that Lee would merely use Longstreet to strengthen Jackson's line, not extend it south of the turnpike. Pope's solution was to redouble his attacks against Jackson the next day.

On Stuart's Hill, south of the turnpike and below Stony Ridge, Lee established his field headquarters. There he decided that in the morning he would yield the initiative to Pope, to see what the Union general would do. At Pope's headquarters on Buck Hill, just north of the Stone House, the Union commander also decided to wait and see what happened.

At dawn on Saturday, August 30, Union observers on Dogan Ridge watched a long column of infantry and artillery marching away west on the Warrenton Turnpike. Quickly they dispatched the news to Pope: the Confederates were retreating! (What they actually saw was an

View east from Stuart's Hill, site of Lee's headquarters. VIRGINIA DEPARTMENT OF HISTORIC RESOURCES, JOHN S. SALMON

infantry division and an artillery battalion moving back to a safer position, after going too far forward in the predawn darkness.) Maj. Gen. Fitz John Porter then rode to headquarters from the Union left to report large numbers of Confederates south of the turnpike. Pope despised Porter as a McClellan cohort. For the moment Pope would wait and watch; he ordered no attack against the Confederate left.

The warm morning dragged into the hot and humid afternoon. At about 2 P.M., Jackson ordered one of his batteries to fire on some Union guns opposite Starke's front; the fire drove away the enemy cannons. Pope thought that this barrage signaled a retreat by Jackson and ordered a wholesale attack against Jackson's line. At 3 P.M. a lone Federal cannon fired to announce the advance. Some 12,000 men of Porter's and McDowell's corps—thirty-seven regiments in battle order—marched toward Starke's position. Unknown to the Union commanders, Stephen Lee had placed some eighteen guns in front of the railroad grade to sweep the Federal left and center. When the attackers closed on the Confederate line, the carnage wrought by cannon and rifle fire was awesome. Still, Porter's men kept coming.

At the Dump, Jackson's misfits faced some of the heaviest Federal assaults. Soon they and the brigades on either side began running out of ammunition. When the 24th New York Regiment threatened to overrun them, dozens of Confederates started hurling rocks. Shocked by the unlikely barrage, some of the New Yorkers dropped their loaded rifles and threw the stones back instead. (The famous Rock Fight lasted only a few minutes, long enough to become a Southern legend.) Confederate reinforcements arrived to strengthen the line at the Dump and elsewhere, and the Federal attack stalled. Porter's corps began falling back; the Federal left flank was in disarray. Lee's moment had come.

Lee, Jackson, Longstreet, and Stuart had conferred at Lee's headquarters on Stuart's Hill that morning, planning what they would do if Pope attacked—or if he did not. Now was the time to act. First, Longstreet's artillery blasted the Federal left flank, shredding it. Then came a brief but ominous lull as the guns fell silent. At 4 P.M. Longstreet's infantry boiled up out of the woods at the base of Stuart's Hill and swept across the battlefield, crushing a Union brigade and closing on Chinn Ridge as the Confederates surged eastward. For ten minutes one regiment, the 5th New York, stood alone against Hood's Texas Brigade at the center of the onslaught. In those ten minutes the regiment's 500 men were reduced to 200—all the rest shot dead or wounded.

After the initial rout caused by the shock of Longstreet's attack, the Federal soldiers slowly regrouped and stiffened their resistance as they struggled to hold back the onrushing Confederate tide. The Union line held on Chinn Ridge for more than an hour, then Longstreet's men pushed it off. To the north of the Warrenton Turnpike, Jackson's corps finally began to move forward from the railroad grade, pressing Sigel. At about 6 P.M. the Union army fell back to its final line of defense on Henry Hill. The Federal soldiers fought tenaciously, knowing that their survival was at stake. And darkness, followed by rain, finally ended the Confederate assaults.

During the night, Pope pulled his army back into the strong entrenchments at Centreville, six miles east. At dawn on Sunday, August 31, the victorious Confederates awoke to a steady rain and a battlefield covered with some 15,000 wounded and 3,000 dead. The total numbers of killed, wounded, and captured for the three-day battle were staggering. They reflected the large numbers of troops actually engaged, as opposed to the Peninsula and Seven Days' campaigns, for example, where large armies engaged only relatively small parts at any one time. The Confederates lost 8,350 at Second Manassas, while the Federals suffered 13,830 casualties.

Most of the battlefield, and virtually every important site, lies within Manassas National Battlefield Park and is therefore protected for future generations. In 1988 Stuart Hill, the site of Lee's field headquarters, became the focus of what has been called the "Eighth Battle of Manassas" when development threatened it. The U.S. Congress ordered a "legislative taking" of the approximately 550-acre tract in order to preserve it—a decision that galvanized nationwide support for battlefield preservation on the one hand and the "property rights" movement on the other. ■

In the early afternoon of Sunday, August 31, 1862, Maj. Gen. Thomas J. "Stonewall" Jackson and his weary corps trudged off the Manassas battlefield while rain fell steadily. They marched north on the Sudley Springs road (present-day Featherbed Lane, Rte. 622), crossed over Catharpin Run, a tributary of Bull Run, and followed Gum Springs Road (Rte. 659) north, bivouacking around Pleasant Valley Church after turning southeast on the Lit-

tle River Turnpike (U.S. Rte. 50) at Gum Springs.

That morning, Jackson and Gen. Robert E. Lee had reconnoitered ground east of the stone bridge at Bull Run, over which Maj. Gen. John Pope's Army of Virginia had retreated after its defeat at the second battle of Manassas the day before. Lee sought to execute another turning movement to draw Pope eastward and out of his Centreville works. He therefore

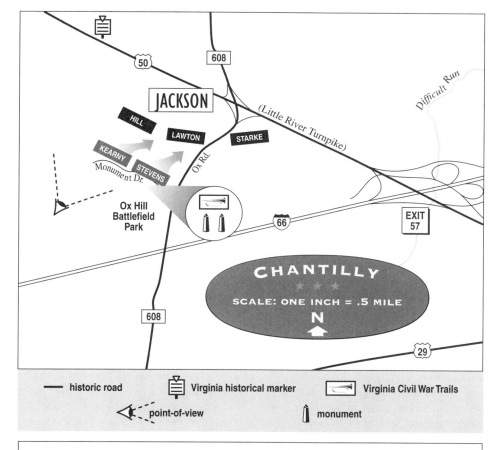

DIRECTIONS: I-66 Exit 57B (U.S. Rte. 50 West, Winchester), w. on U.S. Rte. 50 about 1 mile to exit for Rte. 608 (Ox Rd.); s. on Rte. 608 .3 mile to Monument Dr.; w. (right) on Monument Dr. .1 mile to Ox Hill Battlefield Park on left (includes Virginia Civil War Trails marker); return to I-66.

ordered Jackson north and then southeast on the Little River Turnpike, sweeping around Pope's right flank. Maj. Gen. J. E. B. Stuart's cavalry screened Jackson's movement. Longstreet, presently occupied with tidying up the battlefield and reassembling his corps, gave Jackson a half-day's lead and then followed.

The next morning, September 1, Jackson and his forces marched down the turnpike toward Fairfax Court House, where he planned to intercept Pope's line of retreat. Stuart galloped up from the east to report that he had swept small numbers of Federal troops off the road between a plantation called Chantilly and Germantown, where he had found a larger enemy body. Jackson now knew that the element of surprise was lost. He and his men marched on, and a little before noon Jackson called a halt at a crossroads near Chantilly and waited for Longstreet to close the gap between their corps.

Jackson's halt worked to the advantage of Pope, who sent Brig. Gen. Isaac I. Stevens's small IX Corps—which was about division size—hurrying up the Warrenton Turnpike toward Germantown. Within a couple of hours he had the rest of his army in motion, abandoning the Centreville works for the Germantown line.

Shortly after noon, learning that Longstreet was only a couple of hours' march behind him, Jackson resumed his march down the Little River Turnpike. After about two hours he came upon Stuart near the intersection of West Ox Road (Rte. 608) at Ox Hill and was informed that Federal troops lay ahead. Jackson and Stuart probed the Union line and found it strong. Jackson settled down to wait for Longstreet and Lee, arranging a semicircular defensive line to the south of the turnpike on the southern crest of Ox Hill. Brig. Gen. William B. Starke's division took the left flank, Brig. Gen. Alexander R. Law-

ton's division held the Confederate center, and Brig. Gen. A. P. Hill's division formed the right flank. Thick woods covered the ground south of the turnpike except for some cleared farm fields. The Confederate commanders pushed skirmishers out in front of their divisions to the south, just as Stevens and his corps arrived on a hill overlooking the fields.

Behind Stevens, Pope's army marched slowly toward Germantown—Pope had issued confusing orders, delaying and disordering his army's retreat. Some commanders whom Pope intended to go to Stevens's aid never got the word; one who did, Maj. Gen. Philip Kearny, hurried up West Ox Road as Stevens surveyed the scene to his front. The line of skirmishers appeared to foretell an impending attack against the troops and wagon trains just a mile and a half to Stevens's rear. Immediate action was called for if the Confederate strike was to be stopped. The time was shortly after 4 P.M.

Stevens assembled a battle line, with the 79th New York Infantry on the right and the 28th Massachusetts on the left. A second line followed, with the 8th Michigan on the right and the 50th Pennsylvania on the left, and the third, smaller line consisted of the 46th New York and 100th Pennsylvania Regiments. The 51st New York and 21st Massachusetts Regiments filed into the dense woods to the right of the fields, where they would encounter Starke's division on the Confederate left. At 4:30 P.M., Stevens launched his attack, and soon left his position near his artillery to follow behind the 79th New York.

Suddenly, a wave of fire issued from the woods to Stevens's front as the 79th New York neared Lawton's line. Volley after Confederate volley stalled the Federal advance, and the 79th wavered under the onslaught as five successive color bearers fell dead or wounded. Stevens wrestled

Battle of Chantilly as seen from Maj. Gen. Samuel P. Heintzelman's headquarters, Sept. 1, 1862.
VIRGINIA HISTORICAL SOCIETY, RICHMOND, VA.

the regimental flag from its fallen bearer and raced to the front of the line, leading the charge. The regiment ran after him, knocking down a fence and plunging into the woods. Stevens, as he reached the fence, fell dead with a bullet through his skull. Soldiers from the 79th carried his body to the rear.

At that moment, about 5:30 P.M., a violent thunderstorm burst. Visibility, especially in the woods, was reduced to a few yards. The thunder was so loud that many could not hear the cannons over it, much less the orders of commanders. For the next two hours, each side fought blind and deaf, in what amounted to a disorganized brawl.

Kearny arrived on the field as Stevens's regiments retreated to their jumping-off point. Just as Stevens had done, Kearny threw together his battle line and advanced. He arranged his regiments in echelon, with each following to the right rear of the one ahead. Kearny—regarded by many as the

best field commander in the Army of the Potomac—seemed to be everywhere at once. At about 6 P.M. his attack began; by then the rain and gloom had so obscured the battlefield that the opposing lines could not be seen until they opened fire on one another at a distance of a few yards.

While Kearny followed his line forward, the 21st Massachusetts of Stevens's division staggered out of the woods and onto the eastern part of the field, having lost a hundred casualties in its encounter with Starke's division. Its senior surviving officer, Capt. Charles F. Walcott, was reorganizing the men when Kearny galloped up and ordered Walcott immediately to the left. Walcott tried to explain the situation, but Kearny uttered some cutting remarks about the 21st's courage that enraged Walcott, who finally moved the remnants of the regiment forward, and Kearny rode off. When Walcott encountered heavy fire from the wood line, he halted his men to probe the front and question captured

Confederates. Just then Kearny rode up, again roused to fury by Walcott's halt. Unimpressed with the captain's explanation, Kearny rode forward to see for himself.

In the darkness of the woods, at about 6:15 P.M., Kearny made out armed figures through the leaves. He challenged them to identify themselves, and when they responded that they were the 49th Georgia, Kearny wheeled his horse and raced through the woods as the Georgians opened fire. A bullet struck him in the buttock, passed into his chest, and killed him.

On Jackson's side of the battle, Hill's division bore the brunt of the Union attacks. The brigades of Col. Edward L. Thomas and Brig. Gens. Lawrence O'B. Branch, William D. Pender, and Maxcy Gregg were heavily engaged. At the height of the conflict and the downpour, Hill sent word to Jackson that his line was in danger because the rain had soaked his ammunition. Jackson, sitting hunched on Little Sorrel, replied that the Yankee ammunition was as wet as Hill's and to stay put. Hill stayed. Longstreet did not reach the battlefield until between 6:30 and 7 P.M., when the day's fighting ended, along with the rain.

The Confederate advance that killed Kearny struck the 21st Massachusetts hard, coming so close that the Federals could reach out and touch their opponents' rifles. For five or ten minutes a wild melee ensued, with men on both sides killed with bayonets and clubbed rifles. Finally, at about 6:30 P.M., both sides withdrew when darkness prevented them from telling friend from foe. The battle of Chantilly was over, and Pope and his army had escaped Lee's grasp.

Some 2,100 men were casualties of a battle that ended in a draw. The Confederates lost 800; the Federals, 1,300. Worst of all for the Union, the gallant Stevens and the fearless Kearny were dead—two generals killed within an hour of each other.

On October 2, 1915, at an impressive ceremony attended by survivors of the battle from both sides, two stone monuments to Stevens and Kearny were dedicated near the sites of their deaths. The quarter-acre piece of land on which the markers stand was donated by John N. Ballard, a former Confederate, a member of Mosby's Rangers, in a spirit of reconciliation. The remainder of the Chantilly battlefield has been obliterated by commercial and residential development. ■

FREDERICKSBURG AND CHANCELLORSVILLE CAMPAIGNS, 1862–1863

During the night of September 18–19, 1862, the Army of Northern Virginia forded the Potomac River after its unsuccessful foray into Maryland and the bloody battle of Antietam on September 17. The army's commander, Gen. Robert E. Lee, stationed the second of his two corps at Winchester, in the northern Shenandoah Valley, and the first in Culpeper, in the northern Piedmont. He selected these positions to defend the Valley from attack by Maj. Gen. George B. McClellan, commander of the Army of the Potomac, and to defend central Virginia and Richmond, the capital of the Confederacy, should McClellan make a thrust south from northern Virginia instead.

Lee's corps commanders, Thomas J. "Stonewall" Jackson and James Longstreet, were promoted to the rank of lieutenant general in October 1862 when Lee restructured his army and formalized the corps arrangement. In contrast, McClellan fared badly. Most of the Army of the Potomac was encamped near Warrenton, about twenty miles northeast of Culpeper, while McClellan's headquarters was located in Rectortown, some fifteen miles northwest of Warrenton. Late in the night of Friday, November 7, as McClellan sat in his tent, two general officers (Maj. Gen. Ambrose E. Burnside and Brig. Gen. Catharinus P. Buckingham) entered with a letter from Pres. Abraham Lincoln that relieved McClellan of command and appointed Burnside in his place. The next day, after McClellan's farewell proclamation was

read to the army, he departed. He never again held a military command but ran for president—and lost—against Lincoln in 1864 on the Democratic ticket. He then resumed his career as a civil engineer, served three terms as governor of New Jersey, and later wrote his memoirs.

Ambrose Burnside was a hearty, likeable man who had declined offers of high command before, feeling ill-suited for the responsibility. He had performed well in a North Carolina coastal campaign and, rewarded with promotion to major general, seemed adequate as a subordinate commander. At Antietam, however, his determination to cross the creek there at a stone bridge—since called Burnside's Bridge—delayed his entry into the battle and perhaps prevented a clear Union victory. However, while most of the officers and men were angered by McClellan's removal, they bore Burnside no grudge and resolved to soldier on under his leadership.

Burnside's tenure began well enough, with a reorganization of his 130,000-man army's command structure and plans to seize the initiative from Lee with an aggressive late autumn campaign. Maj. Gen. Edwin V. "Bull" Sumner commanded the Right Grand Division; Maj. Gen. Joseph "Fighting Joe" Hooker, the Center Grand Division; and Maj. Gen. William B. Franklin, the Left Grand Division. Sumner, a courageous, blustery old soldier whose bellow could be heard above the din of battle, was regarded as a good follower of orders but utterly lacking

FREDERICKSBURG
& CHANCELLORSVILLE
CAMPAIGNS

and enable the Army of the Potomac to get between him and the Confederate capital. The ruse depended, unfortunately, on speed of execution—a talent that this army had not exhibited during earlier campaigns.

Lee's Army of Northern Virginia, on the other hand, possessed precisely that talent as well as tactically superior cavalry that served as the commander's eyes and ears. Nonetheless, Lee was surprised when, on November 15, the Union army suddenly began disappearing from his front. Sumner's Grand Division covered the distance to Falmouth, just north of Fredericksburg, in two days, and by November 19 the whole army was in place on the hills east and north of Fredericksburg, with only the Rappahannock River to cross. Unfortunately, Burnside's brilliant maneuver then stopped dead, for the pontoons needed to cross the river that were to be sent from Washington were nowhere in sight, thanks to logistical bungling in the capital. While Burnside stewed, Lee moved, and by the time the pontoons arrived on November 25, Longstreet's corps occupied the high ground on the opposite bank, overlooking the town. Now Burnside faced two choices: withdraw or fight a battle where he had not planned to fight one.

Although Burnside was not responsible for the pontoon delay, he erred when he did not allow Sumner to force a crossing and establish a foothold on the opposite bank before Longstreet's vanguard arrived there. Burnside probed the downstream fords but found them all covered by Confederates, so he reverted to his original plan: Cross at the town despite the guns bristling on the heights, where Lee waited.

The first battle of Fredericksburg began in a foggy dawn on Thursday, December 11. Federal engineers struggled to lay five pontoon bridges across the Rappahannock River, three at Fredericksburg and two downstream. Confederate sharpshooters

in imagination. Hooker, an aggressive field commander, was also known for his overweening ambition; in addition, allegations of low moral character that had surfaced during the Mexican War resurfaced during the Civil War. Franklin, a staunch McClellan partisan, shared his hero's reputation for slowness on the battlefield. Burnside would be challenged to whip these subordinates, and the demoralized men under them, into fighting shape.

Burnside's plan—a turning movement—called for a rapid march by his army from Warrenton southeast to Fredericksburg, a distance of roughly forty miles, in order to get around Longstreet's right flank and march on Richmond. As Richmond lay to the south of the Rappahannock River, Burnside planned to cross the river at Fredericksburg using pontoon bridges. His maneuver, he reasoned, would impel Lee to waste time changing his front

on the southern bank, some concealed in buildings in the town, drove them off there. As the fog slowly lifted, Union gunners began a daylong bombardment of Fredericksburg that failed to dislodge the sharpshooters. Eventually Union infantry crossed the river in boats and drove the Confederates from the town, and the engineers finished their work. The next day most of Sumner's and Franklin's grand divisions (Hooker's remained in reserve) passed over the pontoon bridges, and Burnside gave orders for an assault.

By then the 78,000-man-strong Confederate line stretched for some seven miles, with Longstreet on the left, overlooking the town from a series of hills collectively named Marye's Heights, and Jackson on the right, downriver atop Prospect Hill. At dawn on Saturday, December 13, fog again blanketed the ground. Franklin's Left Grand Division struck Jackson's line and almost broke through a gap created by swampy ground, but reinforcements plugged the opening and drove the Federals back. On the Confederate left, wave after wave of Sumner's and Hooker's men spent themselves in brave but futile assaults against Marye's Heights; the slaughter evermore haunted the participants on both sides. Burnside's generals persuaded their distraught commander to cancel his plans to resume the assaults the next day. Lee, contemplating the large number of Federal cannons on Stafford Heights north of the river, refused to attack Burnside, and the day following the battle passed with some skirmishing. During the night of December 15, the Union army withdrew across the river, and the Fredericksburg campaign ended. Federal casualties totaled 12,600; the Confederates lost 5,300.

A Congressional investigation followed this crushing defeat, and Joseph Hooker used the opportunity to advance his own cause while criticizing Burnside, who finally tendered his resignation to Lincoln; in March, Lincoln assigned him command of the Department of the Ohio. The president appointed Hooker in Burnside's place on January 25, 1863, praising the new commander's military skill while chastising him for undermining his former superior. Hooker set to work at once, reorganizing the army yet again, giving each corps its own badge, and helping to restore Union morale and pride. He also created a separate cavalry corps, first commanded by Maj. Gen. George Stoneman and then, after June 7, Brig. Gen. Alfred Pleasonton. Placing the cavalry under a single command enhanced its performance and soon ended the days of Confederate domination.

Hooker was admired for his courage and aggressiveness, as his nom de guerre, "Fighting Joe," suggested. He also had a reputation, however, as a hard drinker and a man of loose morals. (The nickname for prostitutes has been ascribed to him, when in actuality, the name was derived from a section of New York City called the Hook, known for its brothels. It was coincidence that Hooker's name became famous about the same time as the slang term.)

For the rest of the winter, Hooker's Army of the Potomac trained and refitted while keeping an eye on the Army of Northern Virginia across the Rappahannock. Hooker used elements of his cavalry corps to annoy the Confederates and probe their lines, and Maj. Gen. J. E. B. Stuart responded in kind. At dawn on Tuesday, March 17, Brig. Gen. William W. Averell led about 2,100 troopers from his division across the river at Kelly's Ford to attack Brig. Gen. Fitzhugh Lee's cavalry brigade near Culpeper Court House. Pickets at the ford sent word to Lee, who soon rode to the river with some 800 cavalrymen; Stuart and his brilliant young artillery chief, twenty-four-year-old Maj. John Pelham ("The Gallant Pelham," Robert E. Lee called him), rode along to see the action. The fighting started about noon and continued until the Federals withdrew across the ford about dusk. For the first time the Union cavalry had fought its Confederate counterparts almost to a standstill in what was until then the largest all-cavalry battle in the East. The combined casualties amounted to about 200. Tragically, one of them was John Pelham, mortally wounded by a shell fragment. Stuart wept bitterly at the news, as did many others in the army, for Pelham was much loved by all who knew him.

During the late winter and early spring of 1863, Hooker devised a strategy not only for getting around Lee but for beating him in battle and then marching on to Richmond. Taking a page from Lee's book, Hooker would send his cavalry corps sweeping around the Confederate left flank to cut Lee's communications with the Confederate capital. Then he would assault Lee's left flank and rear by marching north with three corps of his army, crossing the Rappahannock and Rapidan Rivers, and driving southeast. Three other corps would attack directly across the river at Fredericksburg, largely as a diversion, while the remaining ones stayed conspicuously in sight across from Fredericksburg and at Banks's Ford. After whipping Lee, Hooker told Lincoln, he would march on to Richmond. It was a solid plan, and it very nearly succeeded.

In February 1863 Lee unintentionally assisted Hooker by reducing the size of his army near Fredericksburg to about 60,000. Responding to Federal threats in Tidewater Virginia and North Carolina, Lee dispatched Longstreet to southeastern Virginia with instructions to counter any Union initiatives and gather supplies for the main army. Accompanied by major generals George E. Pickett and John Bell Hood and their divisions (some 20,000

men), Longstreet departed on February 17 on his assignment and from April 11 to May 4 conducted the Siege of Suffolk while Maj. Gen. D. H. Hill operated against the Federals in coastal North Carolina. Longstreet's siege of the town and its 25,000 Union defenders under Brig. Gen. John Peck produced two engagements. The first, at Norfleet House, occurred on April 14–15, when Union gunboats on the Nansemond River attempted to run past the Confederate battery just downriver from the town. The attempt failed when the battery crippled the gunboat *Mount Washington.* Overnight the Federals built their own batteries across the river, concealed behind brush and small trees. On April 15 they unmasked their guns and drove the Confederates from the Norfleet House position. The second engagement took place downriver at Hill's Point, where the Confederate left flank rested in an old river fortification dating from the War of 1812, renamed Fort Huger. On April 19 Union gunboats raced past the fort and landed an infantry force just upstream; it attacked the defenders and drove them off, thereby reopening the river to Federal shipping. The two sides suffered fewer than 200 casualties in these engagements. At the end of April, Lee ordered Longstreet to break off his unproductive siege and return to the main army. The last of Longstreet's task force left the area on May 4.

On Monday, April 27, Hooker launched his campaign against Lee. He left 40,000 troops at Fredericksburg under Maj. Gen. John Sedgwick to make a diversionary attack that would freeze the Confederates in their works and marched with the remainder of his army northwest from Falmouth to Kelly's Ford on the Rappahannock River. Part of his force remained on guard downstream at Scott's Ford and United States Ford while the rest crossed at Kelly's Ford and marched south to pass over the Rapidan River at Germanna and Ely's Fords. Stoneman's cavalry corps had departed on April 13 on its largely ineffective raid against Lee's communications with Richmond, which would deprive Hooker of essential flank protection. By the evening of April 30, three of Hooker's seven infantry corps were concentrated near the Chancellor family home on the Orange Plank Road called Chancellorsville. A few miles east, at Zoan Church, in a desperate attempt to prevent the envelopment of the Army of Northern Virginia, Maj. Gen. Richard H. Anderson dug in across the plank road and the Orange Turnpike. Lee divided his army and ordered Jackson to march to Chancellorsville and challenge Hooker; Maj. Gen. Jubal A. Early and 12,000 men remained behind to occupy the Fredericksburg line and thereby block Sedgwick from reinforcing Hooker. Thus far Hooker's plan had succeeded brilliantly: He had virtually enveloped Lee, who had divided his force—already outnumbered two to one—into yet smaller components; victory lay within Hooker's grasp.

Jackson collided with Hooker on Friday, May 1. Hooker's men had emerged from the Wilderness, a tangle of brush and small, second-growth trees, when Jackson confronted them, and a firefight ensued. The sound of battle reached Hooker, who had occupied Chancellorsville as his headquarters. In the early afternoon, with success seemingly assured, Hooker ordered his army to fall back and assume defensive positions. The prospect of directly facing Lee in battle with sole responsibility for the outcome may have been more than Hooker could bear. His generals received his orders with stunned disbelief, then anger. One rode to headquarters for confirmation, threatening to shoot the messenger if he found the orders to be false.

Hooker had passed the initiative to Lee, who reacted with breathtaking audacity. During the night of May 1–2, he and Jackson sat on hardtack boxes at the intersection of the Orange Plank Road and a smaller road that led westward past Catharine Furnace and around the Federal right flank, which Stuart reported to be "in the air"—not anchored on a natural defensive feature, such as a river, swamp, or eminence. The generals pored over a map and discussed the situation. Lee made his decision: He would divide his army yet again and send Jackson and 32,000 men on a wide movement to outflank Hooker's envelopment. Lee, meanwhile, would remain in Hooker's front with 14,000 soldiers and distract his 70,000-man army.

Jackson's march—a twelve-mile-long sweep to the west, south, and north, then east—got under way at about 7:30 A.M. on May 2. It occupied most of the day and remained a secret only for an hour. Hooker, like Pope before him, thought it augured a retreat by Lee. He did warn his right-flank commander, and he also sent a force toward Catharine Furnace to find out what was happening, but the warning largely went unheeded, and the expedition merely drew needed troops away from his line. By 5 P.M. Jackson was in position, his battle line formed in a north-south direction across the turnpike and plank road in the Wilderness. A few minutes later he launched the assault.

An acoustical shadow hung over the Wilderness, like that at Seven Pines during the Peninsula campaign the previous year. The soldiers on the Union right flank heard nothing of the approaching Confederates, but suddenly deer, rabbits, and wild turkeys came racing through their camps, driven by the onrushing line. The Confederates followed fast behind, rolling up the Federal flank. As so often happened, Jackson's sudden success resulted in as much confusion among the attackers as the attacked. By dark both the Union and the Confederate lines were in wild disarray, in some cases intermingled, and little firefights broke out here and there along the front as units collided with one another.

In the early evening Jackson and several others rode toward the Union line to reconnoiter in anticipation of continued attacks that night. Jackson turned to reenter his own lines at about 9:30 P.M. Just then another burst of shooting erupted, and the 18th North Carolina Infantry opened fire on the horsemen riding down on them in the dark. Three bullets struck Jackson, and several in his party were killed. Helped down from his horse, Jackson lay on the ground with his left arm shattered; he was nearly captured before his men got him to a safe area, where Dr. Hunter H. McGuire amputated his arm. Soon he was aboard a train to Guiney Station on the Richmond, Fredericksburg & Potomac Railroad, where his condition improved slowly.

Stuart assumed command of Jackson's corps. Starting at dawn on May 3, he pounded the Union line relentlessly from the west and southwest, driving the Federals back east toward Chancellorsville. The Union soldiers fought tenaciously, and casualties mounted on both sides. By 9 A.M. the Federal line was almost a perfect circle around Hooker's headquarters, where the general stood on the porch to receive a report. A Confederate solid shot struck one of the columns, shattering it and slamming half of it onto Hooker, who fell to the porch floor unconscious. Although he soon regained his senses, Hooker never regained his offensive momentum, and when Lee pressed his army from the south about 10 A.M., Hooker ordered it to fall back toward the Rappahannock into prepared positions. A sturdy defense by Hooker's artillery held off the oncoming Confederates long enough for the infantry to move back as ordered. With Stuart attacking from the

west and southwest and Lee from the southeast, the commander of the Army of Northern Virginia had accomplished by noon what he tried to do at the second battle of Manassas—crush the opposing army in the jaws of a vise—and achieved his greatest victory.

Lee's victory was not quite complete, however, for trouble lurked behind him. In what has been called the second battle of Fredericksburg, Union general John Sedgwick overwhelmed Jubal Early and threatened to attack the rear and right flank of Lee's force. In the morning Sedgwick had attacked Marye's Heights twice without success, but the third time proved the charm. Early fell back to the south, and word of Sedgwick's breakout reached Lee at noon. Again, audaciously, Lee divided his army; leaving 20,000 men to keep Hooker in his works, he headed east on the turnpike with two divisions. At Salem Church, atop a long north-south ridgeline, the Confederates blocked the Federal advance, and the next day, Lee hemmed them in on three sides and pushed them back toward the river. The next morning he found that Sedgwick had led his army back across the Rappahannock at Scott's Ford; at Chancellorsville two days later, Hooker retreated, as well. Now Lee's victory was complete.

The victory came at a terrible cost in casualties. About 60,000 Confederate soldiers had fought some 135,000 Union soldiers; 12,764 Confederates were killed, wounded, or captured, compared with 17,287 Federals. One casualty loomed larger than all the rest in consequences: Stonewall Jackson. After a few days of seeming improvement, Jackson began a steady decline. His wife and baby daughter were rushed to his side from Richmond. Despite Dr. McGuire's best efforts, infection and possibly pneumonia set in; Jackson sank into delirium. Finally he grew quieter, calmer. The great warrior's last words were of peace: "Let us cross over the river and rest under the shade of the trees." He died at 3:15 P.M. on May 10, a Sunday. He had always wished to die on a Sunday, he had said that morning.

The effects of Jackson's death on the Confederate cause are impossible to overstate. The soldiers, particularly those in his corps and his old brigade, were devastated. When the news reached the camps, men wept openly, heaving with sobs. When Lee learned of Jackson's death, he wept for the passing of his friend as well as his lieutenant and could not speak of it. In the midst of their greatest victory, Lee and the Army of Northern Virginia had suffered their greatest loss.

The war went on, of course. Having defeated the Army of the Potomac, Lee convinced Pres. Jefferson Davis that the time was right for another invasion of the North. His army needed fresh supplies, and Virginia's storehouses were empty. It was the North's turn to feed his men. Lee's blood was up; he would invade Pennsylvania. ◼

FIRST BATTLE OF FREDERICKSBURG

When Maj. Gen. Ambrose E. Burnside assumed command of the Army of the Potomac from Maj. Gen. George B. McClellan on November 7, 1862, he immediately reorganized it by dividing it into three grand divisions. He placed Maj. Gen. Edwin V. "Bull" Sumner in charge of the right; Maj. Gen. Joseph "Fighting Joe" Hooker, the center; and Maj. Gen. William B. Franklin, the left. Next, Burnside planned an aggressive campaign against the Army of Northern Virginia and the Confederate capital at Richmond. He would march from Warrenton some forty miles around Lee's right flank to Fredericksburg, cross the Rappahannock River there on rapidly constructed pontoon bridges, and bring the Confederates to battle somewhere between there and Richmond. On November 15 Burnside put his plan and his 130,000-man army in motion away from the Army of Northern Virginia.

At first, Burnside's scheme worked well. Lee wondered where the Union army was headed as it melted away from his front. For once the normally slow-moving Army of the Potomac marched quickly and smoothly, its Right Grand Division reaching Falmouth, just north of Fredericksburg, in two days. Then Burnside's plans fell apart, for the pontoons were nowhere in sight, delayed by a bureaucratic foul-up in Washington. By the time the pontoons appeared on November 25, so had Longstreet's corps of the Army of Northern Virginia, taking post on the southwestern side of the Rappahannock to challenge Burnside's crossing.

Once Lee guessed what his opponent was up to, he shifted Longstreet and his corps to the heights overlooking Fredericksburg and the river. He would hamper the crossing by forcing Burnside to fight his way through the town, then repel the Federals if they attacked the main army to the west. Maj. Gen. Lafayette McLaws's division held the strongest defensive position, Marye's Heights; Maj. Gen. Richard H. Anderson's division stood to his left. The divisions of Maj. Gen. George E. Pickett and Maj. Gen. John Bell Hood were posted to McLaws's right. Brig. Gen. Robert Ransom, Jr., and his division, at first designated the reserve, were later directed to support McLaws.

Jackson and his corps began their march from Winchester on November 24 and arrived at Fredericksburg on December 3.

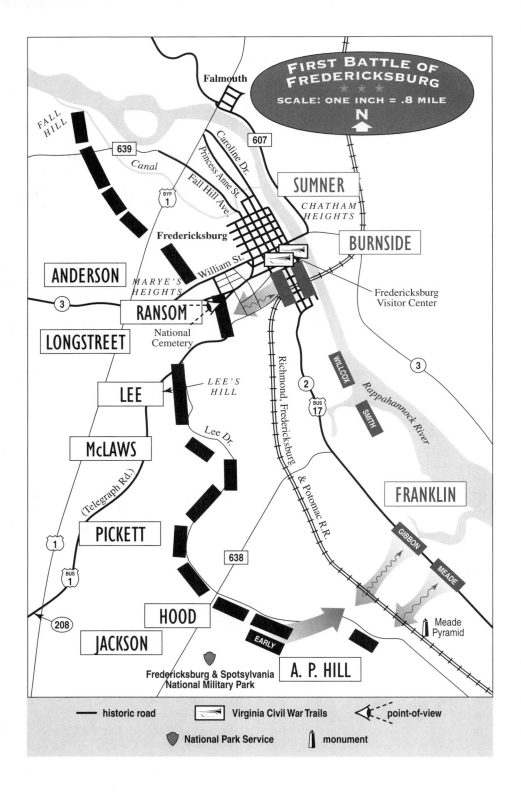

FIRST BATTLE OF FREDERICKSBURG

SCALE: ONE INCH = .8 MILE

N

Falmouth

FALL HILL

639

Canal

607

BYP 1

Caroline Dr.

Princess Anne St.

Fall Hill Ave.

Fredericksburg

SUMNER

CHATHAM HEIGHTS

BURNSIDE

William St.

ANDERSON

MARYE'S HEIGHTS

3

RANSOM

Fredericksburg Visitor Center

LONGSTREET

National Cemetery

LEE

LEE'S HILL

Richmond, Fredericksburg

2

BUS 17

WILLCOX

SMITH

Rappahannock River

3

Lee Dr.

McLAWS

(Telegraph Rd.)

& Potomac R.R.

FRANKLIN

1

PICKETT

GIBBON

MEADE

BUS 1

638

HOOD

EARLY

Meade Pyramid

208

JACKSON

A. P. HILL

Fredericksburg & Spotsylvania National Military Park

——— historic road

Virginia Civil War Trails

point-of-view

National Park Service

monument

DIRECTIONS: I-95 Exit 130A (State Rte. 3 East, Fredericksburg), e. on State Rte. 3 (William St.) and follow signs to Fredericksburg Visitor Center about 1.1 miles to left on William St. downtown; continue on William St. 1.2 miles to Princess Anne St.; s. (right) on Princess Anne St. 3 blocks to Charlotte St.; e. (left) on Charlotte St. 1 block to Fredericksburg Visitor Center parking lot and Virginia Civil War Trails markers; return to Princess Anne St.; s. (left) on Princess Anne St. 2 blocks to Lafayette Blvd. (U.S. Rte. 1 Bus.); w. (right) on Lafayette Blvd. .5 mile to Fredericksburg National Battlefield Park Visitor Center on right (driving tour brochures available at center); to tour battlefield, from visitor center continue w. on Lafayette Blvd. .6 mile to Lee Dr.; s. (left) on Lee Dr. 4.8 miles to end of driving tour; return to visitor center. To return to I-95 from center, turn e. (left) on Lafayette Blvd. 3 blocks to Littlepage St.; n. (left) on Littlepage St. 7 blocks to William St.; w. (left) on William St. 2 miles to I-95. Visit the National Park Service Web site at nps.gov/parks.html for a virtual tour of this and other national parks.

Within ten days his divisions occupied Prospect Hill. Maj. Gen. A. P. Hill's division was posted at the foot of the hill, with the divisions of Maj. Gen. Jubal A. Early and Brig. Gen. William B. Taliaferro behind him, and Maj. Gen. D. H. Hill's division was farther to the rear in reserve. Maj. Gen. J. E. B. Stuart's cavalry division patrolled the army's right flank, which terminated at the south end of the hill; the left flank, Anderson's division, was anchored on the Rappahannock River. Stuart's artillery chief, Maj. John Pelham, commanded a battalion of horse artillery.

Burnside decided to cross the river at three places. His engineers would lay two pontoon bridges over the water at the north end of Fredericksburg, one downstream from the demolished railroad bridge, and three about two miles farther downstream. He would force crossings at all locations—Sumner's Right Grand Division would capture the city—but his primary attack would be by Franklin's Left Grand Division around the Confederate right flank at Prospect Hill. Hooker's Center Grand Division would stand in reserve.

On the morning of Thursday, December 11, Burnside's engineers crept forward to the river under cover of a dense fog. On the other side, along the waterfront and in the buildings behind them, lurked sharpshooters from Brig. Gen. William Barksdale's Mississippi Brigade and a regiment of Floridians, attracted by the sounds of boats and men. As the fog slowly lifted to reveal the Federal engineers at work, the riflemen opened fire and drove the bridge builders away. Rifle fire from both sides had little effect compared to the artillery barrage laid down by Union gunners atop Stafford Heights on the northeastern side of the river. Late in the afternoon the Federal engineers finally completed their bridges. Some of his subordinates, convinced that the Confederate position was impregnable, argued against Burnside's plan, but he was determined to proceed.

Burnside intended to launch his attack shortly after dawn on Saturday, December 13, under cover of the fog that again blanketed the low ground. Franklin, however, dawdled until almost 10 A.M. Maj. Gen. George G. Meade led the advance with his division but stopped when rapid artillery fire came from what he thought was a battery of four guns to his left, on the Confederate right flank. In reality, Meade faced only John Pelham and two guns, which the artillerist deployed so quickly in one place and then another that it brought the Federal attack to a standstill. After one gun was disabled, Pelham dueled a Union battery with his remaining cannon.

Finally the attack lurched forward, but then Maj. Reuben L. Walker's guns on Prospect Hill opened fire, causing another hour's delay before they were neutralized by Franklin's artillery fire. When the infantry resumed its advance, it was not around Lee's and Jackson's right as Burnside had intended. Instead, Franklin's grand division pulled to his right into a wooded marsh that ironically led to the

Marye House (present-day Brompton, residence of the president of Mary Washington College), with C.S.A. rifle pits. LIBRARY OF CONGRESS

one weak spot in the seven-mile-long Confederate line. One brigade was posted to the left of the morass, and another to the right, but a 600-yard gap existed between them. Through the wet ground marched Meade's division with Brig. Gen. John Gibbon's division on his right, threatening the heart of Jackson's line and Lee's right flank. Early's division, with brigades from Taliaferro's, rushed into the breach and stopped the Federal penetration. By mid-afternoon the crisis was over, and Lee's right flank was secure.

On the Confederate left Longstreet prepared for Sumner's onslaught by improving his corps's position, particularly at Marye's Heights. He had posted his artillery on the crest, with infantry behind the guns and in the sunken Telegraph Road, which ran along the base of the hill. A stone wall protected the soldiers in the road. When Sumner's first line approached at about noon, the Confederate fire was devastating, and Confederate rifle-muskets and cannons slaughtered whole brigades of Union soldiers in front of the stone wall.

Late in the day Burnside elected to throw Hooker's Center Grand Division and the V Corps into the fray. Hooker,

who opposed the order, nonetheless complied, sending Brig. Gen. Andrew A. Humphreys's division against the stone wall shortly after 4 P.M. It met the same fate as its predecessors, and after a final, desperate bayonet charge failed, it fell back and left the field to the victorious Confederates.

The brave but futile assaults cost the Federals 12,600 casualties, while the Confederates lost 5,300. Burnside wanted to resume the attack on December 14, but his subordinates talked him out of it. Lee likewise considered attacking his beaten foe, but foresaw that the Union artillery lining Stafford Heights could do unto his forces what his had done to Burnside's and decided to stay put. During the night of December 15, the Army of the Potomac recrossed the Rappahannock River, and the battle for Fredericksburg ended.

Burnside has been roundly condemned, beginning with a Congressional investigation following the battle, for making repeated attacks against Marye's Heights and causing the slaughter of his men. However, Burnside's tactics were virtually the same as Lee's at Gaines's Mill. Also, Burnside's attacks were premeditated while Lee's occurred during his pursuit of the Union army. The major difference, of course, is that Lee succeeded and Burnside did not.

More than 1,500 acres of the battlefield—a small portion of the total—lie within the Fredericksburg and Spotsylvania National Military Park. The parklands include part of Marye's Heights, the sunken road and stone wall, Lee's Hill, a narrow strip containing five miles of Confederate earthworks, and Chatham (Sumner's headquarters). The Civil War Preservation Trust also owns property on the battlefield. Much has been lost to development, however, including the ground over which Sumner and Hooker attacked the stone wall. Likewise, some of the land that constituted the Confederate right flank (Jackson's position) and the scene of Franklin's attack has been built on. Large portions of this ground remain open, but most of it is privately owned, some scheduled for future development. The core of old Fredericksburg is a historic district; two walking tours cover the part of the town affected by the Union shelling and the route of the Federal advance to Willis Hill and Marye's Heights. Once a quiet college town, Fredericksburg is a growing city and a bedroom suburb for northern Virginia and Washington due to Interstate 95 and a commuter rail connection. Continued expansion and a resulting loss of battlefield features are imminent. ■

KELLY'S FORD

In mid-January 1863, seeking to overcome the Army of the Potomac's decline in morale following its disastrous defeat at Fredericksburg on December 13, 1862, Maj. Gen. Ambrose E. Burnside planned a winter campaign against Gen. Robert E. Lee and the Army of Northern Virginia. He would strike Lee's army's rear after feigning attacks at several Rappahannock River fords and crossing the river in force at Banks's Ford, roughly a five-mile march west of the city.

Some of Burnside's officers argued that the army needed to rest and rebuild, not fight Lee again so soon after its loss. Burnside, however, refused to alter his plan, and the march began on January 19. That evening the weather suddenly changed, and a cold front brought fog and forty-eight hours of pouring rain. The march quickly bogged down in mud. Finally, on January 23 Burnside canceled the expedition, and the army marched back to Fredericksburg. Two days later, Pres. Abraham Lincoln relieved him of command and appointed Maj. Gen. Joseph Hooker in his place.

Hooker immediately set about reorganizing and training his army. He abolished Burnside's grand divisions and reinstituted the corps arrangement. Most importantly, he gathered all the army's cavalry under one command and appointed Maj. Gen. George Stoneman to head the new corps. To boost the cavalry's esprit, Hooker used it to probe the Confederate line.

Until this time the Confederate cavalry under Maj. Gen. J. E. B. Stuart had whipped its Union counterparts whenever they encountered them. An innovator of cavalry tactics, he drilled his men hard, understood the importance of setting a personal example and tone, led them into battle boldly, and improvised quickly when necessary. He brought his chief valuable, reliable intelligence, struck Federal outposts, cut Union lines of communication and supply, and generally raised havoc with the enemy.

The tide was about to turn, however. The Union army supplied Northern troopers with a seemingly endless string of mounts, whereas Southern cavalrymen owned their own horses and had to serve on foot when their animals were killed or disabled. In addition, the Federal cavalry swelled with recruits in numbers that the Confederates just could not match. All Hooker's cavalry needed was some training and experience to give Stuart a fight.

On February 25, 1863, Confederate and Union cavalry clashed near Hartwood Church in Stafford County, nine miles

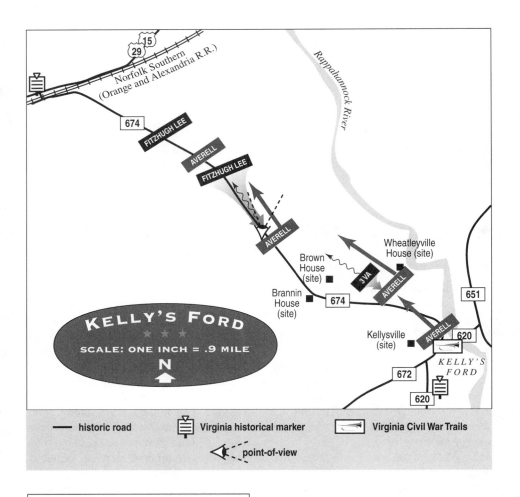

KELLY'S FORD
★ ★ ★
SCALE: ONE INCH = .9 MILE
N

— historic road   Virginia historical marker   Virginia Civil War Trails

point-of-view

DIRECTIONS: I-95 Exit 130B (State Rte. 3 West, Culpeper), w. on State Rte. 3 about 23.2 miles to Rte. 669 (Carrico Mills Rd.); n. (right) on Rte. 669 .8 mile to Rte. 610 (Maddens Tavern Rd.); e. (right) on Rte. 610 1.7 miles to Rte. 724 (Youngs Lane); n. (left) on Rte. 724 1.6 miles to Rte. 672 (Stones Mill Rd.); n. (right) on Rte. 672 2.5 miles to Rte. 620 (Edwards Shop Rd.); s. (right) on Rte. 620 .3 mile to state historical marker J-36, Battle of Kelly's Ford; return to Rte. 672; e. (right) on Rte. 620 .2 mile to Rte. 620; e. (right) on Rte. 620 to Kelly's Ford Bridge and Virginia Civil War Trails marker; return to Rte. 672; right on Rte. 674 (Kelly's Ford Rd.) .7 mile to view of battlefield to e. (right); continue 4.2 miles on Rte. 674 to U.S. Rte. 15/29 at Elkwood and state historical marker (F-10, Where Pelham Fell) on left; retrace route to State Rte. 3.

northwest of Fredericksburg. About 400 of Brig. Gen. Fitzhugh Lee's troopers on a thrust behind Union lines captured some 150 Federal cavalrymen in a surprise attack. Lee, one of Stuart's ablest subordinates and a nephew of Gen. Robert E. Lee, was a graduate of the United States Military Academy at West Point. By coincidence, one of his classmates and closest friends at the academy, Brig. Gen. William W. Averell, commanded a division of Union cavalry and the prisoners belonged to that division.

Hooker was furious. He wanted such forays by the Confederates stopped, and he threatened to relieve Stoneman of his command if he did not put an end to them. Averell's scouts found Lee about three weeks later near Culpeper Court House. Averell organized an expedition and left the Union lines on March 16 with 2,100 cavalrymen and an artillery battery, bound for Kelly's Ford on the Rappahannock River between Fauquier and Culpeper Counties.

On the western or Culpeper County side of Kelly's Ford, the Kelly farmhouse—Kellysville—sat atop a knoll overlooking the ford and a fork in the road that crossed the ford. The southwestern fork (present-day Rte. 672) led to Stevensburg; the northwestern fork (Rte. 674) curved around the base of the knoll almost directly west before turning abruptly northwest toward the Orange & Alexandria Railroad. Really a farm lane, the road passed through the Wheatley, Brown, and Brannin farms on its way to the railroad.

Confederate pickets learned of Averell's advance, and when he attempted to cross the ford about dawn on Tuesday, March 17, they delivered such a volume of fire that it took him two hours to force a crossing. Averell moved cautiously; by noon he had progressed only two miles up the farm lane to the vicinity of the Wheatley farm. The delay enabled Fitzhugh Lee to assemble 800 cavalrymen and ride to the attack from Culpeper Court House. He struck Averell's line about noon, and for the next five hours the battle raged back and forth over the countryside.

Stuart, in Culpeper Court House to attend a court-martial, decided to ride out to Kelly's Ford and watch the action. His artillery chief, Maj. John Pelham, joined him on a borrowed horse. The two men arrived at the scene of the battle to find it had not gone well for Lee. Outnumbered more than two to one and facing a battery of artillery, Lee's horsemen had suffered severe losses. The 2nd Virginia Cavalry had even fled in the face of a Union

Kelly's Ford battlefield, looking northeast near site of Pelham's mortal wounding. VIRGINIA DEPARTMENT OF HISTORIC RESOURCES, JOHN S. SALMON

charge, for the first time in the war. Pelham and Stuart reined in to watch as Lee sent the 3rd Virginia Cavalry south toward the Federal position; the Union left was in a woodlot, while the right passed through a field and farmyard behind a stone wall. Pelham cantered forward with Lee's men, looking for an opening in the wall as Union artillery shells began to burst nearby. As he waved the cavalrymen through a gate, a shell exploded over Pelham's head, and a tiny fragment drove into his brain. He died a few hours later.

Technically, the Confederates won the Kelly's Ford battle since Averell failed to destroy Lee's smaller force and withdrew across the ford at dusk under pressure. To the Federal cavalrymen, however, the battle constituted a moral victory for they had more than held their own against Stuart's vaunted horsemen. About 170 of Lee's horsemen were killed, wounded, or captured, while Averell lost 78.

The Kelly's Ford battlefield is in an excellent state of preservation, an area of farms, fields, woods, and historic roadways. A late-nineteenth-century dwelling occupies the site of Kellysville, and although the Wheatley house is gone, the stone wall can still be identified. Part of the battlefield along the river, the Phelps Wildlife Management Area, is owned by the Virginia Department of Game and Inland Fisheries; the rest is privately owned. ■

The winter of 1862–1863 was not a particularly good one for Gen. Robert E. Lee and the Army of Northern Virginia. Lee fell ill in March 1863, likely due to the onset of angina pectoris or a mild heart attack. Lee also had the health of his soldiers on his mind. Piedmont Virginia had been plundered repeatedly by both armies in their search for food and forage. The soldiers of the Army of Northern Virginia were showing signs of malnutrition and scurvy.

In mid-February Lee had sent Lt. Gen. James Longstreet with the divisions of major generals George E. Pickett and John B. Hood (a total of about 20,000 troops) to southeastern Virginia to gather supplies and counter Union forces. Longstreet also was to guard the eastern approaches to Richmond and explore the possibility of capturing strategically important Suffolk.

Suffolk is located at the head of navigation on the Nansemond River, a tidal river with many sandbars and tributary creeks, which empties into the James River at Hampton Roads. Also, two railroads intersected near the town: the Norfolk & Petersburg and the Seaboard & Roanoke. The former ran east-west, while the latter led into North Carolina. Federal troops garrisoned the town; their commander, Brig. Gen. John J. Peck, assumed command in October 1862 and oversaw the construction of the earthworks that encircled Suffolk. Union gunboats supported Peck's 25,000 soldiers by patrolling the river between Suffolk and Hampton Roads.

By mid-March 1863, Longstreet had decided to besiege Suffolk after determining that Peck's defensive works were too strong to be taken by direct assault. On April 11, after several probes, Longstreet determined that Suffolk's defenses were

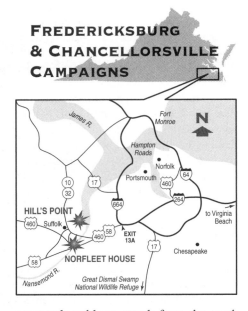

FREDERICKSBURG & CHANCELLORSVILLE CAMPAIGNS

most vulnerable to attack from the north (the Great Dismal Swamp protected the town on the east). On Monday, April 13, Confederate sharpshooters on the west side of the river fired at several Union gunboats; in the evening the vessels, on their way downriver (north) to Hampton Roads, steamed back toward Suffolk, but two of them, *Stepping Stones* and *Mount Washington,* ran aground near the Norfleet farm, some two and a half miles north of the town. That night Confederate artillerymen constructed a battery, and infantrymen dug a line of rifle pits near the farmhouse.

In the morning, the rising tide refloated the gunboats, which continued south toward Suffolk. As they rounded a sharp bend in the river, the sailors noticed the new earthworks at Norfleet House but decided to run past them, anticipating only sharpshooters. As the gunboats approached, however, the Confederate gunners pushed their pieces out of conceal-

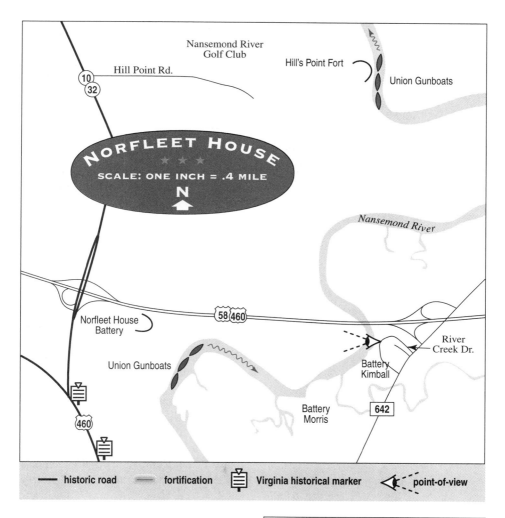

NORFLEET HOUSE
★ ★ ★
SCALE: ONE INCH = .4 MILE
N

Nansemond River
Golf Club

Hill Point Rd.

Hill's Point Fort

Union Gunboats

Nansemond River

Norfleet House
Battery

Union Gunboats

River
Creek Dr.

Battery
Kimball

Battery
Morris

642

58 460

10
32

460

— historic road   — fortification   🏛 Virginia historical marker   ◁⋯ point-of-view

ment in the woods and into the battery, opening fire. Mount Washington was hit and ran aground as did West End, but Stepping Stones pulled both vessels free. The gunboats made their way downstream, towing the disabled Mount Washington, until they were opposite Hill's Point, where at about 11:30 a.m. Mount Washington lodged on a sandbar. During the morning's action the Confederates had moved six cannons into the old War of 1812–era Hill's Point fort, renamed Fort Huger, and placed another four nearby. As soon as Mount Washington grounded, they opened

DIRECTIONS: I-664 Exit 13A (U.S. Rtes. 13/58/460, Suffolk), w. on U.S. Rtes. 13/58/460 about 6 miles to U.S. Rtes. 13/58/460 Bus.; w. on U.S. Rtes. 13/58/460 3.2 miles to Rte. 642 (Wilroy Rd.); n. (right) on Rte. 642 1.8 miles to Rte. 1870 (River Creek Dr.); e. (left) on River Creek Dr. 1 block to River Creek Landing; left on River Creek Landing 1 block to River Creek Crescent; right on River Creek Crescent and proceed to turnaround in play area (provides view of river and general area of engagement).

fire, hitting and damaging the vessel. The gunboat Commodore Barney raced upriver to assist, and the gunboats returned fire until the Confederate pieces fell silent at

Nansemond River in vicinity of Norfleet House engagement. VIRGINIA DEPARTMENT OF HISTORIC RESOURCES, JOHN S. SALMON

about 1:30 p.m. They resumed firing at about 3 p.m., when the tide rose; by 6 p.m. the tide had floated Mount Washington, and Stepping Stones towed it to safety downriver. The Union gunboats suffered 5 killed, 14 wounded, and 1 missing; Confederate casualties, if any, are unknown.

During the morning engagement, Brig. Gen. George W. Getty observed the Confederate battery at Norfleet House from a concealed position across the river and considered ways to neutralize it. He located two sites, each covered with brush and small trees, that were ideal for "masked" batteries. During the night of April 14–15, when rain muffled the sounds of construction, Battery Morris was built in the first position (with rifle pits in front) and Battery Kimball in the second.

At dawn on Wednesday, April 15, the artillerymen in Battery Morris chopped down the trees and bushes that concealed it and opened fire on the Norfleet House battery. A lively duel ensued, and when the Union battery had gotten the range, the screen of vegetation that masked Battery Kimball suddenly vanished and the gunners there joined in with enfilading fire. For three hours the artillerymen dueled, supported by sharpshooters in the Battery Morris rifle pits. Eventually the Confederate guns fell silent, and during the night they were withdrawn, not to return. The Confederate casualty figures are unknown; the Federals suffered three wounded, one mortally.

The Norfleet House battery kept Union gunboats out of the upper Nansemond River for a few days, but Getty's quick response drove the Confederates away. Downstream, however, the Confederate gunners continued to occupy the Hill's Point battery and threaten Federal vessels.

The Norfleet battery was destroyed by March 1971 for a borrow pit for highway construction. Residential development has obliterated the Morris and Kimball battery sites, as well. ■

HILL'S POINT (SIEGE OF SUFFOLK)

In the hours before dawn on Sunday, April 19, Capt. David L. Smoot and his Alexandria Battery built a new earthwork about two-thirds of a mile north (downriver) from Fort Huger, the Hill's Point fortification, on a high spot today called Knob Hill. The work was screened, or "masked," from Federal observation by natural vegetation. Sharpshooters dug rifle pits near the battery, which had been built to help protect Fort Huger and prevent Union gun-boats from steaming upriver (south) from Hampton Roads to Suffolk. Fort Huger had two 24-pounder howitzers and three 12-pounder Napoleons (also smoothbores). Infantry support was provided by about 150 men from the 44th Alabama.

At about 10 A.M., five Union gunboats came within range of the Knob Hill battery, which opened fire. The Federal gunners responded in kind, and the resulting duel lasted some five hours. Although the

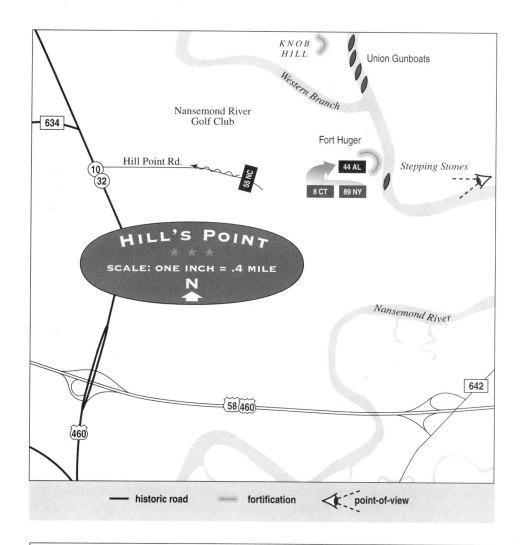

KNOB HILL

Union Gunboats

Western Branch

Nansemond River
Golf Club

634

Fort Huger

Hill Point Rd.

10
32

55 NC

44 AL

Stepping Stones

8 CT   89 NY

HILL'S POINT
★ ★ ★
SCALE: ONE INCH = .4 MILE
N

Nansemond River

642

58 460

460

historic road   fortification   point-of-view

DIRECTIONS: I-664 Exit 13A (U.S. Rtes. 13/58/460, Suffolk), w. on U.S. Rtes. 13/58/460 about 6 miles to U.S. Rtes. 13/58/460 Bus.; w. on U.S. Rtes. 13/58/460 3.2 miles to Rte. 642 (Wilroy Rd.); n. (right) on Rte. 642 3.5 miles to Long Point Lane; w. (left) on Long Point Lane (semi-private, winding dirt road) .55 mile to observation point just across wooden bridge (no railings) at edge of pond; see Hill's Point fort area in trees to w. (left) across marsh; cross pond and at next right turn around and return to Rte. 642.
  Alternative route: I-664 Exit 13A (U.S. Rtes. 13/58/460, Suffolk), w. on U.S. Rtes. 13/58/460 about 6 miles to U.S. Rtes. 13/U.S. Rte. 460/32/10 Bus. 1.5 miles to Rtes. 10 West/32 North and state historical marker K-258, Siege of Suffolk; n. (right) on Rtes. 10 West/32 North 1.7 miles (at Elephant Fork intersection, observe state historical marker K-259, Siege of Suffolk) to Hill Point Rd.; e. (right) on Hill Point Rd. .3 mile to stop sign; turn s. (right) .5 mile to Nansemond River Golf Club (public course) clubhouse. The fort is behind the 17th tee; to see it you must play a round of golf.

Confederates thought that the gunboats were attempting a run up the Nansemond River to Suffolk, the Federals had another objective in mind—to capture Fort Huger.

At 5 P.M., Union infantrymen boarded the gunboat *Stepping Stones:* 130 men from the 8th Connecticut Regiment, 140 from the 89th New York Regiment, and 40

View west across Nansemond River toward site of Hill's Point engagement. VIRGINIA DEPARTMENT OF HISTORIC RESOURCES, JOHN S. SALMON

other men to drag four boat howitzers ashore when the time came. Lt. Roswell H. Lamson commanded the force.

Stepping Stones got under way at 5:30 and steamed upriver; the other gunboats fired to give her cover as she ran past the Knob Hill and Fort Huger batteries, and the Confederate infantry ducked for cover to escape the barrage. About 300 yards beyond Fort Huger, Lamson ordered *Stepping Stones* to turn in to the swampy ground on the west bank of the river. Capt. Hazard Stevens was the first into the muck, and the rest of the infantry followed him ashore. Stevens hurried his men across a cornfield toward the open rear of Fort Huger, which was vulnerable to infantry attack. The Alabamians spotted them and opened fire with small arms and artillery, but the Federals were in the fort so quickly that only 4 men were killed and 10 wounded. The Confederates lost 1 man killed (supposedly shot by his commander for trying to run away). All the others, some 130 soldiers and 7 officers, as well as 5 cannons, were captured; the Federals had attacked with bayonets fixed and had not fired a shot.

Lamson spent the night consolidating his position and preparing for an expected counterattack. He posted his howitzers to sweep the fields south and west of the fort, dug rifle pits, and threw out pickets in the direction of the Confederates. Then he reinforced the fort with infantry and sent artillerymen to serve the captured guns, which were turned around to be used against any attackers. His men dug new gun emplacements and rifle pits to the west of the fort. No attack came, however, except for a probe soon after dark by skirmishers from the 55th North Carolina Infantry, which was repulsed easily. Fort Huger remained in Union hands.

Without Fort Huger, Longstreet could not hope to obstruct Union vessels on the river and carry on an effective siege. Both armies continued to probe each other's lines, to little effect. Before the month was out, Longstreet, who at least had accomplished that part of his mission that called for resupplying the army with foodstuffs, ended the siege and departed. The last of his reduced corps left Suffolk on May 4—too late to take part in the great battle being fought just west of Fredericksburg at a place called Chancellorsville.

The miles of Union earthworks that once surrounded Suffolk have been obliterated by residential and commercial development or by the return of the land to farming operations. The battery at Knob Hill appears to be gone, but as the only access is by water, its condition is not positively known. Fort Huger, on the other hand, still stands on Hill's Point on the grounds of the Nansemond River Golf Club. In Suffolk, Riddick's Folly, which served as Peck's headquarters, is operated as a house museum and visitors center. ∎

CHANCELLORSVILLE

When Pres. Abraham Lincoln appointed Maj. Gen. Joseph "Fighting Joe" Hooker commander of the Army of the Potomac on January 25, 1863, he instructed the general: "Beware of rashness, but with energy, and sleepless vigilance, go forward, and give us victories."

Hooker certainly intended to give Lincoln victories. He had developed a plan for attacking Gen. Robert E. Lee and his Army of Northern Virginia, defeating it, and marching on to Richmond. He would send the cavalry corps on a wide sweep around Lee's left flank and rear to cut his communications with Richmond, leave part of his army at Fredericksburg to demonstrate against the Confederates there and hold them in place, and take the rest of his army around Lee's flank, strike Lee in the rear, and crush his army. The plan was bold, and depended for its success on the effectiveness of the cavalry, the courage of the infantry, and the nerve of the army's commander.

Hooker had numerical superiority over Lee in every department. The Army of the Potomac counted more than 133,000 men, while the Army of Northern Virginia opposite Fredericksburg had been reduced to about 60,000 after Lt. Gen. James Longstreet and two divisions of his corps departed for southeastern Virginia in February (the third division had gone earlier to North Carolina). Hooker's cavalry numbered about 11,500 to Lee's 4,450; his artillery pieces added up to 413 versus Lee's 220. Lee's advantages were less tangible but nonetheless significant: prepared defensive positions, knowledge of the ground, an army renowned for its rapid maneuvers in the field, and such legendary commanders as Lt. Gen. Thomas J. "Stonewall" Jackson.

The Rappahannock River flows generally southeastward and is joined by several tributaries, most notably the Rapidan River fourteen miles northwest of Fredericksburg. Several fords and other crossings on both rivers were strategically important during the Chancellorsville campaign. From the fords a network of roads led southward to the two principal east-west thoroughfares, the Orange Turnpike and the newer Orange Plank Road. The turnpike and the plank road were one (present-day Rte. 3) from Fredericksburg west for about five miles, past Salem Church to Tabernacle Church; there, the turnpike continued west some five miles to Chancellorsville, while the plank road (Rte. 610) swung off to the southwest and then northwest to intersect the pike again at Chancellorsville. Other roads, trails, paths, and tracks crisscrossed the area.

On Monday, April 27, Hooker put his army in motion toward Kelly's Ford, marching north of the Rappahannock River over present-day U.S. Rte. 17 and Rte. 651. Maj. Gen. Oliver O. Howard led the way with XI Corps, followed by Maj. Gen. Henry W. Slocum and XII Corps, and Maj. Gen. George G. Meade and V Corps. Maj. Gen. Darius N. Couch and II Corps, Maj. Gen. John Sedgwick and VI Corps, Maj. Gen. John F. Reynolds and I Corps, and Maj. Gen. Daniel E. Sickles and III Corps remained closer to Fredericksburg to demonstrate against the Confederate defensive line.

Opposite Fredericksburg, the division of Maj. Gen. Lafayette McLaws, of Longstreet's corps, occupied Marye's Heights and northwest to Taylor's Hill. Brigades from the other remaining division of Longstreet's command, led by Maj. Gen. Richard H. Anderson, guarded Scott's,

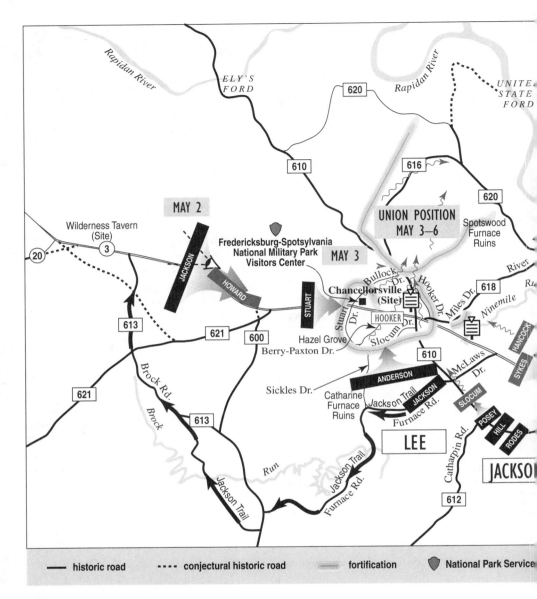

Banks's, and United States Fords on the Confederate left flank. Jackson's corps occupied Prospect Hill south of Fredericksburg, with Maj. Gen. Jubal A. Early's division just to the right of McLaws's. South of Early along the high ground, the divisions of Maj. Gen. A. P. Hill, Brig. Gen. Robert E. Rodes, and Brig. Gen. Raleigh E. Colston completed Lee's right

flank. Maj. J. E. B. Stuart's cavalry patrolled Culpeper County in the vicinity of Kelly's Ford beyond Lee's left flank.

By the night of April 27, Hooker's flanking force had reached Hartwood Church in Stafford County, some nine miles northwest of Fredericksburg. By the next evening Couch's II Corps (less Brig. Gen. John Gibbon's division) had marched

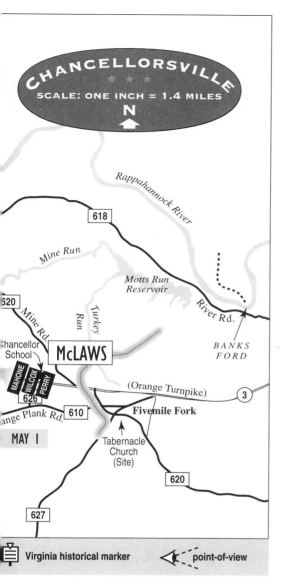

CHANCELLORSVILLE
★ ★ ★
SCALE: ONE INCH = 1.4 MILES
N

Rappahannock River

618

Mine Run

Motts Run
Reservoir

620

Mine Rd.

Turkey Run

River Rd.

BANKS
FORD

Chancellor
School

McLAWS

MAHONE
WILCOX
PERRY

626

(Orange Turnpike)

3

Orange Plank Rd.

610

Fivemile Fork

MAY 1

Tabernacle
Church
(Site)

620

627

Virginia historical marker   point-of-view

DIRECTIONS: I-95 Exit 130B (State Rte. 3 West, Culpeper), w. on State Rte. 3 about 6.4 miles to state historical marker J-39, Wounding of Jackson; continue 1.4 miles farther to Chancellorsville Visitor Center entrance, Fredericksburg and Spotsylvania National Military Park. Visit the National Park Service Web site at nps.gov/parks.html for a virtual tour of this and other national parks.

communications with Richmond. Stuart could not tell immediately how many Federal troops were on the move, or their destination.

On the morning of April 29, the picture became a little clearer for Stuart as Howard and Slocum marched the eleven miles south from Kelly's Ford to Germanna Ford on the Rapidan River (Rtes. 672, 724, 610, 647, and 3), while Meade took a road to the east (Rtes. 620, 682, and 610) that led to Ely's Ford. When Stuart's cavalrymen captured a few foot soldiers from XI Corps, he realized that a large movement was under way, but he still did not know where it was headed. He quickly sent word to Lee.

Meanwhile, at Germanna Ford, Slocum pushed on across the swift-flowing river. Meade crossed at Ely's Ford, while Couch, across the Rappahannock, approached United States Ford. Confederate couriers galloped from one ford to another on the south sides of the rivers, alerting the infantry brigades guarding the crossings. At United States Ford, brigade commanders William Mahone and Carnot Posey moved to block the Ely's Ford road and the Orange Turnpike and Orange Plank Road, down which Howard and Slocum were marching from Germanna Ford. Men were posted just west of the intersecting roads where Chancellorsville stood, a large brick house named for the family that owned it. Inside the house, several men and women would witness—and survive—the battle.

southwest toward United States Ford on present-day Rte. 655, while the rest of the column reached Kelly's Ford and awaited the construction of pontoon bridges; the men crossed in the night. Word reached Stuart, who rode to investigate and collided with one of the four Union cavalry regiments not with Stoneman on his ultimately futile effort to sever Confederate

Chancellorsville • 175

Back in Fredericksburg, at Franklin's Crossing, Sedgwick's and Reynolds's corps forced their way across the Rappahannock in boats and on hastily constructed bridges. By nightfall the bridgeheads were firmly established, and at least one division from each corps was over the river confronting Early.

Hooker's maneuver had succeeded brilliantly. Lee was stunned to hear of the river crossing. He ordered Anderson with a third brigade to reinforce Mahone and Posey at Chancellorsville. When a message from Stuart confirmed that all the Union troops that crossed the Rapidan were heading south, Hooker's intentions became clear to Lee, who wired Pres. Jefferson Davis in Richmond for additional troops.

Anderson arrived at Chancellorsville to word that Couch had crossed United States Ford and was approaching the intersection from the northeast. Anderson, concerned that Union troops on Ely's Ford road would move down Mine Road and cut him off, pulled his division back to a more defensible position east of Chancellorsville, between Zoan and Tabernacle Churches.

Hooker's columns, meanwhile, were marching slowly through the seventy-square-mile area just west of Chancellorsville called the Wilderness, a nasty, dense thicket of stumps, scrub pine, briers, and brambles with visibility of only a few feet, which made military maneuvering virtually impossible. Here and there clearings offered some relief, but most of the Wilderness was barely penetrable.

The morning of Thursday, April 30, came with a cool drizzle. Anderson's division marched east to its new position near the churches as the head of Meade's column approached Chancellorsville on the Ely's Ford road. The Confederate rear guard fought several sharp skirmishes with Meade's vanguard to hold off the Federals temporarily. At about 11 A.M. Meade himself arrived at the house to find four of the Chancellor women perched on the upper floor of the two-story front porch, castigating the Union soldiers as they marched by.

Soon the main Federal force—Howard's and Slocum's corps—began to arrive at the intersection after its march through the Wilderness. Hooker originally had ordered the column to march on to Banks's Ford, but he changed his mind and told the commanders to halt at Chancellorsville, regroup and rest, and be prepared to resume the initiative the next day. Two divisions of Couch's II Corps established positions just north of the house on the road to United States Ford. Meade's V Corps set up across the turnpike east of the intersection, facing Anderson, while Slocum's XII Corps formed an arc south of the road and Howard's XI Corps formed on the turnpike west of Slocum. Hooker rode to Chancellorsville in the late afternoon to his new headquarters in the house (the Chancellor family was confined to a back room). That evening dozens of officers came to the house to celebrate their successful flanking movement. Hooker assured a newspaper reporter that Lee and his army were now Army of the Potomac property. Hooker thought his victory was all but won.

Meanwhile, near Fredericksburg, Lee, like Hooker, had issued new orders that day—orders that violated the principle that a commander does not divide his army in the face of a numerically superior foe. Instead, Lee adopted Napoleon's principle: Take the offensive before your adversary becomes fully prepared, and strike the first blow. Lee split his army, ordering McLaws to leave only one brigade (Brig. Gen. William Barksdale's) on Marye's Heights and Stonewall Jackson to leave one division (Early's) on Prospect Hill to confront the Union corps: roughly 11,000 soldiers to face 45,000. The rest of the force would march on toward Chancellorsville, with

McLaws reinforcing Anderson. Lee would have some 40,000 men; Hooker, 80,000.

Jackson's corps began its westward march at about 2 A.M. on Friday, May 1. When dawn came, neither the Confederate nor the Union force at Fredericksburg could see the other because of thick fog along the river. After the fog lifted near midmorning, it became clear to Sedgwick that something was up by the clouds of dust and trains of wagons. But the meaning of the activity remained obscured: a lateral movement along the river, a retreat, or something else? Sedgwick ordered his troops to stand fast while he figured it out.

Hooker, meanwhile, ordered an advance eastward, back toward Fredericksburg, against Anderson's position. This movement would turn Lee's flank. Once Anderson had been swept aside, Hooker would move his headquarters to Tabernacle Church and press the attack against Lee's flank. Hooker delayed his advance until Sickles's corps arrived.

Jackson joined Anderson at about 8 A.M. and found his men building strong earthworks in a good defensive position. With most of his corps still on the road behind him, however, Jackson realized that if Hooker chose to attack with the majority of his army, the Confederates would only have about 10,000 men in the earthworks to oppose him. Jackson therefore continued to take the offensive although logic suggested that he remain on the defensive. Jackson would proceed south and west on the plank road to strike Hooker's right flank. By 11 A.M. the march got under way, and within twenty minutes the battle of Chancellorsville began.

A brisk firefight developed along McLaws's front as his vanguard collided with Meade's men. Maj. Gen. George Sykes commanded Meade's right division, and he launched a counterattack that recovered most of the ground taken by McLaws in the opening engagement.

Sykes sent word to Hooker and began an orderly retreat with Maj. Gen. Winfield Scott Hancock's division covering when skirmishers discovered the advance of Jackson's command on his right flank. Hooker ordered Couch to send Hancock east to Sykes's left and help him repulse the Confederate attack.

And then . . . as Fighting Joe Hooker later allegedly put it, he suddenly lost confidence in Joe Hooker. By the time Hancock found Sykes, at about 1 P.M., a new order had arrived from Hooker: Pull back to the previous night's bivouac, and prepare defensive positions. Hancock was furious as were Couch and Sykes. Hooker later issued a new order, urging his generals to hold their positions until 5 P.M., but by the time it arrived, the retreat was in full swing and the new order only angered them further.

Jackson's advance encountered Maj. Gen. Alpheus S. Williams's division of Slocum's corps, and the sound of gunfire rippled through the dense woods south of the turnpike. Jackson's men pushed forward until they found the main Federal line, then halted at his order. Lee, meanwhile, had ridden west from Fredericksburg to join Jackson, and the two generals puzzled over the Union army's slow advance and sudden retreat.

As darkness fell on May 1, the Federals felled trees and dug up the soil around Chancellorsville to construct a line of breastworks. At midday they had been prepared to conquer the Army of Northern Virginia. That evening they were on the defensive, awaiting attack. With his men subdued and his generals angry, Hooker's situation posed more problems to him than Lee's gathering army alone.

As the sun set, Lee and Jackson conferred, examining a rough map of the country in the dwindling light and discussing their options. Jackson expected Hooker to withdraw across the Rappahannock River by morning; Lee disagreed, convinced that a movement as massive as Hooker's would not be abandoned so soon. If Hooker was still there in the morning, Lee would attack—but where? He could attack the Union army directly, or he could go around it and strike a flank. Hooker's left flank was too close to the river, but perhaps his right was vulnerable. At just that moment, Stuart galloped up the furnace road (Rte. 613) to report that Hooker's right flank was out in the open on the turnpike. Now, how to get there? Stuart cantered off into the night to search out the narrow woodcutters' paths that wound through the Wilderness, while Lee's and Jackson's aides scattered to question local civilians. The aides returned intermittently to report their findings; at dawn the two generals resumed their consultation. They agreed on the roads Jackson would take to Hooker's right flank, roads that were wide enough—barely—to allow artillery to pass and far enough away from Hooker's lines to conceal the movement. It was time for a decision.

Lee asked Jackson what he proposed, and Jackson answered that he would make the movement with his whole corps—leaving Lee with the divisions of Anderson and McLaws.

Lee was momentarily taken aback. Certainly a flanking attack meant dividing his army yet again, but Jackson's proposal would leave Lee with only 14,000 men with which to face Hooker's 80,000 immediately before him, and at any time Sedgwick might push through Early's thin line with his 40,000 soldiers and strike Lee's back. Still, if Jackson and his 28,000-man corps maintained secrecy, marched quickly, and attacked aggressively, the risk would be worth the results. Lee agreed to Jackson's plan.

Jackson alerted his subordinates. He had promised Lee at midnight that his corps would move at 4 A.M., but now the night was gone and with it the opportunity for an early start. The first units got under way at 8 A.M. on Saturday, May 2. Lee told Anderson and McLaws to make a lot of noise to cover Jackson's movement. Then he stood beside the furnace road as the head of Jackson's column approached. The two generals held a brief conversation, Lee on foot, Jackson astride Little Sorrel. Jackson gestured toward the west and Lee nodded; Jackson rode on. They had spoken together for the last time.

Jackson's column stretched for more than six miles as it wound through the narrow tracks cut through the Wilderness. The last of Jackson's men would not join the march until the front of the column neared its objective that afternoon.

Jackson lost the advantage of secrecy within an hour of starting his march when Union observers in the trees near Hazel Grove saw sunlight glinting on metal as the Confederates marched west. Hooker was out inspecting his lines; when he returned to Chancellorsville at about 9 A.M., he found word of Jackson's movement. Was Lee retreating—or maneuvering for an attack against the Union right flank? To be safe, Hooker sent messages to Howard and Sickles, warning against a flank attack (historians have since debated whether Howard ever received word). Hooker also sent orders to Sedgwick in Fredericksburg, informing him that only a detachment (Early's division) remained to oppose him and instructing him to attack if there was reasonable prospect of success. As worded, Hooker's order left the decision to attack up to Sedgwick; in his own mind, Hooker had given Sedgwick a command, with the expectation that his subordinate would immediately drive through Early's line and come to Hooker's support. The expectation went unfulfilled. Finally, Hooker ordered Reynolds to cross back over the Rappahannock River, march over United States Ford, and join the main army at Chancellorsville. That order, at least, was executed.

Maj. Gen. Daniel E. Sickles commanded the portion of Hooker's line centering on Hazel Grove. After watching Jackson's column pass for almost three hours, Sickles decided it was a retreat and talked Hooker into allowing him to attack. For his part, Jackson realized that his men could be seen through breaks in the woods, and when he noticed a track that entered the Catharine Furnace road from the north, he detached the 23rd Georgia Infantry Regiment and sent it up the road to block it. Sickles attacked the Georgians around noon, and Lee sent Posey's and Brig. Gen. Ambrose R. Wright's brigades to strike Sickles's left flank. The Confederate defense enabled the rear of Jackson's column to get beyond the reach of Sickles's infantry if not his artillery, which fired a few shells as the column disappeared to the southwest.

By 2 P.M. Jackson and the head of his column had reached the Orange Plank Road, south of the old turnpike, as the rear was marching past Catharine Furnace. Several encounters with Federal units prompted officers to report the Confederate movement up the chain of command, where it was ignored or laughed away. Brig. Gen. Fitzhugh Lee galloped up to Jackson and announced that a better position for the attack was located a mile and a half north, on the Orange Turnpike. Jackson followed him to a knoll and looked north; there, the soldiers of Howard's XI Corps relaxed behind their earthworks, their arms stacked and their cannons unattended.

Jackson returned to his column and urged the men into position for the attack. He ordered the 2nd Virginia Cavalry commanded by Col. Thomas T. Munford, a Virginia Military Institute graduate, to cover his left flank with the words,

"Colonel, the Institute will be heard from today." It took almost three hours for the lines to form: Rodes's division in front, Colston's next, and A. P. Hill's brigades of Brig. Gen. Dorsey Pender and Brig. Gen. James H. Lane behind Colston. By 5 P.M. approximately 25,000 men were in place, with Jackson watching quietly from Little Sorrel. At 5:15 P.M. Jackson told Rodes to begin the attack.

At Chancellorsville an hour before, Hooker had sent another in a series of messages to Sedgwick, urging him to advance and asserting that the enemy was fleeing. In the XI Corps bivouac, the men began to cook their suppers. Suddenly, from the west, wildlife bolted into the camp. Small-arms fire erupted, and many of the soldiers wondered what the pickets were up to. They found out seconds later: Stonewall was upon them.

Here and there, valiant officers and soldiers struggled to form ranks and face the onslaught, but many men of the XI Corps ran for their lives as the gray waves swept forward. In the road, two guns of the 1st Ohio Light Artillery Battery held their position, unleashed several volleys of their own, then limbered up and raced east to a new site. Jackson's corps pressed on without hesitation.

The Confederate soldiers pursued the XI Corps through thickets and across fields. At Howard's headquarters, the corps commander leaped into the saddle and tried desperately to stem the flight, to no avail.

Soon Jackson's corps was in a state of disarray almost as great as Howard's. The cohesion of the attacking lines disintegrated not long after the assault began, as some regiments got tangled in underbrush while others charged unimpeded across open fields. Pockets of Federal resistance and the obstacles created by Union earthworks at Wilderness Church slowed the

Howard's troops scrambling to form a line of battle as Jackson's corps sweeps toward them from the distant tree line. LIBRARY OF CONGRESS

assault along parts of the line, while other parts met no such challenges. The sight of the fleeing Federals excited the Confederates, and they rushed forward, heedless of their officers' demands to reform their lines and control their blood lust.

Jackson's attack went on for an hour before Hooker learned of it. As at Seven Pines, an acoustical shadow covered part of the battlefield, including the Chancellor house, so that Hooker heard little. Lee heard a vague murmur to the west that he assumed was Jackson's assault. Lee pressed Hooker's line with Anderson's and McLaws's divisions. In the early evening, Hooker lounged on the porch of Chancellorsville with his aides, listening to Lee's demonstration, when suddenly a mob of blue-clad soldiers raced toward and then past the Chancellor house in wild flight. Hooker mounted his horse and strove unsuccessfully to stem the flow—a nearby band even started playing every patriotic tune it knew—but finally Hooker realized that nothing but an infusion of fresh, calm troops could hope to form a line and hold it.

At about 6:30 P.M., John Reynolds rode up to Chancellorsville in the midst of the confusion to report that his corps had crossed United States Ford and now stood ready, albeit some four miles away, to engage the enemy. Hooker ordered Reynolds to occupy part of the line abandoned by Howard and gave him directions. Unfortunately, Hooker thought Howard had been farther north than he was, so Reynolds obediently took up a position that left him out of the battle. To the south, however, Sickles, who had assailed the rear of Jackson's column earlier in the day, now turned around and hastened to counterattack. The 8th Pennsylvania Cavalry, riding to join Howard, stumbled into the Confederates and charged in desperation. The collision produced many casualties on both sides.

Darkness and confusion ended the infantry battle for the day. Having been driven from one series of earthworks, the Federals began digging a second, west-facing line that extended roughly north from Sickles's position at Hazel Grove, across the plank road, and up to Little Hunting Run on Bullock Road, a narrow trail that entered the plank road about a mile west of Chancellorsville. The rest of the Federal line, which extended south and east of Chancellorsville, remained intact. To the west, Jackson's corps struggled to regroup and dug trenches hastily in case Hooker counterattacked.

Jackson wanted to conduct a night attack to keep pressure on the Federals.

However, he needed fresh, organized troops at the front. Hill's division moved forward to take Rodes's place in the Confederate line, with Lane's North Carolina brigade in the vanguard. Pender's brigade later formed to Lane's left, creating a half-mile-long front.

At about 9 P.M. Jackson led a reconnaissance toward the Union lines, to scout them personally before Hill attacked. Eight men accompanied Jackson. Behind Jackson's party, Hill followed with nine members of his staff. The two groups passed through Lane's left-flank unit, the 18th North Carolina Regiment. None of the 18th's officers were informed of the reconnaissance.

Jackson rode forward for several hundred yards, until he heard noises a couple hundred yards ahead. He listened quietly for a few minutes, and then, satisfied that he had heard the sounds of Federal soldiers entrenching, started back toward his own lines. His staff followed. It was almost 9:30 P.M.

To the 18th North Carolinians, the sudden appearance of horsemen in their front signaled a Federal cavalry probe. They opened fire: first some scattered shots, then a full volley. Hill and his staff raced back toward them, shouting at them to cease firing at their own men. Maj. John D. Barry of the 18th North Carolina shouted back for his men that the order was a lie and to pour on the firepower. Another volley followed, wounding and killing horses and men in both reconnaissance parties.

Three bullets crashed into Jackson, one breaking two fingers of his right hand, another passing through his left forearm, and the third splintering the bone three inches below his left shoulder. Finally, a staff officer caught up with him, reined in Little Sorrel, and helped Jackson off. When Federal artillery began to unlimber a short distance down the plank road,

Jackson was carried rearward on a litter and helped into an ambulance that took him the few miles west to Wilderness Tavern. There Dr. Hunter Holmes McGuire amputated Jackson's left arm in an operation that ended about 3 A.M.

The volleys in the night not only had removed Jackson from the scene, they had cut to pieces his and Hill's staffs. Four of Jackson's aides were killed, three of Hill's were wounded, and three men were captured when their horses bolted into the Union lines. Of the nineteen men in the two groups, ten besides Jackson thus became casualties—Hill was wounded as he oversaw Jackson's removal from the battlefield. Although the command of Jackson's corps, which Hill had assumed, should have devolved on Rodes as the next senior officer, Hill instead appointed Stuart. Rodes yielded for the good of the service at that crucial moment.

Jackson's proposed night attack was canceled, of course. The Union line had been fully roused by all the gunplay, Federal artillery fire halted the Confederate advance, and Stuart needed time to plan his course of action. The Confederates would also have to deal with Daniel Sickles in a night attack that demonstrated why such assaults were seldom tried, and seldom succeeded, during the war.

Hoping to recapture some cannons, Sickles launched his attack just after midnight on Sunday, May 3. The moon was high, and the Confederates saw the Federal troops coming down the road toward their positions in captured Union earthworks. Their fire forced the attacking Federals into the woods and ever farther right, where the Union soldiers found themselves taking fire from the front and rear as other Federals, thinking they were the enemy, opened up on them. Sickles did succeed in attaching his corps to the main Union line—once the occupants of the line had stopped shooting at his soldiers—and forming a sort of salient at the southwestern corner of Hooker's defenses.

Lee sent Stuart a message at 3 A.M., ordering a dawn attack to give the Federals no time to assemble. They had to be pressed so that the two wings of Lee's army could be unified. Again, as at the second battle of Manassas, Lee sought to close the jaws of the vise, this time with Stuart striking from the west and himself from the southeast, to crush the Army of the Potomac.

It would not be that simple, of course, principally because Sickles's salient projected southwest beyond Stuart's line, blocking a direct approach to Lee's left flank near Catharine Furnace. Lee's right was anchored on the turnpike some two miles northeast; the forces at his disposal numbered about 14,000. Stuart's three divisions amounted to some 30,000 men; all three divisions straddled the plank road on a roughly north-south axis, but Brig. Gen. Henry Heth's was bent back sharply toward the southwest just below the road, so as to face Sickles at Hazel Grove. Neither Stuart nor Lee could reach the other on a direct line; one or the other would have to get around Sickles to the west.

Jeb Stuart took command of Jackson's corps. Lee, Jackson, and Longstreet had recognized his leadership qualities and knew that they could rely on his information and on his skill as a cavalry commander in battle. But now he would lead an infantry corps, an entirely different proposition. He himself knew that he did not completely grasp the military situation in front of Jackson's corps, for he had spent most of Saturday away from that part of the field. However, he trusted his division commanders, and he understood that the momentum of the previous evening's successful onslaught should not

be lost. Stuart gave orders for a general advance at dawn.

Sickles, meanwhile, spent part of the night trying to persuade Hooker to extend his lines so that Hazel Grove would be incorporated into them. Hooker, however, wished to shrink his lines, not extend them. He ordered Sickles to abandon Hazel Grove and march to the Chancellorsville defenses. Reluctantly, Sickles complied; at dawn, only his rear guard remained at Hazel Grove.

Stuart's attack began as planned, but the Wilderness and the reinforced Federal defenses quickly fragmented his assaulting line. Heth's division splintered into its component parts and attacked the Federals piecemeal. Bursting through three lines of Union earthworks, Heth's men took heavy casualties before they were thrown back by Federal counterattacks. Stuart realized that a single division could not accomplish his goal and ordered Colston and Rodes into the attack. He also brought most of his available artillery, some thirty guns at Hazel Grove, to bear on Hooker's southwestern flank; the result was some of the most effective supporting fire executed by either side during the war. Union cannons responded, often at point-blank range, against the Confederate infantry, inflicting numerous casualties and dreadful carnage.

By shortly after 9 A.M., Stuart's men had pushed Hooker's southwestern flank back to Fairview, half the distance to Chancellorsville, Hooker's headquarters. The Union commander stood on the front porch of the house as one of Sickles's aides rode up with a plea for reinforcements. Suddenly a solid shot from a Confederate cannon struck a column and split it in half, striking Hooker on his head and knocking him senseless for a while. He remained in a daze for the rest of the day, and about midmorning, he turned command of the army over to Couch, at the same time ordering Couch to effect a withdrawal to Chancellorsville from the forward positions.

As the fighting raged on Stuart's front, Lee ordered Anderson's and McLaws's divisions to attack from the south and east. At 10 A.M., the two wings of the army united at Hazel Grove, turned northeast in a single if ragged line, and drove toward Chancellorsville despite heavy Federal rearguard opposition. The house became a target for Confederate gunners, unaware that it had become a hospital treating the wounded of both sides. Soon the dwelling was afire, its chimneys blown to bits, and a Union officer led the Chancellor family to safety down the road to United States Ford. Around the house, Federal artillerymen fought gallantly to hold back the gray tide long enough for the infantry to escape to Hooker's new line a mile and more toward United States Ford.

Long before noon the last Union defenders had fled Chancellorsville. Dead horses, dead soldiers, abandoned cannons, shattered wagons, and all the detritus of battle lay scattered along the roads and around the flaming house. In the Wilderness, a new horror: Flames raced through the dry brush, burning to death many of the wounded of both sides despite efforts to drag them to safety.

Shortly before noon, Lee rode into the Chancellorsville clearing. When his men saw him, they erupted into wild cheering and pressed around him, some reaching out to touch him or his horse. Four miles away, in a hospital tent near Wilderness Tavern, Stonewall Jackson received the news of the great victory with words of praise to the Almighty.

The battle of Chancellorsville was over, although other fighting was occurring, or would occur, at Fredericksburg and Salem Church. Indeed, until the news of the Federal breakout at Fredericksburg reached him about 12:30 P.M., Lee had been expecting to continue the attack against Hooker's new line. Now he had to turn his attention to events going on behind him. Lee had won his greatest victory at the cost of some 10,000 dead, wounded, and captured out of 57,000 Confederates engaged. Hooker lost 14,000 of the 97,000 men he had engaged.

Chancellorsville is arguably the most important Civil War battlefield in Virginia, an evaluation that rests on two facts: It is the site of Lee's greatest victory and of Jackson's mortal wounding, and it had greater consequences for the Confederacy than any other battle fought on Virginia soil. Lee's masterstroke was born of desperation following Hooker's successful movement around his left flank; the tactics the Confederate commander employed exemplified his audacity and aggressiveness. Lee divided his army not once but three times in the face of vastly superior numbers, countered and then outflanked Hooker's attempted envelopment, achieved near-total surprise with Jackson's assault on Hooker's right flank, and destroyed the confidence of the Army of the Potomac in its leader and itself. In the wake of this success, Lee and his Army of Northern Virginia left the Chancellorsville battlefield with an intense love between them, which, together with confidence in each other's abilities, would continue for the remainder of the war and beyond. As a result of his victory, Lee decided to invade the North once again—a decision that would have disastrous consequences at Gettysburg.

One might expect to find that the Chancellorsville battlefield, the site of the Confederacy's true high-water mark, is as well-preserved and well-marked as Gettysburg. Quite to the contrary, however, this most important of all Virginia Civil War battlefields is being devoured on all sides by sprawl. Much of the core area lies within the Fredericksburg and Spotsylvania Battlefields National Military Park, but most of the remainder of the field has disappeared beneath development, is in private hands in an increasingly suburban region, or is currently being developed. A planned expressway to connect I-95 with Rte. 3 for the convenience of commuters to and from Northern Virginia undoubtedly will accelerate development. Within the next decade or two, barring heroic actions to preserve it, most of the battlefield outside the park will vanish. ■

SECOND BATTLE OF FREDERICKSBURG

Beginning late in the afternoon of Saturday, May 2, 1863, Maj. Gen. John Sedgwick received one message after another from Maj. Gen. Joseph Hooker ordering him to drive through the Confederate defenses at Fredericksburg and come to Hooker's aid at Chancellorsville. Yet Sedgwick, a thoroughly professional and dependable soldier, kept delaying his advance.

Part of his slowness was due to the wording of Hooker's dispatches, some of which implied that the proposed movement was up to Sedgwick's discretion. Sedgwick also could not grasp just how his single reinforced corps could turn the tide of battle when Hooker already greatly outnumbered Lee and Jackson. Finally, Sedgwick feared that Hooker did not appreciate the situation in Fredericksburg, where he faced a Confederate force in strong defensive positions atop Marye's Heights and Prospect Hill, the scene of Federal disaster the previous December.

In fact, Sedgwick outnumbered his opponent, the irascible Maj. Gen. Jubal A. Early, by a margin of two to one. But Early had ordered his brigade commanders to stir up a lot of dust to delude the Federals into thinking his numbers were large, and they had succeeded.

Sedgwick had missed a window of opportunity that opened on Saturday after-

DIRECTIONS: I-95 Exit 130A (State Rte. 3 East, Fredericksburg), e. on State Rte. 3 (William St.) about 1.1 miles to left on William St. downtown; continue on William St. 1.2 miles to Princess Anne St.; s. (right) on Princess Anne St. 3 blocks to Charlotte St.; e. (left) on Charlotte St. 1 block to Fredericksburg Visitor Center parking lot and Virginia Civil War Trails markers; return to Princess Anne St.; s. (left) on Princess Anne St. 2 blocks to Lafayette Blvd. (U.S. Rte. 1 Bus.); w. (right) on Lafayette Blvd. .5 mile to Fredericksburg National Battlefield Park Visitor Center on right (driving tour brochures available at center); to tour battlefield, from visitor center continue w. on Lafayette Blvd. .6 mile to Lee Dr.; s. (left) on Lee Dr. 4.8 miles to end of driving tour; return to visitor center. To return to I-95 from center, turn e. (left) on Lafayette Blvd. 3 blocks to Littlepage St.; n. (left) on Littlepage St. 7 blocks to William St.; w. (left) on William St. 2 miles to I-95. Visit the National Park Service Web site at nps.gov/parks.html for a virtual tour of this and other national parks.

noon when Early had all but abandoned his lines, leaving only a token force, to march west toward Chancellorsville. At about 11 A.M., Early had received a verbal order from Lee, delivered by Lee's chief of staff, Col. Robert H. Chilton, to march to Chancellorsville immediately with all his force except a brigade and a few cannons. Early was thunderstruck; if he abandoned his works now, Sedgwick's corps could attack his rear and destroy his reinforced division in the open. Surely there was some mistake. Chilton was adamant, however, and Early issued the orders. Partway

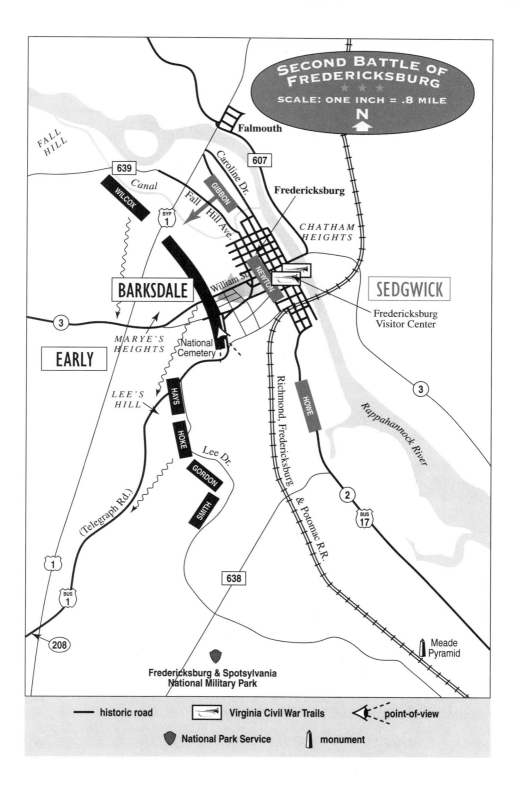

SECOND BATTLE OF
FREDERICKSBURG
★ ★ ★
SCALE: ONE INCH = .8 MILE
N

Falmouth

FALL
HILL

639

607

Caroline Dr.

Canal

WILCOX

GIBBON

Fall Hill Ave.

BYP
1

Fredericksburg

CHATHAM
HEIGHTS

BARKSDALE

William St.

NEWTON

SEDGWICK

3

Fredericksburg
Visitor Center

MARYE'S
HEIGHTS

EARLY

National
Cemetery

3

LEE'S
HILL

HAYS

Richmond, Fredericksburg

HOWE

Rappahannock River

HOKE

Lee Dr.

GORDON

(Telegraph Rd.)

SMITH

& Potomac R.R.

2

BUS
17

1

BUS
1

638

208

Meade
Pyramid

Fredericksburg & Spotsylvania
National Military Park

—— historic road   Virginia Civil War Trails   point-of-view

National Park Service   monument

to Chancellorsville, however, he received a written note from Lee, making it clear that Chilton indeed had garbled Lee's orders: Early was to join the main army only when he thought it was safe to do so.

Now what? Should Early press on to Chancellorsville or return to Fredericksburg? While he pondered his choices, a message arrived from Brig. Gen. William Barksdale, commanding his trailing brigade. The Federals were threatening the force left behind on Marye's Heights and might overrun the artillery; Barksdale had turned back to help the defenders. That decided the issue for Early. It was more important to hold the high ground at Fredericksburg, thereby blocking a vastly superior Union force, than to add a few thousand men to Lee's divisions fighting at Chancellorsville. Early turned his men around and marched east, closing the window on Sedgwick.

On the morning of Sunday, May 3, however, Sedgwick finally moved. Clear instructions from Hooker had arrived late the previous night: He was to begin his march immediately. Hooker's chief engineer came in person to describe the Chancellorsville situation in candid detail. Sedgwick ordered pontoons into the river in front of Fredericksburg to cross those units that were not already on the west bank. The movement started at about 2 A.M. but Barksdale's sharpshooters held it up, much as they had in December, until daylight. Soon after 7 A.M., all four divisions of Sedgwick's force were across and ready to attack along a four-mile front. Sedgwick's plan of attack called for Maj. Gen. John Newton's division to demonstrate in front of Marye's Heights while Brig. Gen. John Gibbon and two brigades from Couch's corps swung around the northern end of the hill and Brig. Gen. Albion P. Howe's division attacked the other end, on his left.

The Confederate defenses stretched even farther than the Federal line. Brig. Gen. Cadmus M. Wilcox's brigade of Maj. Gen. Richard H. Anderson's division formed the left flank, facing Gibbon and anchored on the high ground overlooking the river to the north. Early's division occupied almost all the rest of his miles-long line, with the brigades of Brig. Gen. Harry T. Hays, Brig. Gen. Robert F. Hoke, Brig. Gen. John B. Gordon, and Brig. Gen. William Smith extending from left to right. Brig. Gen. William Barksdale and his Mississippi Brigade from Maj. Gen. Lafayette McLaws's division held the strongest position in Early's line, Willis Hill and Marye's Heights and the famous stone wall at its base.

Sedgwick's attack, which was launched soon after 7 A.M., quickly bogged down. Gibbon and his men crossed a bridge over a millrace but unexpectedly encountered another canal in the flats below Wilcox's position. As they attempted to bridge the obstacle, Confederate artillery found the range and sent the men scurrying for cover. At the south end of Willis Hill and Marye's Heights, meanwhile, Howe found that Hazel Run effectively blocked his route of approach; to maneuver around it would expose his men to flanking fire from Hoke's and Hays's brigades. With his plans stymied, Sedgwick decided that his only hope of dislodging Early lay in a frontal attack against the heights while Howe assaulted Lee's Hill straight ahead. He ordered Newton to move forward against Barksdale.

Newton's attack began at 10:30 A.M., ninety minutes before the last of Hooker's men abandoned Chancellorsville. He directed his men to double-time in assault columns toward the heights with bayonets fixed and forbade them to fire a shot. Images of the previous winter's slaughter were on everyone's minds, especially

C.S.A. dead behind the stone wall on Marye's Heights, believed to have been photographed a few minutes after the battle. LIBRARY OF CONGRESS

when they saw Confederate soldiers and artillery behind the stone wall and on the heights above. As the Federals drew closer, the artillery began to play on their lines, while the men in gray behind the wall took aim but held their fire. At a distance of about forty yards, the wall erupted in a sheet of flame, and the attackers collapsed in rows.

Peeking through a board fence around a house just in front of the stone wall, soldiers of the 7th Massachusetts Infantry thought they saw a gap in the Confederate line. When one of their officers sent forward a flag of truce during a lull in the action to request a brief cease-fire to retrieve the wounded, Col. Thomas M. Griffin of the 18th Mississippi Infantry gallantly but foolishly gave permission. The Federal party got close enough to the wall to see that the Confederate line was only one soldier deep at most. They finished their work and passed the word up

the chain of command. On order, the 7th Massachusetts crashed through the fence and surged toward the stone wall. Others followed, with one officer giving the command to start at double-quick, not fire a shot, and not stop until they got the order to halt—which order they would never get. When the signal came, the men charged and did not halt.

The fighting at the stone wall was hand-to-hand but brief. The thin Confederate line quickly collapsed as the survivors of the attack clambered up Willis Hill and Marye's Heights to the relative safety provided by the artillery. Soon even that line was overrun, and many of the cannons fell into Federal hands because the gunners had moved most of their horses to the reverse slope to protect them from shellfire.

With his center—the strongest part of his line—now breached, Early needed to extract his command before the Federals attacked his flanks. Most of his forces were closer to Telegraph Road (present-day U.S. Rte. 1 Bus.), which led southwest to Spotsylvania Court House, than to the Orange Plank Road (Rte. 3), the direct route west to Chancellorsville. Early fell back slowly down Telegraph Road, establishing strong lines of defense. To the north, on the Orange Plank Road, Wilcox and his brigade alone blocked Sedgwick's route to Chancellorsville. Like Early, Wilcox fell back slowly, causing Sedgwick to halt while he brought fresh divisions forward from Fredericksburg.

The second battle of Fredericksburg, a Union victory, cost the two sides about 2,000 casualties. The battlefield essentially covers the same ground as the December 1862 engagement and therefore is mostly covered by residential and commercial development. The Fredericksburg and Spotsylvania National Military Park owns part of Marye's Heights, the sunken road and stone wall, Lee's Hill, and some five miles of Confederate earthworks to the southeast. The Civil War Preservation Trust also owns property on the battlefield. ■

SALEM CHURCH

Lt. Andrew L. Pitzer, a member of Maj. Gen. Jubal A. Early's staff, informed Gen. Robert E. Lee of the fall of Fredericksburg at about 12:30 P.M. on Sunday, May 3, 1863. Lee had just pushed most of Maj. Gen. Joseph Hooker's Army of the Potomac into prepared defensive positions covering United States Ford on the Rappahannock River, just north of Chancellorsville. Lee, having won the three-day battle there, was preparing to attack Hooker again when Pitzer arrived with the news that Lee's rear was in danger. If Maj. Gen. John Sedgwick moved rapidly, and Hooker came out of his works and attacked boldly, the Union commander's original plan to crush Lee between the two wings of his army might still be accomplished.

Lee already had divided his army twice in the face of a numerically superior foe: the first time at Fredericksburg and the second time near Catharine Furnace. Now he would do it a third time, leaving 25,000 men at Chancellorsville to keep Hooker in his earthworks while he dealt with Sedgwick.

Riding to the side of Maj. Gen. Lafayette McLaws, Lee instructed him to

send the brigades of Brig. Gen. William Mahone (of Maj. Gen. Richard H. Anderson's division) and Brig. Gen. Joseph B. Kershaw at once toward Fredericksburg. After they left, Lee ordered McLaws to follow with his two remaining brigades, commanded by Brig. Gen. William T. Wofford and Brig. Gen. Paul J. Semmes. Lee then ordered Brig. Gen. Raleigh E. Colston to march his division up the United States Ford road (present-day Rte. 616) and Maj. Gen. Richard H. Anderson with his division up River Road (Rte. 618) to its intersection with Mine Road (Rte. 620). Colston would test Hooker's defenses, while Anderson would block any move to aid Sedgwick.

On the Orange Plank Road (Rte. 3) west of Fredericksburg, as McLaws's men marched rapidly east, Brig. Gen. Cadmus M. Wilcox and his brigade fought a textbook delaying action against Sedgwick's advancing forces. Wilcox had fallen back down the adjacent plank road while the rest of Early's command had withdrawn southwest down Telegraph Road (U.S. Rte. 1 Bus.). Using his infantry, cavalry, and artillery well, Wilcox fought one small

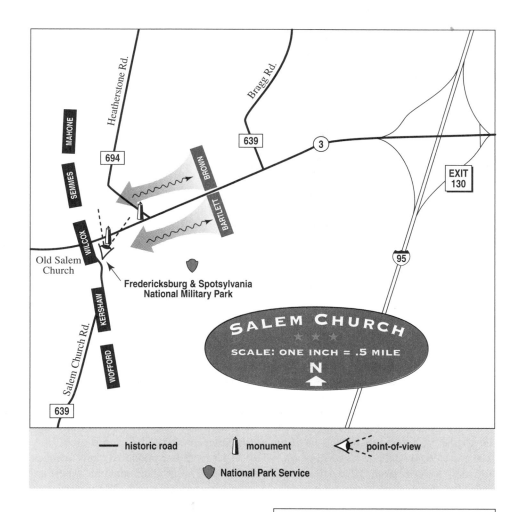

historic road   monument   point-of-view

National Park Service

engagement after another as Sedgwick's corps marched west on the plank road with Brig. Gen. William T. H. Brooks's division in the vanguard. As he encountered each obstacle placed in his way by Wilcox, Brooks laboriously deployed skirmishers, called up artillery, and cleared the path ahead. Finally, at Salem Church (about four miles west of Fredericksburg and six miles east of Chancellorsville), Wilcox found a strong defensive position along a wooded north-south ridgeline. There he would make his stand.

Just before he reached Salem Church—which sat on the south side of Orange

DIRECTIONS: I-95 Exit 130B (State Rte. 3 West, Culpeper), w. on State Rte. 3 about 1.4 miles to Rte. 639 (Salem Church Rd.); s. (left) on Rte. 639 .2 mile to first traffic light; e. (left) into Old Salem Church unit, Fredericksburg and Spotsylvania National Military Park. Visit the National Park Service Web site at nps.gov/parks.html for a virtual tour of this and other national parks.

Plank Road and was the dominant feature on the ridge—Wilcox got word that McLaws was on his way with reinforcements. Wilcox sent word back to McLaws to halt his columns out of sight behind the church. Then he began to march his own

At the Salem Church battlefield, only the old church, a small parcel of undeveloped land, and two monuments survive intact. VIRGINIA DEPARTMENT OF HISTORIC RESOURCES, JOHN S. SALMON

men into rifle pits dug in back of the building by Maj. Gen. George E. Pickett's division the previous January.

Wilcox placed the 11th and 14th Alabama Regiments on the north side of the road, the 8th and 10th Alabama on the south, and four artillery pieces in the road between them. He put one company of the 9th Alabama in the church, a second in the frame schoolhouse that stood about sixty yards east of the building, and the remainder of the regiment just behind the 10th Alabama. When Mahone's and Kershaw's brigades arrived from Chancellorsville, they filed into the line to the left and right of Wilcox's. Soon McLaws appeared with Semmes and Wofford; he shifted Mahone farther to the left and inserted Semmes between him and Wilcox, and sent Wofford around to the right of Kershaw. At about 4:30 P.M., Federal artillery began peppering the ridgeline from a tollgate half a mile east.

At 5 P.M., Brooks stopped the artillery fire and deployed skirmishers who moved forward to test the Confederate line. After a few minutes Brooks sent two brigades against Wilcox: Col. Henry W. Brown's New Jersey regiments on and north of the plank road, and Brig. Gen. Joseph J.

Bartlett's New Yorkers south of it. The 16th New York Infantry bore the brunt of the attack but finally succeeded in capturing the schoolhouse and the company inside it. Soon it was back in Confederate hands after a brutal counterattack supported by sharpshooters in Salem Church.

The fighting north of the road was equally vicious, with Semmes's Georgia Brigade at the center of the action. The Confederates finally charged and drove Brown's New Jersey Brigade back. Behind Brown, three regiments from Newton's division swung north to strike the Confederate flank but were driven back by the onrushing Georgians. With Brooks's line now in retreat, the Confederates pursued them past the tollgate but were stopped by Union artillery fire and their own exhaustion as the sun set behind them.

Theoretically, Sedgwick should have won at Salem Church. He outnumbered Wilcox and McLaws with some 20,000 men to their 10,000. But the Confederates concentrated more troops at the point of contact, where their 10,000 on the ridgeline stopped the 5,000 Federals.

That night Lee pondered plans to attack the next day. Early had sent him a message proposing to repossess Willis Hill and Marye's Heights, then strike west against the rear of Sedgwick's column. Lee then approved the plan, directing McLaws to press Sedgwick hard from the west. Lee, meanwhile, would continue his aggressive containment of Hooker.

At dawn on Monday, May 4, Anderson opened up with his artillery on the Federal left flank from his blocking position on River Road. Maj. Gen. Henry W. Slocum sent skirmishers forward from the Union line, as though to capture the guns, but Anderson's men beat them back. Orders came to Anderson from Lee: Brig. Gen. Henry Heth's division will occupy your position; march quickly toward Fredericksburg, and unite your division with McLaws's to attack Sedgwick.

Near Fredericksburg, Early moved to reoccupy Willis Hill and Marye's Heights. In the morning he sent Brig. Gen. John B. Gordon and his brigade across Telegraph Road and the Orange Plank Road to strike Sedgwick's left flank, the rear of his column. Brig. Gen. William Smith and his brigade would follow, while Brig. Gen. William Barksdale and his men would occupy the heights and the stone wall for the third time since December 1862. The brigades of Brig. Gen. Harry T. Hays and Brig. Gen. Robert F. Hoke would move to the right along Hazel Run.

Early's plan succeeded sooner than he thought it would, after Gordon jumped off ahead of the rest of the force and Barksdale reoccupied the heights more easily than expected. Early hesitated, listening for the sound of McLaws's guns, but heard nothing.

Couriers rode back and forth between Early and McLaws. Early wanted McLaws to strike Sedgwick's right flank, but McLaws preferred that Early start first. McLaws sent a message requesting reinforcements to Lee, who replied that Anderson was on his way. McLaws decided to wait for Anderson before attacking, so Early continued to hold his position. A little before 11 A.M., Lee himself turned his back on Hooker and rode to Salem Church to oversee the attack on Sedgwick and crush him.

Lee organized the attack himself. Anderson would approach from the south while the other two divisions assaulted Sedgwick from the west and east respectively. Although the plan seemed simple, it was executed in slow motion. The terrain played a role, and McLaws, especially, seemed less than eager to offer battle. But

most of the men had been marching and fighting for a week with little sleep and less food; they were at the end of their endurance.

Just before 6 P.M., finally, the attack began. Sedgwick had clearly drawn in his lines before the onslaught, forming an attenuated U with his back to the Rappahannock on the north, and the Federals put up a stiff defense after the initial shock. Soon the Confederate attack bogged down in deep woods and encroaching dusk, and the attackers settled down to keep what they had taken.

Lee was not happy. After some deliberation, he ordered a night attack, not knowing that Sedgwick already had directed his army to withdraw to Scott's Ford. Soon fog descended over the battlefield, mercifully ending the possibility of executing Lee's orders.

During the night, Hooker and his staff sent poor Sedgwick a barrage of contradictory orders: Withdraw, hold your position, prepare to attack. At the same time, Hooker called a council of war and put the question of whether to attack or retreat to his corps commanders. They recommended attacking Lee in the morning. Hooker, however, ordered them to withdraw across United States Ford in the darkness, thereby further angering his subordinates. Sedgwick, disgusted, conveniently got so many of his men across the river that when he received an order countermanding the movement, he simply ignored it and informed Hooker later.

Lee awoke on the morning of Tuesday, May 5, to find Sedgwick gone. He turned his divisions toward Chancellorsville, but they arrived there too late in the day to attack Hooker. That night Hooker's army crossed the Rappahannock, and the Chancellorsville campaign was finished. The two days of battles around Salem Church and the recaptured Willis Hill and Marye's Heights cost the combatants about 5,000 casualties, with the Union forces no doubt taking the heavier losses.

The Salem Church battlefield is gone, buried beneath a sea of parking lots, shopping centers, and traffic lanes. Besides two Federal monuments, only the church, still pocked by the bullets of 1863, and its graveyard remain in a little island of green amid the asphalt. Salem Church is part of the Fredericksburg and Spotsylvania National Military Park. ■

GETTYSBURG CAMPAIGN, 1863

Gen. Robert E. Lee began his march to Pennsylvania on June 3, 1863, within two weeks of his return from Richmond to his field headquarters near Fredericksburg after the battle of Chancellorsville, by moving two of his three infantry corps from the banks of the Rappahannock River to Culpeper Court House. Lt. Gen. A. P. Hill was left temporarily in strong earthworks above Fredericksburg to block any Federal attack in the Confederate rear. Maj. Gen. Joseph Hooker, commander of the Army of the Potomac, probed Lee's line to find out what was happening but did not succeed. Rumors ran rampant that Lee planned a big cavalry raid by Maj. Gen. J. E. B. Stuart, a flanking movement to get between Hooker and Washington, or even an invasion of Maryland and Pennsylvania. Finally ascertaining that the head of the Army of Northern Virginia was concentrating in Culpeper County, on June 7 Hooker ordered Brig. Gen. Alfred Pleasonton to conduct a spoiling raid there, "disperse and destroy" the column and its supplies, and generally disrupt Confederate plans.

Lee arrived in Culpeper the same day, responding to an invitation from Stuart to attend a grand review of his cavalry corps on June 8—the third such since May 23. The second, on June 5, had been a grand affair indeed, with mock combats, special trains from the town bearing bevies of beauteous belles, and Stuart's horse bedecked in flowers. The third performance was scaled back, but even so both cavalrymen and newspaper reporters groused that the reviews did little more than exhaust the horses and feed Stuart's ego.

After the review, Stuart and his horsemen bivouacked in and around Brandy Station. Lee intended for Stuart to begin the next morning to screen the infantry's march toward the Blue Ridge Mountains and the Shenandoah Valley by crossing the Rappahannock River and striking the Union army's advance posts. While Stuart slept atop Fleetwood Hill overlooking the depot, however, Pleasonton slipped into position at Beverly's and Kelly's Fords, two important river crossings just a few miles northwest and southeast of Stuart's headquarters.

The battle of Brandy Station on June 9 came as a surprise on both sides of the river. Pleasonton had divided his 11,000-man force (seven cavalry brigades, two infantry brigades, and six artillery companies) in two. Brig. Gen. John Buford, commanding the first part, approached Beverly's Ford stealthily over two days, bivouacking about a mile from the ford in Fauquier County on June 8. Brig. Gen. David M. Gregg's division encamped farther away from Kelly's Ford, about six miles downstream from Beverly's, and arose before dawn to ride to the crossing. Pleasonton's plan called for both commands to cross simultaneously at dawn, unite at Brandy Station, and ride to Culpeper Court House.

Pleasonton knew the fords would be guarded by Confederate pickets on the western bank of the Rappahannock, hence

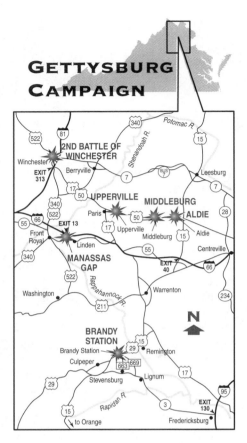

GETTYSBURG CAMPAIGN

drove through Stuart's pickets and charged down the Beverly's Ford road toward Fleetwood Hill but were stopped at Saint James's Church by Jones's hastily assembled defense and effectively driven back up the road. The Federals gradually pushed Jones's men back to the church, but Hampton arrived to lengthen and strengthen the line there, and Rooney Lee threatened the Union right flank at the northern end of Fleetwood Hill, in an area known as the Yew Hills. Buford was forced to fight on two fronts: the combat on his right flank, focused on a stone wall seized by Lee's men on the Cunningham farm, soon reached a stalemate; the fighting straight ahead (south) around the church resulted in Jones's and Hampton's cavalrymen falling back slowly southwest to Fleetwood Hill. Their evacuation exposed Rooney Lee's right flank, and he was compelled to abandon the stone wall and retire toward Farley as Buford pressed west.

Gregg, meanwhile, crossed at Kelly's Ford; the Confederate pickets raced to Brandy Station to bring the news to Stuart, who at first disbelieved them. He sent Robertson and his brigade toward the ford, and they encountered a Union infantry brigade there. Robertson formed his men in a blocking position across the road from Brandy Station (Rte. 674) on the Brown and Brannin farms, the scene of the battle of Kelly's Ford on March 17. There the two brigades faced each other all day, scarcely firing a shot, while Gregg rode off in the direction of Stevensburg (on present-day Rte. 672) with his cavalry force.

Gregg divided his command near Carrico Mill. He and about 2,400 of his men rode northwest toward Brandy Station (on today's Rte. 669) while Col. Alfred N. A. Duffié led a smaller number toward Stevensburg. There, Duffié was to turn north and ride to Brandy Station (on present-day Rte. 663).

his method of approach. He did not know, however, that Stuart's entire corps, some 9,500 men, was bivouacked close by. Brig. Gen. Fitzhugh Lee's brigade was at Oak Shade Church, a few miles northwest of Brandy Station; Brig. Gen. William H. F. "Rooney" Lee's was around the Welford house, Farley; Brig. Gen. William E. "Grumble" Jones's slept around Saint James's Church on the Beverly's Ford road (present-day Rte. 677); Brig. Gen. Beverly H. Robertson's was around the Barbour house, Beauregard; and Brig. Gen. Wade Hampton's legion had encamped just north of Stevensburg, a village about four and a half miles south of Brandy Station.

Buford's crossing took place on time; Gregg's did not. Buford's cavalrymen

At about noon, as Jones's and Hampton's cavalrymen held their own along the Saint James's Church line, Gregg's column arrived at Brandy Station and surprised Stuart for the second time that day. Stuart's adjutant, Maj. Henry B. McClellan, held off Gregg with a single cannon long enough for some of Jones's troopers to reach the crest of Fleetwood Hill at the same time as Gregg's. A classic cavalry confrontation ensued: mounted charges and countercharges, horse against horse and saber against saber. First one side and then the other swept across the broad hilltop. The arrival of Hampton's brigade finally tipped the scales for the Confederates.

When Hampton raced to Jones's aid early that morning, he left Col. Matthew C. Butler and the 2nd South Carolina Cavalry to guard the road from Stevensburg to Brandy Station. Butler learned of Duffié's approach and rode through Stevensburg to form a mile-long blocking line across the road and along the eastern crest of Hansborough Ridge. Meanwhile, Col. Thomas T. Munford, who commanded Fitz Lee's brigade that day, ordered Col. Williams C. Wickham's 4th Virginia Cavalry to assist Butler. Wickham arrived just as Duffié charged Butler's thin line, and the 4th Virginia broke and ran for the rear. Pursued through Stevensburg, Butler formed a new line facing south across Mountain Run, about a mile north of the village. A lucky shot from a Federal cannon seriously wounded Butler and killed Will Farley, one of Stuart's favorite scouts. Butler's troopers, and Wickham's, pulled back another mile to Jonas Run; Duffié, receiving orders to hasten to Gregg's assistance, rode to Brandy Station along Gregg's path but arrived too late to pitch into the fray.

As the afternoon wore on, Stuart at last organized an effective counterattack using reinforcements from Fitz Lee's brigade. While Rooney Lee charged Buford across

the Yew Hills, pushing the Union commander back toward Beverly's Ford, another Confederate charge swept the Federals from Fleetwood Hill. As the sun set, Pleasonton's command crossed to safety at Beverly's, Norman's, and Kelly's Fords. Pleasonton reported some 900 casualties, Stuart, 500.

Tactically, the battle of Brandy Station—the largest mounted cavalry fight of the war—ended in a draw, but both sides claimed victory. Strategically, the advantage went to the Union cavalrymen, although they had failed in their immediate mission as defined by Hooker. Instead, they had surprised Stuart twice, battled his vaunted troopers effectively all day long, and withdrawn from the field under their own steam, not because they had been defeated. (Many Southern newspapers pilloried Stuart, relishing his comeuppance. Stuart's narrow escape and the presumed damage to his ego are thought by some historians to have influenced his behavior on the remainder of the Gettysburg campaign, causing him to miss the first day's battle in Pennsylvania while attempting to recover his former glory by riding around the Union army—and thereby contributing to Lee's defeat.)

Lee professed pleasure over the outcome at Brandy Station and complimented Stuart on his quick reactions. Then he continued his infantry's march toward the Shenandoah Valley unimpeded by Hooker. Because of the army's size, about 75,000 men, the three corps took different routes west to the Valley and north to Pennsylvania. Lt. Gen. Richard S. Ewell and his corps, leading the advance, materialized south and east of Winchester on June 13. Maj. Gen. Edward "Allegheny" Johnson's division approached from the south and east the next day while Maj. Gen. Jubal A. Early's attacked from the west; Ewell ordered Maj. Gen. Robert E. Rodes and his division first to Berryville and then to Martinsburg, north of Winchester. Now the Federal garrison, commanded by Maj. Gen. Robert H. Milroy, was effectively surrounded.

The second battle of Winchester began at about 6 P.M., when Confederate artillery opened on the Union positions as a prelude to Early's infantry assault at 6:45 P.M. An earthwork was overrun before darkness fell, and Milroy decided—as he should have done days earlier—to retreat. The withdrawal began at 1 A.M. on June 15, and Ewell moved swiftly to block it. Although Rodes could cut off Milroy's retreat into Maryland, Ewell wanted to stop Milroy before he got that far, so he ordered Johnson to march quickly around Winchester and intercept the Federals. At 3:30 A.M., in a rare night attack, Johnson struck Milroy's column near Stephenson's Depot on the Winchester & Potomac Railroad four miles northeast of Winchester. The intense fighting resulted in a humiliating Union defeat as about half of Milroy's force soon surrendered (Milroy himself escaped). Some 4,000 Federals were captured and about 450 killed or wounded; Ewell lost 50 killed or missing and about 200 wounded. The Confederates also captured 23 cannons, 300 wagons and horses, and a large quantity of stores. More importantly, Ewell had cleared the way for Lee's advance into Maryland and Pennsylvania without the threat of attack by Union forces in the Valley or northern Virginia. Rodes's command led the way across the Potomac River the same day.

Stuart, meanwhile, continued to screen the army's march. On June 17 Pleasonton sent three brigades under Gregg to Aldie, a milling village at the intersection of three highways, to search out the Confederate army. The first highway at Aldie, Little River Turnpike (U.S. Rte. 50), led east

through Fairfax Court House to Alexandria. The second, Snicker's Gap Turnpike (Rte. 734), ran northwest to the gap, where other roads continued to Berryville and Winchester. The third, Ashby's Gap Turnpike (U.S. Rte. 50), extended southwest to the Valley Turnpike just south of Winchester. Since the Army of Northern Virginia was marching by way of, or crossing, the latter two of these roads, driving Gregg out of Aldie and eastward became a priority for Stuart.

Gregg's command consisted of the brigades led by Duffié, Brig. Gen. H. Judson Kilpatrick, and Col. J. Irvin Gregg. He ordered Duffié to march to Middleburg on a roundabout route, then rode to Aldie, located some five miles east of Middleburg, with his other brigades and accompanied by Pleasonton. They arrived at the village at about 4 P.M., just as Fitz Lee's brigade, temporarily commanded by Munford, prepared to bivouac there overnight. The result was a short, sharp fight.

The engagement at Aldie surprised both combatants. The Confederates approached the village from the west while the Federals passed through it from the east, and the two forces collided just northwest of the village on the Snicker's Gap Turnpike. The Federals suffered heavy casualties in this four-hour-long engagement.

Duffié, meanwhile, arrived south of Middleburg in the late afternoon and drove in the Confederate pickets there. Stuart, who was in the town, evaded Duffié, while Munford's and Robertson's brigades attacked and routed Duffié's command in an early morning assault on June 18 as he tried to break out toward Aldie. The principal engagement at Middleburg occurred the next day, June 19, when Col. J. Irvin Gregg's brigade advanced west from Aldie. Stuart formed his command in a line just west of Middleburg along a ridgetop and repulsed Gregg's charge. Stuart counterattacked, then fell back to another defensive position a half-mile farther west.

Little skirmishing occurred the next day, but at about 7 A.M. on June 21 Pleasonton made a concerted effort to pierce Stuart's screen by advancing on Upperville, nine miles west of Middleburg. Col. Strong Vincent marched with his infantry brigade directly down the Ashby's Gap Turnpike, along with Col. J. Irvin Gregg's and Brig. Gen. H. Judson Kilpatrick's cavalry brigades, while Brig. Gen. John Buford led his cavalry division north and west in the main attack against Stuart's left flank. Buford's maneuver bogged down when he encountered Jones's and Col. John R. Chambliss's brigades; Stuart withdrew, fighting furiously, to take a strong defensive position in Ashby's Gap.

The week of cavalry combat resulted in some 800 Union casualties and about 240 on the Confederate side. Stuart, heartened by his success at screening the Army of Northern Virginia, now made a fateful decision. He received vaguely worded discretionary orders from Lee the next day, June 22, and early on June 25 began his ride through and east of the Army of the Potomac. After raiding Union supply lines, Stuart finally rejoined Lee at Gettysburg, but not until the day after the two armies had blundered into one another on July 1 and become fully engaged.

Joseph Hooker had submitted his resignation as commander of the Army of the Potomac on June 27, and Lincoln had appointed Maj. Gen. George G. Meade in his place early the next morning. After Meade's victory at Gettysburg, the Union army was hardly in a condition to rush into another fight. The casualty figures after three days of combat were enormous: on the Union side, 3,155 killed, 14,529 wounded, and 5,365 missing; on the Confederate, 3,903 killed, 18,735 wounded, and 5,425 missing. Both sides needed to recuperate.

Lee crossed the Potomac River into Virginia at Falling Waters and Williamsport, Maryland, on July 13–14 and withdrew up the Shenandoah Valley. Meade crossed east of the Blue Ridge and paralleled Lee's route. On July 23 Meade ordered the III Corps under Maj. Gen. William H. French to force a passage through Manassas Gap and cut off the retreating Confederate columns at Front Royal. Brig. Gen. Henry H. Walker's Confederate brigade guarded the gap; at first light, French began pushing Walker back slowly. At about 4:30 P.M., a strong Union attack drove Walker's men until they were reinforced by Maj. Gen. Robert E. Rodes's division and artillery. By dusk the Federals abandoned their poorly coordinated attacks, and during the night the Confederate forces withdrew into the Luray (Page) Valley. The next day the Union army occupied Front Royal, but Lee's army was safely beyond pursuit.

Lee's invasion of the North accomplished some of his objectives, disrupted Federal plans for a summer campaign in Virginia, and enabled his men to subsist on Union supplies instead of Virginians'. But the cost was far too high. The Army of Northern Virginia had received a blow from which it would never recover, Vicksburg had fallen to Grant, Maj. Gen. William S. Rosecrans had maneuvered Gen. Braxton Bragg's army out of middle Tennessee, and the dream of European recognition had vanished. The Confederate tide had crested at Chancellorsville; it began running out at Gettysburg. ■

A month after his victory at Chancellorsville, Gen. Robert E. Lee began marching the Army of Northern Virginia northwest to the Shenandoah Valley to invade the North. To prevent Maj. Gen. Joseph Hooker, the commander of the Army of the Potomac, from finding out what he was doing, Lee ordered Maj. Gen. J. E. B. Stuart to screen the army's movement by interposing his cavalry between the two forces. Specifically, Stuart was to cross the Rappahannock River on June 9, 1863, and raid Union forward positions. After a cavalry review for Lee, Stuart ordered his cavalry corps into bivouac in and around Brandy Station and the Rappahannock River, to be ready to cross at the various fords the next day.

The terrain around Brandy Station was (and remains) generally open, rolling farmland with several forested areas and three significant pieces of high ground: Fleetwood Hill, a broad prominence just north of the tracks at the station; the Yew Hills, which actually constitute the northern end of Fleetwood Hill just south of Hazel River; and Hansborough Ridge, a few miles south of Brandy Station. Watercourses include the Rappahannock River, flowing southeast about five miles east of Brandy Station, and several tributaries flowing east to the river. Two fords permitted crossing of the Rappahannock in the area: Beverly's Ford and Kelly's Ford. The Orange & Alexandria Railroad ran northeast and crossed the river at present-day Remington, then the site of the Rappahannock railroad bridge. The principal roads included one from Brandy Station to Kelly's Ford (present-day Rtes. 685 and 674); Beverly's Ford Road (Rte. 677); the road from Kelly's Ford to Stevensburg (Rte. 672); and the road from Stevensburg to Brandy Station (Rte. 663).

Across the Rappahannock, Hooker sought vainly to learn what Lee was up to. On June 7, realizing that the Confederates were concentrating their forces in Culpeper County, he ordered Brig. Gen. Alfred Pleasonton to conduct a spoiling raid just in case Lee and Stuart planned to strike east into Fauquier County. Pleasonton's mission was to vanquish as much of Lee's cavalry corps as possible.

The Federal plan of attack called for Pleasonton's cavalry corps—some 7,900 horsemen plus two brigades of infantry (about 3,000 men) and six artillery companies—to cross simultaneously at dawn on June 9 at Beverly's Ford and Kelly's Ford. Brig. Gen. John Buford commanded the first division (Pleasonton accompanied him), which bivouacked near Beverly's Ford on the night of June 8, and Brig. Gen. David M. Gregg the second, which approached Kelly's Ford in two columns during the night. Buford's command was arranged, for the purposes of the raid, into the First Cavalry Division (led by Buford), the Reserve Brigade (led by Maj. Charles Whiting), and the Infantry Brigade under Brig. Gen. Adelbert Ames. Gregg's command was arranged into the Second Cavalry Division (led by Col. Alfred A. N. Duffié), the Third Cavalry Division (led by Gregg), and the Infantry Brigade under Brig. Gen. David A. Russell.

On the Culpeper County side of the Rappahannock, Stuart's cavalry corps, about 9,500 men, was divided into five brigades plus the six-battery Stuart Horse Artillery. The brigades were commanded by Brig. Gen. Beverly H. Robertson, Brig. Gen. Wade Hampton, Col. Thomas T. Munford (during the absence due to rheumatism of Brig. Gen. Fitzhugh Lee, nephew of Robert E. Lee), Brig. Gen. William H. F. "Rooney" Lee (Robert E.

Lee's second son), and Brig. Gen. William E. "Grumble" Jones. The brigades were widely dispersed throughout the area. Stuart himself slept in the yard at Fleetwood, at the southern end of Fleetwood Hill overlooking Brandy Station.

Confederate pickets from Jones's and Robertson's brigades guarded the fords, and Buford and Gregg approached the crossings differently. Buford's command slipped quietly into a forest that grew just over the ridge line in Fauquier County above Beverly's Ford. Gregg's command was divided and approached Kelly's Ford in the wee hours from different, distant bivouacs. He intended to unite his force and cross at dawn, but Duffié's division got lost and delayed him for a couple of hours.

In the predawn darkness on Tuesday, June 9, Buford and his men assembled quietly on the Fauquier County side of Beverly's Ford. At 4 A.M. the First Cavalry Division, with Col. Benjamin F. "Grimes" Davis and the 8th New York Cavalry in the lead, splashed across the ford and burst through the picket line with blazing revolvers and charging horses. Pleasonton had achieved surprise.

The division pressed on for about a thousand yards before it encountered Jones's troopers, who had scrambled onto their horses and then charged up the Beverly's Ford road toward the river. The onrushing Confederate column stalled the Union advance momentarily; Davis was shot and killed. The Federals slowly pushed the Confederates back until they formed a strong defensive line to the northwest of Saint James's Church.

Hampton and his brigade formed a line on a ridge occupied by the Gee house. At the same time, Rooney Lee's men attacked the Union right flank across the northern end of Fleetwood Hill. Lee's brigade raced the oncoming Federals for a stone wall on the Cunningham farm, reached it first, and held it.

View south toward St. James Church site and first C.S.A. line. VIRGINIA DEPARTMENT OF HISTORIC RESOURCES, JOHN S. SALMON

Buford sent the First Cavalry Division to the east of the Beverly's Ford road, forming the Union left; he ordered Ames's infantry to positions on both sides of the road; and he moved Whiting's reserves to the west of the road. Most of the morning's heavy fighting took place to the west of the road, where Confederate artillery took its toll.

While the battle developed northeast of Brandy Station, Gregg's command finally crossed Kelly's Ford and drove in the pickets at the Kelly farm on the west bank. Some of the pickets fled to Brandy Station and reported to Stuart, who sent Robertson's brigade to the ford. Robertson arrived in time to see the dust of Gregg's main column rise above the Kelly farm ridge as Gregg rode down the road to Stevensburg. The Union commander left Russell's infantry brigade to guard the ford; Russell and Robertson faced each other for the rest of the day, scarcely firing a shot.

Gregg, meanwhile, divided his force near Carrico Mill. He and the Third Cavalry Division turned northwest up a road (Rte. 669) leading to Brandy Station, while Duffié continued with the Second Cavalry Division toward Stevensburg, there to turn north and ride to the station on present-day Rte. 663.

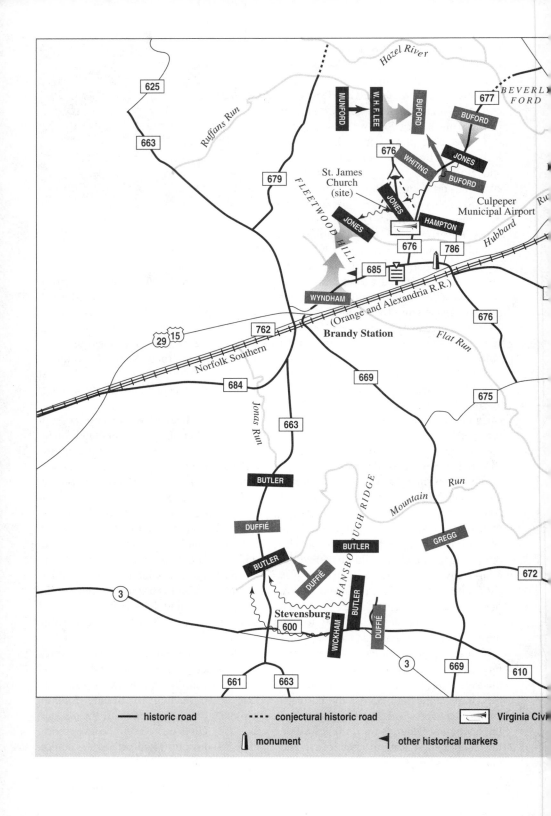

625

663

679

MUNFORD W. H. F. LEE BUFORD

677 BEVERLY FORD

BUFORD

676 WHITING BUFORD

JONES

St. James
Church
(site)

JONES HAMPTON

Culpeper
Municipal Airport

Hazel River

Ruffians Run

FLEETWOOD HILL

JONES

676 786

685

Hubbard *Ru*

WYNDHAM

(Orange and Alexandria R.R.)

676

29 15 762 Brandy Station *Flat Run*

Norfolk Southern

684

Jonas Run

663

669 675

676

BUTLER

DUFFIÉ

BUTLER BUTLER DUFFIÉ *Mountain* *Run* GREGG

672

HANSBOROUGH RIDGE

3

Stevensburg 600 WICKHAM BUTLER DUFFIÉ

3 669 610

661 663

— historic road   ···· conjectural historic road   Virginia Civi

monument   ◀ other historical markers

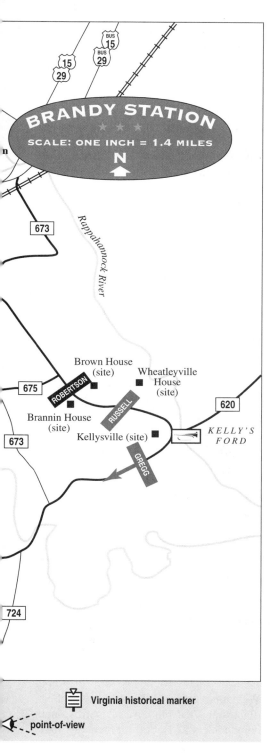

BRANDY STATION ★★★
SCALE: ONE INCH = 1.4 MILES
N

Rappahannock River

673

673

675

ROBERTSON

RUSSELL

GREGG

Brown House
(site)

Wheatleyville
House
(site)

Brannin House
(site)

Kellysville (site)

620

*KELLY'S
FORD*

724

🏛 **Virginia historical marker**

◀ **point-of-view**

DIRECTIONS: I-95 Exit 130B (State Rte. 3 West, Culpeper), w. on State Rte. 3 about 23.2 miles to Rte. 669 (Carrico Mills Rd.); n. (right) on Rte. 669 .8 mile to Rte. 610 (Maddens Tavern Rd.); e. (right) on Rte. 610 1.7 miles to Rte. 724 (Youngs Lane); n. (left) on Rte. 724 1.6 miles to Rte. 672 (Stones Mill Rd.); n. (right) on Rte. 672 2.6 miles to Rte. 674 (Kelly's Ford Rd.) at Kelly's Ford Bridge; n. (left) on Rte. 674 .7 mile to view of battlefield to e. (right); continue 4.2 miles on Rte. 674 to U.S. Rte. 15/29 at Elkwood; w. (left) on U.S. Rte. 15/29 .3 mile to Rte. 676 (Beverly Ford Rd.); n. (right) on Rte. 676 .2 mile to Rte. 786 (Airport Dr.) and Rte. 685 (Fleetwood Heights Rd.); n. (right) on Rte. 676 .5 mile to Rte. 677 (Beverly Ford Rd.); w. (left) on Rte. 676 (St. James Church Rd.) and Virginia Civil War Trails marker; return to Rte. 677; n. (left) on Rte. 677 2.3 miles to Beverly Ford turnaround; return to Rte. 676; w. (right) on Rte. 676 (St. James Church Rd.) 1.2 miles to end of road at farm gate; return to intersection of Rte. 786 and Rte. 685; w. (right) on Rte. 685 1.3 miles to United Daughters of the Confederacy marker on left at crest of Fleetwood Hill, and continue .5 mile farther to Rte. 663 (Alanthus Rd.); Beauregard visible on right; n. (right) on Rte. 663 1.2 miles to Rte. 679 (Farley Rd.); n. (right) on Rte. 679 .9 mile to end of state maintenance; return to Rte. 663/685 intersection; continue s. on Rte. 663 .1 mile to U.S. Rte. 15/29; cross U.S. Rte. 15/29 through Brandy Station on Rte. 663 .2 mile to Rte. 700 (Brandy Rd.); e. (left) on Rte. 700 .1 mile to Rte. 669 (Carrico Mills Rd.); s. (right) on Rte. 669 .2 mile to Rte. 663 (Stevensburg Rd.); s. (right) on Rte. 663 3.3 miles to site of wounding of Butler and Farley just north of Mountain Run; continue .8 mile to Rte. 600 (York Rd.) in Stevensburg; e. (left) on Rte. 600 .6 mile to State Rte. 3; e. (left) on State Rte. 3 .8 mile to Rte. 739 (Clay Hill Rd.) and view to w. (rear) of Hansborough Ridge; continue on State Rte. 3 about 24.8 miles to I-95.

Gregg reached Brandy Station at about noon and paused to study the terrain ahead. Up on Fleetwood Hill, Stuart's adjutant, Maj. Henry B. McClellan, sent word to Stuart, then opened fire on Brandy Station with the only cannon on Fleetwood Hill. Uncertain as to how many guns he faced, Col. Percy Wyndham, commander of Gregg's lead brigade, hesitated to advance, buying Stuart time to redeploy his men to meet this threat. The Federals, finally determining that McClellan's cannon posed little threat, raced for the hilltop from one side as two of Jones's units charged up from the other. The two forces collided on the crest, with charges and countercharges going on almost without letup into the afternoon. Gregg sent couriers racing south to find Duffié and hurry him along. At the northern end of the battlefield, meanwhile, Buford compelled Rooney Lee to retire from the stone wall after Jones's and Hampton's sudden withdrawal exposed his right flank.

As Duffié's column approached Stevensburg, he unexpectedly encountered Col. Matthew C. Butler and his 2nd South Carolina Cavalry guarding the Confederate rear. Butler, learning that a Federal force was on its way to Stevensburg, had led his command to the village. Stationing some of his men in the road, Butler spread the rest along the eastern crest of Hansborough Ridge, which rose just north of the road and extended for a mile and a half toward Brandy Station. Col. Williams C. Wickham's 4th Virginia Cavalry soon followed and came down onto the road just as Duffié ordered a charge. The Federals drove the outnumbered Confederates westward through Stevensburg and beyond. Soon the pursuing Federals fell back to join the main body, and Butler began to rally his men behind Mountain Run.

Duffié and his force, including his artillery, emerged on the west slope of the ridge and saw a small group of mounted men about half a mile northwest, in the road and just across Mountain Run, west of the ridge. When other men rode up to the group and then galloped away, Duffié knew that he was observing his Confederate counterpart, Butler. A Union artilleryman fired a solid shot, which cost Butler a foot. The Confederates withdrew a mile up the road toward Brandy Station, but as Duffié prepared to charge them, a dispatch arrived from Gregg ordering him to withdraw and march to Brandy Station by

Gregg's Carrico Mill route. Duffié complied, arriving at the station too late to play a role in the battle there.

As the afternoon waned, the momentum slowly shifted to the Confederates at Brandy Station. Three regiments from Fitz Lee's brigade arrived at Farley under the command of Col. Thomas T. Munford. About the same time, Gen. Robert E. Lee and his staff rode from Culpeper to the Barbour house, Beauregard, to survey the situation from a cupola on the roof. Stuart ordered Rooney Lee, reinforced by Munford, to counterattack Buford. Under pressure from the Virginians, but at the price of a severe leg wound for Lee, Buford withdrew toward Beverly's Ford.

At the southern end of Fleetwood Hill, a Confederate charge swept the Union horsemen off the hill and through Brandy Station. Back at Beauregard, Lee ordered infantry to march to the battlefield and assist. Gregg, who thought he saw them coming, withdrew his command toward the Rappahannock railroad bridge. At about sunset, the last elements of the Union expedition crossed over the Rappahannock River, bringing the day-long battle to an end. The Federals suffered about 900 casualties, the Confederates 500.

Technically, one could argue, as Stuart did, that the battle was a Confederate victory since he held the field at the end of the day and had frustrated Pleasonton's "spoiling" attack. In fact, however, the battle was a draw tactically. Twice Stuart had been surprised, first at Beverly's Ford by Buford and then at Brandy Station by Gregg. The Federal horsemen had withdrawn more on their own initiative than because they were driven off. For the first time, not counting the battle of Kelly's Ford, they had given as good as they got. Were it not for the skills of Stuart's subordinates and the initiative shown by such commanders as Butler, the Federals may well had swept him from the field and discovered Lee's infantry.

Lee praised Stuart's adept handling of the situation, politely overlooking the fact that he literally had been caught sleeping, with near-disastrous consequences for the Army of Northern Virginia. But never again would the advantage in battle automatically go to Stuart's cavalrymen. The tide had turned.

Most of the Brandy Station battlefield is in an excellent state of preservation. The major developmental intrusions are the four-lane U.S. Rte. 29, the Culpeper County airport, an adjacent industrial park, and scattered modern dwellings and businesses. Much of the terrain is little changed, however, with historic roads, fields, woodlots, fence lines, watercourses, dwellings, and other features still intact. The Brandy Station Foundation and the Civil War Preservation Trust have purchased some of the core area of the battlefield to preserve and interpret it for future generations. ■

SECOND BATTLE OF WINCHESTER

The battle of Brandy Station barely disrupted the march of Gen. Robert E. Lee's 75,000-man Army of Northern Virginia west and north into the Shenandoah Valley, Maryland, and Pennsylvania. Lee had reorganized his army after the battle of Chancellorsville in May 1863. Besides Stuart's cavalry division (usually referred to as a corps), Lee created three infantry corps. Lt. Gen. James Longstreet commanded the first, Lt. Gen. Richard S. Ewell the second (formerly Stonewall Jackson's), and Lt. Gen. A. P. Hill the third. Because of the large number of men—plus the long trains of supply wagons—each corps took a different route of march on the campaign or followed its predecessor at some distance.

Ewell led the way, marching with his corps through the Blue Ridge Mountains at Chester Gap, then through Front Royal toward Winchester. Longstreet's corps, which Lee accompanied, entered the Valley at Ashby's and Snicker's Gaps. Hill followed Ewell's route through Chester Gap but waited until after Hooker had abandoned Fredericksburg on June 14 to begin pursuing Lee. Stuart's cavalry remained on the east side of the Blue Ridge in the Loudoun Valley to screen the army from Hooker's view.

Although safe from Hooker, the Confederates had to confront Federals in the Shenandoah Valley. Maj. Gen. Robert H. Milroy commanded 7,000 men in three brigades, two stationed in Winchester and one about ten miles east of Winchester at Berryville. Milroy's command was the Second Division of Maj. Gen. Robert C. "Fighting Bob" Schenck's Middle Department and VIII Corps. Schenck had scattered his divisions across the valleys of the Shenandoah and Potomac Rivers to guard transportation routes, but the Union general in chief, Henry W. Halleck, thought that they were too widely dispersed. Ewell soon would prove Halleck right.

Milroy had strengthened his position at Winchester by constructing a system of forts and interconnecting trenches west of the town. The forts or redoubts occupied the ridges overlooking Winchester and included West Fort (south of Pughtown Road, present-day Rte. 522), Star Fort (north of Rte. 522), and Fort Milroy (just north of Bower's Hill).

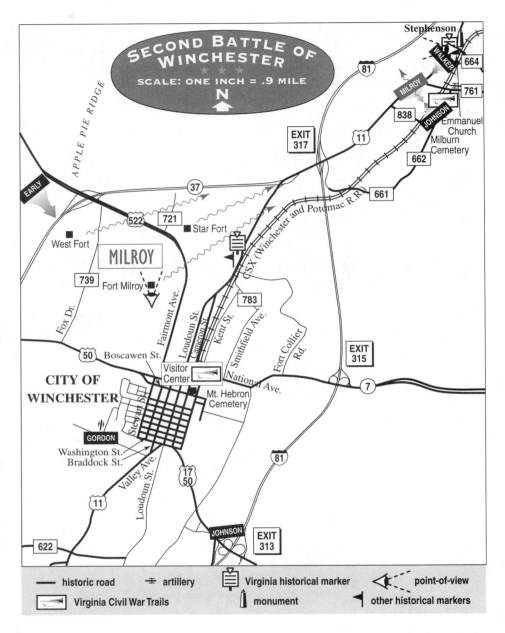

Halleck began warning Schenck in January that Milroy's position was untenable despite his fortifications. On May 8 he instructed Schenck to withdraw all but a handful of troops from Winchester, but Schenck, regarding the instruction as one of Halleck's countless suggestions rather than an unequivocal order, ignored it. Finally, on June 14, Halleck threatened to dismiss Schenck if he did not obey his command.

It was too late. On the previous day, a Saturday, Ewell suddenly appeared just south of Winchester. He dispatched Maj.

Gen. Robert E. Rodes and his division to capture the Federal garrisons at Berryville and Martinsburg, but owing to poor Confederate reconnaissance and effective Union maneuvering, Rodes arrived at Berryville the next day to find the Federals gone to join Milroy at Winchester. On

June 14 Rodes discovered the same situation at Martinsburg. He had to content himself with relieving the Federal depots at both places of their stores; he also was positioned to block any northward retreat by Milroy.

Ewell then led his other two divisions under Maj. Gen. Edward "Allegheny" Johnson and Maj. Gen. Jubal A. Early toward Winchester. He ordered Johnson to march north on the Front Royal road (Rte. 522) and feign an attack against the town from the southeast. Meanwhile, Ewell and Early marched north on the Valley Turnpike (U.S. Rte. 11) toward Winchester and Brig. Gen. John B. Gordon's brigade seized Bower's Hill (scene of the climax of the first battle of Winchester) at dawn on June 14. Ewell and Early conferred there, and when Early suggested a plan for capturing fortified West Fort Ridge, which commanded Milroy's other fortifications, Ewell agreed.

Leaving Gordon's brigade and two batteries on Bower's Hill, Early marched west on Cedar Creek Grade (Rte. 622), then north to the North Western Turnpike (U.S. Rte. 50), where he rode to the top of Apple Pie Ridge to reconnoiter. Back on Bower's Hill, Gordon used his cannons to start an artillery duel with Fort Milroy, while Johnson feinted against the Union line with his skirmishers, thereby drawing the attention of the Federals away from Early's flank march.

Early reached the northern end of Apple Pie Ridge undetected by the Union occupants of West Fort, located atop the next ridge to the east. He concealed his artillery pieces on a farm northwest of the fort and in an orchard to the southwest. At 6 P.M., as the sounds of gunfire died away to the south and east, Early opened up on West Fort with his guns while Brig. Gen. Harry T. Hays led his brigade stealthily toward West Fort Ridge through wheat and corn

This photograph may show the interior of Fort Milroy with captured U.S. cannons, June 1863, or may have been taken later at Star Fort. HANDLEY REGIONAL LIBRARY, WINCHESTER, VA.

fields. After an artillery barrage of almost an hour, Hays led his men in a rush across 300 yards of open ground and up the west slope of the ridge. A brief but bloody hand-to-hand fight took place, and the Confederates captured the fort and a Union battery when two more brigades arrived to reinforce Hays.

By the time the fighting ended and the Confederates had secured their position, nightfall was approaching, and Early had no time to make additional gains. Behind his few remaining fortifications, Milroy decided—far too late—to retreat. Ewell, anticipating him, ordered Johnson to march northwest and block Milroy's route of withdrawal on the Martinsburg and Winchester Turnpike (U.S. Rte. 11) and the old Charles Town Road (Rte. 761). Johnson took with him three brigades, with the Stonewall Brigade joining the column after midnight. He marched to the Berryville Turnpike (Rte. 7), where he left one brigade to block any eastward Federal retreat. With his remaining three brigades, he proceeded to Stephenson's Depot, four miles northeast of Winchester on the Winchester & Potomac Railroad.

Milroy, meanwhile, withdrew his men from their works so quietly that Early did not realize they were gone until morning. With cannons spiked and caissons destroyed, Milroy and his division wended their way north along the turnpike and railroad. In the predawn darkness, at about 3:30 A.M. on June 15, the head of Milroy's column approached the intersection of the turnpike and the Charles Town Road, one mile south of Stephenson's Depot. Suddenly, gunfire blazed as skirmishers from Johnson's column challenged the Federals. Milroy ordered his command to face right and fight its way out of the situation.

Johnson deployed his troops along Milburn Road (Rte. 662) and placed part of his artillery at the junction of the Charles Town Road and the tracks, with the rest east of Milburn Road. When the Stonewall Brigade arrived just after dawn to cut the turnpike to the north, Milroy's command began to throw down their arms and surrender. Milroy himself, his staff, and a few units escaped to the west, but about half of his force became prisoners.

The second battle of Winchester, a humiliating Federal defeat, cost the Union about 4,000 soldiers captured and 450 killed or wounded out of 7,000 engaged, as well as 23 cannons, 300 wagons and horses, and a large quantity of supplies.

The Confederates lost some 50 killed or missing and 200 wounded out of about 12,500 engaged. It was one of their best-executed battles of the war and opened the way for Lee to cross into Maryland and Pennsylvania.

Much of the battlefield has succumbed to development as Winchester has expanded in all directions. The site of Early's attack on West Fort is largely undisturbed, however, and portions of the fort still exist. Some of Fort Milroy remains, and Star Fort is well preserved. The Stephenson's Depot site is also in good condition. Many of the routes over which Early and Johnson maneuvered are public roads in rural settings and can be traveled today. Other parts of the battlefield are fragmented, and the site is under increasing development pressure. ∎

ALDIE

Maj. Gen. Joseph Hooker, commander of the Army of the Potomac, became increasingly frustrated as June 1863 wore on with no clear indication of the whereabouts and intentions of Gen. Robert E. Lee and the Army of Northern Virginia. The Confederate cavalry chief, Maj. Gen. J. E. B. Stuart, continued to stymie the commander of the Federal cavalry corps Brig. Gen. Alfred Pleasonton and his attempts to penetrate the screen. As Pleasonton felt the sting of Hooker's displeasure, he resolved to punch through.

Pleasonton acted on Hooker's orders on Wednesday, June 17, by sending three cavalry brigades under Brig. Gen. David M. Gregg westward from Manassas Junction on the Little River Turnpike (present-day U.S. Rte. 50) toward the Blue Ridge Mountains. Gregg's object that day was Aldie, a village with a large brick mill. Strategically important, Aldie stood at the intersection of three highways: Little River Turnpike, Snicker's Gap Turnpike (Rte. 734), and Ashby's Gap Turnpike (U.S. Rte. 50). The latter two roads connected with other routes that led to highways and towns in the Shenandoah Valley, the immediate destination of Lee's army.

Much of that army still was located east of the Blue Ridge, marching down or across the turnpikes west of Aldie. Stuart could not allow Federal cavalry to come that close to the Confederate infantry. Once he found out quite by accident that Gregg occupied Aldie, Stuart was compelled to drive him out.

Gregg approached the village from the east with two of his brigades, those commanded by Brig. Gen. H. Judson "Kilcavalry" Kilpatrick and Col. J. Irvin Gregg. He sent the 1st Rhode Island Cavalry, led by Col. Alfred A. N. Duffié, northward in a sweep to Middleburg, about four miles west of Aldie. There, Duffié was to send word to Gregg on what he found and await further orders.

Meanwhile, Col. Thomas T. Munford, temporarily commanding Brig. Gen. Fitzhugh Lee's brigade, had led his troopers on a reconnaissance and foraging expedition between Aldie and Middleburg. Late in the afternoon, Munford led his own regiment, the 2nd Virginia, plus the 3rd Virginia about four miles up the Snicker's Gap Turnpike to obtain corn. The 4th Virginia, the 1st, and the 5th all followed. Munford planned to bivouac his regiments northwest of Aldie for the night, with his right flank about a mile and a half west of Aldie. His plans were disrupted when a courier rode up at about 4 P.M. to

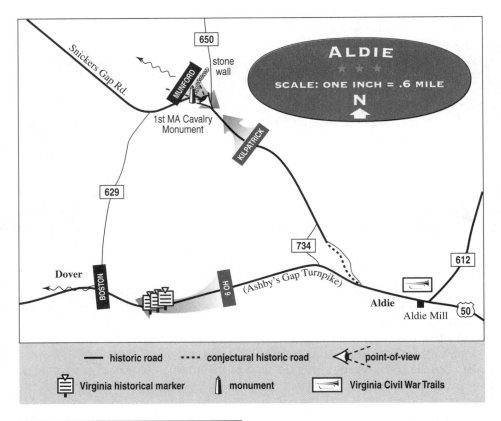

DIRECTIONS: I-66 Exit 40 (U.S. Rte. 15 North, Leesburg), n. on U.S. Rte. 15 North about 10.8 miles to U.S. Rte. 50 at Gilbert's Corner; w. (left) on U.S. Rte. 50 1.75 miles through Aldie to Rte. 734 (Snickersville Tpke.); n. (right) on Rte. 734 1.3 miles to 1st Mass. Cav. monument on right; continue on Rte. 734 .4 mile to Rte. 629 (Cobb House Rd.); s. (left) on Rte. 629 1.1 miles to U.S. Rte. 50; e. (left) on U.S. Rte. 50 1.3 miles to Rte. 734; return to U.S. Rte. 15 and I-66.

announce that Federal cavalry was approaching the milling village.

Heading Gregg's column, Kilpatrick led his brigade (2nd and 4th New York, 6th Ohio, and 1st Massachusetts) through Aldie on the Ashby's Gap Turnpike. The 1st Massachusetts, in the advance, encountered Munford's pickets west of the village and drove them back. Col. Thomas L. Rosser arrived on the scene with his 5th

Virginia and pushed the lead elements of the 1st Massachusetts back on the main body, but Union sharpshooters dismounted and formed a line to the north of the turnpike on high ground. Rosser withdrew west but left Capt. Reuben Boston and some fifty sharpshooters concealed in a ravine just west of the intersection of the Ashby's Gap and Snicker's Gap Turnpikes.

A charge by the 1st Massachusetts against the seemingly fleeing Virginians brought on a quick countercharge. The Bay Staters regrouped and pressed forward again, augmented by the 4th New York. Rosser formed his regiment to the right of Boston and charged as the sharpshooters fired, driving back the Federals and securing his hold on the Ashby's Gap Turnpike. The 1st Virginia, hearing the shooting, had come up the road to cover Rosser's rear.

Rosser had placed pickets behind some stone walls about a mile northwest of town on the Snicker's Gap Turnpike to cover his left flank. Now Kilpatrick turned his attention there. The pickets withdrew a short distance, but Col. Williams C. Wickham brought part of his 4th Virginia and a battery of Breathed's Artillery up in support. An artillery duel drove Munford back, leaving Boston unsupported on the Ashby's Gap Turnpike and exposing the center of the Confederate line.

Kilpatrick, reinforced with the 1st Maine Regiment, sent his troopers to assault Munford's center. The Union battle line was spearheaded by the 1st Massachusetts, with the 4th New York to its right, the 1st Maine on its left, and the 2nd New York and 6th Ohio close behind in reserve. Munford, meanwhile, had ordered sharpshooters from the 2nd and 3rd Virginia into the gap, and they closed up his line behind the stone walls and awaited Kilpatrick.

The sharpshooters' withering fire stalled the Union attack, and the rest of the 2nd Virginia charged with drawn sabers. The 1st Massachusetts fell back, and the 2nd Virginia regrouped and charged again, against the 4th New York. The 3rd Virginia joined in, driving the 1st Massachusetts into the 1st Maine. Behind the two Virginia regiments came two squadrons of the 4th Virginia as well as the entire 5th.

On the Ashby's Gap Turnpike, meanwhile, Boston kept up his fire whenever he observed Federal targets. Unfortunately he attracted the attention of the 6th Ohio, which finally overran his position and captured or killed most of his men.

With night coming on, at about 8 P.M. both sides pulled back to defensive posi-

Stone wall on the site of the cavalry engagement near Aldie, June 17, 1863. VIRGINIA DEPARTMENT OF HISTORIC RESOURCES, JOHN S. SALMON

tions. South of Middleburg, meanwhile, Duffié had arrived at about 4 P.M. with his 275 troopers. There he received orders to spend the night, then ride north and west the next morning to Snickersville. Duffié drove in Confederate pickets before he bivouacked, thereby alerting Stuart, who was in the town with two squadrons of the 4th Virginia Cavalry. The stage was set for another engagement the next day.

About 1,500 Confederates engaged roughly 2,000 Federals in the battle of Aldie. Casualties for the two sides totaled about 250. Most of the dead and wounded were Federals, and most of the prisoners (close to 100) were Confederates.

The Aldie battlefield retains much integrity. The village and mill still appear much as they did in the nineteenth century. On the former Snicker's Gap Turnpike, the stone walls still stand amid farmsteads and old houses. Some road-widening and realignment activities have occurred, especially on U.S. Rte. 50 and near the intersection with Rte. 734, but otherwise the terrain is little changed. ■

The engagement at Aldie, four miles west of Middleburg, on Wednesday, June 17, 1863, alerted Maj. Gen. J. E. B. Stuart that the Union cavalry was closing in on him. Stuart's mission was to screen the march of Gen. Robert E. Lee's Army of Northern Virginia from prying Union eyes, and he had sent his cavalry brigades roaming the countryside to accomplish that mission. Col. John R. Chambliss, temporarily in command of Brig. Gen. W. H. F. "Rooney" Lee's brigade (Lee had been wounded at Brandy Station on June 9), was south of Aldie near Thoroughfare Gap, while Brig. Gen. Beverly H. Robertson was near Rectortown, southwest of Aldie.

Col. Alfred A. N. Duffié prepared to bivouac for the night south of Middleburg but first sent word to Brig. Gen. H. Judson Kilpatrick at Aldie that he had been informed (erroneously, it turned out) that Stuart was on his way from Middleburg with 2,000 horsemen. Instead, Stuart had sent word to Munford, as well as Robertson and Chambliss, to converge on Mid-

dleburg. As he realized his predicament, Duffié dismounted half his force to fight as infantry behind some of the many stone walls that ran through the area, and sent Capt. Frank Allen to Aldie to plead for help from Kilpatrick. Kilpatrick spoke to Brig. Gen. David M. Gregg, who went off to find Brig. Gen. Alfred Pleasonton, commander of the Union cavalry corps, and discuss the situation. Duffié, in other words, was on his own.

Back at Middleburg, the Union situation deteriorated rapidly. Robertson's brigade struck Duffié's hard in the evening, but the Federals put up a stiff resistance, then withdrew south to a relatively safe bivouac. On the morning of Thursday, June 18, however, Duffié's force was effectively surrounded, as Munford had arrived from Aldie. Duffié invoked the rule of "every man for himself," and his command scattered through the countryside, pursued by Chambliss. Duffié, accompanied by four officers and twenty-seven men, reached the Union lines early

1st Maine Cavalry fighting dismounted as skirmishers, June 19, 1863. LIBRARY OF CONGRESS

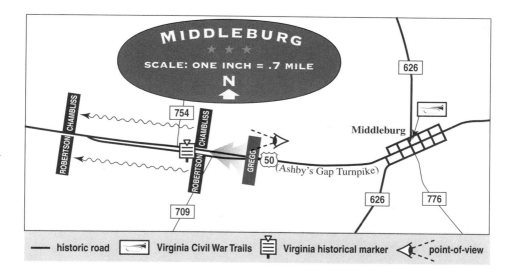

that afternoon. Over the next two days five officers and sixty men trickled into the lines, but roughly 300 officers and men were casualties in Duffié's disaster.

Despite that defeat, Pleasonton pressed on against Stuart at Middleburg, ordering Gregg's division forward the next morning, Friday, June 19. Robertson and Chambliss withdrew west of the town to a position on Mount Defiance and posted sharpshooters behind a stone wall there along a wood line, where they repulsed a Union charge. Supported by additional cavalry, the Federals regrouped and charged again, forcing the Confederates through woods and an open field to a second defensive position on the next hill to the west.

Chambliss and Robertson charged but failed to drive the Federals east. Stuart withdrew his cavalry yet another half mile west, and the fighting ended for the day. Pleasonton held Middleburg, while Stuart remained ensconced between that town and Upperville, some six miles west of his line. Though pushed back, the Confederates still blocked Pleasonton's path to Lee's army.

The three days' fighting around Middleburg cost both sides some 390 casualties, and the Federals suffered the heavier

DIRECTIONS: I-66 Exit 40 (U.S. Rte. 15 North, Leesburg), n. on U.S. Rte. 15 North about 10.8 miles to U.S. Rte. 50 at Gilbert's Corner; w. (left) on U.S. Rte. 50 7.7 miles through Middleburg (detour 1 block north at Red Fox Inn to Virginia Civil War Trails marker) to Rte. 709 (Zulla Rd.) on left about .4 mile after beginning of divided highway; continue w. on U.S. Rte. 50 .6 mile to Rte. 754 (Kirk Branch Rd.) on n. (right), site of first Confederate position on reverse (w.) slope of hill; state historical marker B-31, Battle of Middleburg, on s. side of divided highway at Loudoun/Fauquier Co. line; continue w. on U.S. Rte. 50 .3 mile to second Confederate position (hill just past end of divided highway) at Easton and Bittersweet Lanes; return to U.S. Rte. 15 and I-66.

losses. On the Confederate side, one significant casualty was Maj. Heros von Borcke, a Prussian adventurer and officer who served Stuart as an aide. Seriously wounded with a bullet in his neck, Von, as he was known, spent many months recovering and never fought again.

The Middleburg battlegrounds, situated for the most part on large farms in the midst of Virginia's hunt country, have fared well since the war. Some road widening and straightening has occurred along U.S. Rte. 50, the former Ashby's Gap Turnpike, but most of the terrain remains unchanged. ■

Middleburg • 211

A lull in the fighting on Saturday, June 20, 1863, gave Maj. Gen. J. E. B. Stuart an opportunity to consolidate and strengthen his position about six miles east of Upperville, where he faced two divisions from Brig. Gen. Alfred Pleasonton's Union cavalry corps on the Ashby's Gap Turnpike (present-day U.S. Rte. 50) just west of Middleburg. Stuart placed Col. Thomas T. Munford's brigade on his left, guarding the Snicker's Gap Turnpike (Rte. 734) and the gap itself. Brig. Gen. William E. "Grumble" Jones stationed his brigade to Munford's right, Col. John R. Chambliss posted his brigade to Jones's right, and Brig. Gen. Beverly H. Robertson and his brigade were near Ashby's Gap Turnpike. Brig. Gen. Wade Hampton's brigade straddled the pike to form Stuart's right flank.

Pleasonton, determined to locate the infantry of Gen. Robert E. Lee's Army of Northern Virginia, attacked at about 7 A.M.

on Sunday, June 21. Under the command of Brig. Gen. David M. Gregg, Col. J. Irvin Gregg's and Brig. Gen. H. Judson Kilpatrick's cavalry brigades trotted down the Ashby's Gap Turnpike toward Upperville, with Col. Strong Vincent's 1,550-man Third Infantry Brigade in support to handle Stuart's dismounted sharpshooters. Brig. Gen. John Buford, meanwhile, led his cavalry division out of Middleburg to strike Stuart's left flank. Buford's would be the main attack; Gregg's advance was a feint.

DIRECTIONS: I-66 Exit 40 (U.S. Rte. 15 North, Leesburg), n. on U.S. Rte. 15 North about 10.8 miles to U.S. Rte. 50 at Gilbert's Corner; w. (left) on U.S. Rte. 50 13.7 miles through Middleburg to Rte. 719 (Greengarden Rd.), then .3 mile to Virginia Civil War Trails marker on left at first Confederate position; continue w. on U.S. Rte. 50 1 mile to Rte. 712 (Delaplane Grade Rd.); return to U.S. Rte. 15 and I-66.

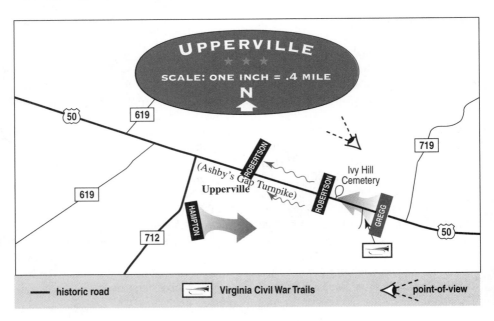

historic road   ◁═ Virginia Civil War Trails   ◀⋯ point-of-view

U.S. cavalry charge near Upperville, June 21, 1863. LIBRARY OF CONGRESS

The plan changed, however, when Buford, unable to cross Goose Creek a few miles north of Middleburg, swerved from his first objective, and Jones's and Chambliss's brigades halted his advance (along present-day Rte. 619). On the turnpike, Gregg unleashed Vincent's infantry against Stuart's skirmishers, which had moved east to Mount Defiance (Rtes. 1220 and 709). Under pressure, the Confederates withdrew west toward Upperville.

Stuart's line frayed as Gregg pressed the attack. Munford held his position while Chambliss fell back and Jones formed a rear guard to protect the withdrawal north of the turnpike. Robertson retreated through Upperville with Gregg in pursuit, but Hampton struck Gregg's left flank, thereby stopping the Federal advance. By sunset Stuart's brigades held the line between Ashby's Gap in the south and Snicker's Gap in the north.

After a day-long fight, Pleasonton declared victory and withdrew eastward to Aldie the next day. Lee, somewhat concerned about the blows Stuart had sustained, ordered Maj. Gen. Lafayette McLaws's division from Lt. Gen. James Longstreet's corps to guard Ashby's Gap.

The two sides suffered about 400 casualties during the engagement at Upperville. Pleasonton claimed to have captured two of Stuart's cannons (Stuart admitted to one) and 250 Confederate prisoners. Stuart had accomplished his screening mission, but again the Union cavalry had done well in fighting his horsemen. Now both armies would march north into Maryland and Pennsylvania, where they would blunder into battle at Gettysburg.

The battlefields around Upperville, which like Middleburg lies in the Virginia hunt country, consist of well-kept large horse farms. Little change has occurred, except along U.S. Rte. 50, and the significant parts of the battleground are easily observed from rural roads. ■

When the Army of Northern Virginia marched into Pennsylvania in June 1863, a brigade was detached from Maj. Gen. George E. Pickett's division to remain in Virginia. Brig. Gen. Montgomery D. Corse commanded the brigade, which spent most of the month and early July guarding bridges and rail junctions in central Virginia. On July 7 Corse received orders to march from Gordonsville to Winchester, to help cover the main army's retreat after its defeat at Gettysburg. On July 20 the brigade marched back to Front Royal, and then east to Manassas Gap, which the 17th Virginia Infantry Regiment was assigned to hold.

As Lee's army retreated south up the Shenandoah Valley, Maj. Gen. George G. Meade and the Army of the Potomac pursued it on a roughly parallel course on the eastern side of the Blue Ridge. Various Confederate units guarded the many gaps in the ridge to prevent penetration by the Federals.

On Tuesday, July 21, Brig. Gen. Wesley Merritt, commanding the Reserve Cavalry Brigade, probed Manassas Gap and encountered the 17th Virginia Regiment at its western exit. Lt. Col. Arthur Herbert, commander of the regiment, had thought another Confederate unit already occupied the gap, but when he walked forward in advance of his regiment to find it, he found Merritt's skirmishers instead. He raced back and quickly deployed his men, who opened fire and halted a charge by the 1st United States Cavalry Regiment. Merritt pressed the attack again, but Herbert was reinforced with the remnants of Brig. Gen. Lewis A. Armistead's brigade, and the narrow defile prevented Merritt from bringing up his artillery. Sharpshooters at a

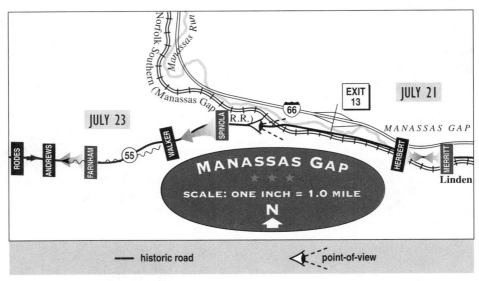

DIRECTIONS: I-66 Exit 13 (Rte. 79 to State Rte. 55, Linden), s. on Rte. 79 about .1 mile to State Rte. 55; w. (right) on State Rte. 55 .6 mile to Southern Railway bridge; continue .1 mile farther to turnaround on left.

cut made by the Manassas Gap Railroad held off a thrust by Herbert. That night the 17th Virginia was ordered to advance at dawn, but by daylight it received new orders to withdraw when relieved by Maj. Gen. John B. Hood's division.

On Wednesday, July 22, Meade ordered Maj. Gen. William H. "Old Blinkey" French to march his III Corps to Manassas Gap, break through, and attack Lee's column in the Shenandoah Valley. It was a good plan, but French was not very competent. Notoriously slow, he crept forward with Brig. Gen. Henry Prince's division in the lead. Part of Maj. Gen. Richard H. Anderson's Confederate division guarded the gap, and some skirmishing occurred throughout the day. During the night, elements of French's corps secured a portion of the gap, while the rest bivouacked about four miles east.

At 4 A.M. on July 23, Brig. Gen. Francis B. Spinola led the Excelsior Brigade (70th–74th and 120th New York) west from Markham toward the gap, with the remainder of Prince's division following. First composed of five regiments raised in 1861 (the 120th was added later), the Excelsior Brigade suffered from poor generalship, although competent colonels commanded several of its regiments. Spinola, like French slow and hesitant, was one of the brigade's less effective leaders.

The 70th New York, commanded by Col. J. Egbert Farnum, marched at the head of the column, which stopped at about 1 P.M. at Linden Station on the Manassas Gap Railroad. Prince sent the 120th New York as a skirmish line to the left of the road (present-day Rte. 55) running through the gap. Just short of Wapping Station, about a mile west of Linden Station, the column stopped again and reorganized. The 70th marched down to the railroad at Wapping Station, then followed the 120th New York skirmishers west to

View east at Manassas Gap. VIRGINIA DEPARTMENT OF HISTORIC RESOURCES, JOHN S. SALMON

another hill. There the division halted yet again at about 4 P.M. to allow stragglers, such as the 74th New York, to catch up.

An hour later, Prince ordered Spinola to advance the Excelsior Brigade against the Confederate position on the next hill west. Col. Edward J. Walker, commander of the 3rd Georgia Infantry Regiment, had posted it on that hill under Capt. C. H. Andrews, opposite the 70th New York. He also stationed the 22nd Georgia on a hill behind the 3rd and the 48th Georgia to the right of the 22nd. Walker deployed two of the four companies comprising the 2nd Georgia Battalion in front of the 22nd as skirmishers and the other two a mile and a half in the rear to guard a road junction. Observing the advancing Federal corps, Walker sent a message to Lt. Gen. Richard S. Ewell requesting reinforcements.

Before they arrived, Spinola attacked. The 70th New York and the 3rd Georgia bore the brunt of the combat. Soon the 70th overwhelmed the Georgians, who fell back and joined the rest of Walker's brigade in a thin line that extended almost two miles. Both Walker and Spinola were wounded during the engagement; Andrews took over for Walker and Farnum for Spinola.

Ewell arrived on the field with Maj. Gen. Robert E. Rodes, who was leading his division to reinforce Andrews. After heavy fighting, the center of Andrews's line began to give way. He ordered his brigade to retire to the position occupied by Rodes's division, some 600 yards to the rear. About that time Farnum received orders to halt and hold his ground for the night. The fighting ended at sunset.

The next morning Farnum found the road to Front Royal clear of Confederates. The Army of Northern Virginia had marched south and escaped in the night.

The engagement at Manassas Gap, also known as Wapping Heights, cost Wright's brigade 168 killed, wounded, and missing.

The Excelsior Brigade reported 75 killed and wounded. The Confederates' successful defense of Manassas Gap can be attributed in large part to the nearly twelve hours it took for French, Prince, and Spinola to march the five or so miles from Markham to Wapping Station, giving Walker plenty of time to prepare his positions and make good use of the terrain.

The battlefield at Manassas Gap generally retains good integrity. Interstate 66 now cuts through the gap, together with a widened Rte. 55, and some commercial and residential development has occurred in and around Linden, as well as north of the highways on the western side of the gap. The hills to the south where most of the combat took place remain little altered, however, and are about as difficult to access now as they were then. ∎

BRISTOE STATION AND MINE RUN CAMPAIGNS, 1863

The Army of Northern Virginia and its commander, Gen. Robert E. Lee, were never the same after the Gettysburg campaign. Of the 75,000 soldiers who marched to Pennsylvania in the summer of 1863, some 28,000 were killed, wounded, captured, or missing by the end of the campaign. The departure in September of Lt. Gen. James Longstreet and his corps for Georgia and Tennessee reduced the army's strength to 45,000.

Lee's army faced critical shortages of manpower, horses, and supplies. Desertion threatened the life of the army, and to keep his men in the ranks, Lee resorted to both carrots and sticks—furloughs and exhortations to patriotism on the one hand, courts-martial and executions on the other—with modest success. The supply shortage, which included the slow replacement of arms and equipment lost at Gettysburg, caused morale to suffer, which in turn increased the desertion rate.

On the Union side, Maj. Gen. George G. Meade's Army of the Potomac faced desertion problems, too, mostly among new conscripts, and Meade tried tactics similar to Lee's, with similar results. Meade also faced shortages of cavalry horses—mounts sturdy enough to withstand the approaching summer's heat and humidity—and supplies. The supply problem, however, concerned food for Meade's horses, not his men. And the numbers of his men kept increasing, from roughly 68,000 (Gettysburg had reduced their ranks by 23,000), to about 81,000 in the fall. Many of the new men were draftees, mostly Irish and German immigrants, and ethnic and social conflicts ran high. Meade worried about the battlefield effectiveness of this new army.

Despite these problems, both commanders were under pressure to resume field operations. Meade did not enjoy the full support of Pres. Abraham Lincoln and his cabinet members, many of whom thought that his pursuit of Lee after Gettysburg had been dilatory. Although Meade had several excellent military reasons for proceeding cautiously, his detractors assumed that Meade suffered from the same "disease" that had infected other Union commanders: reluctance to face Robert E. Lee in combat. This was not true of Meade, but as usual perceptions were more important than reality, and Meade realized that he would have to take to the field soon.

Lee, too, felt the pressure, although he received Jefferson Davis's unflinching support and encouragement. It was Lee's own nature and the growing predicament facing the army that hurried him toward combat. He could not afford to wait for Meade to attack his smaller force; outnumbered and poorly supplied, Lee knew that inaction meant death for the Army of Northern Virginia. He had to attack.

The Confederate army concentrated in Culpeper and Orange Counties in Piedmont Virginia, north of the Rapidan River and west of the Rappahannock River. The Army of the Potomac occupied much the

BRISTOE STATION & MINE RUN CAMPAIGNS

Lee had three objectives: Drive Meade back toward Washington, defeat his army, and prevent the transfer of any more Federal troops to the western theater. The Confederate victory at Chickamauga on September 19–20 had heartened Lee, the condition of the roads and the weather were conducive to campaigning, and the soldiers of the Army of Northern Virginia had recovered physically from the effects of the Gettysburg campaign. These conditions favored Lee's plans.

Several facts militated against it, however. Longstreet, Lee's ablest corps commander, was in the West. Neither of the other two was Old Pete's equal. Lt. Gen. Richard S. Ewell's reputation had suffered after the defeat at Gettysburg, while Lt. Gen. A. P. Hill often was impetuous and since Gettysburg seemingly ill whenever a crisis threatened. Horses remained in short supply, many of Lee's soldiers lacked shoes, and Meade's army outnumbered Lee's 76,000 to 45,000.

After considering all the factors, Lee chose to take his army into the field and employ much the same strategy as he had late in August 1862: Leave a rear guard on the Rapidan River, and execute a turning movement toward Washington with the rest of his troops, thereby forcing the Federals to defend the capital and fight the Confederates on ground favorable to the Army of Northern Virginia. The plan had worked once before; it might work again. But Lee did not have Stonewall Jackson to lead the march around Meade's army, nor Longstreet on the Rapidan, nor an entire corps to station there. Instead, he would leave Maj. Gen. Fitzhugh Lee's three-brigade cavalry division and three infantry brigades to guard the riverfront crossings and accompany Ewell and Hill as they swept around the Union right. Maj. Gen. J. E. B. Stuart would lead Maj. Gen. Wade Hampton's cavalry division ahead of the infantry to clear the way.

same positions on the north bank of the Rapidan as it had the year before when Maj. Gen. John Pope commanded it. Both armies were stripped of divisions or corps to meet the demands of the war in the West. Longstreet and two divisions departed for Georgia and Tennessee in September (and helped secure the victory at Chickamauga), and Meade's XI and XII Corps were ordered late in September to the Chattanooga area, to help secure Middle Tennessee for the Union. (Later, that gateway town would serve as a base of operations for Maj. Gen. William T. Sherman's Georgia campaign.) Meade sent more troops to Tennessee when he learned of Longstreet's reassignment, and Lee decided to resume the offensive when he discovered that the Army of the Potomac had lost two entire corps.

On Thursday, October 8, Hill's Third Army Corps began its march north from Orange Court House through Madison Court House. The corps consisted of three divisions: Maj. Gen. Richard H. Anderson's five brigades, Maj. Gen. Henry Heth's four brigades, and Maj. Gen. Cadmus Wilcox's four brigades. Ewell's Second Army Corps, like Hill's corps, consisted of three divisions. The first, commanded by Maj. Gen. Jubal A. Early, included four brigades; the second, under Maj. Gen. Edward "Allegheny" Johnson, consisted of four brigades; and the third, Maj. Gen. Robert E. Rodes's, contained five brigades. Stuart's cavalry corps, which had been reorganized on September 9, contained two divisions. The first, commanded by Hampton (who had been wounded at Gettysburg and was away recuperating), consisted of three brigades and the second, commanded by Fitz Lee, also consisted of three brigades. Maj. Robert F. Beckham commanded Stuart's Horse Artillery, while the rest of the army's artillery was organized into two five-battalion divisions to support Ewell's and Hill's infantry corps, with Brig. Gen. Armistead L. Long commanding one division and Col. Reuben L. Walker the other.

Meade's Army of the Potomac consisted of five infantry corps (I, under Maj. Gen. John Newton; II, Brig. Gen. Gouverneur K. Warren; III, Maj. Gen. William H. French; V, Maj. Gen. George Sykes; VI, Maj. Gen. John Sedgwick), each with its own artillery brigade; a cavalry corps commanded by Maj. Gen. Alfred Pleasonton; and an artillery reserve with six brigades under Brig. Gen. Henry J. Hunt. Each infantry corps, as well as the cavalry corps, contained three divisions. In I Corps, they were commanded by Brig. Gen. Lysander Cutler, Brig. Gen. John C. Robinson, and Brig. Gen. John R. Kenly; II Corps, Brig. Gen. John C. Caldwell, Brig. Gen. Alexander S. Webb, and Brig. Gen. Alexander

Hays; III Corps, Maj. Gen. David D. Birney, Brig. Gen. Henry Prince, and Brig. Gen. Joseph B. Carr; V Corps, Brig. Gen. Charles Griffin, Brig. Gen. Romeyn B. Ayres, and Col. William McCandless; VI Corps, Brig. Gen. Horatio G. Wright, Brig. Gen. Albion P. Howe, and Brig. Gen. Henry D. Terry; Cavalry Corps, Brig. Gen. John Buford, Brig. Gen. David M. Gregg, and Brig. Gen. H. Judson Kilpatrick.

Lee's march did not go undetected by Meade and his generals. Not only were Union spies more numerous and their reports more accurate than before, but watchers with telescopes occupied observation posts atop such heights as Cedar Mountain in Culpeper County. In addition, the Federal signal corps had cracked its Confederate counterpart's code; by October 6, Union signal officers knew an offensive was imminent. On October 8–9 they reported Lee's troops on the march, and Federal soldiers were issued five days' rations in preparation for the coming campaign. Meade himself climbed Cedar Mountain on October 9 to peer through a telescope at his enemy.

Meade remained uncertain, however, about just what the Confederate activity signified. Was Lee attempting a turning movement against the Union right flank, or was he about to fall back toward Richmond? The Union commander ordered Buford to seize Morton's Ford on the Rapidan River in case a push to Orange Court House might be productive against a Confederate retrograde toward Richmond. He also strengthened Kilpatrick, who held James City (present-day Leon) on the Union right flank, by dispatching Prince's infantry division to him in support. By October 10 Meade had positioned troops to counter either move by Lee without overcommitting his forces.

Lee launched his campaign at 3 A.M. on Saturday, October 10, when Stuart began a diversionary attack down the road to

James City with Brig. Gen. James B. Gordon's brigade in the lead. His troopers struck at Russell's Ford on the Robertson River at about 6:30 A.M., just after dawn, and broke through the Federal cavalry guarding the crossing. This sector of Meade's line belonged to the youngest general in the Union army, twenty-three-year-old Brig. Gen. George Armstrong Custer, who had leaped from captain after his heroic cavalry charges at Aldie and elsewhere. Custer's men withdrew in good order and joined Kilpatrick at James City following a brief engagement with Southern cavalry at Bethsaida Church.

A day-long action at James City followed. Kilpatrick's force occupied a ridge north of the village, and Stuart's men secured one to the south. Each side shelled the other, and skirmishers fired from one crest to the other while villagers huddled between the two heights as rounds buzzed overhead. Neither side assaulted the other; Stuart hesitated to push hard, and Kilpatrick could not persuade Prince to come to his aid. (Prince was relieved of divisional command that winter.)

Buford, meanwhile, had crossed the Rapidan River at Germanna Ford, then circled west to Morton's Ford. The plan called for him to attack the Confederates at the ford on October 11 while Newton's I Corps infantry assailed it from the north. Meade, however, decided that the action at James City meant that Lee intended either to outflank him on the right or withdraw toward the Shenandoah Valley, not Richmond. He canceled Newton's march and ordered the army to new positions north of the Rappahannock River. Word did not reach Buford until 7 A.M. on October 11; he decided to push across the ford and return to Stevensburg, and after a sharp action he succeeded.

When Stuart discovered on the same day that Kilpatrick had withdrawn from James City, he set off in pursuit, headed for Culpeper Court House. Late in the morning he caught up with Kilpatrick at Brandy Station, scene of the great cavalry battle of four months earlier. As the fight developed, other columns converged on the battlefield from the south, and the result was a wild, disjointed engagement with charges and countercharges along the Orange & Alexandria Railroad line between Brandy Station and the Rappahannock River bridge to the east. Stuart, hampered by the exhaustion of his mounts, was unable to trap the Union cavalry as he had hoped, and spectacular charges led by Custer among others enabled the Federals to cross the river to safety. By nightfall Meade's headquarters were at Rappahannock Station, Lee's were at Culpeper Court House, and Hill's and Ewell's corps were marching northeast toward Warrenton.

Meade and his commanders spent part of the night revising orders for the next day's march. Now that scouts reported that Lee was moving roughly northeast, Meade sought to parallel his route along the railroad and attack Lee if the opportunity arose. In the morning, however, Meade received word that Confederate infantry had been engaged at Amissville, about ten miles west of Warrenton and on the route that Jackson had taken to Thoroughfare Gap in August 1862. Was Lee also heading for the gap?

In fact, the infantry at Amissville was Hill's, and it was marching on roads parallel to Ewell. Hill would unite with Ewell at Warrenton, and then both corps would head east.

Meade's misapprehension of Lee's destination caused him to change his plans. He would withdraw up the Orange & Alexandria Railroad to Centreville, there to defend Washington and to prepare a new offensive. He also altered the army's order of march, and the resulting confusion delayed some units for hours. Fortunately for Meade, Lee's army made little progress because of its supply shortages.

On October 13 Stuart reconnoitered toward Catlett's Station on the Orange & Alexandria Railroad to locate the Union left flank. Brig. Gen. Lunsford L. Lomax's brigade left Warrenton and rode southeast toward the station by way of Dumfries Road. Stuart followed an hour or so later with two brigades; Lomax halted at Auburn, a hamlet roughly halfway to his objective, and waited for Stuart to catch up. While he waited, Lomax sent scouts out to check the rolling, wooded countryside for enemy troops. They found a huge wagon park and Buford's cavalry division at Warrenton Junction but failed to reconnoiter Three Mile Station on the Warrenton Branch Railroad, some three miles southwest of Auburn. If they had, they would have found Kilpatrick's and Gregg's cavalry divisions and the II and III Corps.

Stuart rode into Auburn at about 1 P.M., noted Lomax's error, and dispatched a member of his staff and a small escort to check Three Mile Station. Then he turned his attention to the wagons at Warrenton Junction, sent word for Fitzhugh Lee to join him quickly, and prepared to attack. Lee left Warrenton at about 4 P.M. and traced Stuart's route to Auburn, bringing with him two brigades. He was approaching the hamlet at about 4:15 P.M. when he encountered one of Stuart's staff officers riding toward Warrenton with news for Robert E. Lee: A Union army corps was marching up the road directly for Auburn, thereby threatening to get between Stuart and the main army at Warrenton.

The III Corps had blundered down the wrong roads that morning under the leadership of French. Afflicted with facial tics (according to rumor, caused by heavy bouts with the bottle), "Old Blinkey" had

led his column into an unexpected clash with Lomax at Auburn. The brief action took place on the Old Carolina Road just south of Auburn. Lomax charged French's column, was driven back by artillery fire, then held his position briefly with support from Lee and Col. John R. Chambliss before withdrawing to Warrenton. Now Stuart was sandwiched between marching columns of the enemy.

Stuart decided to conceal his two brigades in a wooded ravine just east of Auburn. He dressed half a dozen volunteers in captured Federal uniforms and after dark sent them through French's column (they would have been shot as spies if captured) to inform Lee of Stuart's predicament. All six made it through safely, and Lee ordered Ewell's corps to march to Auburn at dawn. Meanwhile, Stuart and his men passed the night nervously. First French's soldiers marched by in the darkness to bivouac at Greenwich; then Warren's corps pitched camp for the night just a few hundred yards away. An officer later wrote that he had never seen Stuart look so worried.

Lee's plans for October 14 called for dividing his army, then reuniting it. Hill's corps would pursue Meade's army eastward on the Warrenton and Alexandria Turnpike; Ewell's corps would march to Auburn, help free Stuart, then rejoin Hill in time to strike Meade.

At dawn, Hill's corps marched east through Warrenton and set off down the turnpike, with part of Fitzhugh Lee's cavalry division reconnoitering in advance. At about 5 A.M. Ewell began his rescue mission. He split his corps into two wings and sent them to Auburn by different routes: Rodes's and Johnson's divisions marched down from the north while Early's division, supported by the rest of Fitzhugh Lee's cavalry, approached from the west.

Just south of Auburn, meanwhile, Warren's II Corps, which had bivouacked there for the night, prepared to continue its eastward march. French's corps was now out of the way, followed by Kilpatrick's cavalry division, so Warren's route was clear. He knew of the previous day's engagement and understood that Lee was in Warrenton trying to find and attack Meade's army at a vulnerable point. Warren, bringing up the rear of the column, *was* that point, and he took care to protect his line of march against an attack from the north.

Caldwell's division was closest to Auburn, Hays's division camped just south of Caldwell's, and Webb's division was next, about two miles south of Auburn. Warren's corps supply train, more than 200 wagons and ambulances, stretched some two miles in length, and it approached the ford at Cedar Run, just south of Auburn. There, slippery mud and early morning fog bogged down the train; rather than delay the infantry's march, Warren ordered Caldwell to lead the way through fields and woods west and north of the road and cross Cedar Run over a bridge. Once across, Caldwell's men deployed for defense and then settled down for coffee and breakfast on a hill (thereafter called Coffee Hill) on the north side of the stream while Hays followed with his division.

Stuart was thus trapped between Caldwell and Warren's supply train. He knew that Ewell was approaching from Warrenton, and he cautiously deployed seven guns of his horse artillery on a hill some 800 yards east of Caldwell's position. He then waited for rifle fire to tell him that Ewell's skirmishers had made contact with Warren's corps.

The second engagement at Auburn began at about 6:30 A.M., when vedettes from Gregg's cavalry division opened fire on Ewell's skirmish line. Stuart, as soon as he heard the shots, ordered his artillery to fire, as well. Hays sent infantry toward Stuart's artillery while Caldwell moved his division to the reverse slope of Coffee Hill to protect it from the Confederate guns. Warren galloped to Auburn with his staff, having been informed that three enemy columns were converging there (one was Stuart's horsemen, who were attacking only to escape). To the west of Auburn, Gregg's cavalrymen needed assistance, and Warren ordered an infantry brigade to help them. He also ordered Webb's division ahead to support Hays.

Stuart realized that the time had come for his departure. He ordered Gordon to lead his brigade against Hays's infantry approaching from the west while Stuart led Col. Oliver R. Funsten's brigade eastward through the Union line. The maneuver succeeded; Gordon then followed Stuart in a trek south and west around Warren's corps, and Stuart soon reunited his detachment with Fitz Lee's.

Back on Coffee Hill, Union artillery had replaced Caldwell's division to support Hays's infantry marching east against Stuart. To the northwest, Fitz Lee's troopers and the vanguard of Early's infantry column pressed Gregg and the supporting infantry brigade sent by Warren, while Rodes attacked from the west. The Coffee Hill batteries turned around and fired at Rodes's men once Stuart had disengaged and escaped eastward. Confederate guns unlimbered to respond.

By 10 A.M. the Auburn engagement had become an artillery duel. Warren, realizing that the Confederates would not attack with their infantry, used the opportunity to extract most of his own infantry and cavalry and march first southeast to the Orange & Alexandria Railroad, then northwest toward Manassas Junction. The cannon fire died away after an hour, and Warren's artillery pulled out under the protection of a combined rear guard of cavalry and infantry.

For his part, Lee did not plan to fight a battle with Warren. Instead, he likewise quickly disengaged and marched Ewell's infantry and Lee's cavalry (and Stuart) eastward as planned to strike Meade's flank or rear.

Hill had marched down the turnpike from Warrenton with Anderson's division in the lead, followed by Heth's and Wilcox's. By 8:30 A.M. the column had reached New Baltimore, some five miles east of Warrenton. There, Hill received reports of Federal troops marching eastward south of his position; indeed, he claimed he could hear the rumbling of Union wagons. The road the Federals were using crossed the turnpike three or four miles ahead, near Buckland Mills, so he sent Anderson ahead to block the intersection. He also ordered Heth and Wilcox to leave the turnpike at New Baltimore and march southeast on the road to Greenwich, then head northeast back to the turnpike to strike the enemy in the rear.

The enemy, however, was not to be found, except for Kilpatrick's cavalry. Fitzhugh Lee arrived with his reunited cavalry division between 9 and 10 A.M. and hurried to engage Kilpatrick, who withdrew toward Gainesville with Lee in pursuit. Anderson, meanwhile, finding no other Federals, turned south on the road to Greenwich. From that village, Hill marched with Heth's and Wilcox's divisions east on the road leading to Bristoe Station, where he expected to find the elusive rear of Meade's army. He marched blindly, however, for when he most needed it, Hill's reconnaissance capability had almost disappeared. Fitzhugh Lee's cavalry was chasing Kilpatrick while Stuart covered Ewell's right flank several miles behind Hill.

At noon Meade was at Bristoe Station, pleased with the progress his army was making toward Centreville. He wired Warren at Catlett's Station to continue his march up the railroad but to be aware that Lee was on the Warrenton and Alexandria Turnpike and might send a column to intercept him. Meade ordered Sykes, who was approaching Bristoe Station with V Corps ahead of Warren, to wait there until he spotted Warren's column. At about 1:30 P.M. Sykes thought Warren had been sighted, so he ordered the last of his corps to cross Broad Run.

Just then Hill and Heth arrived north of the station and saw the end of Sykes's column passing over the stream. Believing that he had found the rear of Meade's army, Hill ordered an immediate attack, sending Heth forward. Although other Federals were observed near the railroad tracks, Hill assumed they were a small rearguard detachment.

In reality, they were the vanguard of Warren's corps. Most of the Federals were concealed behind the high railroad bed just west of Bristoe Station; when Heth deployed his division to attack the rear of Sykes's column, Warren struck the Confederate right flank. Heth's commanders wheeled the division in a frontal assault against the unexpected threat, but the Confederate line crumpled under the hail of bullets and artillery shells. The stunned survivors stumbled to the rear, leaving hundreds of dead, dying, and wounded on the field.

Although Ewell's corps arrived before dark, Lee decided not to continue the battle. The Federals withdrew across Broad Run in the night, and after dawn on October 15 Lee and Hill surveyed the carnage together. Finally an angry Lee cut off Hill's admission of responsibility with "Well, well, General, bury these poor men and let us say no more about it." The Army of Northern Virginia had suffered some 1,400 casualties to the Federals' 550.

Lee probed the territory between Bristoe Station and Bull Run in the days following the battle but realized the Federal position was too strong to attack. Once again the Army of the Potomac had eluded his grasp. Lee ended the Bristoe Station campaign and on October 16 ordered the Army of Northern Virginia to withdraw to Culpeper Court House.

Lee's campaign was a failure; he had not brought on a decisive battle, and he had not changed Federal strategy regarding the West. He had risked his army by marching beyond its supply line to outflank Meade, who had countered the Confederate maneuver effectively even though it meant pulling the Union army back to the Centreville defenses instead of attacking Lee. The outnumbered Confederates could not hope to drive through Meade's lines to Washington, so there was nothing else for Lee to do but withdraw. Meade, in contrast, was sitting on his supply base, his army had half again as many men as Lee's, and they had suffered far less during the campaign than their Confederate counterparts. Lincoln pressed Meade to attack Lee, but he did not press him too hard. When Meade discovered that Lee was withdrawing down the Orange & Alexandria Railroad, however, he set off at once in pursuit.

Lee had his men tear up track as they went, to hinder the Federals. At about noon on Sunday, October 18, the Confederates began crossing into Culpeper County at Rappahannock Station. Stuart, who had been screening the army's march, fell back to Gainesville as Kilpatrick pressed forward. The next day Kilpatrick found that Stuart had vanished. Under orders to continue to Warrenton, Kilpatrick assumed the route was open.

Stuart had ridden down the Warrenton and Alexandria Turnpike to Buckland Mills, where the road crossed Broad Run. There, on the western bank, he set up a defensive line and sent word to Fitzhugh Lee at Auburn to come protect his right flank. Meanwhile, Custer approached at the head of Kilpatrick's column, and a sharp fight developed. When Custer threatened Stuart's flanks, the Confederates withdrew toward Warrenton. Kilpatrick arrived shortly after noon and set off in pursuit, ordering Custer to follow. Fortunately for the Federals, Custer allowed his men to eat lunch first; for just after they crossed Broad Run, Fitz Lee struck them from the south, causing them to retreat across the stream. Had Custer followed his orders, Lee would have hit him from the rear, catching the entire Federal force between his division and Stuart.

Kilpatrick heard the shooting behind him just as he encountered Stuart's new line at Chestnut Hill, east of Warrenton. Stuart charged and drove Kilpatrick east on the turnpike toward Broad Run. Although the Federals at first fell back fighting, eventually the pressure proved too much, and the retreat became a headlong flight. For some five miles the Confederates pursued them, until the Union cavalry became so scattered that the chase was abandoned. Between them, the two combatants lost about 230 men, most of them captured Federal troopers.

For the rest of October and into November, Lee and Meade faced each other across the Rappahannock River. The Confederates held the crossings at Rappahannock Station and at Kelly's Ford, so Meade decided to reoccupy the ground between the Rappahannock and Rapidan Rivers by forcing passages at the two crossings. Lee, once he divined Meade's scheme, planned to allow him to cross at the ford but hold him at the railroad bridge, then counterattack in force—the Confederate fortifications were on the east side of the river near the railroad bridge but on the west side at the ford.

On November 7 Meade's offensive got under way. French's III Corps seized Kelly's Ford while Sedgwick's VI Corps attacked at Rappahannock Station. Sedgwick encountered resistance at the bridge, where part of Early's division held the Confederate works as the afternoon faded. After some hesitation, Sedgwick decided on a risky attack at dusk; Lee, on the other hand, assuming that the day's fighting would end at sunset, neglected to support the bridgehead.

Sedgwick's attack succeeded, shocking Lee and Early. After vicious hand-to-hand fighting, Sedgwick's men captured the earthworks and about 1,600 defenders who did not swim the river to safety. In addition to the Confederate prisoners, the two sides suffered about 900 other casualties.

Early had the western end of the railroad bridge burned, delaying the Federal crossing, and Lee ordered his army back across the Rapidan River to Orange County, abandoning Culpeper County to the Union army. Lee had crossed that river for the last time.

The Army of the Potomac occupied the Confederates' half-finished winter encampment between Brandy Station and Culpeper Court House, repaired the railroad bridge, and anticipated the end of the campaign season. Pressured by Washington politicians, however, Meade planned another offensive for early winter.

Meade discovered that the right of Lee's line, which was stretched from Verdiersville in the east to Gordonsville in the west, was not anchored on a naturally defensible feature such as a river. He also found that small numbers of defenders held the many Rapidan River fords. The Confederates seemed vulnerable.

Hill's corps constituted Lee's left flank, while Ewell's (temporarily commanded by Early) formed the right. The two principal east-west roads, the Orange Turnpike and the Orange Plank Road, ran behind Ewell's lines, thereby furnishing a route of attack against the Confederate rear. Meade planned to send his corps across several fords simultaneously, drive south to the highways, and sweep west, rolling up Lee's right flank.

Meade's Mine Run campaign, as it became known, encountered a two-day postponement due to rain and high water. Lee, learning of the Union army's maneuvers in the interim, used the delay to prepare his forces for battle. The same roads that afforded the Federals the opportunity to attack gave Lee internal lines of communication and movement.

Stalled by weather and the slowness of French's corps, Union forces had to be shifted from one ford to another, further delaying their progress. Meade bivouacked his army, then resumed the march and got all his corps across the river the next day, November 27.

Lee's lieutenants reacted to the reports of Federal crossings by blocking the avenues of approach. Early sent Hays's (formerly Early's) and Rodes's divisions down the Orange Turnpike to Robinson's Tavern and ordered Johnson's division up the road to Jacob's Ford. Hays and Rodes stopped Warren's and Sedgwick's corps at the tavern, while Johnson encountered French at Payne's Farm. French might have swept Johnson aside, but the Union general allowed the Confederate commander to bring him to a dead halt. Meade was furious, for he realized that Lee would grasp his intentions and act to counter them.

Meade's intended envelopment gave Lee an opportunity to fight a defensive battle and watch the Federal army destroy itself in futile attacks. He withdrew to the western bank of Mine Run, which ran across the highways that Meade intended to take. Throughout the night, the Confederates labored to construct and strengthen earthworks along the stream.

Meade and his generals spent November 28 studying Lee's defenses, and Warren suggested making an attack against the Confederate right the next day. On November 29, however, a Confederate cavalry raid struck Meade's left flank and rear, causing him to wonder whether Lee intended a flanking movement of his own.

During the night, Hill's men strengthened the works on the Confederate right. When dawn came and Warren rode forward to study the terrain, he realized that an assault would fail and cause needless casualties. He canceled the attack and informed Meade, who at first was enraged but ultimately agreed with Warren. Meade held a council of war that night and decided to conclude the campaign and withdraw across the Rapidan during the night of December 1–2.

Lee and his men, meanwhile, waited patiently behind their works for the attack that would never come. On December 1 Lee decided to launch his own attack the next day. When morning arrived, however, Meade and his army were gone, and it was Lee's turn to be angry.

Both armies went into camp for the winter, while Meade soon traveled to Washington to explain himself to Lincoln and his cabinet. The Mine Run campaign had cost him some 1,300 casualties, while the Confederates lost about 700, all to no advantage. Meade's plan was good, but its execution was execrable, in part because of weather-related delays and in part because of French's slowness. French was soon relegated to garrison and administrative duties, whereas most critics eventually forgave Meade. It had taken considerable courage to cancel a campaign when he undoubtedly understood that a storm of outrage would be the consequence, even if his decision did save his army.

Meade went home to Philadelphia on furlough for a rest. Lincoln considered replacing him as commander of the Army of the Potomac but decided against it. Instead, he would promote Ulysses S. Grant, who had engineered the relief of Chattanooga, Tennessee. Grant was the same commander who had captured Vicksburg, Mississippi, on July 4, 1863, and secured the great river for the Union. This man of grim determination, Lincoln believed, might be just the general he had been searching for to lead his military machine to victory. He would promote Grant to lieutenant general, place him in command of all Union armies, and see what he could do when the winter ended. ■

FIRST BATTLE OF AUBURN

When Gen. Robert E. Lee put the Army of Northern Virginia in motion on Thursday, October 8, 1863, he intended to turn the right flank of Maj. Gen. George G. Meade's Army of the Potomac, compelling Meade to face him and, Lee hoped, offer him battle in the open. Lee's strategy depended on secrecy and speed.

Secrecy failed him from the start, and slowness plagued both armies. Union spies watched Lt. Gen. A. P. Hill's Third Army Corps march north from Orange Court House through Madison Court House and Lt. Gen. Richard S. Ewell's Second Army Corps follow. Within hours Meade's army was on alert and ready to march, although at first the Federals were uncertain whether

Lee was heading for northern Virginia or back toward Richmond. Meade provided for either eventuality by ordering spoiling attacks and shifting units around.

Lee left Maj. Gen. Fitzhugh Lee's three-brigade cavalry division and three infantry brigades to guard the Rapidan River fords. Maj. Gen. J. E. B. Stuart's Confederate cavalry corps struck the Union right flank at James City (present-day Leon) on October 10, thus convincing Meade that Lee's objective was either northern Virginia or the Shenandoah Valley. Meade ordered his army to withdraw successively from the Rapidan and Rappahannock River lines and march to Centreville along the Orange & Alexandria Railroad right-of-way, from where Meade could either defend Washington or sally forth to the Valley.

The two armies marched parallel to each other, with Lee's along the Warrenton and Alexandria Turnpike and Meade's along the railroad to the south. Neither commander was certain of the other's location, and both generals sent their cavalry out to discover and harass the enemy's columns.

On Tuesday, October 13, Lee ordered Stuart to find the Federal left flank—the rear of Meade's army. At about 10 A.M., Stuart sent Brig. Gen. Lunsford L. Lomax's brigade south on the Dumfries and Saint Stephen's Roads (present-day Rtes. 605 and 667) from Warrenton. An hour later Stuart followed with two brigades from Maj. Gen. Wade Hampton's division, Col. Oliver R. Funsten's and Brig. Gen. James B. Gordon's.

Lomax stopped at Auburn, a crossroads hamlet, to wait for Stuart and scout the surrounding countryside. The terrain was rolling and wooded, with several steep ridges and ravines; the principal watercourse, Cedar Run, flowed south through Auburn between Saint Stephen's Road and the spur line to the west.

View north from U.S. position near Auburn.

VIRGINIA DEPARTMENT OF HISTORIC RESOURCES, JOHN S. SALMON

Some of Lomax's scouts rode northeast to Saint Stephen's Episcopal Church and then turned on the Bastable's Mill Road. At Warrenton Junction they found Brig. Gen. John Buford's Federal cavalry division, which was guarding the army's principal wagon train spread between the junction and Catlett's Station. None of the scouts rode west on the Old Carolina Road (Rte. 602) to Three Mile Station (today's Casanova) and so did not observe the Union II and III Corps there, as well as Brig. Gen. David M. Gregg's and Brig. Gen. H. Judson Kilpatrick's cavalry divisions, marching toward Auburn.

When Meade changed the route and order of his army's march, he inadvertently caused chaos. As the soldiers maneuvered from one road to another, some of them had to halt and wait for others to cross their paths. Gaps developed between corps that allowed Stuart and his cavalry to pass through and then get caught between columns as the army moved on and the gaps shifted eastward.

Stuart arrived at Auburn at about 1 P.M. He left Lomax to guard Auburn and rode south to reconnoiter Catlett's Station before attacking the wagons there. He concealed two brigades at Saint Stephen's Church and ordered his aide, Capt. William W. Blackford, to scout Three Mile Station with a small escort.

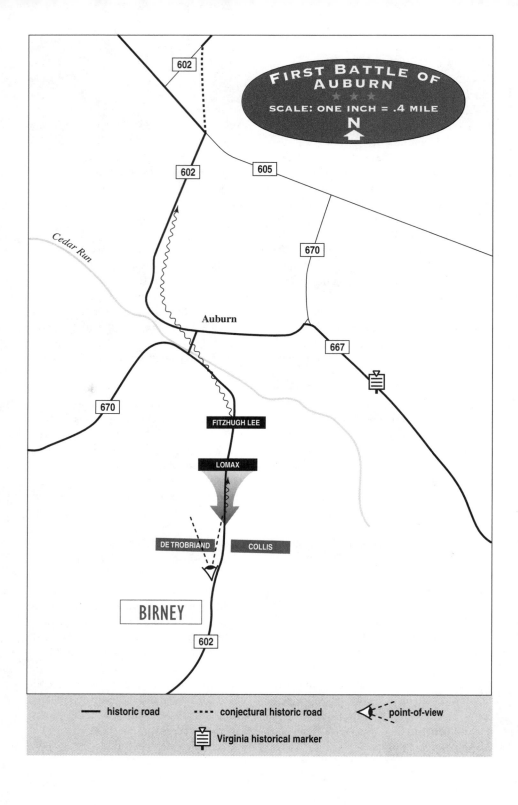

FIRST BATTLE OF
AUBURN
★ ★ ★
SCALE: ONE INCH = .4 MILE
N

602

602

605

670

Cedar Run

Auburn

667

670

FITZHUGH LEE

LOMAX

DE TROBRIAND

COLLIS

BIRNEY

602

——— historic road   ---- conjectural historic road   ◀ point-of-view

Virginia historical marker

Blackford got lost. Stuart, awed by the size of the wagon train, wrote a midafternoon dispatch to Fitz Lee requesting his aid in the attack. Lee left the Warrenton area with his cavalry brigades at about 4 P.M. and retraced Stuart's route to join him at Auburn. Stuart also wrote a message to Robert E. Lee at 3:30 P.M. and entrusted it to an aide, who galloped back toward Warrenton by way of Auburn. He approached Auburn at about 4:15 P.M., just as the shooting started.

Two Union corps marched past Three Mile Station toward Auburn on the Old Carolina Road. Maj. Gen. William H. French and III Corps led the way, with II Corps and Brig. Gen. Gouverneur K. Warren following. French, a man of legendary incompetence and slowness, delayed the army's march by stumbling down the wrong roads. Late in the afternoon, the vanguard of III Corps walked into an engagement at Auburn.

Ordinarily, cavalry would have been at the head of the Union column, but French had ordered Kilpatrick to patrol to the north to guard the infantry's left flank. French himself rode at the head of the corps, and he and his staff fired their revolvers at the Confederates. Maj. Gen. David B. Birney's division led the column, and his first brigade, under Col. Charles H. T. Collis, deployed to the right of the road while the third under Col. Phillipe Régis de Trobriand formed to the left. Both sides brought up artillery, and when Lomax charged the Federal line, a barrage of canister stopped his attack and drove him back.

This initial engagement lasted half an hour and ended about the time Fitz Lee rode in from Warrenton. When he found that he was facing an infantry corps, Lee ordered a withdrawal to Warrenton.

Blackford, meanwhile, had discovered his error and notified Stuart of the Federal presence. Stuart then rode back to Saint Stephen's Church, gathered the two brigades there, and trotted north to Auburn. He was trapped between two marching columns of the Army of the Potomac. There was no time for escape before he was cut off from the roads to Warrenton. Likewise, he could not move south without encountering the Union wagon train. What had been Stuart's target was now a wall blocking his movement. All he could do was hide, send word to Lee, and pray not to be discovered until reinforcements arrived.

Stuart concealed his two brigades—some 3,000 men with their horses—five ordnance wagons, and seven pieces of artillery in a wooded ravine just east of Auburn. About 9:30 P.M., when it was fully dark, half a dozen men dressed in captured Federal uniforms crept out of the ravine and began to pick their way through French's column, marching by just half a mile west. If captured, they would have been executed as spies, but one by one they made it to Warrenton.

The first scout to arrive reported to Lee, who issued orders for Ewell's corps to march at dawn to Auburn and rescue the cavalrymen. Back at Auburn, Stuart spent a sleepless night with Warren's II Corps bivouacked within 300 yards of his hiding place. Although he would try to wait until he heard Ewell's opening shots, Stuart would break out soon after dawn. The night passed slowly.

The first action at Auburn resulted in about fifty casualties on both sides. It was a minor engagement, remarkable mainly for the fact that it ended with Stuart trapped in the middle of the Union army.

Most of the terrain, road networks, and countryside around Auburn remain undeveloped. The routes of march and the site of the engagement are easily discernable. ∎

SECOND BATTLE OF AUBURN

Wednesday morning, October 14, 1863, found Maj. Gen. J. E. B. Stuart and two of his cavalry brigades trapped among enemy columns near Auburn. To the south was the Federal wagon train guarded by Brig. Gen. John Buford's cavalry division. To the north, between Stuart and the Army of Northern Virginia, Maj. Gen. William H. French's III Corps had spent much of the night marching by on the Old Carolina Road (present-day Rte. 602). To the west, Brig. Gen. Gouverneur K. Warren's II Corps—the rear of Maj. Gen. George G. Meade's Army of the Potomac—had bivouacked.

Theoretically, if II Corps did not discover Stuart in his concealed position just off the Old Carolina and Saint Stephen's (Rte. 667) Roads, the Confederate cavalry chief could escape unharmed. With daylight, however, that likelihood was negligible, as Federal stragglers and patrols roamed around the main line of march. Stuart would have to fight his way out, he hoped with help from Gen. Robert E. Lee.

Meanwhile, Lt. Gen. Richard S. Ewell and his corps had been ordered to march at dawn to Stuart's rescue. When the sun rose, they and Maj. Gen. Jubal A. Early's infantry division took the Double Poplars Road (Rte. 670) accompanied by Brig. Gen. Fitzhugh Lee's cavalry division, while Maj. Gen. Robert E. Rodes's division marched down the Dumfries Road (Rte. 605).

Knowing that Lee was in the area, Warren had decided to camp for the night rather than risk blundering into enemy lines by marching down unfamiliar roads in the dark. For his soldiers, the early morning meant breaking camp and resuming the march to Auburn.

The corps's three divisions, spread out over several miles of the Old Carolina Road southwest of Auburn toward Three Mile Station (Casanova), included Brig. Gen. John C. Caldwell's, Brig. Gen. Alexander Hays's, and Brig. Gen. Alexander S. Webb's. Col. Samuel S. Carroll's brigade was detached from Webb's division to guard the corps wagon train at the station. Brig. Gen. David M. Gregg's cavalry division protected the corps's route of march, with the 10th New York Regiment stationed almost two miles northwest of Auburn. Col. John P. Taylor's brigade covered both the Old Carolina Road to Three Mile Station and the Double Poplars Road toward Warrenton.

At about 3 A.M., Carroll began escorting the two-mile-long wagon train toward Auburn on the Old Carolina Road. Once he secured the crossing at Cedar Run just west of the hamlet, the remainder of War-

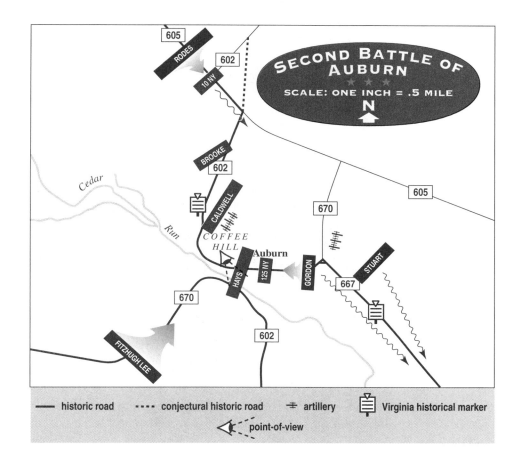

historic road ···· conjectural historic road ⚏ artillery 📷 Virginia historical marker

◁ point-of-view

ren's corps would march across the bridge and continue on to Catlett's Station.

The passage of French's corps had churned the road to a muddy mess, and as Carroll and the wagons approached in the predawn darkness, some of the wagons and artillery caissons slid down the steep grade and overturned. Warren ordered his infantry divisions to keep moving while Carroll guarded the rear. Caldwell marched his division across the stream, where he deployed his brigades on a hill to guard the bridge and road while the other divisions and the wagons continued to Catlett's Station. Since Caldwell's men would be stopping for a while, many of them lit campfires for coffee and breakfast.

DIRECTIONS: I-95 Exit 133 (U.S. Rte. 17 North, Warrenton), n. on U.S. Rte. 17 about 27 miles to intersection with U.S. Rtes. 15/29 at Opal; n. (right) on U.S. Rtes. 15/29 4.6 miles to U.S. Rtes. 15/17/29 Bus.; stay on U.S. Rte. 17 North (Washington, DC), 2.3 miles to U.S. Rtes. 15/29 North (Leesburg, Washington); continue on U.S. Rtes. 15/29 North 1.8 miles to Rte. 605 (Dumfries Rd.); e. (right) on Rte. 605 4 miles to Rte. 602 (Rogues Rd.); s. (right) on Rte. 602 .7 mile to state historical marker CL-9, Battle of Coffee Hill; continue .3 mile to stop sign at Rte. 670 (Old Auburn Rd.); e. (straight) on Rte. 670 .5 mile to Rte. 667 (Old Dumfries Rd.); s.e. (right) on Rte. 667 .25 mile to Pembridge Lane on left (Stuart's ravine) and state historical marker CL-8, Stuart's Bivouac; return to stop sign at Rtes. 670 and 602; n. (right) on Rte. 602 and return to U.S. Rtes. 17/29 by Rtes. 602 and 605.

House and mill at Auburn, drawn shortly after engagement and Stuart's escape. VIRGINIA HISTORICAL SOCIETY, RICHMOND, VA.

Most of Caldwell's division formed a line facing northwest, toward Warrenton. In front of the line rode the 10th New York cavalry vedettes. At about 6:15 A.M., at full light, the advance of Ewell's corps (Rodes's division) approached the Federal vedettes. Fifteen minutes later the opposing skirmish lines clashed, and the sound of gunfire carried back to the Cedar Creek bridge, where Hays's division was crossing, and half a mile farther east to the ravine where Stuart and his men stood waiting. Stuart, reconnoitering quietly, had spotted Caldwell's men on what the Federals would ever after call Coffee Hill and posted the seven guns of Maj. Robert F. Beckham's Horse Artillery on a height some 800 yards east. Hearing gunshots in the distance, Stuart ordered Beckham to open fire on Coffee Hill.

The Confederate artillery barrage caught Caldwell's men by surprise. However, the officers quickly turned their artillery batteries around to face the new threat. Soon nineteen Union guns dueled Stuart's seven, and Hays's division deployed to attack the horse artillery. Caldwell moved his men to the reverse

slope of Coffee Hill, at once protecting them from Beckham's guns and positioning them to confront Ewell.

Hays ordered Brig. Gen. Joshua T. Owen to deploy the 125th New York Infantry Regiment as skirmishers on the Saint Stephen's Road and advance with the rest of his brigade toward Stuart's guns. Stuart saw them coming just as he ordered Beckham to limber up his guns and fall back. To buy time for Beckham, Stuart pushed forward Col. Oliver R. Funsten's brigade as dismounted skirmishers and ordered Brig. Gen. James B. Gordon to charge the oncoming Federals.

Gordon charged with part of his brigade, and the New Yorkers fell back. Owen quickly formed a stronger skirmish line with the 126th New York to the right (south) of the road and part of the 125th to the left. He also deployed the 8th and 111th New York as well as the rest of the 125th north of the road on a hill behind the skirmishers.

While the New Yorkers took their positions, Stuart instructed Gordon to make one more charge while he started the rest of his command southeast. Gordon led Col.

Thomas Ruffin and his 1st North Carolina Regiment against Owen's line. The cost was high—Gordon was wounded, while Ruffin was shot and taken prisoner—but the charge worked, and Stuart raced away from Auburn. Soon he and his command, with Ruffin's regiment following, galloped across Cedar Run and north to Double Poplars Road, where he found Early and Fitzhugh Lee.

Soon after Stuart's escape, Ewell's part of the engagement resumed in earnest with increased skirmishing. As Ewell's lead division, Rodes's, closed in on Coffee Hill from the northwest, the artillerymen there who had been dueling with Stuart's Horse Artillery to the southeast received the command to turn their cannons around, thus reversing to face Rodes.

Meanwhile, Hays marched south on the Saint Stephen's Road. Warren's orders, after all, were to march to Catlett's Station and up the Orange & Alexandria Railroad, not to engage the enemy at Auburn. Soon all of the corps and its wagons had passed through Auburn except for Caldwell's division atop Coffee Hill covering the withdrawal, and Gregg's troopers guarding Double Poplar Road.

Rodes pressed his attack down Dumfries Road between 8 and 9 A.M., and Early and Fitz Lee did likewise on Double Poplar Road. The Coffee Hill batteries shelled the Confederate skirmish lines, while Ewell's artillery commander deployed his guns in response. By 10 A.M. both sides were locked in an artillery duel that lasted for an hour, providing cover for the last of the Federal infantry and cavalry to leave for Catlett's Station.

Ewell likewise began extracting his corps, although Rodes pursued the Federals a short distance down Saint Stephen's Road. Ewell, like Warren, had other orders for the day. Neither side had looked for a battle at Auburn. By 1 P.M. Ewell's corps was marching northeast toward Greenwich, while Warren's had reached Catlett's Station and prepared for the next leg of its march, which would take it northeast to Bristoe Station. The second engagement at Auburn cost the combatants little more than a hundred casualties.

Most of the terrain, road networks, and countryside around Auburn remain undeveloped. The routes of march, Stuart's hiding place, and the sites of the engagements are easily discernable. ■

BRISTOE STATION

While Lt. Gen. Richard S. Ewell's corps hurried to Auburn on the morning of Wednesday, October 14, 1863, to rescue Maj. Gen. J. E. B. Stuart and his cavalrymen, Lt. Gen. A. P. Hill's corps continued its eastward march. Gen. Robert E. Lee had ordered Hill to pursue Maj. Gen. George G. Meade's retreating Army of the Potomac and attack its rear. Lee and Ewell would catch up later and, once the Army of Northern Virginia was reunited, fight and crush Meade's force.

Hill's corps left its bivouac and headed east on the Warrenton and Alexandria Turnpike (present-day U.S. Rte. 29). By 8:30 A.M. the front of the column had reached New Baltimore, five miles east of Warrenton. There Hill received word of Federal troop movements in the area. One report had the enemy's wagons trundling north toward the turnpike on a road (Rte. 604) from Greenwich that intersected the highway just east of Buckland Mills. Hill ordered Maj. Gen. Richard H. Anderson's infantry division to continue on the turnpike to intercept the enemy column near

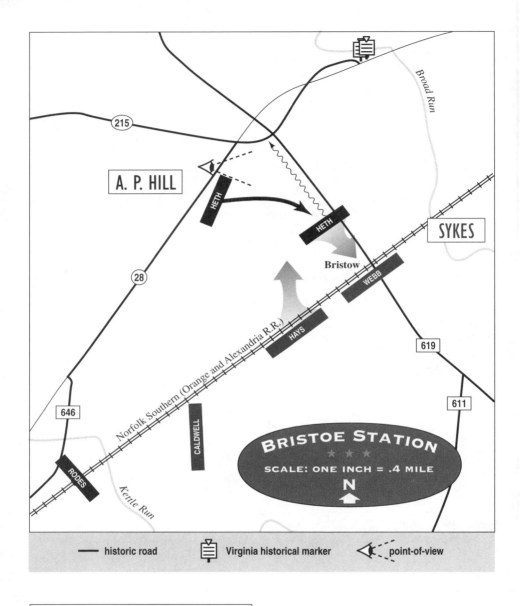

215

A. P. HILL

HETH

HETH

SYKES

Bristow

WEBB

HAYS

Broad Run

28

Norfolk Southern (Orange and Alexandria R.R.)

619

646

611

CALDWELL

RODES

Kettle Run

BRISTOE STATION
★ ★ ★
SCALE: ONE INCH = .4 MILE
N

—— historic road   Virginia historical marker   point-of-view

DIRECTIONS: I-66 Exit 43A (U.S. Rte. 29 South, Gainesville-Warrenton), s. on U.S. Rte. 29 about .4 mile to Rte. 619 (Linton Hall Rd.); s.e. (left) on Rte. 619 6 miles to Rte. 28; cross Rte. 28 on Rte. 619 (Bristow Rd.) .8 mile to Norfolk Southern track; continue on Rte. 619 .4 mile to New Hope Baptist Church on left at top of hill; return to State Rte. 28; e. (right) on State Rte. 28 .5 mile to state historical markers G-19, Action at Bristoe Station, and G-20, Battle of Bristoe Station; continue e. to I-66.

the mills, and Maj. Gen. Henry Heth's and Maj. Gen. Cadmus Wilcox's divisions down the road from New Baltimore to Greenwich (Rtes. 600 and 215), thereby striking the Federals front and rear simultaneously and destroying them.

Hill's information, it turned out, was false. The rumble Hill had heard was not wagons but cavalry—Brig. Gen. H. Judson

Kilpatrick and his division. Fitz Lee attacked Kilpatrick and spent most of the rest of the day pushing him toward Gainesville. Consequently, Hill lacked his principal reconnaissance arm as he led his infantry eastward.

Hill reached Greenwich at about 10 A.M. and found the still-smoldering campfires left by French's corps. From supplies and clothing abandoned by the retreating Federals, it was clear that French had marched southeast on the road to Bristoe Station (Rte. 215) on the Orange & Alexandria Railroad. Hill's corps set off in pursuit.

Soon Hill's skirmishers encountered stragglers from French's corps, who confirmed that the Federals were in retreat. A couple of miles later, they encountered stiff resistance in the form of French's rear guard, which slowed the Confederate advance and bought time for the rest of the Union corps to cross over Broad Run at Milford, a hamlet just northeast of Bristoe Station.

Brig. Gen. Gouverneur K. Warren and his II Corps formed the rear of the Federal column closest to the railroad. At noon Warren still occupied Catlett's Station, about eight miles southwest of Bristoe Station, while the head of the line was well beyond Bristoe, Meade's noontime headquarters. Meade wired Warren to urge him to close up the column by making haste to Bristoe Station, where only one corps— Maj. Gen. George Sykes's—remained to cross Broad Run. Meade ordered Sykes to wait until Warren was in sight after he crossed, so he could come to Warren's assistance if he was attacked.

Warren marched up the railroad right-of-way with Brig. Gen. Alexander S. Webb's division on the north side of the tracks, Brig. Gen. Alexander Hays's on the south side, and Caldwell behind the wagons and ambulances on both sides. Two

Northern Virginia sprawl may soon engulf the Bristoe Station battlefield. VIRGINIA DEPARTMENT OF HISTORIC RESOURCES, JOHN S. SALMON

brigades from Brig. Gen. David M. Gregg's cavalry division guarded Warren's left and rear.

Hill approached Bristoe Station from the northwest with Heth's division in the lead (including Brig. Gen. John R. Cooke's unattached brigade), Wilcox's following, and Anderson's coming down a different road. A mile-wide gap existed between Heth and Wilcox, and Anderson was still three or four miles away as Hill neared the station.

At about 1:30 P.M. an impatient Sykes believed an erroneous report that the head of Warren's column was drawing near. He ordered his rear guard to continue to Centreville. At the same time, Heth and Hill mounted a rise north of the station that gave them a view of the Broad Run bridge and the fields beyond, which were full of Union soldiers. Observing the last of Sykes's men crossing the bridge, Hill concluded that he had found the rear of Meade's army and decided to attack.

Hill ordered Heth forward, and Heth deployed Cooke's brigade just north of the tracks on the right, Brig. Gen. William W. Kirkland's on the left, Brig. Gen. Henry H. Walker's about a hundred yards behind Kirkland, and Brig. Gen. Joseph R. Davis's and Brig. Gen. James J. Archer's brigades behind Walker in reserve. The Confederates faced east—unfortunately for them not in the direction of Warren's approach. As Heth's division advanced, a battery from Maj. William T. Poague's Artillery Battalion opened on the Federals from a hill. It was 2 P.M.

At the same time, an officer on Cooke's right reported seeing Federal units by the tracks on the west side of Broad Run, where they were not supposed to be. Cooke informed Hill, who ordered him to continue his attack as Anderson would arrive soon. Both Hill and Cooke assumed that the Union force was a small rear guard; in fact, it was the head of Warren's column, the lead regiments in Webb's division.

Webb had been marching some distance west of Bristoe Station. From high ground Webb could see Heth's division preparing to attack. He sent a regiment through pine woods to strike Heth's right flank, deployed an artillery battery below him on the slope of the hill (it soon shifted to another hill across Broad Run), and ordered the rest of the brigade up to the elevated rail bed, which provided concealment as well as a ready-made fortification, just west of the railroad bridge over Broad Run.

Webb's men poured a heavy skirmish fire into Heth's flank over the next half hour. More of Warren's corps marched up to lengthen and strengthen the line behind the tracks, shielded from Hill's view by the elevated bed, the rolling terrain, and thickets of scrub pine. Additional Union batteries occupied positions overlooking the field. By 2:45 P.M. the roar of gunfire had become deafening as Cooke led the Confederate attack against what he thought was a strong skirmish line behind the railroad; he also thought that the main Union force was concealed on the reverse slope of Webb's ridge. At about 3 P.M., as his and Kirkland's brigades closed on the railroad, he discovered his mistake.

The Federal fire devastated the attacking Confederates. Cooke himself fell wounded with a bullet through his leg. Despite assistance from Anderson's brigades, the attack was a bloody failure, and within half an hour the Confederate survivors fell back to regroup.

Over the next two hours most of the Army of Northern Virginia assembled on the field as the rest of Hill's corps arrived, and then Ewell's. Across the tracks, Warren extended his front two miles west to Kettle Run, a tributary of Broad Run. As the afternoon wore on he became increasingly concerned that his line, thin as it was, would not withstand a concerted attack, and that his left might be outflanked. But an assault never came. Darkness fell at last, and Warren withdrew east of Broad Run during the night.

Lee arrived on the battlefield just before sunset, and Hill reported his failure. The two generals met again the next morning to survey the wreckage and the dead. Southern newspapers later excoriated Hill, and his reputation never recovered. The casualties amounted to 1,980, all but about 550 of them Confederate.

Most of the Bristoe Station battlefield remains intact, especially the historic road network, the railroad bed, and the patterns of open and wooded land. Some residential development has taken place along the roads, however, and much more is planned around and on the battlefield. Although preservation efforts have begun, most of the battlefield is at risk. ■

BUCKLAND MILLS

After the disaster at Bristoe Station on October 14, 1863, Gen. Robert E. Lee spent the next several days trying to salvage his campaign. Finding the Union defenses at Centreville too strong to attack, Lee decided to withdraw across the Rappahannock River to Culpeper County and encamp for the winter.

Maj. Gen. J. E. B. Stuart, screening the Confederate army's march from the Federals, and Lt. Gen. Richard S. Ewell had some of their men tear up the Orange & Alexandria Railroad tracks to hamper the Union army while Lee withdrew to Rappahannock Station and crossed the river into Culpeper County about noon on Sunday, October 18. Early that morning Stuart was pushed west by Brig. Gen. H. Judson Kilpatrick's reconnaissance to Groveton and Haymarket. By dark Stuart, commanding Maj. Gen. Wade Hampton's divi-

sion, faced Brig. Gen. George A. Custer's brigade and part of Brig. Gen. Henry E. Davies's east of Gainesville.

The next morning, Maj. Gen. Alfred Pleasonton, head of the Union cavalry corps, ordered Kilpatrick to ride southwest along the Warrenton and Alexandria

DIRECTIONS: I-95 Exit 133 (U.S. Rte. 17 North, Warrenton), n. on U.S. Rte. 17 about 27 miles to intersection with U.S. Rtes. 15/29 at Opal; n. (right) on U.S. Rtes. 15/29 4.6 miles to U.S. Rtes. 15/17/29 Bus.; stay on U.S. Rte. 17 North (Washington, DC), 2.3 miles to U.S. Rtes. 15/29 North (Leesburg, Washington); continue on U.S. Rtes. 15/29 North about 1.2 miles to Virginia Civil War Trails marker in Park & Ride lot on n. side of highway; continue 5.3 miles to Rte. 215 (Vint Hill Rd.); continue on U.S. Rtes. 15/29 North .9 mile to U.S. Rte. 15; return on U.S. Rtes. 15/29 North to Rte. 215; s. (left) on Rte. 215 .3 mile to Custer's position; continue on Rte. 215 .4 mile farther to Fitzhugh Lee's position (left-hand bend in road); return to U.S. Rtes. 15/29.

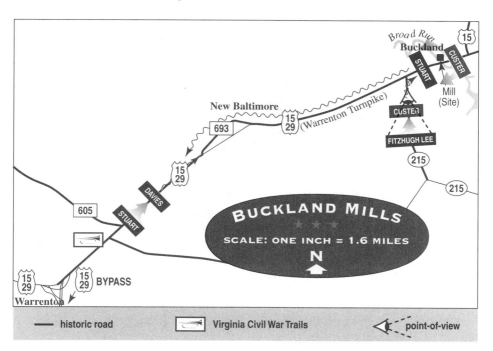

View south along Fitzhugh Lee's route of attack. VIRGINIA DEPARTMENT OF HISTORIC RESOURCES, JOHN S. SALMON

noon. He ordered Custer to follow as they pursued Stuart, but instead Custer rested his men and horses and allowed them to eat. About a mile west of Broad Run, after encountering Confederate skirmishers, Davies left a small force to guard the crossroads and pressed on until he came to Chestnut Hill, about two and a half miles east of Warrenton, at 3:30 P.M. Suddenly he heard cannons firing behind him and realized that Custer was under attack.

Fitz Lee had struck Custer on his left flank, at the intersection of the turnpike and the road to Greenwich (Rte. 215). Recovering quickly from the initial shock, Custer reformed his line and fell back to the Broad Run bridge. He soon withdrew across the bridge to the east bank, then retreated to Gainesville with Lee in pursuit.

Back at Chestnut Hill, Stuart charged as Davies and Kilpatrick turned back toward Broad Run, now some five and a half miles away. Davies organized effective rearguard actions until word reached him that the Broad Run bridge was in Confederate hands. Kilpatrick then divided his command, sending part of it north to Thoroughfare Gap with the wagons and artillery while the remainder continued its fighting retreat east on the turnpike. At last, however, Davies told every man to save himself, and a wild flight began. Many Union cavalrymen became prisoners; others escaped by fording Broad Run north of the bridge. Kilpatrick had his horse killed under him but quickly remounted. The two sides lost about 230 men between them, mostly captured Federals.

Stuart crossed the Rappahannock River at Fauquier White Sulphur Springs the next morning to join the rest of the Army of Northern Virginia. Despite the destruction of the Orange & Alexandria Railroad, the line soon was repaired by the indefatigable U.S. Military Railroads Construction Corps, the creation of superintendent Her-

Turnpike to Warrenton. Kilpatrick found Stuart gone from his front; scouting reports suggested that he would have little opposition en route to his objective.

In fact, Stuart had withdrawn down the turnpike to the ruined bridge over Broad Run at Buckland Mills. He posted sharpshooters as well as artillery on the west bank of the rain-swollen creek and sent orders to Maj. Gen. Fitzhugh Lee, south of Auburn, to cover his right flank with his division. Lee started north toward Stuart.

Early in the morning, Custer led Kilpatrick's advance down the turnpike. Confronted at Broad Run by Stuart's men on the opposite bank, Custer returned fire and finally bridged the stream on Stuart's right and left flanks. Stuart fell back fighting toward Warrenton.

Kilpatrick, with Davies's first brigade, arrived at Buckland Mills shortly after

man Haupt. For the remainder of October and early November the two armies faced each other across the river, familiar terrain for both combatants.

Most of the Buckland Mills battlefield remains undeveloped, although the widening of U.S. Rte. 29, the construction of Lake Manassas, and the building of new roads and houses have impinged on the edges of the site. The visitor can still follow the routes of advance and retreat on the public roads, however, and much of the area remains in farms and woodlands. ■

RAPPAHANNOCK STATION

To keep Maj. Gen. George G. Meade, commander of the Army of the Potomac, at arm's length and to encourage him to abandon the pursuit and instead encamp at Centreville for the winter, Gen. Robert E. Lee's Army of Northern Virginia destroyed railroad track as it retreated after the defeat at Bristoe Station on October 14, 1863. The Confederates soon crossed the Rappahannock River and held the important fords and bridges between it and the Union army, including Kelly's Ford and the site of the demolished railroad bridge near Rappahannock Station, about four miles downstream. The Union commander decided to force his way across at the ford and bridge site simultaneously, but Lee soon discerned Meade's plans and devised a strategy to counter them. He would allow Meade to cross at Kelly's Ford but hold him back at Rappahannock Station; once Meade's force was split by the river, Lee would strike at the ford.

On Saturday, November 7, Meade launched his attack. Maj. Gen. William H. French's III Corps assaulted at Kelly's Ford while Maj. Gen. John Sedgwick's VI Corps, supported by Maj. Gen. George Sykes's V Corps, threatened the bridge site near Rappahannock Station. At Kelly's

C.S.A. fortifications on the Rappahannock River. VIRGINIA HISTORICAL SOCIETY, RICHMOND, VA.

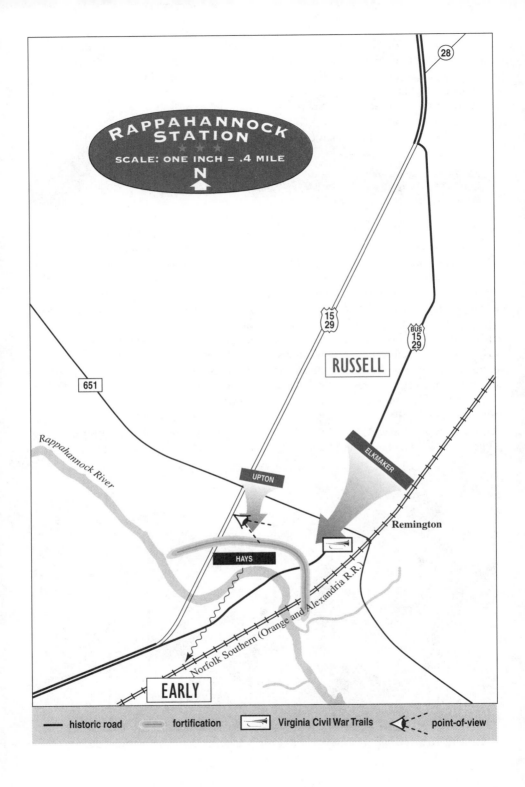

RAPPAHANNOCK STATION

SCALE: ONE INCH = .4 MILE

N

28

15
29

BUS
15
29

RUSSELL

651

Rappahannock River

ELKMAKER

UPTON

Remington

HAYS

Norfolk Southern (Orange and Alexandria R.R.)

EARLY

— historic road   fortification   Virginia Civil War Trails   point-of-view

DIRECTIONS: I-95 Exit 133 (U.S. Rte. 17 North, Warrenton), n. on U.S. Rte. 17 about 23.8 miles to Rte. 28; w. (left) on Rte. 28 2 miles to U.S. Rtes. 15/29 South; s.w. (left) on U.S. Rtes. 15/29 South 2 miles to Rte. 651 (Freemans Ford Rd.); e. (left) on Rte. 651 .6 mile to U.S. Rtes. 15/29 Bus. (Remington Rd.); s. (right) on Remington Rd. .1 mile to Virginia Civil War Trails marker on left; continue s. on Remington Rd. .8 mile over Rappahannock Bridge to U.S. Rte. 15/29.

Ford, Union artillery and sharpshooters combined effectively to blast and overwhelm the Confederate defenders there. By late afternoon French held an enclave on the west bank of the river.

Downstream at Rappahannock Station, however, Sedgwick ran into strong opposition from two brigades of Maj. Gen. Jubal A. Early's division (commanded by Brig. Gen. Harry T. Hays while Early temporarily commanded Lt. Gen. Richard S. Ewell's corps) posted in front of the earthworks that ran between Sedgwick and the river. The brigades had crossed the river on a pontoon bridge constructed just upstream from the destroyed railroad bridge. The Union general pushed the Confederates back into their works, then pounded them with artillery before launching an all-out assault. Some 2,000 of Early's men faced about 30,000 Federals.

Three hours of Union shelling failed to obliterate the Confederates or drive them from their works. As darkness fell, Sedgwick decided to make a twilight assault with infantry, assigning the task to Brig. Gen. David A. Russell's division. Such attacks succeeded rarely, so Sedgwick made his decision only after some hesitation. Lee, assuming that combat would end at nightfall, did not order that Early's infantry be reinforced.

The assault came quickly and succeeded after vicious hand-to-hand fighting. Within minutes the Federals not only had captured the eastern end of the railroad bridge site but the nearby pontoon bridge, as well, in addition to hundreds of Confederates. Across the river, Lee and Early were unaware of the desperate struggle until survivors swam the river to tell them. Early sent volunteers to burn the western end of the pontoon bridge to prevent a Federal crossing.

The Rappahannock Station engagement did not reflect well on Lee's generalship. The two sides lost a total of some 2,500 men, of whom 1,600 were captured Confederates. Worse, the Union success compelled the Army of Northern Virginia to withdraw to Orange County instead of encamping around Culpeper Court House, which passed to the Union army. Never again during the war would Lee cross the Rappahannock.

Meade's 85,000-man army moved over the river and into the former Confederate encampment between Brandy Station and Culpeper Court House. The troops soon repaired the Orange & Alexandria Railroad bridge for use in resupplying the army, as well as the half-completed huts abandoned by Lee's men, and settled in for the winter.

Although most of the Kelly's Ford segment of the battlefield remains undeveloped, road and building construction has destroyed part of the Rappahannock Bridge site. Portions of the Confederate earthworks remain on the south and north banks of the river at each place respectively, however, and the visitor can still understand the progress of the battle over the terrain. ■

Although the 85,000-man army of Maj. Gen. George G. Meade had settled in for the winter in the former Confederate encampment abandoned by Gen. Robert E. Lee's Army of Northern Virginia after November 7, 1863, important Washington politicians made it clear that the campaign season had not ended as far as they were concerned. Meade took the hint and planned an early winter offensive.

Lee's army, some 50,000 strong, was encamped from Gordonsville to Verdiersville, paralleling the Rapidan River, with Lt. Gen. A. P. Hill's corps on the left and Lt. Gen. Richard S. Ewell's (temporarily commanded by Maj. Gen. Jubal A. Early) on the right. Meade soon learned from cavalry probes that the Confederate right flank was vulnerable to attack. Meade's plan called for Maj. Gen. George Sykes and Maj. Gen. John Newton, commanding V and I Corps respectively, to cross the Rapidan River at Culpeper Mine Ford, march south to the Orange Plank Road—which ran behind Ewell's line—then turn west. Brig. Gen. Gouverneur K. Warren would lead II Corps across Germanna Ford, south to the Orange Turnpike (present-day Rte. 20)—also behind Ewell—and then west. Maj. Gen. John Sedgwick and Maj. Gen. William H. French, commanders of VI and III Corps, would cross at Jacob's Ford and drive south directly into the Confederate right flank.

Meade's advance was scheduled to begin on November 24, but heavy rain and high water persuaded him to postpone it until Thursday, November 26, Thanksgiving Day. Lee discovered the Union army's preparations and placed his troops on alert. He could use the same highways that threatened his army's flank to march men to where they were most needed.

DIRECTIONS: I-95 Exit 130B (State Rte. 3 West, Culpeper), w. on State Rte. 3 about 12.2 miles to Rte. 20; w. (left) on Rte. 20 4.8 miles to Locust Grove at Rte. 611 and state historical marker JJ-15, Robinson's Tavern; continue on Rte. 20 1.8 miles to state historical marker JJ-10, Mine Run Campaign, located just e. of Mine Run at U.S. position; continue on Rte. 20 1.7 miles to Rte. 692 (Grasty Gold Mine Rd.); s. (left) on Rte. 692 2 miles to Rte. 621 (Mine Run Rd.); e. (left) on Rte. 621 4.9 miles to Rte. 604 (Golddale Rd.); n. (left) on Rte. 604 2 miles to Rte. 611 (Golddale Rd.); n.w. (left) on Rte. 611 1.3 miles to Rte. 20; cross Rte. 20 on Rte. 611 (Zoar Rd.) 1.1 miles to Rte. 602 (Old Office Rd.); continue straight on Rte. 611 1.4 miles to Rte. 603 (Indiantown Rd.); n. (right) on Rte. 603 1.2 miles to Rte. 685 (Russel Rd.); turn around and return to Rte. 611 and Rte. 602; w. (right) on Rte. 602 (cross Mine Run at 1.7 miles; Confederate left flank earthworks visible in woods to left .65 mile past Mine Run) 3.1 miles to Rte. 692 (Burr Hill Rd.); s. (left) on Rte. 692 1.4 miles to Rte. 20; return to State Rte. 3 and I-95.

Nature's delay foreshadowed other impediments that soon befell Meade's Mine Run campaign, as it came to be called. French failed to start his march on time, then found that he was one pontoon short of a bridge to span the high water at Jacob's Ford. He also discovered that the steep, muddy south bank of the Rapidan at Jacob's Ford made it virtually impossible to get his artillery and wagons across the bridge and up the road. An exasperated Meade ordered French to cross instead at Germanna Ford. Darkness fell before all five corps had passed over the river, and reluctant to stumble through the Wilderness in the night, Meade called a halt until daylight came.

The Wilderness, seventy square miles of cut-over thickets of stumps, broken limbs, underbrush, vines, and scrub pine and oak, was a soldier's nightmare, with nearly impenetrable tangles that reduced

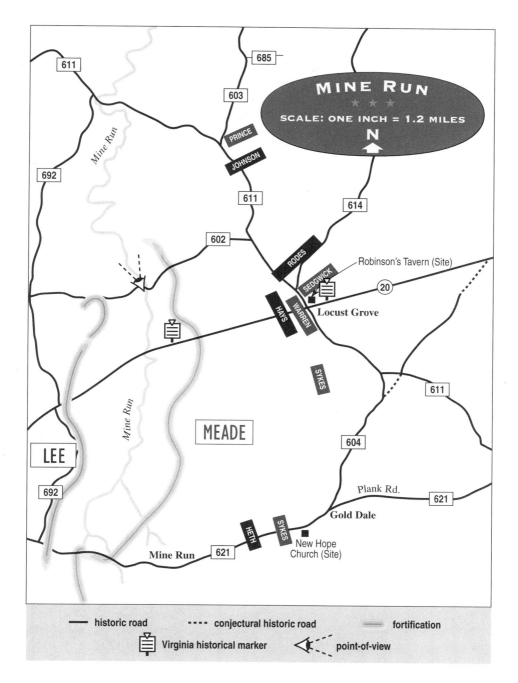

MINE RUN
★ ★ ★
SCALE: ONE INCH = 1.2 MILES
N

611

685

603

692

PRINCE

JOHNSON

611

614

602

RODES

Robinson's Tavern (Site)

SEDGWICK

20

HAYS

WARREN

Locust Grove

SYKES

611

MEADE

604

LEE

Plank Rd.

621

692

Gold Dale

HETH

SYKES

New Hope
Church (Site)

Mine Run

621

Mine Run

Mine Run

— historic road   ---- conjectural historic road   fortification

Virginia historical marker   point-of-view

visibility to inches and rendered unit cohesion in an attack almost impossible.
Meade had been there before, at the battle
of Chancellorsville, and knew that pene-

trating it would be difficult enough during
daylight and virtually suicidal at night.

Although Lee knew that Meade had
launched an attack, the same Wilderness

Mine Run, no-man's-land between Lee and Meade. VIRGINIA DEPARTMENT OF HISTORIC RESOURCES, JOHN S. SALMON

that slowed the Federals' march hid their approach from view. Early, on Lee's right flank, redeployed his corps to meet the threat he perceived to be coming from the east and north, based on the vedettes' reports. Maj. Gen. Edward "Allegheny" Johnson marched his division northeast toward the slow-moving French; the two forces collided at Payne's Farm, about halfway down the road from Jacob's Ford to the turnpike. Brig. Gen. Harry T. Hays and Maj. Gen. Robert E. Rodes encountered Warren's and Sedgwick's corps at Robinson's Tavern at about the same time. Farther south, on the Orange Plank Road (Rte. 621), Hill rushed Maj. Gen. Henry Heth's division forward to relieve Stuart and to engage the vanguard of Sykes's corps at New Hope Church (in present-day Gold Dale).

On the Union right, French stalled the Federal advance by twice ordering Brig. Gen. Henry Prince, commanding the lead division, to halt rather than push through Johnson's lines at Payne's Farm. The day dwindled into night, and the Federals went nowhere.

Lee now knew that Meade intended an attack against his army, not a flanking maneuver toward Richmond. Delighted, he saw an opportunity to crush the Army of the Potomac. After dark, he ordered his forces to fall back to the high western bank of Mine Run, a tributary of the Rapidan River, and entrench. By dawn the men had constructed imposing fortifications.

On November 28, Meade studied Lee's defenses, uncertain of his next move. Warren, positioned on the Union left, suggested a flank attack around the Confederate right, the most lightly defended part of the line. Meade agreed, and the attack was scheduled for the next day. A cavalry skirmish in Warren's rear on November 29 caused him to hesitate, however. By dusk, having determined that the engagement did not indicate a turning movement by Lee, Warren's opportunity to attack had dissipated;

the assault would occur the next morning. Hill used the respite to reinforce the Confederate right during the night, so that when Warren reexamined it after dawn, it was far more formidable.

Confederates mounted their works, which now bristled with abatis and cannons, and taunted the Federals. Warren canceled the attack.

The news reached Meade at his headquarters, and ultimately he agreed with Warren: An attack would result in a slaughter. That night Meade held a council of war and, after considering the strength of Lee's line and his own dwindling supplies, canceled the campaign and ordered his army to withdraw north across the Rapidan on the night of December 1–2.

Meanwhile Lee, who saw another Fredericksburg in the making, waited eagerly for Meade's attack. When by December 1 it did not come, he ordered his own attack for the next morning. He awoke to find Meade gone. Angry at letting the enemy get away, he ordered his men back to their former camps for the winter. Meade's army returned to Culpeper County.

The Mine Run campaign cost the Federals about 1,300 casualties and the Confederates some 700. Although Meade at first suffered heavy criticism, most members of Lincoln's administration gradually accepted his reasons for aborting the campaign. Lincoln retained him as head of the Army of the Potomac, realizing that although cautious, Meade was solid, dedicated, and especially effective in the defense. Before spring came, however, Meade would find himself under the command of a general suited to the offense: the conqueror of Vicksburg, Mississippi, Ulysses S. Grant.

Little remains of the network of fortifications along Mine Run. Many of the Union works were destroyed by the Confederates, and most of the Confederate works have been obliterated by subsequent development or may be hidden in the woods. The battle sites, such as Payne's Farm, remain intact, and a few historic structures, such as Robinson's Tavern, still stand. ■

OVERLAND CAMPAIGN, 1864

Pres. Abraham Lincoln summoned a forty-two-year-old Ohioan, Ulysses Simpson Grant, to Washington in March 1864. About five feet eight inches tall and weighing around 135 pounds, Grant was as silent as he was spare, and rather than converse, he preferred to chew on a cigar. He was a mystery to everyone who encountered him during that late winter, a bit seedy and unkempt in appearance but bearing an aura of unshakable determination.

Rumors surrounded Grant, including whispers of drunkenness and emotional instability. Yet none could deny that this obscure West Point graduate—a failed businessman who once was reduced to peddling firewood in the streets of Saint Louis—had given the Union two of its greatest victories in the West: Vicksburg and Chattanooga. The first, with the surrender of Port Hudson four days later, had secured the Mississippi River for the United States and split the Confederacy in two. The second had ensured that the vitally important rail center in east Tennessee would supply Maj. Gen. William T. Sherman's army group as he marched through northwest Georgia and on to Atlanta in 1864.

When Grant met with Lincoln on March 9, the president demonstrated his respect for his new lieutenant general's reputation and demeanor by promising to let Grant handle his own affairs. Lincoln declared his absolute confidence in him and added, "The particulars of your plans I neither know nor seek to know." Lincoln went on to offer Grant, now general-in-chief of the Federal armies, every assistance at the government's disposal to help him succeed.

Lincoln's willingness not to rein in Grant may have been due to the simplicity of the general's plan for the spring campaign: Attack everywhere at once, and keep attacking until the Confederate armies were defeated. He would pit Sherman against Gen. Joseph E. Johnston in the Deep South and Maj. Gen. George G. Meade against Lee in Virginia. His goal would be to destroy the opposing armies, not to capture and hold cities or territory. Grant himself would accompany Meade and the Army of the Potomac.

Grant's decision to remain in Virginia perhaps arose in part from the confidence he felt in his old friend Sherman's ability to command independently. Grant already knew the western armies and their officers intimately; rumor had it that he thought them superior to the eastern armies. In addition, Grant knew of Meade's reputation as a dedicated but plodding leader who lacked aggressiveness, and no doubt thought he could supply the deficiency. On March 10, Grant arrived at Brandy Station to confer with Meade, who had steeled himself to be replaced. Instead, Grant confirmed him in his position as commander of the Army of the Potomac.

How the monosyllabic, dour Grant could charm and win over the prickly, sarcastic Meade is one of the war's great mysteries, but he did—at least temporarily. The

OVERLAND CAMPAIGN

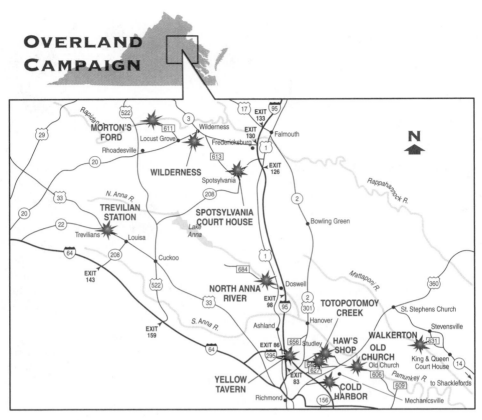

soldiers were less sure. To them he looked ordinary, indeed—mud-spattered, careless of his appearance—not like the commanding sort of general that the Army of the Potomac was used to, even astride Cincinnati, a magnificent bay Thoroughbred. Furthermore, he had paid little attention to the welcoming band at the station. Although the troops did not know it, Grant was tone deaf. He admitted that he could recognize only two tunes. One of them was "Yankee Doodle," and the other wasn't.

Lee's appearance contrasted sharply with Grant's. Almost four inches taller (just under six feet), Lee looked handsome with his well-groomed gray hair and beard and made a striking and dignified appearance in his spotless gray uniform, especially when mounted on his gray horse, Traveller. But both men shared certain

traits, however different their appearance. Each was determined and aggressive. Neither would quit until circumstances forced them to do so.

Each general also rode at the head of a great army. Lee's, the Army of Northern Virginia, numbered about 60,000. Many of the men were experienced, battle-hardened veterans with unshakable confidence in themselves and in Lee. They had fought the Army of the Potomac time and time again over three years and, except at Gettysburg, had either beaten it or fought it to a draw despite always being outnumbered. Now, in the spring of 1864, with their numbers down and their supplies short, they still had each other and Lee, a lethal combination. Devotion and aggression could be worth divisions.

But would they be enough? Meade's

army, with Maj. Gen. Ambrose E. Burnside's IX Corps (which until the fourth week of May reported directly to Grant), contained some 120,000 men, a two-to-one advantage. Many of the soldiers, however, were new, foreign-born recruits; some spoke no English. And despite the army's superiority in numbers and supplies, serious self-doubts plagued its officers. Discounting the victory in Pennsylvania the year before, many of them doubted that they would meet with easy success on Lee's home ground.

Other Federal officers, however, realized that their new commander had brought a different attitude with him to the Army of the Potomac. A defeat or two or ten would not deter him.

The opposing armies were organized along similar lines. The Army of the Potomac initially contained three infantry corps, each with three or four divisions, as well as the remnants of I Corps, commanded by Maj. Gen. John Newton, which was disbanded on March 23, 1864, and absorbed by V Corps. Maj. Gen. Winfield Scott Hancock commanded II Corps, and Brig. Gen. Francis C. Barlow led the 1st Division, Brig. Gen. John Gibbon the 2nd, Maj. Gen. David B. Birney the 3rd, and Brig. Gen. Gershom Mott the 4th, with Col. John C. Tidball in charge of the artillery brigade. Maj. Gen. Gouverneur K. Warren led V Corps, which contained Brig. Gen. Charles Griffin's 1st Division, Brig. Gen. John C. Robinson's 2nd, Brig. Gen. Samuel W. Crawford's 3rd, Brig. Gen. James S. Wadsworth's 4th, and Col. Charles S. Wainwright's artillery brigade. Maj. Gen. John Sedgwick commanded VI Corps, and the 1st Division was led by Brig. Gen. Horatio G. Wright, the 2nd by Brig. Gen. George W. Getty, the 3rd by Brig. Gen. James B. Ricketts, and the artillery brigade by Col. Charles H. Tompkins. Maj. Gen. Ambrose E. Burnside led

IX Corps, which included Brig. Gen. Thomas G. Stevenson's 1st Division, Brig. Gen. Robert B. Potter's 2nd, Brig. Gen. Orlando B. Willcox's 3rd, and Brig. Gen. Edward Ferrero's 4th (Ferrero's division, which was not engaged, contained six regiments of United States Colored Troops). Maj. Gen. Philip H. Sheridan, who Grant brought with him from the western army, commanded the cavalry corps. It contained three divisions, led respectively by Brig. Gen. Alfred T. A. Torbert, Brig. Gen. David M. Gregg, and Brig. Gen. James H. Wilson.

Three infantry corps, commanded by Lt. Gen. James Longstreet, Lt. Gen. Richard S. Ewell, and Lt. Gen. A. P. Hill, and Maj. Gen. J. E. B. Stuart's cavalry corps comprised the Army of Northern Virginia. Each corps contained three divisions and an artillery brigade. Longstreet's First Corps included divisions commanded by Brig. Gen. Joseph B. Kershaw, Maj. Gen. Charles W. Field, and Maj. Gen. George E. Pickett, and Brig. Gen. E. Porter Alexander's artillery brigade. Ewell's Second Corps contained the divisions of Maj. Gen. Jubal A. Early, Maj. Gen. Edward "Allegheny" Johnson, and Maj. Gen. Robert E. Rodes as well as the artillery brigade of Brig. Gen. Armistead L. Long. The divisions in Hill's Third Corps were commanded by Maj. Gen. Richard H. Anderson, Maj. Gen. Henry Heth, and Maj. Gen. Cadmus M. Wilcox, while Col. Reuben L. Walker led the artillery brigade. Stuart's cavalry divisions were led by Maj. Gen. Wade Hampton, Maj. Gen. Fitzhugh Lee, and Maj. Gen. William H. F. "Rooney" Lee; Maj. Robert F. Chew commanded Stuart's Horse Artillery.

For most of the winter, the armies had faced each other across the Rapidan River while each one trained, resupplied, and conducted limited operations. Perhaps the boredom of camp life—and the knowledge that the war was about to enter its third year—encouraged dreamers and schemers in the Union army to concoct plans to capture or raid Richmond.

In February 1864, Maj. Gen. Benjamin F. Butler requested approval from Washington for a surprise raid up the Peninsula to Richmond. Butler reasoned that because recent operations in North Carolina had left Richmond lightly defended, he might seize the city with little difficulty. To distract the Confederates and prevent the capital from being reinforced, he requested that Meade's army make a demonstration along the Rapidan. Over the objections of Sedgwick, the army's temporary commander while Meade was on leave, the plan was approved.

On February 6, II Corps (temporarily commanded by Warren) led the way to Morton's Ford while Newton's I Corps bombarded Raccoon Ford a few miles upstream and Brig. Gen. Wesley Merritt's cavalry division crossed Robertson's River and Barnett's Ford on the Rapidan. Brig. Gen. Alexander Hays's division spearheaded the assault at Morton's Ford, which at first was successful and caught the Confederates by surprise. Ewell's corps guarded this reach of the Rapidan, and it reacted quickly. By sunset the Federals were effectively pinned down. The fighting continued into the night, with each side seizing prisoners under cover of darkness. When no headway was made the next morning, however, the Union force withdrew across all the fords to safety. The affair cost both sides some 700 casualties. Ironically, Butler already had aborted his raid after learning that a deserter had revealed his scheme to the Confederates.

At roughly the same time, Brig. Gen. H. Judson Kilpatrick hatched another plan, this time to raid Richmond, free Union prisoners, and burn the city, among other acts. Kilpatrick, a self-promoting, reckless cavalry division commander whose high casualty rate earned him the nickname "Kilcavalry," found a coconspirator in the person of Col. Ulric Dahlgren, an adventurous twenty-two-year-old aide to successive commanders of the Army of the Potomac.

The Kilpatrick-Dahlgren Raid began on the evening of February 28 when Kilpatrick led some 4,000 horsemen across Ely's Ford on the Rapidan and then south through Spotsylvania Court House to Mount Pleasant in the southern part of the county. There the force divided. Dahlgren took about 500 cavalry with him southwest to Goochland Court House, roughly twenty miles west of Richmond, while Kilpatrick led the remainder south toward Richmond. The plan called for Dahlgren to cross the James River and enter the city from the south while Kilpatrick executed a diversionary attack from the north.

Each part of the force made good progress through February 29, but the next day the raid began to fall apart. Kilpatrick's nerve failed him as he approached Richmond's lightly held intermediate defenses, and he quickly withdrew. Assaulted himself from the north by some 300 of Hampton's cavalry that had been pursuing him, Kilpatrick ordered a retreat down the Peninsula toward Federal lines.

Meanwhile, high water prevented Dahlgren from crossing the James River, and he decided to enter the city from the west instead. He had not even reached the outskirts, however, when the home guard confronted him on the afternoon of March 1; in the ensuing skirmish, he and about 100 horsemen got separated from the remainder of his force. Hoping to find Kilpatrick, he galloped in a wide arc around the city to the north and east.

On March 2 Dahlgren and his men crossed the Mattaponi River into King and Queen County and rode east past the hamlet of Walkerton toward King and Queen Court House. About three miles northwest of the courthouse, at a junction today called Dahlgren's Corner, the home guard and a detachment of the 9th Virginia Cavalry ambushed Dahlgren. In a brief firefight Dahlgren was killed instantly, and most of his command was captured.

The raid cost the Federals about 300 casualties, and the Confederates far fewer. Although the raid itself was a fiasco, it caused a great uproar in the South when Dahlgren's body was examined and papers were recovered that called for the murder of Pres. Jefferson Davis and his cabinet as well as the burning and looting of Richmond. In response to a letter from Lee demanding an explanation, Meade and Kilpatrick disavowed any knowledge or sanctioning of the burning of Richmond and the killing of Davis and his cabinet. Northerners claimed the papers were Southern forgeries calculated to inflame the citizenry. Recent tests have led knowledgeable historians to conclude that the documents were indeed Dahlgren's work; however, they appear to reflect Dahlgren's wishful thinking, not orders from higher authorities. The failure of the Kilpatrick-Dahlgren Raid put an end to such schemes, whether authorized or not. For the rest of the winter, the Army of the Potomac instead prepared for the approaching campaign season.

In May 1864 the two armies faced each other across the Rapidan River. The Army of Northern Virginia was encamped south of the river, with Longstreet's headquarters at Gordonsville, Lee's and Hill's at Orange Court House, and Ewell's near Morton's Ford. The Army of the Potomac, whose camps were visible from the Confederate observation post atop Clark's Mountain south of the river, was sprawled across eastern Culpeper County from Culpeper Court House to Rappahannock Station in

Fauquier County. Lee ascended the mountain on Monday, May 2, with his generals and studied the peaceful-looking scene north of the river.

Unknown to Lee, Grant had selected Wednesday, May 4, to begin his spring offensive. On or about that same date, Union forces all over the country would launch attacks. Sherman would strike southeast from Chattanooga against Johnston's army in Georgia. In Virginia, Maj. Gen. Franz Sigel would drive south up the Shenandoah Valley. Butler would lead the Army of the James on transports up the James River from Hampton Roads to City Point and Bermuda Hundred, a first step on the road to Petersburg and Richmond, which Gen. Pierre G. T. Beauregard defended. Earlier, in southwestern West Virginia and Virginia, Brig. Gen. William W. Averell and Brig. Gen. George Crook would launch a series of infantry and cavalry raids against the Virginia & Tennessee Railroad. In a matter of days the Confederacy would find itself under attack everywhere.

For Meade's Army of the Potomac, Grant set the task of crossing the Rapidan River and destroying the Army of Northern Virginia in battle. The Federals faced enormous logistical challenges to accomplish their goals. The army could stretch for thirty miles if its soldiers were placed in double columns, and its 6,000 supply wagons could occupy fifty miles of roads. Grant's plan of attack called for Warren's V Corps and Sedgwick's VI Corps to cross the Rapidan at Germanna Ford at dawn on May 4, with Hancock's II Corps crossing half a dozen miles east at Ely's Ford. The wagon train would cross at Ely's and Culpeper Mine Fords, and Burnside's IX Corps would follow Warren's and Sedgwick's corps across Germanna Ford after detaching Ferrero's division to guard the trains. Warren and Sedgwick would encamp beyond Wilderness Tavern while Hancock would head for Chancellorsville and then on to Todd's Tavern and Spotsylvania Court House.

Grant sought to lure Lee into the open by threatening both the Confederate right flank and the capital at Richmond. At the same time, by keeping his army between Lee and the Rappahannock River, Grant would protect his army's projected supply route via the river and the Richmond, Fredericksburg & Potomac Railroad. The plan had only one obvious weakness: the challenge of getting the huge force safely through the seventy-square-mile Wilderness and out onto open ground to maneuver effectively against Lee. Many of the soldiers remembered vividly the horrors of the place from the previous years' battle there—the tangled terrain that destroyed unit coherence, the enemy invisible in the thick undergrowth, the fires ignited by exploding gunpowder that burned alive the helpless wounded. No one wanted to fight there again.

Lee knew that Grant planned to attack. But having the smaller army, and possessing a ready-made defensive line constructed in December 1863 along Mine Run during Meade's aborted campaign, Lee was content to let Grant make the first move. If Grant waited too long, however, Lee planned to strike the Federals.

The vanguard of Warren's corps, preceded by Wilson's cavalry, left its camp at about 3 A.M. on May 4 and splashed across Germanna Ford, driving away the Confederate pickets there. Sedgwick's corps followed. The advance of Hancock's corps repeated the scene at Ely's Ford, and the campaign was under way.

When dawn came at about 5 A.M., great clouds of dust revealed the Union troop movement to Confederate observers atop Clark's Mountain. They sent word to Lee that the Federal objectives appeared to be Germanna Ford and then perhaps Fredericksburg. By midmorning Confederate columns prepared to march as the Union columns, slowed by the trains, were compelled to halt in the Wilderness, well short of the day's goals.

Ewell's corps, encamped near Morton's Ford on the Rapidan River, headed southeast to the Orange Turnpike at Verdiersville, then turned east toward Wilderness Tavern. Hill's corps, accompanied by Lee, moved east from Orange Court House to the Orange Plank Road and then marched toward Parker's Store. Longstreet's corps approached the Wilderness from the southwest near Gordonsville. By late morning elements of each army were in striking distance of the other, with Lee ready to smite Grant's line of march on its right flank the next morning if it remained in the Wilderness.

At about 6 A.M. on May 5, Ewell's column made contact with Warren's corps and began entrenching at the edge of Saunders's Field. At midday the fighting began in earnest as the Federals unsuccessfully attacked Ewell. The tinder-dry Wilderness undergrowth caught fire, and much of the fighting took place amid smoke and flames.

To the south, the main conflict erupted around the intersection of the Orange Plank Road and Brock Road as both sides contended for this crucial junction. Hill's corps fought elements of Hancock's corps and Getty's division of Sedgwick's corps through the late afternoon and evening, but at the end of the day the place remained in Federal hands. During the night, each corps strengthened its position and fed more troops into its line.

Soon after dawn on May 6, the Federals charged out of their hastily constructed Plank Road works and struck Hill's corps, pushing it back. Lee watched his artillery buy time for Longstreet and his corps to march to the front. When the head of Longstreet's column, the Texas Brigade, approached Lee, he joined it and cheered the men forward. Suddenly realizing that Lee intended to lead the counterattack himself, the horrified soldiers refused to advance unless he rode to the rear. One of Lee's aides at last persuaded him to withdraw. Satisfied, the brigade charged and, reinforced by other brigades, soon pushed the Federals back. Longstreet's counterattack culminated in an effective assault on the Union left flank.

By 12:30 P.M., after a morning of brutal fighting, Hancock's corps had been driven into its earthworks, and Lee planned to take advantage of the Confederate momentum. At this crucial moment Longstreet suffered a serious wound in a "friendly fire" episode reminiscent of Jackson's mortal wounding a year earlier. Unlike Stonewall, however, Lee's "Old War Horse" would recover in four months' time.

Ewell authorized an attack for 6 P.M. that evening. At first successful, his attempt soon failed as Grant fed troops into the fray to reinforce Sedgwick's corps. By nightfall the fighting ended with neither side having gained or lost ground, and the next day only desultory skirmishing occurred. Essentially a draw, the battle of the Wilderness had cost the Federals some 18,000 in dead, wounded, and missing and the Confederates about 11,000 casualties.

Early in the morning on May 7, when Lee's past opponents would have retreated, Grant instead ordered Meade to make a night march to occupy Spotsylvania Court House; accordingly, Meade sent Warren's corps southeast on Brock Road past Lee's right flank. Grant's decision surprised the men in his army—and doubtless some of his own aides—who did not think the Army of the Potomac measured up to the Federal force in the West. Grant had not intended to fight a battle in the Wilderness

and therefore refused to alter his strategy of compelling Lee to fight in the open.

Lee and his men considered the battle of the Wilderness a strategic victory, expecting Grant to follow the example set by Maj. Gen. Joseph Hooker the year before at Chancellorsville and retreat. By the early morning of May 7, however, Lee concluded after the Federals took up their pontoons at Germanna Ford that Grant was executing a flanking movement, either toward Fredericksburg or Spotsylvania Court House. Lee ordered Anderson, now commanding Longstreet's corps, to march to the courthouse village and defend its important road junction.

Anderson won the ensuing "race" to the courthouse, although neither side, marching on parallel roads in the dark, knew that a contest existed until it was over. Meade was furious when he found out that the Confederates already were building fortifications across Brock Road. Disjointed Federal attacks in the afternoon failed to dislodge them.

The battle of Spotsylvania Court House consisted of engagements fought over a two-week period while the Confederates built and strengthened their earthworks. Lee's men could erect incredibly strong fieldworks in a matter of hours. At Spotsylvania, however, they made an error in placement that soon cost them dearly. Moving into a new position under cover of darkness and digging in at the edge of a wood line on a plateau, Ewell's corps built a section that projected beyond the neighboring works, thereby forming a salient. In addition, it was located so far up the slope that in places the view of the bottom was obscured. Because of its odd shape, this salient was nicknamed the Mule Shoe; a short time later, part of it became known as the Bloody Angle.

On May 9 elements of each army continued to trickle into the area north of the courthouse. By evening Hancock's II Corps had marched around Lee's left flank to the vicinity of Block House Bridge, a crossing over the Po River on the Shady Grove Church Road. That night Lee ordered units from Heth's division and Brig. Gen. William Mahone's division—formerly Anderson's—to block and attack Hancock's corps. The attack took place on May 10 as Hancock received orders to withdraw and assault the Confederate line elsewhere.

Piecemeal Federal attacks occurred in several places that day, most significantly at the Mule Shoe. Col. Emory Upton, commander of the 121st New York Infantry, led the assault, which breached the Confederate line. The attack involved twelve regiments taken from Sedgwick's VI Corps, commanded by Brig. Gen. Horatio G. Wright since Sedgwick's death from a sharpshooter's bullet on May 9. The assault ultimately failed for lack of support.

Heartened by Upton's initial success, Grant decided to attack the Mule Shoe with Hancock's entire corps, holding Wright in support. Hancock's soldiers would charge across an open field at dawn on May 12, storm the Confederate works, and shatter the center of Lee's line. Grant sent a telegram to Washington on May 11, "I propose to fight it out on this line if it takes all summer."

During the night of May 11–12, Ewell's men heard Union soldiers and wagons marching across their front from west to east. Anticipating a Federal flanking movement, Lee ordered the artillery out of the Mule Shoe and to the rear. Then, near dawn, the noise stopped. Frantic, the occupants of the salient sent word to bring back the cannons, but before they returned, Hancock's corps charged. The time was 4:35 A.M., and for the next twenty-three hours there would be almost constant combat at the Mule Shoe.

Most Civil War actions were over in minutes or a few hours, and hand-to-hand combat was rare since one side or the other usually gave way quickly. The fight for the Mule Shoe was unique, not only for its length but also for the carnage it wrought as both sides slaughtered each other with every resource available. Later, some of the survivors tried and failed to put the experience into words in their letters home. Men who had lived through Antietam and Gettysburg could only report that this battle surpassed them both in its viciousness and gore.

At first Hancock's attack succeeded. Protected from Confederate fire by a swale at the foot of the ridge, his men were able to assault en masse and overwhelm the Mule Shoe's defenders. The Federals drove through to Ewell's rear, but Lee reacted swiftly and threw reinforcements into the breach to push them back, even trying on two occasions to lead the men forward himself until they compelled him to withdraw. Soon most of Hancock's men were driven back to the line of entrenchments first captured, but they refused to retreat any farther. Both sides fought with shot and shell and bayonets and clubbed muskets, and with fists and knives when the ammunition ran low. The combat lasted far into the night. (At about 2 A.M. on May 13, an oak tree some twenty inches in diameter, its trunk cut through by Union bullets, crashed to the ground behind the Mule Shoe.)

The battle for the Mule Shoe left both sides sickened and exhausted. During the night, the Confederates withdrew to a second, more easily defended line. Two days of drenching rain, coupled with the severe losses and the tasks of burying the dead and caring for the wounded, brought a brief pause in the fighting. Casualty estimates vary, but the Federals may have lost between 6,000 and 9,000 killed, wounded, and missing to the Confederates' 6,000 to 8,000, many of whom were captured in the initial attack.

As horrific as the casualty figures were, and as ominous as they were for the Confederate army, no single death affected Lee as much as one that was reported to him in the midst of the Spotsylvania battle. On May 12, in Richmond, J. E. B. Stuart died of a mortal wound he received the day before at Yellow Tavern.

After the battle of the Wilderness, Grant had decided to turn Sheridan loose to attack Lee's communications lines with Richmond and see if he could draw Stuart out. On May 9, accordingly, Sheridan and some 10,000 cavalrymen circled east and then south around Lee's right flank and that evening struck Beaver Dam Station on the Virginia Central Railroad, then headed for the northern outskirts of Richmond.

Stuart, once he had divined Sheridan's intentions, countered by dividing his cavalry corps and sending part of it to attack the Federal rear while he led the rest to intercept Sheridan near the capital. The two forces collided on May 11 at Yellow Tavern, an old unpainted stagecoach stop a few miles north of the city. Brig. Gen. George A. Custer's dismounted cavalrymen charged through Stuart's line before the Confederates pushed them back. Stuart, astride his horse, was shouting and firing his huge LeMat revolver at the retreating Federals when one of them, Pvt. John A. Huff, of the 5th Michigan Cavalry, turned and fired his pistol. The bullet struck Stuart in the abdomen and he reeled in the saddle. Led away from the action, Stuart was placed in an ambulance and taken to Richmond.

He died in agony, at the home of his brother-in-law, Dr. Charles Brewer, on May 12. Stuart had hoped to survive long enough to see his wife one last time, but she arrived just minutes too late.

Excepting Stuart's death, the battle of Yellow Tavern was a small affair that cost the two sides some 800 casualties. Sheridan's expedition did little damage, but it deprived both armies of their "eyes and ears" when they were needed by Grant and Lee in Spotsylvania County.

The battles around Spotsylvania Court House ground on, as the Federals lengthened their left flank by shifting the II, V, and VI Corps to the east on May 14–15, to the left of the IX Corps. This maneuver realigned Grant's line along the Fredericksburg Road. Two Union corps attacked Lee's new line behind the Mule Shoe on May 18 but were repulsed. The next day, Ewell attempted to locate the new position of the Union right flank on the Fredericksburg Road. His corps collided with some heavy artillerymen newly arrived from the defenses of Washington. After a vicious and bloody engagement in which the gallant gunners fought as infantry, Ewell withdrew. The battle of Spotsylvania Courthouse had ended. Two days later Grant disengaged his army and marched it south, continuing to maneuver around Lee.

Lee followed suit, marching the Army of Northern Virginia south on roads paralleling the route taken by the Army of the Potomac. On the afternoon of May 22, the Confederate vanguard arrived at the North Anna River and stopped to bathe and rest while the rest of the army caught up. Lee expected Grant and his men to pause to regroup after two and a half weeks of near-constant combat, but the Federal commander surprised him by pressing on to the North Anna and attempting to cross the next day.

The battle for the North Anna River began on the afternoon of May 23, when Hancock's II Corps captured a redoubt guarding Chesterfield bridge on Telegraph Road. The Confederates attempted to burn the bridge that night but failed. They succeeded, however, in destroying the Richmond, Fredericksburg & Potomac Railroad bridge just downstream. Upstream at Jericho Mill, meanwhile, Warren's V Corps forded the river with little opposition. Hill launched a counterattack, but Union artillery and infantry reinforcements drove his men back.

That night Lee and his generals conferred at Hanover Junction. With Union forces across the river at two points, a defensive line on the high south bank alone was not tenable. If he withdrew south toward Richmond, Lee would not have room to maneuver his army and would be forced to retreat behind the city's defensive works. But he had to keep his army between Grant and Richmond.

The Confederates still held Ox Ford, so Lee decided to make that the center of his new line. Hill's corps was assigned the left flank, opposing Warren. Anderson's corps formed the center, while Ewell's held the right flank. Grant, Lee reasoned, would have to divide his army to attack either flank or hold back long enough to capture Ox Ford. Lee hoped to stall Grant and then launch his own attack against either Warren or Hancock.

On May 24, finding Lee's forces pulled back from the II Corps and V Corps fronts, Grant assumed that they were retreating to Richmond and ordered a pursuit, strengthening Warren with Wright's VI Corps. The Army of the Potomac pressed forward and ran into a hail of lead. Burnside's IX Corps failed to capture Ox Ford when, during a thunderstorm, a drunken Brig. Gen. James H. Ledlie led his brigade in a futile charge against the Confederate works. Along Telegraph Road, a Confederate skirmish line fought with such tenacity that it stopped a II Corps division in its tracks. As darkness fell, Grant realized that Lee's position was virtually impregnable and ordered his men to entrench.

For the next two days, the armies skirmished but did not engage in heavy fighting. The North Anna campaign had cost the Federals some 2,600 casualties; the Confederates, about 1,800. During the night of May 26–27, Grant withdrew to the north side of the river, then swung east and continued south around Lee's right flank. Why did Lee not execute an attack on one of Grant's flanks? On May 24 he fell so ill with diarrhea that he kept to his tent; Hill and Ewell also were unwell. Though Lee was determined that the Federals would never pass the Confederates again, Grant did pass him, and Lee ordered his army to fall back toward Richmond.

As the Army of Northern Virginia retreated, the Army of the Potomac advanced with two of Sheridan's cavalry divisions and an infantry division in the lead. The force marched east along the North Anna and then crossed the Pamunkey River. On May 28 Lee and Grant sent part of their cavalry on reconnoitering missions to locate the opposing army. The horsemen collided at Haw's Shop, a machine shop that stood at the intersection of three roads in eastern Hanover County.

The Federal expedition consisted of Gregg's division, with Torbert's following in support. Hampton and Fitzhugh Lee rode toward them from the west with parts of their divisions, while two newly arrived South Carolina regiments trailed behind. At about 10 A.M., Gregg reached the intersection and established a dismounted skirmish line. Half a mile west, Hampton's men arrived at about the same time. Hampton attacked but was driven back by a Federal counterattack and formed a defensive line near Enon Church. For some seven hours the combatants fought a bloody, indecisive engagement. Finally Hampton withdrew, since he had learned from prisoners that Union infantry had indeed crossed the Pamunkey—the information he had been sent to gather. Just as he began to disengage, however, Custer led the Michigan cavalry in a final assault. The tally of casualties for the day's action amounted to about 340 Federals and perhaps 400 Confederates. It had been the largest and bloodiest eastern cavalry engagement since Brandy Station in June 1863.

On May 28 Lee set up a new blocking line on the south bank of Totopotomoy Creek, a tributary of the Pamunkey River. More a series of swamps than a clear-cut watercourse, the sluggish creek lay only nine miles north of Richmond in eastern Hanover County. On May 29 the Federals took up positions on the north side of the creek with the intention of dislodging Lee.

For two days Lee and Grant traded attacks and counterattacks. The Union corps commanded by Hancock, Warren, and Burnside probed across the creek to Lee's lines on May 29. Wright's VI Corps maneuvered the next day to strike Lee's left flank but bogged down in swampy Crump's Creek and failed to get into position. On May 30 Hancock's II Corps breached the first line of Lee's earthworks; the main Confederate line held, however. Burnside's IX Corps drove in Confederate pickets on the Shady Grove Road, while Early launched an attack against Warren's V Corps at Bethesda Church. Although Early failed to crush Warren's vanguard, the attack spoiled plans for an overall Federal advance, and Warren fell back to Shady Grove Road. The two days of fighting resulted in an equal number of casualties (about 1,100) on each side, but neither combatant gained any advantage.

On May 30 Torbert's cavalry division began searching for a way around Lee's right flank. Grant had ordered the Federal horsemen to clear a route to Cold Harbor, a hamlet where five roads intersected, and from which one road led to the Union supply base at White House on the Pamunkey River. Torbert found his path blocked near Old Church and Matadequin Creek, a tributary of the Pamunkey. There Torbert confronted the South Carolinians commanded by Brig. Gen. Matthew C. Butler, who defended the steep crossing point. However, they soon fell back to Cold Harbor, from where, although reinforced by Fitz Lee, they were driven the next day by more of Sheridan's cavalry. The capture of the crossroads meant that Grant could change his front to face Lee's right flank on a north-south line, thereby compelling Lee to do likewise. The fighting at Old Church and Matadequin Creek cost the Federals 90 casualties; the Confederate losses are not known.

Cold Harbor (actually Old Cold Harbor) consisted of little more than an ancient tavern set among fields and woods and a network of roads. Grant and his staff never got the hang of the hamlet's seemingly nonsensical name, rendering it variously as "Coal Harbor" and "Cold Arbor." There was no harbor there, and it is not particularly cold except at certain times of the winter. The name instead may have derived from an old English term for a tavern that did not offer hot food. Regardless of the placename's meaning, within a few days Cold Harbor would be known for a battle that was as hot as the weather from which the men of both armies suffered as they filed wearily into their positions on May 31.

Sheridan's cavalrymen had seized the crossroads earlier that day, driving the Confederates west and repelling several counterattacks. During the night, both sides entrenched and extended their lines north and south as additional troops arrived (including Maj. Gen. Robert F. Hoke's Confederate division from the Richmond defenses), a trend that continued for two days. On June 1 Lee ordered Anderson to recapture the ground in coordination with Hoke, but Sheridan's horse soldiers—fighting dismounted and using Spencer repeating carbines—repelled the attempt, and around noon Wright's VI Corps replaced the cavalrymen.

Grant realized that his best hope for holding Cold Harbor and defeating Lee lay in attacking before the entire Army of Northern Virginia assembled and entrenched. He ordered Wright to lead an assault as soon as the XVIII Corps of Maj. Gen. William F. Smith arrived from Bermuda Hundred, south of Richmond. The attack was delayed for hours, however, when Smith was misdirected by orders issued by Grant's headquarters; finally, at about 5 P.M., the Federals charged Anderson's and Hoke's position. At first they succeeded in breaking through the Confederate line, but soon countercharges erased most of their gains.

Grant decided to launch a coordinated attack at dawn on June 2 and ordered Hancock's II Corps to march all night to join in the assault. When Hancock's march did not end until well after the hour appointed for the attack, Grant postponed the charge until late in the afternoon and then, when delay followed delay, until 4:30 the next morning.

The postponements gave Lee the opportunity he needed. Lee was a master at moving his army quickly, and his men were experts at entrenching. By dawn on June 3, the Confederates had constructed the strongest network of fortifications they had yet built in Virginia. Extending for almost seven miles, the trenches were several lines deep, with interconnecting works to protect the soldiers, large batteries, and interlocking fields of fire. Sensing that capturing them would be no easy task, many Federal soldiers wrote their names on scraps of paper and stitched them to their uniforms so that their bodies might be identified later.

At 4:30 A.M. almost 50,000 men of the II, VI, and XVIII Corps attacked the Confederate entrenchments along a three-mile front. Withering fire from rifles and cannons greeted the Federals, and they fell in heaps. In a short time, 5,500 of them lay dead or wounded. Later in the day attacks and counterattacks along Warren's and Burnside's front cost the Federals another 1,500 casualties. The Cold Harbor battles, from start to bloody finish, cost the Federals some 12,000 casualties and the Confederates about 2,500.

In retrospect, Grant admitted that the attack had been a dreadful mistake. But he had believed that one grand assault, launched before Lee was fully prepared, might have ended the war, and in that he may have been correct. Grant's mistake was Lee's last major victory of the war.

Both sides reeled from the butchery, and little action occurred for the next several days. On June 12 Grant used the cover of darkness to slip away, intent on moving far around Lee and threatening Richmond from the south, from the direction of Petersburg. To distract the Confederates, Grant had ordered Sheridan to ride westward and destroy track along the Virginia Central Railroad, which connected Richmond with the Shenandoah Valley. Sheridan departed on June 7 with some 6,000 cavalrymen. Lee, as usual, soon learned of the Federal movement and sent Hampton and roughly 5,000 troopers in pursuit. On June 11 Hampton caught up with Sheridan near Trevilian Station, just west of Louisa Court House.

The two forces had bivouacked within five miles of each other the night before. On the morning of June 11, opposing patrols encountered each other and the battle began. At first Sheridan drove a wedge between Hampton's and Fitzhugh Lee's divisions and pushed the former back to the station, where Custer attacked the Confederate rear. Hampton's men quickly regrouped, however, and soon had Custer surrounded on three sides. He and his troopers cut their way out, and the action ended as much from mutual exhaustion and ammunition shortages as from the approaching darkness.

On June 12 the fighting resumed in the morning with an unsuccessful attack by Sheridan. When he tried again in the afternoon, Sheridan's assault was broken by Hampton's strong counterattack, which nearly shattered the Union force. Again darkness ended the fighting, and by dawn the next day Sheridan and his men were withdrawing toward White House on the Pamunkey River.

The two-day battle at Trevilian Station was the bloodiest all-cavalry encounter of the war. Sheridan suffered 1,000 casualties; Hampton, somewhat fewer. The expedition had resulted in little damage to the railroad, although it had accomplished its goal of drawing most of the Confederate cavalry away from the action at Cold Harbor. Given the nature of the fighting in Hanover County, the absence of the cavalry meant little, but after the battle, the Confederate cavalry's absence helped Grant move south undetected by Lee. Sheridan and Hampton rejoined their armies just after Grant and Lee began to maneuver toward Petersburg.

Grant's Overland campaign had failed in its goals of drawing Lee into open battle and crushing him, then capturing the Confederate capital. However, Lee assumed the defensive—a role he kept for the remainder of the war while searching unsuccessfully for opportunities to attack Grant—whereas the Federal commander continued to maneuver around Lee's right flank toward Richmond, thereby reinforcing Lee's defensive posture.

The cost was ghastly, with each side losing about 45 percent of its strength. Grant began the campaign on May 4 with about 120,000 men, Lee with about 60,000. By June 12, when Grant disengaged his army at Cold Harbor and began the march that would take him to Petersburg, he had suffered about 55,000 casualties. Lee's losses amounted to roughly 27,000. The total number of effectives for the Army of the Potomac stood at about 65,000 by mid-June; the Army of Northern Virginia had about 33,000. Both sides soon received reinforcements.

The Overland campaign ended in a stalemate, but the horrific losses were far more serious for Lee than for Grant, especially since Grant's overall strategy had proven effective. Sherman was thrusting into northwestern Georgia, while Maj. Gen. David Hunter was marching through the Shenandoah Valley. Lee could do nothing to help Johnston against Sherman, but he could and did divide his army and send first Maj. Gen. John C. Breckinridge and then Early to counter Hunter. This decision virtually eliminated any possibility that Lee could maneuver against Grant and attack him successfully. For the rest of the war, Lee and the Army of Northern Virginia would be restricted to trench warfare; eventually, a desperate flight from Petersburg would end at Appomattox Court House. ▓

MORTON'S FORD

The February 1864 engagement at Morton's Ford on the Rapidan River resulted from a scheme by Maj. Gen. Benjamin F. Butler to conduct a surprise raid on Richmond. Butler assumed that the capital's defenses had been stripped to support Confederate operations in North Carolina during the winter of 1863–1864, making for an easy capture of the city by a small Federal force. Butler's idea caught on among the politicians in Washington.

Maj. Gen. George G. Meade, the permanent commander of the Army of the Potomac, was home on leave. Maj. Gen. John Sedgwick, the acting commander, was appalled when he learned of the plan and the role he was to play in it. Sedgwick was ordered to stage a diversion along the Rapidan, where his army faced Lee's on the other side, while Butler raced west to Richmond.

Reluctantly, Sedgwick drew up plans for executing his orders. Maj. Gen. Gouverneur K. Warren, temporarily commanding II Corps, would cross the Rapidan

DIRECTIONS: I-95 Exit 130B (State Rte. 3 West, Culpeper), w. on State Rte. 3 about 12.2 miles to Rte. 20; w. (left) on Rte. 20 4.8 miles to Locust Grove at Rte. 611 (Zoar Rd.); n. (right) on Rte. 611 7.2 miles to Rte. 620 (Horseshoe Rd.); n. (right) on Rte. 620 4.1 miles through Confederate line to Hays's U.S. line at apex of loop overlooking Morton's Ford (not visible because of vegetation) to north, then back to Rte. 611 (Raccoon Ford Rd.); w. (right) on Rte. 611 3.7 miles to U.S. Rte. 522 (at 2 miles pass Raccoon Ford at Rocky Branch); s. (left) on U.S. Rte. 522 5.9 miles to Rte. 20; e. (left) on Rte. 20 and return to I-95.

from Culpeper County at Morton's Ford on February 6. Simultaneously, Brig. Gen. Wesley Merritt's cavalry division would cross Robertson's River and Barnett's Ford on the Rapidan, while part of Maj. Gen. John Newton's I Corps would threaten and bombard Raccoon Ford. On the Orange County side of the Rapidan, Lt. Gen. Richard S. Ewell's corps held the eastern part of the Confederate line, and pickets guarded the fords in shifts. In addition, the Richmond Howitzers occupied a battery on a bluff overlooking Morton's Ford.

U.S. night attack at Morton's Ford. LIBRARY OF CONGRESS

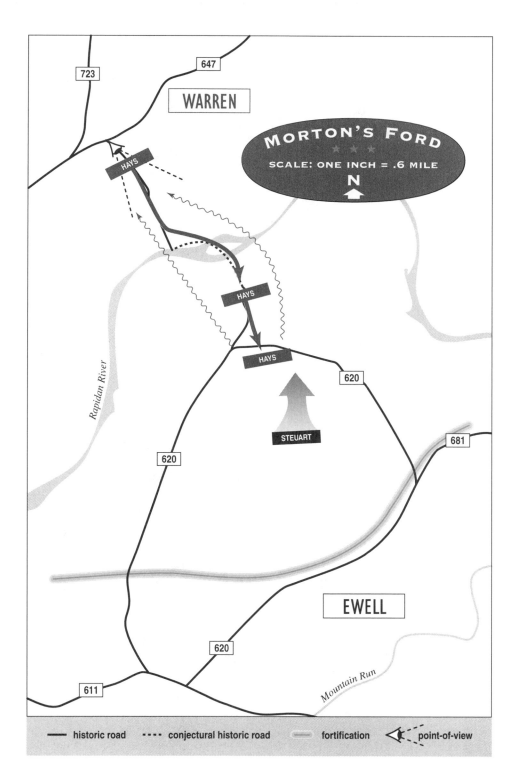

723

647

WARREN

MORTON'S FORD
★ ★ ★
SCALE: ONE INCH = .6 MILE
N

HAYS

Rapidan River

HAYS

HAYS

620

STEUART

620

681

EWELL

620

611

Mountain Run

historic road ···· conjectural historic road ═══ fortification ◄··· point-of-view

On Saturday, February 6, Warren's II Corps marched to the ford in a steady drizzle of freezing rain. Despite the discomfort, fortune favored the Federals at first, for they caught the pickets between shifts and the ford nearly unguarded except for the Howitzers.

Three batteries of Federal artillery—Ricketts's, Arnold's, and Thompson's—fired from the north side of the river, and the divisions commanded by Brig. Gen. Alexander S. Webb and Brig. Gen. John C. Caldwell remained in reserve while Brig. Gen. Alexander Hays's led the attack. The Confederates huddled in their camps behind the ford and tried to stay warm, but word that the Federals were crossing the river and making for the battery caused the Howitzers to hurry back to save their guns.

The sound of the cannons reached Ewell at his headquarters at nearby Morton Hall, and he galloped to the ford to find that one brigade from Hays's division had crossed the river but had not advanced beyond the flood plain. Ordering the Howitzers and pickets to hold the enemy for ten minutes, Ewell returned to the rear to send Brig. Gen. George H. Steuart's brigade forward. Soon Hays's men huddled against the bluffs as they sought cover from the fire from the Confederate earthworks above them on three sides.

Some of the Federals pressed forward to the brick Buckner house and a wooden outbuilding that stood on an eminence within the semicircle of earthworks. The house became yet another trap, however, as the Confederates concentrated their fire on it, as well as on the bottomland, then captured the building around sunset. Shooting, charges, and countercharges continued until after dark, when Hays's men withdrew across a rude bridge to safety. By sunrise the Confederates had secured the ford, and the Federals had departed after suffering some 200 killed and many more wounded; the losses for both sides totaled 700.

From Warren's point of view, the casualty figures may have been worth it if Butler had succeeded in capturing Richmond. Unknown to him and to the other commanders, however, Butler had aborted the raid after he learned that a deserter had disclosed his plan to Confederates on the Peninsula.

The attack served as a wake-up call to Gen. Robert E. Lee and his army. Lee ordered new batteries constructed along the Rapidan, and soon his defensive line became strong enough to deter any future attacks. ■

WALKERTON

Brig. Gen. H. Judson Kilpatrick, the commander of a cavalry division, and Col. Ulric Dahlgren, a young aide serving at the Army of the Potomac headquarters, hatched a scheme to capture Richmond during the winter of 1863–1864. Kilpatrick fancied himself a brave and dashing cavalier on the scale of his sometime subordinate, Brig. Gen. George A. Custer. His men, however, considered him reckless, inept, and of low moral character. Dahlgren, twenty-two years old, brave, earnest, and adventurous, often volunteered for hazardous duty. During the pursuit that followed the victory at Gettysburg, Dahlgren had joined Kilpatrick's men in street fighting in Hagerstown, Maryland, been severely wounded, and lost a leg. After recuperating, he rejoined Kilpatrick to execute his plan against Richmond.

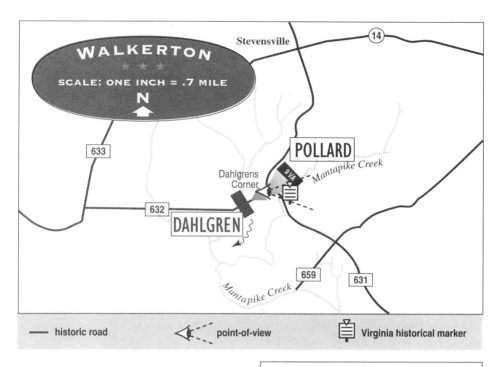

Kilpatrick, like Maj. Gen. Benjamin F. Butler before him, believed the city to be lightly defended. He proposed to lead his division south, then divide it and attack Richmond from two directions: himself from the north and Dahlgren from the south. While Kilpatrick distracted the city's defenders, Dahlgren would slip in and free the thousands of Union prisoners held on Belle Isle and in Libby Prison and other warehouses, then create as much havoc as possible before fleeing to safety.

The expedition got under way on the evening of Sunday, February 28, 1864, when Kilpatrick crossed the Rapidan River at Ely's Ford and brushed aside Confederate pickets. The pickets spread word of the advance, and soon Confederate cavalry was in pursuit of Kilpatrick's 4,000-man force.

The next day, Kilpatrick divided his command at Mount Pleasant in southern Spotsylvania County. While he led about 3,500 men against the Richmond defenses from the north, Dahlgren rode southwest with 500 troopers to Goochland Court

DIRECTIONS: I-64 Exit 220 (State Rte. 33 East, West Point), n.e. on State Rte. 33 about 2.6 miles to State Rte. 30; continue n.e. on State Rte. 30/33 8.7 miles through West Point to Rte. 14 at Shackleford's; n.w. (left) on Rte. 14 14.1 miles past King and Queen Court House to Rte. 631 (Bunker Hill Rd.); n.w. (left) on Rte. 631 2.6 miles to Rte. 632 at Dahlgren's Corner and state historical marker OB-8, Where Dahlgren Died; n. (right) on Rte. 631 (Stevensville Rd.) 1.4 miles to Rtes. 14 and 633; continue n. on Rte. 14 10.8 miles to U.S. Rte. 360 at St. Stephen's Church, or: e. (right) on Rte. 14 19.6 miles to State Rte. 30/33 at Shackleford's and return to I-64.

Alternative route: I-64 Exit 227 (State Rte. 30, West Point, Toano), n. on State Rte. 30 2.3 miles to Barhamsville and Rte. 633; n. (right) on Rte. 633 .5 mile to Rte. 273 (Farmer's Dr.); n.e. (right) on Rte. 273 5.2 miles to State Rte. 30/33 at Eltham; n.e. (right) on State Rte. 30/33 5.7 miles through West Point to Rte. 14 at Shackleford's; continue as above.

House to cross the James River. He then intended to lead his force to Manchester, just south of Richmond, recross the river at Belle Isle, free the prisoners, and carry out the rest of his mission.

Nature failed to cooperate, however. Two days of rain and sleet had raised the

Site of Dahlgren's death. VIRGINIA DEPARTMENT OF HISTORIC RESOURCES, JOHN S. SALMON

water level of the James River. A plantation slave, Martin Robinson, escorted the troopers to a ford he said they could cross; when they arrived, however, the water was too high. Enraged, and suspecting deliberate trickery, Dahlgren hanged the unfortunate Robinson. Abandoning his plan to cross the river, he instead decided to enter Richmond from the west on March 1.

Meanwhile, Kilpatrick closed in from the north. Harried by some 300 of Maj. Gen. Wade Hampton's troopers, Kilpatrick also encountered unexpectedly strong opposition from Richmond's Home Guard, which had been warned of his coming. Finding the situation in front of him tougher than anticipated and harassed by Hampton at his back, Kilpatrick abandoned his plan for the safety of the Federal lines on the Peninsula. Dahlgren, unaware, was now on his own.

Just west of the city, Richmond's Home Guard and its Armory Battalion intercepted and repulsed Dahlgren's advance after heavy skirmishing. Dahlgren's forces scattered, and the young colonel and about a hundred horsemen looked in vain for Kilpatrick. About 300 Union troopers eventually found their way first to Kilpatrick's camp and then back to the Army of the Potomac.

On Wednesday, March 2, Dahlgren led the remnants of his command across the Mattaponi River into King and Queen County, pursued and harassed by cavalry from Maj. Gen. Fitzhugh Lee's division. As darkness fell, Dahlgren's force rode east past Walkerton on the River Road (present-day Rtes. 634, 633, and 632) toward King and Queen Court House. Lt. James Pollard and the 9th Virginia Cavalry paralleled Dahlgren's route on roads to the north and east (Rtes. 14 and 631) and succeeded in getting in front of him on River Road. There, at a junction even today known as Dahlgren's Corner (Rtes. 632 and 631), Pollard laid an ambush.

Shortly before midnight Dahlgren and his troopers approached the intersection and saw men in the road in front of him. Demanding their surrender, Dahlgren fired his pistol. The Confederates returned a volley, and Dahlgren toppled from his horse dead. His men scattered, but most were rounded up and sent to the prisons in Richmond that they had hoped to liberate.

The casualties resulting from this Federal fiasco were light on both sides, amounting to some 300 Union cavalrymen, most of them captured, and far fewer Confederates killed or wounded. What made the raid memorable, however, were documents found on Dahlgren's body after his death that caused an uproar that reverberated all the way to Gen. Robert E. Lee and Pres. Jefferson Davis.

One document was an address to the officers and men of Dahlgren's detachment, the other a rough draft of that address—both acknowledged as Dahlgren's handwriting. In the first he exhorted his troopers to destroy and burn Richmond and not allow Davis and his cabinet to escape. The second paper was even more specific about destroying the city and killing Jefferson Davis and his cabinet.

In the mid-nineteenth century, guerilla warfare was widely viewed as a violation of the rules of civilized combat. For a military officer to go a step further and deliberately wreak death and destruction on civilians, especially by killing the political leaders of the enemy, was regarded as what today would be called a war crime.

On March 5, just a few days after the raid, Confederate Secretary of War James A. Seddon sent copies of the Dahlgren papers to Lee, urging publication in the newspapers and advocating that at least some of the captured raiders be executed for such a diabolical plot. Lee agreed with the former suggestion but not the latter, concluding that not only was such a penalty too harsh, any executions would force retaliation.

On April 1 Lee sent Maj. Gen. George G. Meade, commander of the Army of the Potomac, copies of Dahlgren's papers and asked whether Dahlgren's stated intentions had been authorized and sanctioned by the Federal government or his superior officers. It was potentially of great propaganda value to the Confederacy: Had the political and military leaders of the United States planned to commit war crimes? Had they plotted the murder of civilians?

Meade ordered Kilpatrick to examine the papers and interrogate surviving members of Dahlgren's detachment. All the men testified that Dahlgren gave them no speech or instructions of the character set forth in the papers. Kilpatrick admitted that Dahlgren had shown him the text of a proposed address and that he had approved and signed it, but it contained none of the inflammatory remarks quoted by Lee. Furthermore, he noted that the copies sent by Lee did not contain Kilpatrick's endorsement. In conclusion, Kilpatrick wrote that Dahlgren had received no orders from him or his superiors to pillage, burn, or kill.

Meade wrote Lee on April 17, stating formally that neither the U.S. government nor any officers had authorized or sanctioned the burning of Richmond and the killing of Davis and his cabinet. There the matter ended, as far as Lee and the leaders of the Confederacy were concerned. Although Kilpatrick implied that the Dahlgren papers were forgeries, it is probable that they were authentic. Most likely, however, they indicate Dahlgren's overheated imagination rather than an authorized plot.

Today most of the sites around Richmond associated with the Kilpatrick-Dahlgren Raid have been developed and obliterated. The site of the Walkerton engagement in King and Queen County, however, remains rural and unchanged. ∎

WILDERNESS

The battle of the Wilderness was another of those unintended battles that the opposing armies' commanders had not planned to fight. No one who had been in the Wilderness, especially the veterans who had fought at Chancellorsville in 1863, ever wanted to see the place again, much less engage in combat there.

Some seventy square miles in size— twelve miles wide and six miles from south to north—the Wilderness sprawled west of Chancellorsville and south of the Rapidan River. A repeatedly cut-over tangle of scrub trees and briar patches, the thick undergrowth limited visibility to ten feet or less in places and threw military maneuvers into confusion. The Wilderness was nightmarish terrain to be gotten through as quickly as possible, not fought in.

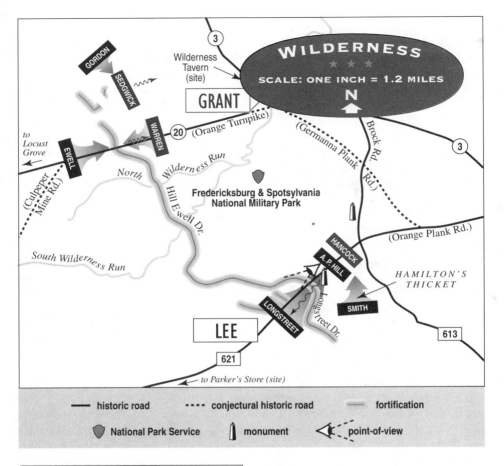

WILDERNESS
★ ★ ★
SCALE: ONE INCH = 1.2 MILES
N

GORDON
SEDGWICK
Wilderness Tavern (site)
GRANT
to Locust Grove
EWELL
WARREN
(Orange Turnpike)
20
North
(Culpeper Mine Rd.)
Wilderness Run
Hill Ewell Dr.
Fredericksburg & Spotsylvania National Military Park
(Germanna Plank
Brock Rd.
Rd.)
3
South Wilderness Run
(Orange Plank Rd.)
HANCOCK
A. P. HILL
HAMILTON'S THICKET
LONGSTREET
Longstreet Dr.
SMITH
LEE
613
621
to Parker's Store (site)

— historic road   ···· conjectural historic road   fortification

🛡 National Park Service   ▯ monument   ◁ point-of-view

DIRECTIONS: I-95 Exit 130B (State Rte. 3 West, Culpeper), w. on State Rte. 3 about 7.8 miles to Chancellorsville Visitor Center entrance, Fredericksburg and Spotsylvania National Military Park, and follow Wilderness battlefield tour with park brochure. Visit the National Park Service Web site at nps.gov/parks.html for a virtual tour of this and other national parks.

When, on Wednesday, May 4, 1864, Lt. Gen. Ulysses S. Grant and Maj. Gen. George G. Meade launched the Army of the Potomac south on its spring offensive across the Rapidan, they planned to march their 120,000 men through the Wilderness and onto open ground around the road hub of Spotsylvania Court House and thereby threaten both the Confederate right flank and the capital at Richmond. Gen. Robert E. Lee, they believed, would then have to lead his 60,000-man Army of Northern Virginia into combat on their terms.

Lee, realizing that he was vastly outnumbered, had no intention of fighting on any terms other than his own. A master at using terrain to his advantage, he saw the Wilderness as a potential ally. His soldiers had a ready-made defensive line available: the earthworks built along the western bank of Mine Run the previous autumn to stop Meade's ill-advised campaign.

Lee had posted Lt. Gen. James Longstreet's corps around Gordonsville, Lt. Gen. A. P. Hill's at Orange Court House, and Lt. Gen. Richard S. Ewell's near Morton's Ford. Longstreet formed the army's left flank on the west, Ewell's the right on the east. Grant's attack came to the east of Ewell's position.

Maj. Gen. Gouverneur K. Warren led V Corps, preceded by Brig. Gen. James H. Wilson's cavalry and followed by Maj. Gen. John Sedgwick and VI Corps, across the Rapidan at Germanna Ford at dawn on May 4, and headed for the assigned encampment site southeast of Wilderness Tavern. At the same time, Maj. Gen. Winfield Scott Hancock and II Corps escorted the army's huge wagon train across Ely's Ford about six miles farther east; Maj. Gen. Ambrose P. Burnside and IX Corps followed as a rear guard. Chancellorsville was Hancock's immediate destination.

The Confederates observed the Federal movement almost the instant it began. By noon Confederate soldiers were on the march, and Lee's front was changing to face east instead of north. By late afternoon, it was Grant whose right flank was vulnerable.

The thickets and narrow roads of the Wilderness slowed the Union advance and bought time for Lee to put his troops in motion. By the end of the day, Ewell had passed Verdiersville and reached Locust Grove or Robertson's Tavern on the Orange Turnpike (present-day Rte. 20), while Hill camped half a dozen miles behind him between Verdiersville and New Verdiersville, on the Orange Plank Road (Rte. 621).

Warren's corps had bivouacked five miles in front of Ewell. Thick undergrowth separated the two corps, and the Federals slept unaware of their enemy's proximity. Maj. Gen. J. E. B. Stuart's cavalry, however, had spotted their Union counterparts forward of Warren's position and alerted Lee. Meade, meanwhile, had received reports that some of Stuart's cavalry was behind the Union army, between it and Fredericksburg. Based on this misinformation, Grant and Meade altered their plans,

ordering most of the Federal cavalry to the east to counter Stuart's imagined threat while the infantry set up a new line facing west. Sedgwick's, Warren's, and Hancock's corps would hold this line in the Wilderness at least long enough for Burnside and the wagon trains to catch up with the rest of the army. Then Grant would attack Lee, whom he expected to occupy the old Mine Run works.

However, since Lee knew the general position of the Army of the Potomac, he would bring on a battle, with Ewell's and Hill's corps marching east on their respective roads to find the Federals and pin them down. Then he would repeat his tactics of the year before (but with Longstreet instead of Jackson) and sweep around the Union line to strike its flank.

The next morning, May 5, both armies maneuvered as planned, but the Federal infantrymen, absent most of their cavalry scouts, groped along blindly on the narrow, brushy roads. Ahead of Warren's corps on the Orange Turnpike, Brig. Gen. Charles Griffin had posted three regiments from his division as pickets. An hour after dawn, after V Corps had marched by on its way south to Parker's Store, the pickets were preparing to abandon their position when the head of Ewell's column swung into view. It took the pickets and several officers a couple of tries to convince Warren that Lee was not safely ensconced behind Mine Run but instead was probing toward the Federal right flank. Once convinced, Warren passed the word along to Meade and Grant and quickly realigned his corps for combat. The commanding generals hastened troops to Warren's aid—they hoped before Lee had disposed his own men for the attack.

Their hopes were quickly dashed. Ewell and Hill were prepared to engage piecemeal if they could not get their entire corps to the front at once. And the Federals struggled forward through the brush and briars. The Wilderness was on the Confederates' side.

Warren sent the divisions commanded by Brig. Gen. James S. Wadsworth and Brig. Gen. Samuel W. Crawford probing the underbrush between the turnpike and the plank road to locate the Confederates while Griffin's division moved west on the Orange Turnpike. From Sedgwick's corps, Brig. Gen. Horatio G. Wright's division protected Griffin's right flank, while Brig. Gen. George W. Getty's division hurried to secure the intersection of Brock Road (Rte. 613) and the Orange Plank Road.

The first engagements took place on the Orange Turnpike as Ewell's men encountered a regiment of Wilson's cavalry. At Saunders's Field, the action intensified as the Confederates entrenched and withstood repeated Federal assaults. Late in the afternoon, Sedgwick's corps arrived to augment the Union force, but the result by evening was a stalemate.

Soon after the Orange Turnpike engagement began, Getty's VI Corps division raced south on the Germanna Ford Road (Rte. 3) to seize the important Orange Plank Road and Brock Road (Rte. 613) intersection. By nightfall the Federals firmly held the ground. Under cover of darkness, both sides dug in and added troops to their lines. Lee assured a nervous Hill that Longstreet would arrive early to support him, while Grant ordered dawn attacks on the turnpike and the plank road.

At first Grant's attacks succeeded. Lee's left flank—Ewell's corps on the Orange Turnpike—was threatened, and Hill was driven back on the right, but then Ewell's defense stiffened and held. On the plank road at the Tapp farm, however, Hill's line collapsed. Lee rode forward to help Hill stop the rout and guide the placement of artillery, then sent couriers to find Longstreet and urge him forward. Just after 6 A.M., when all seemed lost, the Texas Brigade hove into view, marching at the head of Longstreet's corps.

Lee, his face flushed, rode to greet the brigade. Informed of its identity, he stood in his stirrups, waved his hat over his head, and shouted, "Texans always move them!" The brigade answered with a roar and hustled forward toward the oncoming Federals. Suddenly the men slowed, aware that Lee had not remained behind but instead was riding with them, intent on leading the counterattack himself. Appalled, many of them shouted "Go back, General Lee, go back!" and "Lee to the rear!" and clutched at Traveller's reins. Lee still rode on until the men mobbed him so that he could no longer advance, and Brig. Gen. John Gregg, commander of the Texas Brigade, argued him into turning around. Just then, Longstreet rode near and Lee trotted over to confer with him. After they separated, one of Lee's aides told Longstreet of the incident and urged him not to let it happen again. Longstreet rode up to Lee and with difficulty persuaded him to retire and leave the details to "Old Pete." Lee's "blood was up," or, as Longstreet later put it, he was "off his balance." But he yielded to Longstreet and withdrew.

Longstreet greeted each of his regiments as it marched forward. While he formed them into columns for a mass assault, the Texas Brigade charged ahead alone. It smashed through the first Federal line and bent the second one back before almost being overwhelmed by numbers. For twenty minutes the brigade held its ground before falling back; of the 800 who went into battle, only some 250 escaped unhurt.

The rest of Longstreet's corps entered the fray, and for the next six hours the fighting raged back and forth through the tangled undergrowth of the Wilderness. North of Hill's line, Ewell's men engaged Warren's and Sedgwick's in much the same manner. Grant ordered Burnside to

Fighting in the woods: part of Brig. Gen. James S. Wadsworth's division near the spot where he was mortally wounded. LIBRARY OF CONGRESS

lead IX Corps to Hancock's aid against Longstreet. Burnside complied slowly, stopping to allow his men to cook breakfast, then bogging down in the thickets after an unexpected attack by Brig. Gen. Stephen D. Ramseur's brigade slowed his two lead divisions to a crawl. The Federal attack had run out of steam, and the initiative passed to Lee.

The Confederate commander sought a way to outflank his opponents. At about 10 A.M. Longstreet found it. Hancock's left flank was exposed south of the plank road, and Longstreet organized an impromptu attack by sending his aide, Lt. Col. G. Moxley Sorrel, who with Maj. Gen. Martin L. Smith, Lee's chief engineer, was to lead the men against Hancock. The ploy worked. Soon Hancock's right was collapsing as well under the onslaught of fresh Confederate brigades sent to augment Sorrel. Longstreet rode toward the fighting to launch the final attack that might bring victory.

Although the Federals were retreating, Longstreet's men were in almost as much disarray as their opponents. Some regiments were moving into the fight as others marched out of it to reorganize. Just as Longstreet gained the front, Brig. Gen. Micah Jenkins led his fresh brigade forward. In the smoke and limited visibility of the Wilderness, the 12th Virginia Regiment, emerging from the thickets, mistook Jenkins's men for Federals and opened fire, mortally wounding Jenkins. A bullet also ripped into Longstreet's neck and emerged from his right shoulder, but he would survive. The next day Lee appointed Maj. Gen. Richard H. Anderson to temporarily lead Longstreet's corps.

The loss of Longstreet devastated Lee; only Longstreet knew his plan of combat. In the early afternoon, Lee and the other Confederate generals struggled to regain control of Longstreet's and Hill's corps, locate the Federals, and continue the attack. Hancock's men, meanwhile, fell back in disarray to their earthworks along Brock Road behind its intersection with the Orange Plank Road. By 2 P.M. it appeared as though Longstreet's corps was about to resume its assault, and Hancock's men braced for it.

Instead, they heard the sound of gunfire to their right, not to their front. It was Burnside, some eight hours behind schedule, supporting Hancock by attacking Longstreet's left flank. Suddenly the tables had turned on the Confederates, or so it seemed. Then Alabama troops challenged Burnside's attack, and after heavy fighting brought it to a halt. Now the way was clear for Lee to secure the victory that Longstreet had handed him.

Shortly after 5 P.M. he launched his assault against Hancock's corps at the intersection. Hancock's men had made good use of the delay by strengthening their fortifications, especially by adding abatis—trees felled with their tops interlocking and pointing toward the Confederates. As Longstreet's men struggled through this natural "barbed wire," they were met by a deafening roar of rifle fire. At about the same time, Burnside renewed his assault on Longstreet's flank but again made little progress. By 6 P.M. the fighting throughout the southern sector had died out.

To the north, however, Ewell's corps launched another attack as dusk fell, with Brig. Gen. John B. Gordon turning the Union right flank with his brigade. At first the Confederates succeeded. Gordon rolled up part of Sedgwick's VI Corps line, and his men came close to capturing the Union general as he attempted to rally his panic-stricken troops, but soon the Federal flight slowed as reinforcements held firm. The Confederate attack faded away with the last of the light, and the battle of the Wilderness came to an end.

The battle concluded as a tactical draw, with each army in about the same position it had occupied at the beginning. After two days of combat, the exhausted men counted their casualties. The Federals had lost some 18,000 killed, wounded, and missing and the Confederates about 11,000.

The Wilderness battlefield, like that of Chancellorsville, has been affected by the sprawl of development from Fredericksburg and an exponential increase in house construction as the area has become a bedroom suburb of Northern Virginia. Although portions of the battlefield lie within the Fredericksburg and Spotsylvania National Military Park, much of it is private property and, like the Chancellorsville battlefield, threatened with obliteration. ■

SPOTSYLVANIA COURT HOUSE

The heaviest fighting in the battle of the Wilderness ended on the evening of May 6, 1864. The next morning, at the beginning of a day of skirmishing that gained no territory for either side, the commanding general of each army issued orders that would affect the course of the spring campaign. Lt. Gen. Ulysses S. Grant ordered Maj. Gen. George G. Meade, commander of the Army of the Potomac, to secure the strategically important intersection at Spotsylvania Court House. Meade detached Maj. Gen. Gouverneur K. Warren and V Corps to accomplish the mission.

Gen. Robert E. Lee deduced that Grant might move his army there, or perhaps to Fredericksburg. Lee therefore detached from the Army of Northern Virginia the corps formerly commanded by Lt. Gen. James Longstreet and now led by Maj. Gen. Richard H. Anderson and ordered it to the same location. Anderson's infantry would march to Shady Grove Church Road (present-day Rte. 608), while his artillery moved south from Parker's Store to the church road, where the two wings would unite and march east to the courthouse.

The most significant engagements of the day took place about three miles south of the armies at Todd's Tavern, which stood at the intersection of the Brock and Catharpin Roads. As the Federals were to march down Brock Road (Rte. 613) to Spotsylvania Court House, Maj. Gen. Philip H. Sheridan and his cavalry were dispatched to the road junction by way of the Catharpin Road (Rte. 612), which took them around the infantry's left flank. At the same time, Lee dispatched Maj. Gen. J. E. B. Stuart and his cavalry to secure the same intersection and prevent any incursions westward on the Catharpin Road. The opposing cavalry corps clashed at the junction in a series of engagements that continued until nightfall. At dusk Sheridan retired to Todd's Tavern, satisfied to hold the intersection. This proved a mistake, as the Confederate route of march remained clear while Stuart still threatened the Federal path. Maj. Gen. Fitzhugh Lee had positioned his cavalry division across Brock Road southeast of the tavern, and his men spent much of the night building timber barricades.

Warren's and Anderson's corps marched after dark on May 7, neither aware of the other as they trekked down parallel roads a mile or two apart. At 3 A.M. on Sunday, May 8, first Brig. Gen. Wesley Merritt's cavalry and then Warren's infantry attacked Fitzhugh Lee's roadblocks while Brig. Gen. James H. Wilson led his Federal cavalry division on a wide sweep to Spotsylvania Court House. Fitz Lee fell back down Brock Road slowly, contesting every foot of ground and buying time for Anderson's men, who marched through the countryside west of the courthouse. By 8 A.M. Lee

had occupied Laurel Hill, an eminence overlooking the intersection of Brock Road and Old Courthouse Road (Rte. 648). Just then, the vedettes arrived from Spotsylvania Court House to report Wilson's cavalrymen in the village. Lee ordered the 3rd Virginia Cavalry down Brock Road to retard Wilson's progress. Stuart arrived, and together the Confederate commanders prepared their men and artillery to meet Warren's infantry.

Anderson's corps, meanwhile, had reached the intersection of Shady Grove Church Road and Old Courthouse Road and learned of Stuart's and Lee's situation and of the Federal cavalry in the village. Anderson split his lead division (Brig. Gen. Joseph B. Kershaw's) and sent two brigades to the courthouse and two to Laurel Hill. The latter arrived at their destination minutes ahead of the lead of Warren's corps, thereby "winning" the race begun the night before.

Warren launched his attack on Laurel Hill, against what many in the Union army believed to be the Confederate rear guard, at about 8:30 A.M. Behind makeshift breastworks of fence rails and small pine trees the 2nd and 3rd South Carolina Infantry Regiments fired successive volleys and drove Warren's men back. Meanwhile, Kershaw's brigades marched into Spotsylvania Court House just as Wilson and his cavalry, forewarned in the nick of time, withdrew. Lee's rear and flank were now secure.

At the end of the day on May 8, Anderson's corps occupied the ground around Laurel Hill with his left flank on the Po River. Ewell's corps filed into place on Anderson's right, extending the Confederate line to the north and east. The men worked through the night to occupy the high ground, erect earthworks, dig traversing trenches, clear fields of fire, and construct artillery emplacements. Most of

DIRECTIONS: I-95 Exit 130B (State Rte. 3 West, Culpeper), w. on State Rte. 3 about 7.8 miles to Chancellorsville Visitor Center entrance, Fredericksburg and Spotsylvania National Military Park. From visitor center, continue w. on State Rte. 3 3.6 miles to Rte. 613 (Brock Rd.); s. (left) on Rte. 613 10.2 miles to Spotsylvania Courthouse Battlefield Exhibit Shelter on left; driving and walking tour information available; return to Rte. 613; s. (left) on Rte. 613 1.8 miles to Spotsylvania and State Rte. 208 (Courthouse Rd.); e. (left) on State Rte. 208 .1 mile to Virginia Civil War Trails markers on left; continue on State Rte. 208 .3 mile to Confederate Cemetery on right; continue 2.3 miles to state historical marker EM-2, Engagement at Harris Farm (Bloomsbury), on left; continue on State Rte. 208 4.1 miles to U.S. Rte. 1; s. (right) on U.S. Rte. 1 about .9 mile to I-95 Exit 126. Visit the National Park Service Web site at nps.gov/parks.html for a virtual tour of this and other national parks.

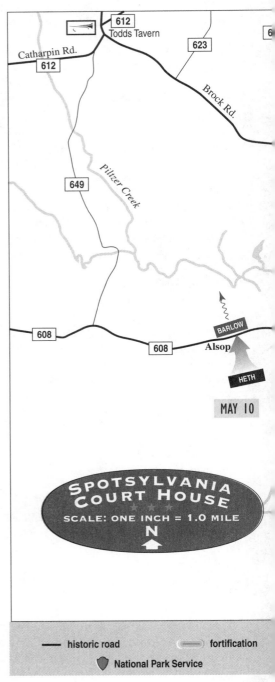

them got no rest until dawn on Monday, May 9. When the sun shone on their night's work, however, they received a shock.

In the dark, following the contours of the land and the tree line, the men had constructed a salient, a portion of the line that projected north toward the Federals. Dubbed the Mule Shoe because of its shape, it was exposed to enfilading Union artillery fire, and should the rest of the line be breached, the occupants of the Mule Shoe could be cut off and attacked front and rear. Furthermore, the apex of the salient had not been built at the military crest of the high ground—the point farthest forward on the slope from which all the ground in front could be covered by gunfire—but farther back, so that part of the field in front was hidden from view. Nothing could be done about the Mule Shoe, however, for on the Union side, Federal soldiers, like their Confederate counterparts, spent the night building earthworks and dodging artillery shells. Morning found Sedgwick's VI Corps facing the Mule Shoe's left flank, with Warren's V Corps on the right opposite the Confederate left.

Sedgwick rode along his line ordering adjustments to the positions occupied by his artillery and infantry, as they were within range of Confederate sharpshoot-

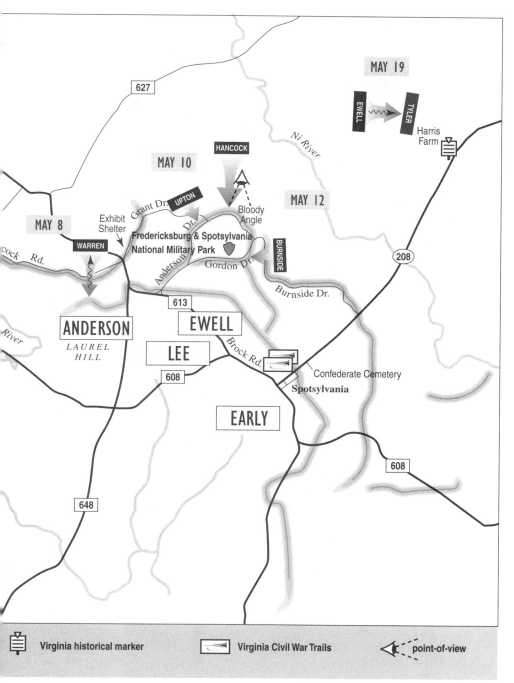

MAY 19

EWELL → TYLER

Harris Farm

627

Ni River

MAY 10

HANCOCK

MAY 12

Grant Dr. UPTON

Bloody Angle

Exhibit Shelter

MAY 8

Fredericksburg & Spotsylvania National Military Park

WARREN

Anderson Dr.

Gordon Dr.

BURNSIDE

cock Rd.

Burnside Dr.

208

613

ANDERSON

LAUREL HILL

EWELL

River

LEE

Brock Rd.

Confederate Cemetery

608

Spotsylvania

EARLY

608

648

Virginia historical marker   Virginia Civil War Trails   point-of-view

ers. Grant paid him a visit about 8 A.M., and Sedgwick, much beloved his troops, assured him that matters were going well in his sector. The commander in chief rode off, and Sedgwick spent the next hour and a half moving troops and teasing the young men who dodged the odd artillery shell and sharpshooter's bullet. At about

9:30 A.M., after he scolded a private who hit the dirt, Sedgwick blustered that the Confederates "can't hit an elephant at that dis—," but was struck by a bullet below the left eye that killed him instantly. Sedgwick's men were inconsolable, and Grant was stunned when he heard the news. Many Confederate officers such as Stuart, who had been friends with the jovial Sedgwick in the "old army," likewise mourned his death.

Brig. Gen. Horatio G. Wright took command of VI Corps. On his left, Burnside and IX Corps marched toward Spotsylvania Court House, seeking to pass Lee's right flank. Their movement was delayed for more than an hour, however, by Sheridan's cavalry crossing their front on its way to threaten Richmond and draw Stuart into combat. Had the Union cavalry remained with the main army to reconnoiter, it would have found that Lee's right flank barely extended east beyond the Mule Shoe and therefore left the courthouse village virtually unprotected.

Grant ordered Hancock to march south on Brock Road (Rte. 613), cross the Po River twice, and attack Lee's left flank. Hancock soon ran into opposition, however, and his progress slowed. By dark he was poised on the banks of the Po at Block House Bridge but decided to wait there until morning. Grant's best opportunity to destroy the Army of Northern Virginia slipped away.

Lee, in contrast, seized the opportunity to go on the offensive when it presented itself. Here suddenly were three divisions of Hancock's corps virtually waiting to be attacked. Lee detached part of Early's corps (Brig. Gen. William Mahone's and Maj. Gen. Henry Heth's divisions) from the vicinity of Spotsylvania Court House and marched them west in the darkness to strike Hancock at first light.

On Tuesday, May 10, none of the commanding generals' plans—which changed almost hourly—went as expected. Mahone and Heth fought Hancock's corps and succeeded in spoiling the Federal assault but did not deliver Lee's hoped-for crushing blow. Grant abandoned his turning movement against Lee's flank and instead launched an attack against the entire Confederate line at 5 P.M. His scheme went awry, however, and the result was a bloody stalemate.

Meade upset the timetable by approving an early (4 P.M.) attack by Warren's corps on the Confederate works atop Laurel Hill. If the works had been strong two days earlier, Anderson's men had since rendered them virtually impregnable. Federal scouts sent forward just before the attack returned to their lines shaking their heads and muttering. By the time the assault commenced, the Federal troops were so demoralized by the reports and the heavy gunfire from the hilltop that their attacks were only halfhearted and easily repulsed. Grant postponed his 5 P.M. attack by an hour to give Hancock time to organize another assault on Laurel Hill with most of II Corps.

In midafternoon Meade approved another plan: attack the left side of the Mule Shoe. Col. Emory Upton, commander of the 121st New York Infantry, would lead a picked command of VI Corps regiments against the salient, burst through the Confederate defenses, and be quickly supported on the left by Brig. Gen. Gershom Mott's division from II Corps. Upton was to step off at 5 P.M. but soon received word to wait until 6 P.M., in accordance with Grant's postponement. Mott, however, never heard of the change of hour and launched his assault at 5 P.M. He was easily repulsed by artillery fire and pulled his men back from the front. No one informed Upton.

At 6:35 P.M., after a brief delay, Upton's men charged their assigned sector of the Mule Shoe, holding their fire despite heavy losses until they were almost in the Confederate works. At first the attack succeeded, but soon an effective counterattack stopped the Federal momentum. Once more Lee tried to lead his men forward but they refused to go until he retired to the rear. Upton's men held on gallantly for as long as they could, waiting for the promised help that never came. Finally, they fled to the rear under overwhelming Confederate pressure.

Meanwhile, Hancock's attack against Laurel Hill was canceled when Confederate troops were spotted making what appeared to be a flanking march around him. After the reports were determined to be incorrect, the cancellation was withdrawn and the attack was rescheduled for 7 P.M. Like Upton's, it at first succeeded despite heavy Confederate fire and the reluctance of some Union regiments to advance. But once again no reinforcements followed up, and Hancock's men fell back.

On the Union left, near Spotsylvania Court House, Burnside led IX Corps in an attack against the Confederate right flank. After an hour-long probe beginning at 6 P.M., however, Burnside withdrew his lead division and disengaged. Darkness soon fell and mercifully ended the day's bloody and fruitless fighting. Grant and his generals had performed poorly but Lee and his subordinates had not. The Union effort had been stymied by miscommunications, delays, and confusion. The Confederates, in contrast, had fought a brilliant defensive battle under Lee's leadership.

The next day, May 11, both sides spent their time probing the other's lines and guessing at intentions. For once Lee guessed wrong. Whereas the Federals commonly misread Lee's preattack maneuvers as signs of impending retreat, now Lee made the same mistake. A driving rainstorm precluded any action that day; instead, Grant decided to follow Upton's temporary success against the Mule Shoe

with a massed attack by Hancock's and Burnside's corps on May 12. He ordered Burnside to march IX Corps north, to prepare to attack the eastern base of the salient—a move that Lee misinterpreted as presaging a march by the entire Federal army to Fredericksburg. Late in the afternoon, Lee directed the artillery to leave the Mule Shoe and form up to set off in pursuit of the Army of the Potomac.

Grant's plan called for a coordinated attack at 4 A.M. While Burnside struck from the east, Hancock would storm the Mule Shoe from the north. Wright's VI Corps would form the reserve to Hancock's right, and Warren was to hold his corps in readiness to assist. To get into position to launch the attack, three divisions of Hancock's corps would march three miles after midnight.

Despite the Federals' best efforts to maintain noise discipline, the Confederates heard them coming. Maj. Gen. Edward "Allegheny" Johnson, of Early's corps, commanded in the Mule Shoe, and he was alarmed to see his artillery heading for the rear as a threatening rumble arose from the woods to his front. Johnson rode to the rear to plead his case to Ewell for the artillery's return. Informed a short time later, Lee reluctantly assented, ordering the artillery back to the salient by first light. Unfortunately, the order did not reach the sleeping gunners until about half an hour before dawn. In drizzle, fog, and predawn darkness, the men limbered up their cannons and started back to the Mule Shoe.

At the appointed hour, Hancock and Burnside and their men stood in the mud and waited for the light to come up so they could see their way over the unfamiliar ground. In the Mule Shoe, Johnson and his men noted the sudden silence in the woods. Finally, at 4:35 A.M., Hancock gave the order, and the attack began.

The oncoming Federals smashed through the Confederate picket lines. The

Confederates pulled the triggers on their rifle-muskets, but instead of a roar and a sheet of flame, there was only the sound of percussion caps popping harmlessly. The incessant rain had soaked their gunpowder, and before they could clear their weapons and reload, the Federals were upon them with bayonets fixed.

Thus began more than twenty-three hours of almost constant combat at the Mule Shoe. From the start, the fighting was hand-to-hand as men stabbed and beat each other to death with bayonets and clubbed rifles. One of Johnson's aides rode to the rear for reinforcements. Amid the chaos, the first of the artillery returned and unlimbered, but the Federal wave was irresistible, and entire Confederate regiments were engulfed and surrendered. In a few minutes both Allegheny Johnson and Brig. Gen. George H. "Maryland" Steuart, commanding the right of the salient, were made prisoners. To the southeast, Burnside sent his corps slamming into the base of the Mule Shoe in Steuart's sector. By a little after 5 A.M., the Confederates in the salient were on the verge of rout, with only

the extreme left and right flanks holding firm for the moment. The center had collapsed, and Lee's army was about to be split in half.

Brig. Gen. John B. Gordon rode to seal the breach, leading what had been Early's division from its reserve position below the Mule Shoe. Brig. Gen. Robert D. Johnston's brigade took the point and slammed into the Federal advance through the salient, bringing it momentarily to a halt. Lee, finding Gordon organizing the rest of his division for the attack, grimly rode to its front and prepared to lead the charge himself. Gordon's soldiers, however, surrounded Lee and forcibly turned Traveller around, some tugging at his bridle and others pushing on his flanks. Finally, Lee retired.

Gordon's men charged into the melee, assaulting the Federals with bayonets, rifles, pistols, and swords. Shots were fired at such close range that the muzzle flashes set uniforms afire. The fighting raged back and forth for several minutes; finally, Ewell sent word to Gordon that if he could hold on for another quarter hour, four brigades of reinforcements would arrive in support.

U.S. soldiers form for another attack on the Mule Shoe (tree line), in a drawing Alfred R. Waud titled "The Toughest Fight Yet." LIBRARY OF CONGRESS

In the Confederate rear, Lee found Ewell trying to stem the flow of Confederates fleeing the front. Raining oaths and sword blows on them in equal amounts, the excitable Ewell galloped around like a man possessed. Lee, in contrast, spoke quietly to the soldiers, who began to turn around and go back to the fight.

On the Confederate left wing in the salient, Ramseur had been holding firm. Now he pulled his command out of its works, turned it around, and sent it against the Federal right flank in the Mule Shoe, leading the charge personally until a bullet struck his right arm below the elbow. His brigade soon recaptured part of the earthworks and continued to fight not only the Federals who were inside the Mule Shoe and occupied traversing trenches but those just across the ramparts who were trying to get in.

By 6 A.M., an hour and a half after it began, Grant's attack had stalled. To turn the tide, Grant ordered Warren's V and Wright's VI Corps—his reserve—into action. Wright attacked the western angle of the Mule Shoe at about 6:30 A.M. Both sides took advantage of natural swales and depressions in the earth to shelter some of the troops while others attacked amid a constant downpour of bullets and shells. This part of the Mule Shoe soon became known as the Bloody Angle.

Warren, ordered to attack the Laurel Hill works to draw off some of the defenders of the Mule Shoe, hesitated. Some of his men, mindful of the earlier assaults that had been bloodily repulsed, refused to advance. Finally, after repeated orders from Grant and Meade, Warren launched his attack at 10 A.M.; it quickly failed under one barrage after another of effective rifle and artillery fire from the Confederate defenders. One division thereby stalled an entire Federal corps.

On the Union far left, Burnside likewise had to be prodded to attack in concert with Hancock's corps. Despite a blizzard of sharply worded messages from Grant, Burnside attacked piecemeal and without linking up with Hancock on his right. As a result, the Confederate right flank clung to its toehold at the base of the Mule Shoe and stopped Burnside's and Hancock's advance. The Confederates there occupied an eastward bulge in the line called Heth's Salient. By 2 P.M. their defense had proven so effective that Lee ordered a counterattack, launched just as Burnside finally got a coordinated attack under way and disrupting his advance. By 3 P.M. both sides had achieved equilibrium.

Grant responded to the stalemate by throwing more divisions against the Bloody Angle to find Lee's weak spot. Federal units at the front were so disorganized by the initial assault and Confederate counterattacks, however, that the reinforcements only added to the confusion. Lee likewise countered with one brigade after another.

The fighting at the angle continued throughout the morning and afternoon, and if anything grew in intensity as additional troops entered the fray. In a few places the Federal assault lines were some ten men deep, and they were matched across the earthworks by hordes of Confederates. The Federals brought artillery up to the works and poured shot and shell across to blast men and horses to pieces. Caissons rolled over the dead and wounded alike and ground them into the mud. Periodically, the men on one side or the other would get word to "clear the trench," and they would hoist the corpses of their fallen comrades and heave them over the ramparts to fall on the enemy beyond. The constant buzz and roar of bullets and shells overhead drowned out officers' orders, and the storm of lead brought instant death to anyone who poked his head over the earthworks.

Even darkness did not stop the slaughter, although it gradually declined. Around midnight, the Federal divisions began to withdraw back to the safety of their wood line. On the Confederate side, Lee had ordered a new set of works dug across the base of the salient, and by dawn on May 13 his men had fallen back and occupied them. Cautiously, Union units crept toward the abandoned Mule Shoe and slipped over the ramparts. There they found the remains of a nightmare.

Bodies were piled up several deep on both sides of the works, and some obviously dead men seemed to squirm and writhe as the wounded beneath them struggled to extricate themselves from the heaps. The survivors were appalled by the mutilation that the dead had undergone from the intensity of the fire. Headless corpses and body parts and unrecognizable chunks of flesh lay everywhere. One Union officer found the body of his friend; it had no area larger than four inches that had not been struck, and eleven bullet holes were in the sole of one shoe alone. The soldiers of each army who had witnessed the ghastly slaughters at Antietam and Fredericksburg and Gettysburg agreed that they paled in comparison to the Mule Shoe.

Only the strength of the Confederate earthworks and the tendency of foot soldiers and artillerists to fire high kept the death toll from being greater than it was. Still, the numbers were appalling: some 9,000 killed, wounded, and captured Federals and about 8,000 Confederate casualties. The Confederates lost several able brigadiers.

Grant's attacks on strongly entrenched positions, however necessary, proved costly. Unlike Lee, he commanded from his headquarters behind the lines rather than getting close enough to the front to understand the obstacles his subordinates faced. (For instance, Grant might not have insisted on Warren's attack against Laurel Hill if he had seen the strength of the Confederate works for himself.) In addition, the piecemeal attacks undertaken by the Union divisions blunted their effectiveness.

On the Confederate side, Lee blundered badly in ordering the artillery out of the Mule Shoe, and his men paid dearly for his mistake. But Lee decisively countered Grant's attacks and inspired his soldiers by his presence.

The soldiers of both armies had seldom fought with greater intensity or courage. For the next two days the survivors nursed their wounds and waited stolidly for the next round of combat. Each had gained respect and admiration for the fighting abilities of his opponents.

Grant ordered the II, V, and VI Corps to shift eastward, thereby lengthening the Federal left flank and realigning the Union position from an east-west to a north-south direction along the Fredericksburg Road (present-day Rte. 208). The shift was accomplished on May 14–15, and on May 18 Grant launched II and VI Corps in an attack on Lee's defenses south of the Mule Shoe. Just after 4 A.M., Federal artillery opened up on the Confederate positions, and the infantry assault soon followed. By 9 A.M., however, the fighting all but ceased when Hancock convinced Grant that Lee's position was impregnable.

On May 19 Ewell led his corps out of the Confederate defenses in a turning movement to the north and east, in an attempt to locate and strike the Federal right flank. The extreme right rested on a hilltop at the Harris farm, manned by several heavy artillery regiments that recently had served in the defenses of Washington. Without their huge guns, the artillerymen were expected to act as infantry, a role foreign to them.

The Confederates approached the Harris farm from the northwest after 4 P.M., with Ramseur's brigade in the lead and Gordon's division just behind. As they turned east to face the Federals, the former stood to the left of the latter. Despite their lack of infantry training, the artillerymen marched to meet the attack. Although they suffered severe casualties, they came close to enveloping Ramseur's and Gordon's commands on either flank. The Confederates soon withdrew, and the last battle of Spotsylvania Court House ended. On May 21, Grant disengaged the army and began marching south once more, again determined to maneuver around Lee.

During the two-week-long battle, approximately 100,000 Federals fought some 52,000 Confederates. Grant's army suffered about 18,000 casualties, or 18 percent of the total engaged, while Lee's army lost roughly 12,000, or 23 percent. In other words, one army lost a fifth, the other a quarter, of its strength. The war in Virginia had entered a phase in which the ability to kill had reached new heights.

Much of the Spotsylvania Court House battlefield lies within the boundaries of the Fredericksburg and Spotsylvania National Military Park. Much, however, also remains in private hands and is therefore susceptible to development. A bypass to be constructed around the county seat may intensify that tendency. ■

YELLOW TAVERN

As the Army of the Potomac maneuvered against the Army of Northern Virginia early in May 1864, a simmering feud between two Union generals boiled over. Maj. Gen. George G. Meade, commander of the army, was noted for his quick temper and sarcastic tongue. Maj. Gen. Philip H. Sheridan, with a fiery temper of his own, was as combative off the battlefield as on it. The two men argued loudly about Sheridan's failure to defeat his Confederate counterpart, Maj. Gen. J. E. B. Stuart, and to stop the Confederate march from the Wilderness to Spotsylvania Court House.

When Meade reported the argument to Lt. Gen. Ulysses S. Grant, the general in chief of United States forces in the field, Grant decided to allow Sheridan to lead his cavalry corps against Stuart and seek the fight he desired. Sheridan eagerly accepted the challenge. At dawn on Monday, May 9, he was in his saddle and waiting at the intersection of the Orange Plank Road

(present-day Rte. 621) and Catharpin Road (Rte. 612). His division commanders—Brig. Gen. Wesley Merritt, Brig. Gen. David M. Gregg, and Brig. Gen. James H. Wilson—had arrived in the night with their horse soldiers, some 10,000 in number. The corps was assembled in one place for the first time during the campaign.

Sheridan planned to ride east far enough to pass Lee's right flank, then turn south on the Telegraph Road (U.S. Rte. 1) to Richmond. He would threaten the Confederate lines of communication and supply and capture or destroy stores where he found them. The purpose of the expedition was not only to raid and harass but also to lure Stuart into combat and then crush him.

Confederate cavalry, in small units, dogged the expedition from the start. Most of Stuart's troopers, however, were on duty near Spotsylvania Court House, and it was not until midday that Brig. Gen. Williams C. Wickham's brigade left the Confederate lines in pursuit. Sheridan, meanwhile, decided to leave Telegraph Road at the Ta River crossing and strike southwest on a road (Rte. 603) that led through Mitchell's Shop and Chilesburg to the North Anna River at Anderson's Ford.

Wickham caught up with Sheridan's rear guard at Jerrell's Mill on the Mat River and fought a series of increasingly sharp actions for the next few hours. Brig. Gen. Henry E. Davies, Jr., of Gregg's division, commanded the rear guard. He and his officers pronounced themselves satisfied that they were keeping Wickham at bay, while the Confederates believed they harried the Federals every step of the way.

At Mitchell's Shop, Davies arranged an ambush. At about 5 P.M. the oncoming Confederates found themselves facing a mere squadron of the 6th Ohio Cavalry blocking the roadway. Wickham ordered part of the 3rd Virginia Cavalry to charge and the Ohioans fled, the Confederates racing after. Suddenly the woods exploded in flame and smoke as the 1st Massachusetts and 1st Pennsylvania opened fire. The surviving Virginians struggled to cut their way out, and Wickham sent the rest of the regiment circling around to strike Davies's force in the rear. The action was heavy for several minutes until the Confederates escaped.

About the same time, the head of Sheridan's column reached the North Anna River. Riding at the front, Brig. Gen. George A. Custer's brigade crossed the river at Anderson's Ford and pressed on to Beaver Dam Station, a stop on the Virginia Central Railroad, while the rest of the corps remained on the north bank and bivouacked. At about 8 P.M., in a violent thunderstorm, Custer and his men attacked the station, where two trains waited to transport Union prisoners to Richmond. The Federal troopers freed the captives, burned the depot, and captured the trains. They also fought a brief engagement with a small Confederate unit that stumbled on

DIRECTIONS: I-95 Exit 83B (State Rte. 73, Parham Rd. West), w. on Parham Rd. about .5 mile to U.S. Rte. 1; n. (right) on U.S. Rte. 1 .6 mile to state historical marker E-7, Yellow Tavern; continue 1.4 miles over I-295 Exit 43C (U.S. Rte. 1 North, Ashland) to state historical markers E-8 and E-9, Stuart's Mortal Wound, and E-51, Battle of Yellow Tavern; continue .2 mile to Virginia Center Pkwy. (first traffic light n. of interchange); e. (right) on Virginia Center Parkway .5 mile to Telegraph Rd.; s. (right) on Telegraph Rd. .2 mile to Stuart monument and Virginia Civil War Trails marker; return to U.S. Rte. 1; n. (right) on U.S. Rte. 1 1.1 miles to Rte. 656 (Sliding Hill Rd.); e. (right) on Rte. 656 .5 mile to I-95 Exit 86 (Atlee/Elmont).

the burning station. The Confederates fled, and Custer led his men and the liberated prisoners back to the North Anna.

Back at Mitchell's Shop, Wickham and Stuart formulated a plan to defeat Sheridan. Brig. Gen. Lunsford L. Lomax soon arrived with his brigade, followed by Brig. Gen. James B. Gordon, of Maj. Gen. William H. F. "Rooney" Lee's division, and his brigade. Although he had only three brigades to face three Union divisions, Stuart planned to strike Sheridan as he crossed the North Anna River. With Lomax's and Gordon's brigades, he would cross the river at Davenport Bridge and attack Sheridan from the south, while Fitzhugh Lee, with Wickham's brigade, would hammer him from the north.

Meanwhile, Sheridan decided on a plan of his own. He would drive south to Mountain Road (U.S. Rte. 33 to the Henrico County line, Mountain Road thereafter), then east to Telegraph Road, then south again to Richmond. He also decided that if Stuart attempted a flanking movement against him, he likely would cross the North Anna at Davenport Bridge. Sheridan ordered Capt. Abraham K. Arnold to lead a detachment to the bridge being reconstructed by Confederate engineers. Arnold arrived there just before Stuart shortly after dawn on May 10, drove off the workmen, and then watched Stuart

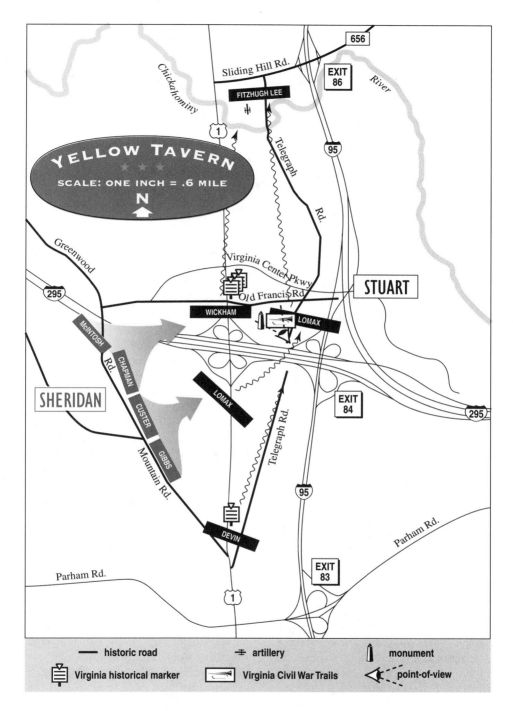

YELLOW TAVERN
★ ★ ★
SCALE: ONE INCH = .6 MILE
N

——— historic road	╪ artillery	⬗ monument
Virginia historical marker	Virginia Civil War Trails	point-of-view

trot west to find another crossing. Arnold sent a detachment upriver to the next ford, then followed himself. After a brief engagement with Stuart's vanguard, Arnold and his detachment galloped back toward Beaver Dam Station to rejoin

Sheridan. They found, however, that the main column had crossed the North Anna and was being harassed by Wickham's brigade. Arnold and his men fought their way past the Confederates and galloped across the Little River bridge to safety just before Union engineers destroyed it.

Stuart reunited his brigades at Beaver Dam Station and devised a new plan. Gordon would press on against Sheridan's rear guard. Stuart and Fitzhugh Lee, meanwhile, would ride east with Lomax's and Wickham's brigades to Hanover Junction, where two important railroads—the Richmond, Fredericksburg & Potomac and the Virginia Central—intersected. They then would proceed south on Telegraph Road to the intersection where Mountain Road entered Brook Turnpike and there ambush Sheridan's vanguard.

Sheridan likewise decided to divide his command. He designated Col. J. Irvin Gregg's brigade of Brig. Gen. David M. Gregg's division the rear guard, ordered Merritt's and Wilson's divisions to proceed down Mountain Road to Telegraph Road as planned, and sent Davies and his brigade to raid Ashland. There Davies was to destroy track and whatever stock he found.

Each side was on its way before dawn on Wednesday, May 11. However, whereas Sheridan's men had ridden at a leisurely pace and were essentially well rested, Stuart's troops approached exhaustion, having pursued and fought the larger Federal force several times, ridden miles on futile flanking missions, and slept little.

Shortly after sunrise Gordon attacked Gregg's brigade at Ground Squirrel Bridge, where Mountain Road crossed the South Anna River. A brisk skirmish and hand-to-hand mounted combat ended when the Federals fled toward Sheridan's main force, then acted as the rear guard for Wilson and Merritt. At about the same time, Davies engaged Wickham's brigade

at Ashland Station, then withdrew before 6:30 A.M.

By 8 A.M. Lomax had reached the intersection. Just below the intersection, on the eastern side of Brook Turnpike, stood the Yellow Tavern, a dilapidated, unpainted-pine building.

Lomax positioned the 6th Virginia Cavalry near the intersection, and the 5th and 15th Virginia to the north along Telegraph Road. Stuart and Fitzhugh Lee soon rode up and approved Lomax's dispositions. Once Wickham arrived, Stuart placed his brigade on a hill just north of Turner's Run that overlooked the intersection from the north. When Sheridan appeared, Stuart planned to let him approach the road junction and strike him on his left flank and rear. Stuart dispatched his aide, Maj. Henry B. McClellan, to Richmond to ascertain whether infantry could be spared from the defenses to join in the impending combat.

At about 9 A.M., the Federals drew near, with Merritt's division leading the way. When the 6th Pennsylvania Cavalry encountered the 6th Virginia's pickets, the engagement began. Soon Merritt's division was in battle formation along the Brook Turnpike, with Col. Thomas C. Devin's brigade on the right near the tavern, Col. Alfred Gibbs's in the middle, and Custer's on the left near Mountain Road. Custer dismounted half his force and sent it forward against the skirmishers, who drove back the Federals. Custer's men charged once more, but Confederate artillery forced them back again.

On Custer's right, Gibbs and Devin had better success. Building momentum, they pushed their way north on Telegraph Road. The Confederates joined Wickham's line to the left. By late morning the fighting subsided, and each side studied the other's situation.

Stuart's men occupied a strong defensive position, but Merritt's division had succeeded in interposing itself between the Confederates and their capital. Sheridan, unable to overcome Stuart with a single division, settled down to wait for Wilson before renewing the fight. For his part, Stuart was in no hurry to leave his position before reinforcements arrived. He hoped for infantry from Richmond to strike Merritt's rear. Anticipating that very eventuality, Sheridan dispatched Devin and two regiments down the turnpike. They rode as far as the second line without encountering significant opposition. Returning to Sheridan, Devin reported finding no Confederate troops.

At about 2 P.M. McClellan returned to Stuart's line from Richmond and informed the general that infantry reinforcements were about to march to his aid. Within the hour, however, Wilson arrived and formed his division on Merritt's left. Now two divisions faced two brigades, and Sheridan launched his attack.

Custer led the assault himself at 4 P.M., just as a violent thunderstorm broke over the battlefield. While the 5th and 6th Michigan Cavalry advanced on foot toward Wickham's position, the 1st and 7th Michigan Cavalry and the 1st Vermont Cavalry charged the Confederate artillery battery on horseback. Stuart quickly realized that the guns were the principal objective and called for the 1st Virginia Cavalry to mount a countercharge.

Suddenly the Federals began surging the other way as the 1st Virginia charged into them and pushed them off the hilltop. Stuart, mounted on horseback, shouted encouragement. As the 5th Michigan streamed by in retreat, a forty-eight-year-old trooper turned and fired a single shot from his pistol at the big, bearded rider. Pvt. John A. Huff, an expert marksman, hit his target squarely in the stomach.

The battle ended soon after, with Stuart's cavalry in full flight. Sheridan made

Site of Stuart's mortal wounding, with monument erected by former comrades. VIRGINIA DEPARTMENT OF HISTORIC RESOURCES, JOHN S. SALMON

good on his boast to "whip Stuart"—although he might have been of more benefit to Grant had he and his troopers remained at Spotsylvania Court House.

Stuart was transported to Richmond by ambulance and brought to the house of a kinsman on East Grace Street. He lingered in excruciating pain, hoping to speak to his wife one last time, before expiring shortly after 7:30 P.M. on Thursday, May 12. Flora Stuart arrived after a long and harrowing ride just a few minutes too late. J. E. B. Stuart was buried the next day.

Stuart's brilliant career had lasted some three years. As Lee's "eyes and ears," he never gave his commander a piece of false information. He had led the Confederate cavalry through its years of glory and had been struck down as its inevitable decline began.

The battle of Yellow Tavern cost the two sides some 800 casualties. It is most significant, of course, as the engagement in which Stuart was mortally wounded. Otherwise, neither side gained any advantage.

The battlefield has been almost obliterated by subsequent residential and commercial development. A stone monument in the midst of a residential neighborhood marks the site where Stuart fell. ■

When it became clear to Gen. Robert E. Lee on May 21, 1864, that Lt. Gen. Ulysses S. Grant was marching Maj. Gen. George G. Meade's Army of the Potomac past his right flank, the Confederate commander expected that Grant would do what his other opponents had done after sustained combat against the Army of Northern Virginia: retreat. Grant, on the other hand, expected Lee to attack. When he did not, but instead maneuvered south toward the vital rail intersection at Hanover Junction, a disappointed Grant suspected that the Confederate army was too debilitated to fight. Each general misjudged the other.

Most of the Army of Northern Virginia marched south on Telegraph Road while the Army of the Potomac followed on parallel roads to the east. On the morning of May 22, the Confederate advance guard approached the North Anna River about a quarter mile west of present-day U.S. Rte. 1 and crossed the Chesterfield bridge. The soldiers rested and bathed in the river while the remainder of the army crossed. Lee, certain that Grant would not attack, left only a light guard to protect the bridge as well as the railroad bridge a short distance to the east.

The next day the vanguard of the Union army surprised the Confederate pickets. Grant quickly deployed Maj. Gen. Winfield Scott Hancock's II Corps to capture the Chesterfield bridge and ordered Maj. Gen. Gouverneur K. Warren's V Corps upriver to cross the North Anna at Jericho Mill. After a Federal artillery barrage, at about 6 P.M. two Union brigades attacked the single brigade Lee had stationed at the bridge and captured the structure intact. That night, the Confederates tried to burn it; they failed but did destroy the railroad bridge downstream.

Upstream, Warren's Corps forded the river at Jericho Mill at about 1:30 P.M. with no opposition. Once across, the 22nd Massachusetts Infantry encountered the 1st South Carolina Rifles, and a brief firefight ensued. Soon, however, the area became quiet, and the Federals spent the afternoon constructing pontoon bridges and establishing headquarters on the south side of the North Anna River.

View from Jericho Ford toward C.S.A. works on distant ridge. LIBRARY OF CONGRESS

The Confederates, meanwhile, had not been idle. Lt. Gen. A. P. Hill, who had resumed command of his corps, ordered Maj. Gen. Cadmus M. Wilcox to lead his division north to Jericho Mill. At about 5:45 P.M., just as the Federals were cooking their suppers, Wilcox struck. At first the Confederates, who had the advantage of surprise, succeeded in jolting the Union line, but soon the superior Federal numbers (15,000 against the Confederates' 6,000) began to tell. By 6:30 Wilcox's division was withdrawing. Nightfall ended the fighting.

Lee and his subordinates met at Hanover Junction to ponder the situation. The Federals had crossed the river in force at Jericho Mill, on the Confederate left flank, but had only established a bridgehead at the Chesterfield bridge on the right. Lee's army could not defend every crossing point between the mill and the bridge, but neither could it simply withdraw toward Richmond, for the army would be compelled to take shelter behind the city's defenses—an option Lee believed would mean the death of the Army of Northern Virginia.

Lee decided to make the best of the circumstances by altering his defensive line into an inverted V. He ordered Hill to pull most of his corps back from the North Anna River to a new left flank running from Ox Ford southwest to the Little River. Lt. Gen. Richard S. Ewell's corps would secure the right flank facing Telegraph Road, the Chesterfield bridge, and Hancock's II Corps. Lt. Gen. Richard H. Anderson's corps would hold the center, which extended from Ox Ford southeast along the North Anna for half a mile, then swung back from the river to join Ewell near Telegraph Road.

Lee's rearrangement of his line was masterful. It forced Grant to choose his point of attack carefully, for to support an assault by Warren or Hancock on either of Lee's flanks, his remaining corps would have to march for miles. Lee, on the other hand, had a relatively short distance to shift troops between flanks and occupied a remarkably strong defensive position at Ox Ford.

Grant, misinterpreting Lee's pullbacks on the morning of Tuesday, May 24, decided that the Confederates were retreating to Richmond and ordered a general pursuit, supplementing V Corps with Maj. Gen. Horatio G. Wright's VI Corps. It soon became apparent that Ox Ford was heavily defended. Now Grant was compelled to slow his advance on the flanks and await the capture of the stronghold at the ford.

Maj. Gen. Ambrose E. Burnside's IX Corps faced Ox Ford in the center of the Union line. Burnside pushed his corps forward steadily throughout the day as he sought to cross the ford and bring his command even with V and VI Corps. By 3 P.M., Maj. Gen. Thomas L. Crittenden's IX Corps division had forded the river above Ox Ford and established contact with Brig. Gen. Samuel Crawford's division of V Corps. Crittenden's first brigade, commanded by Brig. Gen. James H. Ledlie, pressed forward alone despite cautionary orders and attacked the western flank of the Ox Ford defenses.

Ledlie, drunk, sent his men into the teeth of an artillery barrage. When the shattered Union line got within range of the Confederate entrenchments, the defenders opened up with small-arms fire and further ravaged the Federals.

On Ledlie's right, elements of Crawford's division tried to render assistance but were stopped short by a withering fire. At about 6 P.M. the Confederates finally realized that the attacking force was so small that it might be surrounded and crushed. Three regiments issued from the fortifications to attack Ledlie's flanks as a

DIRECTIONS: I-95 Exit 98 (State Rte. 30, Doswell), w. on State Rte. 30 about .7 mile to U.S. Rte. 1; n. (right) on U.S. Rte. 1 1 mile to Rte. 688 (Doswell Rd.) at Doswell; e. (right) on Rte. 688 .4 mile to Hanover Junction and Virginia Civil War Trails marker; return to U.S. Rte. 1; continue w. on Rte. 688 .5 mile to Rte. 602 (Mount Hope Church Rd.); n. (right) on Rte. 602 1.6 miles to Rte. 684 (Verdon Rd.); w. (left) on Rte. 684 .6 mile to state historical marker EA-4, Attack at Ox Ford, and North Anna Battlefield Park on right; walking tour maps, trails, and markers in park; return by Rte. 684 2.6 miles to U.S. Rte. 1; s. (right) on U.S. Rte. 1 1.3 miles to State Rte. 30; e. (left) on State Rte. 30 .6 mile to I-95.

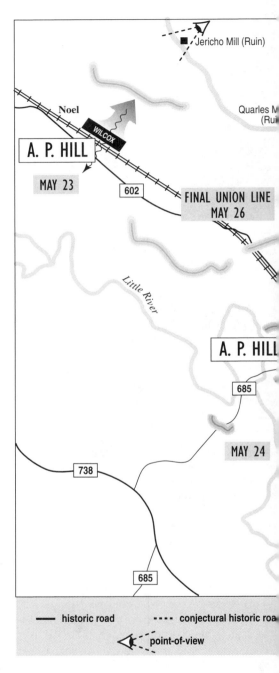

thunderstorm erupted over the battlefield. The sudden assault and the storm sent the Federals retreating in near panic. The survivors reached the safety of the division's earthworks; Ledlie turned over command of his brigade to a junior officer for the night.

While Ledlie's ill-fated attack stalled in the afternoon, Hancock's II Corps advanced cautiously from the Chesterfield bridge down Telegraph Road and the railroad tracks toward the vital rail intersection at Hanover Junction. Col. Thomas A. Smyth's brigade led the way at about 3 P.M., reconnoitering for the corps. Maj. Gen. Robert E. Rodes's division of Ewell's corps and Maj. Gen. Charles W. Field's division of Anderson's corps guarded the junction, with Rodes's division facing east along the tracks and Fields's facing north behind a farm road.

A few hundred yards north of the farm road, some of Field's troops formed a strong line of skirmishers and sharpshooters. Protected by rifle pits and trenches and supported by a two-gun section of the Richmond Howitzers, the skirmishers brought the Federal advance to a halt. Smyth assaulted the skirmish line repeatedly and soon captured its rifle pits, but the Confederates counterattacked. Suddenly the same thunderstorm that had

drenched Ledlie's men burst over the battleground, soaking the soldiers. The combatants glared at each other from a few feet away but held their fire, fearing that

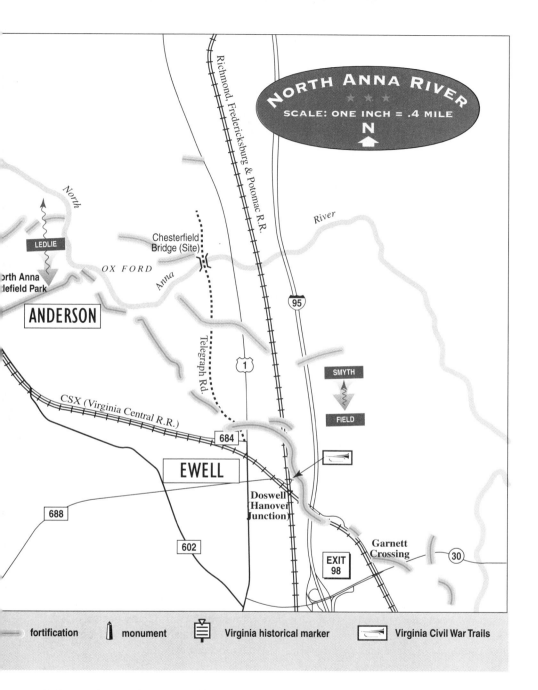

NORTH ANNA RIVER
★ ★ ★
SCALE: ONE INCH = .4 MILE
N

Richmond, Fredericksburg & Potomac R.R.

River

North

LEDLIE

Chesterfield
Bridge (Site)

OX FORD

North Anna
Battlefield Park

Anna

95

ANDERSON

Telegraph Rd.

1

SMYTH

FIELD

CSX (Virginia Central R.R.)

684

EWELL

688

Doswell
Hanover
Junction

602

Garnett
Crossing

EXIT
98

30

fortification | monument   🖹 Virginia historical marker   [▱] Virginia Civil War Trails

their powder would get wet if they fired and then attempted to reload. When the storm passed, the fighting resumed. The Confederates soon breached their former works, and Smyth's men retreated. By then, darkness was falling, and Grant ordered a halt for the night.

That night and the next day, Grant

learned the extent and strength of the Confederate defenses. He ordered his army to entrench and spent May 25–26 skirmishing and probing for a weakness. Finding none, on the night of May 26–27 he disengaged his army and began maneuvering once more around Lee's right flank. Lee, confined to his tent by a debilitating attack of diarrhea, could do little but counter Grant's probes and flanking march.

The North Anna River campaign cost the Army of Northern Virginia 1,800 casualties and the Army of the Potomac 2,600. Surprisingly, the drunken James Ledlie was promoted to division commander. Grant also placed Burnside and XI Corps under Maj. Gen. George G. Meade's authority, thereby eliminating the divided command that had blurred the lines of responsibility.

Much of the North Anna River battlefield remains in farmland, but development is an ever-present threat. The Confederate earthworks at Ox Ford, some of the most impressive remaining anywhere, were donated to Hanover County by General Crushed Stone, Inc., which owns a large quarry and extensive acreage adjoining them. ■

HAW'S SHOP

When Lt. Gen. Ulysses S. Grant disengaged the Army of the Potomac from the North Anna River line on May 26–27, 1864, to begin its march around the Army of Northern Virginia's right flank, Maj. Gen. Philip H. Sheridan led the way. This vanguard consisted of cavalry divisions commanded by Brig. Gen. Alfred T. A. Torbert and Brig. Gen. David M. Gregg as well as Brig. Gen. David A. Russell's infantry division, which was detached from VI Corps.

To block Grant's approach to Richmond from the east, Gen. Robert E. Lee ordered Lt. Gen. Richard S. Ewell's corps to march south to Ashland, a station on the Richmond, Fredericksburg & Potomac Railroad. Both Lee and Ewell suffered severely from the diarrhea that also plagued the army; Lee rode in a carriage and Ewell in an ambulance, while Maj. Gen. Jubal A. Early assumed command of Ewell's corps.

Lee, uncertain of Grant's intentions, ordered Maj. Gen. Wade Hampton and his cavalrymen to reconnoiter into eastern Hanover County and locate the Union army on Saturday, May 28. Hampton's reconnaissance force consisted of Maj. Gen. W. H. F. "Rooney" Lee's division, Brig. Gen. Williams C. Wickham's brigade from Maj. Gen. Fitzhugh Lee's division, Hampton's brigade (commanded by Brig. Gen. Thomas L. Rosser), and the 4th and 5th South Carolina regiments—recent arrivals who had tasted little combat.

Grant ordered a similar reconnaissance to learn the whereabouts of the Confederate army. Gregg led his division west on the Hanovertown Road, followed some time later by Torbert and his division. At about 10 A.M., Gregg arrived at the intersection of three roads. Haw's machine shop was located just west of the intersection, and Enon Church stood just less than a mile farther west. Gregg posted pickets to guard the junction just as Hampton's force rode into view.

The 10th New York Cavalry had advanced beyond the main Federal body; Wickham's and Rosser's brigades charged and drove the New Yorkers back. Almost simultaneously, the 1st Pennsylvania Cavalry struck the Confederates, who then

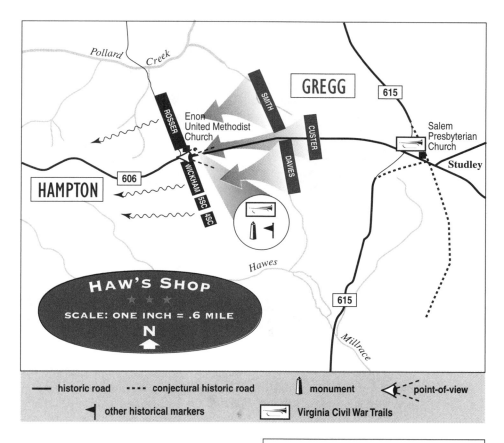

Pollard Creek

ROSSER

Enon
United Methodist
Church

SMITH

GREGG

615

CUSTER

Salem
Presbyterian
Church

Studley

WICKHAM

DAVIES

HAMPTON

606

5SC

4SC

Hawes

HAW'S SHOP
★ ★ ★

SCALE: ONE INCH = .6 MILE

N

615

Millrace

—— historic road   · · · · conjectural historic road   ⚑ **monument**   ◁ **point-of-view**

◀ **other historical markers**   **Virginia Civil War Trails**

retreated to Hampton's defensive line, centered on the white-frame church. Rosser's division formed the Confederate left, Wickham's brigade the center, and the 4th and 5th South Carolina the right. For some seven hours the horse soldiers fought a dismounted engagement between the church and Haw's Shop.

After the initial attacks were repelled by the Confederates, the Federal right flank was strengthened by part of Col. J. Irvin Gregg's brigade. Despite the additional men, however, the fighting remained a bloody stalemate as the two sides struggled for the possession of fence lines and ditches. From Union prisoners Hampton learned that the Union army had crossed the Pamunkey River—the information Lee had sent him to gather.

DIRECTIONS: I-295 Exit 41A (Rtes. 2/U.S. 301 North, Hanover), n. on Rtes. 2/U.S. 301 North about .3 mile to state historical marker ND-11, Lee's Headquarters; continue about 1.5 miles to Rte. 640 (Shady Grove Rd.); s. (right) on Rte. 640 .5 mile to Rte. 606 (Studley Rd.); e. (left) on Rte. 606 4.9 miles to Enon United Methodist Church and Virginia Civil War Trails marker and Richmond Battlefield Markers Association marker (Enon Church); continue on Rte. 606 1.1 miles to Salem Presbyterian Church and Virginia Civil War Trails marker at Rte. 615 (Williamsville Rd.); return to I-95.

Toward dusk, Brig. Gen. George A. Custer, of Torbert's division, arrived. His troopers deployed on both sides of the Mechanicsville road (present-day Rte. 606), and Custer led them toward the Confederate line just as Hampton ordered his men to withdraw. The inexperienced South

View east from Enon Church on route of Custer's attack. VIRGINIA DEPARTMENT OF HISTORIC RESOURCES, JOHN S. SALMON

Carolinians lingered and bore the brunt of Custer's assault. After some hard fighting, both sides withdrew to tend their wounded.

The Haw's Shop engagement was inconclusive, a collision between reconnaissance parties. Some 4,000 Federal cavalrymen engaged about 2,500 Confederates. Gregg's command suffered 344 casualties (among the mortally wounded was Pvt. John A. Huff, who had fired the shot that mortally wounded Maj. Gen. J. E. B. Stuart) and Hampton's lost an estimated 400 men.

Haw's Shop itself has long since vanished, but Enon Church still stands, its shell holes covered with patches. Most of the battleground remains in farms and woodlots and in private hands. ■

TOTOPOTOMOY CREEK

On Saturday, May 28, 1864, Gen. Robert E. Lee deployed the Army of Northern Virginia to meet the threat posed by the southeastward movement of the Army of the Potomac as ordered by Lt. Gen. Ulysses S. Grant. Lee's infantry shifted to a new line on the south bank of Totopotomoy Creek, a swampy tributary of the Pamunkey River some nine miles north of Richmond that formed a natural obstacle for the Union army. (Lee himself, still suffering from diarrhea and possibly angina, occupied the Clarke family house near Atlee Station on the Virginia Central Railroad. His reluctant decision to move out of his cherished tent and into a private dwelling indicated the severity of his illness.)

The Totopotomoy Creek line sliced across the principal roads and railroads that led south and southwest to Richmond. If Grant's true intention was to attack directly toward the Confederate capital, then his troops would have to charge across the low, swampy ground, scale the

bluffs to the south, and assault well-prepared earthworks. At first it appeared that Grant would take the bait Lee offered him, as the Federal commander spent almost two days probing the Confederate lines.

By May 29–30 Lt. Gen. A. P. Hill's corps occupied the Confederate left, with Hill's own left flank resting on the high ground above the Pamunkey River. Lt. Gen. Jubal A. Early's corps filled the center of the line from about Opossum Creek east toward Polly Hundley's Corner. At that intersection, the Confederate line bent to the south, with Lt. Gen. Richard H. Anderson's corps constituting the right flank.

Opposing the Confederates on the north side of Totopotomoy Creek, ready to attack, stood Maj. Gen. Winfield S. Hancock's II Corps, Maj. Gen. Ambrose E. Burnside's IX Corps, and Maj. Gen. Gouverneur K. Warren's V Corps. They probed across Totopotomoy Creek to Lee's lines on Sunday, May 29, but with little result. On Monday, May 30, Maj. Gen. Horatio

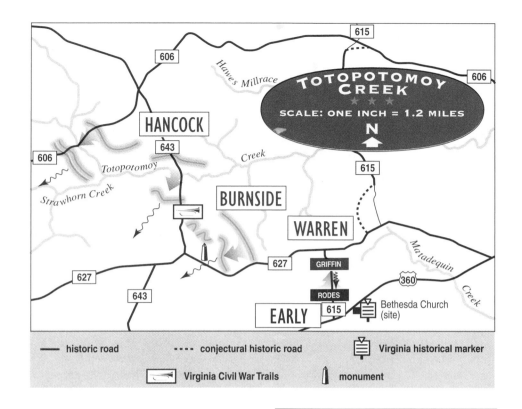

| historic road | ---- conjectural historic road | 🏛 Virginia historical marker |
| 🔲 Virginia Civil War Trails | ⬆ monument |

G. Wright's VI Corps worked its way west to assault Hill on the Confederate left flank. However, it floundered through Crump's Creek and did not arrive at its assigned position until almost dark, too late to attack.

Elsewhere along the Totopotomoy on May 30, the Federals initially experienced modest successes. Burnside crossed the creek and pushed back Confederate pickets near Polly Hundley's Corner and Pole Green Church. Just north of Strawhorn Creek, part of Hancock's corps captured the forward fieldworks occupied by Early's pickets; digging furiously, the Federal soldiers "turned" the trenches so that they faced the main Confederate line to the west instead of the Totopotomoy. The Union attacks developed slowly, however, and failed to make much headway against the strong Confederate defenses.

DIRECTIONS: Recommend first visiting the Richmond National Battlefield Park Visitor Center (open 9–5 daily) at Tredegar Iron Works in downtown Richmond: I-95 Exit 74C (U.S. Rte. 33 West/U.S. Rte. 250 West, Broad St.) and follow blue-and-green signs to visitor center, Brown's Island, and Belle Isle, w. on Broad St. about .4 mile (5 blocks) to 8th St.; s. (left) on 8th St. 5 blocks to Canal St.; w. (right) on Canal St. 3 blocks to 5th St.; s. (left) on 5th St. 2 blocks to Tredegar St.; w. (right) on Tredegar Street .1 mile to visitor center and parking lot. Visit the National Park Service Web site at nps.gov/parks.html for a virtual tour of this and other national parks. To visit the battlefield directly: I-295 Exit 41A (Rtes. 2/U.S. 301 North, Hanover), n. on Rtes. 2/U.S. 301 North about 1.8 miles to Rte. 640 (Shady Grove Rd.); s. (right) on Rte. 640 .5 mile to Rte. 606 (Studley Rd.); e. (left) on Rte. 606 3.7 miles to Rte. 643 (Rural Point Rd.); s. (right) on Rte. 643 1.7 miles to Virginia Civil War Trails marker; continue .4 mile to Rte. 627 (Pole Green Rd.); e. (left) on Rte. 627 .2 mile to 36th Wisconsin Volunteer Infantry monument on left; continue 3.8 miles to U.S. Rte. 360 (Mechanicsville Tpke.); w. (right) on U.S. Rte. 360 2 miles to state historical marker O-12, Bethesda Church; continue w. on U.S. Rte. 360 2.7 miles farther to Rte. 643 (Lee-Davis Rd.); n. (right) on Rte. 643 1.8 miles to Rte. 627 (Meadowbridge Rd.); e. (left) on Rte. 627 1.8 miles to I-295 Exit 38A (Rte. 627 East, Pole Green Rd.).

Remains of U.S. and C.S.A. earthworks still are found in the woods around Totopotomoy Creek. VIRGINIA DEPARTMENT OF HISTORIC RESOURCES, ASHLEY M. NEVILLE

At about noon, Lee—now substantially recovered from his illness—reconnoitered with Early and realized that Warren's corps on the Union left flank was still moving into position near Bethesda Church, a small edifice near Shady Grove Church Road. He ordered Early to lead an attack against that point. He also ordered Anderson to assist Early if the opportunity arose.

The attack was disjointed and piecemeal. Maj. Gen. Robert E. Rodes's division, at the head of Early's assault, struck a division of Warren's corps at about 2 P.M. but was driven back. Early had expected Brig. Gen. Stephen D. Ramseur to lead his division quickly to Rodes's support, but Ramseur arrived almost four hours later. Anderson's corps never did reinforce the attack, which Brig. Gen. Charles Griffin's division soon repelled.

By the end of the day, Lee and Grant each had lost about 1,100 men killed, wounded, and missing. The bloody results exemplify the Overland campaign: chronic combat fatigue, loss of command control, and decimated ranks. Grant learned that a direct assault along the Totopotomoy would be costly and that his best policy was to continue slipping east and south around Lee's right flank. Rather than face swamp and field fortifications, Grant determined to realign his corps on an east-west axis to attack Lee's flank directly.

Most of the extensive Totopotomoy Creek earthworks erected by Federals and Confederates have been obliterated by the renewed farming operations that followed the war and by more recent residential development. A few fieldworks remain intact in some heavily wooded tracts, but eventually most of them may disappear beneath new housing subdivisions. The Association for the Preservation of Virginia Antiquities owns thirty-five acres with extensive earthworks at Bethesda Church. Lockwood, the Clarke house, was disassembled in 1990 by Richmond Newspapers, Inc., and moved from its historic site despite widespread public opposition after the corporation bought the land to construct a printing plant. ■

OLD CHURCH

After the Totopotomoy Creek engagements, Lt. Gen. Ulysses S. Grant ordered a cavalry reconnaissance to locate the right flank of Gen. Robert E. Lee's Army of Northern Virginia. He also sought to secure the important intersection at Old Cold Harbor. Brig. Gen. Alfred T. A. Torbert's division of Maj. Gen. Philip H. Sheridan's cavalry corps was encamped near the Haw's Shop battleground; on Monday, May 30, 1864, Torbert led his men toward the Confederate flank, with Col. Thomas C. Devin and his brigade in front, followed by the brigades of Brig. Gen. George A. Custer and Brig. Gen. Wesley Merritt.

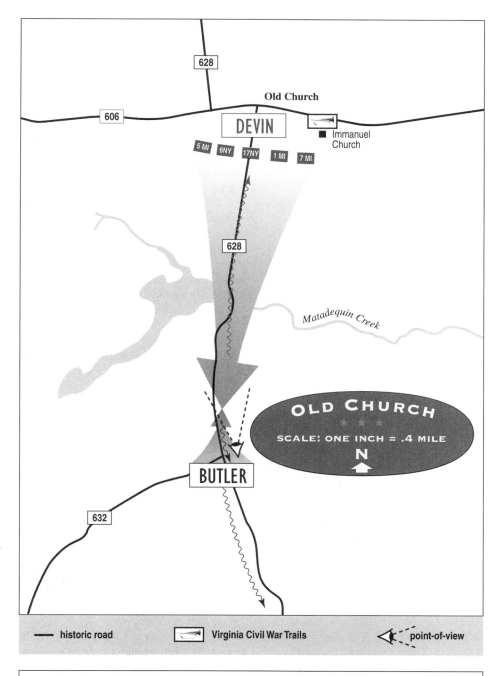

628

Old Church

606

DEVIN

Immanuel
Church

5 MI 6NY 17NY 1 MI 7 MI

628

Matadequin Creek

OLD CHURCH
★ ★ ★
SCALE: ONE INCH = .4 MILE
N

BUTLER

632

━━━ historic road   Virginia Civil War Trails   ◀ point-of-view

DIRECTIONS: I-295 Exit 37A (U.S. Rte. 360 East, Tappahannock), e. on U.S. Rte. 360 about 7.1 miles to Rte. 606 (Old Church Rd.); right on 606 1.4 miles to Rte. 628 (McClellan Rd.) at Old Church intersection; continue .3 mile to see Immanuel Episcopal Church; return to intersection; s. (left) on Rte. 628 .9 mile to Matadequin Creek and continue up hill to turn around and return to I-295.

View north along route of Butler's advance.
VIRGINIA DEPARTMENT OF HISTORIC RESOURCES, JOHN S. SALMON

At Old Church they turned south (present-day Rte. 628) toward the Chickahominy River. Not quite a mile beyond, the road descended steeply to Matadequin Creek, then ascended sharply over bluffs. Devin secured the crossing and posted pickets on the south side of the creek while he awaited the rest of the division.

To the southwest, Brig. Gen. Matthew C. Butler was leading his brigade of Confederate cavalry toward Matadequin Creek. Lee, assuming that Grant would continue maneuvering around his right flank, had ordered a reconnaissance to locate the Union left flank. Butler and his men rode northeast on Parsley's Mill Road

(Rte. 609) to the Black Creek Church road, then turned north toward the creek.

At about 2 P.M. Butler struck Devin's picket line, a squadron of the 17th New York Cavalry. Two Federal squadrons hurried to support the pickets, and Butler withdrew to regroup. An hour later he resumed the attack and pushed the reinforced pickets north across the creek. Devin strengthened his line by dismounting the 9th New York to the left of the 17th and the 6th New York to its right. He also ordered three regiments of Custer's brigade to dismount, positioning the 5th Michigan on the right of the Black Creek Church road and the 1st and 7th Michigan on the left. Charging across the creek, his troopers compelled Butler's smaller force to fall back toward Old Cold Harbor.

The next day, May 31, after a struggle, the Federal cavalry seized Old Cold Harbor, Grant's objective, and secured Grant's supply line. The engagement at Old Church, or Matadequin Creek, cost the combatants some 90 casualties.

At present, the engagement site is in a good state of preservation under private ownership. There has been some residential development along Rte. 628, however, and more is likely to occur. ▪

COLD HARBOR

The occupation of the road intersection at Old Cold Harbor on Tuesday, May 31, 1864, placed the Army of the Potomac in a position to turn the right flank of the Army of Northern Virginia. Lt. Gen. Ulysses S. Grant ordered his corps commanders to form a new line of attack along an east-west axis centered on the intersection. Gen. Robert E. Lee, realizing the danger this posed to his army, issued similar orders to his subordinates. The race

was on: Would Lee's men fortify their positions in time to resist an attack, or would Grant's soldiers stage an assault before they could dig in?

Both Lee and Grant needed fresh troops. Lee had written a stream of messages to Richmond, arguing that if his field operations failed for want of reinforcements, then the city would fall regardless of how many men manned the defenses. In response, Maj. Gen. Robert F. Hoke's divi-

C.S.A. lines at Cold Harbor were breached briefly in a few places; here the commander of the 164th New York falls at the head of his regiment. LIBRARY OF CONGRESS

sion was detached from the Confederates' Howlett line and transported by train to Atlee Station on the Virginia Central Railroad, arriving after noon on May 31. Grant, meanwhile, on May 30 ordered Maj. Gen. William F. "Baldy" Smith, commander of the XVIII Corps, to join the main army near Cold Harbor. Grant's numbers soon would swell to 108,000, Lee's to 62,000.

Frustration plagued Grant, however. First, Smith's corps got lost as it marched on June 1, thereby delaying a planned assault until late in the afternoon; the attack failed. The next day, after Maj. Gen. Winfield S. Hancock's II Corps arrived exhausted from a night-long march, a co-ordinated attack planned for dawn was postponed until the morning of June 3.

Lee's men, meanwhile, made the most of these delays to construct some of the most comprehensive earthworks they had yet built. By daylight on June 3, the fortifications extended for almost seven miles

from Totopotomoy Creek south to the Chickahominy River. They were several trenches deep, with lateral works connecting them to protect soldiers marching to or from the front line, and provided enfilading fields of fire. At the Chickahominy, Maj. Gen. Fitzhugh Lee's cavalry division watched the river for any sign of a Federal flanking movement.

Grant, however, was determined to execute his straight-ahead attack against Lee planned for two days earlier, now that he had all of his corps in position at last. On the Union right flank, Maj. Gen. Ambrose E. Burnside's IX Corps faced Lt. Gen. Jubal A. Early, with Maj. Gen. Gouverneur K. Warren's V Corps next. Smith's XVIII Corps occupied the center of the Federal line opposite Lt. Gen. Richard H. Anderson. Maj. Gen. Horatio G. Wright's VI Corps and Hancock's II Corps completed the Union left flank opposite Maj. Gen. Henry Heth's division of Lt. Gen. A. P. Hill's corps.

The evening before the attack, Col. Horace Porter, one of Grant's aides, was delivering final orders to the front when he noticed several soldiers bent over their uniform jackets, apparently intent on patching tears in the cloth. When he looked more closely, however, Porter saw that the men had written their names and regiments on pieces of paper and were pinning them to the backs of their jackets. They expected to be killed in the morning, and wanted their bodies identified.

Dawn came at about 4:30 A.M. on Friday, June 3. Federal artillery opened the attack, followed by an infantry charge in an all-out mass assault on the Confederate line. Within a short time, according to many accounts, the attack had ended in failure and some 5,500 Union soldiers lay dead or wounded. In the afternoon the Federal V and IX Corps lost another 1,500 men in battling Heth and Early on the Confederate left.

The II, VI, and XVIII Corps attacked the Confederate center and right flank with some 50,000 men. Most of the ground had not been reconnoitered, and several regiments floundered in creeks or swamps or ravines slick with mud from the previous night's rain. Many men were killed or wounded by cannon and rifle fire from the Confederate fieldworks before they got within a hundred yards of the opposing lines.

Only a handful of II Corps regiments succeeded in penetrating the Confederate works and then only for a moment. They belonged to Brig. Gen. Francis C. Barlow's division and included the 7th New York Heavy Artillery and 2nd Delaware Infantry, both of Col. John L. Brooke's brigade. They struck Maj. Gen. John C. Breckinridge's division on the Confederate right and engaged in hand-to-hand combat with the 26th Virginia Regiment, pushing the Confederates back. Brig. Gen. Joseph Finegan's Florida brigade rushed to the

DIRECTIONS: Recommend first visiting the Richmond National Battlefield Park Visitor Center (open 9–5 daily) at Tredegar Iron Works in downtown Richmond: I-95 Exit 74C (U.S. Rte. 33 West/U.S. Rte. 250 West, Broad St.) and follow blue-and-green signs to visitor center, Brown's Island, and Belle Isle, w. on Broad St. about .4 mile (5 blocks) to 8th St.; s. (left) on 8th St. 5 blocks to Canal St.; w. (right) on Canal St. 3 blocks to 5th St.; s. (left) on 5th St. 2 blocks to Tredegar St.; w. (right) on Tredegar Street .1 mile to visitor center and parking lot. Visit the National Park Service Web site at nps.gov/parks.html for a virtual tour of this and other national parks. To visit the battlefield directly: I-295 Exit 38A (Rte. 627 East, Pole Green Rd.), e. on Rte. 627 about 4.2 miles to Rte. 615 (Walnut Grove Rd.); s. (right) on Rte. 615 1.1 miles to Rte. 1507 (Colts Neck Rd.); s. (left) on Rte. 1507 .8 mile to Rte. 635 (Sandy Valley Rd.); s. (left) on Rte. 635 .5 mile to Rte. 633 (Beulah Church Rd.); s.e. (right) on Rte. 633 1.4 miles to State Rte. 156 (Cold Harbor Rd.) at Old Cold Harbor; w. (right) on State Rte. 156 .5 mile to Garthright House; continue .1 mile farther on State Rte. 156 to Cold Harbor National Cemetery; continue .1 mile farther on State Rte. 156 to Richmond Battlefield Markers Association marker (Battle of Cold Harbor, Position of the Federal Sixth Corps); continue .4 mile farther on State Rte. 156 to Richmond National Battlefield Park Cold Harbor Unit and Richmond Battlefield Markers Association marker (Battle of Cold Harbor, The Confederate Main Line); return on State Rte. 156 to Old Cold Harbor; s. (right) on State Rte. 156 3.9 miles to I-295 Exit 31A (State Rte. 156 North, Cold Harbor).

Virginians' rescue, and recovered the forward trenches. The surviving Federals retreated, and the battle effectively ended.

The assault gave Lee one of his most lopsided victories. The battles around Cold Harbor, including the one on June 3, cost the Federals some 12,000 casualties and the Confederates about 2,500. Desultory skirmishing and sharpshooting continued for a few days, and both armies continued digging in, but on the night of June 12, the Army of the Potomac began to march again, toward Petersburg. Grant had abandoned the idea of a direct attack on Richmond; Lee had won his last major victory.

The Cold Harbor battlefield is among the most threatened in Virginia. Much of it already has been obliterated by residential

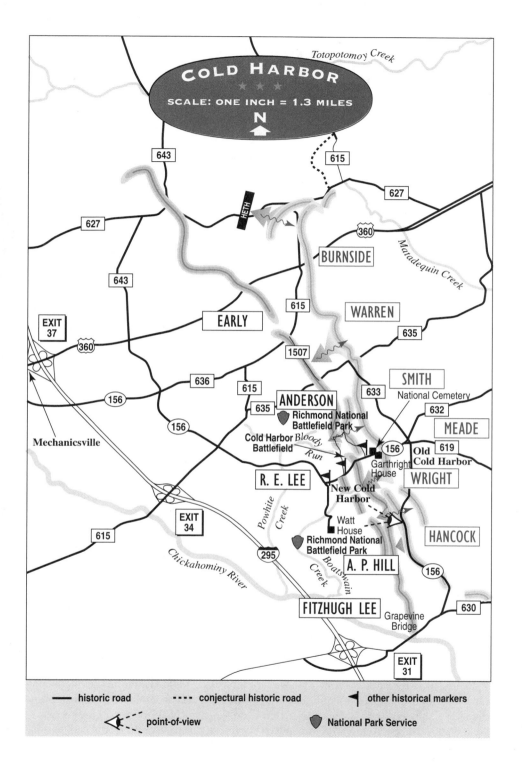

development, and more of the same is likely to happen. Only fragments have been preserved within the 150-acre unit of Richmond National Battlefield Park in Hanover County. The county owns 50 acres, however, as a park around the Garthright House and has constructed an interpretive trail to guide visitors to the earthworks there. ■

TREVILIAN STATION

Following the Confederate victory at Cold Harbor on June 3, 1864, Lt. Gen. Ulysses S. Grant contemplated other options for the Army of the Potomac. He observed that the Federal forces had met with some success in the Shenandoah Valley, where Maj. Gen. David Hunter had defeated Brig. Gen. William E. "Grumble" Jones at Piedmont in Augusta County on June 5. To further harry the Confederates and disrupt any plans to resupply their troops in the Valley, Maj. Gen. Philip H. Sheridan was ordered to lead two cavalry divisions west from Cold Harbor, destroy track along the Virginia Central Railroad, join Hunter at Charlottesville, and then return with him to the main army.

Sheridan and some 6,000 men departed their camp on June 7. Brig. Gen. Alfred T. A. Torbert and Brig. Gen. David M. Gregg commanded the divisions. Torbert's consisted of three brigades led by Brig. Gen. George A. Custer, Col. Thomas C. Devin, and Brig. Gen. Wesley Merritt, while Gregg's contained two brigades commanded by Brig. Gen. Henry E. Davies, Jr., and Col. J. Irvin Gregg. Four batteries of horse artillery and a supply train of some 125 wagons accompanied the force.

Lee quickly learned of the expedition and dispatched Maj. Gen. Wade Hampton with his own division and that of Maj. Gen. Fitzhugh Lee in pursuit. Hampton's division included three brigades: Brig. Gen. Pierce M. B. Young's (commanded temporarily by Col. Gideon J. Wright),

Brig. Gen. Thomas L. Rosser's, and Brig. Gen. Matthew C. Butler's. Lee's division consisted of two brigades, one commanded by Brig. Gen. Lunsford L. Lomax and the other by Brig. Gen. Williams C. Wickham. The Confederate force, under Hampton's overall command, amounted to some 4,700 cavalrymen as well as three batteries of horse artillery. It broke camp on June 8.

Sheridan, slowed by his wagons, marched along the north bank of the North Anna River, then turned southwest into Louisa County and bivouacked around Clayton's Store (present-day Oakland) on June 10. Hampton led his force south of Sheridan's along the Virginia Central Railroad (today's CSX) and reached the vicinity of Louisa Court House in the evening of June 10. Hampton's men bivouacked along the Gordonsville Road (Rte. 33). Lee's division, east of Louisa Court House; Butler's and Wright's brigades at Trevilian Station, and Hampton and Rosser's brigade three miles west of the station.

Soon after sunrise on Saturday, June 11, the 4th South Carolina Cavalry of Butler's brigade probed north on a road (present-day Rte. 613) leading from Trevilian Station to Clayton's Store. Southwest of the store, in woods, the regiment encountered pickets from Merritt's brigade and drove them back, but quickly the rest of Merritt's brigade counterattacked, and the South Carolinians retreated. Butler then formed a strong defensive line blocking the road about half a mile north of Trevilian Station.

About the same time, Custer led the 1st and 7th Michigan Cavalry down the road (Rte. 669) to Louisa Court House. Partway there, he encountered Wickham's brigade and a brief fight ensued. Wickham withdrew, and Lee led Lomax's brigade toward Trevilian Station. Custer also withdrew and followed a narrow track that led to Mildred Crossing, about a mile and a half east of Trevilian Station. Accidently, Custer found himself in the rear of the Confederate force, with Hampton's lightly guarded wagon train lying west of his position. Custer sent Col. Russell A. Alger and the 5th Michigan Cavalry against the train, and Alger's men captured some 800 prisoners, 90 wagons, 6 artillery caissons, and 1,500 horses.

Despite this easy success, Custer soon found himself surrounded on three sides by Rosser, Hampton, and Lee. Alger's regiment and its booty quickly were overwhelmed and the Confederate prisoners liberated by Rosser, while Lee's division captured Custer's supply train and his headquarters wagon. Custer formed the remainder of his brigade into a defensive circle in a grassy clearing near Trevilian Station and countered the Confederate attacks with both dismounted fighting and mounted charges.

Northeast of the station, meanwhile, Butler had been holding off Merritt's brigade and two regiments from Devin's brigade. Then Colonel Gregg's brigade joined in, and the Federal line charged and drove through Butler's force to Custer's position. Custer sent the 7th Michigan Cavalry in a breakout charge that also recaptured some of his wagons and caissons. Lee's division fell back toward Louisa Court House, and Hampton's

View west toward the Ogg house behind the C.S.A. position, scene of heavy fighting on the second day at Trevilian Station. VIRGINIA DEPARTMENT OF HISTORIC RESOURCES, JOHN S. SALMON

retreated west of Trevilian Station, which was occupied by Sheridan.

That night Lee maneuvered south to join Hampton. Sheridan, meanwhile, learned that Hunter was not bound for Charlottesville. He therefore decided to return to the main army at Cold Harbor.

On Sunday morning, June 12, Sheridan prepared to withdraw. Colonel Gregg's men destroyed Trevilian Station and several rail cars as well as a mile or more of track to the east. Torbert and Merritt led their brigades west on the Gordonsville Road to locate the Confederates and act as a rear guard. They found their adversaries about two miles west of Trevilian Station.

The Confederates had formed an L-shaped line at the Ogg and Gentry farms. Torbert's division took up a position in the woods around the Gentry farm and east of the Ogg house, north of the railroad tracks, and Torbert launched one attack after another against Butler and the short leg of the L. The South Carolinians repulsed some seven dismounted assaults and inflicted heavy losses. Finally, Lee detached his division and marched behind Hampton's lines, striking the Federal right flank and ending the all-day engagement. Torbert's division hastened east to rejoin Sheridan.

DIRECTIONS: I-64 Exit 143 (Louisa, Ferncliff), n. on State Rte. 208 about 8.8 miles to State Rte. 22/U.S. Rte. 33 at Louisa; w. (left) on State Rte. 22/U.S. Rte. 33 .2 mile to Rte. 669 (Ellisville Dr.) at CSX track; n. (right) on Rte. 669 1.7 miles to Wickham-Gregg engagement site, then 4.25 miles farther to Rte. 613 (Oakland Rd.); w. (left) on Rte. 613 4.9 miles to Merritt-Butler engagement site (about .7 mile past Rte. 692); continue 2 miles to State Rte. 22/U.S. Rte. 33; w. (right) .5 mile to state historical marker W-210, Trevilian Station Battle, on north side of road; continue .1 mile to United Daughters of the Confederacy marker and state historical marker W-209, Battle of Trevilians, on south side of road; continue .1 mile to triple intersection of U.S. Rte. 33, State Rte. 22, and Rte. 613; n. (right) on U.S. Rte. 33 1.3 miles to Merritt-Hampton engagement site at Ogg Farm on left side of road; return to State Rte. 22/U.S. Rte. 33 and return to Rte. 208 and I-64.

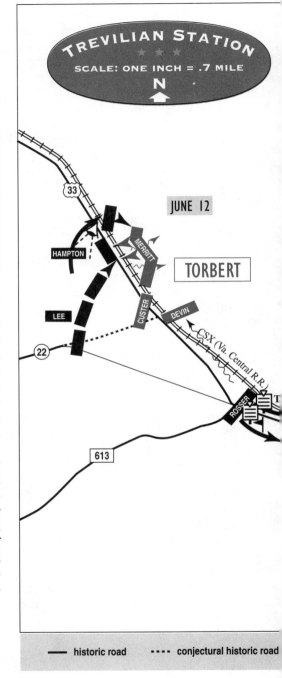

The battle of Trevilian Station was the bloodiest and largest all-cavalry engagement of the war, primarily because so much of the fighting was conducted by dismounted troops. Each side lost more than 1,000 killed, wounded, or captured, or between 15 and 20 percent of the forces engaged. The battle ended as a Confederate victory, as Sheridan failed to accomplish his mission of linking his force with Hunter's.

The battlefield has been minimally affected by residential development and road-widening activities. Although it is privately owned, it currently appears under little threat of obliteration. Most of the land is heavily wooded, as it was at the time of the battle. The Trevilian Station Battlefield Foundation has purchased part of the battlefield, and efforts are underway to establish a state park there. ■

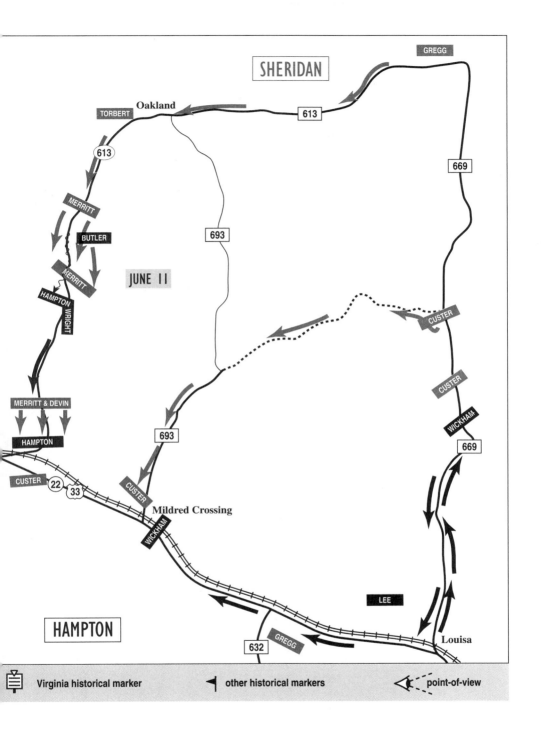

GREGG

SHERIDAN

Oakland

TORBERT

613

613

MERRITT

BUTLER

MERRITT

JUNE 11

693

669

HAMPTON
WRIGHT

CUSTER

CUSTER

WICKHAM

669

MERRITT & DEVIN

HAMPTON

CUSTER
22
33

CUSTER

693

Mildred Crossing

WICKHAM

LEE

HAMPTON

GREGG

632

Louisa

Virginia historical marker   other historical markers   point-of-view

BERMUDA HUNDRED CAMPAIGN, 1864

When Lt. Gen. Ulysses S. Grant assumed command of the armies of the United States on March 10, 1864, he initially favored a major advance on Richmond from Suffolk by way of Raleigh, North Carolina, reasoning that this strategy would cut Gen. Robert E. Lee's supply lines and compel him to fight a major battle to restore them. Eventually, however, Grant abandoned this plan in favor of an overland campaign south from the Army of the Potomac's winter encampment in Culpeper County.

Besides the new campaign, Grant ordered two other offensive operations in Virginia. Maj. Gen. Franz Sigel would lead a force through the Shenandoah Valley, and another army would operate against Richmond from the south. This also would sever the Confederate lines of supply and oblige Lee either to fight in the open or retreat behind the Richmond defenses. To lead this force, Grant was compelled to appoint Maj. Gen. Benjamin F. Butler, the commander of the Department of Virginia and North Carolina.

Butler was perhaps the most politically well-connected general in the Union army. Many professional soldiers heartily despised Butler, but although he was widely regarded as incompetent in the field, his political associations and his acknowledged administrative skills rendered him impossible to ignore and all but impossible to remove. Grant would have preferred Maj. Gen. William F. "Baldy" Smith as commander of what would soon be called the Army of the James, but after conferring with Butler on April 1–2, 1864, he assigned him the direction of the campaign up the Peninsula.

The conference established Butler's plan of attack, which would begin at the same time as Grant's overland campaign. The Army of the James would ascend the James River and establish a supply base about nine miles east of Petersburg at City Point as well as two defensive posts downriver—Fort Powhatan opposite Weyanoke, and Fort Pocahontas at Wilson's Wharf—to protect Federal vessels and the depot. Butler's army would then establish its base of operations at Bermuda Hundred, a peninsula above City Point between the James and Appomattox Rivers. After entrenching there, Butler would threaten Petersburg, send cavalry against the railroads to the south, and move on Richmond. If all went well, both armies would link up somewhere west of Richmond after ten days or so.

Although Grant's strategy seemed clear, Butler misinterpreted a key element of it. Naturally cautious, Butler assumed that Grant wanted him first to take the time to strongly fortify Bermuda Hundred so as to secure his base, then march against Richmond. Grant, on the contrary, intended Butler to entrench sufficiently to protect himself but get to Richmond as quickly as possible. Many of the subsequent difficulties between Grant and Butler can be traced to this misunderstanding.

The 39,000-man Army of the James consisted of two corps: X Corps, commanded by Maj. Gen. Quincy A. Gillmore,

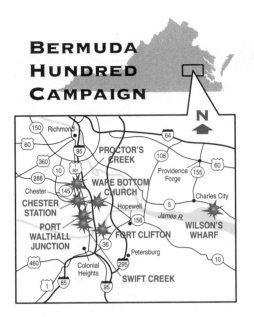

BERMUDA HUNDRED CAMPAIGN

and XVIII Corps, by Smith. Each corps contained three infantry divisions, each of which was supported by an artillery brigade, plus a cavalry division consisted of two brigades and unattached troops.

Opposing Butler was the Confederate garrison at Petersburg commanded by Maj. Gen. George E. Pickett. Pickett was not a happy general. After his division had been badly cut up at Gettysburg, he had been appointed head of the Department of North Carolina, which included southern Virginia. His principal task, defending Petersburg and the rail connections with the rest of the South, was rendered virtually impossible for the lack of troops. As April wore toward May and rumors arose of Federal activity aimed in his direction, Pickett grew even more frustrated, especially when his urgent messages to Richmond frequently were ignored.

On April 15, 1864, Gen. P. G. T. Beauregard was appointed department head to replace Pickett. Beauregard, however, was instructed to proceed to Weldon, North Carolina, not Petersburg, to await further orders, while Pickett marked time in the

Virginia city until Beauregard arrived to relieve him. Beauregard's command was as spread out as the two commanders. Some elements were en route to Richmond from Charleston, South Carolina, others from Wilmington, North Carolina, while still others were engaged in an operation against New Bern, North Carolina.

After it finally assembled near Petersburg in mid-May, Beauregard's army consisted of four infantry divisions commanded by Maj. Gen. Robert Ransom, Jr., Maj. Gen. Robert F. Hoke, Brig. Gen. Alfred H. Colquitt, and Maj. Gen. W. H. Chase Whiting. Ransom's and Hoke's divisions contained four brigades, Colquitt's and Whiting's two. Brig. Gen. James Dearing commanded the cavalry brigade, and other units moved in and out of the command at various times during the campaign. Probably the total never amounted to more than 18,000 troops.

On May 5, Butler's army sailed up the James River in a wide variety of military and civilian vessels. Elements of the force boarded transports at various wharves en route, gunboats escorted the flotilla, and the 1st and 2nd U.S. Colored Cavalry Regiments trotted parallel to the fleet on the north bank of the river. At Wilson's Wharf, half of Brig. Gen. Edward A. Wild's brigade disembarked to construct Fort Pocahontas there. The remainder of Wild's brigade disembarked at Fort Powhatan several miles upstream on the south bank to occupy and improve the abandoned Confederate fortification there.

At about 4 P.M. the lead elements of the Army of the James stormed ashore at City Point, achieving tactical surprise and capturing several prisoners. The rest of the army steamed a mile and a half upriver to Bermuda Hundred Landing, which it likewise occupied without resistance. There, the Army of the James disembarking continued throughout the evening and well into the night. In Petersburg, meanwhile, Pickett sent a steady stream of telegrams to Richmond to inform the Confederate government of Butler's progress and beg for instructions and assistance. The wire traffic only flowed one way, however. He had better luck with his telegrams to Beauregard, who immediately began rounding up troops to send him.

While Pickett and Beauregard struggled to scrape together a defensive force, Butler, flush with the expedition's early success, considered a night march on Richmond. Cooler heads prevailed among his subordinates, however, and the advance was put off until dawn on May 6, when the Army of the James marched west from Bermuda Hundred Landing.

The XVIII Corps led the way, with Brig. Gen. Charles A. Heckman's brigade of Brig. Gen. Godfrey Weitzel's division in the vanguard. Two miles inland, at Enon Church, the road forked. The XVIII Corps took the left-hand fork toward Petersburg while the X Corps continued straight ahead. At Ware Bottom Church, some four miles farther on, Gillmore's men halted and began construction of the northern half of Butler's defensive line. To the south, Smith's XVIII Corps eventually would build its half of the line, which would extend from the James to the Appomattox River. In midafternoon Butler ordered Heckman to advance to the junction of the Richmond & Petersburg Railroad and an abandoned branch line that led east to Port Walthall.

Pickett, meanwhile, struggled to anticipate Federal troop movements and block them with his scattered forces. He stationed Brig. Gen. Johnson Hagood's brigade, recently arrived from South Carolina, at Port Walthall Junction; the men had barely settled into place when Heckman attacked late in the afternoon. As Hagood himself had not yet arrived, Col.

Robert Graham coordinated the defense, which held off Heckman until he withdrew for lack of support and the belief that he faced two Confederate brigades.

That night Butler ordered another attack to seize the junction and destroy track, while Pickett strengthened the defenses there with Brig. Gen. Bushrod R. Johnson's brigade called up from eastern Tennessee, bringing the total number to about 2,600. Some 8,000 Federals under the command of Brig. Gen. William T. H. Brooks marched west on the morning of May 7. They encountered stiff opposition from the Confederates at first but almost collapsed the line with an envelopment of Johnson's left flank. The defenders rallied and held, however, and at the end of the day Brooks withdrew after destroying very little of the railroad. The Federals suffered some 300 casualties and the Confederates 200.

The Confederates were jubilant over their victory, but their high spirits subsided quickly as late that night Pickett ordered Johnson to withdraw south from Port Walthall Junction across Swift Creek. Pickett, assuming that Butler's ultimate objective was Petersburg, feared he did not have enough troops to protect the city and sought to tighten his defensive perimeter. He fretted over Beauregard's continued absence and Richmond's silence and increasingly felt abandoned. His decision to withdraw Johnson left the rail line to Richmond unprotected, although it did strengthen the Petersburg defenses.

South of the city, in contrast to Brooks's foray, the Petersburg Railroad (also called the Weldon Railroad) suffered serious if temporary damage as the result of a raid by 2,500 cavalrymen led from Portsmouth by Brig. Gen. August V. Kautz. The raid, which began on May 5 and ended five days later when Kautz's troopers entered the Union lines at City Point, disrupted the transportation of Beauregard's reinforcements. As a result, the force opposing Butler remained vulnerable.

Fortunately for Pickett and Richmond, Butler failed to exploit his opportunity. Concerned about the fate of the Army of the Potomac—at that moment fighting the Army of Northern Virginia in the Wilderness—and his own army should the Confederates concentrate their forces against him, Butler spent the next day improving his fortifications across the neck of Bermuda Hundred.

On May 9 Butler resumed his attempt to cut the rail link between Richmond and Petersburg. Several divisions from both corps marched to Port Walthall Junction and Chester Station on the Richmond & Petersburg Railroad, then turned south toward Petersburg. At Swift Creek, they encountered Hagood's and Johnson's strong line. The Confederates launched a counterattack across the creek that was overwhelmed by superior Federal numbers, but Butler did not follow up on his success.

In coordination with the Swift Creek attack, five Union vessels shelled Fort Clifton, located on the Confederate right flank overlooking the Appomattox River downstream and north of Petersburg. Counterfire from the battery there damaged a gunboat and foiled a planned assault by Brig. Gen. Edward W. Hincks's division of U.S. Colored Troops. The casualties for the day, probably all suffered at Swift Creek, numbered about 140 for each side.

During the night, having received optimistic reports of Grant's progress toward Richmond after the battle of the Wilderness, Butler decided to withdraw his corps inside the Bermuda Hundred line and await Grant's seemingly imminent arrival. To protect the route of withdrawal for the troops destroying track at Chester Station, on May 9 a small blocking force had been placed at the intersection of the Richmond

Turnpike and the road leading to Bermuda Hundred (today's U.S. Rte. 1 and Rte. 10) and another at Ware Bottom Church.

On May 10 Maj. Gen. Robert Ransom, Jr., led two of his brigades south toward the Bermuda Hundred road to reconnoiter in force. Just west of the turnpike intersection, they encountered the Federal blocking detachment, which had been reinforced almost to brigade strength. Fresh Union regiments were fed into the engagement, and the Federal line was extended, eventually threatening to outflank the Confederates. Late in the afternoon Ransom broke off the engagement, and the Union troops withdrew to Bermuda Hundred, while the Confederates retired toward Drewry's Bluff. The Federals suffered some 280 casualties and the Confederates about 250.

On the day of the battle, Beauregard, who had been delayed in part by illness, finally arrived in Petersburg. To the north of Richmond, meanwhile, Maj. Gen. Philip H. Sheridan was leading most of his cavalry command on a raid against the Confederate defenses, a raid that culminated in the battle of Yellow Tavern on May 11. Anxious to relieve the pressure and prevent an attack on the capital from two directions, Pres. Jefferson Davis and his military advisers urged Beauregard to attack Butler. Beauregard appeared eager to oblige, but complications in the deployment of his command delayed a general advance.

While Butler's men washed clothes and strengthened their entrenchments on May 11, Maj. Gen. Robert F. Hoke led his division north from Petersburg to reconnoiter and to make contact with Ransom's division. Late in the day he united with Ransom near Drewry's Bluff and bivouacked his troops near Proctor's Creek. There he formed the left wing of the Confederate line; Ransom, the right.

Butler, meanwhile, had decided to demonstrate in the direction of Richmond.

At dawn on May 12, Smith led the XVIII Corps through the Bermuda Hundred line to the Richmond Turnpike, then north toward the capital city. About a mile up the road, at Redwater Creek, Smith encountered a Confederate skirmish line; it delivered such a stiff fire that he halted to reconnoiter. After some additional skirmishing, he stopped for the night.

Gillmore and X Corps, meanwhile, followed Smith out of the works and then marched west on the road to Chester Station and likewise bivouacked. At dawn on May 13, Gillmore marched on in the rain through Chester Station to Chesterfield Court House, then north to the western end of the Confederate defensive line above Proctor's Creek. Smith, meanwhile, cautiously crept up the turnpike toward the main part of the line near Drewry's Bluff. Late in the afternoon, while Smith reconnoitered, Gillmore struck the Confederate left flank. Ransom's troops crumpled under the onslaught, rallied and counterattacked, and finally fell back to the main line. The next day, Smith and Gillmore launched coordinated attacks that drove through the first defensive line but stopped short of the second, which appeared stronger. The Federals dug in.

On the Confederate side, meanwhile, Beauregard planned an all-out counterattack for May 16. While Hoke demonstrated against the Federal center and left, Ransom would attack and turn the Union right flank. Whiting, who had been left in charge of the troops in Petersburg when Beauregard rode to the front on May 13, was to attack the rear of Butler's army.

Shortly before 5 A.M. on May 16, Beauregard's offensive began despite a thick fog that had rolled in during the night. Ransom attacked first, driving the Federal right flank south to Butler's headquarters at Half-Way House, an eighteenth-century tavern midway between Richmond and Petersburg. Butler repeatedly urged Gillmore, holding the Union left, to attack Hoke, but Gillmore delayed until he got orders to withdraw late in the morning. The Federals began to fall back toward the safety of Bermuda Hundred.

Whiting's force had advanced from Petersburg as ordered but halted at Port Walthall Junction in the face of slight opposition. There Whiting, who was ill and also had gone without sleep for three days (Brig. Gen. Henry A. Wise thought he was drunk), became increasingly befuddled and uncertain of what to do. While he dallied and Beauregard waited impatiently, Butler and his army slipped out of the Confederate trap. Each side lost about 3,000 men killed, wounded, and captured.

Once within the Bermuda Hundred stronghold, Gillmore's X Corps occupied the right half of the works; Smith's XVIII Corps, the left. Beauregard looked for an opportunity to attack, but Jefferson Davis ordered him to send several brigades north to reinforce the Army of Northern Virginia, then embroiled at Spotsylvania Court House. The troops began departing in the evening of May 19. The next morning at dawn, Beauregard launched a limited attack against the Federal lines to secure ground that could be defended with a relatively short line of entrenchments and limited troops.

Most of the combat took place near Ware Bottom Church in Gillmore's sector. Whiting's division drove in Gillmore's pickets, captured their rifle pits, and pressed forward in some places for more than half a mile. In the afternoon Gillmore counterattacked and regained some of the lost ground. At the end of the day, however, Beauregard decided that his goals had been accomplished. The Confederates suffered about 800 casualties, the Federals some 700. Soon Beauregard's men would construct fieldworks called the Howlett line for the farm of Dr. John Howlett that was located near the northern end of the line. Butler's Bermuda Hundred campaign had ended.

In the opinion of some observers, the Howlett line effectively bottled up Butler at Bermuda Hundred, but although any movement overland to the west was inhibited, Butler remained able to cross both the Appomattox and the James Rivers. Butler's natural caution and his conclusion that he had accomplished most of the goals established when he met with Grant in April contributed more to his decision to remain on the peninsula than any immediate Confederate threat. Finally, as Lee fell back toward Richmond, Butler was well positioned to threaten either Petersburg or Richmond or to take the field and assist Grant.

The outpost at City Point gained in importance, too, in mid-June when it became Grant's principal supply depot—indeed, one of the largest "ports" in the country—for the Army of the Potomac. Likewise, the fortifications strengthened or erected at Fort Powhatan and Wilson's Wharf (Fort Pocahontas) protected the vessels carrying troops and supplies to City Point.

On May 24, however, the Confederates launched an attack on Wilson's Wharf. Incensed by largely contrived reports in the Richmond newspapers of "atrocious outrages" committed by the U.S. Colored Troops there against white civilians in the neighborhood, and anxious to clear the north bank of the James River of Federal forces, Maj. Gen. Fitzhugh Lee led some 2,500 cavalrymen against the place. After Lee's initial attack was repulsed, he sent forward a flag of truce to demand surrender, with the promise that the black soldiers would be treated as prisoners of war—and an implied threat that if they resisted, they might be slaughtered as at Fort Pillow. Brig. Gen. Edward A. Wild, commander of the 1,500-man garrison, refused to surrender and repulsed Lee's second attack. The Confederates withdrew during the night, having suffered almost all the 165 casualties.

Bermuda Hundred, and the James River below it, remained in Federal hands. Soon, Grant would arrive to launch the next phase of his campaign against Richmond and Petersburg. ■

PORT WALTHALL JUNCTION

When Maj. Gen. Benjamin F. Butler's Army of the James began landing at City Point and Bermuda Hundred on May 5, 1864, it threatened the security of the railroad system that supplied Richmond and Petersburg as well as Gen. Robert E. Lee's Army of Northern Virginia. To Maj. Gen. George E. Pickett, responsible for the defense of Petersburg, that city seemed the most obvious Federal objective. Pickett scrambled to organize his widely scattered forces and begged the

Confederate government in Richmond for more troops. That evening, soldiers arrived in Petersburg by train, and Pickett ordered Brig. Gen. Johnson Hagood's Charleston, S.C., brigade to Port Walthall Junction due west of Bermuda Hundred, where part of the 21st South Carolina Infantry already was posted.

Despite Pickett's concerns for Petersburg, Butler was more interested in consolidating his army on the Bermuda Hundred peninsula and damaging the

C.S.A. position along railroad looking south. VIRGINIA DEPARTMENT OF HISTORIC RESOURCES, JOHN S. SALMON

nearby railroad than in storming the city. About midafternoon on Friday, May 6, Butler ordered Brig. Gen. Charles A. Heckman's brigade from Brig. Gen. Godfrey Weitzel's division of XVIII Corps to advance to Port Walthall Junction and destroy the track there.

Confederate units, meanwhile, also began marching to the junction. The rest of the 21st South Carolina Infantry and half of the 25th South Carolina arrived just as Heckman's brigade prepared to attack. The Confederate commander, Col. Robert Graham, positioned his troops in a sunken road just east of the junction; shortly after 5 P.M., Heckman's brigade advanced against them, but a stiff fire pushed the Federals back. Heckman ordered a withdrawal to the Ware Bottom Church line. The Confederates fell back to the junction itself.

Butler and his generals decided to attack again the next day with a force composed of five brigades, one from each division at Bermuda Hundred, to capture the junction and destroy the railroad there. Under the overall command of Brig. Gen. William T. H. Brooks, the 8,000-man detachment consisted of five brigades as well as an artillery battery and the 1st New

York Mounted Rifles. At the junction, meanwhile, the South Carolinians were augmented by Brig. Gen. Bushrod R. Johnson's Tennessee brigade, bringing the total number of Confederates to about 2,600. Maj. Gen. D. H. Hill rode out from Petersburg to observe.

At about 10 A.M. on Saturday, May 7, while the Tennesseans waited behind the railroad bed, Hagood led his brigade forward on the Old Stage Road (present-day Rte. 620) to probe for the Federal line. Barely a mile down the road, Hagood's skirmishers encountered the New York cavalry, the advance of Brooks's force, and drove it back on the Union infantry. After some further skirmishing, Hagood's brigade withdrew to the railroad, where it occupied the line to the left of Johnson; both brigades faced northeast.

By early afternoon, three of the Federal brigades formed the center of the Union line, most of which was positioned to the west of the Old Stage Road and north of the Confederates. A fourth advanced on the Federal left along the abandoned rail line to Port Walthall, while the fifth marched by Col. William B. Barton on the right to strike the Confederate left flank from the north.

Happy Hill Rd.

619

CSX (Richmond and Petersburg R. R.)

BARTON

95

PLAISTED

BURNHAM

HAGOOD

746

(Richmond Turnpike)

(Port Walthall Junction)

EXIT 58

JOHNSON

1
301

620

——— historic road   ⊣⊢ artillery

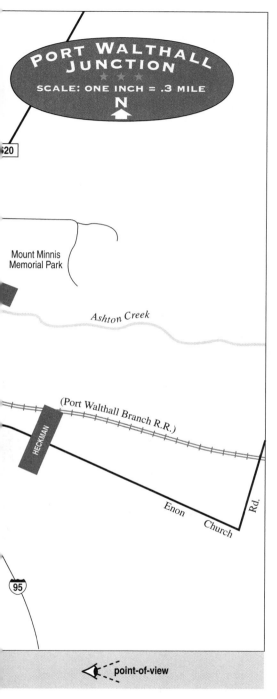

PORT WALTHALL JUNCTION
★ ★ ★
SCALE: ONE INCH = .3 MILE
N

620

Mount Minnis
Memorial Park

Ashton Creek

(Port Walthall Branch R.R.)

HECKMAN

Enon Church Rd.

95

point-of-view

DIRECTIONS: I-95 Exit 58 (Rte. 620, Woods Edge Rd.; Rte. 746, Ruffin Mill Rd.), w. on Rte. 620 (Woods Edge Rd.) about .8 mile to U.S. Rte. 1/301; n. (right) on U.S. Rte. 1/301 .5 mile to Rte. 746 (Indian Hills Rd.); continue on U.S. Rte. 1/301 n. .3 mile to CSA left flank position at CSX railroad overpass; return s. .3 mile to Rte. 746 (Ruffin Mill Rd.); e. (left) on Rte. 746 .4 mile to CSX railroad track (site of Port Walthall Junction); continue on Rte. 746 .4 mile over the overpass to Rte. 620 (Woods Edge Rd.); n. (left) on Rte. 620 .1 mile to stop light, then n. (left) again .1 mile to continuation of Rte. 620; n. (right) on Rte. 620 .2 mile to Mount Minnis Memorial Cemetery on right (US artillery position); return to I-95.

The ploy worked, and at about 2:30 P.M. Hagood's flank began to crumble. Hagood and Hill stopped the rout and formed a new line. Some of the Federal troops, meanwhile, set about tearing up track.

In the midst of seeming success, someone ordered Brooks's provisional division to withdraw. The Federals slowly disengaged and retired to the Ware Bottom Church line. Only a hundred feet of track had been damaged, at a cost of more than 300 casualties. The Confederates lost almost 200 men, most of them from Hagood's brigade. (The Federals wondered how long it would take to capture Richmond if they marched only two miles every day and then returned to their starting point every night.)

Since the battlefield covered a relatively small area, a substantial amount of it still survives, especially around the site of the junction. Most of the Federal position is occupied by residential development, but the Confederate position is reasonably intact. The battlefield is threatened, however, by continuing development along U.S. Rte. 1 to the west and the Interstate 95 interchange to the east. ■

Despite the Confederate success at Port Walthall Junction on May 7, 1864, Maj. Gen. George E. Pickett expected another concerted Federal attack to occur the next day. He therefore ordered Brig. Gen. Bushrod R. Johnson to withdraw overnight to a stronger defensive position on the high ground south of Swift Creek.

Ironically, it was Maj. Gen. Benjamin F. Butler's failure to keep the pressure on that enabled Pickett to further concentrate his forces and strengthen his new line, which extended from Brander's Bridge on

the Richmond Turnpike east along the south bank of Swift Creek to about half a mile west of Fort Clifton, which overlooked the Appomattox River north of

> **DIRECTIONS:** I-95 Exit 54 (Temple Ave., State Rte. 144); n. (left) on Temple Ave. about .6 mile to U.S. Rte. 1/301; n. (right) on U.S. 1/301 .8 mile to Ellerslie Rd. (Hagood's position); continue n. on U.S. 1/301 .6 mile to state historical marker S-31, "Brave to Madness," and .2 mile farther to state historical marker S-25, Union Army Checked; continue .3 mile farther to US position at State Rte. 144 (Harrowgate Rd.); return to I-95.

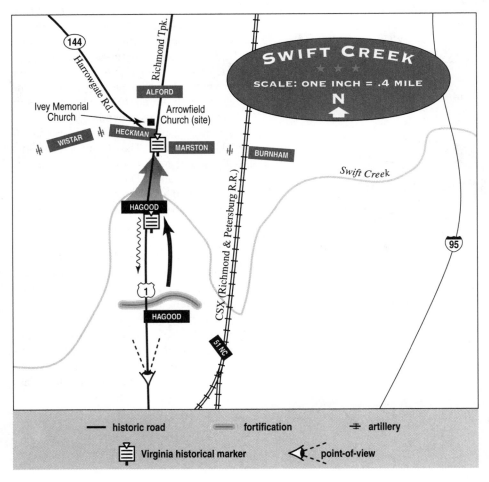

Petersburg. Meanwhile, Gen. P. G. T. Beauregard, on his way from North Carolina to relieve Pickett, was shipping additional brigades north to Pickett by train, although their progress was slowed by a Union cavalry raid against the railroads led by Brig. Gen. August V. Kautz.

On May 8, while his troops constructed earthworks across the neck of Bermuda Hundred, Butler ordered an advance for dawn the next day by both corps. Maj. Gen. William F. Smith would lead XVIII Corps against Port Walthall Junction, while Maj. Gen. Quincy A. Gillmore's X Corps attacked both the Richmond Turnpike and the railroad at Chester Station. In contrast with the Port Walthall Junction expedition, the Federals were prepared to destroy track and equipment. The navy, meanwhile, would attack Fort Clifton.

The enterprise went much as planned on the morning of Monday, May 9, and met no Confederate opposition. Spotting enemy observers to the south of Port Walthall Junction, however, Smith suggested to Butler that Gillmore wheel south from Chester Station and crush the Confederates; Smith would follow suit. Butler approved the plan, and by early afternoon XVIII Corps approached Swift Creek from the north, following the turnpike and railroad.

North of Swift Creek on the turnpike, near Arrowfield Church, Hagood had posted the 11th South Carolina Infantry and part of the 25th. In midafternoon, those units engaged the approaching Federals, who stopped, uncertain whether to press on or not. Likewise, Johnson hesitated to rush more troops forward to reinforce the South Carolinians, as he was under orders to protect the crossings, not to bring on a general engagement. Back in Petersburg, however, Pickett had received a telegram from Gen. Braxton Bragg, Pres. Jefferson Davis's military adviser, order-

Commercial development has affected most of the Swift Creek battlefield. View north along route of Hagood's attack. VIRGINIA DEPARTMENT OF HISTORIC RESOURCES, JOHN S. SALMON

ing him to recover the ground lost the day before. Pickett ordered Johnson to reconnoiter; Johnson transmitted the order to Brig. Gen. Johnson Hagood, the only officer in that communication chain on the scene. Hagood knew that what was needed was an assault not a reconnaissance, and ordered the 21st South Carolina Infantry, already marching toward the turnpike bridge, to aid their comrades across the creek. Over there, Col. F. Hay Gannt sent the 11th South Carolina against the Federals, assuming from all the activity that the time had arrived for a general battle.

Opposing the onrushing South Carolinians was Brig. Gen. Charles A. Heckman's brigade. The Federal commanders ordered their men to prepare to fire by volley and gave the command when the Confederates were but fifty yards away. Suddenly the South Carolinians were scrambling back down the hill toward the turnpike bridge. The 25th South Carolina formed a rear guard until all the survivors were safely across, then withdrew, as well.

Heckman's and Brig. Gen. Isaac J. Wistar's brigades occupied the ground evacuated by the Confederates, and soon an artillery duel erupted. By then evening was fast approaching, and the mutual shelling dwindled away. Both sides bivouacked on the battlefield in their fortifications. The combatants each lost about 140 killed, wounded, and captured.

The Swift Creek battlefield has been obliterated by commercial and residential development, although the contours of the hills are apparent as are the crossing points of the turnpike (U.S. Rte. 1) and the railroad. Old Arrowfield Church has been replaced by a modern structure. Swift Creek Mill operates as a restaurant and stage theater. ■

FORT CLIFTON

On Monday, May 9, 1864, as elements of Maj. Gen. Benjamin F. Butler's Army of the James maneuvered south toward Swift Creek, United States naval vessels commanded by Brig. Gen. Charles K. Graham made their way to the mouth of the Appomattox River to protect the army's left flank as well as the right flank of Brig. Gen. Edward W. Hincks's detachment of 1,800 U.S. Colored Troops from City Point. The subject of the gunboats' attention was Fort Clifton, a large Confederate earthwork constructed to protect Petersburg and commanded by Capt. S. Taylor Martin. The Federals planned to reduce the fort with artillery fire, then capture it and its three 30-pounder guns and two pieces of field artillery with Hincks's infantry.

The naval flotilla ultimately consisted of the armed side-wheel steamers *General Putnam* and *Skokokon* and the wooden

DIRECTIONS: I-95 Exit 54 (Temple Ave., State Rte. 144); s. (right) on Temple Ave. about .35 mile to Conduit Rd. (first traffic light); n. (left) on Conduit Rd. 2.15 miles to state historical marker S-33, Fort Clifton, at Brockwell Lane; e. (right) on Brockwell Lane .25 mile past Tussing Elementary School to Fort Clifton Park; return to I-95.

gunboats *Brewster, Chamberlin,* and *Commodore Perry.* The shelling of Fort Clifton began about 8:30 A.M. and continued until 6 P.M., with the heaviest bombardment occurring between 11 A.M. and 2 P.M. Although the gunboats and steamers expended several hundred rounds of all types, the damage to the fort appeared slight. The gunboats were hampered by the elevation of the fort above the river, which resulted in most of their shots passing over the heads of the defenders.

Battery B, 2nd U.S. Artillery, in foreground; Fort Clifton across Appomattox River on right.
LIBRARY OF CONGRESS

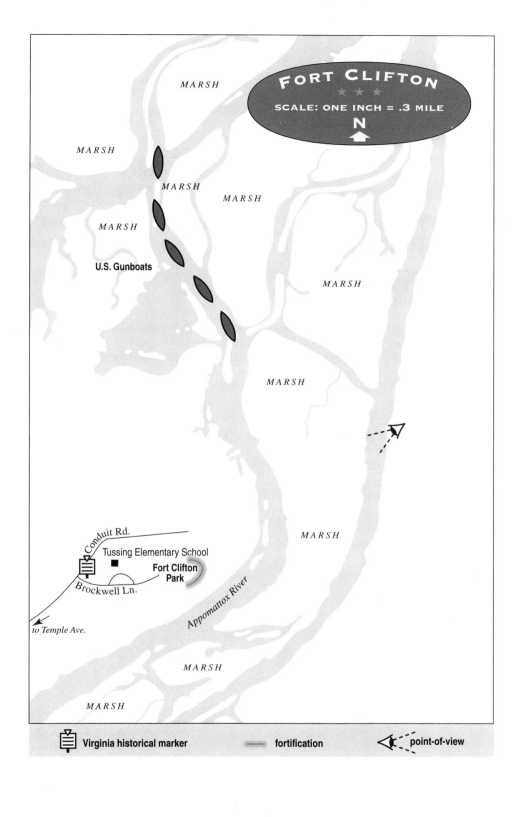

FORT CLIFTON
★ ★ ★
SCALE: ONE INCH = .3 MILE
N

MARSH

MARSH

MARSH

MARSH

MARSH

MARSH

MARSH

U.S. Gunboats

MARSH

MARSH

MARSH

Conduit Rd.
Tussing Elementary School
Fort Clifton Park
Brockwell Ln.

Appomattox River

to Temple Ave.

MARSH

MARSH

Virginia historical marker   fortification   point-of-view

For their part, the fort's gunners were frustrated by the limited range of their cannons. Between 1 and 2 P.M., however, a shot struck *Brewster* and exploded the magazine; the crew burned and abandoned the wreckage. At about 1:30 P.M., *Chamberlin* ran aground, and *General Putnam* towed her into the channel. Late in the afternoon, the flotilla retired down the Appomattox.

On the opposite bank of the river, meanwhile, Hincks's detachment accomplished little. It drew even with Fort Clifton but could only watch as the gunboats failed to neutralize it. Unable to find an accessible road to Petersburg, Hincks retired that afternoon to City Point.

No casualty figures are available for the futile attack on Fort Clifton. The fort stands, very well preserved, in Fort Clifton Park in the city of Colonial Heights. The principal threat to the fort is presented by visitors walking on the earthworks. Fort Clifton is listed on the National Register of Historic Places and the Virginia Landmarks Register. ∎

CHESTER STATION

When Maj. Gen. Benjamin F. Butler next launched an expedition against the Richmond & Petersburg Railroad on May 9, 1864, Maj. Gen. Quincy A. Gillmore led X Corps to Chester Station to destroy track there. After the battle at Swift Creek, he and XVIII Corps commander Maj. Gen. William F. Smith conferred with Butler about the next day's plans. Butler at first decided to continue toward Petersburg but changed his mind after receiving telegrams reporting that Gen. Robert E. Lee's army was retreating with the Army of the Potomac in pursuit. Since Butler's primary mission was to join with Grant when the opportunity arose to attack Lee and Richmond, he ordered a withdrawal to Bermuda Hundred to prepare for Grant's arrival.

Gillmore's route to Chester Station had taken him west on the principal road from Bermuda Hundred (present-day Rte. 10) and past the Old Stage Road (Rte. 732) and the Richmond Turnpike (U.S. Rte. 1) a mile farther west. Col. Joshua Howell's brigade was detailed to protect these junctions and the Bermuda Hundred road, with three regiments stationed at Ware Bottom Church, the 67th Ohio under Col. Alvin C. Voris at the turnpike, and a section of the 1st Connecticut Light Battery supporting Voris's regiment.

To the north of Chester Station, meanwhile, Maj. Gen. Robert Ransom, Jr., ordered a reconnaissance to locate the Federal rear guard. Two brigades probed but did not dislodge the forces at the intersections. Ransom scheduled a stronger thrust for the next morning, while Voris urgently requested reinforcements from Gillmore.

The Confederate reconnaissance in force began shortly after 5 A.M. on Tues-

View north from 13th Indiana Infantry position. VIRGINIA DEPARTMENT OF HISTORIC RESOURCES, JOHN S. SALMON

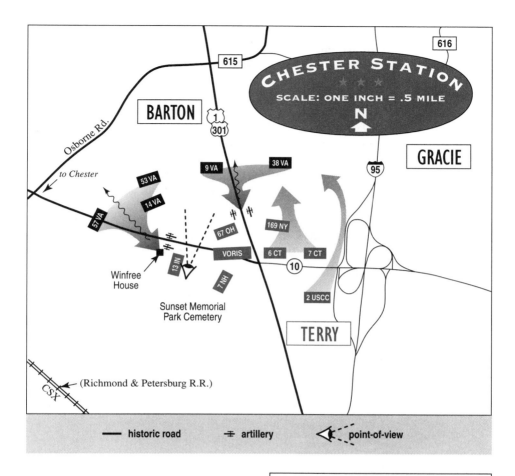

day, May 10. Each brigade advanced with a regiment deployed as skirmishers in front, one on the left flank from the James River to the Richmond Turnpike, and one covering the right between the turnpike and the Richmond & Petersburg Railroad. Because of the divergence of the railroad and the turnpike, a gap opened in the middle of the skirmish line; in addition, heavy woods impaired the commanders' line of sight and the coordination of the advance.

The Confederate skirmishers emerged from dense woods west of the turnpike intersection. They were greeted by bullets fired by the Ohioans, positioned in a crescent-shaped line that extended almost to the house of Henry A. Winfree. They also

> **DIRECTIONS:** I-95 Exit 61B (State Rte. 10 West, Chester), w. on State Rte. 10 about .5 mile to Rte. 804 (Rock Hill Rd.); continue w. on State Rte. 10 for .9 mile through center of battlefield to Rte. 616 (Osborne Rd./Curtis St.); return to I-95. Note Winfree house on left (s.) side of State Rte. 10 .2 mile w. of Rte. 804 (just w. of Sunset Memorial Park).

encountered the 13th Indiana Infantry to the west of the 67th Ohio and the 169th New York across the turnpike. Both regiments had arrived about daybreak to reinforce Voris. Two guns of the 4th New Jersey Battery were positioned on either side of the turnpike, while the Connecticut section was placed on an east-west road just in front of the Winfree house.

At about 11 A.M., Brig. Gen. Seth M. Barton formed the 38th and 9th Virginia Regiments on the east and west side of the turnpike respectively and charged the New Jersey guns. The Virginians captured one gun and scattered the New York regiment. The charge soon collapsed under an artillery bombardment from Howell's guns at Ware Bottom Church. On the Confederate right, the 53rd and 57th Virginia Regiments pressed the Connecticut battery and the 13th Indiana Infantry in front of the Winfree house, but their attack ended when reinforcements arrived under the command of Brig. Gen. Alfred H. Terry and Col. Joseph R. Hawley. Terry quickly ordered the 7th New Hampshire to support the Indiana regiment at Winfree's and the 6th and 7th Connecticut Regiments to countercharge the Virginia regiments east of the turnpike. A short time later the 2nd U.S. Colored Cavalry arrived and fought as infantry with the Connecticut regiments. At Winfree's, the other two sections of the 1st Connecticut Light Battery, which had come up with Terry, raced to relieve the exhausted cannoneers who had been facing the 53rd and 57th Virginia Regiments.

Facing an ever-increasing number of Federal reinforcements, Ransom withdrew toward Drewry's Bluff. Indeed, as Butler's divisions were marching north from the Swift Creek battlefield to Bermuda Hundred, Ransom soon would have faced an overwhelming force.

By late afternoon the last Union forces departed for Bermuda Hundred, and the fighting near Chester Station faded away. Some 3,400 Federal troops had been engaged during the day; about 280 became casualties. On the Confederate side, Barton's brigade—fewer than 2,000 in number—had lost about 250 men.

Most of the Chester Station battlefield has been obliterated by commercial and residential development, particularly around the intersection of U.S. Rte. 1 and Rte. 10. The Winfree house and farm lane still exist, and their setting is somewhat protected by a large cemetery (Sunset Memorial) just to the east. ■

PROCTOR'S CREEK

After the battles that resulted from Maj. Gen. Benjamin F. Butler's attacks on the Richmond & Petersburg Railroad and the demonstrations toward Petersburg, the Army of the James retired to the safety of the Bermuda Hundred lines on May 10, 1864. Butler decided to make a demonstration in the direction of Richmond, which he believed would soon be attacked from the north by the Army of the Potomac under the direction of Lt. Gen. Ulysses S. Grant and Maj. Gen. George G. Meade.

Meanwhile, the Confederates were consolidating their forces and refining their defensive strategy. In Petersburg, Gen. P. G. T. Beauregard labored to coordinate troop movements in response to the changing military situation and the often contradictory orders from Richmond. By the evening of May 11, Maj. Gen. Robert F. Hoke's division had arrived from Tidewater North Carolina. It joined the division commanded by Maj. Gen. Robert Ransom, Jr., to form the left and right wings of the Confederate line blocking the way north to Richmond. The divisions occupied fortifications guarding a height on the James River called Drewry's Bluff.

The works consisted of an outer and an inner line; Hoke stationed one brigade on the right flank of the outer line. Next, he posted four other brigades from west to east. Ransom positioned one brigade to the east, then anchored the left flank a mile west of the James River with another brigade. Two others were positioned behind these east and west flanks. Brig. Gen. Alfred H. Colquitt's division assumed a reserve position.

A mile south of the right flank of the outer Confederate line, a section of fieldworks snaked across Wooldridge's Hill, which overlooked Crooked Branch to the west as well as the Richmond & Petersburg Railroad to the east. Brig. Gen. Matt W. Ransom's brigade held the position.

Butler's force consisted of parts of two corps commanded by Maj. Gen. William F. Smith and Maj. Gen. Quincy A. Gillmore. Two divisions of Smith's XVIII Corps, one commanded by Brig. Gen. Godfrey Weitzel and Brig. Gen. William T. H. Brooks, were reinforced by Brig. Gen. John W. Turner's division of Gillmore's X Corps to lead the demonstration. The remainder of X Corps formed the expedition's reserve and rear guard.

The Federal demonstration began at dawn on Thursday, May 12. Weitzel led the way, followed by Turner and Brooks. The advance soon bogged down in rain, mud, and aggressive skirmishing by a Confederate picket line located barely a mile up the Richmond Turnpike. Smith ordered Weitzel to deploy east of the turnpike, with two brigades of Brooks's division to the west and the third behind Weitzel as a reserve. Once on line, the men slogged their way to high ground just south of Proctor's Creek. Because the Confederate defenses north of the creek appeared strong, and because his own line was thin and the day was waning, Smith ordered his men to bivouac. Part of Gillmore's division came forward and camped behind Smith's command around Chester Station.

Looking north along route of Hagood's attack from Brooks's position. VIRGINIA DEPARTMENT OF HISTORIC RESOURCES, JOHN S. SALMON

At about 6:30 A.M. on Friday, May 13, Butler sent Gillmore's X Corps to envelop the Confederate right flank while Smith attacked from the south. Elements of Col. Harris M. Plaisted's brigade led the march, followed by Col. Joseph R. Hawley's brigade, Col. Richard White's, and Brig. Gen. Gilman Marston's. Two regiments were left to make a diversionary attack up the Richmond & Petersburg Railroad and two were posted near Chesterfield Court House as a rear guard.

In Petersburg, meanwhile, Beauregard put Maj. Gen. W. H. Chase Whiting in command of the garrison and made his way to Drewry's Bluff. Whiting, just arrived from North Carolina, was both physically ill and mentally unprepared to assume command.

During the morning, Smith's XVIII Corps pressed forward slowly. When he confronted the main line of Confederate fieldworks north of Proctor's Creek early in the afternoon, Smith ordered a halt. To the west, Gillmore maneuvered toward Ransom's brigade at Wooldridge's Hill. At about 4 P.M., having achieved complete surprise, Gillmore struck.

Three regiments of Hawley's brigade attacked across Crooked Branch and up Wooldridge's Hill from the west and gained the rear of Ransom's line. The stunned Confederates quickly rallied,

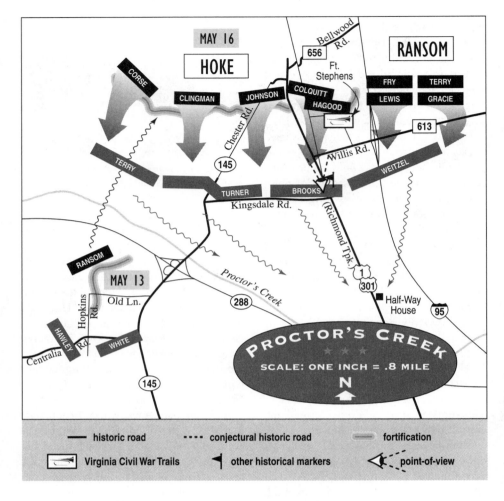

MAY 16

HOKE

RANSOM

656

Ft. Stephens

Bellwood Rd.

CORSE

CLINGMAN   JOHNSON   COLQUITT

HAGOOD

FRY   TERRY

LEWIS   GRACIE

Chester Rd.

613

TERRY

145

Willis Rd.

WEITZEL

TURNER   BROOKS

Kingsdale Rd.

RANSOM

MAY 13

Old Ln.

Proctor's Creek

288

(Richmond Tpk.)

1

301

Half-Way House

95

Hopkins Rd.

HAWLEY   Rd.   WHITE

Centralia

145

PROCTOR'S CREEK

★ ★ ★

SCALE: ONE INCH = .8 MILE

N

— historic road   ···· conjectural historic road   fortification

Virginia Civil War Trails   ◄ other historical markers   ◄··· point-of-view

however, and drove the Federals back. As Hawley debated his next move, White's regiments attacked up the railroad line from Chester Station and pushed Ransom off his hill. The defenders slipped away from the outer defensive line and regrouped at the inner line.

Because of the lateness of the day, the Union corps bivouacked once more in the steady downpour while their commanders laid plans. To the north, Beauregard rode into the Drewry's Bluff defenses at about 3 A.M. There he learned of the Federal gains and began to formulate his own plans to take the offensive.

At dawn on Saturday, May 14, Smith's and Gillmore's corps cautiously crept forward to the outer Confederate line, which they found abandoned. While they consolidated their position and skirmished with the Confederates, Gen. Braxton Bragg arrived at Drewry's Bluff to confer with Beauregard, followed in the afternoon by Jefferson Davis. Davis dictated plans to Beauregard: Whiting was to march from Petersburg west around Butler and join Beauregard at Drewry's Bluff, after which Beauregard would attack.

Davis and Bragg returned to Richmond while Beauregard revised his plans. He

DIRECTIONS: I-95 Exit 62 (State Rte. 288 North, Chesterfield); n. on State Rte. 288 to third exit (State Rte. 145, Chester Rd.); s. (left) on State Rte. 145 about .7 mile to State Rte. 145 West (Centralia Rd.); w. (right) on State Rte. 145 West .2 mile to site of Gillmore advance and fight, May 16, 1864; continue .2 mile to Rte. 637 (Hopkins Rd.); n. (right) on Rte. 637, paralleling Confederate works and around sharp right curve .4 mile to Old Lane; straight ahead on Old Lane .4 mile to State Rte. 145 (Chester Rd.); n. (left) on State Rte. 145 beneath State Rte. 288 overpass .8 mile to Rte. 1495 (Kingsdale Rd.); e. (right) on Rte. 1495 .9 mile along Federal line to U.S. Rte. 1/301; n. (left) on U.S. 1/301 .1 mile to Richmond Battlefield Markers Association marker (Drewry's Bluff Battlefield) on right (identifies outer line of Confederate earthworks); continue n. .8 mile to Rte. 656 (Bellwood Rd.) and inner line of Confederate earthworks; return on U.S. Rte. 1/301 .6 mile to Rte. 613 (Willis Rd.); e. (left) on Rte. 613 .2 mile to Pams Ave.; n. (left) on Pams Ave. .2 mile to Fort Stephens (Chesterfield County Parks & Recreation) and Virginia Civil War Trails marker on left; return to Rte. 613; left on Rte. 613 .2 mile to I-95 interchange (Exit 64).

quickly realized that although Davis wanted him to help relieve the pressure on Richmond from the north, Whiting could not possibly reach Drewry's Bluff until May 18. When Beauregard reported this to Richmond on Sunday, May 15, he received orders to the contrary: Attack immediately. Beauregard then took it on himself to order Whiting to march to Port Walthall Station and there to stand ready to attack the rear of Butler's army the next morning.

Butler, meanwhile, had canceled an assault on the Confederate inner line scheduled for dawn on May 15. Reconnoitering to the rear of the army, Brig. Gen. Charles A. Heckman discovered unguarded roads near the James River between the army and Bermuda Hundred and posted a detachment to protect them. Weitzel's division held the Union right flank, with Heckman's brigade on the eastern end near the James River and Brig. Gen. Isaac J. Wistar just west of Heckman. Two brigades of

Brooks's division occupied the center of the Union line, and a third brigade held the extreme left. Gillmore's X Corps occupied the rest of the left flank, with Terry's division on the far left and Turner's between it and Brooks's.

Beauregard spent the rest of the day preparing detailed instructions for his division commanders. Hoke's men were to demonstrate against the Federal center and left while Ransom's division attacked the right flank. Beauregard scheduled the assault for dawn.

On Monday, May 16, at 4:45 A.M., Ransom ordered his division forward; Brig. Gen. Archibald Gracie's and Brig. Gen. William G. Lewis's brigades led the way. A thick fog had rolled in that would virtually blind the combatants until midmorning. Soon the opposing troops clashed, firing blindly into the fog. After just a few minutes, Ransom's attack began to stall because of the rapid depletion of ammunition and the stiff opposition offered by Heckman's brigade. Gracie pressed on, however, and the Union right flank crumbled. Heckman, trying to sort matters out in the fog, rode into Confederate hands and by 9 A.M. was confined in Libby Prison in Richmond. Soon the Confederates became disorganized in the fog, and the action ground to a halt.

Awakened by the gunfire, Butler and Smith strove to gain control. Smith ordered the artillery to the rear and summoned infantry reinforcements. Butler assessed the situation and ordered Gillmore to attack the Confederate right flank, hoping to disrupt any planned advance in that quarter. Gillmore hesitated, however, as he feared that an attack on his front was imminent.

The center of the Union line suddenly erupted in gunfire as Hoke's division struck. Hoke, who could see no more than a few yards in the fog, assumed that Ransom's attack had succeeded and his men would encounter Federals ready to flee from the onslaught. Wistar's and Brig. Gen. Hiram Burnham's brigades, however, had been spared any action and were ready to fight; because of the fog, they may not even have known that their right was crumbling. Soon both sides were locked in a bloody stalemate.

Smith, persuaded by Ransom's and Hoke's attacks that his line could not hold, ordered a retreat at about 7:45 A.M. A short time later, the fog began to lift and Smith realized that his forces were not as threatened as he had feared. He ordered an about-face, but the troops became intermingled and confused. Smith gave up and ordered his corps to form a new defensive line at the Half-Way House, Butler's headquarters.

The opposing generals became increasingly frustrated as the fog burned off to reveal a relatively quiet battlefield. Butler wondered why Gillmore still had not launched his assault. And Beauregard sent urgent messages to Whiting: Come fast and strike the Union rear, and victory will be ours.

Gillmore, lightly challenged by skirmishing to his front as Hoke began probing his lines shortly after dawn, lost his nerve in the fog. Despite Butler's repeated orders to attack, Gillmore essentially delayed until circumstances compelled Butler to change his orders. About midmorning, Gillmore finally received a message from Butler instructing him to retire to the rear of the Half-Way House and defend the route of retreat to Bermuda Hundred.

Whiting, meanwhile, had made slow progress north from the Swift Creek line with his command. Encountering Federal skirmishers, Whiting deployed his brigades in battle formation, thereby further slowing his advance through the thick woods lining the Richmond Turnpike and the Old Stage Road. By 8:30 A.M., the force arrived at Port Walthall Junction, where Whiting confronted Brig. Gen. Adelbert Ames with part of his X Corps division. Although Ames withdrew almost immediately, Whiting still directed his brigades as though he was encountering serious opposition. Convinced that his force could be annihilated at any moment, Whiting was incapable of advancing as Beauregard demanded. Instead, he spent the remainder of the morning at Port Walthall Junction dueling Ames's skirmishers at long range. In the afternoon he began a slow, halting retreat to Swift Creek.

Beauregard had delayed his advance during the late morning hours while he awaited some sign that Whiting was closing in on the Federal rear. The fighting faded away to light skirmishing as Gillmore and Smith prepared to withdraw to Bermuda Hundred. Finally Beauregard ordered Hoke to press the Army of the James, which obviously was retreating to its lines. A heavy thunderstorm hampered the movement, however, and the Federals made good their escape late in the day.

Although the battle at Proctor's Creek was a Confederate victory, it was hardly the success it might have been. The weather, Whiting's failure to advance, and Confederate confusion all combined to enable the equally confused Federals to evade Beauregard's grasp. The battle cost each side more than 3,000 men.

The battlefield has been largely altered by much residential and commercial development, although parts of it remain intact. Half-Way House is now a popular restaurant, and Chesterfield County has preserved Fort Stevens and erected interpretive markers there. ■

After the fighting at Proctor's Creek concluded on May 16, 1864, Gen. P. G. T. Beauregard continued to look for an opportunity to attack the Federals. North of Richmond, however, Gen. Robert E. Lee had been bombarding the Confederate government with urgent requests for more troops with which to combat the Army of the Potomac, which outnumbered the Army of Northern Virginia almost two to one.

On May 19, Pres. Jefferson Davis directed Gen. Braxton Bragg, his military adviser, to order Beauregard to detach four infantry brigades, an artillery battalion, and a cavalry regiment from his command and send them north to Lee. As this order stripped Beauregard of fully one-third of his infantry, he argued unsuccessfully for a delay while he shortened his lines that faced the Federal defenses. Without enough men to cover the entire Union front, which extended roughly three miles, Beauregard sought to push the Federals

back far enough to seize a narrower part of the Bermuda Hundred peninsula.

The commander of the Union army, Maj. Gen. Benjamin F. Butler, had posted Maj. Gen. Quincy A. Gillmore's X Corps on the right, or northern, sector of the Bermuda Hundred line, and Maj. Gen. William F. Smith's XVIII Corps on the left. Some distance in front of the main line, pickets manned a series of rifle pits to provide early warning of a Confederate attack.

Beauregard struck at about 9 A.M. on Friday, May 20, by attacking the northernmost part of Gillmore's sector. First, Beauregard's troops set fire to the woods and brush in their line of advance, creating a natural smoke screen to obscure their movements. Then they charged. Within half an hour, the Confederates had seized most of the rifle pits in front of Brig. Gen. Alfred H. Terry's and Brig. Gen. Adelbert Ames's positions. In Ames's sector, the Confederate brigades pushed almost three-quarters of a mile into Union territory.

Parker's Battery unit of Richmond National Battlefield Park preserves the largest undisturbed piece of the Ware Bottom Church battlefield. VIRGINIA DEPARTMENT OF HISTORIC RESOURCES, JOHN S. SALMON

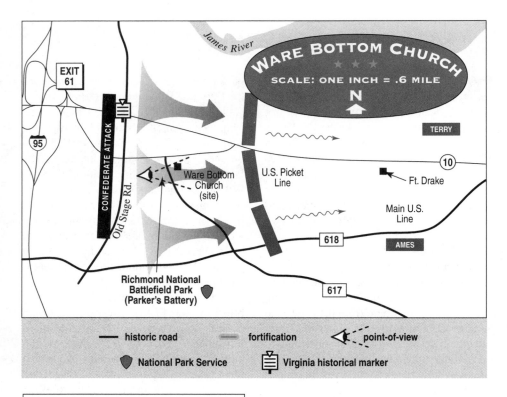

WARE BOTTOM CHURCH

★ ★ ★

SCALE: ONE INCH = .6 MILE

N

James River

EXIT 61

95

CONFEDERATE ATTACK

Old Stage Rd.

Ware Bottom Church (site)

U.S. Picket Line

TERRY

10

Ft. Drake

Main U.S. Line

618

AMES

Richmond National Battlefield Park (Parker's Battery)

617

—— historic road   ▭▭ fortification   ◁⋯ point-of-view

🛡 National Park Service   🏛 Virginia historical marker

DIRECTIONS: Recommend first visiting the Richmond National Battlefield Park Visitor Center (open 9–5 daily) at Tredegar Iron Works in downtown Richmond: I-95 Exit 74C (U.S. Rte. 33 West/U.S. Rte. 250 West, Broad St.) and follow blue-and-green signs to visitor center, Brown's Island, and Belle Isle, w. on Broad St. about .4 mile (5 blocks) to 8th St.; s. (left) on 8th St. 5 blocks to Canal St.; w. (right) on Canal St. 3 blocks to 5th St.; s. (left) on 5th St. 2 blocks to Tredegar St.; w. (right) on Tredegar Street .1 mile to visitor center and parking lot. Visit the National Park Service Web site at nps.gov/parks.html for a virtual tour of this and other national parks. To visit the battlefield directly: I-95 Exit 61A (State Rte. 10 East, Hopewell), e. on State Rte. 10 about .3 mile to Virginia historical markers K-201, Battery Dantzler, and S-6, The Howlett Line, on right *(Caution!: To read these markers you must stop in a right turn lane near a busy intersection at Old Stage Rd., so pull over as far as you can and turn on your emergency flashers; check behind you thoroughly before proceeding);* s. (right) on Old Stage Rd. (Rte. 732) .2 mile to Ware Bottom Spring Rd. (Rte. 828); e. (left) on Ware Bottom Spring Rd. .1 mile to Parker's Battery Unit of Richmond National Battlefield Park; return to Ware Bottom Spring Rd. and then to I-95.

NOTE: Parker's Battery was not constructed until a month after the battle, but it stands on the only undeveloped, accessible part of the battlefield.

Gillmore counterattacked in the afternoon and recaptured some of the lost ground. Col. Joshua B. Howell led two regiments and part of a third in a costly assault that reclaimed Terry's picket line on the Union right flank. Ames, however, was compelled to establish a new picket line to the east.

The day's fighting cost the Federals about 700 in killed, wounded, and missing, while the Confederates lost some 800. Beauregard achieved at least part of his goal to establish a defensible line across the Bermuda Hundred neck to block Butler's exit to the west and "bottle up" the Army of the James on the peninsula. The fortifications were named the Howlett line after Dr. John Howlett, whose dwelling marked the Confederate left flank.

Although much of the battlefield has been covered with residential development, some survives relatively intact. ■

WILSON'S WHARF

While the greater part of the Army of the James landed at Bermuda Hundred on May 5, 1864, elements of it had already disembarked to establish strongholds to protect Federal shipping on the James River. Half of Brig. Gen. Edward A. Wild's brigade—the 1st and 22nd Regiments of U.S. Colored Troops (USCT) and two two-gun sections of Company B, 2nd U.S. Colored Artillery Regiment—landed some twenty miles downriver from the rest of the army at Wilson's Wharf. Just two miles from Sherwood Forest, the home of John Tyler, the late former president of the United States, Wilson's Wharf was an

ancient plantation dock located at a strategic bend in the river, overlooked by high bluffs. The black troops immediately set about constructing an earthwork soon named Fort Pocahontas, while Wild estab-

---

DIRECTIONS: I-64 Exit 214 (Providence Forge, State Rte. 155), s. on State Rte. 155 about 11.3 miles to State Rte. 5 at Charles City Court House; e. (left) on State Rte. 5 3.2 miles to Sherwood Forest on right. Alternate route: e. on State Rte. 5 30.8 miles from eastern boundary of Richmond city to Sherwood Forest on right.

NOTE: Wilson's Wharf Battlefield is entirely on private property and access can be gained only through the ticket office at Sherwood Forest, which is open to the public.

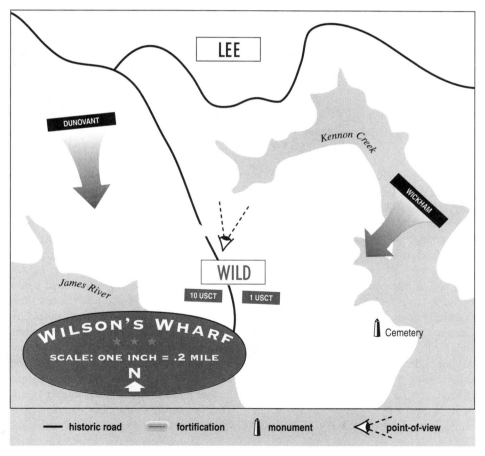

lished his headquarters in Dr. John C. Wilson's house, whose farmland spread over the plateau to the north.

The presence of African American troops sent shock waves all the way to the Confederate capital some thirty miles west. Blacks bearing arms struck at the core of slave owners' fears. Officially, the Confederate government refused to recognize the legitimacy of black soldiers, treated captives as slaves in rebellion not prisoners of war, and turned a blind eye to atrocities committed against black prisoners. The most notorious of such atrocities, the "Fort Pillow Massacre" in Tennessee and the Poison Springs fight in Arkansas, had occurred the month before the landing at Wilson's Wharf. At the former, Confederate soldiers allegedly slaughtered black prisoners after they had surrendered; at the latter, Indians and whites had done the same to soldiers of the 1st Kansas Colored Infantry.

Soon, reports of "atrocious outrages" committed by Wild's soldiers began appearing in Richmond newspapers. Wild helped fan the flames of Confederate anger, particularly when he authorized the public whipping of a civilian, William H. Clopton, for his cruelties to his slaves. Wild turned the tables on Clopton. He was stripped, and four of his slaves whipped him by turns. When the Richmond newspapers reported the incident, however, Clopton had been transformed into three white men and the slaves into Wild's soldiers.

The Confederate government responded, motivated in part by military considerations and in part by anger over the presence of black troops. Gen. Braxton Bragg, Pres. Jefferson Davis's military adviser, ordered Maj. Gen. Fitzhugh Lee to capture the black garrison at Wilson's Wharf. Lee and his cavalry division left their camp at Atlee's Station on the Richmond, Fredericksburg & Potomac Railroad

north of Richmond at about 4 P.M. on Monday, May 23. They rode all night, covering the forty miles to Wilson's Wharf, where they finally arrived at about 11 A.M. on Tuesday, May 24.

Lee's division consisted of about 2,500 cavalrymen from the commands of Brig. Gen. Lunsford L. Lomax, Brig. Gen. Williams C. Wickham, and Col. John A. Baker. Lomax's brigade included the 5th, 6th, and 15th Virginia Regiments, Wickham's the 1st, 2nd, 3rd, and 4th Virginia Regiments, and Baker's the 1st, 2nd, 3rd, and 5th North Carolina Regiments. In addition, Col. John Dunovant's 5th South Carolina Regiment was attached to the force, and one artillery piece accompanied it. Lomax remained at Atlee's Station to command the camp there.

At Fort Pocahontas, Wild's garrison consisted of the 1st Regiment U.S. Colored Troops, four companies of the 10th USCT, and a two-gun (10-pounder rifled Parrott guns) section of Company M, 3rd New York Artillery Regiment. The gunboat *Dawn* lurked nearby in the river.

When Lee's division came within sight of Fort Pocahontas, he and his men observed a work still in progress but already formidable. More than half a mile in length, the crescent-shaped fort faced north; its left flank rested on a bluff above a small, swampy inlet on the James River, while its right faced a branch of Kennon Creek. Two bastions with artillery emplacements faced north across the Wilson farm fields. An old plantation road penetrated the center of the fort between the two bastions and led south to the wharf. A deep, broad ditch fronted the steep face of the fort, with abatis—trees felled so that their interlocked branches faced the enemy—beyond the ditch. More progress had been made east of the plantation road. The western half was less complete, but the attackers would have to cross broad,

USCT reenactors hold off C.S.A. attackers once more on May 20, 2000. VIRGINIA DEPARTMENT OF
HISTORIC RESOURCES, JOHN S. SALMON

deep fields to assault it. Each section of the fort offered its special protections and dangers to the defenders.

About noon, Lee mounted a charge and drove in Wild's pickets, who were posted near the Charles City Road a mile or so north of the fort. Lee separated his division into two detachments: Wickham's brigade in one and Lomax's and Baker's brigades and the 5th South Carolina in the other. The Confederates quickly dismounted and invested the fort, maneuvering to cut off its communications with the river to prevent reinforcement from Fort Powhatan. Lt. Julius M. Swain, the Union signal officer, managed to maintain communications and direct fire from the *Dawn* despite Lee's efforts.

At 1:30 P.M. Lee sent a flag of truce to the fort with a message. He demanded the surrender of the garrison, promising that the black soldiers would be taken to Richmond and treated as prisoners of war. If they did not surrender, Lee would not be responsible for the consequences. Wild and his men understood the implications of the threat. Wild's reply: "We will try it."

Lee ordered continued skirmishing while Wickham led his detachment to the right flank of the fort. Meanwhile, Dunovant's men would demonstrate against the western half to draw the defenders there; then Wickham would charge up the ravines, across the ditch, and over the eastern face of the fort.

Lee's plan was executed flawlessly but failed. Dunovant's detachment reached the abatis and ditch but was driven back by heavy fire. On the Union right, Wickham's men were observed, and when they charged up the ravines, they met a vicious crossfire, as the eastern section of earthworks zigzagged to provide interlocking fields of fire.

During the skirmishing as well as during the general attack, *Dawn* shelled Wickham's men, adding to their woes, and by late afternoon the Confederates withdrew out of range, as reinforcements and additional gunboats arrived from Fort Powhatan. Lee and his division bivouacked at Charles City Court House, then rode back to Atlee's Station the next morning. Fort Pocahontas was not attacked again, and soon white troops replaced black.

(Ironically, it was the white soldiers who later committed attacks on civilian households, including nearby Sherwood Forest.)

Lee acknowledged 10 killed, 48 wounded, and 4 missing, but the Federals reported the Confederate casualties as approaching 180. On the Union side, Wild reported 7 killed and 40 wounded. Most of those killed were among the pickets overrun by Lee. The Union victory at Fort Pocahontas helped ensure the continued passage of Federal vessels on the James River.

The Wilson family abandoned their farm after the war, and the land and the fort soon were covered in trees. The foliage protected the fort from erosion and helped ensure its survival. Fort Pocahontas is in an excellent state of preservation today, thanks to the efforts of Harrison Tyler, the grandson of President John Tyler and present owner of Sherwood Forest. He purchased the tract with the fort in 1996 and since then has cleared trees selectively and opened the fort for public tours. Of the several Virginia battlefields that are associated with African American troops—including The Crater, New Market Heights, and Saltville—Wilson's Wharf is the only one that is in virtually pristine condition. ■

SHENANDOAH VALLEY CAMPAIGNS, 1864–1865

When Lt. Gen. Ulysses S. Grant planned his campaign strategy for spring 1864, he decided on two major Union thrusts: Destroy Gen. Joseph E. Johnston's Army of Tennessee and occupy Atlanta, the South's most important railroad hub; and crush Gen. Robert E. Lee's Army of Northern Virginia and capture Richmond, the capital of the Confederate States of America. The Virginia campaign consisted of an attack toward Richmond, an advance up the James River to threaten the rail center at Petersburg, and the destruction of the railroad at Staunton and Lynchburg to sever Confederate links with the fertile Shenandoah Valley. To accomplish the third objective, Grant ordered Maj. Gen. Franz Sigel to lead a small army south through the Valley, in what Grant considered a sideshow compared to the thrust south from Germanna Ford.

Sigel and his 9,000-man army marched south from Winchester on the Valley Turnpike on May 2, 1864, their progress impeded by Brig. Gen. John D. Imboden's cavalry brigade, which harassed the column. Imboden's tactics bought time for Maj. Gen. John C. Breckinridge, a former vice president of the United States and former senator from Kentucky, who had been assigned the task of stopping Sigel with a makeshift Confederate force. By the second week of May, as Sigel marched into Shenandoah County, Breckinridge had scraped together a 5,300-man army, which included 247 teenage boys from the Virginia Military Institute, the entire corps of cadets.

On May 15 the two forces confronted each other at New Market, a farming village at the southern edge of Shenandoah County on the Valley Turnpike. Sigel blocked the turnpike a mile north of town, but Breckenridge, although outnumbered, attacked. Putting his infantry and a regiment of dismounted cavalry in line of battle, Breckinridge ordered his force to advance through New Market. Sigel ordered a withdrawal to a hill half a mile farther north and deployed his cannons effectively against the oncoming Confederates. Reluctantly, Breckinridge gave the command to "Put the boys in" to attack the Union artillery position just as a battery was withdrawn to replenish its ammunition. The cadets advanced in battle line with the rest of the Confederates and then charged the guns under heavy fire. At a cost of 10 killed and 47 wounded, some 20 percent of their number, the corps raced up the hill and captured a cannon abandoned by the fleeing Federal artillerists. His right flank endangered, Sigel retreated across the North Fork of the Shenandoah River to Strasburg and abandoned his campaign. For the moment the Valley was secure for the Confederates. The battle of New Market cost Sigel about 840 casualties, Breckinridge, 540.

Maj. Gen. David Hunter replaced Sigel four days later. On May 26 Hunter led his army, now strengthened to about 12,000, up the Valley from Cedar Creek. He planned to rendezvous near Staunton with Brig. Gen. George Crook's and Brig. Gen. William W. Averell's forces. By May 29

**SHENAN-
DOAH VALLEY
CAMPAIGNS
1864–1865**

RUTHERFORD'S FARM
3RD BATTLE OF WINCHESTER — Berryville
(OPEQUON) — Winchester
Middletown
2ND BATTLE OF KERNSTOWN — (522)
Strasburg — (823)
CEDAR CREEK — Woodstock — 11
GUARD — Front
TOM'S BROOK — Mt. Jackson — 81 — Edinburg — HILL — Royal
211
NEW MARKET — New Market — BERRYVILLE
Luray

New Market
Battlefield — Harrisonburg — FISHER'S
Park — HILL — COOL
Weyers Cave — (340) — SPRING
PIEDMONT — 612
Verona — 33
Staunton — 608 — Skyline Dr
New Hope
Lexington — WAYNESBORO — 64
Waynesboro

64
HANGING — 81
ROCK — James R.
11 — Blue Ridge Pkwy

LYNCHBURG — **N**
Salem
Bedford
to Roanoke — Lynchburg — 460

Hunter's army was at New Market, where it paused to rest and reinter in deeper graves the dead from the earlier battle there.

Once again the Confederates scrambled to meet the Union threat, Breckinridge having been summoned to the North Anna River. Brig. Gen. William E. "Grumble" Jones's infantry brigade hurried north from Bristol, while Imboden's cavalry blocked Hunter's advance at Mount Crawford. Augmented by local militia, Jones's command amounted to some 5,600 troops.

Hunter sidestepped the Confederate blocking force by marching around it and crossing the North River at Port Republic. Jones and Imboden, with reinforcement by Brig. Gen. John C. Vaughn's cavalry, countered by marching southeast and occupying ground around Piedmont, about

seven miles southwest of Port Republic. The infantry formed a defensive line of fence rails and felled trees in an arc northwest of Piedmont, while Vaughn's cavalry held a position southeast of the community.

On June 5 Hunter crossed the river at Port Republic and encountered Imboden's cavalry outposts at Mount Meridian. Hunter's cavalry forced the Confederates back to Piedmont, where they dismounted and joined Vaughn's men. Shortly after noon, Hunter launched the first of a series of attacks against Jones that revealed a gap in his line. A Union brigade assaulted the gap while Jones repositioned and rallied his men. At the height of the battle, a bullet to the head killed Jones instantly, and the Confederate line collapsed. Only a stiff rearguard action on the road south of Piedmont held off the Union pursuit. The Confederate defeat was costly: 1,600 casualties (including more than 1,000 captured) versus 875 for the Federals. Now the upper Valley lay unprotected before the Union columns.

Hunter occupied Staunton the next day, and Crook joined him two days later, swelling his force to some 20,000. Hunter then embarked on a campaign of destruction and pillaging (Grant had ordered him to live off the land) south to Lexington. Hunter's army ransacked the town and burned many buildings, including the Virginia Military Institute. Then he focused on his primary objective, Lynchburg, and marched east through the Blue Ridge Mountains.

East of the mountains, meanwhile, Lee's Army of Northern Virginia had been locked in combat with the Army of the Potomac throughout May and the first half of June. While Breckinridge fought Sigel at New Market on May 15, the eastern armies had been struggling at Spotsylvania Court House. The news of Jones's defeat at Piedmont on June 5 reached Lee soon after the battle of Cold Harbor. Then came Sheridan's raid against the Virginia Central Railroad and the Confederate victory at Trevilian Station, which saved the line at least temporarily. Now Hunter was rampaging through the upper Valley and threatening Lynchburg, the rail and canal center of the Virginia Piedmont.

In consultation with Pres. Jefferson Davis and Gen. Braxton Bragg, Davis's military adviser, Lee first returned Breckinridge's division to the Valley and then sent an entire corps of his army to save both Lynchburg and the Valley. The tactic entailed great risk for his army, but Lee had to act with vigor to preserve the western rail links and take some of the pressure off Richmond.

Lt. Gen. Jubal A. Early commanded this corps, formerly Stonewall Jackson's. Early, it has been pointed out, was no Jackson, but neither was anyone else. "Old Jube's" aggressiveness earned him the enthusiastic support of his troops, but his rashness, abrasiveness, and feelings of insecurity caused him to mistrust his most capable subordinates. Known for his profane language and acid tongue, Early provoked strong emotions in those who knew him; few were impartial.

Lee and Early conferred on June 12. Early was to defeat Hunter, march north down the Valley into Maryland, and threaten Washington. Early's corps, with Breckinridge's division attached to it, numbered about 14,000.

On June 13 the corps began its westward march by foot and rail to Lynchburg, while Hunter and his army approached the city from the west. Both armies reached their objective on June 17, with Hunter confronting the southern defensive works while the vanguard of Early's army rode railroad cars into the north side of town. Early's corps rushed forward to man the earthworks while Hunter probed cautiously. After several skirmishes, Hunter ordered a retreat the next day, in part because he was short of supplies. His army fled southwest toward Big Lick (present-day Roanoke) with Early in pursuit.

The Confederates caught up with the Federals on June 21 just north of Salem at Hanging Rock. In a small, sharp engagement confined to a narrow valley by steep hills, Early delivered the final blow to Hunter that hastened his retreat into West Virginia. The route Hunter chose to reach the relative safety of Harpers Ferry ensured that he and his army would be out of the war for a month.

Now Early was free to carry out the remainder of Lee's orders: Invade Maryland and attack Washington. The Confederates marched north down the Shenandoah Valley and on July 9, near Frederick, Maryland, defeated a Union force under Maj. Gen. Lew A. Wallace at the battle of Monocacy. Two days later, to the astonishment of the capital's inhabitants, Early's army appeared before the northwestern defenses of Washington. Pres. Abraham Lincoln rode out for a look, while Grant ordered two divisions north from the Petersburg siege lines. Early found the Federal lines unassailable by his relatively small force and withdrew shortly after midnight on July 12.

Maj. Gen. Horatio G. Wright pursued Early with elements of three army corps, some 25,000 men. Early's army crossed the Potomac River at White's Ford and marched west through the Blue Ridge at Snicker's Gap. Roughly three miles beyond the gap, where the road crossed the Shenandoah River at Castleman's Ferry, Early was brought to bay at a farm on the western side called Cool Spring. After Union cavalry confronted Confederate cavalry at one river crossing on July 17 and another the next day, Wright decided that Early's infantry had retreated to Winchester, so the Federal infantry might successfully force its way across. Early's infantry divisions were just out of sight to the west, however, and they quickly moved east to block Wright's advance under Crook. Col. Joseph Thoburn's Federal division, which had crossed the river and expected reinforcements that never came, found itself pinned down near the riverbank. He and his men held out until darkness permitted them to retreat across the river. A night artillery duel ended the engagement, which cost the Federals 422 casualties and the Confederates 397.

Early continued his retreat west to Winchester and then south to Strasburg, while Wright's force followed slowly. Then Early learned that a combined Federal detachment of cavalry supported by infantry and commanded by Averell was marching south from Martinsburg, West Virginia, to join Wright. Early detailed Maj. Gen. Stephen D. Ramseur's division to defend the northern approaches to Winchester. On July 20, as Ramseur was getting into position to attack Averell at John Rutherford's farm northeast of Winchester, the Federals suddenly struck Ramseur's flank. Overwhelmed by the onslaught, Ramseur's division fled in a rout, and some 300 Confederates were taken prisoner.

Because of this defeat and Wright's slow approach, Early withdrew his army to Fisher's Hill, south of Strasburg. Wright concluded that the Confederates no longer posed a threat to Washington and ordered most of his detachment back to the capital preparatory to a return to the Petersburg front. He left Crook at Winchester to defend the northern end of the Valley.

No sooner had Wright departed than Early struck back at the second battle of Kernstown. There, at the site of Jackson's defeat more than two years earlier, Early's cavalry skirmished with Averell's through-

out the day on July 23. The engagement was renewed the next day, in part to screen the march of Early's infantry north from Strasburg at first light. Crook met Early's initial probe, which developed into a strong demonstration in Crook's front. Breckinridge, meanwhile, led his division in an envelopment of Crook's left flank, which soon crumbled. Crook's command fled north through Winchester and crossed the Potomac River near Williamsport, Maryland. The Federals lost some 1,200 men in the battle, the Confederates about 600.

Early quickly took advantage of his victory. He ordered an expeditionary force commanded by Brig. Gen. John McCausland to seize Chambersburg, Pennsylvania. McCausland and his troopers rode into town on July 30 and demanded $100,000 in gold or $500,000 in paper currency in retribution for Hunter's destruction of Lexington. When the town fathers refused, his men burned the center of town and destroyed more than 400 buildings, almost 300 of them private dwellings.

Crook's defeat and the subsequent burning of Chambersburg galvanized Grant as well as Lincoln. The two men met at Fort Monroe on July 31 to discuss the organization of an army to reoccupy the Shenandoah Valley and the appointment of its leader. Maj. Gen. George G. Meade, commander of the Army of the Potomac, and Maj. Gen. William B. Franklin, the commander of the Left Grand Division at Fredericksburg, were considered and rejected. Lincoln departed for Washington with the matter unsettled, leaving the decision to Grant, and the next morning Grant wired Maj. Gen. Henry W. Halleck, the Federal chief of staff, with his choice: Maj. Gen. Philip H. Sheridan, Meade's cavalry commander.

Barely five foot three, Sheridan was called "Little Phil" by his troops. His bullet-shaped head, accentuated by his close-cropped hair, was remarked on by many.

Sheridan was naturally combative; he was also intense and energetic, giving an impression of being in perpetual motion. On horseback Sheridan became particularly animated and charismatic, and few in the Federal army were as adept at inspiring men on the verge of battle.

Sheridan's 43,000-man army, called the Army of the Shenandoah, consisted of Wright's VI Corps, two divisions of the XIX Corps commanded by Maj. Gen. William H. Emory, the XIII Corps led by Crook, a dozen artillery batteries, and three cavalry divisions under Brig. Gen. Alfred T. A. Torbert. On August 7, when Sheridan arrived to take command, the army was encamped at Halltown, West Virginia, about three miles southwest of Harpers Ferry. There, almost 5,000 troops under Brig. Gen. John D. Stevenson also were available to Sheridan.

Early and his Army of the Valley, as he styled it, were camped at Bunker Hill, West Virginia, on the Valley Turnpike some fourteen miles west of Halltown. The army consisted of about 14,000 men in three infantry divisions, five cavalry brigades, and three artillery battalions totaling nine batteries. Early's force was outnumbered by better than three to one.

Grant's orders to Sheridan were clear: Push the Confederates south, away from Washington, and strip the Valley of provisions that the enemy would find useful. Whatever could not be used should be destroyed. Grant added that it was not desirable to destroy buildings—a suggestion that Sheridan later would ignore.

The Federals began marching up the Valley on August 10, and by August 13 they were at Cedar Creek, with the Confederates ensconced on Fisher's Hill four miles south. Word reached Sheridan of Confederate troop movements from Petersburg to the Valley; on Grant's recommendation he withdrew his force to Winchester. Although Sheridan feared that

Lt. Gen. James Longstreet's corps had reinforced Early, in fact Lee had dispatched only Maj. Gen. Joseph B. Kershaw's infantry division, Maj. Gen. Fitzhugh Lee's cavalry division, and Lt. Col. Wilfred E. Cutshaw's artillery battalion under the overall command of Lt. Gen. Richard H. Anderson. On Grant's advice, Sheridan began withdrawing through Winchester back to Halltown.

On August 14 Anderson reached Front Royal, where the north and south forks of the Shenandoah River converge. There, Anderson threatened the Federal line of retreat, which Brig. Gen. Wesley Merritt's cavalry division guarded just north of the rivers. On August 16, when Merritt began moving north, Anderson ordered Brig. Gen. William T. Wofford's infantry brigade and Brig. Gen. Williams C. Wickham's cavalry brigade to move across the rivers to Guard Hill to watch the roads and river fords.

In midafternoon Wickham advanced from Guard Hill against Merritt, but two regiments of Brig. Gen. Thomas C. Devin's brigade counterattacked, and the Confederates retreated across the rivers. Brig. Gen. George A. Custer led another Federal attack on Guard Hill; again the Confederates retreated, and many drowned or were captured as they crossed the river. Having confirmed the presence of Confederate infantry and cavalry in Front Royal, Merritt's cavalry followed the main Federal army toward Halltown. The two sides suffered a total of some 550 casualties in the Guard Hill engagement.

For the next several weeks, Early probed the Union lines around Halltown, and Sheridan likewise skirmished with the Confederates. Considerable maneuvering occurred in Jefferson County, West Virginia, and Clarke County, Virginia. On September 3 most of Sheridan's army advanced to Berryville in Clarke County and took up defensive positions north of the town on rolling ground. The Confederates occupied a parallel line about a mile west. As part of Crook's corps settled down for the night on the Union left flank, Kershaw's division attacked and met with initial success but lacked the manpower to continue. During the night, Early brought up the remainder of his army, but when daylight revealed entrenchments too strong to attack, he withdrew that night beyond Opequon Creek. The two sides suffered about 500 total casualties, and the maneuvering continued with little interruption.

As the armies appeared to be stalemated, in mid-September Early agreed that Anderson would depart with Kershaw's division and Cutshaw's artillery battalion and rejoin Lee at Petersburg, leaving Early with some 12,500 men against Sheridan's 40,000. On September 15 Anderson and his men began their march out of the Valley, a movement observed by Federal spies. The next day Grant arrived at Charlestown to confer with Sheridan. Asked if he could move on Early in four days, Sheridan replied that he could do so in three. "Go in," Grant ordered.

Early approved Anderson's departure in part because he thought Sheridan timid. In case he was wrong, however, Early ordered a withdrawal to Winchester. He also scattered his infantry divisions and resumed raiding the Baltimore & Ohio Railroad at Martinsburg, West Virginia. At about 1 A.M. on September 19, Sheridan's Army of the Shenandoah was roused from its bivouac and marched west on the Berryville Turnpike. The third battle of Winchester (called Opequon by the Federals) was about to begin, and Early would discover just how wrong he was about Sheridan's aggressiveness.

Just before dawn, Brig. Gen. James H. Wilson's cavalry division trotted across Opequon Creek, followed by Sheridan's infantry. The army successfully negotiated the narrow, two-mile-long defile called

Berryville Canyon because Ramseur, defending this sector, only posted pickets at the eastern entrance.

Ramseur's division blocked the western end of the turnpike and formed the Confederate right flank. Maj. Gen. Robert E. Rodes's division held the center, and Maj. Gen. John B. Gordon's division secured the left. The Federal forces deployed with Brig. Gen. William Dwight's and Brig. Gen. Cuvier Grover's divisions forming the right flank, Brig. Gen. James B. Ricketts's division the center, and Brig. Gen. George W. Getty's the left. Brig. Gen. David A. Russell's division was held in reserve.

The Union attack began at about 11:40 A.M. Grover's division suffered heavy losses against Gordon, and Dwight's was pinned down. Ricketts and Getty, however, almost collapsed Ramseur's right flank before Rodes counterattacked at about 1:30 P.M. Sheridan ordered all of his reserves, including the cavalry, to strike the Confederate flanks, and that action turned the tide. Early's line dissolved, and the men fled in panic up the Valley Turnpike to Kernstown, where a hastily organized rearguard action saved the army from destruction.

The battle was hideously costly, with the Confederates losing some 3,600 killed, wounded, or captured—almost 25 percent of the force engaged—and the Federals about 5,000, or 13 percent. The Union XIX Corps suffered 40 percent casualties and lost every regimental commander among the killed or wounded during the fighting in Second Woods and Middle Field. Suddenly, Sheridan found himself in control of the northern end of the Valley, and he set off in pursuit of Early.

Early's army wended its way south to Fisher's Hill, a ridge south of Strasburg that spanned the turnpike and provided the Confederates with a natural stronghold that provided the best chance of stopping Sheridan's progress. On September 20 Early deployed his force, now reduced to about

9,500, in a line that extended almost five miles, with skirmishers on the hills just to the north. Although infantry held the Confederate center and right flank, Early stationed Maj. Gen. Lunsford L. Lomax's cavalry division alone on the fragile left as little more than a skirmish line.

Sheridan's force of some 30,000 arrived at Hupp's Hill north of Strasburg as Early completed his deployment. The Federals entrenched on a series of hills just north of Early's skirmishers. The next day, shortly after noon, Sheridan mounted three assaults that succeeded in capturing Flint Hill, one of Early's forward positions near the center of his line. During the night and early on the morning of September 22, others of Sheridan's units pushed ahead until they occupied virtually all the ridges and hills overlooking Tumbling Run in front of Early's position.

In the meantime, Crook secretly marched his two divisions to the base of Little North Mountain and around Early's left flank. At about 4 P.M. Crook ordered his men to charge; they rushed pell-mell through Lomax's thin line and rolled up the Confederate left flank until they encountered stiffening resistance by Ramseur's division. Simultaneous with Crook's charge, the rest of Sheridan's force attacked, and soon Early's line collapsed and the men fled south in disarray. Early withdrew to Rockfish Gap near Waynesboro, having suffered some 1,200 casualties (mostly captured) to Sheridan's 530.

The rout meant that most of the Shenandoah Valley lay open to Sheridan. Having accomplished the first part of Grant's orders by driving Early far away, Sheridan proceeded to execute the second part, destroying the Valley's ability to sustain the Confederate army. For the next several weeks, the Union army incinerated barns, mills, and crops between Strasburg and Staunton in what became known locally as "The Burning" or "Red October."

Sheridan's activities did not go unchallenged, particularly by Lt. Col. John S. Mosby, the "Gray Ghost," and his Partisan Rangers (officially, the 43rd Virginia Battalion). In operation since late in 1862, the Rangers harassed the Federals in northern Virginia so successfully that Fairfax, Fauquier, Loudoun, and Prince William Counties were known as Mosby's Confederacy. As soon as Sheridan's army entered the area in August 1864, Mosby waged a relentless and effective campaign against its lines of supply and communication, continuing into the winter. An exasperated Grant finally ordered captured Rangers summarily executed, but when Mosby responded in kind, he canceled the order. Mosby was a problem with no solution.

Suddenly in October, Early demonstrated that he had not been "solved" by Sheridan, either. After the defeat at Fisher's Hill, Early asked Lee to send additional cavalry to his aid and for the return of Kershaw's infantry and Cutshaw's artillery. Lee complied and also dispatched Brig. Gen. Thomas L. Rosser and his brigade from Petersburg. They arrived just as Sheridan began withdrawing north down the Valley early in October. Assigning Rosser the command of all his cavalry, Early ordered him to pursue and harass the Federals. By the evening of October 8, Sheridan, fed up, angrily ordered Torbert with his cavalry command to "start out at daylight and whip the rebel cavalry or get whipped."

The Confederate cavalrymen had bivouacked just south of Tom's Brook, a stream that flowed across the Valley and emptied into the North Fork of the Shenandoah River. Lomax's division held the right flank on the Valley Turnpike north of Woodstock, while Rosser's occupied the left almost two miles west on the Back Road. Merritt's division encamped a mile across the stream opposite Lomax, while Custer bivouacked north of Rosser's camp.

Torbert ordered a dawn attack for October 9. While Merritt pressed Lomax, Torbert sent a brigade to Custer's assistance. The reinforced Custer soon overwhelmed Rosser and forced a retreat. Once the Confederate left gave way, Lomax could only follow suit. Despite brief rearguard actions by Lomax and Rosser, the Union cavalry routed their once-vaunted opponents. The Confederates lost 11 cannons and some 350 men killed, wounded, and captured, the Federals fewer than 60. Once again Sheridan dominated the Valley.

For the next week and a half, Sheridan and Early played cat-and-mouse. Despite frequent skirmishes, Sheridan believed Early's army finished as an offensive force; it had reoccupied the Fisher's Hill works and appeared to be on the defensive. The same engagements, however, caused Sheridan to postpone his plan to detach part of his army to reinforce Grant at Petersburg. In addition, Grant preferred that Sheridan establish a fortified position near Manassas Gap, a proposal that contributed to the impasse. On October 13 Secretary of War Edwin Stanton wired Sheridan to suggest that he come to Washington for a conference with chief of staff Henry W. Halleck. Sheridan departed for Washington on October 16. At the conference he gained support for his plan to leave a small defensive force in the Valley and send the bulk of the army to Grant. On October 18 Sheridan returned to Winchester.

Sheridan's army was encamped on low hills and ridges north of Cedar Creek about fourteen miles south of Winchester. The terrain dictated the U-shaped encampment, with Col. Joseph Thoburn's division of Crook's corps in front of the main body at the apex. The Union force numbered some 32,000 against the Confederates' 21,000.

Early knew he had to do something to keep Sheridan in the Valley and away from Petersburg. On October 18 he held a council of war with all his generals. Gordon proposed to lead most of the army east to the base of Massanutten Mountain, then north toward Cedar Creek, and finally against Sheridan's left flank. The rest of the army would march by divisions to attack the Federal center and right. The march would take place that night, and the attacks would occur simultaneously at dawn. Early supported this clearly risky plan over a few objections, and Gordon set off with his detachment at 8 P.M.

The audacious scheme succeeded brilliantly in one of the great maneuvers of the war. Leaving behind their canteens, cooking pots, and anything else that might rattle, Early's men marched silently through the night to their assigned attack points. Virtually every unit was in its place at the appointed time. On October 19, aided by a dense fog that had rolled in, Early achieved surprise when the attack began at 5:40 A.M. In a matter of minutes the Federal left and center had crumbled, and the soldiers fled.

Sweeping over the abandoned Union camps, many Confederates stopped to plunder tents and sample the still-warm breakfasts of their adversaries. Additionally, unit cohesion declined in the smoke and fog and rush of combat, whereas Federal resistance stiffened here and there. Slowly Early's attack lost momentum. By 10 A.M. a new Union line had formed some three miles north. For a while, the battle lapsed into an artillery duel.

On the southern edge of Winchester just after dawn, the Union pickets there heard the low rumble of gunfire in the distance and reported it to Sheridan. He mounted his horse and rode up the Valley Turnpike toward Cedar Creek, exhorting fleeing men to rejoin their units. At about 10:30 A.M. Sheridan arrived at the front. After discussing the situation with his generals, Sheridan turned west off the road and galloped along the front of his army, shouting that it would sleep in its camps again that night. The men roared and believed him.

The fog lifted, and Early saw the Federals in their new position. With Union cavalry nipping at his own flanks, he turned cautious. He launched a couple of attacks while the camp plunderers were being rounded up but concluded that the army had accomplished all that it could, given the imbalance of numbers and the Federals' strong position. He did not pull his men back, however, but continued to confront Sheridan.

That was a mistake. At 4 P.M., after his own stragglers had returned to their units, Sheridan launched a counterattack that soon broke Early's left flank and turned his center. Retreat became a rout, and the Confederates fled south. By sundown the Federals held their old campsites.

Early's army suffered almost 3,000 casualties in the battle; Sheridan's, just under 5,700. Though losing fewer men, the Confederate army had been reduced enough to preclude taking the offensive. By mid-November both armies were being broken up as they were recalled piecemeal to Petersburg. In December the remnants went into winter camp, Early's at Staunton and Sheridan's at Winchester.

In late February 1865, Grant ordered Sheridan south to destroy the Virginia Central Railroad and capture Charlottesville. With two cavalry divisions, some 10,000 men, Sheridan left Winchester on February 27 and by March 1 had occupied Staunton, which had been stripped of supplies and was largely empty of inhabitants. Early's force, now reduced to 1,600 men, had abandoned the town and marched east to Waynesboro.

Early set up a defensive line on hills west of the town. The next day Custer led his cavalry division to within reconnoitering distance and spent three hours studying Early's dispositions. Finding a gap in the left flank, Custer sent three dismounted regiments slicing through it at 3:30 P.M. As the Confederate left crumbled, a Federal brigade charged the center, and Early's men fled in panic. Early himself barely escaped, and most of his force was captured. The Valley was in Federal hands for good.

Early eventually reached his home in Franklin County. Sheridan spent March raiding east by way of the Virginia Central Railroad and the James River & Kanawha Canal, destroying each as he progressed. On March 26 he and his cavalrymen joined Grant at Petersburg in time for the last campaign of the war in Virginia.

Much criticism has been heaped on Early's head for his "failure" to hold the Valley, in contrast to Stonewall Jackson's earlier success there. But although Jackson was outnumbered by the totality of the three Federal armies he faced, he engaged each one separately when the superior numbers were on his side. More importantly, his opponents' armies were unseasoned, and the generals themselves were barely competent. Early faced some of the most experienced troops in the Union army, matched wits with the extremely capable Sheridan, and was outnumbered in every battle he fought. In addition, his own men were worn out and ill-supplied, problems the Federals did not experience. Despite the odds against it, Early's army marched farther and fought more large battles than Jackson's and tied up three Union corps for most of the campaign season. The wonder is not that Early ultimately was defeated but that he and his men accomplished as much as they did. ■

NEW MARKET

The Confederates in the Shenandoah Valley were ill-prepared to stop the advance of Union Maj. Gen. Franz Sigel's 9,000-man army when it left Winchester and marched south on May 2, 1864. Gen. Robert E. Lee, his hands full in the Wilderness, assigned the difficult task to Maj. Gen. John C. Breckinridge. Brig. Gen. John D. Imboden's cavalrymen bought time for Breckinridge by harassing the Federal column, slowing Sigel's advance. Sigel's army consisted of an infantry division, two brigades of cavalry, and five artillery batteries.

Breckinridge scrambled to assemble a defensive force at Staunton. By May 12 he had under his command some 5,300 troops, including two infantry brigades, Imboden's cavalry brigade, artillery batteries totaling fourteen guns, and some local militia. With Lee's reluctant approval, 247 cadets from the Virginia Military Institute augmented the army. By May 14 Breckinridge had led his force to Lacy's Spring, located about nine miles south of New Market on the Valley Turnpike (present-day U.S. Rte. 11).

The vanguard of Sigel's army occupied high ground in and west of New Market the same evening. When Imboden informed Breckinridge of Sigel's position, he resolved to march at once to confront him. The Confederates moved north at 1 A.M. on Sunday, May 15, and approached New Market about five hours later.

Breckinridge spent almost two hours reconnoitering the Federal position. A series of hills or ridges lay before him. The closest unoccupied eminence, Shirley's Hill, stood within cannon shot of the next ridge, Manor's Hill, which in turn was succeeded by Bushong's Hill. At 8 A.M. Breckinridge ordered the artillery forward

DIRECTIONS: I-81 Exit 264 (U.S. Rte. 211 West) to Rte. 619; s. on Rte. 619 about .2 mile and turn around for view of battlefield, town, and route of Confederate advance; return to U.S. Rte. 211; cross U.S. Rte. 211 to State Rte. 305 n. 1.1 miles to New Market Battlefield Historical State Park, site of the last principal actions of the battle, including the charge of the Virginia Military Institute cadets (other museums on State Rte. 305 include the Cavalry Museum and the New Market Battlefield Military Museum); return to U.S. Rte. 211; e. (left) on U.S. Rte. 211 .4 mile to U.S. Rte. 11; n. (left) on U.S. Rte. 11 .9 mile n. to second Confederate position; continue .2 mile to Virginia Civil War Commission (Circle Tour) interpretive markers and state historical marker A-28, Battle of New Market, on left; continue .1 mile to second Union position, and 54th Pennsylvania Infantry monument on left; continue 1.3 miles to final Confederate position; continue .5 mile to Rte. 620 (Smith Creek Rd.), site of Union rearguard holding action; proceed .3 mile to Rte. 730 atop Rude's Hill; w. (left) on Rte. 730 .4 mile to I-81 Exit 269. For more information about the battlefield, visit the park Web site at: vmi.edu/MUSEUM/nm/ or call the park at 540-740-3101.

to Shirley's Hill to engage Col. August Moor's infantry troops on Manor's Hill and Union artillery positioned west of the turnpike. Brig. Gen. Julius Stahel then arrived and ordered Moor to withdraw some of his troops to Bushong's Hill.

Breckinridge was in no rush to attack, as not all of his infantry had reached him. Sigel, who rode up at about 11 A.M., had allowed his troops to straggle badly—some found the battlefield after the fighting had ended—and after reviewing the dispositions of those on the field, he pulled back Moor's brigade to Bushong's Hill and to the left of Col. Joseph Thoburn's brigade, ordered fourteen artillery pieces to support Thoburn, and stationed both brigades of Stahel's cavalry on the Union left flank, east of the turnpike. Sigel's line now stretched from the North Fork of the Shenandoah River on the west to Smith's Creek on the east.

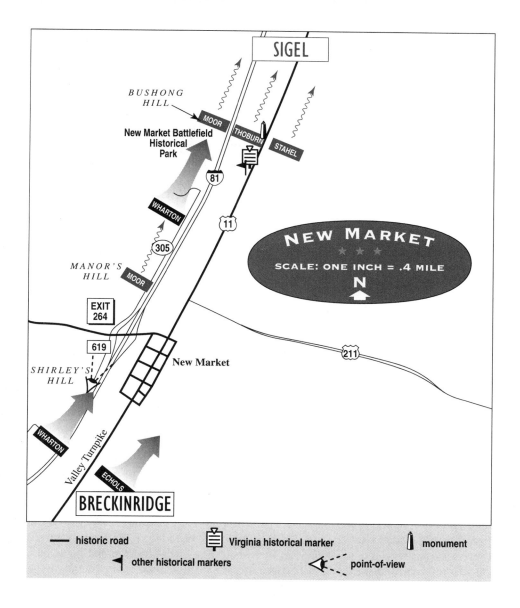

SIGEL

BUSHONG HILL

MOOR

THOBURN

STAHEL

New Market Battlefield Historical Park

81

WHARTON

11

305

NEW MARKET
★ ★ ★
SCALE: ONE INCH = .4 MILE
N

MANOR'S HILL

MOOR

EXIT 264

619

SHIRLEY'S HILL

New Market

211

WHARTON

Valley Turnpike

ECHOLS

BRECKINRIDGE

— historic road   🗎 Virginia historical marker   🮲 monument

◀ other historical markers   ◁---- point-of-view

By 12:30 P.M. Breckinridge had deployed his infantry in a line paralleling Sigel's. Brig. Gen. Gabriel C. Wharton's infantry brigade occupied Manor's Hill west of the turnpike after pushing off Moor's two remaining regiments, and Brig. Gen. John Echols took a position astride the turnpike and to the east. At about 2 P.M. Breckinridge ordered Whar-

ton to advance against the Federals on Bushong's Hill. From the Confederate left to right, four regiments marched down Manor's Hill toward the Bushong farmhouse and Bushong's Hill north of it.

On Bushong's Hill, from the Union right to left, two artillery batteries and three infantry regiments confronted the advancing Confederates with heavy fire.

Wharton's route of advance north from Shirley's Hill to Manor's Hill (left center; New Market on right). VIRGINIA DEPARTMENT OF HISTORIC RESOURCES, JOHN S. SALMON

The attack bogged down around the Bushong house, and Breckinridge finally gave the order to "put the boys in" to bolster the sagging line. On his right flank, meanwhile, Confederate artillery stopped a cavalry charge ordered by Stahel.

At about 3 P.M., Sigel ordered a counterattack against Breckinridge's line, but the Confederates easily repulsed it. When Confederate sharpshooters began picking off the gunners on Bushong's Hill, Sigel directed the batteries to withdraw. When the fire slackened, Breckinridge ordered a general advance.

The Confederates swept up Bushong's Hill, with the cadets in the middle of the line. The Confederates drove the Federals from the hill, and the cadets captured a cannon and many men of the 34th Massachusetts Infantry. With the Union right collapsing, the left quickly began to withdraw.

After falling back two miles, Sigel formed a new line on a ridge at Cedar Grove Dunker Church (now Cedar Grove United Brethren Church) along present-day Rte. 620. Breckinridge halted his pursuing force to reorganize at about 4:30 P.M.

Imboden had led his cavalry across Smith Creek in an unsuccessful attempt to get around Sigel's army and burn the Meem's Bottom Bridge to cut off Sigel's retreat across the North Fork of the Shenandoah. An artillery duel ensued, and then Sigel crossed the bridge at about 7 P.M. and burned it behind him. He reached Strasburg the next day.

The Confederate victory at New Market dealt the Federals an unexpected, albeit temporary, setback. Sigel suffered some 840 casualties, Breckinridge about 540. The Virginia Military Institute cadets maintained coolness under fire despite being placed in the center of the Confederate line; 10 died, and 47 were wounded.

The New Market battlefield has been fragmented by development and Interstate 81, which splits the field in half. Light industrial and residential construction has occurred along Rte. 11 (the Valley Turnpike), and several large structures have been built on Manor's Hill. Still, enough remains that the visitor can understand the course of the battle, and several historic structures stand, as well. At the northwestern end of the field, Virginia Military Institute owns the New Market Battlefield Park and Hall of Valor. There, a self-guided tour leads the visitor through the restored Bushong Farm and up Bushong's Hill to the main Federal position and by tunnel under I-81 to the position and monument of the 54th Pennsylvania Infantry. The Institute also owns an important parcel on Shirley's Hill and may acquire others in the future. Further development is likely to occur, however, near the highway interchanges as well as around the town of New Market, which retains much of its historic fabric and charm nonetheless. ■

Four days after Maj. Gen. Franz Sigel was defeated at the battle of New Market by a patched-together Confederate force led by Maj. Gen. John C. Breckinridge, Maj. Gen. David Hunter replaced Sigel as the commander of the Union army in the Shenandoah Valley. Assuming that their victory had neutralized the threat posed by Sigel, the Confederates were surprised when the 12,000-man Federal army began marching south once more on May 26, 1864.

Hunter was an aggressive commander who heeded Lt. Gen. Ulysses S. Grant's admonition to travel light, live off the land, and strike fast and hard. Hunter planned to unite his forces with those of Brig. Gen. George Crook, en route north from southeastern West Virginia, and Brig. Gen. William W. Averell near Staunton. Then he would lay waste to the Shenandoah Valley, march to Lynchburg, and destroy the railroads there.

The Confederates had few troops available with which to counter Hunter's advance, as Lee had ordered Breckinridge and his command to join the Army of Northern Virginia at the North Anna River thirty miles north of Richmond. While Brig. Gen. John G. Imboden's cavalry brigade delayed Hunter at Mount Crawford, Brig. Gen. William E. "Grumble" Jones's infantry brigade was rushed northeast by rail from Bristol on the Tennessee border. Brig. Gen. John C. Vaughn's mounted infantry brigade brought Imboden's and Jones's combined force to about 5,600 men.

With his advance on the Valley Turnpike blocked, Hunter led his army east to Port Republic, crossed the North River, then proceeded toward Staunton on the East Road (present-day Rtes. 605, 865,

View east across path of Thoburn's second attack. VIRGINIA DEPARTMENT OF HISTORIC RESOURCES, JOHN S. SALMON

and 608). Jones sought to check Hunter by marching his force southeast to the hamlet of Piedmont. There Jones stationed most of his infantry north of the village and west of the East Road behind barricades of felled trees and fence rails, with his left flank (Col. Beuhring Jones's brigade) facing north and resting on the Middle River and the center (Col. William H. Browne's brigade) on the road facing east. He posted Vaughn's dismounted cavalrymen southeast of Piedmont along the Cross Road (Rte. 778) to form the right flank, with artillery supporting his position and Browne's brigade. The reserve Home Guards took up a position west of the artillery and south of Piedmont. Imboden's cavalry occupied Mount Meridian, about four miles north of Piedmont, to warn of Hunter's approach.

Hunter crossed the North River at Port Republic shortly after dawn on Sunday, June 5. Elements of Brig. Gen. Julius Stahel's cavalry division led the way, followed by Brig. Gen. Jeremiah C. Sullivan's infantry division and the artillery. Stahel's division consisted of the brigades commanded by Col. William B. Tibbits and Col. John E. Wynkoop, while Sullivan's contained Col. Joseph Thoburn's and Col.

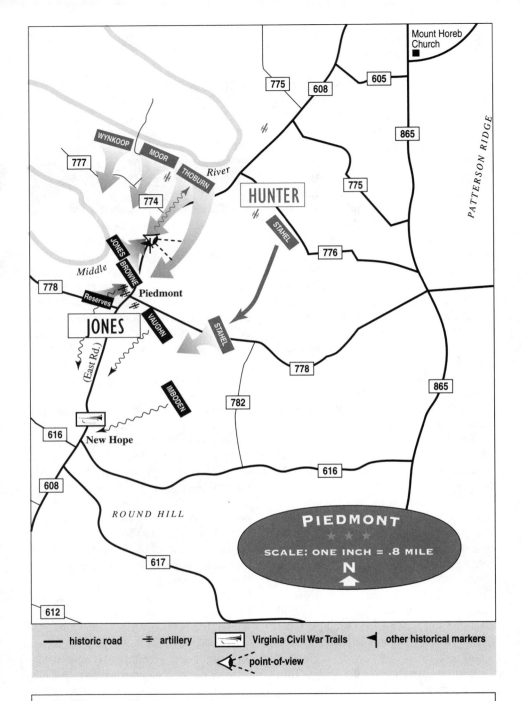

Mount Horeb Church

775 · 608 · 605 · 865

PATTERSON RIDGE

WYNKOOP · MOOR · THOBURN · *River*

777 · 774

HUNTER

STAHEL

775

776

JONES · BROWNE

Middle · Piedmont

778 · Reserves

JONES

VAUGHN

STAHEL

(East Rd.)

IMBODEN

778

782 · 865

616 · New Hope

608

ROUND HILL

616

PIEDMONT
★ ★ ★
SCALE: ONE INCH = .8 MILE
N

617

612

— historic road · ╪ artillery · ◁═ Virginia Civil War Trails · ◄ other historical markers

◄--- point-of-view

DIRECTIONS: I-81 Exit 235 (State Rte. 256, Weyer's Cave–Grottoes); e. on State Rte. 256 about 4.3 miles to Rte. 865 (Rockfish Rd.); s. (right) on Rte. 865 1 mile to Rte. 608 (Battlefield Rd.); s. (right) on Rte. 608 2.1 miles to Rte. 776 (Hatchery Rd.); continue s. on Rte. 608 through Union position .9 mile to United Daughters of the Confederacy marker on left; continue s. on Rte. 608 .5 mile to Rte. 778 on right at Piedmont (Confederate reserve position to w., Vaughn's position to e.); continue s. on Rte. 608 .6 mile to Virginia Civil War Trails marker; continue s. on Rte. 608 1.8 miles to Rte. 612 (Laurel Hill Rd.); right on Rte. 612 about 5.3 miles to I-81.

August Moor's brigades. Capt. Henry A. Du Pont commanded the artillery.

Almost immediately Stahel's troopers encountered Imboden's vedettes. Stahel's men fell back on the main cavalry force, which then advanced with ten field pieces and slowly compelled Imboden to retire toward Piedmont. By 10 A.M. the Confederate cavalry had reached the temporary safety of Jones's lines, where the artillery forced the Federal troopers to withdraw and await the infantry. Imboden's men joined Vaughn's to extend the Confederate right flank farther south.

Moor's brigade arrived first and deployed facing Colonel Jones's brigade, while Thoburn's brigade took its position east of the road. Du Pont arranged his twenty-two guns on high ground and confronted the smaller Confederate contingent in the gap between Browne's and Imboden's brigades; two batteries fell back to the village.

Near 1 P.M. Moor, supported by a regiment of Thoburn's brigade, advanced against Colonel Jones's pickets and then against the Confederate left flank. Grumble Jones reinforced his left flank with troops from Browne's brigade, and ordered a counterattack. The fighting surged back and forth, and Hunter threw Wynkoop's dismounted cavalry brigade into the fray.

In midafternoon Thoburn led the remainder of his brigade in an attack against the gap in Jones's line. Jones ordered the Home Guard reserve to fill the breach; while directing them into position, he fell dead with a bullet through his brain. The Confederate defense collapsed almost immediately.

Fleeing through Piedmont and New Hope, Jones's little army lost all order. Imboden's and Vaughn's cavalry fought a stiff rearguard action just north of New Hope that enabled most of the infantry to escape. Gradually, the Federals abandoned their pursuit.

Besides the death of Jones, the Confederates suffered some 1,600 casualties, most of them prisoners. They also suffered the loss of much of the Shenandoah Valley, which now lay open to Hunter and his army, which had lost about 875 of its number.

The Piedmont battlefield remains one of the most pristine and beautiful sites in the Shenandoah Valley. Most of the residents appear determined to continue their agricultural pursuits and retain the rural character of the area. ■

LYNCHBURG

Following his stunning victory over Brig. Gen. William E. "Grumble" Jones at Piedmont on June 5, 1864, Maj. Gen. David Hunter turned his army toward Lynchburg. His primary objective was the junction of three railroads, the Orange & Alexandria, the South Side, and the Virginia & Tennessee. Once he captured the town, Hunter planned to destroy the railroad facilities there as well as those of the James River & Kanawha Canal, then join his army with Maj. Gen. Philip H. Sheridan's cavalry at Charlottesville and meet up with Lt. Gen. Ulysses S. Grant and the Army of the Potomac near Richmond on June 7.

Learning of Hunter's actions, Gen. Robert E. Lee dispatched Maj. Gen. John C. Breckinridge's division to delay him. Lee detached an entire corps of his army and send it to the Valley, as well, despite being locked in a desperate struggle with Lt. Gen. Ulysses S. Grant. Although he had just dealt Grant a severe blow at Cold

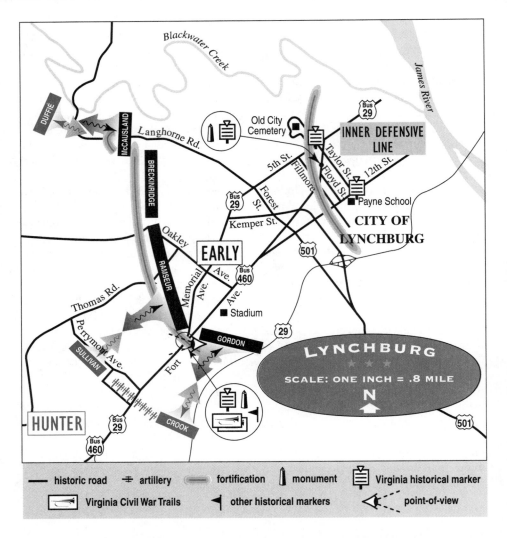

Map Legend:
— historic road   ⚓ artillery   ▬ fortification   🏛 monument   📋 Virginia historical marker   📋 Virginia Civil War Trails   ◀ other historical markers   ◀--- point-of-view

Harbor, Lee had seen the Army of Northern Virginia bled almost dry over the past six weeks, from the Wilderness through Spotsylvania Court House and the North Anna River to Cold Harbor. But the Valley and the railroad had to be defended, and some of the pressure had to be lifted from Lee's army. Lee detailed the assignment to Lt. Gen. Jubal A. Early: Defeat Hunter and threaten Washington.

Early and his corps, which would total 14,000 men counting Breckinridge's 5,000-man division, departed Cold Harbor

on the night of June 12–13 and headed for Lynchburg. Breckinridge arrived in Lynchburg two days later to organize the town's defense. He also ordered his two cavalry brigades under Brig. Gen. John D. Imboden and Brig. Gen. John McCausland to reconnoiter to the west and impede Hunter's advance.

On Thursday, June 16, as Early's corps marched into Charlottesville, the Confederate cavalry encountered the head of Hunter's army at New London, about eleven miles southwest of Lynchburg.

DIRECTIONS: U.S. Rte. 460 Exit (U.S. 501 North, Buena Vista); n. on U.S. Rte. 501 about 1.3 miles to U.S. Rte. 29 Bus. North (Wards Rd.); n. (right) on U.S. Rte. 29 Bus. North 1.6 miles to Fort Early on left (state historical marker Q-6-1, Fort Early, and Jubal A. Early monument on right in median; Virginia Civil War Trails markers, map of battle, and audio presentation in fort on left); bear left on U.S. Rte. 29 Bus. North (Memorial Ave.) and park in median to tour fort; continue n. on U.S. Rte. 29 Bus. North 2 miles to Taylor St. (just past state historical marker Q-6-9, Inner Defences); w. (left) on Taylor St. 1 block to Old City Cemetery, Pest House Medical Museum, Confederate section, Jubal A. Early grave (interpretive plaques, maps, etc., throughout cemetery); from cemetery exit, return left to Taylor St.; e. (right) on Taylor St. .5 mile to 12th St.; s. (right) on 12th St. 2 blocks to Robert S. Payne Elementary School and state historical marker Q-6-3, Inner Defenses, 1864, on left at Floyd St.; continue on 12th St. 4 blocks to Kemper St.; w. (right) on Kemper St. .1 mile (1 long block) to Fort Ave.; w. (right) on Fort Ave. .3 mile to 9th St. and triangular park on right with state historical marker Q-6-8, Inner Defenses, and John Warwick Daniel statue at Floyd St.; e. (right) on Floyd St. 3 blocks to 12th St.; s. (right) on 12th St. 4 blocks to Kemper St.; e. (left) on Kemper St. .3 mile to U.S. Rte. 29 North and South.

Hunter had divided his force at Liberty (now the city of Bedford); while Col. Alfred N. A. Duffié led his cavalry division northeast toward Lynchburg on the Forest Road (present-day U.S. Rte. 221), Brig. Gen. George Crook's infantry division marched just south along the Virginia & Tennessee Railroad, tearing it up as they went. Brig. Gen. William W. Averell led his cavalry division southeast on the Lynchburg & Salem Turnpike (U.S. Rte. 460) to strike Lynchburg from the south, followed by the main force: Brig. Gen. Jeremiah C. Sullivan's infantry division, the artillery, and the supply wagons. Mc-Causland and Imboden briefly blocked Averell's progress at New London, then fell back toward Lynchburg and pitched camp for the night.

Early proceeded to Lynchburg from Charlottesville by train the next morning.

By 7:30 A.M. on Friday, June 17, Maj. Gen. Stephen D. Ramseur's division and part of Maj. Gen. John B. Gordon's division were boarding the only trains available; the remainder of Gordon's division marched with Maj. Gen. Robert E. Rodes's division down the track to board the empty trains on their return after disembarking the others in Lynchburg.

West of Lynchburg, meanwhile, Averell resumed his march on the turnpike and at around 10 A.M. encountered McCausland about eight miles short of the town. McCausland's stiff defense bought time for Early and Lynchburg. By 1 P.M. the locomotive from Charlottesville chugged into Lynchburg with the first elements of Early's corps and Early himself. The troops quickly began strengthening the defensive works.

Hunter closed in on the town by midafternoon. Imboden blocked Averell's advance on the turnpike at the Quaker Church some four miles southwest of Lynchburg, while McCausland delayed Duffié's progress about five miles west of the city near Clay's Mill. In the evening, the Federal infantry bivouacked near Hunter's headquarters at Sandusky, the home of George C. Hutter. Hunter reconnoitered the Confederate defenses and found them stronger than he expected.

Early made his headquarters in the city at the home of his brother William H. Early. He oversaw the hasty construction of an outer line of defense, the second of two that arced around Lynchburg. The first extended just west and south of town along the edge of College Hill. The outer line, which paralleled the first about a mile and a half distant, began at a redoubt on the Forest Road and continued south and then east across the turnpike at another redoubt called Fort Early.

Early deployed his corps and Breckinridge's infantry in the outer works, with

Fort Early stood at the center of Early's thrusts against Crook and Sullivan. VIRGINIA DEPARTMENT OF HISTORIC RESOURCES, JOHN S. SALMON

McCausland anchoring the right flank at the Forest Road redoubt. Breckinridge's division came next. Ramseur's division and Brig. Gen. William G. Lewis held the left center, with Lewis's left flank on the turnpike at Fort Early. Two brigades of Gordon's division occupied the Confederate left flank to the east of the turnpike.

Early knew that Hunter's force outnumbered his own, so during the night he directed an empty railroad train to leave the city and then return from the north while a band played and a crowd cheered. The ruse, repeated more than once, worked. Hunter became convinced that Early was being reinforced and by morning would outnumber the Federals. In fact, Rodes's division and the rest of Gordon's were still on their way to Lynchburg from Charlottesville.

Beginning on the morning of Saturday, June 18, Hunter began tentative probes of Early's line with his infantry. Federal pickets advanced to the turnpike tollgate half a mile south of Fort Early, while artillery bombarded Early's fortifications. The Confederate gunners counterfired and effectively neutralized the Federal batteries. At the same time Crook marched a brigade against Early's left flank but soon deemed an assault impracticable. At about

1 P.M., while Crook was still returning to his former position, Early attacked the Union center opposite Fort Early. Crook rushed to help keep the Federal line from collapsing, then forced the Confederates back into their fortifications. A Union counterattack failed. The Federals tried once more at about 3 P.M. and momentarily drove some of the Confederates from their lines. But they could not sustain their success, and soon the infantry combat on the turnpike ended.

On the Forest Road, meanwhile, Duffié and McCausland similarly engaged each other all day to little effect. When Duffié advanced at about 9 A.M. to the Confederate redoubt, McCausland withdrew to the fortification. Pursuing, Duffié was slowed by Blackwater Creek as well as effective Confederate artillery fire. When Duffié's men charged the Forest Road bridge over the creek, McCausland's troopers drove them back. At about 5 P.M. Duffié's skirmishers were forced across Blackwater Creek. Efforts to envelop the Federal left and right flanks failed, and Duffié held his position; the Confederates withdrew to their earthworks. At the same time, the remainder of Early's corps had arrived.

That night Hunter decided that Lynchburg was too strongly defended to capture and made plans to retire to the Valley. At first unsure whether Hunter's army was retreating or maneuvering to attack another part of his works, Early concluded that the Federals were indeed retreating and at about 4 A.M. on June 19 ordered a pursuit. Lynchburg remained safely in Confederate hands.

The Federals and Confederates suffered some 900 casualties, most of them wounded. Although the battle of Lynchburg amounted to little more than several disjointed skirmishes, it defeated Grant's plan to cripple the Confederate lines of communication and supply with the

Shenandoah Valley. Hunter's retreat also opened the Valley for virtually unimpeded use by the Confederates.

The Lynchburg battlefield has been almost totally obliterated by the growth of the city. Fort Early still stands, however, as does the Quaker Church, Sandusky, and a portion of the Forest Road redoubt. And the visitor can still view the battleground from various hilltop vantage points around the city; the scene, however, is one of houses and shopping malls instead of farmlands and woodlots. ∎

HANGING ROCK

Following his defeat at Lynchburg on June 18, 1864, Maj. Gen. David Hunter marched his army southwest on the Lynchburg & Salem Turnpike (present-day U.S. Rte. 460) during the night of June 18–19. Lt. Gen. Jubal A. Early's reinforced corps got under way shortly after dawn in pursuit, with Brig. Gen. John McCausland's cavalry in the lead.

Uncertain which route Hunter would take, Early divided his corps and sent elements down separate roads. McCausland reportedly got lost; Maj. Gen. Stephen D. Ramseur's infantry division caught up with the rear guard of Hunter's army at Liberty (today's Bedford) and fought a brisk action in the streets. The pursuit continued the next day to the edge of the Blue Ridge, where Early concluded late in the afternoon that Hunter intended to head to Salem and beyond.

Early sent a courier to Maj. Gen. Robert E. Rodes with orders to lead the march to Salem on Tuesday, June 21, but the messenger did not deliver the note soon enough for Rodes to get his division on the road until after sunup. This almost enabled Hunter to make good his escape.

Hunter's army paused for two hours in Salem early in the morning to rest and allow Col. Alfred N. A. Duffié to reconnoiter the Salem & New Castle Turnpike (Rte. 311). When Duffié reported that the way was clear, the baggage train and

View east in direction of McCausland's attack on Hunter's rear, with Gen. George M. Jones statue. VIRGINIA DEPARTMENT OF HISTORIC RESOURCES, JOHN S. SALMON

artillery were ordered up the road with the infantry to follow. What Duffié did not know was that although the Confederate infantry divisions were marching behind Hunter on the Lynchburg & Salem Turnpike, McCausland had led his cavalry on a road that intersected the Salem & New Castle Turnpike northeast of Salem at a natural feature called Hanging Rock. When the Federal wagons and guns rolled

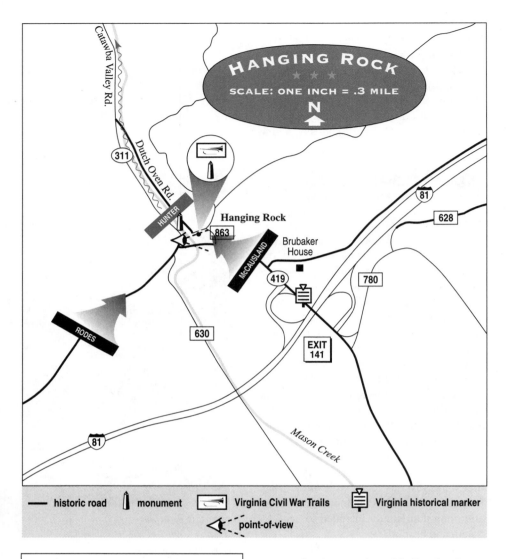

SCALE: ONE INCH = .3 MILE

— historic road   🪦 monument   Virginia Civil War Trails   Virginia historical marker

point-of-view

DIRECTIONS: I-81 Exit 141 (State Rte. 419 to State Rte. 311 North, New Castle); n. on State Rte. 419 about .3 mile to Rte. 863; e. (right) on Rte. 863 .1 mile to Hanging Rock Battlefield Trail, North Trail Head Parking Area and Virginia Civil War Trails marker, George Morgan Jones monument, and other historical markers; continue n. on Rte. 863 (Dutch Oven Rd.) .5 mile to State Rte. 311 (Catawba Valley Rd.); s. (left) on State Rte. 311 .6 mile to State Rte. 419 and United Daughters of the Confederacy monument on left; e. (left) on State Rte. 419 .3 mile to I-81.

up to the intersection, McCausland was waiting for them.

The Confederates captured perhaps a hundred prisoners, several cannons, and many wagons, and they burned the stores and wagons that they could not carry off. The narrow valley and the surrounding high hills prevented the Confederate infantry from assisting the cavalry so the action remained a skirmish rather than a general engagement, especially when the Federal infantry approached the intersection on its march from Salem. McCausland withdrew with his prisoners, guns, and wagons, and Hunter continued his flight into West Virginia.

The engagement at Hanging Rock cost the Federals about a hundred prisoners, while the Confederates suffered few if any casualties. However, with the Union army absent from the Shenandoah Valley, Early had free rein to threaten Washington.

The Hanging Rock battlefield has lost much of its ambience because of the construction of Interstate 81 nearby, the widening of Rte. 311, and commercial and industrial development in the area. The road network and natural features remain, however, and a United Daughters of the Confederacy monument stands near Rte. 311 along Hunter's route of retreat after the fight. The principal threats to the battlefield include additional development and the continuing widening of what is today a major commuter route into and out of the Roanoke metropolitan area. ▨

COOL SPRING

Lt. Gen. Jubal A. Early's "attack" on Washington on July 11–12, 1864, gained the desired results: near-hysteria in the capital and the close attention of the Union army. Early withdrew to the safety of the Shenandoah Valley with Maj. Gen. Horatio G. Wright in pursuit. About three miles beyond Snicker's Gap in the Blue Ridge, Wright caught up with Early.

The Confederates had crossed the Shenandoah River at Castleman's Ferry on the Berryville Turnpike (present-day Rte. 7). On the afternoon of Sunday, July 17, the vanguard of the Union army, the cavalry division commanded by Col. Alfred N. A. Duffié, arrived at nearby Snicker's Ford and attempted a crossing. Across the river, however, two Confederate infantry regiments and two artillery pieces foiled Duffié, who explored upstream for another crossing place. He was again repulsed at Shepherd's Ford, about two miles upriver.

Early in the morning of Monday, July 18, Col. James A. Mulligan led his infantry brigade in another unsuccessful assault on Snicker's Ford. Col. Joseph Thoburn's division of Brig. Gen. George Crook's corps soon arrived nearby. Crook and Wright directed Thoburn's division to cross about a mile downstream at Parker's Ford. They assumed that Early was well on his way to Winchester and had merely left a strong picket guard at the Shenandoah River to slow Wright's progress.

In reality, most of Early's army was just across the river at a farm called Cool Spring, where rolling fields and woodlands kept the men out of sight. The same hills concealed Thoburn's crossing at about 3 P.M. from the Confederates, surprising them.

Thoburn's men captured several Confederate pickets, and Thoburn learned from them that Early's army was nearby, not in Winchester. He signaled the information to Wright, who had Thoburn hold

Shenandoah River, with U.S. positions on east (right) bank prior to crossing. VIRGINIA DEPARTMENT OF HISTORIC RESOURCES, JOHN S. SALMON

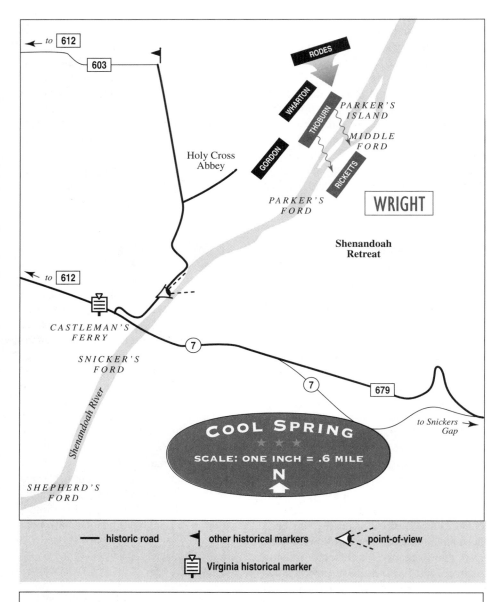

to 612
603
to 612

RODES

WHARTON

THOBURN

GORDON

PARKER'S
ISLAND

MIDDLE
FORD

RICKETTS

Holy Cross
Abbey

PARKER'S
FORD

WRIGHT

Shenandoah
Retreat

CASTLEMAN'S
FERRY

7

SNICKER'S
FORD

7

679

to Snickers
Gap

COOL SPRING
★ ★ ★
SCALE: ONE INCH = .6 MILE
N

Shenandoah River

SHEPHERD'S
FORD

— historic road   ◀ other historical markers   ◀--- point-of-view

Virginia historical marker

DIRECTIONS: I-81 Exit 315 (State Rte. 7, Berryville), e. on State Rte. 7 about 12.8 miles (by Berryville bypass) to Rte. 603 (Castleman Rd.) and state historical marker T-8, Castleman's Ferry Fight, on s. side of State Rte. 7; continue .4 mile across Shenandoah River and turn around; w. on State Rte. 7 .4 mile to Rte. 603; n. (right) on Rte. 603 (note Shenandoah River and Union position on e. bank) 1.2 miles to Holy Cross Abbey entrance; continue w. (left) on Rte. 603 1 mile to United Daughters of the Confederacy marker at sharp left turn; continue w. on Rte. 603 1.2 miles to Rte. 612 (Shepherd's Mill Rd.); s. (left) on Rte. 612 1.5 miles to State Rte. 7; w. (right) on State Rte. 7 to I-81.

NOTE: Almost all of Cool Spring battlefield is located on monastery property and is not open to the public. The monastery maintains a small collection of artifacts found on the battlefield in the course of farming operations. The collection may be viewed by appointment only; call the gift shop at 540-955-1425.

fast until supported by Brig. Gen. James B. Ricketts's division of VI Corps. Thoburn occupied a height in a wheat field and sent forward a picket line.

Meanwhile, Confederate Maj. Gen. John B. Gordon's division marched east to occupy high ground overlooking Thoburn's position. Simultaneously, Brig. Gen. Gabriel C. Wharton's division took its post to Gordon's left, driving back the Federal pickets and confronting the bulk of Thoburn's force. Maj. Gen. Robert E. Rodes's division soon arrived and joined the Confederate line on Wharton's left. Thoburn was now enclosed to his front and right, with the river and its steep bluffs at his back.

Rodes mounted a concerted attack at about 6 P.M. that crushed Thoburn's right flank. Ricketts arrived on the east bank of the river, and after conferring with Crook, he held back his division, citing the strength of the Confederate attack. Wright agreed that the best course was for Thoburn to extricate himself. Thoburn, meanwhile, withstood three Confederate charges with the help of Federal artillery on the eastern bluffs of the river. The fighting finally died down about dark, and Thoburn and his men crossed the Shenandoah to safety.

The battle at Cool Spring cost the Federals 422 casualties and the Confederates 397. It slowed the cautious Wright even further and allowed Early to withdraw to Winchester unhindered.

Most of the Cool Spring battlefield is in very good condition, thanks in no small part to the good stewardship of Holy Cross Abbey, which owns the core battle area. Road widening, a new bridge, and residential construction have taken their toll, but the heart of the battlefield is largely intact. ▪

RUTHERFORD'S FARM

After the combat at Cool Spring on July 17–18, 1864, Lt. Gen. Jubal A. Early continued to withdraw his army west to Winchester, with Maj. Gen. Horatio G. Wright in pursuit at a respectful distance. When Early learned that a second Union force, a detachment composed of cavalry and infantry led by Brig. Gen. William W. Averell, was marching south from Martinsburg, West Virginia, on the Martinsburg & Winchester Turnpike, he directed his army south to Strasburg and on July 19 ordered Maj. Gen. Stephen D. Ramseur's infantry division and Brig. Gen. John C. Vaughn's mounted infantry brigade north of Winchester to block the Federal line of advance.

Ramseur and his division waited two miles north of Winchester while Vaughn

Lewis's position and site of Averell's flanking movement, north of Valley Turnpike. VIRGINIA DEPARTMENT OF HISTORIC RESOURCES, JOHN S. SALMON

led his cavalry northeast on the Martinsburg & Winchester Turnpike to locate Averell. At about noon Vaughn requested an artillery battery from Ramseur, who ordered the guns forward and told Vaughn to push Averell north to Bunker Hill, some

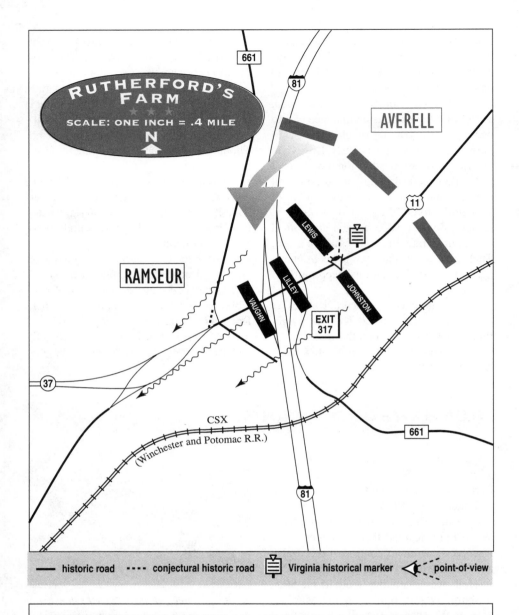

RUTHERFORD'S
FARM
★ ★ ★
SCALE: ONE INCH = .4 MILE
N

AVERELL

RAMSEUR

LEWIS

LILLEY

VAUGHN

JOHNSTON

EXIT
317

CSX
(Winchester and Potomac R.R.)

661

81

11

37

661

81

—— historic road   ···· conjectural historic road   Virginia historical marker   point-of-view

DIRECTIONS: I-81 Exit 317 (U.S. Rte. 11 North); right on U.S. Rte. 11 North (past John Rutherford farmhouse site about .4 mile on left) about .3 mile to state historical marker on right: A-2, Action of Rutherford's Farm.

twelve miles from Winchester. Near 4 P.M. Ramseur heard small-arms fire up the turnpike and immediately marched his men there. After a mile he encountered Vaughn, who reported that Averell was advancing with a regiment each of infantry and cavalry as well as a four-gun battery. Convinced that his own force outnumbered Averell's, Ramseur decided to entice the Federals into combat.

Ramseur's division straddled the turnpike on a ridge just southeast of John Rutherford's farmhouse. He posted Lewis's brigade to the left of the road and Brig. Gen. Robert D. Johnston's to the right, with one brigade held in reserve, and placed Vaughn's cavalry in the rear. Ramseur threw a skirmish line fifty yards forward of his position to lure the Federals.

Ramseur's plan quickly came unraveled as not one but three infantry regiments marched rapidly against the Confederate right flank. Ramseur reoriented his right flank to meet the threat but discovered that his left flank was under attack, as well. He ordered the reserve to Lewis's aid, but Lewis's part of the line crumpled under the Federal onslaught. Despite Ramseur's best efforts to rally his troops, the men fled in near-panic. Almost 300 of them were captured in the rout as well as four pieces of artillery.

Part of the battlefield has been lost to an Interstate 81 interchange. A portain remains intact but is threatened by development encroaching from Winchester. ▨

SECOND BATTLE OF KERNSTOWN

The retreat of Lt. Gen. Jubal A. Early's Army of the Valley to Fisher's Hill near Strasburg convinced Maj. Gen. Horatio G. Wright that Early no longer posed a threat to Washington. Wright marched most of his command toward the capital preparatory to returning to the Petersburg front, while Brig. Gen. George Crook remained at Winchester with his three-infantry-division VIII Corps and a cavalry division.

Early immediately skirmished with Crook's pickets. Confederate cavalry drove out the Federal troopers occupying New-town (present-day Stephens City) on the afternoon of July 23, 1864, then were themselves pushed back. That evening, Crook bivouacked his infantry behind Abrams Creek at Winchester, while a cavalry brigade served as pickets at Kernstown.

At dawn on Sunday, July 24, Early's army advanced on Kernstown by the Valley Turnpike (U.S. Rte. 11) under the immediate command of Maj. Gen. John C. Breckinridge. At Bartonville, just north of Newtown, Early divided his force to strike the Union flanks and rear. Columns of cavalry circled east and west, Ramseur's

Pritchard's Hill from Opequon Church and cemetery. VIRGINIA DEPARTMENT OF HISTORIC RESOURCES, JOHN S. SALMON

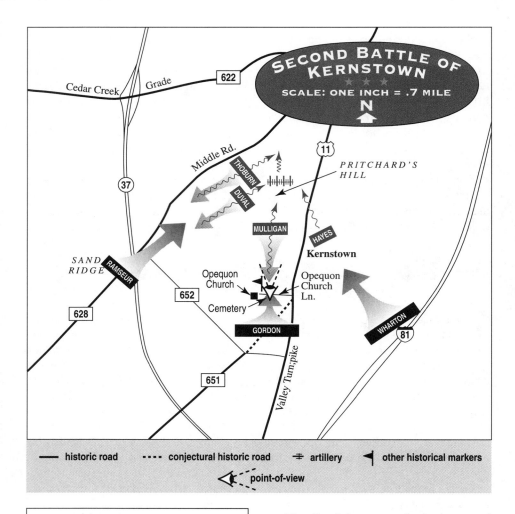

SECOND BATTLE OF KERNSTOWN
★ ★ ★
SCALE: ONE INCH = .7 MILE
N

Cedar Creek Grade — 622

Middle Rd.

37

THOBURN

DUVAL

11

PRITCHARD'S HILL

MULLIGAN

HAYES

Kernstown

SAND RIDGE — RAMSEUR

Opequon Church

Opequon Church Ln.

652

Cemetery

628

GORDON

WHARTON

81

Valley Turnpike

651

—— historic road   ···· conjectural historic road   ⚓ artillery   ◀ other historical markers

◀ point-of-view

DIRECTIONS: I-81 Exit 310 (State Rte. 37 West) .2 mile to U.S. Rte. 11; n. (right) on U.S. Rte. 11 about .7 mile to Rte. 652 (Apple Valley Rd.); w. (left) on Rte. 652 1.3 miles to Rte. 628 (Middle Rd.); n. (right) on Rte. 628 1.9 miles to U.S. Rte. 11; s. (right) on U.S. Rte. 11 1.4 miles to Opequon Church Lane; w. (left) on Opequon Church Lane .2 mile to church, cemetery, and Winchester–Frederick County Historical Society interpretive marker; return to U.S. Rte. 11; s. (right) on U.S. Rte. 11 1.5 miles to State Rte. 37; e. (left) on State Rte. 37 .2 mile to I-81.

infantry went west to the Middle Road (Rte. 628) and against the Union right flank, and the remaining three infantry divisions headed north on the turnpike toward Kernstown and Winchester.

The Confederate cavalry encountered the main Federal position at Kernstown at about 10 A.M., and the three divisions marching down the turnpike reached the village two hours later. Brig. Gen. Gabriel C. Wharton's division deployed east of the highway, Maj. Gen. John B. Gordon's to the west, and Maj. Gen. Robert E. Rodes's division followed a ravine that led east from the turnpike toward the Union left flank. Ramseur's headed farther west across the Middle Road.

Crook deployed two of his own divisions to meet the threat in front of him. Col. James A. Mulligan took the high ground on Pritchard's Hill, facing Gordon, while Col. Isaac H. Duval posted each of his two brigades on Mulligan's flanks. The brigade commanded by Col. Rutherford B. Hayes, the future U.S. president, occupied ground on Mulligan's left flank, and Col. Joseph Thoburn's division took the reserve position behind Mulligan.

Mulligan advanced his skirmish line down Pritchard's Hill to Opequon Presbyterian Church and cemetery, but Gordon's men drove it back. Mulligan counterattacked in force, but soon Gordon's division repulsed him and occupied the churchyard.

During this series of engagements, Duval's brigade on Mulligan's right flank moved even farther west and Thoburn's division marched down Pritchard's Hill to fill the resulting gap. Then, Ramseur arrived and attacked Thoburn; Gordon shifted one of his brigades westward to join the assault. Thoburn gradually fell back to his original position northwest of Pritchard's Hill.

Meanwhile, Wharton's division closed in on Mulligan's left flank. Wharton attacked at about 3 P.M. in conjunction with Ramseur's and Gordon's assaults, dislodging Hayes's brigade and turning Mulligan's flank. Hayes retreated to stone walls atop Pritchard's Hill and held his position long enough for Capt. Henry A. Du Pont to limber up and withdraw his artillery batteries. The Union line collapsed, and Mulligan fell mortally wounded. The Federals streamed north through Winchester, with Early's cavalry and Rodes's division in pursuit on the Front Royal Road (U.S. Rte. 340/522) all the way to Stephenson's Depot. Because the cavalry did not advance as fast as Early hoped, most of Crook's force escaped. Still, the Federals suffered some 1,200 casualties, hundreds of them prisoners, while the Confederate losses amounted to about 600.

The Kernstown battlefield has mostly vanished beneath commercial and industrial development, with the exception of Pritchard's Hill. Opequon Presbyterian Church burned in 1873; a new building was constructed in 1896. The old cemetery and its headstones are still intact, however, and the integrity of the ground between the church and Pritchard's Hill is excellent. ▨

GUARD HILL

When Maj. Gen. Philip H. Sheridan assumed command of the 43,000-man Army of the Shenandoah on August 7, 1864, he planned to push Lt. Gen. Jubal A. Early's Army of the Valley from its camp at Bunker Hill, West Virginia, drive it south, and lay waste to the Breadbasket of the Confederacy. By August 13 the Federals were bivouacked at Cedar Creek and the Confederates some four miles farther south at Fisher's Hill. When Sheridan learned that reinforcements were on their way to Early from the Richmond front north of the James River, however, he withdrew temporarily through Winchester to Halltown, using the Valley Turnpike (present-day U.S. Rte. 11).

Lt. Gen. Richard H. Anderson commanded the entire group of Confederate reinforcements, which included an infantry division, a cavalry division, and an artillery battalion. On August 14 Anderson's force reached Front Royal, where the north and south forks of the Shenandoah River converge to form the main river just south of a steep ridge called Guard Hill. The principal road between Front Royal and Winchester, the Front Royal Road (U.S. Rte. 340/522), passed through a gap in Guard Hill. Anderson's presence in

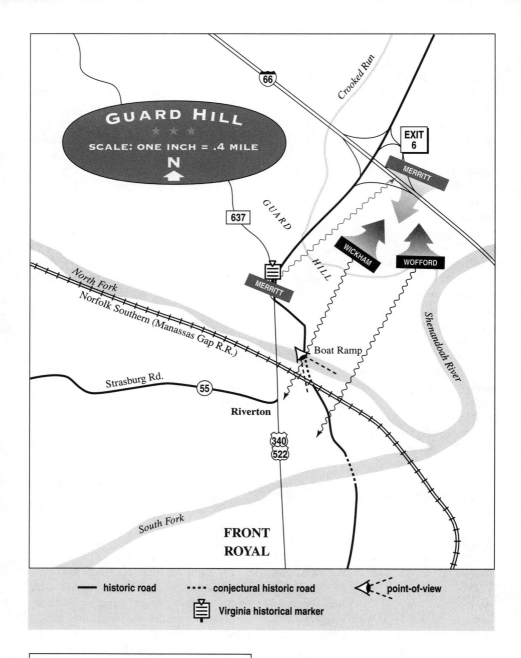

GUARD HILL
★ ★ ★
SCALE: ONE INCH = .4 MILE
N

66

Crooked Run

EXIT 6

MERRITT

637

G U A R D

MERRITT

H I L L

WICKHAM

WOFFORD

North Fork

Norfolk Southern (Manassas Gap R.R.)

Boat Ramp

Shenandoah River

Strasburg Rd.

55

Riverton

340 522

South Fork

FRONT ROYAL

— historic road   ···· conjectural historic road   ◁···· point-of-view

Virginia historical marker

DIRECTIONS: I-66 Exit 6 (U.S. Rte. 340/522, Front Royal), s. on U.S. Rte. 340/522 about .6 mile to Rte. 637 (Guard Hill Rd.); w. (right) on Rte. 637 to state historical marker J-11, Guard Hill Engagement, on right; return to U.S. Rte. 340/522 and cross on Rte. 637 .2 mile to boat ramp area; s. (right) into parking lot and view of Shenandoah River; return to I-66.

Front Royal threatened the main Federal route of retreat on the Valley Turnpike a few miles west; the Strasburg Road (Rte. 55) linked it with the Front Royal Road.

Brig. Gen. Wesley Merritt's cavalry division, located north of the forks, hovered near the intersection of the Front Royal and Strasburg Roads. Merritt began moving south toward Front Royal on Tuesday, August 16. Anderson ordered Brig. Gen. William T. Wofford's infantry brigade and Brig. Gen. Williams C. Wickham's cavalry brigade to move across the rivers to Guard Hill to watch the roads and river fords.

In midafternoon Wickham advanced against Merritt, but two regiments of Brig. Gen. Thomas C. Devin's brigade counterattacked, and the Confederates retreated across the rivers. Brig. Gen. George A. Custer led another Federal attack against Wofford's infantry; again the Confederates retreated, and many drowned or were captured as they crossed the two forks. Having confirmed the presence of Confederate infantry and cavalry in Front Royal, Merritt followed the main Federal army toward Halltown, pressed by the Confederates as far as Cedarville. The two sides suffered a total of some 550 casualties in the Guard Hill engagement.

Site of Wickham's and Wofford's retreat, Shenandoah River, looking east. VIRGINIA DEPARTMENT OF HISTORIC RESOURCES, JOHN S. SALMON

Although Front Royal has expanded north of its Civil War–era boundaries to the Shenandoah River and beyond, and roads have been widened and paved, the road networks in the vicinity of Guard Hill follow much the same routes. Some residential development has occurred on and around Guard Hill itself, and the gap in the hill has been widened along with U.S. Rte. 340/522. The general outlines of the battlefield remain intact, however. ▪

BERRYVILLE

For the remainder of August 1864, the Federal and Confederate armies skirmished with each other in the vicinity of Halltown, West Virginia. By the end of the month, however, Maj. Gen. Philip H. Sheridan's Army of the Shenandoah was on the march into Virginia.

On Saturday, September 3, the Federal column reached Berryville, the Clarke County seat. The countryside around the town was largely open farmland set amid gently rolling terrain containing a series of low ridges. Near the end of the day, Sheridan's army assumed defensive positions on such a ridge just north of Berryville. The army faced west, where about a

View south to U.S. artillery position (left) on VIII and XIX Corps line. VIRGINIA DEPARTMENT OF HISTORIC RESOURCES, JOHN S. SALMON

mile away part of Early's army occupied a similar ridge.

BERRYVILLE
★ ★ ★
SCALE: ONE INCH = .9 MILE
N

RODES

639

639

653

WHARTON

Long Marsh Run

632

654

641

XIX Corps

654

653

611

340

EARLY

RAMSEUR

SHERIDAN

632

7

VII Corps

KERSHAW

BYP 7

Cooley School

BUS 7

VII Corps

636

Berryville

—— historic road   ···· conjectural historic road   ⚌ artillery   fortification

Virginia historical marker   ◁ point-of-view

The Federal position extended south from the intersection of present-day Rtes. 639 and 611 along Rte. 611 and U.S. Rte. 340 almost to Berryville. Part of the VIII Corps occupied a ridge just northwest of the town on the Berryville Turnpike (U.S. Rte. 7).

Toward evening, as the Federal army settled into its bivouac, fighting suddenly erupted on the Berryville Turnpike as the Confederate divisions commanded by Maj. Gen. Stephen D. Ramseur and Maj. Gen. Joseph B. Kershaw launched a surprise attack against the Union left flank. The Confederates were unable to penetrate far, and Federal counterattacks

DIRECTIONS: I-81 Exit 315 (State Rte. 7, Berryville), e. on State Rte. 7 (Berryville Turnpike) about 8.7 miles to U.S. Rte. 340 (stay on State Rte. 7 Bypass); n. (left) on U.S. Rte. 340 along Union VIII Corps line 2 miles to Rte. 641 (Lewisville Rd.); n. (left) on Rte. 641 (note Mansfield, the Mann Page house, on left after about .5 mile and Asbury house on right .2 mile later) 1.4 miles to Rte. 639 (Allen Rd.); w. (left) on Rte. 639 .7 mile to Rte. 611 (Summit Point Rd.); s. (left) on Rte. 611 along XIX Corps line .6 mile to Long Marsh Run bridge; cross bridge and continue s. (noting site of J. L. Van Meter house and Union artillery position on left) 1.1 miles to Rte. 654 (Stringtown Rd.) and note Union artillery position on left; w. (right) on Rte. 654 .7 mile, between Union and Confederate picket lines along ridges on both sides of road, to sharp s. (left) bend (here was posted Rodes's division to the n. and Wharton's to the s.); continue s. (left) on Rte. 654 (behind Wharton's line) .6 mile to sharp w. (right) bend (water tower to s.e. marks position of Kershaw's and Ramseur's divisions); w. (right) on Rte. 654 .3 mile to Rte. 653 (Kimble Rd.); left on Rte. 653 1.4 miles to State Rte. 7 Bypass; e. (left) on State Rte. 7 Bypass 1 mile to State Rte. 7 Bus. (first right); right on State Rte. 7 Bus. .7 mile to state historical marker J-30, Battle of Berryville, at Cooly School (Kershaw's and Ramseur's lines); continue e. .4 mile to bend in road to right (position of Union VIII Corps line); continue .6 mile to U.S. Rte. 340; left on U.S. Rte. 340 .8 mile to State Rte. 7 Bypass.

and encroaching darkness soon ended the combat.

Early brought the remainder of his army to the field during the night. The next morning, however, revealed that the Federals had been digging, not sleeping. Convinced that the fieldworks were too formidable, Early gave orders to withdraw to the west side of Opequon Creek near Winchester. The brief engagement at Berryville resulted in some 500 casualties for both sides.

The scene of the fighting west of Berryville has been altered by commercial and residential development, and a school occupies part of the site on the south side of Rte. 7. If any earthworks survive, they are not visible from public roads. To the north of town, the roads, fields, and wood-lots appear much as they did at the time of the confrontation. Although little or no skirmishing occurred in this area and no fieldworks are extant, the positions of the combatants are still apparent when the terrain is compared with historic maps. ■

THIRD BATTLE OF WINCHESTER (OPEQUON)

After more than a month of stalemate, in September 1864 Maj. Gen. Philip H. Sheridan took the offensive against Lt. Gen. Jubal A. Early's Army of the Valley after Lt. Gen. Richard H. Anderson's command left the Shenandoah Valley to return to the Army of Northern Virginia at Petersburg. The move left Early with about 12,500 men to face Sheridan's 40,000.

Early had withdrawn to Winchester from West Virginia, dispersing his infantry over a large area. Maj. Gen. Stephen D. Ramseur's division guarded the eastern approaches to Winchester by way of the Berryville Turnpike (present-day Rte. 7), which crossed Opequon Creek and led to Winchester through a two-mile-long ravine called the Berryville Canyon. Ramseur posted pickets at the eastern end of the canyon at the stream crossing but held the bulk of his division at the western end.

At daybreak on Monday, September 19, Brig. Gen. James H. Wilson's cavalry division trotted across Opequon Creek at a ford called Spout Spring, followed by Sheridan's infantry. The army immediately entered Berryville Canyon. Had Ramseur posted his men in strength at the canyon's eastern mouth, Sheridan's expedition might have ground to a halt, but since only pickets covered the entrance, Ramseur could not stop the advance. The vanguard

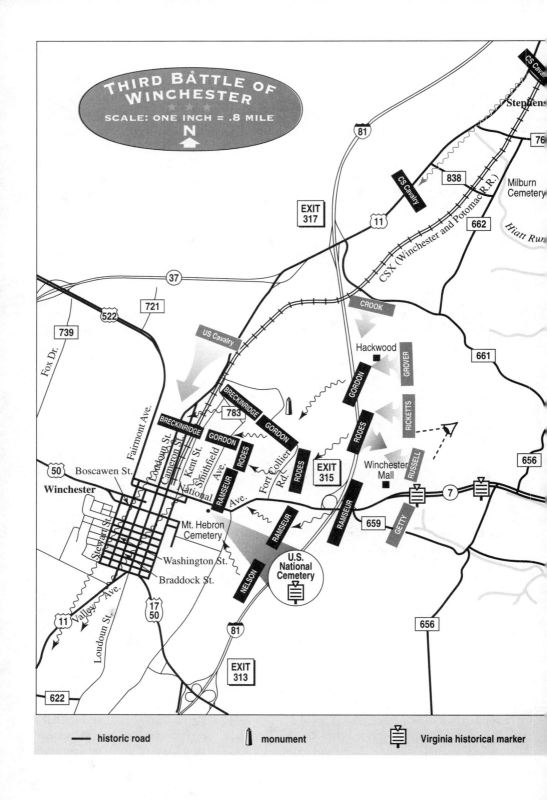

THIRD BÁTTLE OF WINCHESTER
SCALE: ONE INCH = .8 MILE
N

Stephens

81

76

CS Cavalry

838

Milburn Cemetery

EXIT 317

11

CSX (Winchester and Potomac R.R.)

662

Hiatt Run

37

721

522

739

Fox Dr.

US Cavalry

CROOK

Hackwood

GORDON

GROVER

661

BRECKINRIDGE

783

BRECKINRIDGE

GORDON

RODES

RICKETTS

656

Fairmont Ave.

GORDON

RODES

Loudoun St.

Cameron St.

Kent St.

Smithfield Ave.

RAMSEUR

RODES

Fort Collier Rd.

EXIT 315

Winchester Mall

RUSSELL

50

Boscawen St.

National Ave.

Winchester

Stewart St.

Mt. Hebron Cemetery

RAMSEUR

RAMSEUR

659

GETTY

7

Washington St.

U.S. National Cemetery

NELSON

Braddock St.

11

Valley Ave.

17 50

81

Loudoun St.

656

EXIT 313

622

—— historic road   ⌂ monument   Virginia historical marker

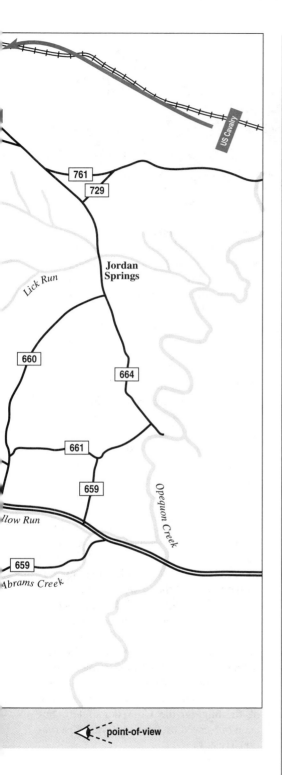

US Cavalry

761

729

Jordan
Springs

Lick Run

660

664

661

659

Opequon Creek

low Run

659

Abrams Creek

◄┅┅ point-of-view

DIRECTIONS: I-81 Exit 315 (State Rte. 7, Berryville), e. on State Rte. 7 (Berryville Turnpike) about .6 mile to state historical marker J-13, Third Battle of Winchester; continue e. .7 mile farther to state historical marker J-3, Third Battle of Winchester; continue e. 1.1 miles farther to Opequon Water Reclamation Facility, noting narrow Berryville Canyon through which Sheridan's army passed marching w.; continue e. .4 mile across Opequon Creek to crossover at Rte. 645; make U turn w. on State Rte. 7 1.7 miles to Rte. 660 (Woods Mill Rd.); n. (right) on Rte. 660 2.1 miles to Rte. 664 (Jordan Springs Rd.); n. (left) on Rte. 664 .8 mile to Rte. 729 (Morrison's Rd.); n.e. (right) on Rte. 729 .4 mile to Rte. 761 (Old Charles Town Rd.); e. (right) on Rte. 761 1.2 miles to Cleridge Farm and Seiver's Ford (US cavalry crossed from e. here and drove CSA cavalry w. from hills to rear; other crossing was at Locke's Ford just n., not accessible); turn around and return to State Rte. 7 by way of Rte. 660; w. (right) on State Rte. 7 .6 mile to Rte. 656 (Morgan Mill Rd.); n. (right) .2 mile to clear area on left for view toward First Woods; continue .45 mile to Wood House and observation point for Crook's advance out of the Berryville Canyon to Redbud Run and w. to First Woods; return to State Rte. 7; w. (right) on State Rte. 7 1.2 miles to Winchester Mall shopping center just w. of I-81 interchange; n. (right) into mall parking lot and drive to n.w. corner for view of ravine used by VI Corps; return to State Rte. 7; w. (right) on State Rte. 7 .8 mile to Ft. Collier Rd.; n. (right) on Ft. Collier Rd. 1 mile to Gen. Russell Hastings monument on right near sharp left turn in road (only monument still on battlefield in original position); continue on Ft. Collier Rd. .25 mile to Brooke Rd.; w. (left) on Brooke Rd. .5 mile to U.S. Rte. 11 (Loudoun St.) and Fort Collier on right; n. (right) on U.S. Rte. 11 and note Virginia Civil War Commission (Circle Tour) interpretive markers and state historical marker A-4, Fort Collier, just w. of intersection on w. side of U.S. Rte. 11 across Fort Collier Rd.; return to Brooke Rd.; e. (left) on Brooke Rd. and immediately turn s. (right) on Rte. 783 (Brick Kiln Rd.; becomes Smithfield Ave.) 1.2 miles to National Ave.; w. (left) on National Ave. 2 blocks to Winchester National Cemetery entrance on right and state historical marker J-4, Third Battle of Winchester; return to National Ave.; e. (right) 2 blocks to Pleasant Valley Rd.; s. (right) on Pleasant Valley Rd. 1 block to Woodstock Lane; w. (right) on Woodstock Lane .4 mile to East Lane; s. (left) on East Lane 1 block to Boscawen St. and Mount Hebron Cemetery entrance on left; left through gate and straight to Stonewall Cemetery; return to Boscawen St. and continue 2 blocks to Old Town Winchester Welcome Center (Kurtz Cultural Center) and Virginia Civil War Trails marker; continue n. on Cameron St. following I-81 signs on U.S. Rte. 11 2.8 miles to I-81 Exit 317 (Stephenson, Rtes. 37/U.S. 522 North/U.S. 50 West), s. on Rte. 661 (Redbud Rd.) .5 mile to railroad tracks at power station, then .2 mile to rise just past stone gates on right to view US attack site near Hackwood; return to I-81.

Sheridan's attack on Winchester, with Berryville Turnpike on left. LIBRARY OF CONGRESS

of Sheridan's force punched its way through to the western end of the canyon.

The Federal infantry, however, soon competed with slow-moving wagons and artillery for space on the same narrow road. It was after 10 A.M. by the time two infantry divisions marched past Sheridan, who was enraged because the delay had given Early time to organize a defense.

Ramseur's division blocked the Berryville Turnpike, while Maj. Gen. Robert E. Rodes's division occupied the Confederate center north of and slightly behind Ramseur. Maj. Gen. John B. Gordon's division held the left flank in a forest. Across a large, grassy field from Gordon, Brig. Gen. William Dwight's and Brig. Gen. Cuvier Grover's divisions held the Federal right flank. Brig. Gen. James B. Rickett's division occupied the middle of the line on open ground to the south and Brig. Gen. George W. Getty's the left, facing west. Brig. Gen. David A. Russell's division was held in reserve to the rear of Ricketts, while Brig. Gen. George Crook's two divisions waited at Spout Spring.

At about 11:40 A.M., Grover, Ricketts, and Getty advanced against the Confederates. On the Union right, Grover's men were hammered by Gordon's determined defense and a series of countercharges. Grover's division collapsed and fled, and when Dwight's advanced in support, it was pinned down in the field by intense Confederate fire. Almost simultaneously, however, the Confederate right gave way as Ramseur was hard pressed by Ricketts and Getty. Then at about 1:30 P.M. Rodes led a devasting counterattack in a gap between the two Union divisions that stalled the Federal thrust. Sheridan ordered Russell's division into the fray against Rodes; both generals died in the subsequent fighting. He also ordered Crook's divisions to strike Gordon's left flank at Hackwood, and the Confederates withdrew to a second line that crossed the site of the present-day U.S. National Cemetery. Sheridan's cavalry thundered down the Valley Turnpike and struck the Confederate left and rear just as the infantry combat reached its climax. The Army of the Valley was routed and fled south to Kernstown and beyond.

Confederate casualties totaled about 3,600 and the Federals lost some 5,000. Sheridan, at great cost, had achieved an enormous victory that made him temporarily the master of the Lower Valley.

The battlefield of Third Winchester—arguably one of the most important actions in the Valley—has virtually disappeared beneath residential and commercial development. Only small portions remain intact. Fortunately, the Hackwood property, one of the more substantial tracts and the scene of fighting on the Confederate left, has been preserved by the Civil War Preservation Trust. ∎

After it was crushed at Third Winchester (Opequon) on September 19, 1864, Lt. Gen. Jubal A. Early's Army of the Valley retreated to Fisher's Hill, an imposing ridge across the Valley Turnpike. Early distributed his 9,500 troops over some five miles. Brig. Gen. Gabriel C. Wharton's division occupied the Confederate right flank, Maj. Gen. John B. Gordon's division held the ground across the Manassas Gap Railroad, Maj. Gen. John Pegram's division came next, and Maj. Gen. Stephen D. Ramseur's division stood on the infantry's left flank on a high hill located south of Tumbling Run. Early stationed Maj. Gen. Lunsford L. Lomax's dismounted cavalry division on his far left flank.

Most of Maj. Gen. Philip H. Sheridan's 30,000-man Army of the Shenandoah neared Hupp's Hill and Strasburg in the afternoon as the Confederates completed their deployment. Brig. Gen. George Crook's corps, however, remained behind in the woods near Belle Grove to conceal it from Confederate observers atop Signal Knob on Massanutten Mountain. Crook and Sheridan had devised a plan for Sheridan to threaten the center and right flank of Early's line while Crook, his infantry, and one of Sheridan's three cavalry divisions struck the Confederate left flank.

Sheridan's remaining corps, the VI commanded by Maj. Gen. Horatio G. Wright and the XIX led by Maj. Gen. William H. Emory, confronted Fisher's Hill. Brig. Gen. James B. Ricketts's division of Wright's corps manned the Union right flank, and Brig. Gen. George W. Getty's and Brig. Gen. Frank Wheaton's the center. Emory's corps occupied the Federal left, with Brig. Gen. William Dwight's division next to Wheaton and Brig. Gen. Cuvier Grover's division on the extreme left by the North Fork of the Shenandoah River.

Sheridan's skirmishers advancing south to Fisher's Hill, presumably in vicinity of Flint Hill.

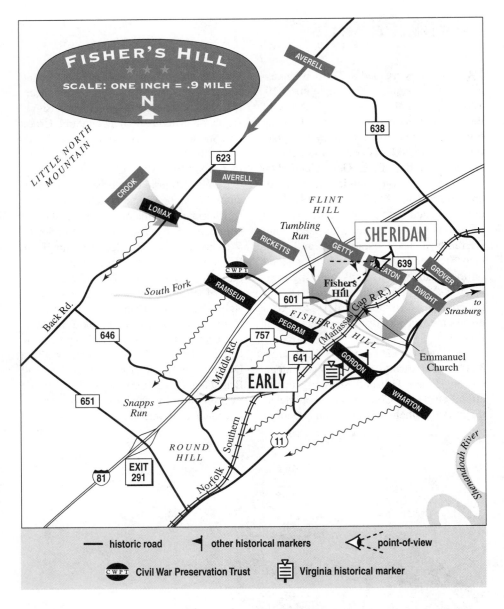

FISHER'S HILL
★ ★ ★
SCALE: ONE INCH = .9 MILE
N

LITTLE NORTH MOUNTAIN

AVERELL

638

623

AVERELL

CROOK

LOMAX

RICKETTS

FLINT HILL

Tumbling Run

GETTY

SHERIDAN

WHEATON

639

GROVER

CWPT

South Fork

RAMSEUR

601

Fishers Hill

Manassas Gap R.R.

DWIGHT

to Strasburg

Back Rd.

FISHER'S HILL

646

Middle Rd.

757

PEGRAM

641

GORDON

Emmanuel Church

651

Snapps Run

EARLY

WHARTON

ROUND HILL

Southern

11

EXIT 291

81

Norfolk

Shenandoah River

— historic road ◄ other historical markers ◄◄◄ point-of-view

CWPT Civil War Preservation Trust ▤ Virginia historical marker

The two sides skirmished throughout the day on Wednesday, September 21. Late in the afternoon, Sheridan directed Wright to press forward and occupy Flint Hill, an eminence just north of Fisher's Hill that Sheridan correctly believed would let him view the Confederates'

main line. It took three attempts, but Ricketts and Getty finally succeeded just before sundown.

That night the Federals realigned their units for the next day's fighting. To the north, Crook's corps crept southward in the darkness and then rested near Hupp's

DIRECTIONS: I-81 Exit 296 (State Rte. 55 South, Tom's Brook and Strasburg), s. on State Rte. 55 about 1.7 miles to U.S. Rte. 11 (Valley Turnpike) 1.2 miles to Rte. 639 (Green Acre Drive); w. (right) on Rte. 639 1 mile to Rte. 757 (Copp Rd.); continue across Rte. 757 .1 mile to clear position from which to observe Flint Hill, just s.w. (here Sheridan ordered capture of Flint Hill); return to Rte. 757; s.w. (right) on Rte. 757 .6 mile to Church Hill Lane; e. (left) on Church Hill Lane to upper parking lot of Emmanuel Evangelical and Reformed Church (from here you can see extent of Confederate position atop Fisher's Hill to s.); return to Rte. 757; s.w. (left) on Rte. 757 .1 mile to Rte. 601 (Battlefield Rd.); w. (right) on Rte. 601 1.1 mile to the Civil War Preservation Trust's Fisher's Hill Battlefield Civil War Site (Ramseur's Hill) on left (self-guided walking tour brochures available at site; tour takes 30–45 minutes; some parts steep); e. (right) on Rte. 601 1.8 miles to U.S. Rte. 11 (just before intersection, look to right to see trace of original Valley Turnpike climbing Fisher's Hill, including abutments for bridge over Tumbling Run; most clearly visible in winter); s. (right) on U.S. Rte. 11 .6 mile to United Daughters of the Confederacy marker; continue .2 mile to Virginia Civil War Commission (Circle Tour) interpretive markers and state historical marker A-27, Battle of Fisher's Hill; continue 2.1 miles to Rte. 651; s.e. (right) on Rte. 651 .8 mile to I-81. To visit Tom's Brook battlefield, continue s. on U.S. Rte. 11 past Rte. 651 1.2 miles to Rte. 653 (see Tom's Brook battlefield tour).

Hill. At dawn on Thursday, September 22, the skirmishing began again all along the front as Crook's corps marched west to Little North Mountain.

At about 11:30 A.M. the Union line struck the Confederates at several points. Early concluded that he could not continue to hold Fisher's Hill with the relatively few troops he had and ordered a withdrawal once darkness fell.

On the Federal right flank, Crook's corps approached the point of attack on Little North Mountain in midafternoon. Maj. Gen. William W. Averell's cavalry division had spent much of the day skirmishing lightly with Lomax's troopers, both to keep them in place and to screen Crook's march. As the Union infantry approached, the Confederates could not ascertain their numbers. When the truth finally dawned on Ramseur, who commanded the infantry division closest to the mountain, it was too late.

Crook's corps swept down onto Lomax's division at about 4 P.M. The impact was immediate and devastating. Ramseur struggled to hold his hill as the Federal tide rolled up its slopes, shifting brigades to meet the assault but in vain. He was under attack not only from Crook but from Ricketts, who pressed forward at the sounds of battle at the foot of the mountain. The remainder of Wright's and Emory's corps followed suit, and quickly the entire Confederate line was in retreat. The controlled withdrawal turned into a rout as the troops fled south. Miles passed before a rear guard could be formed, and skirmishing continued until after dark.

The Confederates lost some 1,200 men, many of them captured in the rout, while the Federals suffered about 530 casualties. Sheridan justifiably concluded that Early was no longer a major threat, although he was unable to stop and crush his army completely. The Federal commander was confident enough to begin the scourging of the Shenandoah Valley. Now the populace would get a taste of war as they had never had before.

Although the Fisher's Hill battlefield is bisected by Interstate 81 and some residential development has occurred there, especially on Flint Hill, much of it remains in good condition. The important sites of combat are intact and the battle is easily interpreted from the terrain. The Civil War Preservation Trust owns Ramseur's position, known as Ramseur's Hill, and maintains a self-guided walking tour of the property. ▪

In September 1864 Lt. Gen. Jubal A. Early wrote Gen. Robert E. Lee requesting additional cavalry. This change of tactics would allow his infantry time to recover from its defeats and slow the Federal advance by using the mounted arm to harass and delay Maj. Gen. Philip H. Sheridan. The decision was ironic, for Early, like Stonewall Jackson before him, had little confidence in his cavalry commanders.

Lee ordered Brig. Gen. Thomas L. Rosser and his "Laurel Brigade" to ride to the Shenandoah Valley from Petersburg. Early appointed the newly arrived Rosser commander of all his cavalry.

Sheridan, who by the first week of October had reached as far south as Staunton, considered his Valley strategy successful and began withdrawing north

DIRECTIONS: I-81 Exit 291 (Rte. 651, Tom's Brook), s.e. on Rte. 651 about .8 mile to U.S. Rte. 11 (Valley Turnpike); s.w. (right) on U.S. Rte. 11 1.2 miles (through Merritt's bivouac) to Rte. 653 (Brook Creek Rd.); n.w. (right) on Rte. 653 (Lomax's bivouac) 2.4 miles to Rte. 623 (Back Rd.); s.w. (left) on Rte. 623 1.5 miles to Rte. 655 (Harrisville Rd.) (Custer's position at .3 mile and Rosser's position .4 mile farther); s.e. (left) on Rte. 655 2.3 miles to Rte. 653; s.e. (right) on Rte. 653 .5 mile to U.S. Rte. 11; n.e. (left) on U.S. Rte. 11 1.2 miles to Rte. 651; n.w. (left) on U.S. Rte. 651 .8 mile to I-81.

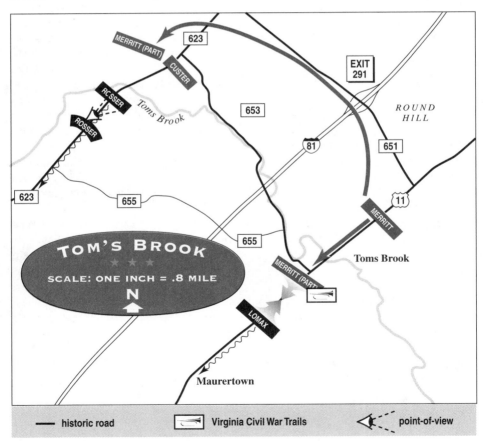

historic road — Virginia Civil War Trails — point-of-view

toward Winchester to join the main body of the Union army at Petersburg. En route, his army burned barns, mills, and fields and seized and ran off livestock. Meanwhile, Early, reinforced by Maj. Gen. Joseph B. Kershaw's infantry division and Lt. Col. Wilfred E. Cutshaw's artillery battalion, now all returned to the Valley, advanced his four infantry divisions from Rockfish Gap to Mount Jackson in Sheridan's wake. When the Confederate cavalry began to harass the rear of the Federal column, Sheridan got fed up.

View north from Rosser's position to route of Custer's attack. VIRGINIA DEPARTMENT OF HISTORIC RESOURCES, JOHN S. SALMON

After skirmishing all day on Saturday, October 8, the Federal and Confederate cavalry bivouacked near each other. A mile north of Tom's Brook, Torbert's command encamped with Brig. Gen. Wesley Merritt's division on the Valley Turnpike to form the Federal left flank, while Brig. Gen. George A. Custer's division held the right flank on the Back Road (present-day Rte. 623) about two miles west. South of Tom's Brook, Rosser disposed his cavalry so that Brig. Gen. Lunsford L. Lomax held the Confederate right flank opposite Merritt, while Rosser's own division camped atop Spiker's Ridge facing Custer.

Torbert attacked at dawn on Sunday, October 9. Custer advanced against Rosser at Spiker's Ridge while two of Merritt's brigades attacked Lomax, and the other rode west to join with Custer. Custer's men advanced dismounted against Rosser's, themselves dismounted behind stone walls and fence rails at the foot of Spiker's Ridge near the south bank of Tom's Brook. The arrival of Merritt's brigade enabled Custer to extend his right flank beyond Rosser's, effectively outflanking the Confederates. Rosser bent the left part of his line back to counter the move but

ordered a retreat when a regiment of Federal cavalry charged the Confederate rear. Custer ordered a charge against the center of Rosser's line, and the retreat quickened.

On the Valley Turnpike, Lomax ordered a charge against the Federal brigade opposing him, but part of the brigade maneuvered around Lomax's left flank, coming between him and Rosser. Now Lomax retreated in haste, with Merritt's men in close pursuit.

The Confederates retreated beyond Woodstock and Columbia Furnace, abandoning their cannons and baggage and giving up roughly 350 casualties, many of them prisoners. The Federals lost about 60 men. From this point on, the Union cavalry maintained a clear superiority over the Confederates.

Although Interstate 81 and residential development have affected parts of the battlefield, much of it remains intact. The road network, open farmland, and Tom's Brook all combine to make the battle easily understandable and interpreted. The Civil War Preservation Trust owns a small parcel of the battlefield near Tom's Brook on the Back Road. ■

CEDAR CREEK

By mid-October 1864, Maj. Gen. Philip H. Sheridan had declared his campaign of destruction in the Shenandoah Valley a success. His army had depleted the Breadbasket of the Confederacy, and—most importantly—inflicted numerous defeats on Lt. Gen. Jubal A. Early's army. Convinced that Early no longer posed a threat to Washington or the North and would not risk another loss by attacking him, Sheridan entrusted his command to Maj. Gen. Horatio G. Wright and left for Washington with few misgivings to meet with Chief of Staff Henry W. Halleck and Secretary of War Edwin M. Stanton on October 17. They planned to reunite most of his command with the main Federal army at Petersburg. Sheridan spent the night in Winchester before rejoining the Army of the Shenandoah on Wednesday, October 19.

Sheridan's 32,000-man army was bivouacked some fourteen miles south, just north of Cedar Creek. The encampments sprawled across the Valley Turnpike (present-day U.S. Rte. 11) and formed a south-facing U west and south of Middletown. Union headquarters were located at Belle Grove, a handsome stone dwelling constructed in 1794–1796 by Revolutionary War veteran Maj. Isaac Hite, Jr. Abundant water made for good camping, although the terrain—cut up by ravines and some steep streambanks—rendered defense deceptively difficult.

Brig. Gen. Alfred T. A. Torbert's two cavalry divisions guarded the Federal right flank. Maj. Gen. Horatio G. Wright's VI Corps held the infantry right flank between Torbert's position and Meadow Brook, a tributary of Cedar Creek. Because it cut a deep ravine, Meadow Brook formed a natural obstacle between

DIRECTIONS: I-81 Exit 302 (Rte. 627, Middletown), w. on Rte. 627 about .4 mile to U.S. Rte. 11 (Valley Turnpike); s. (left) on U.S. Rte. 11 1.25 miles to Cedar Creek Battlefield Visitors Center at 8437 Old Valley Pike, noting Heater House and Virginia Civil War Commission (Circle Tour) interpretive marker on right; from visitors center, continue s. on U.S. Rte. 11 .1 mile to state historical marker A-17, Tomb of Unknown Soldier, on left; continue s. on U.S. Rte. 11 .2 mile to state historical marker A-56, Battle of Cedar Creek, on right; continue s. on U.S. Rte. 11 approximately .7 mile to 128th New York Infantry monument on right just before Rte. 840 intersection; continue past intersection about .5 mile to crossover and 2 Virginia Civil War Trails markers on left at Stickley House; continue s. on U.S. Rte. 11 about 2.9 miles to Rte. 635 (Washington St.) in Strasburg; e. (left) on Rte. 635 1.8 miles to Bowman's Mill Ford; continue e. on Rte. 635 .1 mile to Rte. 611; e. (right) on Rte. 611 2.5 miles to Rte. 840; n. (left) on Rte. 840 1.1 mile to U.S. Rte. 11; n. (right) on U.S. Rte. 11 .7 mile to Rte. 727 and sign for Belle Grove on left; w. (left) on Rte. 727, noting bronze tablet marker, Battle of Cedar Creek, and Ramseur monument at intersection; continue w. on Rte. 727 .5 mile to Belle Grove; continue w. on Rte. 727 .2 mile to Rte. 624 (Hite Rd.); n. (right) on Rte. 624 .8 mile to Rte. 625; w. (left) on Rte. 625 .6 mile to Rte. 635; e. (right) on Rte. 635 .2 mile to Mount Carmel Cemetery, where Getty's division made its stand; continue n. on Rte. 635 .3 mile to Rte. 627; e. (right) on Rte. 627 .1 mile to Rte. 635; n. (left) on Rte. 635 .5 mile to Rte. 634 at Miller's Mill; w. (left) on Rte. 634 .8 mile to Rte. 625; n. (right) on Rte. 625 .9 mile to Rte. 633; e. (right) on Rte. 633 1.2 miles to U.S. Rte. 11; s. (right) on U.S. Rte. 11 .4 mile to state historical marker A-14, End of Sheridan's Ride, on right; continue s. on U.S. Rte. 11 .9 mile to Lord Fairfax Community College on left; e. (left) into parking lot for state historical marker A-15, Battle of Cedar Creek, and a local historical marker on the battle; return to U.S. Rte. 11; s. (left) on U.S. Rte. 11 .3 mile to Rte. 627; e. (left) on Rte. 627 about .4 mile to I-81. For advance information about the battlefield, contact the Cedar Creek Battlefield Foundation, P.O. Box 229, Middletown, VA 22645; call toll-free 888-OCT-1864, or 540-869-2064 (Fax: 540-869-1438); or visit the Foundation's Web site at www.cedarcreekbattlefield.org. For a detailed driving tour of this complex battlefield, purchase a copy of Joseph W. A. Whitehorne's *Self-Guided Tour: The Battle of Cedar Creek* (Strasburg, Va.: The Wayside Museum of American History and Arts, 1987) by telephone, the Web site's online bookstore, or in person at the visitors center.

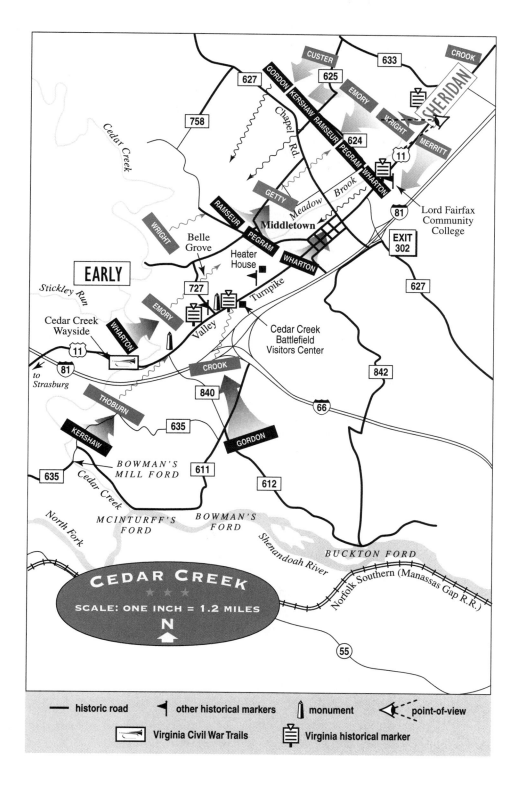

CUSTOM
CROOK
633
625
GORDON
KERSHAW
RAMSEUR
PEGRAM
EMORY
WRIGHT
SHERIDAN
627
758
624
MERRITT
Cedar Creek
Chapel Rd.
11
WHARTON
Meadow
Brook
81
Lord Fairfax
Community
College
GETTY
RAMSEUR
WRIGHT
Middletown
PEGRAM
Belle
Grove
EXIT
302
627
Heater
House
EARLY
WHARTON
Stickley Run
727
Turnpike
Cedar Creek
Wayside
EMORY
Valley
Cedar Creek
Battlefield
Visitors Center
WHARTON
11
CROOK
81
842
to
Strasburg
840
66
THOBURN
635
KERSHAW
635
BOWMAN'S
MILL FORD
611
GORDON
612
Cedar Creek
McINTURFF'S
FORD
BOWMAN'S
FORD
North Fork
Shenandoah River
BUCKTON FORD

CEDAR CREEK
★ ★ ★
SCALE: ONE INCH = 1.2 MILES
N

Norfolk Southern (Manassas Gap R.R.)

55

— historic road ◀ other historical markers 🛆 monument ◀┄ point-of-view

🖾 Virginia Civil War Trails 🖾 Virginia historical marker

Wright's corps and the remainder of the army to the east. Across the stream on a high ridge, Maj. Gen. William H. Emory's XIX Corps occupied the center of the line. Most of Brig. Gen. George Crook's Army of West Virginia and Col. J. Howard Kitching's Provisional Division anchored the army's left flank east of the Valley Turnpike. About a mile south of the main encampment, Col. Joseph Thoburn's division of Crook's army occupied a knoll just north of Cedar Creek. Capt. Henry A. Du Pont stationed part of his artillery brigade within Thoburn's line and the remainder to the rear of it. In front of Thoburn, Massanutten Mountain loomed above the Valley floor just to the southeast.

To the south at Fisher's Hill, Early and his 21,000-man Army of the Valley studied the Federal bivouac carefully. A party of Confederate officers, including Maj. Gen. John B. Gordon and Jedediah Hotchkiss, formerly Stonewall Jackson's cartographer, climbed Massanutten Mountain on the afternoon of October 17, noting the position of each branch of the army, counting cannons, and drawing a detailed map. Then they returned to Early's headquarters and presented him with a bold plan of attack. Gordon would lead three divisions in a night march along the base of Massanutten Mountain to strike the Federal left flank at dawn on October 19. At the same time, Maj. Gen. Joseph B. Kershaw would march with his division to attack Thoburn, and Brig. Gen. Gabriel C. Wharton with his division would drive straight down the turnpike. Rosser's cavalry, minus Col. William H. Payne's brigade, which served as the vanguard of Gordon's column, would keep Torbert occupied. The attack would commence at first light.

The night march began at 8 P.M. Gordon's corps followed a narrow trail along the base of Massanutten Mountain. The darkness was fading and a thick fog covered the ground when the lead elements arrived at Bowman's and McInturff's Fords; Gordon ordered Payne's cavalry across Bowman's Ford, and the Confederate cavalry overran the Federal pickets with only a few shots being fired. Gordon's infantry waded the fords, then assembled in battle formation: Maj. Gen. Stephen D. Ramseur's division on the right, Brig. Gen. Clement A. Evans's on

Sheridan arrives on the field at Cedar Creek from Winchester. LIBRARY OF CONGRESS

the left, and Brig. Gen. John Pegram's behind Evans. Upstream at the turnpike bridge and at Bowman's Mill, Wharton and Kershaw waited in the mist. Half an hour later the attack began.

In the Union camps a few soldiers and officers had become aware of movement to their front, but their reports were dismissed by others as the sounds of a Federal patrol. At 5:40 A.M., however, a gray wave, almost invisible in the fog, proved the reports correct. The attack was surprising, violent, and overwhelmingly successful. Kershaw's division swept over Thoburn's bivouac with little organized resistance. Within an hour the Union center and left flank were in full retreat, and the Confederate tide threatened Wright on the right flank. Du Pont held his ground until the last possible second and deployed his guns effectively to delay the onrushing Confederates long enough to escape with nine cannons out of sixteen.

Although the Federals fled north in confusion and alarm, before long a determination to hold ground somewhere calmed most of them. To the west, Wright's VI Corps had heard the battle and hastened to join in the fray. When the vanguard reached Meadow Brook and Wright learned that Confederates held the opposite bank, he used the watercourse as a natural defensive line.

At the western edge of Middletown stood the town cemetery. There, at about 8 A.M., Brig. Gen. George W. Getty's division of Wright's corps held on while the fragments of Sheridan's army coalesced into a new line a mile and a half north. The hour-long fight was so fierce that Early concluded he was facing Wright's entire corps, not just a division. When Ramseur and Pegram could not dislodge the Federals, Early threw Wharton's division and then all of his artillery to bear on the ridge, to no avail. At about 9:30 A.M., Wharton's

division left to join the rest of the army. The valor of the Union troops not only had bought time for the Federals but had brought the Confederate advance to a virtual standstill. At the same time, just to the east in Middletown, Merritt's Union cavalry blocked the Valley Turnpike and appeared to threaten Early's right flank.

By 10 A.M. Early ordered a halt to reorganize his units, many of which had lost cohesion in the fog, smoke, and hot pursuit—plus looting the Federal camps. Historians have criticized Early for halting and stopping his army's momentum, as well as for ordering wasteful frontal assaults against Getty's division instead of maneuvering around it. However, this was a battle fought by sound, not sight, because fog and smoke blinded Confederate and Federal alike until midmorning. Early was compelled to rely on his subordinates' judgment, and after its pell-mell attack, his army was in almost as much disarray as Sheridan's. More importantly, his men were exhausted, having been on the move since 8 P.M. the night before.

And what of Sheridan? Fourteen miles north, in Winchester, pickets on the southern edge of town reported the sounds of combat to him. Sheridan swung into the saddle and rode up the Valley Turnpike, where he arrived at the new defensive line. In one of the great moments of the war in the Valley, he galloped down the line, shouting at his men that they would sleep in their old camps that night. The Army of the Shenandoah was reborn.

To the south, the Army of the Valley reformed and advanced its line about a mile from the Federals. It extended for almost three miles along Miller's Mill Road (Rte. 634), from the Valley Turnpike westward. Wharton's division held the Confederate right flank, with Pegram to his left, then Ramseur, Kershaw, and Gordon. Sheridan, meanwhile, had placed his cavalry on his flanks, with Brig. Gen. Wesley Merritt's division on the Federal left and Brig. Gen. George A. Custer on the right. The VI Corps was stationed just to the west of Merritt and the XIX Corps to the east of Custer, with Crook's corps to the rear in reserve.

Early probed and skirmished during the afternoon but did not launch an attack. Apparently he believed that the Federals would retreat to Winchester that night. At 4 P.M. Sheridan proved him wrong.

First, however, Sheridan's cavalry put pressure on the Confederate right and left flanks—Merritt advanced at about 3 P.M., Custer at about 3:30 P.M. Early's line was in trouble. Reinforced by elements of the XIX Corps, Custer attacked Gordon's exposed flank. Soon, Gordon and Kershaw began to give way. Then Sheridan struck them hard.

At 4 P.M., as the Confederate left began to fold, Sheridan launched a general attack against Ramseur at the center. Ramseur eventually fell mortally wounded, and his division joined the retreat. With the Confederate left and center in flight, Early's right flank had to withdraw. While Merritt pressed them, Custer continued around and struck the Confederate rear. The retreat turned into a near rout, and when the turnpike bridge across No-Name Run collapsed, the army lost all of its artillery

and most of its wagons. Prisoners were rounded up by the hundreds while the remainder of the army fled south to Fisher's Hill. The Federal pursuit ended with the day, at about 6:30 P.M.

The battle of Cedar Creek was a clear Confederate victory in the morning and a clear Federal victory in the afternoon. The afternoon victory counted more. Although Early lost almost 3,000 killed, wounded, and captured, and Sheridan almost 5,700, Sheridan could afford the casualties. (Ramseur was among the captured and was carried to Federal headquarters at Belle Grove. There, he was visited by old comrades, including Custer, who held his hand while he died.) Early's army was all but destroyed, no longer able to take the offensive against Sheridan, and the Federal victory in the Valley was complete.

The battleground at Cedar Creek, a National Historic Landmark and a huge area, retains much of its integrity despite the growth of Middletown, the construction of Interstate 81 and other roads, and the scattered development of residential areas. Many of the structures that stood at the time of the battle remain, including Belle Grove, and most of the key parts of the battlefield are accessible by vehicle. Increasingly, battlefield sites are being acquired and preserved, and the future of Cedar Creek looks bright. ∎

WAYNESBORO

In late February 1865, Lt. Gen. Ulysses S. Grant directed Maj. Gen. Philip H. Sheridan to complete the mission first assigned to Maj. Gen. David Hunter the preceding June: He should capture Charlottesville and Lynchburg, and at the same time destroy the Virginia Central Railroad

and the James River & Kanawha Canal, thereby severing Gen. Robert E. Lee's rail and canal links with the Shenandoah Valley. The only opposition to Grant's plan would come from Lt. Gen. Jubal A. Early's Army of the Valley, which was now reduced to approximately 1,600 men

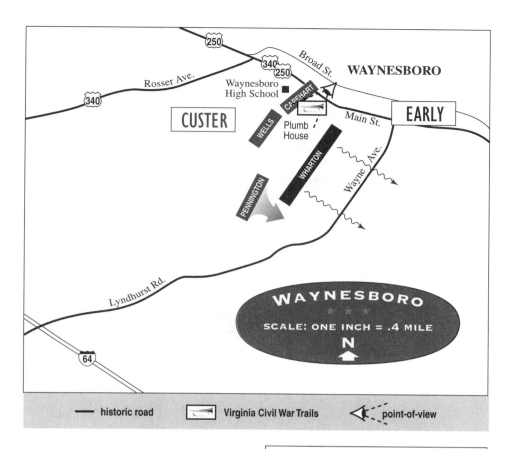

| historic road | Virginia Civil War Trails | point-of-view |

following the battle of Cedar Creek the previous October.

Early had occupied Staunton after the battle, but when Sheridan began his march on February 27, the Confederates abandoned the town after removing all the supplies they could carry. While the 10,000-man Army of the Shenandoah advanced south from Winchester, Early and his men retreated west to Waynesboro, a small town on the western slope of the Blue Ridge Mountains below Rockfish Gap. There they set up a defensive line on low hills west of town while the remnant of Early's cavalry, about 200 in all, struggled to delay Sheridan's progress.

By March 1, Sheridan was in Staunton. The next day Brig. Gen. George A. Custer led the pursuit of Early's army. About

DIRECTIONS: I-64 Exit 94 (U.S. Rte. 340 North, Waynesboro), n. on U.S. Rte. 340 North (Rosser Ave.) about 2.2 miles to U.S. Rte. 250; e. (right) on U.S. Rte. 250 .4 mile following Virginia Civil War Trails signs to Plumb House at 1012 W. Main St. and Virginia Civil War Trails marker; part of battlefield is on Waynesboro High School grounds behind house.
  Alternative route: I-81 Exit 222 (U.S. Rte. 250 East, Waynesboro), e. on U.S. Rte. 250 East 8.4 miles to U.S. Rte. 340; straight through intersection on U.S. Rte. 340 .4 mile following Virginia Civil War Trails signs to Plumb House at 1012 W. Main St. and Virginia Civil War Trails marker.

noon he encountered the Confederate position and spent the next three hours studying it to find its weakness. Brig. Gen. Gabriel C. Wharton, commanding the defenses, had a large front to defend with relatively few men. While he anchored his

Plumb House, behind which the battle took place. VIRGINIA DEPARTMENT OF HISTORIC RESOURCES, JOHN S. SALMON

left flank near the South River, he left a forest-covered gap an eighth of a mile wide between the last man in line and the riverbank, hoping to bluff the Federals into believing that his line extended to the river.

At 3:30 P.M. Custer sent three dismounted cavalry regiments into the gap, where they turned Wharton's flank.

A mounted Federal brigade charged the center of Wharton's line, and in a few minutes the rout was complete. Although Early and a few others escaped, virtually his entire army was made prisoner. In addition, the Federals captured 200 wagons, 14 cannons, and 17 flags. The Civil War in the Shenandoah Valley was over.

In the years since the engagement, the city of Waynesboro has expanded to cover the battlefield with residential neighborhoods. One relic of the battle still survives: the Plumb House, named for the family that owned it at the time. The structure stood in the path of Custer's advance on the road from Staunton, and part of the action swirled around it. ■

SOUTHWEST VIRGINIA CAMPAIGNS, 1862–1865

During the Civil War, Southwest Virginia experienced relatively little military activity, as the most significant campaigns occurred to the east between Richmond and Washington. The region remained strategically important, however, because of its salt and lead mines plus its proximity to Kentucky—which remained in the Union—and the rail center of Chattanooga, Tennessee. Steep hills, poor roads, and remoteness from the primary scenes of activity relegated Southwest Virginia to a secondary role through the first half of the conflict.

Several key transportation corridors passed through the region. In the eighteenth century the Wilderness Road—improved by the frontiersman Daniel Boone—was the historic route of migration into eastern Kentucky through Cumberland Gap. The road was further improved during the antebellum period, when the South Western Turnpike was constructed. During the same era, the Virginia & Tennessee Railroad was built between Lynchburg, Virginia, where it connected with the Orange & Alexandria Railroad and the South Side Railroad, and Bristol, Tennessee, the northeastern terminus of the East Tennessee & Virginia Railroad, which extended to Knoxville, Tennessee. The southwestern railroads would become primary objectives of Federal raids late in the war.

As the gateway between the two principal theaters of operations in Virginia and the west, Cumberland Gap became the immediate objective of both combatants early in the conflict. By September 1861 some 4,000 Confederate troops, initially commanded by Brig. Gen. Felix K. Zollicoffer and then Col. James E. Rains, occupied the gap. On March 16, 1862, a Union brigade some fifty miles northeast captured Pound Gap from entrenched Confederate defenders, thereby threatening Cumberland Gap. Several skirmishes ensued, and on June 18, 1862, Brig. Gen. George W. Morgan's Federal division occupied Cumberland Gap. Brief engagements occurred throughout the summer as each side contended in the surrounding valleys.

In August 1862, to induce Kentucky to embrace the Southern cause, the Confederates launched a two-pronged invasion. Maj. Gen. E. Kirby Smith led a Confederate advance into Kentucky while Gen. Braxton Bragg attacked from Tennessee. Smith crushed a Union force at Richmond, Kentucky, on August 29–30, and a few weeks later a Federal garrison at Munfordville surrendered to Bragg. Brig. Gen. Carter L. Stevenson, who reported to Smith, then besieged Morgan until he evacuated Cumberland Gap on September 17. Soon after Maj. Gen. Don Carlos Buell's Army of the Ohio stopped the combined Southern force at Perryville on October 8, however, the Confederates retreated, and most of Kentucky remained in Union hands.

In September 1863 Maj. Gen. Ambrose E. Burnside, leading the Army of the Ohio, captured Knoxville, Tennessee.

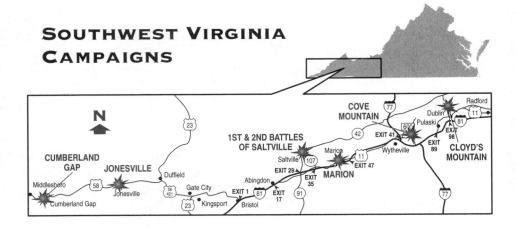

SOUTHWEST VIRGINIA CAMPAIGNS

N

CUMBERLAND GAP

JONESVILLE

COVE MOUNTAIN

CLOYD'S MOUNTAIN

1ST & 2ND BATTLES OF SALTVILLE

MARION

Middlesboro · Cumberland Gap · Jonesville · Duffield · Gate City · Kingsport · Bristol · Abingdon · Saltville · Marion · Wytheville · Dublin · Pulaski · Radford

Brig. Gen James M. Shackelford, leading a cavalry brigade of Burnside's army, approached from the south and, on Burnside's arrival, Union forces then converged on Cumberland Gap and its Confederate garrison led by Brig. Gen. John W. Frazer. The Federals demanded and received the surrender of the smaller Confederate force on September 9 after a three-day siege.

On January 1, 1864, Brig. Gen. William E. "Grumble" Jones led his cavalry brigade toward Cumberland Gap with the intention of seizing it. The next day he learned that Federals under Maj. Charles H. Beeres had defeated Lt. Col. Auburn L. Pridemore's command earlier that day near Jonesville. Jones crossed Powell's Mountain and ordered Pridemore, who had withdrawn from the town, to return and join in an attack on the Federals.

After a night-long march in bitter cold, the Confederates reached Jonesville early on January 3. Jones immediately struck the Union encampment on the western edge of town, having achieved surprise. After capturing Federal artillery in the initial assault, the Confederates abandoned the guns under a Union counterattack. The outnumbered Federals soon retreated to the Milbourn farmhouse and its outbuildings. Jones kept the force pinned down until Pridemore arrived late in the day, then

countered an attempted Federal breakout with a general assault, which was soon followed by the surrender of Beeres's men. The Confederates lost 16 killed and wounded in the engagement, the Federals 12 killed, 48 wounded, and 300 captured.

On March 9, 1864, Pres. Abraham Lincoln appointed Lt. Gen. Ulysses S. Grant commander in chief of all Union armies. Grant's plan for the spring campaign called for massive Federal advances to begin everywhere about May 4, including Piedmont Virginia, the Shenandoah Valley, and Southwest Virginia, where Brig. Gen. George Crook planned to destroy the Virginia & Tennessee Railroad at Dublin in Pulaski County. Later that month Gen. Robert E. Lee ordered Jones and his men north to the Shenandoah Valley to cope with the Federal advance that threatened Lee's left flank.

Crook had marched from the Kanawha River in West Virginia toward Dublin on April 29 with three brigades. After more than a week's march through West Virginia and Virginia, he encountered Brig. Gen. Albert G. Jenkins at Cloyd's Mountain six miles north of Dublin on May 9, 1864.

The Confederates had prepared defensive positions on each side of the road from Dublin to Pearisburg. Shortly after dawn Crook's force crossed the summit of

Cloyd's Mountain and prepared to descend the road toward Jenkins's position. Seeing the Confederates' strength, however, Crook ordered one brigade to march through underbrush east of the road and strike Jenkins's right flank while the other two assaulted the front. After a short but hard fight, Crook stormed the Confederate position and captured a seriously wounded Jenkins. An attempt to rally by Jenkins's second in command, Brig. Gen. John McCausland, was dispersed by a brisk attack. The Federals then marched on to Dublin, where they destroyed the depot and military stores and burned the nearby New River Bridge. On May 11, Brig. Gen. William W. Averell, who had failed to raid Saltville two days earlier, joined Crook there. The battle of Cloyd's Mountain, the largest engagement in Southwest Virginia, resulted in some 538 Confederates killed, wounded, captured, or missing and 745 Federal casualties.

Averell and his brigade had ridden toward Wytheville to prevent the Confederates from concentrating their forces against Crook's and destroy the town's lead works. On the afternoon of May 10, Averell encountered Jones's brigade on the Raleigh & Grayson Turnpike near Cove Mountain, between Wytheville and Dublin. Averell ordered an attack. Jones also advanced, pressing the Union flanks, as he hoped to delay the Federals from reaching Crook. Four hours later, as Averell prepared to renew the attack near nightfall, the Confederates withdrew. The two sides suffered about 300 casualties.

Averell and his brigade marched to the New River on May 11 and crossed on a flatboat while Confederate forces watched from the other side of the river. Averell then joined Crook near Dublin.

During the summer and fall of 1864, the Shenandoah Valley and the vicinity of Petersburg became the focus of military activity in Virginia, while little of note occurred in Southwest Virginia. Grumble Jones was killed and his army defeated at the battle of Piedmont on June 5, thus leaving vulnerable not only the Valley but Southwest Virginia, where Jenkins had been placed in command on May 5 in Jones's absence.

Early in October Federal forces under Brig. Gen. Stephen G. Burbridge attempted to seize Saltville and destroy the nearby saltworks, which produced a large proportion of the salt used to preserve meat and tan leather for the Confederate army. A makeshift Confederate force delayed Burbridge at Clinch Mountain and Laurel Gap on October 1, however, enabling Brig. Gen. Alfred E. "Mudwall" Jackson to amass troops near Saltville. The next morning the Federals attacked Jackson, but Confederate reinforcements continued to arrive during the day and held off successive attacks. As evening fell, Burbridge retired without accomplishing his objective. Afterward, Confederate soldiers under Brig. Gen. Felix H. Robertson massacred an undetermined number of 5th U.S. Colored Cavalry prisoners, many of them wounded. One of the Confederate officers, Capt. Champ Ferguson, would later be captured by Federal forces, tried, and executed for the murders on October 20, 1865. The battle may have cost the two sides as many as 450 casualties.

In November 1864 Maj. Gen. George Stoneman led his cavalry division on raids to destroy iron and lead mines, saltworks, and railroads in East Tennessee and Southwest Virginia. Stoneman's 4,200-man force defeated Confederates under Brig. Gen. Basil W. Duke at Kingsport, Tennessee, on December 4. Two days later, near Bristol, Tennessee, Stoneman prevented a small mounted force commanded by Brig. Gen. John C. Vaughn from joining the main body of the Confederate defenders under Maj. Gen. John C. Breckinridge near Saltville. On December

17–18 Stoneman's force defeated Breckinridge at Marion, thus enabling the Federals to attack Saltville.

Reaching Saltville on December 20–21, the Federals captured and destroyed the saltworks, including between 50,000 and 100,000 bushels of salt. Stoneman then led his troopers through Cumberland Gap to Kentucky and Tennessee. His successful raid cost the Federals and Confederates 275 casualties.

Stoneman returned to Southwest Virginia late in March 1865 on a raid to destroy rail lines and other property of military value to the Confederacy. His men wrecked sections of the Virginia & Tennessee Railroad around Salem and Wytheville as well as the Piedmont Railroad between Danville, Virginia, and Greensborough, North Carolina. Since Confederate resistance in the region had effectively ended with Breckinridge's defeat in December 1864, Stoneman met with little resistance. His raid ended when he learned that Gen. Joseph E. Johnston and the Army of Tennessee had surrendered at Durham Station, North Carolina, on April 26, 1865. ∎

CUMBERLAND GAP

Cumberland Gap—since the late colonial period the gateway from Virginia to Kentucky—became during the Civil War the principal passage between the eastern and western theaters of operation in the Upper South. And whoever controlled the high ground controlled the passage.

Brig. Gen. Felix K. Zollicoffer and his 4,000-man force secured the gap for the Confederates in September 1861 and began to fortify it. Col. James E. Rains replaced Zollicoffer in the winter of 1861. Then in March 1862, Maj. Gen. Don Carlos Buell ordered Brig. Gen. George W. Morgan to occupy and hold the gap for the Union. Morgan's unit, the 7th Division, Army of the Ohio, assembled early in April some fourteen miles north of Cumberland Gap at Cumberland Ford.

Morgan reconnoitered the Confederate position, and found that the strongest fortifications faced north; the southern part of the gap was undefended except for one battery and a line of rifle pits. Morgan decided to bypass his force to the southwest and compel Rains either to fight in the open or evacuate the gap.

Morgan maneuvered various Confederate forces out of his path, including two brigades commanded by Maj. Gen. E. Kirby Smith that were positioned opposite Morgan at Cumberland Ford. Successful in his feints and other deceptive movements, Morgan and three of his four brigades approached the gap from Powell Valley, to the south. In mid-June Rains set fire to the woods near the gap so that the smoke would conceal the evacuation of his position. Morgan took possession of Cumberland Gap unopposed on June 18. During the next three months, his men improved and enlarged the network of fortifications in the gap, constructing additional batteries, rifle pits, and trenches.

Late in the summer of 1862, the focus of the war in the west shifted to Kentucky, a vital border state. Throughout August and September Buell and Gen. Braxton Bragg maneuvered their opposing armies across the state. To protect the Southern armies' right flank, Smith sought to occupy Cumberland Gap.

On August 16 Brig. Gen. Carter L. Stevenson almost encircled Morgan with some 9,000 men. A Federal reconnaissance party sent from the gap to scout Stevenson's position encountered Smith's advance into Kentucky; Smith quickly closed in on Morgan with another 9,000 soldiers. Surrounded, Morgan refused to give up. Smith and Stevenson decided to starve Morgan out.

By September 9 the Federals thought they might hold out another sixty days if they began to slaughter and eat their horses and mules, but soon they ran out of fodder, and the animals started dying. Faced with choosing between surrender and evacuation, a council of war on September 14 unanimously chose evacuation. Two nights later, Morgan sent some of his wagons quietly out of the gap north toward safety (the only route still open). Replying to a flag of truce from the Confederates,

ostensibly to discuss the possibility of surrender, the Federals were merely delaying while Morgan continued his evacuation. When a storehouse burst into flames in the distance, one Union officer coolly told the Confederates that timber was being burned to widen fields of fire for the artillery.

Soon after sundown on September 17, Morgan began the last phase of the evacuation of Cumberland Gap. Leaving a brigade behind to destroy stores and explode mines, Morgan led the remainder of his troops north toward Manchester, Kentucky. By dawn the evacuation was complete and the gap was in Southern hands.

On August 3, 1863, Maj. Gen. Simon B. Buckner ordered Brig. Gen. John W. Frazer to hold the gap for the Confederates

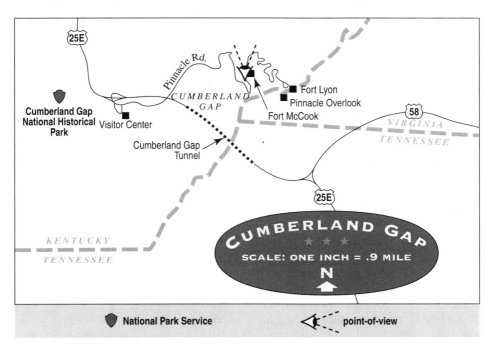

DIRECTIONS: I-81 Exit 1 (U.S. Rte. 58 West), w. about 100 miles through Cumberland Gap Tunnel into Kentucky to Cumberland Gap National Historical Park. A park map is available at the visitor center. Visit the National Park Service Web site at nps.gov/parks.html for a virtual tour of this and other national parks.

View north from U.S. Fort McCook, just over the Virginia line in Kentucky. VIRGINIA DEPARTMENT OF HISTORIC RESOURCES, JOHN S. SALMON

while Buckner's army prepared for what would become the Chickamauga campaign and as Maj. Gen. Ambrose E. Burnside began his march on Knoxville. Frazer occupied the gap with his 2,500-man brigade.

As Burnside marched on Knoxville, he

ordered Col. John F. De Courcy to drive the Confederates from Cumberland Gap. Buckner evacuated Knoxville as Burnside approached, leaving Frazer without close support. Learning early in September that the Confederates still occupied the gap, Burnside ordered Brig. Gen. James M. Shackelford to augment De Courcy. Beginning on September 7, Shackelford besieged Frazer from the south, then informed Burnside that the Confederates were too strongly entrenched to attack. Burnside marched to Shackelford's assistance. De Courcy arrived on September 8 and invested the gap from the north, and Burnside approached the next day.

Every day of the siege, the Federals sent Frazer a demand for surrender as each reinforcement arrived on the scene. Frazer at first refused. When he found his position virtually surrounded, however, he capitulated on September 9.

Most of the contested ground at Cumberland Gap, together with surviving fieldworks, lies within the boundaries of Cumberland Gap National Historical Park. Many of the fortifications remain visible today. ■

JONESVILLE

On January 1, 1864, Col. Wilson C. Lemert, 68th Ohio Infantry, ordered Maj. Charles H. Beeres and his command to Lee County to occupy Jonesville, a small town some thirty miles northeast of Cumberland Gap. Beeres's force consisted of nearly 400 horse soldiers of the 16th Illinois Cavalry and three guns of the 22nd Ohio Battery. He posted about fifty men at the eastern end of the town and bivouacked with the remainder just outside the western end, on the south side of the road to Cumberland Gap (present-day U.S. Rte. 58).

Meanwhile, Brig. Gen. William E. "Grumble" Jones, a native of nearby Washington County, had started from Little War Gap on Clinch Mountain to seize Cumberland Gap for the Confederates. Learning on January 2 that Beeres had occupied Jonesville, Jones decided to drive the Federals out to protect his flank. Jones led his command toward Jonesville from the southwest. He also sent orders to Lt. Col. Auburn L. Pridemore, commander of the 64th Virginia Cavalry, to attack the town from the east. Pridemore's regiment

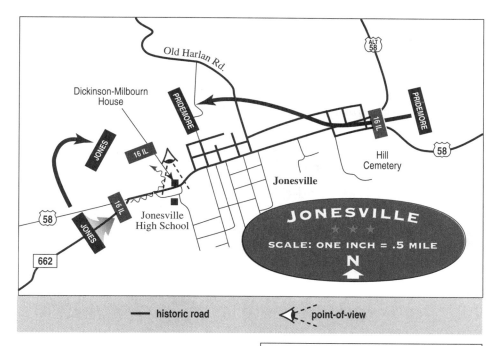

— historic road   point-of-view

had just been driven out of Jonesville by Beeres.

Jones's brigade marched through cold so bitter that one man died of exposure. At dawn on Sunday, January 3, the Confederates reached Jonesville. With the element of surprise in his favor, Jones immediately attacked the Union bivouac at the eastern end of the town without waiting for Pridemore. Although he caught Beeres and his men off guard and captured their artillery, the Federals responded quickly and retook them. Fighting hard, Beeres's force withdrew northward to the Andrew Milbourn farm, taking shelter in and around the farmhouse and outbuildings.

Jones realized that dislodging the Federals would be costly, due to the dominating positions of their artillery, and decided to hold his adversaries in place until Pridemore arrived. As the sun began to set, Pridemore and his regiment finally entered Jonesville from the east. The 64th Virginia quickly overwhelmed the few Union troops remaining in the town and swept

DIRECTIONS: I-81 Exit 1 (U.S. Rte. 58 West), w. about 63 miles to Jonesville. At the time of the battle, Jonesville occupied four blocks or so at the eastern end of the present town; a good view of the historic town may be had from atop Hill Cemetery just to the s. From the Hill Cemetery road, proceed w. on U.S. Rte. 58 .7 mile to Jonesville High School on left. Across the highway on the n. side stands the Dickinson-Milbourn House. Much of the fighting centered around the house and its outbuildings, and the Federal surrender took place in the field n. of the house.

westward to the Milbourn farm. About to be surrounded, Beeres's men fell back to a hill just north of the farmhouse, above a cornfield. Jones, once he was certain that the Federals were too far away from the farm buildings to return, ordered a general assault on the new Union position. Outnumbered, Beeres surrendered.

The Confederates captured some 300 Federals, wounded 48, and killed 12. Jones lost 4 killed and 12 wounded. Because his own ammunition was nearly exhausted, however, Jones had to await the arrival of his wagons before he could

Rear of Dickinson-Milbourne House and U.S. surrender field. VIRGINIA DEPARTMENT OF HISTORIC RESOURCES, JOHN S. SALMON

resume his march to Cumberland Gap; they did not come for two more days. Jones canceled the attack on the gap, reasoning that the Union garrison there had undoubtedly been warned of his approach, so to assault the place would be futile. The Federals held Cumberland Gap for the remainder of the war.

The Jonesville battlefield has been affected by the expansion of the town to the west. The Jonesville High School and grounds occupy the site of the Federal bivouac, but the Milbourn farmhouse still stands, as well as some open space, amid cultivated fields on the north side of U.S. Rte. 58. The house and four acres of land are listed on the National Register of Historic Places. ■

CLOYD'S MOUNTAIN

Lt. Gen. Ulysses S. Grant's offensive plan for the spring of 1864 in Virginia called for two Union armies to advance toward Richmond, a third to occupy the lower Shenandoah Valley, and a fourth to destroy sections of the Virginia & Tennessee Railroad in Southwest Virginia. The latter force of some 6,500 men commanded by Brig. Gen. George Crook marched toward Dublin in Pulaski County early in May from the Kanawha River in West Virginia.

With Maj. Gen. John C. Breckinridge ordered north to counter the Federal threat in the Shenandoah Valley, the command of the scattered Confederate forces in Southwest Virginia fell to Brig. Gen. Albert G. Jenkins. Learning of Crook's approach on May 6, Jenkins labored to assemble a force strong enough to oppose him. Col. John McCausland's infantry brigade and the Ringgold Battery, about to leave for the Shenandoah Valley, were recalled and stationed five miles north of the town.

Jenkins also found other regiments and several local militia companies to reinforce McCausland's position.

Knowing that Crook would march south on the road from Dublin to Pearisburg (present-day Rte. 100), McCausland arranged his force astride the road and on Shuffle Ridge south of Cloyd's Mountain on the James M. Cloyd farm. When Jenkins arrived on the field on the morning of Monday, May 9, he rearranged the Confederate line. He posted the 36th Virginia Regiment in reserve to the west of the road, with Capt. Thomas A. Bryan's battery and a 3-inch rifled gun of Capt. Crispin Dickenson's Ringgold Battery in front. Two of Dickenson's cannons unlimbered just east of the road. The 60th Virginia Infantry formed a line to the right of the cannons, and the third of Dickenson's guns was placed to the infantry's right. The Home Guard companies took up positions on the cannons' right. As skirmishing erupted in front of the line, the 45th

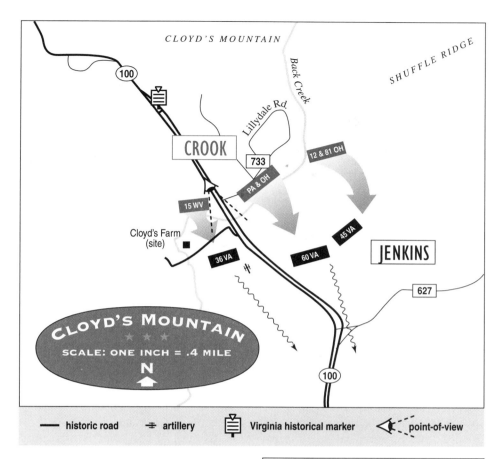

CLOYD'S MOUNTAIN

SHUFFLE RIDGE

Back Creek

100

Lillydale Rd.

CROOK

733

12 & 81 OH

PA & OH

15 WV

45 VA

Cloyd's Farm
(site)

36 VA

60 VA

JENKINS

627

CLOYD'S MOUNTAIN
★ ★ ★
SCALE: ONE INCH = .4 MILE

N

100

—— historic road   ⚏ artillery   📰 Virginia historical marker   ◁ point-of-view

Virginia Infantry Regiment under Col. William H. Browne arrived from Saltville and was posted to the right of the Home Guard, with Col. Alfred Beckley's battalion to the regiment's rear. The infantry quickly threw up fieldworks of fence rails, timber, and earth, creating a half-mile-long defensive line that sheltered some 2,400 soldiers.

Crook's troops, meanwhile, had marched out of their bivouac about two miles north of Cloyd's Mountain and headed south on the road to Dublin at 5 A.M. Crook's force consisted of three brigades: Col. Rutherford B. Hayes commanded the first; Col. Carr B. White, the second; and Col. Horatio G. Sickel, the third. A mile south of their bivouac, the Federals encountered their first Confederate pickets, and a mile farther on, at the

DIRECTIONS: I-81 Exit 98 (State Rte. 100 North, Dublin-Pearisburg); n. on State Rte. 100 about 6.7 miles past Rte. 733 (Lillydale Rd.) .6 mile to median pass-through on left and state historical marker K-38, Battle of Cloyd's Mountain. Marker is located to the right of the center of the Federal line. Facing s., the Confederate position is located across the Back Creek Valley on the next ridge and mostly e. (left) of the highway.

northern base of Cloyd's Mountain, Crook deployed his force to attack the main Confederate position that he expected to find atop the mountain. When he attained the summit, however, Crook discovered the actual location of Jenkins's line.

Crook's attack took advantage of the terrain and natural cover. He directed White's brigade to the Union left, into

From U.S. position, south to Cloyd Farm and 36th Virginia Infantry position on hill (right).
VIRGINIA DEPARTMENT OF HISTORIC RESOURCES, JOHN S. SALMON

thickets of pine at the southern base of the mountain. A local black guide would lead the brigade eastward through the trees and undergrowth to attack the Confederate right flank. Hayes's brigade, meanwhile, would descend the mountain and take its position near the edge of the woods in front of the Confederate line, with Sickel's brigade on its right. All three brigades would thereby be concealed while approaching as close to their objective as possible. Once they were in position, an artillery bombardment would begin; after three volleys, White's brigade would charge the Confederate right flank, and the other two brigades would assault the center and left. However, though it was a good plan, the thick undergrowth impeded its execution.

At about 11 A.M. the Federal bombardment began, and the Confederates responded immediately. On the Union left White quickly lost track of the number of volleys amid all the noise and attacked when he judged the time to be right. The 14th West Virginia (which had never before been in combat) and 12th Ohio led the charge but stalled in the open under heavy Confederate small-arms fire. Browne effectively shifted elements of the 45th Virginia and Beckley's battalion to strengthen the right flank. Meanwhile, Sickel heard the

combat to his left and launched his attack at about 11:30 A.M., not realizing that Hayes's brigade was still getting into position on his right. This attack, too, was stopped with heavy losses by Confederate small-arms and cannon fire.

Hayes, observing a defeat in the making, ordered his brigade to charge by the rear flank; that is, the last regiments filing into position would lead the brigade in an attack across the same ground as Sickel's brigade. The suddenness and determination of the attack carried it to the shelter of a small hill that protected the men from direct fire. Crook impulsively joined in the charge, which further invigorated the Federals. The brigade then edged forward to within twenty yards of the Confederate line and swept aside the Home Guard, capturing the 60th Virginia's fieldworks in a matter of minutes. Close and bloody combat followed for possession of the ground.

On the Confederate right flank, meanwhile, the 12th Ohio and 14th West Virginia fell back. Emboldened, Jenkins ordered Beckley's Battalion to charge. The Confederates rushed after the retreating Federals but ran headlong into the 9th West Virginia and 91st Ohio, waiting out of sight in reserve. The 91st Ohio cut down many in Beckley's Battalion, and then charged the Confederate flank. The 9th West Virginia assaulted the main line and engaged in desperate combat for twenty minutes. Jenkins was wounded by a bullet that shattered his left arm near the shoulder. The command then devolved to McCausland.

On the Confederate left, about the time that the 36th Virginia departed its reserve position to reinforce the right flank, the 15th West Virginia, which had remained behind in reserve when Sickel's brigade charged, attacked Bryan's battery. Learning of the attack, McCausland ordered the 36th Virginia to halt and return to counter the attack on the left. Confused by the change of orders, the 36th began to fall back. Suddenly the rest of the Confederate line collapsed and retreated to a second crest south of Shuffle Ridge. There McCausland fought a brief but bloody holding action to save his artillery and enable the walking wounded to escape to Dublin. Crook marched on to Dublin, destroyed the railroad depot and the supplies stored there, and burned the New River Bridge that night.

For a battle that lasted little more than an hour, Cloyd's Mountain devastated both sides. The Confederates lost 538, or 23 percent of the force engaged, while the Federals suffered 688 casualties, or 10 percent. Surgeons amputated Jenkins's arm; he was captured and then paroled, dying of his wound on May 21.

The Cloyd's Mountain battlefield retains much of its integrity, particularly the Confederate positions. The battlefield may be threatened, however, by a planned industrial park. A residential community occupies most of the initial Federal position east of Rte. 100. The roadway has been widened to four lanes. ■

COVE MOUNTAIN

As Brig. Gen. George Crook marched toward Dublin early in May 1864, Brig. Gen. William W. Averell led some 2,000 men of his cavalry division from Logan Court House, West Virginia. His objective was Saltville, located seventy miles away, where Virginia's largest saltworks were located. After destroying the works, he was to unite his force with Crook's, then join Maj. Gen. Franz Sigel at Staunton.

When Averell reached Tazewell Court House on May 8, he was informed that Confederate infantry and cavalry under Brig. Gen. William E. "Grumble" Jones and Brig. Gen. John Hunt Morgan were defending Saltville. Concluding that the combined force was too strong to attack successfully, Averell turned southeast to Wytheville to prevent Confederate forces from concentrating against Crook, and to destroy the nearby lead works.

Morgan soon learned that Averell had changed plans and rode toward Wytheville. To Averell's surprise, Jones already was there, having utilized the railroad to move his men, blocking the

View south to Allan Crockett house and route of Jones's attack. VIRGINIA DEPARTMENT OF HISTORIC RESOURCES, JOHN S. SALMON

Raleigh & Grayson Turnpike (present-day Rtes. 600 and 610) northeast of the town near the foot of Cove Mountain. The two forces engaged in midafternoon on Tuesday, May 10.

Averell's division was composed of two brigades, one commanded by Brig. Gen. Alfred N. A. Duffié and the other by Col. James M. Schoonmaker. The latter, the 14th Pennsylvania and the 1st West Virginia Cavalry, skirmished with the Confederates while Duffié's brigade deployed, then formed the Federal right. The 2nd

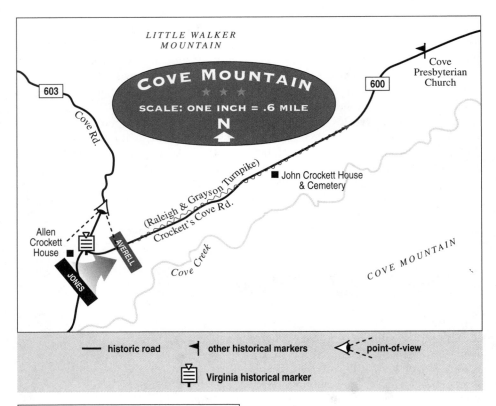

LITTLE WALKER MOUNTAIN

COVE MOUNTAIN
★ ★ ★
SCALE: ONE INCH = .6 MILE
N

603

Cove Rd.

600

Cove Presbyterian Church

(Raleigh & Grayson Turnpike)
Crockett's Cove Rd.

■ John Crockett House & Cemetery

Allen Crockett House ■

AVERELL

JONES

Cove Creek

COVE MOUNTAIN

—— historic road   ◀ other historical markers   ◀⋯ point-of-view

Virginia historical marker

DIRECTIONS: I-81 Exit 72 (I-77 North, Bluefield-Charleston, W.Va.), n. on I-77 North to Exit 41 (Rte. 610, Pepper's Ferry Rd.); e. (right) on Rte. 610 about .8 mile to Rte. 603 (Cove Rd.) on top of hill to right; n. (right) on Rte. 603 4.5 miles to Rte. 600 (note Allen Crockett house on left just before intersection); e. (right) on Rte. 600 (Crockett's Cove Rd.) and state historical marker KD-9, Crockett's Cove, immediately on right; continue 1.2 miles to John Crockett house and family cemetery on right; continue 1.3 miles to Cove Presbyterian Church and United Daughters of the Confederacy marker (if gate is unlocked); return to I-77.

West Virginia Cavalry was positioned on the Union left, the 34th Ohio Mounted Infantry (dismounted) on the right, and the 3rd West Virginia Cavalry on the extreme left.

Jones maneuvered against each of Averell's flanks after Morgan arrived, but the Federals held firm. When Schoonmaker's brigade wavered under the Con-

federate attack on the Union right, the 34th Ohio filled the breach and enabled the brigade to reform. Likewise, the 2nd West Virginia returned fire effectively and held off the Confederates. The engagement continued for four hours until darkness ended. The next day Averell marched east to join Crook.

Averell reported that he lost 114 officers and men killed and wounded; Jones's and Morgan's losses may have amounted to almost 200. Some of the Federal wounded were left behind at Cove Presbyterian Church, where local citizens cared for them.

The Cove Mountain battlefield retains most of its integrity; two historic houses, a cemetery, and Cove Presbyterian Church are extant. Some development is creeping east from Wytheville, but at present it is located to the west of this pristine agricultural valley. ■

In the South during the Civil War, salt was essential to preserve meat as well as tan leather for saddles and shoes. Saltville, Virginia, located five miles north of the Virginia & Tennessee Railroad, produced 200 million pounds of salt in 1864, more than all the other saltworks in the Confederacy combined. Late in September 1864, Brig. Gen. Stephen G. Burbridge commanded a Federal expedition to destroy the strategically important saltworks there. To divert Confederate attention from his raid, he ordered Brig. Gen. Jacob Ammen to secure Bull's Gap in Tennessee while Brig. Gen. Alvan C. Gillem attacked nearby Jonesborough. Burbridge, meanwhile, would lead Brig. Gen. Nathaniel C. McLean's division to seize Saltville.

DIRECTIONS: I-81 Exit 35 (Chilhowie, State Rte. 107 North), n. on State Rte. 107 North about 7.1 miles to scenic overlook on left *(Exercise caution: overlook is located on a curve on a downhill grade)* and state historical marker K-28, Saltville History; continue n. on State Rte. 107 (Worthy Blvd.) 1.4 miles to State Rte. 91; n.e. (right) on State Rte. 91 .3 mile to Buckeye St.; n. (right) on Buckeye St. and turn left at first intersection .3 mile to town park and Virginia Civil War Trail marker on left; return to State Rte. 91; right on State Rte. 91 .4 mile to Rte. 632 (Cedar Branch Rd.); e. (right) on Rte. 632 1.1 miles to Federal position; retrace route to State Rte. 91; s.w. (left) on State Rte. 91 1 mile to stoplight at Rte. 634 (Allison Gap Rd.); n. (right) on Rte. 634 .4 mile to parking area on left at railroad track just before Loretta C. Norris Bridge over Holston River; to visit site of saltworks, return to State Rte. 91 on Rte. 634; s.w. (right) on State Rte. 91 .1 mile to Y intersection with Rte. 610 (Palmer Ave.); s. (left) on Rte. 610 .5 mile to Wellfields Recreation Park (saltworks were located on right); return to I-81.

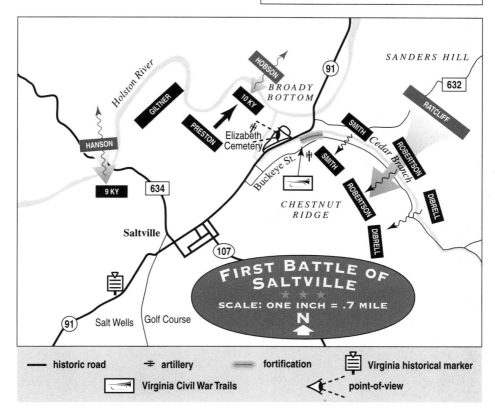

Burbridge's command consisted of three brigades of Kentucky cavalry, several regiments of mounted infantry, and three sections of mountain howitzers. The force would be joined en route by the 5th United States Colored Cavalry Regiment, then being organized. Ammen and Gillem also would join in the attack with their 2,450 men once they had accomplished their diversionary missions. Absent their detachments, Burbridge's command numbered about 5,200.

The Confederates soon discovered Burbridge's operation and moved to counter it. Brig. Gen. John Echols, administrator of the Department of Southwest Virginia, sent telegrams far and wide to organize an army to defend Saltville. It included Col. Henry L. Giltner's cavalry brigade, Col. Robert T. Preston's regiment of Virginia reserves, and Brig. Gen. John S. "Cerro Gordo" Williams's cavalry division. He also ordered Brig. Gen. John C. Vaughn's cavalry brigade to Bull's Gap to impede Ammen and Gillem. Most of the regiments and brigades were well below full strength.

Already in Saltville, under the command of Lt. Col. Robert Smith, was the 13th Battalion Virginia Reserves, made up of under- and overaged local men. Most of the officers and soldiers, however, were away on leave of one kind or another. Making do with the men he had available, Smith began erecting earthworks under the direction of Brig. Gen. Alfred E. Jackson. Skirmishing erupted about three miles northeast of Saltville on the morning of Sunday, October 2, on the main road (present-day Rte. 91) guarded by Giltner's pickets. Burbridge's third brigade, under the command of Col. Robert W. Ratliff, forced them back to the hills just east of the town. About the same time, a makeshift Confederate cavalry brigade arrived in Saltville under the command of Col. Felix H. Robertson. Additional reinforcements also trickled in, until by midmorning perhaps 2,800 had arrived. As the senior brigadier, Williams took command and made the final troop dispositions.

Saltville is located in a narrow part of Rich Valley, on a small plain southeast of Holston River. Little Mountain and Allison Gap are located across the river just northwest of the town. A cluster of steep hills called Chestnut Ridge looms over the northeastern end of Saltville. There Williams positioned most of his troops behind earthworks prepared by Smith and Jackson, to block the Federal approach from the northeast.

The 9th Kentucky Cavalry guarded the Allison Gap road (Rte. 634) at Holston River. To the regiment's right, Williams placed Giltner's brigade and the 10th Kentucky Cavalry Battalion, which covered a Holston River ford at Broddy's Bottom on the brigade's right flank. Next came Smith's 13th Battalion Virginia Reserves, which was posted forward of the main line across Cedar Creek, a tributary of Holston River. On the right flank and also across the creek were Robertson's brigade and Col. George G. Dibrell's Tennessee brigade. Williams stationed Capt. John W. Barr's three-gun battery behind Giltner's right flank and put Capt. Hugh L. W. McClung's four-gun Tennessee battery atop Chestnut Ridge facing northeast to cover the main Federal route of approach.

At about 11 A.M. the battle opened with Col. Robert W. Ratcliff's brigade on the Union left, Brig. Gen. Edward H. Hobson's brigade in the center, and Col. Charles Hanson's brigade en route to the right. Burbridge's six mountain howitzers, posted on the south slope of Little Mountain overlooking Broddy's Bottom engaged in a futile duel with the Confederate guns while Hanson marched west behind them and Hobson got in position below them in the bottom. On the Federal left, Col. Robert W. Ratcliff deployed his brigade: the 5th U.S. Colored Cavalry (which included parts of the 6th U.S. Colored Cavalry as well as new recruits from other black units) on his left flank, the 12th Ohio Cavalry in the center, and the 11th Michigan Cavalry on the right. They drove Smith's battalion back across Cedar Creek and pressed Dibrell and Robertson. The Confederates had heard rumors that Burbridge's force included black soldiers; seeing them infuriated many in Robertson's and Dibrell's commands.

Elizabeth Cemetery, site of C.S.A. battery and counterattack. VIRGINIA DEPARTMENT OF HISTORIC RESOURCES, JOHN S. SALMON

Hard pressed, the Confederate right drew slowly back across Cedar Creek to the first of its successive lines of prepared earthworks on the hill there. When the Federals emerged from the undergrowth bordering the creek, the 5th U.S. Colored Cavalry had shifted to the front of the other regiments and led the attack. The fighting had raged back and forth for three hours when Robertson withdrew his brigade from the first line of fieldworks back to the second, leaving a gap between his and Dibrell's brigade. The 12th Ohio Cavalry charged into the gap, and Dibrell's brigade fell back to join Robertson's. Both sides began running out of ammunition. At about 5 P.M. Dibrell and Robertson retired once more to a new line on the eastern edge of town, and Ratcliff took possession of Chestnut Ridge.

While the principal combat was taking place on the Union left, at about 1 P.M. Hobson charged across Broddy's Bottom Ford and scaled the bluff on the south side to attack the 10th Kentucky Cavalry Battalion commanded by Lt. Col. Edwin Trimble. The attack failed, despite Trimble's being killed, when reinforcements rushed to the position. Hobson retreated across the river after fifteen minutes of hard fighting.

On the Federal right, Hanson's brigade likewise crossed the river shortly after noon, hoping to climb the high bluffs and turn the Confederate left. The Confederate artillery, however, quickly pinned down the Union brigade at the base of the bluffs, and after a couple of hours it, too, withdrew to the north side of Holston River.

With both sides out of ammunition, the fighting ended soon after 5 P.M. When two small Confederate cavalry brigades rode into Saltville to further strengthen the garrison, Burbridge abandoned the fight. The Federals withdrew in the night, leaving their dead and many of their wounded on the field.

What happened next has been the subject of debate among historians, but there seems to be little question that some Confederates murdered wounded black soldiers from the 5th U.S. Colored Cavalry. A newspaper later reported that 150 black soldiers were massacred. This number exceeds, however, the total number of casualties reported for the 5th U.S. Colored Cavalry: 22 killed in action, 37 wounded (most of whom presumably joined in the retreat if they were able), and 53 missing. Four of the total were white officers. According to the most reliable eyewitness accounts, the number of soldiers murdered was between five and a dozen. (Late in 1999, Radford University archaeologists and geologists began combining field surveys with high-altitude photographs produced by NASA to identify and excavate alleged mass grave sites.)

The first battle at Saltville thus ended in failure for the Federals, who suffered about 350 casualties to the Confederates' 108. The Confederate salt supply, there-fore, was safe for the time being.

The Confederate earthworks at Saltville on the west side of Cedar Creek have largely been obliterated by residential development. The initial positions on the east side remain agricultural, however, and the battlefield is still "readable" as such. ■

MARION

The Federal raids against the Confederate infrastructure in East Tennessee and Southwest Virginia continued into the fall of 1864. In November Maj. Gen. George Stoneman and his 4,200-man cavalry division, part of it commanded by Brig. Gen. Stephen G. Burbridge, set out to destroy iron and lead mines, saltworks, and railroads throughout the region; reinforced by Brig. Gen. Alvan C. Gillem's brigade, the force numbered about 5,500. After Stoneman defeated the Confederate defenders of Kingsport and Bristol, Tennessee, Maj. Gen. John C. Breckinridge evacuated his fortifications at Saltville to pursue him.

Breckinridge's force consisted of the understrength cavalry brigades of Brig. Gen. Basil W. Duke, Col. Henry L. Giltner, and Brig. Gen. George B. Cosby, about 900 men in all. Breckinridge separated Lt. Col. Vincent A. Witcher's cavalry brigade from the main body and sent it in pursuit of Stoneman. The 34th harassed the Federal rear guard almost to Wytheville, where Stoneman destroyed the lead works and most of the public buildings. The Federals then turned on Witcher and forced him back about a mile east of Marion, where Breckinridge was waiting.

Stoneman and Burbridge closed on the Confederates late in the afternoon of Saturday, December 17. Breckinridge had posted Giltner to the left of a covered

View west to Cosby's position and Holston River. VIRGINIA DEPARTMENT OF HISTORIC RESOURCES, JOHN S. SALMON

bridge over the river, Duke on the right, and Cosby in front of the bridge. Aside from skirmishing, combat had to wait for daylight.

The next day the Federal attacks began in earnest. Although outnumbered four to one, the Confederates beat back repeated assaults. At about 3 P.M. Gillem marched to envelop Breckinridge's flank but retired in a confusion of orders.

That night, his ammunition almost exhausted, Breckinridge decided to retreat to Mount Airy, North Carolina. His force

MARION
★ ★ ★
SCALE: ONE INCH = .3 MILE
N

714

Holston River

11

81

EXIT 47

GILTNER

STONEMAN

Marion

COSBY

BRECKINRIDGE

DUKE

11

WITCHER

Middle Fork

81

——— historic road   Virginia historical marker   point-of-view

DIRECTIONS: I-81 Exit 47 (Marion, U.S. Rte. 11); w. (left) on U.S. Rte. 11 about .4 mile to state historical marker K-26, Battle of Marion, on left; return to U.S. Rte. 11 and I-81.

slipped away from Marion undetected, handing the victory to Stoneman. The next day, however, he found his way blocked by Col. Harvey M. Buckley's 54th Kentucky Mounted Infantry and therefore turned away from North Carolina toward Wytheville. Stoneman, unimpeded, marched toward Saltville. The two sides suffered perhaps 300 casualties altogether at Marion.

A state historical marker notes the vicinity of the battlefield on U.S. Rte. 11 at the eastern limits of Marion. Residential and commercial development have crept out from the town, but the area is not so heavily developed that the battle cannot be understood. ▪

SECOND BATTLE OF SALTVILLE

After his victory by default at Marion on December 18, 1864, Maj. Gen. George Stoneman and his 5,500-man force turned toward Saltville. The main Federal force, commanded by Brig. Gen. Stephen G. Burbridge, marched northwest from Chilhowie along present-day Rte. 107. Stoneman then sent Brig. Gen. Alvan C. Gillem's brigade circling westward to approach from the southwest.

The Confederate garrison had considerably strengthened the fortifications around Saltville since the October battle. Whereas the original fieldworks had been built east of town, additional works had been constructed on hills to the south and west to protect the saltworks themselves. South of the saltworks, Fort Statham overlooked Burbridge's route. Southwest of town, Fort Breckinridge had been erected on a high hill. West of Saltville and northwest of

DIRECTIONS: I-81 Exit 35 (Chilhowie, State Rte. 107 North); left on State Rte. 107 North about 7.1 miles to scenic overlook on left *(Exercise caution: overlook is located on a curve on a downhill grade)* and state historical marker K-28, Saltville History; continue n. on State Rte. 107 1.4 miles to State Rte. 91; s.w. (left) on State Rte. 91 .4 mile to Rte. 610 (Palmer Ave.); s. (left) on Rte. 610 .5 mile to Wellfields Recreation Park (saltworks were located on right) and Lake Dr.; w. (right) on Lake Dr. .7 mile to State Rte. 91; w. (left) on State Rte. 91 .1 mile to Salt Park and Virginia Civil War Trails markers; return to State Rte. 91; e. (left) on State Rte. 91 .7 mile to state historical marker KB-6, Saltville; continue e. on State Rte. 91 and retrace route to I-81.

Fort Breckinridge, Fort Hatton likewise guarded the road.

On Tuesday, December 20, the Federals approached Saltville late in the rainy, foggy afternoon. Confederate skirmishers below Fort Statham fell back to the fort when Burbridge drove forward. Burbridge

View from scenic overlook north to saltworks site (center and left) and Saltville (right). VIRGINIA DEPARTMENT OF HISTORIC RESOURCES, JOHN S. SALMON

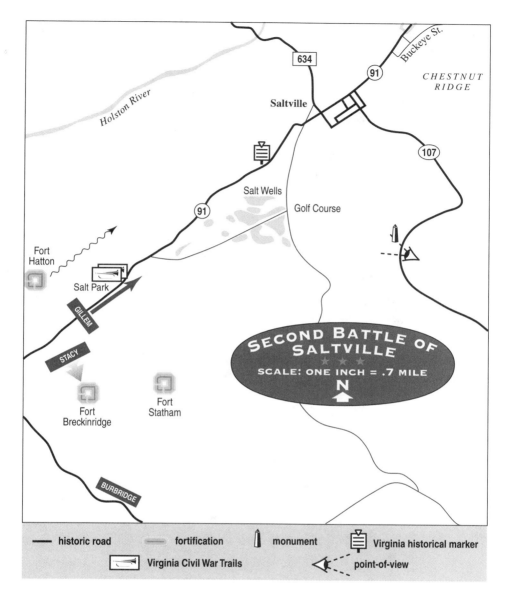

— historic road	— fortification	▮ monument
	▤ Virginia Civil War Trails	◀⋯ point-of-view

historic road   fortification   monument   Virginia historical marker

Virginia Civil War Trails   point-of-view

suggested a coordinated attack with Gillem, who was in position about a mile west, but darkness was falling too quickly to implement it. On his own, however, Gillem sent two of his battalions under Lt. Col. Brazilliah Stacy around Fort Breckinridge. In the gloom, they passed the Confederate pickets unnoticed and turned east toward Saltville. Finally detected as they led their horses up the hill, they remounted and charged over the crest into the fort. The defenders fled, as did the troops in nearby Fort Hatton. Stacy led his men out of Fort Breckinridge, reunited them with the rest of Gillem's command, and marched to the saltworks. By midnight the buildings there were in flames, and Fort Statham also was in Union hands. The town's local defense forces had vanished into the darkness.

The Federals spent the remainder of the night destroying the saltworks, finishing their task about dawn on December 21. Although the Confederates later made some repairs, the saltworks were effectively out of production for the rest of the war. The second engagement at Saltville cost the two sides an estimated 275 casualties.

Remnants of the Confederate fortifications survive on the hills surrounding Saltville, but they are wooded and largely inaccessible. The saltworks site is a public park. For exhibition purposes, parts of the saltworks have been reconstructed. ■

Richmond and Petersburg Campaign, 1864–1865

From early May to early June 1864, the Army of the Potomac and the Army of Northern Virginia bled each other white to little advantage for either side. Lt. Gen. Ulysses S. Grant had not defeated Gen. Robert E. Lee, nor had Lee vanquished Grant. Despite enormous casualties, neither side had achieved its goals; in particular, Grant had not captured Richmond. After all the maneuvering and fighting, Lee and Grant were stalemated.

While the two main armies contended from the Wilderness to Cold Harbor, Maj. Gen. Benjamin F. Butler's Army of the James fought a series of desultory actions and then withdrew behind its fortifications on the Bermuda Hundred peninsula. The Confederate defense force commanded by Gen. P. G. T. Beauregard constructed a system of fieldworks called the Howlett line that paralleled the Federal works and—assisted by Butler's willingness to sit and wait for further orders—effectively "bottled up" his army there for several weeks.

On June 9, Butler finally acted, attacking Petersburg with some 4,500 cavalry and infantry from City Point under Maj. Gen. Quincy A. Gillmore. Petersburg's 2,500 Confederate defenders—most of them Home Guards—were sheltered behind the so-called Dimmock line, a ten-mile-long series of fortifications named for their designer, Capt. Charles H. Dimmock. The line extended around the eastern, southern, and western approaches to the city on the Appomattox River, and Brig. Gen. Henry A. Wise, a former governor of Virginia, commanded the garrison.

While Gillmore and the infantry demonstrated against the northeastern part of the line, Brig. Gen. August V. Kautz led his cavalry division south to the Jerusalem Plank Road, then north to the underbelly of the Dimmock line. He drove through a redoubt designated Battery 27 that was defended by the city militia, but was stopped at the city limits by reinforcements sent from Bermuda Hundred. By midafternoon Butler's thrust at Petersburg had ended in failure, and the Federals withdrew. The two sides suffered about 120 casualties.

To the north, meanwhile, Grant was faced with two choices: Continue to pound Lee's army directly and attempt to drive through to Richmond, or bypass Lee's right flank to the James River and points south, thereby threatening both Richmond and Petersburg, and perhaps engage Lee on more favorable ground. Confronting the prospect of another bloody but fruitless engagement like that at Cold Harbor on June 3, Grant chose the indirect approach and issued orders to Maj. Gen. George G. Meade, the commander of the Army of the Potomac. During the night of June 12, the army disengaged from the Cold Harbor line and marched south to the James River at Wilcox's Landing and Windmill Point.

This logistical feat left Lee seething when he found his adversary vanished on the morning of June 13. After a few days Lee discovered that Grant was crossing the river rather than massing his army behind McClellan's old earthworks. The Confederate commander must have reached his

RICHMOND & PETERSBURG CAMPAIGN, 1864–1865

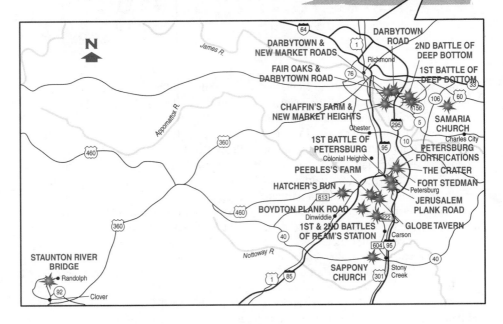

conclusion with some trepidation since earlier he had determined to destroy Grant's army before it got to the James River. If that happened, it would be only a question of time for the Army of Northern Virginia.

The Army of the Potomac crossed the James River in four days beginning June 14, using transport vessels and a 2,200-foot-long pontoon bridge hastily constructed at Weyanoke Point. Even before the entire army had passed over the river, however, Grant ordered an assault on the Petersburg fortifications. His subordinates carried out a series of attacks that lasted four days.

Maj. Gen. William F. "Baldy" Smith led XVIII Corps from Point of Rocks Landing on the Appomattox River and began the attacks in the evening of June 15. He breached the northeastern part of the Dimmock line and forced Wise's men

back to Harrison's Creek, where darkness ended the day's combat. After sundown Maj. Gen. Winfield Scott Hancock's II Corps, which had just arrived at Petersburg after the march from Cold Harbor, relieved Smith's men. Hancock captured another part of the Dimmock line the next day, and Maj. Gen. Ambrose E. Burnside's IX Corps did the same on June 17.

The Confederates, meanwhile, strove mightily to bolster the city's defenses. Beauregard stripped the Howlett line at Bermuda Hundred of every available resource, and Lee rushed troops south to reinforce the garrison at Petersburg. On June 18 Maj. Gen. Gouverneur K. Warren's V Corps joined the II and IX Corps in an all-out attack, but it was repulsed with frightful casualties. Grant then abandoned the effort and began what he believed would be a short siege of Petersburg. The four days of combat resulted in 8,150 Federal and 3,236 Confederate casualties.

Several intermediate objectives eventually comprised Grant's overall strategy during the siege: Cut the city's lines of communication and supply, divert Lee's attention and resources by attacking Richmond's defenses, and stretch the Confederate defenses to the breaking point by extending the Federal lines south- and westward. Initially, Grant concentrated on the first objective by attempting to destroy the three railroads that served Petersburg and Richmond that were not in Union hands. As the Federals extended their lines, they also constructed the U.S. Military Railroad to transport food and ammunition from City Point to distribution areas near the front. This remarkable engineering accomplishment was constructed with little grading, with ties and rails laid directly on the ground.

On June 21 Hancock's II Corps (led temporarily by Maj. Gen. David B. Birney), supported by Maj. Gen. Horatio G. Wright's VI Corps and preceded by Brig. Gen. James H. Wilson's cavalry division, struck at the Petersburg Railroad. One day later, assisted by Maj. Gen. Cadmus Wilcox's division, Maj. Gen. William Mahone's division of Lt. Gen. A. P. Hill's corps counterattacked and drove the II Corps back east to the Jerusalem Plank Road. The Federals had to abandon their advanced positions but still gained ground—at a cost of about 4,000 casualties for the two combatants.

On the north side of the James River, meanwhile, Maj. Gen. Philip H. Sheridan and his cavalry division were returning to the Army of the Potomac after their unsuccessful attack on the Virginia Central Railroad at Trevilian Station on June 11–12. Maj. Gen. Wade Hampton's cavalry division pursued the Federals and attempted to intercept them at Samaria (Saint Mary's)

Church in Charles City County. Sheridan fought a delaying action there on June 24 to protect his supply train, then rejoined the Union army at Bermuda Hundred. This engagement produced some 630 total casualties.

The attack on the Petersburg Railroad on June 21 signaled the beginning of what has come to be called the Wilson-Kautz Raid of June 22–30. Brig. Gen. James H. Wilson and Brig. Gen. August V. Kautz led their respective divisions, some 3,300 troopers, down the South Side Railroad, then southwest along the Richmond & Danville Railroad to destroy track. On June 25 at Staunton River Bridge, their principal objective located just south of Roanoke Station, the cavalrymen encountered a makeshift defense force under Capt. Benjamin L. Farinholt. Repeated attacks failed to dislodge the Confederate defenders, which included civilians as well as regular troops, and the Federals withdrew. They lost 42 killed, 44 wounded, and 30 missing or captured, while Farinholt lost 10 killed and 24 wounded.

Maj. Gen. William H. F. "Rooney" Lee's cavalry division pursued the raiders. At Sappony Church in Sussex County, elements of Lee's division and then Hampton's attacked the Federals on June 28. During the night, Kautz and Wilson disengaged and rode north toward Petersburg, eager to return to Union lines.

They thought they would be secure once they reached Ream's Station, expecting to find Union infantry. However, Kautz, who arrived there first while Wilson fought a rearguard action against Lee, found Mahone's Confederate division occupying the place instead. The Federals were virtually surrounded, and Mahone attacked their front while Lee threatened their left flank. Abandoning their artillery and burning their wagons, Kautz and Wilson cut their way out of the trap and fled.

Kautz and his men reached the Union lines by dark, while Wilson swung east and then north, eventually reaching safety on July 2. Even though the Wilson-Kautz Raid succeeded in tearing up some sixty miles of track, a heavy price was paid in horses and men—about 1,800 human casualties for the raid.

Grant concentrated on the siege for the next month but grew increasingly frustrated when no results seemed apparent. He decided to attack the Petersburg defenses on July 30 after forcing Lee to weaken his lines there by expending troops in the defense of Richmond. During the night of July 26–27, II Corps and two divisions of Sheridan's cavalry under Hancock's overall command crossed to the north side of the James River at Deep Bottom to threaten the Confederate capital. The defenders quickly reinforced their lines, however, and foiled Union attempts to capture positions at New Market Heights and Fussell's Mill. Hancock recrossed the river during the night of July 29 but left a garrison at Deep Bottom. The expedition cost some 1,000 casualties.

The attack on Petersburg began as scheduled, but in a shocking manner. One day near the end of June, Lt. Col. Henry Pleasants, a civil engineer and commander of the 48th Pennsylvania Regiment, had studied the Confederate lines from his own about two hundred yards away. It occurred to him that a gallery could be dug from his lines to the enemy's, filled with gunpowder, and ignited; the explosion would produce a gap large enough to push a division through. He took his idea to Burnside, who approved it. At noon on June 25, the digging began, with Pennsylvania coal miners turned soldiers doing the work. They finished excavating on July 23, packed the far end of the tunnel with four tons of gunpowder, and waited for the day of the attack. At 4:44 A.M. on July 30, the powder exploded in a great burst of flame and smoke, killing or wounding 278 of the 330 Confederate soldiers and gunners located above the gallery and creating an enormous crater.

After that initial success, virtually everything went wrong for the Federals in the battle of the Crater. A plan to send troops around the sides of the opening had been disapproved by Meade in favor of a direct assault through the gap. The folly of the new plan quickly became apparent when the attacking brigades bogged down in the loose soil of the crater, unable to gain footholds to climb out. On the other side Mahone rushed troops forward to the rim of the crater, which soon became a death trap, and the Union breakthrough was repulsed. The United States Colored Troops (USCTs) that were ordered to attack even after it became obvious that the assault would fail suffered especially heavy casualties. When the fighting ended in the afternoon, some 5,300 men lay dead or wounded, the Confederates had recovered all the ground, and Grant's best chance of ending the siege by a coup du main had evaporated.

Grant, disgusted, relieved Burnside of command and returned to his strategy of combining demonstrations against Richmond with raids on the railroads that served Petersburg. On the night of August 13–14, Hancock led the II and X Corps and Brig. Gen. David M. Gregg's cavalry division back across the James River to Deep Bottom. After sunrise, X Corps approached New Market Heights with II Corps to the right near Fussell's Mill. The next day Union assaults near the mill initially succeeded, but Confederate counterattacks drove the Federals out of a line of captured works. Hancock began to withdraw, and heavy skirmishing continued until his command crossed to the south side of the river on August 20, once again leaving a garrison at Deep Bottom. Some 4,600 men had become casualties during this diversion.

The purpose of the expedition had been to divert Lee's attention from yet another attack on the Petersburg Railroad. Warren led the V Corps, with elements of the II and IX Corps following, on the railroad raid. On August 18 he attacked near Globe Tavern and drove in Confederate pickets. A subsequent Federal attack was repulsed, and both sides entrenched during the night. The next day Mahone attacked and rolled up Warren's right flank, but Warren counterattacked and with help from IX Corps recaptured the ground lost earlier. With the two sides effectively stalemated, Warren improved and extended his entrenchments on August 20 until they were connected with the main Union line from the Jerusalem Plank Road and paralleled the Petersburg Railroad. Hill probed the new lines the next day but could not penetrate them. The Globe Tavern engagement resulted in the extension of the Federal siege lines south and west, securing a stranglehold on the Petersburg Railroad about five miles south of the town. Henceforth, the Confederates would have to offload supplies from North Carolina at the Stony Creek depot some twenty miles south of the city and haul them to Petersburg by wagon on the Boydton Plank Road. About 6,055 men were killed or wounded during the four days of fighting.

Not every Federal expedition met with success. On August 23 Gregg's cavalry division led Brig. Gen. Nelson A. Miles's division of Hancock's II Corps south along the Petersburg Railroad to destroy track. The objective was Rowanty Creek, about ten miles from the Union lines and five miles beyond Ream's Station. Brig. Gen. John Gibbon's division joined Miles's men the next day, by which time Lee had dispatched eight brigades of infantry under

Hill and two cavalry divisions under Hampton to attack the outpost. The Federals had begun improving the old earthworks that had been built there in June near the station, but they made little headway before they were attacked. Hill, who was unwell, turned over tactical control of the battle to Maj. Gen. Henry Heth, whose foot soldiers were supported by Hampton's cavalry and Col. William J. "Willie" Pegram's artillery. Near dark on August 25, almost encircled, Hancock gave orders to withdraw. By 9 P.M. the Federals had disengaged and headed back to the Union lines east of Petersburg, but not before losing some 2,600 men, most of them captured. Heth and Hampton lost about 800.

During the next month, Grant's army improved its siege lines and prepared for the coming round of combat. On the night of September 28–29, Butler led most of the Army of the James across the river for another assault on Richmond's defenses. At dawn he launched a two-pronged attack against the outer Confederate fieldworks at Chaffin's Farm and New Market Heights. The principal objective was the stronghold of Fort Harrison at Chaffin's Farm. The attack on the works at the foot of New Market Heights was designed to protect the right flank of the main force as it turned toward the fort. (The USCTs, whose combat role Butler had long championed, performed especially well. Fourteen of the sixteen Medals of Honor awarded to black soldiers during the war were awarded for gallantry in this action.) Fort Harrison fell to the Federals, who held it despite a counterattack on September 30 overseen by Lee himself. With Butler's men firmly established in the captured lines, Lee had no choice but to post troops north of the James to guard against a renewed Union advance on the city. Now it was up to Grant to keep the pressure on Lee.

The Army of Northern Virginia had lost its ability to maneuver, unless it abandoned Richmond and Peterburg to the Federals and took to the field again. Politically, it was not possible to flee the capital; strategically, Lee lacked the manpower to defeat Grant or break through the Union lines into the open; tactically, Lee could only delay the inevitable collapse of his own lines as Grant's manuevers extended them to the breaking point.

Scarcely had the Federals captured Fort Harrison than they moved against the Confederate lines of communication southwest of Petersburg. On September 30 two divisions of Maj. Gen. John G. Parke's IX Corps, two divisions of Warren's V Corps, and Gregg's cavalry division marched by Poplar Spring Church to reach Vaughan Road. The initial Federal attack overran Fort Archer, and the Confederates abandoned their Squirrel Level Road line. Late in the afternoon Confederate reinforcements arrived and soon slowed the Federal advance. The next day the Federals repulsed a counterattack directed by Hill. Reinforced by a II Corps division, the Federals resumed their advance on October 2 and extended their left flank and fieldworks west to Arthur's Swamp. The two sides suffered some 4,200 casualties; once again, the Union lines crept westward.

Hopeful of recapturing Fort Harrison, Lee countered Grant's tactics with his own actions. On October 7 he launched an offensive against the Union right flank that resulted in combat on the Darbytown and New Market Roads. The attack met with success as the divisions commanded by Maj. Gen. Charles W. Field and Maj. Gen. Robert F. Hoke routed Kautz's cavalrymen on Darbytown Road and then assaulted the main Union line on New Market Road. There the attack stalled and then collapsed as the well-entrenched Federals held their ground and the Confederates withdrew. The casualties totaled some 1,750.

A week later, on October 13, Brig. Gen. Alfred H. Terry led two divisions of his corps against the Confederate defenses newly constructed along Darbytown Road. One of Terry's brigades assaulted what appeared to be a weak point in the fortifications and was repulsed with heavy losses. Suffering most of the nearly 500 casualties, the Federals then retired to their own lines.

Grant initiated a combined attack on the defenses of both Petersburg and Richmond on October 27 with little success. Hancock, leading divisions from the II, V, and IX Corps, as well as Gregg's cavalry division, marched west across the Boydton Plank Road toward the South Side Railroad. Although the Federals gained a lodgment on the plank road, an afternoon counterattack by Heth's division of Hill's corps and Hampton's cavalry forced a retreat that was completed the next day at a cost of 3,000 total casualties. North of the James River, Butler attacked the Confederate lines on Darbytown Road and at Fair Oaks. The defenders counterattacked and easily repulsed the Federals. The two sides lost some 1,750 men.

For the next three months, each army concentrated mostly on conserving its resources and strengthening its lines around the two cities. Early in February 1865, however, Grant broke the stalemate with vigorous drives to extend the Petersburg lines westward and cut off Lee's supply lines for good. The first operation occurred on February 5 in the vicinity of Hatcher's Run, when Gregg led his cavalry division to the Boydton Plank Road by way of Ream's Station and Dinwiddie Court House in order to intercept a wagon train reputedly hauling Confederate supplies (none were found). To protect Gregg, Warren led the V Corps across Hatcher's Run to block Vaughan Road while two divisions of Maj. Gen. Andrew A. Humphreys's II Corps (he had replaced the wounded Hancock in November 1864) covered Warren's right flank at Armstrong's Mill. Late in the day Maj. Gen. Henry Heth tried to turn Humphreys's right flank near the mill but was repulsed. During the night, two divisions reinforced the Federals, and Gregg returned to Gravelly Run on Vaughan Road from his unsuccessful raid. The next day a division of Warren's corps was attacked near the site of Dabney's steam sawmill. Although this attack checked the Union advance, the Federals nonetheless extended their fieldworks to the Vaughan Road crossing of Hatcher's Run.

His lines now stretched to the point of rupturing, Lee tried a desperate gamble on March 25. He assembled half of his available forces in an attempt to break through the northeastern portion of the deep Federal works and threaten Grant's supply depot at City Point. Before dawn Gordon led an attack that overwhelmed Fort Stedman and nearby Batteries X, XI, and XII in the IX Corps sector, but the Confederate drive soon sputtered to a halt amid a murderous crossfire and furious counterattacks. More than 1,900 Confederates were captured, another 1,000 were killed or wounded against 950 Federals, and Lee's last hope was dashed. Late in the afternoon Wright's VI Corps drove the Confederate pickets from their trenches north of Fort Fisher, thereby advancing the Federal line closer to its objective. Lee's prophecy about the outcome of the siege had come true. Time was running out for the Army of Northern Virginia. ■

FIRST BATTLE OF PETERSBURG

In 1862 Capt. Charles H. Dimmock had superintended the construction of a ten-mile-long series of fortifications—the Dimmock line—including fifty-five batteries connected by infantry parapets, to protect Petersburg. Two years later, Gen. P. G. T. Beauregard's Confederate defense force there included the troops that kept Maj. Gen. Benjamin F. Butler's Army of the James confined to the Bermuda Hundred peninsula northeast of the city. Brig. Gen. Henry A. Wise, formerly governor of Virginia, led the thousand or so veterans and local militia assigned to the Dimmock line. Since it required some twenty-five times that number to man the entire length of the line, Wise stationed most of them in the northeastern portion, the probable location of a Federal assault.

On Thursday, June 9, 1864, Butler sent a 4,500-man force of cavalry and infantry under Maj. Gen. Quincy A. Gillmore against Petersburg from City Point (pres-

On a battlefield otherwise obliterated, this monument stands as the only visible sign of its existence. VIRGINIA DEPARTMENT OF HISTORIC RESOURCES, JOHN S. SALMON

ent-day Hopewell). Gillmore's division was divided into three columns. The first demonstrated in front of the northeast quadrant of the Dimmock line, the second—United States Colored Troops—did the same against the eastern portion, and the third—led by Brig. Gen. August V. Kautz and composed of his 1,300-man cavalry division—assaulted the line where

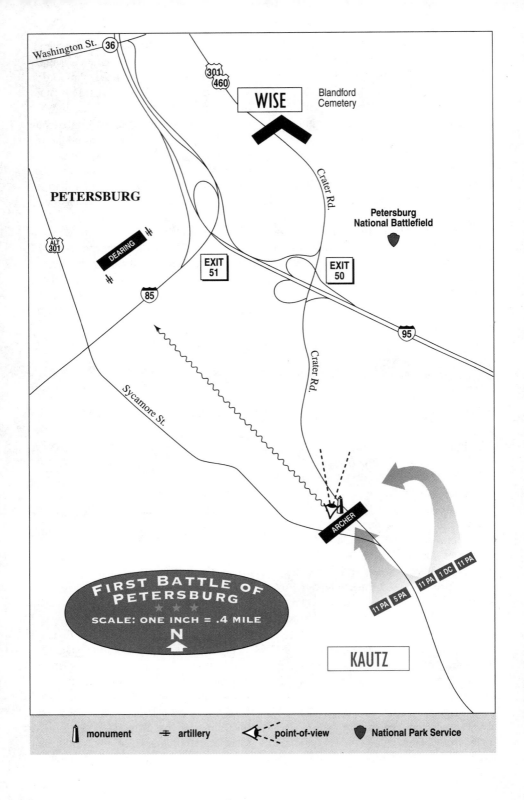

Washington St. 36

301
460

WISE

Blandford Cemetery

PETERSBURG

Crater Rd.

Petersburg National Battlefield

ALT 301

DEARING

EXIT 51

EXIT 50

85

95

Crater Rd.

Sycamore St.

ARCHER

FIRST BATTLE OF PETERSBURG
★ ★ ★
SCALE: ONE INCH = .4 MILE
N

11 PA   5 PA   11 PA   1 DC   11 PA

KAUTZ

monument   artillery   point-of-view   National Park Service

DIRECTIONS: I-95 Exit 50 (U.S. Rte. 301, Crater Rd.), left on exit road about .1 mile to U.S. Rte. 301; s. (right) on U.S. Rte. 301 .6 mile to monument on right marking Rives's Salient in the heart of the battlefield; return to I-95.

it crossed the Jerusalem Plank Road (present-day U.S. Rte. 301).

Gillmore's demonstrations, intended to fix the thin line of Confederates in place, ended about noon. Around the same time, Kautz's division began its attack at Battery 27 (also called Rives's Salient) in the Dimmock line. After an hour spent probing with skirmishers who engaged Maj. Fletcher H. Archer's militiamen there, Kautz launched his main attack at about 1:15 P.M. and overwhelmed the Home Guards, who fell back to the city with heavy losses. The hour, however, had enabled Beauregard to dispatch the 4th North Carolina Cavalry, the Petersburg Battery, and a part of the 7th Confederate States Cavalry from the Bermuda Hundred line to the southwestern edge of the city and repulse a Federal cavalry assault. This second Confederate line held, and the first battle of Petersburg came to an end. The Confederates lost about 80 killed, wounded, or captured, while the Federals lost around 40.

The site of the battle was obliterated by the commercial development and expansion of Petersburg years ago. A historical marker notes the site of the initial contact. ■

PETERSBURG FORTIFICATIONS

L t. Gen. Ulysses S. Grant had ordered a concerted attack on Petersburg before the city's garrison could be reinforced. While unsuccessful, Maj. Gen. Benjamin F. Butler's assault of June 9, 1864, revealed the weaknesses of the Dimmock line as well as the small size of the defending force, and Grant wanted to seize the opportunity.

Alerted to the danger, Gen. P. G. T. Beauregard, the Confederate commander of Petersburg, stripped the Howlett line of troops to defend the city, thereby releasing Butler's Army of the James from its confinement on the Bermuda Hundred peninsula to the northeast. Shortly after dawn on Wednesday, June 15, Maj. Gen. William F. "Baldy" Smith led XVIII Corps across the river toward the northeastern part of the Dimmock line. The corps disembarked from transport vessels not only at Smith's preferred landing site but at others selected at random by the ship captains. Smith wasted much of the morning reassembling his force, which consisted of three infantry divisions and Brig. Gen. August V. Kautz's cavalry division, which would precede the infantry and sweep all resistance from its line of advance. Brig. Gen. William T. H. Brooks's and Brig. Gen. John H. Martindale's divisions, having crossed on the Broadway Landing pontoon bridge, were to march toward the city down the City Point Railroad. Brig. Gen. Edward W. Hincks's United States Colored Troops (USCTs) would approach on the Jordan Point Road.

Like the disembarkation, the march did not go smoothly. At about 6 A.M., Kautz struck an unexpected Confederate stronghold at Baylor's Farm a few miles northeast of Petersburg, in Hincks's sector. The black troops launched two assaults on the place before they overran it and captured a cannon. Although the attack succeeded, it delayed Smith until early afternoon; he

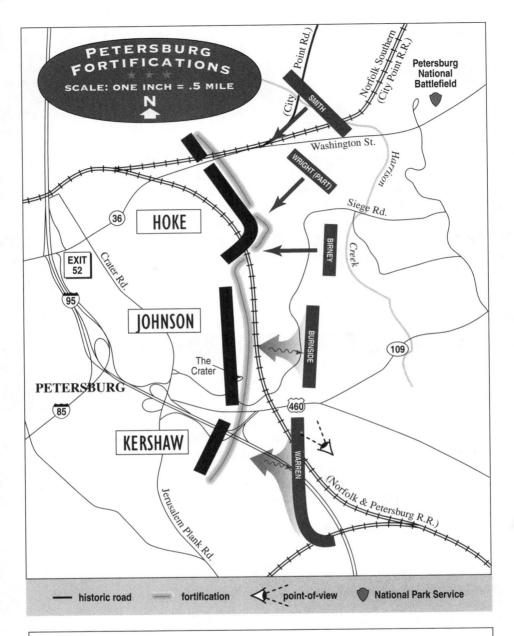

PETERSBURG FORTIFICATIONS
SCALE: ONE INCH = .5 MILE
N

(City Point Rd.)

Norfolk Southern (City Point R.R.)

Petersburg National Battlefield

SMITH

Washington St.

WRIGHT (PART)

Harrison

Siege Rd.

HOKE

36

BIRNEY

Creek

EXIT 52

95

JOHNSON

Crater Rd.

The Crater

BURNSIDE

109

PETERSBURG

85

460

KERSHAW

WARREN

Jerusalem Plank Rd.

(Norfolk & Petersburg R.R.)

— historic road   fortification   ◁ point-of-view   National Park Service

DIRECTIONS: I-95 Exit 52 (Washington St., Wythe St., from n.; Bank St. from s.), e. on Wythe St. and follow signs about 2.5 miles to Petersburg National Park entrance. From I-85 Exit 69 (U.S. Rte. 301 South, Wythe St./ Rte. 36), e. on U.S. 301 South, Wythe St., about 2.4 miles to Petersburg National Park entrance. Walking and driving tour information available at park visitor center. Visit the National Park Service Web site at nps.gov/parks.html for a virtual tour of this and other national parks.

Capt. James H. Cooper (left), Battery B, 1st Pennsylvania Light Artillery, studies Petersburg through a telescope while Mathew B. Brady strikes a pose in the left foreground. Photo taken by one of Brady's photographers on June 21, 1864. LIBRARY OF CONGRESS

fretted about the sounds of trains arriving in Petersburg with what he feared were Confederate reinforcements.

Smith decided, after a reconnaissance, that the works still were lightly defended and might be carried by a strong skirmish line. He briefed his division commanders on the new plan. Once more, however, the attack was delayed, for the artillery commander had taken his guns to the rear and unhitched the horses to water them. The assault did not begin until about 7 P.M.

As Smith had predicted, his powerful skirmish line swept over the earthworks along a three-and-a-half-mile front, capturing Batteries 3 and 5–11, and the defenders fell back to a feebler line at Harrison's Creek. Petersburg lay ahead, devoid of opposition, but night was coming, and Smith decided to wait until dawn to press forward. When he returned to his headquarters, he found Maj. Gen. Winfield Scott Hancock waiting for him. Smith remained determined to attack in the morning, and merely asked Hancock to replace Smith's II Corps divisions with his own.

Beauregard made the most of the delay, bolstering the Dimmock line with men from the Howlett line. Outnumbered three to one, the Confederates still repulsed the Federal attacks on Thursday, June 16, although driven from Batteries 4, 12, 13, and 14. Smith's corps demonstrated on the Union right while Hancock's men pressed forward from Prince George Court House Road. The Harrison's Creek line held, however, and the Federals suffered heavy casualties. Meanwhile, Butler led the remainder of his army out of Bermuda Hundred and began tearing up the Richmond & Petersburg Railroad track between the two cities, believing that a Confederate evacuation of Petersburg was imminent.

Smith's and Hancock's corps had been joined by Maj. Gen. Ambrose E. Burnside's IX Corps to reinforce the attacks scheduled for Friday, June 17. But the day was filled with delays, strong Confederate counterattacks, and little progress. Beauregard constructed a final line of earthworks that extended south from the Appomattox River to rejoin the Dimmock line at the Jerusalem Plank Road (present-day U.S. Rte. 301). Beauregard finally convinced Gen. Robert E. Lee that most of the Army of the Potomac was attacking Petersburg, and Lee sent his army southward, the vanguard entering Petersburg about 7:30 A.M. on Saturday, June 18.

About the same time, the Federals—directed by Maj. Gen. George G. Meade, commander of the Army of the Potomac—launched their morning attack against the northeastern part of the secondary line. However, they found the trenches abandoned and a new line in their front and were compelled to regroup and reassess. Meade hoped to initiate another attack around noon. Instead of a unified assault, however, the XVIII, II, IX, and V Corps launched a series of uncoordinated, piecemeal advances that did little but swell the casualty rolls. By 6:30 P.M. Meade called a halt to the fruitless attacks and gave the order to entrench.

The four days of battles for Petersburg resulted in 8,150 Federal and 3,236 Confederate casualties. With all of Lee's army in the city, the fate of the Confederacy in Virginia would be decided by a siege, not a single battle.

Many of the sites related to the battles for the Petersburg fortifications are included in Petersburg National Battlefield, although commercial and residential development have covered some others. The park units are well interpreted and accessible by car from the visitor center. ■

JERUSALEM PLANK ROAD

Lt. Gen. Ulysses S. Grant decided that the quickest way to force Gen. Robert E. Lee either to surrender or evacuate Petersburg was to cut the Confederate lines of communication and supply. Grant concentrated on seizing or destroying the three unsecured rail lines that served the city: the Petersburg Railroad (also called the Weldon Railroad), which led south to Weldon, North Carolina; the South Side Railroad, which extended west to Lynchburg; and the Richmond & Petersburg Railroad. Late in June 1864 Grant planned a combined infantry and cavalry expedition designed to achieve his goals.

The opening engagement of what became known as the Wilson-Kautz Raid of June 22–30, 1864, began on Tuesday, June 21, when elements of Maj. Gen. Winfield S. Hancock's II Corps (under the temporary command of Maj. Gen. David B. Birney) probed toward the Petersburg Railroad. Even as skirmishing erupted, the main Union lines received a special visitor: Pres. Abraham Lincoln, who arrived by steamer from Washington to confer with Grant and review the troops. The next morning, with Brig. Gen. James H. Wilson's and Brig. Gen. August V. Kautz's cavalry divisions in advance of the infantry, which included Maj. Gen. Horatio G. Wright's VI Corps in support, the attempt to sever the railroad links began in earnest.

According to the plan, the II and VI Corps would advance to the Jerusalem Plank Road (present-day U.S. Rte. 301, or Crater Road), then sweep over it and pivot northwest to the railroad not quite two miles beyond. Difficult terrain, however, impeded the smooth progress of the Federal force. By midmorning on June 22, a gap opened between II and VI Corps as the soldiers struggled through swamps and thickets. By noon II Corps had begun to pivot as planned, but VI Corps encountered Maj. Gen. Cadmus Wilcox's division of Lt. Gen. A. P. Hill's corps and began to entrench rather than advance. The gap between the two Federal corps widened.

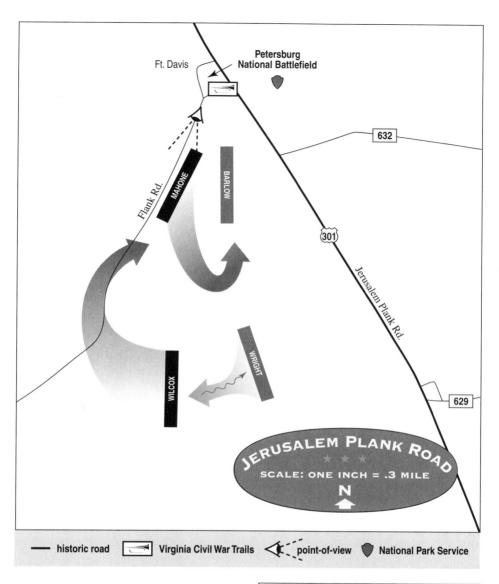

Ft. Davis

Petersburg
National Battlefield

632

MAHONE

BARLOW

Flank Rd.

US 301

Jerusalem Plank Rd.

WILCOX

WRIGHT

629

JERUSALEM PLANK ROAD
★ ★ ★
SCALE: ONE INCH = .3 MILE

N

— historic road   Virginia Civil War Trails   point-of-view   National Park Service

Maj. Gen. William Mahone of Hill's corps observed the Union error from behind Confederate lines. Lee joined him, and when Mahone described a ravine some distance to the front that would conceal his division while he advanced to strike the exposed Federal flank, Lee approved his plan. By 3 P.M. Mahone's men were in position, and when they emerged from the ravine, they found themselves in the rear of

DIRECTIONS: I-95 Exit 50 (U.S. Rte. 301, Crater Rd.); left on exit road about .1 mile to U.S. Rte. 301; s. (right) on U.S. Rte. 301 1.5 miles to Flank Rd. and Fort Davis on right and Virginia Civil War Trails marker; w. (right) on Flank Rd. .7 mile to heart of core area; return on Flank Rd. to U.S. Rte. 301 and I-95. Visit the National Park Service Web site at nps.gov/parks.html for a virtual tour of this and other national parks.

Brig. Gen. Francis C. Barlow's division of Hancock's corps, which quickly collapsed before their onslaught. Mahone sent a frantic message to Wilcox urging him to join the attack, but Wilcox hesitated, concerned that Wright might attack at any time. Soon II Corps found earthworks from which to fight after the initial shock subsided. Darkness ended the day's combat with both sides withdrawing, Mahone to the Confederate lines and II Corps to the Jerusalem Plank Road. The Confederates lost about 400 in the battle, the Federals considerably more, including 1,700 prisoners.

The Jerusalem Plank Road battlefield is heavily blanketed with residential and commercial development. Pockets of fields and woods survive, however, and with some imagination it is possible to reconstruct part of the action from the existing terrain. ■

View south along Mahone's line, southwest of Fort Davis. VIRGINIA DEPARTMENT OF HISTORIC RESOURCES, JOHN S. SALMON

SAMARIA (SAINT MARY'S) CHURCH

In June 1864, Maj. Gen. Philip H. Sheridan, acting on Lt. Gen. Ulysses S. Grant's earlier orders, had led an unsuccessful raid on the Virginia Central Railroad at Trevilian Station. After two days of hard combat with the cavalry divisions of Maj. Gen. Wade Hampton and Maj. Gen. Fitzhugh Lee, Sheridan decided to return to the safety of the Federal lines.

Sheridan's objective was White House depot on the Pamunkey River in New Kent County, a principal Federal supply center. When he arrived on the north bank of the river opposite the White House on June 20, however, he found the bluffs occupied by Confederate pickets. The next day Sheridan sent Brig. Gen. David M. Gregg's division and Brig. Gen. Alfred T. A. Torbert's division to drive the Con-

federates away from the White House as well as Tunstall's Station a few miles west on the Richmond & York River Railroad. Upon completing that task, Sheridan received orders to break up the depot and guide the supply wagons—some 900 of them—southwest to Bermuda Hundred.

On June 22 Torbert led his division south approximately on present-day Rte. 155 while Gregg protected the Federal right flank by following a parallel route to the west, probably along present-day Rte. 106. In the meantime, Hampton closed in from the west, and the next day Brig. Gen. John R. Chambliss's brigade attacked Torbert's pickets on the Long Bridge Road. After driving off the Confederates, Torbert learned from prisoners that they constituted the vanguard of Hampton's force.

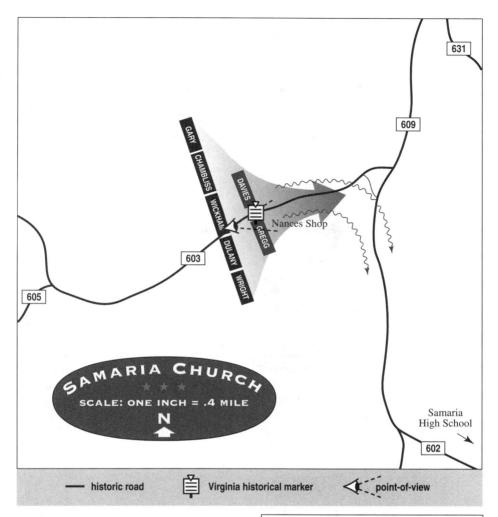

SAMARIA CHURCH
★ ★ ★
SCALE: ONE INCH = .4 MILE
N

Samaria
High School

—— historic road   🏛 Virginia historical marker   ◀ ⋯ point-of-view

The following day, Friday, June 24, Torbert continued escorting the wagons toward Harrison's Landing at Berkeley plantation. Finding Brig. Gen. Lunsford L. Lomax's brigade near the Charles City Court House, Torbert drove it west and concentrated his own force west of the courthouse to protect the train.

Meanwhile, at about 8 A.M., Brig. Gen. Henry E. Davies, Jr., led his brigade out of its bivouac three miles northwest of the courthouse and rode west to the vicinity of Samaria Church (misnamed in Federal accounts as Saint Mary's Church), which

DIRECTIONS: I-64 Exit 211 (State Rte. 106, Prince George), s. on State Rte. 106 (Emmaus Church Rd.) about 4.4 miles to Rte. 609 (Barnett's Rd.); e. (left) on Rte. 609 2.6 miles to Rte. 603 (Union Rd.) near Nance's Shop; w. (right) on Rte. 603 .7 mile to engagement site at state historical marker PH-6, Action of Nance's Shop; return to Rte. 609; s. (right) on Rte. 609 1.1 miles to Samaria Church site at Rte. 602 (Lott Cary Rd.); s.e. (left) on Rte. 602 .8 mile to Samaria Baptist Church at Rte. 630 (Samaria Lane); retrace route to I-64.

stood at the junction of three roads. One (Rte. 609) led north to Long Bridge over the Chickahominy River; the second (Rte.

Gregg's position (right), looking east. VIRGINIA DEPARTMENT OF HISTORIC RESOURCES, JOHN S. SALMON

609 south) southwest to the James River Road; and the third (Rte. 602) southeast to Charles City Court House. Riding up the courthouse road, Davies encountered Confederate pickets near the church and pushed them north with a charge by the 2nd Pennsylvania Cavalry, advancing his force west of the intersection. There the brigade entrenched and erected artillery positions. Davies held the right flank of the Federal line while Col. J. Irwin Gregg's brigade occupied the left.

Hampton deployed his cavalry brigades to attack Gregg's division and also entrenched. Between 3 and 4 P.M., Hampton pressed the attack, with his troopers fighting dismounted as infantry.

Since Hampton outnumbered Gregg at least five brigades to two, the Federals began to give way from their breastworks after a couple of hours of combat. They retired in good order down the Charles City Court House road (Rte. 602), leap-frogging their rearguard lines of defense, and finally arrived near the village at about 8 P.M. Skirmishing continued until 10 P.M. as Hampton's troopers sought out Federal stragglers and probed Gregg's lines.

The Federals reported 339 killed, wounded, and missing (mostly captured), while the Confederates lost fewer than 300. Although Gregg's men were trounced, they nonetheless succeeded in screening the wagon train, which continued unscathed on its way to rejoin the Army of the Potomac near Petersburg.

The Samaria Church battlefield has experienced little development of any kind. However, most of the landmarks of the battle, such as the church itself, have long since disappeared and the Federal and Confederate earthworks have been plowed under. The road patterns remain intact, but much of the battle is conjectural because of the loss of other landmarks. ■

STAUNTON RIVER BRIDGE

L t. Gen. Ulysses S. Grant was determined to destroy the railroads that served Petersburg and supplied Gen. Robert E. Lee's troops there. On June 22, some 5,500 cavalrymen under Brig. Gen. James H. Wilson, Army of the Potomac, and Brig. Gen. August V. Kautz, Army of the James, rode south along the Petersburg Railroad (also called the Weldon Railroad) to Ream's Station, then west and northwest to the South Side Railroad near Ford's Station. Tearing up track as they went, Kautz's men proceeded west to

DIRECTIONS: U.S. Rte. 360 to State Rte. 92 (Clover Rd.) at brown sign for Staunton River Battlefield State Park; n.w. (right) on State Rte. 92 about 4.6 miles to Rte. 600 (Black Walnut Rd.) at Clover; n. (right) on Rte. 600 2.9 miles following Virginia Civil War Trails and brown state park signs to Rte. 855 (Fort Hill Trail) and park entrance; e. (right) on Rte. 855 .25 mile to Rte. 975; n. (left) on Rte. 975 to Clover Center (currently closed Mon.–Tues.) and Virginia Civil War Trails marker; to tour site, follow signs and trails by car and on foot; return to U.S. Rte. 360. For more information about the battlefield, visit the Department of Conservation and Recreation's state parks Web site at dcr.state.va.us/parks or call the park at 804-454-4312.

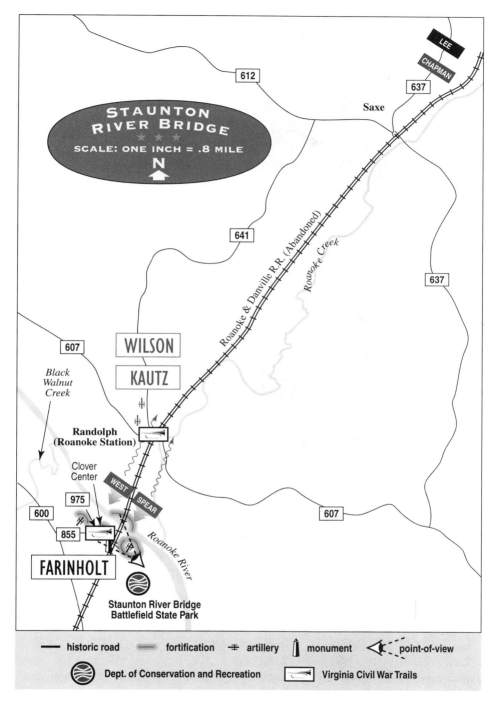

STAUNTON RIVER BRIDGE
★ ★ ★
SCALE: ONE INCH = .8 MILE
N

LEE
CHAPMAN

612

637

Saxe

641

Roanoke & Danville R.R. (Abandoned)

Roanoke Creek

637

607

WILSON

KAUTZ

Black
Walnut
Creek

Randolph
(Roanoke Station)

Clover
Center

WEST

SPEAR

975

600

855

FARINHOLT

Roanoke River

607

Staunton River Bridge
Battlefield State Park

— historic road   fortification   ╪ artillery   ⬙ monument   ◁┈┈ point-of-view

Dept. of Conservation and Recreation   Virginia Civil War Trails

Burkeville Junction (Burke's Station), then turned southwest on the Richmond & Danville Railroad. Wilson and Kautz planned to burn the Staunton River railroad bridge almost seventy miles southwest of Petersburg, then return to the

Interior of principal fortification, facing west. VIRGINIA DEPARTMENT OF HISTORIC RESOURCES, JOHN S. SALMON

Union lines near the city. On Saturday, June 25, the raiders approached Roanoke Station (present-day Randolph), about a mile north of the bridge.

Meanwhile, Lee had dispatched Maj. Gen. William H. F. "Rooney" Lee's cavalry division to pursue and attack the raiders and wired Capt. Benjamin L. Farinholt, who guarded the bridge with 296 men, to warn him of the Union operation. Farinholt called for reinforcements, and about 650 more men came to his aid. Over the next two days his troops built artillery emplacements on the bluffs on the south side of the river and dug two lines of rifle pits below them. Col. Henry E. Coleman, of the 12th North Carolina Infantry, persuaded Farinholt to entrench on either side of the rail bed at the north end of the bridge. Capt. James A. Hoyt and two Danville companies occupied the right flank; Coleman commanded civilians known as the "Old Men and Boys" on the left.

At 2 P.M. on Saturday, June 25, the Union cavalry arrived at Roanoke Station. After spotting Farinholt's defenders, Wilson and Kautz planned their attack. By 6 P.M. the Union artillery had unlimbered on

the hills near the station and Kautz's division had dismounted to attack the bridge. Farinholt's cannons fired on the Union guns, starting an artillery duel.

Kautz launched a frontal assault; Col. Robert M. West led his troops on the right of the rail bed, while Col. Samuel P. Spear commanded on the left. Farinholt thought his troops north of the river were hidden, but West saw them and ordered a charge. The defenders, however, let fly a volley that stalled the assault. The attackers took cover in a dry streambed about 200 yards from the north end of the bridge. Three more assaults, none coming closer to the bridge than seventy or eighty yards, were driven back before sundown. At about 9 P.M. the Union troops retreated to the depot.

Just before the battle, Maj. Gen. W. H. F. "Rooney" Lee's cavalry division appeared north of the depot and skirmished with Wilson's rear guard. After Farinholt repulsed the attacks at the bridge, Wilson and Kautz decided to abandon their mission. During the night the Federals rode east toward Christianville (now Chase City). The Union casualties at the Staunton River Bridge were 42 killed, 44 wounded, and 30 missing or captured. The Confederates lost 10 killed and 24 wounded.

Because of Farinholt's sturdy defense and Lee's timely arrival, Wilson and Kautz failed to burn the Staunton River Bridge. They disrupted Lee's supply lines for a time, but the railroads were repaired so rapidly that the raid was only partially successful.

Today the battlefield retains very good integrity, and many of the key landmarks are easily recognized. Most of the land on the north side of Staunton River, formerly privately owned and well preserved, has been donated to Staunton River Bridge Battlefield State Park; that on the south side, including the surviving portion of Farinholt's earthworks, is also in the park. Just to the south of the battlefield stands the enormous Clover electric generating plant. Two electric companies helped create the park visitor center, which contains an excellent exhibit about the battle, brochures for the battlefield walking and driving tour, and an exhibit on electric power generation. ■

SAPPONY CHURCH

The extended railroad raid led by Brig. Gen. James H. Wilson and Brig. Gen. August V. Kautz from June 22–30, 1864, entered its final phase after the defeat at the Staunton River Bridge. With Maj. Gen. William H. F. "Rooney" Lee's cavalry division threatening their rear, Kautz and Wilson rode east toward the Union lines at Petersburg.

Maj. Gen. Wade Hampton's cavalry division had been shadowing Maj. Gen. Philip H. Sheridan's cavalry since the battle of Trevilian Station on June 11–12. Soon after Sheridan rejoined the Army of

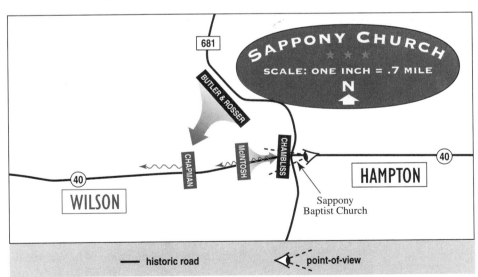

DIRECTIONS: I-95 Exit 31 (Stony Creek, Rte. 40); w. on Rte. 40 about 3.4 miles to Rte. 681 (Flowers Rd.) at Sappony Baptist Church; n. (right) on Rte. 681 .7 mile to site of CSA flanking march through field on left; return to Rte. 40; w. (right) on Rte. 40 .6 mile to US position; return to I-95.

View west through C.S.A. position toward U.S. route of advance. VIRGINIA DEPARTMENT OF HISTORIC RESOURCES, JOHN S. SALMON

the Potomac on June 26, however, Gen. Robert E. Lee ordered Hampton to find and attack Kautz and Wilson.

The Federal raiders crossed the Petersburg (a.k.a. Weldon) Railroad at the Stony Creek Station about twenty miles south of Petersburg. To Wilson's surprise, however, on Tuesday afternoon, June 28, he found the approach to the depot blocked by Confederates. They straddled present-day Rte. 40 about three miles west of the station

near Sappony Church. Hampton soon arrived in support as Wilson tried unsuccessfully to punch his way through. The Federals fell back when Brig. Gen. Matthew C. Butler and Brig. Gen. Thomas L. Rosser led their brigades in an envelopment that threatened Wilson's left flank.

Kautz, whose division had been in the rear of Wilson's, came under attack by the remainder of Rooney Lee's division late in the day. Under the cover of darkness, however, Kautz and Wilson slipped out of the trap and rode north toward Petersburg and the Federal outpost at Ream's Station. Casualty figures for the engagement are not available but probably were light on both sides.

The Sappony Church battlefield has retained much of its integrity despite some scattered residential development along Rte. 40. Woods probably cover more of the area today than at the time of the battle, but enough open space remains to convey an understanding of the troop movements. ∎

FIRST BATTLE OF REAM'S STATION

Having escaped from near-entrapment at Sappony Church (Stony Creek Station) on the Petersburg (a.k.a. Weldon) Railroad on June 28, 1864, Brig. Gen. James H. Wilson and Brig. Gen. August V. Kautz led their cavalry divisions north to the supposed safety of Ream's Station on the same line. There they expected Federal infantry would help them against attacks by the cavalry divisions led by Maj. Gen. Wade Hampton and Maj. Gen. William H. F. "Rooney" Lee, which were pursuing them closely.

On Wednesday morning, June 29, the Federals approached Ream's Station from the west with Kautz in the lead while Wil-

son fended off Lee to the rear. However, they found Confederate, not Union infantry there: Maj. Gen. William Mahone's division of Lt. Gen. A. P. Hill's corps. Brig. Gen. John C. C. Sanders's brigade was astride the Depot Road (present-day Rte. 606), and Brig. Gen. Joseph Finegan's brigade was on the Confederate right flank. Kautz pushed forward a line of skirmishers followed by Col. Samuel P. Spear's brigade, with the 1st District of Columbia Cavalry to the north of the road and the 11th Pennsylvania to the south, and three artillery batteries behind the horse soldiers. The 2nd Ohio and the 5th New York Cavalry were on the Stage Road

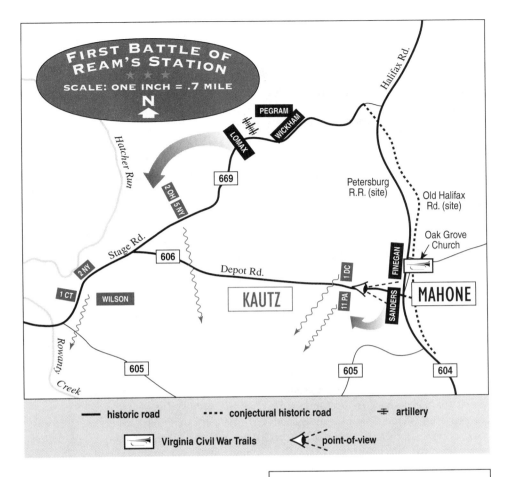

FIRST BATTLE OF REAM'S STATION

★ ★ ★

SCALE: ONE INCH = .7 MILE

N

PEGRAM

WICKHAM

LOMAX

Halifax Rd.

Hatcher Run

2 OH 5 NY

669

Petersburg
R.R. (site)

Old Halifax
Rd. (site)

Oak Grove
Church

Stage Rd.

2 NY

606

Depot Rd.

FINEGAN

1 DC

1 CT

WILSON

KAUTZ

11 PA

SANDERS

MAHONE

Rowanty

Creek

605

605

604

— historic road   ···· conjectural historic road   ‡ artillery

⊏◁⊐ Virginia Civil War Trails   ◀ point-of-view

(Rte. 669) to the northwest, and the 2nd New York and 1st Connecticut guarded the supply train in the rear.

About noon Mahone attacked the right flank of the 11th Pennsylvania Regiment, threatening to get past the dismounted cavalry to the artillery batteries. At the same time, Brig. Gen. Lunsford L. Lomax's brigade, followed by Brig. Gen. Williams C. Wickham's brigade, arrived from the north on the Stage Road. Lomax maneuvered around the 2nd Ohio and 5th New York, thereby enveloping the Federal left flank. Virtually surrounded, Wilson and Kautz gave orders to burn the wagons, spike and abandon the artillery, and flee. At least 300 escaped slaves were aban-

DIRECTIONS: I-95 Exit 41 (Courtland, State Rte. 35); n.w. on State Rte. 35/622 (Providence Rd.) about 2.5 miles to Rte. 606 (Ream's Rd.); w. (left) on Rte. 606 1.8 miles to Rte. 604 (Halifax Rd.) at site of Ream's Station (Rte. 604 on bed of Petersburg R.R.); s. (left) on Rte. 604 .3 mile to Rte. 606; w. (right) on Rte. 606 2 miles to Rte. 669 (Old Stage Rd.); n.e. (right) on Rte. 669 2.5 miles to Rte. 604; s. (right) on Rte. 604 1.2 miles to Rte. 606; e. (right) on Rte. 606 1.8 miles to Rte. 622; s.e. (right) on Rte. 622 and return 2.5 miles to I-95.

doned by the Federals in their retreat as well as most of their wounded.

The Wilson-Kautz Raid achieved modest success, with some sixty miles of track destroyed that took the Confederates several weeks to repair. The cost was high,

From 11th Pennsylvania Cavalry position, looking east to Sanders's line. VIRGINIA DEPARTMENT OF HISTORIC RESOURCES, JOHN S. SALMON

however: about 1,800 casualties for little more than a week's activity.

Little development has occurred on the battlefield itself. The area is heavily wooded, however, which makes it difficult to understand the battle from the terrain. The problem is exacerbated by the realignment of the railroad a mile or more to the east of its historic bed; Rte. 604 now covers the old rail bed. The Conservation Fund owns 217 acres of the battlefield. ■

FIRST BATTLE OF DEEP BOTTOM

While the Wilson-Kautz railroad raid was under way, Lt. Gen. Ulysses S. Grant's siege of Petersburg began in earnest. Grant planned to attack the city's defenses on July 30, 1864; first, however, he proposed to weaken them by compelling Gen. Robert E. Lee to detach troops for the defense of Richmond. He ordered Maj. Gen. Winfield Scott Hancock, commander of II Corps, to lead his corps and two divisions of Maj. Gen. Philip H. Sheridan's cavalry across the James River and attack the Confederate capital.

Hancock's corps would cross a newly built pontoon bridge from the northern tip of Jones Neck, a part of the Bermuda Hundred peninsula, to Deep Bottom in Henrico County. Another pontoon bridge had been constructed just upstream, and Brig. Gen. Robert S. Foster's X Corps division had crossed over to hold a bridgehead on the north bank of the river.

About three miles west of Deep Bottom stood the outer line of Confederate fieldworks guarding Richmond, manned by Lt. Gen. Richard S. Ewell's command. Additional works extended eastward from the main line to threaten the flank of an attacking force, beginning just north of Fort Harrison on New Market Road (present-day Rte. 5) just south of New Market Heights; a Confederate signal station stood on the western end of the plateau. The works followed the contours northwest, overlooking Bailey's Creek, for more than a mile to Fussell's Mill.

Hancock's and Sheridan's forces crossed the lower pontoon bridge beginning at 3 A.M. on Wednesday, July 27. They massed behind a grove of oaks southeast of the bridge until dawn, when Hancock sent his corps toward Fussell's Mill and broke through the Confederate line on New Market Road. Sheridan, meanwhile, led his horse soldiers from Darbytown Road to strike the Confederate left flank near Fussell's Mill.

Lee, having learned of Hancock's move, ordered the Richmond lines reinforced to a total of some 16,500 men. Maj. Gen. Joseph B. Kershaw and Maj. Gen. Cadmus M. Wilcox led their divisions east on New Market Road and behind the Confederate works atop the eastern face of New Market Heights. In the afternoon an artillery duel developed between the Federal gunners and their Confederate coun-

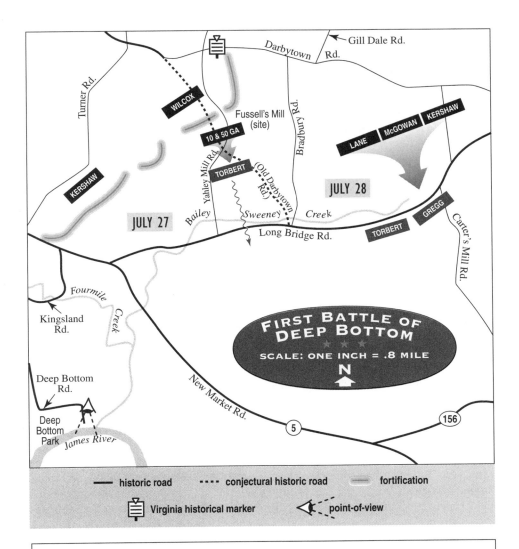

historic road   •••• conjectural historic road   fortification

Virginia historical marker   point-of-view

DIRECTIONS: Recommend first visiting the Richmond National Battlefield Park Visitor Center (open 9–5 daily) at Tredegar Iron Works in downtown Richmond: I-95 Exit 74C (U.S. Rte. 33 West/U.S. Rte. 250 West, Broad St.) and follow blue-and-green signs to visitor center, Brown's Island, and Belle Isle, w. on Broad St. about .4 mile (5 blocks) to 8th St.; s. (left) on 8th St. 5 blocks to Canal St.; w. (right) on Canal St. 3 blocks to 5th St.; s. (left) on 5th St. 2 blocks to Tredegar St.; w. (right) on Tredegar Street .1 mile to visitor center and parking lot. To visit the battlefield directly: I-295 Exit 22A (State Rte. 5 East, Charles City), e. on State Rte. 5 East about 1.8 miles to Long Bridge Rd.; n.e. (left) on Long Bridge Rd. .8 mile to Yahley Mill Rd.; n. (left) on Yahley Mill Rd. 1.5 miles to Darbytown Rd.; e. (right) on Darbytown Rd. .1 mile to state historical marker W-72, 39th Illinois Veteran Volunteers, then 1.7 miles to Carter's Mill Rd.; s. (right) on Carter's Mill Rd. .6 mile to Long Bridge Rd.; s.e. (right) on Long Bridge Rd. 2.8 miles to State Rte. 5; e. (right) on State Rte. 5 1.8 miles to I-295.

terparts on the heights. To the right of the Union infantry, the first cavalry division captured high ground near Fussell's Mill but were driven back when the 10th and 50th Georgia Infantry counterattacked. Farther east, on the road to Riddell's Shop

Jones Neck, from north bank of James River at Deep Bottom. LIBRARY OF CONGRESS

that passed through the old Malvern Hill battleground (Rte. 156), the Federal cavalry encountered one Confederate obstacle after another and made slow progress toward its objective. That evening the Confederates strengthened and extended their earthworks north from Fussell's Mill along the western edge of a ravine and across Darbytown Road.

Late the next morning the second Federal cavalry division left its camp on Strawberry Plains and rode north and east around Fussell's Mill, attempting to turn the Confederate left flank more directly than the previous day's expedition. The plan failed when three Confederate brigades struck the division short of its objective at Gravel Hill. The Confederates captured a Federal cannon before withdrawing to their earthworks.

Hancock ordered the operation abandoned and crossed his corps over the lower pontoon bridge to the safety of Chesterfield County. A garrison held the bridgehead at Deep Bottom to support further operations north of the James.

The first battle of Deep Bottom cost the Federals 488 killed, wounded, and missing; Confederate casualties are estimated at 650. Much of the battlefield remains undeveloped and heavily wooded. ■

THE CRATER

Lt. Gen. Ulysses S. Grant had scheduled an attack against the Confederate lines at Petersburg for dawn on Saturday, July 30, 1864. Instead of a conventional assault by infantry supported by artillery, however, this attack would depend on the success of a plan that both Grant and Maj. Gen. George G. Meade, the commander of the Army of the Potomac, doubted would succeed.

The plan was hatched by Lt. Col. Henry Pleasants, a civil engineer who commanded the 48th Pennsylvania Regiment: Dig a tunnel from his line to a Confederate artillery salient about 200 yards to his front, and pack it with enough explo-

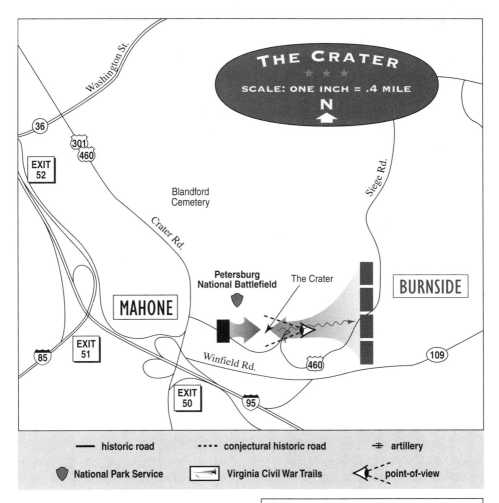

—— historic road	···· conjectural historic road	⚞ artillery
🛡 National Park Service	🖼 Virginia Civil War Trails	◁ point-of-view

sives to blow a huge hole in the opposing line. He reasoned that an immediate division-sized assault, properly supported, should result in the capture of Petersburg.

Maj. Gen. Ambrose Burnside, commander of the IX Corps, approved the scheme, and Meade and Grant allowed it to proceed. Pleasants assigned the task of digging the tunnel to Pennsylvania soldiers who had been miners in civilian life. In one month they constructed a 511-foot-long shaft about 5 feet in height, with two lateral passages or galleries at the end that totaled about 75 feet in length and lay 20 feet beneath the Confederate works. Four

DIRECTIONS: I-95 Exit 52 (Washington St., Wythe St., from n.; Bank St. from s.), e. on Wythe St. and follow signs about 2.5 miles to Petersburg National Park entrance. From I-85 Exit 69 (U.S. Rte. 301 South, Wythe St./ State Rte. 36), e. on U.S. Rte. 301 South, Wythe St., about 2.4 miles to Petersburg National Park entrance. Walking and driving tour information available at park visitor center. Visit the National Park Service Web site at nps.gov/parks.html for a virtual tour of this and other national parks.

magazines in each gallery were packed with four tons of gunpowder (some 320 barrels), a long fuse was spliced together, and the main shaft was tamped with earth

USCTs hurry toward the Crater, July 30, 1864. LIBRARY OF CONGRESS

for 38 feet to contain the explosion and direct it upward.

Once the mine exploded, according to the plan, Brig. Gen. Edward Ferrero's division of United States Colored Troops would lead the charge through the breach. Meade, however, changed the plan. Since the black troops had not been in combat before—and to avoid any suggestion that he offered them up as cannon fodder—he wanted one of the battle-tested white divisions to lead the way. When the three division commanders in Burnside's corps drew lots, the dubious honor fell to Brig. Gen. James Ledlie, arguably the worst division commander in the Army of the Potomac.

On July 30 at 3:30 A.M., Pleasants lit the fuse and then hurried out of range to await the explosion. Minutes passed and nothing happened. Pleasants, in a rage, knew what had caused the failure. He had ordered one long continuous fuse but instead had received several shorter ones that had to be spliced together, and one of the splices had broken. Two men crawled into the tunnel, found the break, relit the fuse, and scrambled out. It was 4:44 A.M.

The explosion felt like an earthquake. The fort was lifted off the hill as flame shot 200 feet into the air. Debris of every kind—timbers and planks, men and guns—rained down on the ground.

Some 278 of the 30 Confederate artillerymen and 300 South Carolina infantrymen stationed in the salient died in the explosion, which stunned all who witnessed it. The dust slowly settled, and where the salient had been there was now a huge hole roughly 200 feet long, about 60 feet wide, and some 30 feet deep. Wounded Confederates writhed on the smoke-filled floor. Leading the way for Ledlie's division, Col. Elisha G. Marshall's brigade plunged into the abyss while Federal artillery pounded the Confederate lines.

When the mine exploded, the earth was hurled high in the air, and although some of it was flung a considerable distance, much of it fell back into the crater, turning what had been solid earth into a mash that trapped the floundering Federals. In addition, the crater's steep sides made it difficult for them to climb out. The Confederates recovered and began shooting into the pit as reinforcements hurried forward to plug the gap.

At about 9 A.M., more than four hours after the explosion, the two sides had reached a horrible equilibrium. Hundreds of Confederates had been blown to smithereens. Now the resulting crater had turned into a slaughter pen for Union soldiers. When Ferrero's black troops marched forward on Burnside's orders and began to push through the jam, fresh Confederate forces under Brig. Gen. William Mahone struck them like a whirlwind. The fighting became hand-to-hand, and some blacks who attempted to surrender were gunned down. Soon the orders came— Grant had issued them before Ferrero's men attacked—for the Federals to withdraw. A second Confederate assault at 1 P.M. gave the retreat added impetus. By midafternoon the surviving Federals had either surrendered or fled, and by early evening the Confederates once more controlled their entire front.

The attack through the crater had been a disaster. A subsequent investigation by the U.S. Congress's Joint Committee on the Conduct of the War placed the blame squarely on Burnside, Ledlie, and Fererro. Burnside was relieved of his command, while Ledlie went on sick leave and never received orders to return, but Ferrero retained his divisional command. Some 3,798 Federals and 1,491 Confederates were killed, wounded, or captured in the fighting.

The Crater battleground lies within the Petersburg National Battlefield. The site is well-interpreted and preserved, although the parklike setting gives few hints of the horrors of that day. The crater itself remains impressive, but the settling of the earth since the engagement makes it seem less terrible than it was. Signs of the tunnel still are visible. ■

SECOND BATTLE OF DEEP BOTTOM

After the failed attack at the Crater, Lt. Gen. Ulysses S. Grant feared that his best opportunity to capture Petersburg had eluded him. He resorted to his earlier strategies, striking the rail lines that supplied the city and making feints against Richmond to drain defensive troops from his real targets. During the night of August 13–14, 1864, he launched another diversion at the Confederate capital designed to lure Gen. Robert E. Lee into thinning his Petersburg defenses.

The movement resembled that of July 26–27. Once again Maj. Gen. Winfield S. Hancock led the expedition, which consisted of Maj. Gen. David B. Birney's X Corps and Brig. Gen. David M. Gregg's cavalry division as well as his own II Corps. Once again, the soldiers of X Corps

Residential development comes to the ridge above the Fussell's Mill site. VIRGINIA DEPARTMENT OF HISTORIC RESOURCES, JOHN S. SALMON

crossed the James River at Jones's Neck over pontoon bridges to Deep Bottom and Strawberry Plains on the north bank, while Hancock's II Corps disembarked from steamships a short distance downstream.

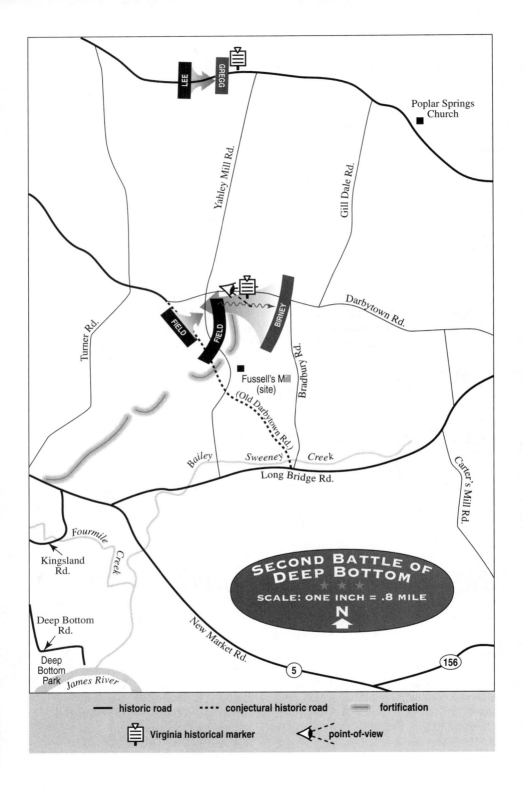

Poplar Springs
Church

Yahley Mill Rd.

Gill Dale Rd.

LEE → GREGG

Turner Rd.

FIELD   FIELD   BIRNEY

Darbytown Rd.

Bradbury Rd.

Fussell's Mill
(site)

(Old Darbytown Rd.)

Carter's Mill Rd.

Bailey   Sweeney   Creek

Long Bridge Rd.

Fourmile Creek

Kingsland
Rd.

**SECOND BATTLE OF
DEEP BOTTOM**
★ ★ ★
SCALE: ONE INCH = .8 MILE
N

Deep Bottom
Rd.

New Market Rd.

Deep
Bottom
Park

James River

5   156

——— historic road   ···· conjectural historic road   ～～ fortification

▤ Virginia historical marker   ◁⋯ point-of-view

DIRECTIONS: Recommend first visiting the Richmond National Battlefield Park Visitor Center (open 9–5 daily) at Tredegar Iron Works in downtown Richmond: I-95 Exit 74C (U.S. Rte. 33 West/U.S. Rte. 250 West, Broad St.) and follow blue-and-green signs to visitor center, Brown's Island, and Belle Isle, w. on Broad St. about .4 mile (5 blocks) to 8th St.; s. (left) on 8th St. 5 blocks to Canal St.; w. (right) on Canal St. 3 blocks to 5th St.; s. (left) on 5th St. 2 blocks to Tredegar St.; w. (right) on Tredegar Street .1 mile to visitor center and parking lot. To visit the battlefield directly: I-295 Exit 22A (State Rte. 5 East, Charles City), e. on State Rte. 5 East about 1.8 miles to Long Bridge Rd.; n.e. (left) on Long Bridge Rd. 1.4 miles to Bradbury Rd.; n. (left) on Bradbury Rd. 1.4 miles to Darbytown Rd.; e. (right) on Darbytown Rd. .2 mile to Gill Dale Rd.; n. (left) on Gill Dale Rd. 1.7 miles to Charles City Rd.; e. (right) on Charles City Rd. .4 mile to Poplar Spring Church; return w. on Charles City Rd. 1.3 miles to state historical marker PA-251, Sad Reunion; return e. on Charles City Rd. .15 mile to Yahley Mill Rd.; s. (right) on Yahley Mill Rd. 1.75 miles to Darbytown Rd.; e. (left) on Darbytown Rd. .4 mile to Fussell's Ridge Dr. and state historical marker PA-153, Second Battle of Deep Bottom; return to Yahley Mill Rd.; s. (left) on Yahley Mill Rd. 1.5 miles to Long Bridge Rd.; s.e. (right) on Long Bridge Rd. .8 mile to State Rte. 5; e. (right) on State Rte. 5 1.8 miles to I-295.

Once again Hancock's objective was to outflank the Confederate defenses from the south and east.

Birney pushed the X Corps north from the bridgehead soon after dawn on Sunday, August 14. Brig. Gen. Robert S. Foster's brigade overran the Confederate picket lines between Deep Bottom and New Market Heights and captured four howitzers, then continued north. Maj. Gen. Charles W. Field, the commander of the Confederate forces north of the James River, strengthened his lines atop the heights in anticipation of a Federal attack.

The next day, August 15, Hancock kept II Corps in place north of Deep Bottom and southeast of New Market Heights while X Corps outflanked and attacked the Confederate left. The maneuver, in the dreadful heat and humidity of the Virginia

summer, took more than a day as the corps marched north and east on Darbytown and Bradbury Roads. Not until Tuesday, August 16, were the units in position. By that time the Confederates were prepared.

At first the attack went well for X Corps, as Brig. Gen. Alfred H. Terry's division broke through the Confederate line. Field, however, quickly filled the breach with all the reinforcements he could assemble. Lee himself arrived on the field late in the day to observe the recapture of the line and the repulse of the Federals.

Gregg's cavalry, meanwhile, made a sweep around the infantry battlefield, riding east and north on New Market and Willis Church Roads (present-day Rte. 156) to Glendale, then northwest on Charles City Road toward Richmond. Early in the morning, Gregg found Maj. Gen. William H. F. "Rooney" Lee's cavalry division blocking Charles City Road, and the two forces engaged each other in what became a day-long series of combats. At first Gregg pushed as far west as White's Tavern, but soon he was forced back toward Glendale. During the initial engagements, Confederate brigadier general John R. Chambliss was killed on Charles City Road about two miles north of the infantry battleground. (Gregg, who had attended West Point with Chambliss early in the 1850s, took charge of his body and later sent it through the lines to Chambliss's widow.)

Once again a Federal onslaught, as at the first battle of Deep Bottom, had ground to a halt in the face of a rugged Confederate resistance. On the other hand, the attack had compelled Lee to detach a brigade from Petersburg and three regiments from the Howlett line at Bermuda Hundred in order to contain the Federal advance. Several days of inconclusive skirmishing followed the August 16 engagement. Finally, on the night of August 20–21, Hancock's force quietly disengaged and crossed to the south side of the James River.

The Federals lost some 2,900 men, some due to heatstroke. Confederate casualties amounted to about 1,300. The second Deep Bottom battlefield, like the first, remains heavily wooded but with increasing residential development. ■

GLOBE TAVERN

Lt. Gen. Ulysses S. Grant launched the second phase of his two-pronged August 1864 offensive operation by ordering Maj. Gen. Gouverneur K. Warren's V Corps to withdraw from the Petersburg entrenchments and then move against the Petersburg Railroad (a.k.a. the Weldon Railroad), south of Petersburg in Dinwiddie County. Warren advanced to the south and west at dawn on Thursday, August 18, drove back Confederate pickets, and reached the railroad at Globe Tavern at about 9 A.M.

Once the railroad was seized, parts of Brig. Gen. Charles Griffin's division were detailed to destroy track. Meanwhile, Brig. Gen. Romeyn B. Ayres's division formed in line of battle and marched slowly north along the railroad to thwart any attack from that direction.

At about 1 P.M., as intermittent showers turned into a steady downpour, Ayres engaged a Confederate skirmish line. Warren ordered Brig. Gen. Samuel W. Crawford to advance his division on Ayres's right and thereby outflank the Confederate left. The rain, the terrain, and opposing artillery fire made the maneuver more difficult and time-consuming than expected. At 2 P.M., as the reinforced line began to advance once again, it suddenly was struck by an onslaught of Confederates.

Gen. P. G. T. Beauregard commanded the defense of Petersburg. As reports of the Federal expedition reached Beauregard, he notified Lee, requesting cavalry reinforcements, and dispatched two brigades of Maj. Gen. Henry Heth's division (soon followed by a brigade of Maj. Gen. Robert F. Hoke's division) to contain the Union advance. Heth's strong attack flung back the Federals almost three-quarters of a mile to a clearing north of Globe Tavern. Warren counterattacked, recaptured much of the lost ground, and entrenched as darkness fell.

During the night each side reinforced its lines. Maj. Gen. John G. Parke led IX Corps to Warren's aid, while Lee ordered Maj. Gen. William H. F. "Rooney" Lee's cavalry division and three infantry brigades of Maj. Gen. William Mahone's division to augment Heth. The Federals were determined to hold the railroad, while the Confederates were just as determined to take it back.

The rain continued unabated throughout the night and all the day on August 19. Each side skirmished intermittently with the other, but heavy combat did not occur until late in the afternoon. Mahone believed that the Federals had not extended their right flank through an area of thick woods and dense undergrowth and would be exposed to a flank attack from the

> **DIRECTIONS:** I-95 Exit 50 (U.S. Rte. 301 South, Crater Rd.); s. (right) on U.S. Rte. 301 1.5 miles to Flank Rd. and Fort Davis on right; w. (right) on Flank Rd. 3.3 miles to Rte. 604 (Halifax Rd.) at Fort Wadsworth; right on Rte. 604 1.2 miles to intersection of Rte. 604 and Rte. 675 (Vaughan Rd.); return to I-95.

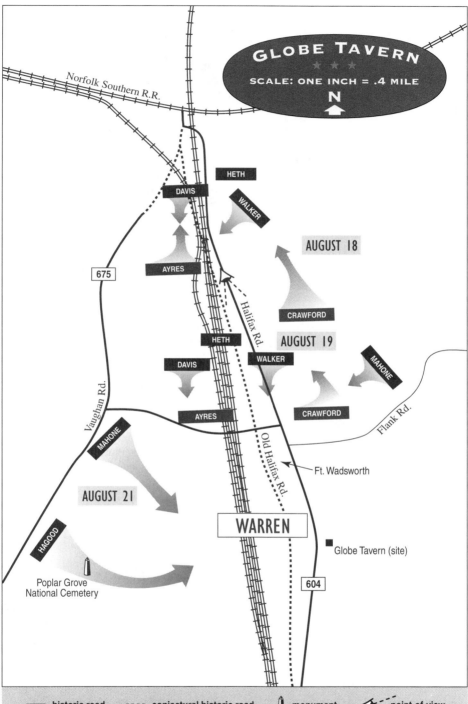

GLOBE TAVERN
★ ★ ★
SCALE: ONE INCH = .4 MILE
N

Norfolk Southern R.R.

HETH

DAVIS

WALKER

AUGUST 18

675

AYRES

Halifax Rd.

CRAWFORD

HETH

AUGUST 19

DAVIS

WALKER

MAHONE

Vaughan Rd.

AYRES

CRAWFORD

Flank Rd.

MAHONE

Old Halifax Rd.

Ft. Wadsworth

AUGUST 21

HAGOOD

WARREN

Globe Tavern (site)

Poplar Grove
National Cemetery

604

── historic road   ···· conjectural historic road   monument   ◁···· point-of-view

The heart of the Globe Tavern battlefield.

VIRGINIA DEPARTMENT OF HISTORIC RESOURCES, JOHN S. SALMON

northeast. He was correct; at about 5 P.M. his detachment succeeded for a time in rolling up the Union right flank. Four Federal brigades virtually ceased to exist, the men either killed or captured. A IX Corps counterattack and the confusion of battle in the woods and briar patches finally checked Mahone's attack at dusk.

Little fighting occurred while the rain continued to fall. During the soggy night of August 20–21, Warren pulled his troops back to a second, stronger line of fieldworks that the men continued to strengthen. They also connected it with the main Federal lines at Jerusalem Plank Road (present-day U.S. Rte. 301). Mahone, meanwhile, led his detachment opposite the Federal left flank. Then at last the sun appeared.

Confederate artillery bombarded the Union works beginning at 9 A.M., and the infantry attack began under its umbrella. Mahone struck the Federal left while Heth assaulted the center. This time, however, the Confederates were attacking strong positions that were well defended. The results were devastating, as Mahone's and Heth's units were thrown back with heavy losses. Brig. Gen. John C. C. Sanders was shot in both thighs and quickly bled to death. The Confederate assault was over by 10:30 A.M. The Federals had held, the railroad north and south of Globe Tavern for several miles was irretrievably in their hands, and soon the Union siege lines would be extended farther to secure the area. The Confederates were now forced to off-load rail cars at Stony Creek Station for a twenty-mile wagon haul up the Boydton Plank Road (U.S. Rte. 1) to reach Petersburg.

The days of battle at Globe Tavern cost the Federals some 4,455 casualties (more than 2,700 of them captured). The Confederates lost about 1,600.

An industrial park occupies part of the Globe Tavern battlefield. Elsewhere, farming operations continue, and the remainder of the ground is wooded. ▪

SECOND BATTLE OF REAM'S STATION

The Federal success at Globe Tavern on August 18–21, 1864, severed Gen. Robert E. Lee's supply line to North Carolina. To exploit his victory, Maj. Gen. George G. Meade ordered elements of Maj. Gen. Winfield S. Hancock's II Corps to march south along the railroad and assist in destroying the fourteen miles of track from Globe Tavern through Ream's Station to Rowanty Creek.

Brig. Gen. David M. Gregg's cavalry division preceded Brig. Gen. Nelson A. Miles's infantry division on August 22 and drove off Confederate skirmishers and pickets lurking near the rail line. By evening, Miles's men had wrecked the railroad to within two miles of Ream's Station, which the cavalry then occupied. Cavalry skirmishing continued well into the night.

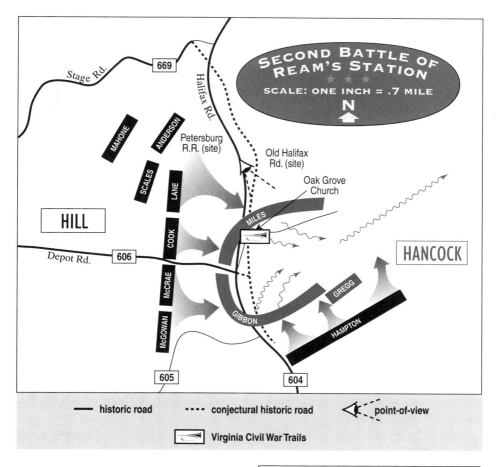

SECOND BATTLE OF REAM'S STATION
★ ★ ★
SCALE: ONE INCH = .7 MILE
N

Stage Rd.

669

Halifax Rd.

MAHONE

ANDERSON

Petersburg
R.R. (site)

Old Halifax
Rd. (site)

Oak Grove
Church

SCALES

LANE

MILES

HILL

COOK

Depot Rd. 606

HANCOCK

McCRAE

GREGG

McGOWAN

GIBBON

HAMPTON

605

604

—— historic road   ···· conjectural historic road   ◄··· point-of-view

Virginia Civil War Trails

Brig. Gen. John Gibbon's II Corps division followed Miles's and occupied Ream's Station beginning in the predawn hours of August 23. The infantrymen filed into the nearby earthworks that had been constructed by Brig. Gen. James H. Wilson's and Brig. Gen. August V. Kautz's horse soldiers late in June. The fieldworks were half-collapsed, and water stood in the ditches, yet the soldiers made little effort to improve them.

Gen. Robert E. Lee, meanwhile, considered the Federals at Ream's Station a threat to his supply line, which (because of the destruction of the Petersburg Railroad) wound northwest from Stony Creek depot to Dinwiddie Court House and thence

DIRECTIONS: I-95 Exit 41 (Courtland, State Rte. 35); n.w. on State Rte. 35/622 (Providence Rd.) about 2.5 miles to Rte. 606 (Ream's Rd.); w. (left) on Rte. 606 1.8 miles to Rte. 604 (Halifax Rd.) and site of Ream's Station (Rte. 604 on bed of Petersburg R.R.); s. (left) on Rte. 604 1.9 miles to Rte. 668 (Brick Rd.); right on Rte. 668 2 miles to Rte. 703 (Carson Rd.); right on Rte. 703 3.3 miles to Rte. 670 (Dabney Mill Rd.); right on Rte. 670 2.5 miles to Rte. 669 (Old Stage Rd.); right on Rte. 669 1.3 miles to Rte. 606; right on Rte. 606 2 miles to Rte. 604; n. (left) on Rte. 604 .3 mile to Rte. 606; e. (right) on Rte. 606 1.8 miles to Rte. 622; s.e. (right) on Rte. 622 and return 2.5 miles to I-95.

northeast to Petersburg. From Ream's Station, the Union force could attack the county seat, fewer than a dozen miles

View southeast along axis of C.S.A. attack against center of Miles's line. VIRGINIA DEPARTMENT OF HISTORIC RESOURCES, JOHN S. SALMON

west, and compel Lee to abandon Petersburg and Richmond. Lee ordered Maj. Gen. Wade Hampton, his cavalry commander, to drive off the Federals, and sent Hampton's two divisions as well as infantry units: Maj. Gen. Cadmus M. Wilcox's division, part of Maj. Gen. Henry Heth's division, and part of Maj. Gen. William Mahone's division, with Lt. Gen. A. P. Hill in overall command of the expedition. Hill, indisposed, placed Heth in charge.

Hancock himself soon arrived at Ream's Station to oversee the operation. By the evening of August 24, the Federal wrecking crew had destroyed track to a point three miles south of Ream's Station. On Thursday, August 25, the men left the earthworks to continue their task. Hancock recalled them, however, when word came that Confederate cavalry was approaching from the west.

The more serious threat, however, arose from Wilcox's infantry, which closed in on the Union position from the west while Hampton's cavalry swept to the south. At about 2 P.M. Wilcox twice assaulted the western face of Hancock's line and was driven back by Miles's division. South of the works, meanwhile, detachments from Gibbon's division were holding Hampton's cavalry at bay.

During the late afternoon, Heth's and Mahone's divisions reinforced the Confederate infantry. Col. William J. "Willie" Pegram's artillery softened up the Federal position, and the final attack began about 5:30 P.M. This time the Confederates broke through the northwest corner of the Union works, while Hampton pressed hard against Gibbon's sector in the southern portion. Gibbon's men either fled in panic or surrendered. Miles, barely holding on to the north, found himself flanked by Hampton. Over the next hour and a half, the Union generals labored to avoid having a defeat turn into a rout. Hancock organized a counterattack that bought time for an orderly withdrawal to the Petersburg lines. Only darkness and a violent rainstorm ended the fighting.

The Confederates lost about 800 in the battle; the Federals suffered more than 2,700, about 2,000 of them captured. The Hancock-Gibbon team that had spelled disaster for the Confederates at Gettysburg—and which was under stress since the Wilderness—ruptured, and the two generals went their separate ways.

Little development has occurred on the battlefield itself. The area is heavily wooded, however, which makes it difficult to understand the battle from the terrain. The problem is increased by the realignment of the railroad a mile or more to the east of its historic bed; Rte. 604 now covers the old rail bed. The Conservation Fund owns 217 acres of the battlefield. ∎

CHAFFIN'S FARM AND NEW MARKET HEIGHTS

On September 29, 1864, Maj. Gen. Benjamin F. Butler's Army of the James crossed the James River from Bermuda Hundred for the third Federal incursion of the year against the defenses of Richmond. Lt. Gen. Ulysses S. Grant had ordered the attack to induce Gen. Robert E. Lee to weaken further his Petersburg garrison and, if possible, to penetrate the line and capture Richmond.

The axis of attack was two-pronged. Maj. Gen. David B. Birney's X Corps, augmented by Brig. Gen. Charles J. Paine's black division from XVIII Corps, would form the right wing and assault the Confederate line just south of New Market Road. They would breach the line and capture New Market Heights behind it, a bluff on which Confederate artillery was posted. They would thus protect the right flank of Maj. Gen. Edward O. C. Ord's XVIII Corps, which would form the left wing

and simultaneously attack Fort Harrison, the stronghold of the Confederate line, from the southeast. Once the New Market Road line was neutralized, the Federals there would assist Ord's assault by attacking Fort Gregg and Fort Gilmer, north of Fort Harrison.

Butler had long been a champion of the black soldier. On May 24 the first brigade's 1st United States Colored Troops (USCT), which with part of the third brigade's 10th USCT had garrisoned Fort Pocahontas (Wilson's Wharf) in Charles City County, had repulsed successive attacks by dismounted Confederate cavalry. Under Butler's plan of attack, they and the other men in their division would test their mettle against Confederate fieldworks on September 29.

Ord's corps crossed the James River at Aiken's Landing, a few miles upstream from Deep Bottom, using a hastily

Capture of Fort Harrison. LIBRARY OF CONGRESS

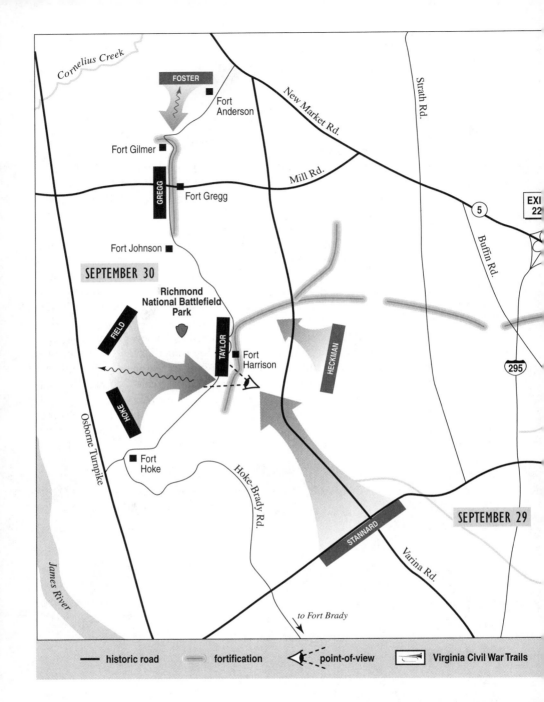

Cornelius Creek

FOSTER

Fort Anderson

New Market Rd.

Strath Rd.

Fort Gilmer

Mill Rd.

GREGG

Fort Gregg

EXIT 22

5

Fort Johnson

Buffin Rd.

SEPTEMBER 30

Richmond National Battlefield Park

FIELD

TAYLOR

Fort Harrison

HECKMAN

295

HOKE

Osborne Turnpike

Fort Hoke

Hoke-Brady Rd.

SEPTEMBER 29

STANNARD

Varina Rd.

James River

to Fort Brady

— historic road   — fortification   ◁ point-of-view   Virginia Civil War Trails

constructed pontoon bridge on Thursday, September 29. Before dawn the corps had gained the opposite shore without a shot being fired. The Deep Bottom crossing did not go as smoothly, however. Paine's division led the way, but Birney's corps straggled badly as it marched up Jones's Neck.

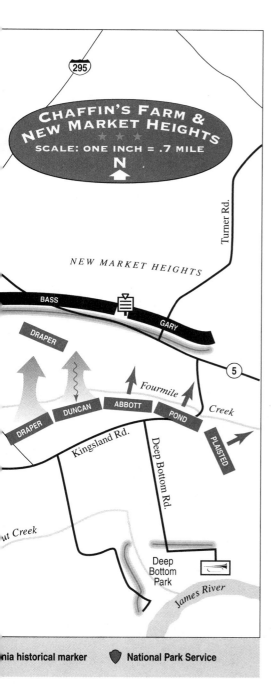

CHAFFIN'S FARM &
NEW MARKET HEIGHTS
★ ★ ★
SCALE: ONE INCH = .7 MILE
N

295

Turner Rd.

NEW MARKET HEIGHTS

BASS

GARY

DRAPER

DUNCAN

ABBOTT

POND

DRAPER

Fourmile

Creek

PLAISTED

5

Kingsland Rd.

Deep Bottom Rd.

ut Creek

Deep
Bottom
Park

James River

nia historical marker   ● National Park Service

DIRECTIONS: Recommend first visiting the Richmond National Battlefield Park Visitor Center (open 9–5 daily) at Tredegar Iron Works in downtown Richmond: I-95 Exit 74C (U.S. Rte. 33 West/U.S. Rte. 250 West, Broad St.) and follow blue-and-green signs to visitor center, Brown's Island, and Belle Isle, w. on Broad St. about .4 mile (5 blocks) to 8th St.; s. (left) on 8th St. 5 blocks to Canal St.; w. (right) on Canal St. 3 blocks to 5th St.; s. (left) on 5th St. 2 blocks to Tredegar St.; w. (right) on Tredegar Street .1 mile to visitor center and parking lot. Visit the National Park Service Web site at nps.gov/parks.html for a virtual tour of this and other national parks. To visit the battlefield directly: I-295 Exit 22A (State Rte. 5 East, Charles City), e. on State Rte. 5 East (main battlefield on s. side of road) about .8 mile to state historical marker V-26, Battle of New Market Heights, and view of CSA earthwork remnant on s. side of road; continue on State Rte. 5 .6 mile to Kingsland Rd.; s. (right) on Kingsland Rd. .7 mile to Deep Bottom Rd.; s. (left) on Deep Bottom Rd. 1.4 miles to Deep Bottom Park and Virginia Civil War Trails marker; return to Kingsland Rd.; e. (left) on Kingsland Rd. .8 mile to Buffin Rd.; n.w. (right) on Buffin Rd. 2.1 miles to State Rte. 5; w. (left) on State Rte. 5 1.7 miles to Richmond National Battlefield Park Fort Harrison Unit at Battlefield Park Rd. and Richmond Battlefield Markers Association marker, Fort Gilmer; s. (left) on Battlefield Park Rd. to tour unit; return to State Rte. 5; e. (right) on State Rte. 5 2.3 miles to I-295.

Confederate pickets observed the crossings and passed the word to their commanders. Telegraphed immediately in Petersburg, Lee ordered reinforcements

north from the Howlett line. Other troops were dispatched from Richmond, but by 6 A.M. only 4,500 Confederates manned the New Market Road and Fort Harrison lines.

Fewer than 300 soldiers garrisoned Fort Harrison, the strongest point in the north-south defensive line. The fort itself appeared awesome, with twenty-foot-high parapets, a deep ditch in front, and six cannons, but the stronghold was undermanned, and four of the large-caliber guns were inoperable. Maj. Richard Taylor commanded the troops there (Lt. Gen. Richard S. Ewell had overall responsibility), and reinforcements arrived just before the battle began.

The garrison faced an entire 3,000-man division, Brig. Gen. George J. Stannard's command of Ord's corps. The division advanced after 6 A.M. across ground freshly cleared to provide fields of fire for Fort

Chaffin's Farm and New Market Heights • 431

Harrison's guns. At first the artillerists aimed high, but soon they found the range, and a single shell killed and maimed a dozen or more soldiers in the compact ranks. After crossing the field, the division took cover in a depression a hundred yards short of the objective, then charged up and over the ramparts. The commander of the brigade spearheading the attack, Brig. Gen. Hiram Burnham, was killed. The fort's garrison, overwhelmed by superior numbers, fled to the second, intermediate line.

The commander of the corps' second division, Brig. Gen. Charles A. Heckman, supported Stannard's attack but struck the line north of Fort Harrison. His division's frontal assaults against Forts Johnson, Gregg, and Gilmer were repelled by the defenders there, despite having been reinforced by Birney's corps from New Market Heights. Ord was wounded seriously.

While the left wing attacked Fort Harrison, the right wing struggled against the New Market Road works, which contained fewer than 1,800 defenders. Several obstacles aided the Confederates, however: Four Mile Creek, a boggy watercourse that the Federals had to cross, two lines of abatis, or trees felled so that the intertwined branches faced the enemy—a predecessor of barbed wire—and a dense, concealing ground fog.

Brig. Gen. Alfred H. Terry formed his X Corps division on the Union right. The 2nd USCT Cavalry, dismounted, linked Terry's left flank with Paine's right flank. Col. Samuel A. Duncan's USCT brigade of Paine's division led the attack on the Confederate left just after dawn. It forded Four Mile Creek, drove in the pickets, and attacked the New Market Road line only to become entangled in the abatis. Some struggled through while others were shot down; Duncan himself fell wounded. Few of the black soldiers reached the trenches, and those who did were killed or captured.

Col. John W. Ames, of the 6th USCT, called for a retreat.

Paine ordered Col. Alonzo G. Draper, commanding the second brigade, to follow up Duncan's attack, and sent the 22nd USCT to screen the brigade's left flank, with Col. John H. Holman's brigade following in support. By this time, the ground fog had dissipated, and the Federals took casualties as soon as they began to cross Four Mile Creek. When the troops struck the abatis, they stopped to exchange shots with the Confederates rather than continue their assault on the works. Draper finally convinced them to stop shooting and charge, which they did in the face of continued heavy fire. As they struck the Confederate works, the defenders fled, having received orders to retire to the Fort Harrison line. Draper's brigade swept over the works and up New Market Heights, assisting Terry's division in driving off the Confederate artillery.

Brig. Gen. Robert S. Foster's X Corps division, which had been held in reserve, marched forward at about 8:30 A.M. to take the lead in carrying the attack westward to the Fort Harrison line. Having borne the brunt of the New Market Road fighting, Paine's brigades rested while Foster's and Terry's divisions marched by to support the futile attacks against Forts Johnson, Gregg, and Gilmer. The 7th USCT of Brig. Gen. William Birney's attached X Corps brigade spearheaded the attack on Fort Gilmer's eastern front. By the end of the day, the Federals had to settle for overrunning the New Market Road line, sweeping New Market Heights clean, and occupying Fort Harrison.

They had no time to rest on their laurels, however. Anticipating a Confederate counterattack, the soldiers labored to "turn around" Fort Harrison: that is, they constructed and strengthened earthworks on the western, or Richmond, side of the fort and prepared to defend them. From Petersburg, Lee rode north to take charge of the counterattack himself. He also ordered two divisions and four regiments to reinforce Brig. Gen. John Gregg, who was commanding in the field.

Maj. Gen. Charles W. Field and Maj. Gen. Robert F. Hoke led their divisions, accompanied by four of Maj. Gen. George E. Pickett's regiments, north of the James River. On September 30, about noon, a half-hour bombardment of the new Federal works began, followed at 1:45 P.M. by what was supposed to be a coordinated infantry attack. But the artillery fired high and long, and the infantry assault quickly fell apart. The Federals shot down Brig. Gen. George T. Anderson's Georgia brigade of Field's division as it approached the fort. Brig. Gen. John Bratton's South Carolina brigade and two brigades of Hoke's division were likewise torn to pieces. Finally, near dusk, Lee stopped the attacks. Grant at last had the foothold he had sought north of James River.

Two days of bloody combat had cost both sides dearly. The Confederates lost about 1,750, mostly on the second day, while the Federals suffered most of their 4,150 casualties on the first day in capturing Fort Harrison and New Market Heights. For the black soldiers, the New Market Heights and Chaffin's Farm combats meant glory and respect. Persevering despite nearly being cut to ribbons, their individual acts of heroism were so frequent that fourteen of them (and two white officers) later received Medals of Honor. Sixteen black soldiers altogether were awarded the medal for heroism during the war.

Some 310 acres of the Chaffin's Farm battlefield, primarily Fort Harrison and related parts of the Confederate lines, are preserved in the Fort Harrison unit of Richmond National Battlefield Park. Housing developments and individual residences are scattered up and down the roads through the battlefields. Most of the New Market Heights battlefield remains under private ownership and part may soon be developed. In 2000, plans were afoot to honor the African Americans who served there. ◼

PEEBLES'S FARM

Gen. Robert E. Lee had weakened his Petersburg defenses by ordering 10,000 troops northward in vain counterattacks against the Federals, and Lt. Gen. Ulysses S. Grant seized the opportunity, hoping to extend his left flank to the South Side Railroad, Lee's final rail link into Petersburg from the west. Grant ordered Brig. Gen. David M. Gregg's cavalry division and two infantry divisions each from Maj. Gen. Gouverneur K. Warren's V Corps and Maj. Gen. John G. Parke's IX Corps to cut the railroad and extend the Union lines westward. At about 9 A.M. on

View south from behind C.S.A. position toward U.S. route of attack. VIRGINIA DEPARTMENT OF HISTORIC RESOURCES, JOHN S. SALMON

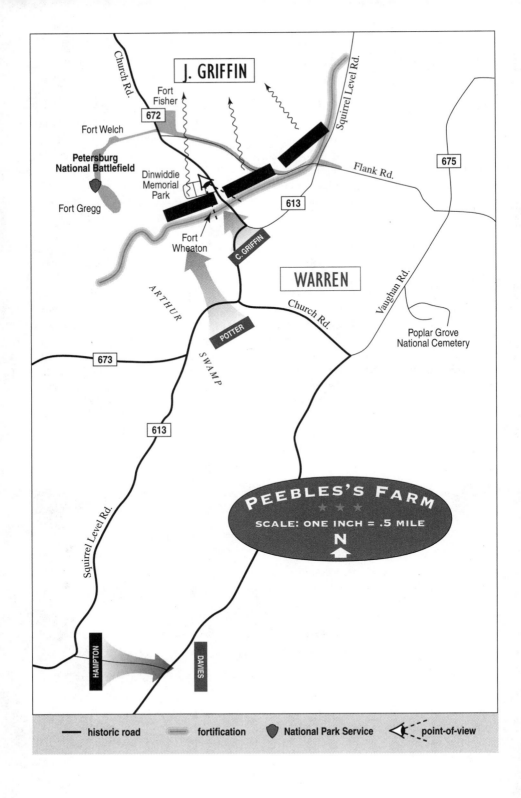

J. GRIFFIN

Church Rd.

Fort Fisher

672

Fort Welch

Squirrel Level Rd.

Petersburg
National Battlefield

Flank Rd.

675

Fort Gregg

Dinwiddie
Memorial
Park

613

Fort
Wheaton

C. GRIFFIN

WARREN

ARTHUR

Church Rd.

Vaughan Rd.

POTTER

Poplar Grove
National Cemetery

673

SWAMP

613

PEEBLES'S FARM

★ ★ ★

SCALE: ONE INCH = .5 MILE

N

Squirrel Level Rd.

HAMPTON

DAVIES

— historic road   fortification   National Park Service   point-of-view

DIRECTIONS: I-85 Exit 61 (Sutherland), e. on U.S. Rte. 460 about .3 mile to U.S. Rte. 1; s.e. (right) on U.S. Rte. 1 2.4 miles to Rte. 613 East (Dabney Mill Rd.); e. (left) on Rte. 613 East 3 miles to Rte. 613/670 (Dabney Mill Rd.); s.e. (right) on Rte. 613/670 .5 mile to Rte. 613 (Squirrel Level Rd.); n.e. (left) on Rte. 613 .8 mile to Rte. 674 (Wheaton Rd.); do not turn but continue on Rte. 613 past Rte. 674 into heart of battlefield 3.4 miles to Rte. 672 (Church Rd.); n. (left) on Rte. 672 .3 mile to Dinwiddie Memorial Park on left; turn around in cemetery and return .8 mile to Rte. 741 (Fort Emory Rd.); e. (right) on Rte. 741 .6 mile to Rte. 675 (Vaughan Rd.); s. (right) on Rte. 675 3.8 miles to Rte. 670 (Duncan Rd.) (you will reenter battlefield after about 2 miles); n.w. (right) on Rte. 670 .6 mile to Rte. 613/670 (Duncan Rd.); n.w. (left) on Rte. 613/670 (Dabney Mill Rd.) .5 mile to Rte. 613 East (Dabney Mill Rd.); w. (left) on Rte. 613 East 3 miles to U.S. Rte. 1; n.e. (right) on U.S. Rte. 1 2.7 miles to I-85.

September 30, 1864, Brig. Gen. Charles Griffin's and Brig. Gen. Romeyn B. Ayres's V Corps divisions led the way behind a small cavalry screen. Brig. Gen. Robert B. Potter and Brig. Gen. Orlando B. Willcox followed about an hour later with their IX Corps divisions, while Gregg's cavalrymen protected the Federal left flank.

The Union force, some 20,000 strong, marched northwest on Poplar Grove Road (present-day Rte. 741). As the three infantry divisions approached Fort Archer in the Confederate line along Squirrel Level Road (Rte. 613) north of the Peebles's farm, the fort's artillery opened on them at long range. The guns themselves and the Confederate defenders were hidden from direct Federal observation by heavy woods and thickets. Warren therefore deployed his force with deliberate care.

At 1 P.M., Griffin's division attacked Fort Archer. The fort's defenders were overwhelmed by the enormous Federal force within fifteen or thirty minutes, despite firing several volleys with small arms and artillery. The Confederates abandoned Fort Archer and the remainder of their works on Peebles's farm, and retreated northwest to their inner line at the Jones farm. The Federals spent more than an hour preparing to continue the attack to the Boydton Plank Road (present-day U.S. Rte. 1).

Lt. Gen. A. P. Hill, meanwhile, rushed elements of Maj. Gen. Wade Hampton's cavalry division and Maj. Gen. Cadmus M. Wilcox's infantry division to the area as Confederate reinforcements. When the Federal advance began late in the afternoon, the Confederates were ready for it, and the thrust was dispersed by a strong counterattack. On the right, another Confederate attack drove back Brig. Gen. Charles Griffin's division of V Corps. By dusk the Federals had retreated to the Peebles's farm works, which they spent the night strengthening.

The next day Maj. Gen. Henry Heth's division of Hill's corps attacked southwest on Squirrel Level Road against the Federal position, but two charges failed to dislodge them. South of Peebles's farm at Poplar Springs Church, meanwhile, Hampton led three of his brigades in an effort to flank the Federal position on Vaughan Road. Brig. Gen. Henry E. Davies's cavalry brigade, however, entrenched and blocked Hampton's path. A bloody fight began at about 3 P.M. that stymied Hampton's maneuver.

On Sunday, October 2, Warren, reinforced by Brig. Gen. Gershom Mott's II Corps division, advanced west toward the Boydton Plank Road, with units of the V and IX Corps on his right. Perceiving the strength of the Confederate position, however, Mott did not attack. The Federals instead consolidated their lines and extended their entrenchments west from the Petersburg Railroad.

At a cost of almost 2,900 casualties, Warren had extended the Union left flank from the Globe Tavern to within striking distance of the Boydton Plank Road. In denying the Federals that objective and in protecting the South Side Railroad, the Confederates lost some 1,300 men.

Portions of the battlefield, excluding Peebles's farm, are in Petersburg National Battlefield. These segments consist mostly of trenches and fortifications constructed after the battle. Fort Archer, renamed Fort Wheaton, is in the park. The remainder of the battlefield is in private hands, and a steel-recycling plant has obliterated a large portion of it. Part of the area still consists of small farms and woods. ■

DARBYTOWN AND NEW MARKET ROADS

Although the Federals' numerical superiority compelled Gen. Robert E. Lee to remain on the defensive, he struck back whenever possible. In early October 1864 he designed a plan to retake Fort Harrison.

The right flank of Maj. Gen. Benjamin F. Butler's Army of the James, Brig. Gen. August V. Kautz's cavalry division, rested on Darbytown Road. In military parlance, the flank was "in the air": It did not rest on a natural obstacle as a safeguard and therefore was subject to envelopment. Lee's scheme called for most of Maj. Gen. Charles W. Field's infantry division to attack the front of Kautz's division while Brig. Gen. Martin W. Gary's cavalry brigade and one of Field's infantry brigades attacked from the north. Together, the two forces would crush Kautz and drive south toward New Market Road (Rte. 5). Maj. Gen. Robert F. Hoke's infantry division would then join in the assault to force the Federals to evacuate Fort Harrison and retreat to Deep Bottom.

Launched near dawn on Friday, October 7, the attack at first succeeded despite being detected by some of Kautz's scouts and by Col. Samuel P. Spear's spoiling attacks to counter the Confederate offensive. The sheer numbers overwhelmed Kautz's flank and sent his horse soldiers fleeing south toward Maj. Gen. David B. Birney's X Corps. Birney and his officers organized three brigades of Brig. Gen.

DIRECTIONS: Recommend first visiting the Richmond National Battlefield Park Visitor Center (open 9–5 daily) at Tredegar Iron Works in downtown Richmond: I-95 Exit 74C (U.S. Rte. 33 West/U.S. Rte. 250 West, Broad St.) and follow blue-and-green signs to visitor center, Brown's Island, and Belle Isle, w. on Broad St. about .4 mile (5 blocks) to 8th St.; s. (left) on 8th St. 5 blocks to Canal St.; w. (right) on Canal St. 3 blocks to 5th St.; s. (left) on 5th St. 2 blocks to Tredegar St.; w. (right) on Tredegar Street .1 mile to visitor center and parking lot. Visit the National Park Service Web site at nps.gov/parks.html for a virtual tour of this and other national parks. To visit the battlefield directly: I-295 Exit 22B (State Rte. 5 West, Varina), w. on State Rte. 5 West about .5 mile to Doran Rd.; n. (right) on Doran Rd. 2.1 miles to Darbytown Rd.; n.w. (left) on Darbytown Rd. 1.4 miles to Strath Rd.; s. (left) on Strath Rd. 2.4 miles to State Rte. 5; e. (right) on State Rte. 5 .9 mile to I-295.

Alfred H. Terry's division north of New Market Road to meet the threat.

Field's attack, after its initial success, lost momentum amid the woods and watercourses south of Darbytown Road. By the time his men reorganized and prepared to advance, Terry was ready to receive them. The Confederate line, from right to left, consisted of the brigades commanded by Brig. Gen. John Gregg, Brig. Gen. John Bratton, and Col. William F. Perry. The Federal line, in the same order, included the brigades of Col. Harris M. Plaisted, Col. Joseph C. Abbott, and Col. Francis B. Pond. To tip the scales in favor of the Confederates, Hoke's division was

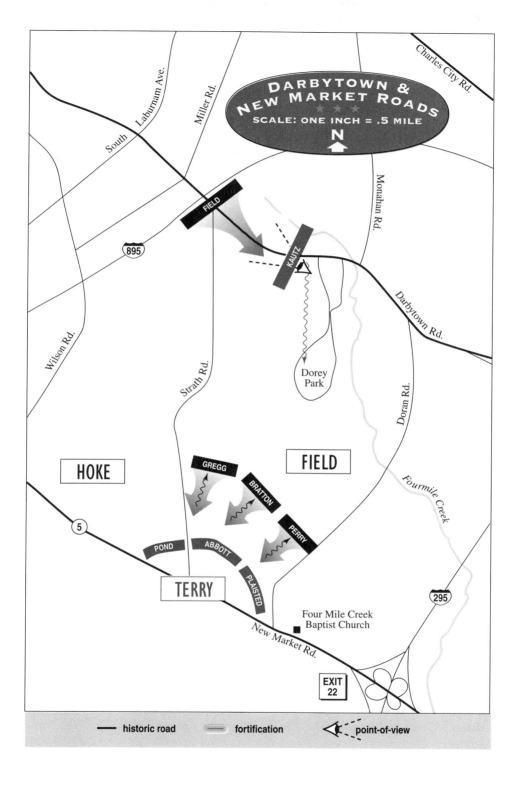

DARBYTOWN &
NEW MARKET ROADS
★ ★ ★
SCALE: ONE INCH = .5 MILE
N

Charles City Rd.

South
Laburnam Ave.

Miller Rd.

Monahan Rd.

Darbytown Rd.

895

FIELD

KAUTZ

Wilson Rd.

Strath Rd.

Dorey
Park

Doran Rd.

HOKE

FIELD

GREGG

BRATTON

PERRY

Fourmile Creek

5

POND

ABBOTT

PLAISTED

TERRY

295

Four Mile Creek
Baptist Church

New Market Rd.

EXIT
22

— historic road   ▱ fortification   ◀ point-of-view

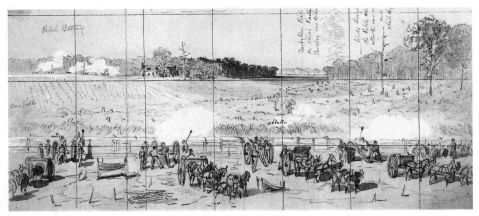

Kautz faces Field's attack on Darbytown Road. LIBRARY OF CONGRESS

to join the attack on Gregg's right. In addition, Brig. Gen. Edward Porter Alexander's artillery brigade fired over the Confederate right, using a maneuver called fire advancing by half battery (one-half of a battery fired while the other moved forward). The effect on the Federal artillery was devastating.

The infantry assault, however, foundered. Hoke's division remained in place on Darbytown Road instead of supporting Field. The Union left, protected by strong earthworks, easily repulsed Gregg's Texas Brigade; Gregg himself died in the futile assault. Lee's last offensive action north of the James River shuddered to a halt, and he soon ordered a withdrawal. By mid-afternoon the Federals had recovered all their lost ground to Darbytown Road.

The Confederates suffered about 700 casualties in the battle, while the Federals lost 458. The battlefield is almost entirely in private hands, except for part of the Darbytown Road segment, which is in Henrico County's Dorey Park. Much of the battlefield near New Market Road has been covered by a housing development, while small parts remain wooded and inaccessible. The site of Gregg's death, located west of the intersection of Strath and Lampworth Roads, remained intact in the late-1990s as a soybean field and woodlot. The destruction of the battlefield through development, however, seems imminent. ∎

DARBYTOWN ROAD

A week after the Confederate defeat at Darbytown and New Market Roads on October 7, 1864, Brig. Gen. Alfred H. Terry led two Union X Corps divisions out of the Federal works north of New Market Road (present-day Rte. 5) to "develop"— i.e., locate and reconnoiter—the new Confederate defensive positions. The force would deploy in woods and advance its skirmish line against the fortifications, not attempt to capture them. Indeed, most of the combat that day would take place between opposing skirmish lines.

At 4 A.M. on Thursday, October 13, the Federals marched on two parallel routes. While Brig. Gen. August V. Kautz's horsemen protected the force's right flank, Brig. Gen. Adelbert Ames's first division and

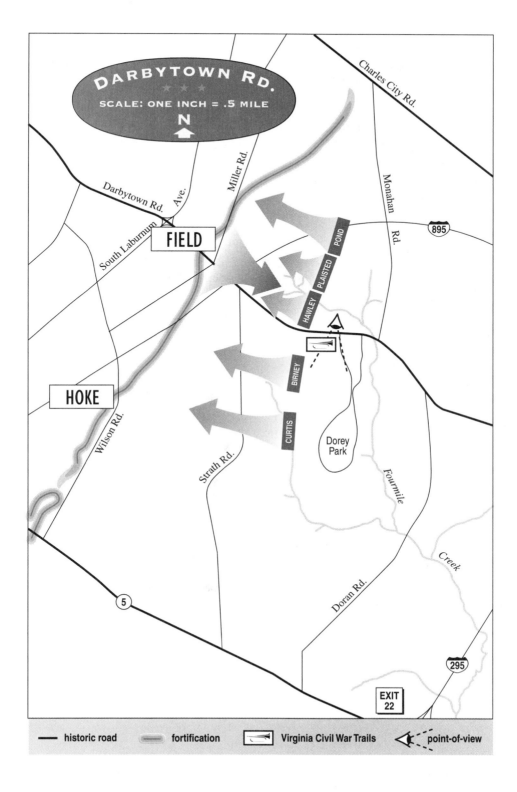

DARBYTOWN RD.

★ ★ ★

SCALE: ONE INCH = .5 MILE

N

Charles City Rd.

Miller Rd.

Monahan Rd.

895

Darbytown Rd.

Ave.

South Laburnum

FIELD

POND

PLAISTED

HAWLEY

BIRNEY

HOKE

Wilson Rd.

CURTIS

Dorey Park

Fourmile

Creek

Strath Rd.

5

Doran Rd.

295

EXIT 22

— historic road   fortification   Virginia Civil War Trails   point-of-view

DIRECTIONS: Recommend first visiting the Richmond National Battlefield Park Visitor Center (open 9–5 daily) at Tredegar Iron Works in downtown Richmond: I-95 Exit 74C (U.S. Rte. 33 West/U.S. Rte. 250 West, Broad St.) and follow blue-and-green signs to visitor center, Brown's Island, and Belle Isle, w. on Broad St. about .4 mile (5 blocks) to 8th St.; s. (left) on 8th St. 5 blocks to Canal St.; w. (right) on Canal St. 3 blocks to 5th St.; s. (left) on 5th St. 2 blocks to Tredegar St.; w. (right) on Tredegar Street .1 mile to visitor center and parking lot. Visit the National Park Service Web site at nps.gov/parks.html for a virtual tour of this and other national parks. To visit the battlefield directly: I-295 Exit 22B (State Rte. 5 West, Varina), w. on State Rte. 5 West about 2.3 miles to Wilson Rd.; n. (right) on Wilson Rd. 1.4 miles to Miller Rd.; n.e. (right) on Miller Rd. 2.3 miles to Charles City Rd.; s.e. (right) on Charles City Rd. .6 miles to Monahan Rd.; s. (right) on Monahan Rd. 1.7 miles to Darbytown Rd.; w. (right) on Darbytown Rd. .25 mile to Virginia Civil War Trails marker on left at Dorey Park entrance; then .7 mile to Strath Rd.; s. (left) on Strath Rd. 2.4 miles to State Rte. 5; e. (right) on State Rte. 5 .9 mile to I-295.

View south behind center of U.S. line. VIRGINIA DEPARTMENT OF HISTORIC RESOURCES, JOHN S. SALMON

Brig. Gen. William Birney's third division formed the right and left flanks of the Federal expedition. The Union force began to deploy its skirmish line, one regiment in front of each brigade, at about 7 A.M.

For the Confederates, Brig. Gen. Martin W. Gary's dismounted cavalry brigade occupied the left flank opposite Kautz. Maj. Gen. Robert F. Hoke's infantry division formed the Confederate right flank. Maj. Gen. Charles W. Field's infantry division occupied the center and faced most of the Federal infantry. Between 8 and 10 A.M., the Confederate skirmishers in the woods were driven in to the fieldworks by the Union advance.

Skirmishing continued until midafternoon, when the Federals attacked Field's position and were repulsed with heavy losses. Field counterattacked an hour later with a series of probes against Col. Harris M. Plaisted designed to keep the Union divisions at bay. Between 4 and 5 P.M., having developed the Confederate defenses to his satisfaction, Terry returned his divisions to their lines on New Market Road.

The Confederates, well entrenched, only suffered an estimated 50 casualties in the day's combat. The Federals lost 437.

Most of Kautz's position and the site of the Confederate left flank has been obliterated by Richmond International Airport and the commercial and residential development that has been constructed nearby. Most of the Confederate fieldworks likewise have been destroyed by residential neighborhoods. The site of Pond's attack is in woods, and some earthworks may survive there. The battlefield may disappear within a few years, given the rate of new construction. ■

On Thursday, October 27, 1864, Lt. Gen. Ulysses S. Grant launched simultaneous attacks against the Confederate lines at Petersburg and Richmond, intending the Richmond thrust to prompt Gen. Robert E. Lee to deplete the Petersburg defenses to protect the capital. The main blow would fall at Petersburg, in the form of an attack on the South Side Railroad southwest of the city.

Maj. Gen. John G. Parke's IX Corps would attack the incomplete Confederate line directly west of the Peebles's farm. If he broke through the line, he would pivot north and strike the inner line near Petersburg; if not, he would continue to threaten the line to distract the Confederates. Maj.

Gen. Gouverneur K. Warren's V Corps would march from the Petersburg Railroad and support IX Corps' movements. Maj. Gen. Winfield S. Hancock's II Corps would attack southwest of Warren from Vaughan Road (present-day Rte. 675), cross Hatcher's Run, then drive northwest on the Boydton Plank Road (U.S. Rte. 1)

DIRECTIONS: I-85 Exit 61 (Sutherland), e. on U.S. Rte. 460 about .3 mile to U.S. Rte. 1; s.w. (right) on U.S. Rte. 1 2.1 miles to state historical marker S-51, Burgess Mill (on e. side of road), then continue .3 mile farther to Rte. 613 East (Dabney Mill Rd.); e. (left) on Rte. 613 East .8 mile to site of Mahone's flank attack (just past second sharp right curve in road); return to I-85.

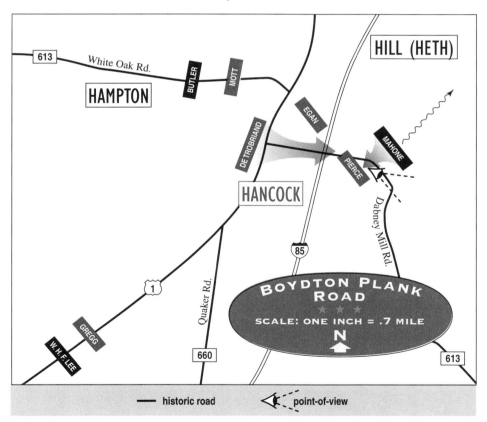

Looking east through Mahone's route of attack against Hancock. VIRGINIA DEPARTMENT OF HISTORIC RESOURCES, JOHN S. SALMON

to the South Side Railroad. Brig. Gen. David M. Gregg's cavalry division, meanwhile, would protect the infantry's left flank.

The movements got under way at 3 A.M. in a drizzle that turned into a steady rain. Roads became muddy, artillery limbers and caissons bogged down, and the infantrymen's progress—impeded anyway by Confederate skirmishers—slowed to a crawl. When IX Corps and V Corps soldiers approached the Confederate works six hours later, they found strongly defended lines, for the element of surprise was gone.

Hancock's II Corps, meanwhile, advanced over Hatcher's Run and threatened to separate two of Maj. Gen. Wade Hampton's cavalry divisions from the Confederate lines. Hampton left Maj. Gen. William H. F. "Rooney" Lee's division on Boydton Plank Road to counter Gregg's cavalry, then withdrew north to block White Oak Road (Rte. 613 west of U.S. Rte. 1) with Brig. Gen. Matthew C. Butler's division. Brig. Gen. Gershom Mott's infantry division moved against Butler. At the same time, Lt. Gen. A. P. Hill hastened to strike the Federals.

Hill's plan called for Hampton to block Gregg while Heth's and Maj. Gen.

William Mahone's infantry divisions cut Dabney Mill Road (approximately Rte. 613 east of U.S. Rte. 1) and isolated II Corps from the rest of the Federal infantry. In reality, that separation had already occurred, as V Corps had failed to link its left flank with II Corps' right flank across the heavily wooded Hatcher's Run. Mahone, recognizing his opportunity, attacked across the stream at 4:30 P.M.

Hancock and his men fought back effectively against Mahone, who had advanced unsupported. Brig. Gen. Régis de Trobriand's brigade counterattacked Mahone's right flank, while Col. Michael Kerwin's dismounted cavalry brigade struck his center and left. Mahone abruptly retreated across Hatcher's Run. The Confederate cavalry attack likewise failed when the Union horse soldiers, fresh from their victory over Mahone, held Hampton in check.

Hancock, despite his strategic victory, decided to withdraw to his original line. His corps had never linked up with V Corps, his men were low on ammunition, and both V and IX Corps had been stymied by the unexpectedly strong Confederate defense. Indeed, Grant had canceled the offensive at 1 P.M., following the poor Federal showing in the morning.

This last major Virginia battle of 1864 cost the Federals 1,758 casualties, while the Confederates suffered about 1,300. It was also Hancock's last battle of the war. He took sick leave, and when he returned to duty, it was as head of the Invalid Corps.

Despite the construction of Interstate 85, the widening of U.S. Rte. 1, and light residential and commercial development along major roads, much of the Boydton Plank Road battlefield retains good integrity. None of it, however, is publicly owned and therefore remains threatened. ∎

FAIR OAKS AND DARBYTOWN ROAD

L t. Gen. Ulysses S. Grant, still seeking to stretch Gen. Robert E. Lee's lines to the breaking point, launched additional attacks on Thursday, October 27, 1864. Maj. Gen. Benjamin F. Butler assaulted Confederate lines east of Richmond in the hope that Lee would detach forces from Petersburg to defend the capital city.

The Federal plan called for Maj. Gen. Alfred H. Terry's X Corps to demonstrate before the Confederate line as far north as Charles City Road while Maj. Gen. Godfrey Weitzel led XVIII Corps around Terry's right flank to turn the Confederate left. Weitzel would accomplish the task by following Brig. Gen. August V. Kautz's cavalry division north, then attacking west on Williamsburg Road (present-day U.S. Rte. 60) near Fair Oaks.

Lt. Gen. James Longstreet commanded the troops defending Richmond. Maj. Gen. Charles W. Field's infantry division held the Confederate left flank, with Brig. Gen. Martin W. Gary's dismounted cavalry brigade extending south from the Chickahominy River bluffs and Brig. Gen. John Bratton's infantry brigade stationed on Gary's right. Maj. Gen. Robert F. Hoke commanded the division to the right of Fields's troops.

Although Grant intended the attack merely to distract Lee, Butler hoped to carry the thrust to Richmond itself and reap the glory of capturing the Confederate capital. His offensive got under way at 4 A.M., as Terry's corps marched north from the Union works at New Market Road (State Rte. 5). Brig. Gen. Adelbert Ames's division led the way, with Brig. Gen. Robert Foster's division next and Brig. Gen. William Birney's all-black brigade last. The corps would advance over the same ground it had covered during the Darbytown Road engagement on October 13. The X Corps executed its part of the plan effectively, despite being hampered by woods and brush.

The same was not true of Weitzel and Kautz. Weitzel could not advance until Terry cleared his front, then had to cover several miles by a roundabout route. Kautz's cavalry, which was to continue to Williamsburg Road, instead halted on Charles City Road, roughly two miles short of its objective, to skirmish with the Confederates and await further orders. Weitzel found Kautz blocking his path and sent to Butler to learn if plans had changed; it was 1 P.M. before he reached Williamsburg Road.

Butler and staff in foreground during battle; Darbytown Road in middle ground, in front of house.
LIBRARY OF CONGRESS

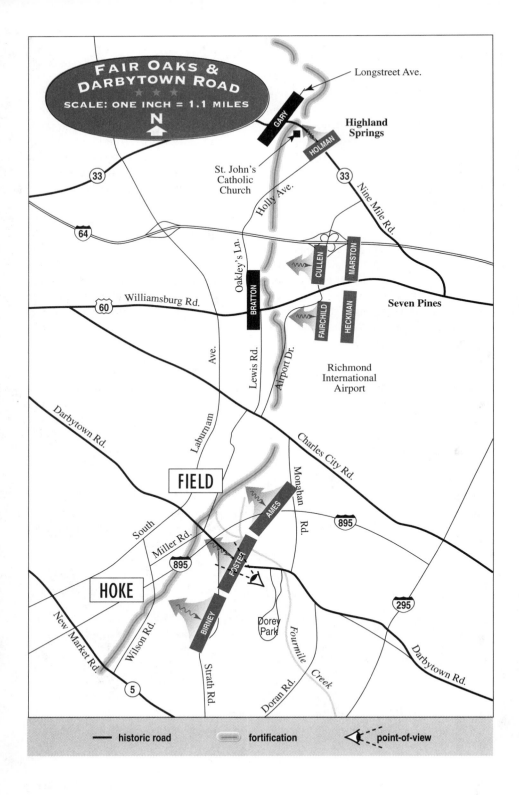

FAIR OAKS &
DARBYTOWN ROAD
★ ★ ★
SCALE: ONE INCH = 1.1 MILES
N

Longstreet Ave.

GARY

HOLMAN

Highland
Springs

St. John's
Catholic
Church

33

Nine Mile Rd.

33

Holly Ave.

64

Oakley's Ln.

CULLEN

MARSTON

BRATTON

Williamsburg Rd.

60

FAIRCHILD

HECKMAN

Seven Pines

Lewis Rd.

Airport Dr.

Richmond
International
Airport

Ave.

Darbytown Rd.

Laburnum

Charles City Rd.

FIELD

Monahan
Rd.

AMES

895

South

Miller Rd.

895

FOSTER

HOKE

Wilson Rd.

BIRNEY

Dorey
Park

Fourmile

Creek

295

New Market Rd.

Strath Rd.

Doran Rd.

Darbytown Rd.

5

historic road   fortification   point-of-view

The long delay between Terry's opening volleys and anything further developing told Longstreet that the Federals' real objective lay elsewhere. About midmorning he ordered Field to pull out his division and march to Williamsburg Road while Hoke extended his line to cover Field's front.

Despite Longstreet's rapid response, Weitzel found the Confederate works on Williamsburg Road lightly defended. However, he had lost contact with Terry's right flank and hesitated to advance before knowing that his own left was protected. For more than two hours, Weitzel reconnoitered and deployed his divisions.

Longstreet, meanwhile, shuttled sol-diers to his left flank by every available means, including putting two or three on a single horse. By the time the remainder of Field's division arrived, at about 3:30 P.M., Weitzel had at last launched his attack. Amazingly, he sent only two brigades— Col. Edgar M. Cullen's on the north side of the road and that of Col. Harrison S. Fairchild on the south side—attacking across 600 yards of open ground. Field's men hastened into position and formed a thin but effective line behind the field-works. Confederate artillery rolled up and unlimbered, and as Cullen's and Fairchild's men approached, they encountered an increasingly violent storm of fire. Some defenders left the earthworks to assault the Union brigades' flanks and capture about 300 soldiers. Soon the Federals retreated to Weitzel's main line, and the attack came to an end. After dark Weitzel and Terry disengaged their corps and retired to the Union works on New Market Road.

Col. John H. Holman's USCT brigade, meanwhile, skirmished with Confederate cavalry but eventually located Gary's field-works. The 1st USCT charged and occupied a section of the works, while the 22nd USCT became entangled in underbrush, was cut up by heavy small-arms fire, and broke for the rear. Gary recaptured his works with a mounted cavalry charge, and the black troops joined the general Union retreat.

The Union demonstration cost Butler 1,603 casualties. The Confederates lost fewer than 100. Richmond did not fall.

The site of Weitzel's attack has been obliterated by Richmond International Airport, and the works captured by the USCTs have likewise succumbed to development. The remainder of the battlefield is likely to be developed in the next few years. ∎

After the battles of October 27, 1864, the Union and Confederate armies dug in for the winter, except for periodic raids. The Federals brooded about their lack of success in severing the South Side Railroad, Gen. Robert E. Lee's last rail communication from Petersburg. Because the Federals had cut the Petersburg Railroad, wagons hauled the much-needed supplies to the city from Stony Creek depot by way of a military road east of Dinwiddie Court House.

Early in February 1865 a spell of relatively mild weather led Maj. Gen. George G. Meade to launch another offensive on the South Side Railroad, which was defended by Lt. Gen. A. P. Hill's corps. On Sunday, February 5, Maj. Gen. David M. Gregg's cavalry division rode into Dinwiddie Court House, interrupting traffic over the Boydton Plank Road from Stony Creek to Petersburg. Simultaneously, Maj. Gen. Gouverneur K. Warren's V Corps marched west to support Gregg by blocking Vaughan Road (present-day Rte. 675).

Maj. Gen. Andrew A. Humphreys, now commanding II Corps, led it west to Armstrong's Mill, north of Hatcher's Run.

By 9:30 a.m. II Corps had secured its position facing the same Confederate works that had stopped the Federal right wing and center in October 1864. This time, however, Humphreys posted Brig. Gen. Thomas A. Smyth's brigade on the Union left and Brig. Gen. Gershom Mott's division on the right and waited for the Confederates to attack him rather than assaulting their strongly defended earthworks.

Gen. Robert E. Lee, informed of the Federal movements, quickly laid plans to counter them. Maj. Gen. Henry Heth observed Humphreys's corps to determine its intentions; late in the afternoon, he decided that Humphreys was not going to attack. Heth's scout had located a gap in Humphreys's line—a gap that Humphreys had also noticed and partially plugged with a regiment from Col. Robert McAllister's brigade. At 4 P.M., as another brigade filed

Armstrong's sawmill, north of Dabney's Mill, and C.S.A. earthworks on Hatcher's Run battlefield.
LIBRARY OF CONGRESS

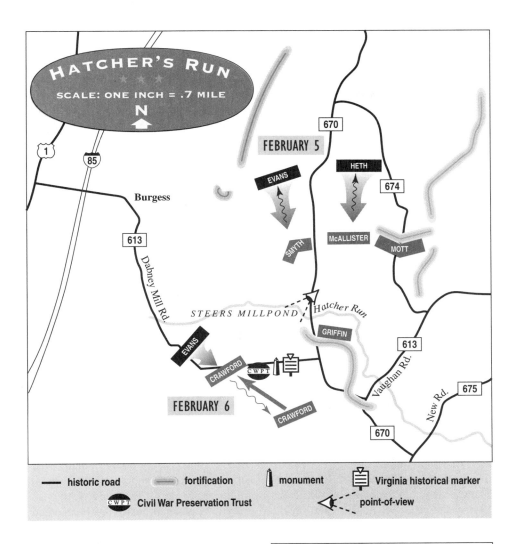

HATCHER'S RUN

SCALE: ONE INCH = .7 MILE

N

FEBRUARY 5

670

HETH

EVANS

674

Burgess

613

McALLISTER

SMYTH

MOTT

Dabney Mill Rd.

STEERS MILLPOND

Hatcher Run

GRIFFIN

EVANS

613

CRAWFORD

CWPT

Vaughan Rd.

FEBRUARY 6

675

CRAWFORD

New Rd.

670

— historic road   fortification   monument   Virginia historical marker

CWPT Civil War Preservation Trust   point-of-view

into place to relieve McAllister, Heth attacked. The combat lasted for an hour and a half until dusk, but McAllister's men held firm, and the Confederates retreated with heavy losses to their right flank.

During the night, in light of Heth's strong attack, Meade ordered Gregg's division back to the Federal lines. The horsemen rejoined the infantry at 4 A.M. on Monday, February 6. Warren's V Corps likewise had pulled back and linked up with II Corps near the Vaughan Road crossing of Hatcher's Run.

DIRECTIONS: I-85 Exit 61 (Sutherland), e. on U.S. Rte. 460 about .3 mile to U.S. Rte. 1; s.w. (right) on U.S. Rte. 1 2.1 miles to state historical marker S-50, Hatcher's Run (on e. side of road), then continue .3 mile farther to Rte. 613 East (Dabney Mill Rd.); e. (left) on Rte. 613 East 2.4 miles to state historical marker S-63, Battle of Hatcher's Run, and Brig. Gen. John Pegram monument at Civil War Preservation Trust Hatcher's Run Battlefield Civil War Site; return to I-85.

The morning passed with little activity aside from limited Union reconnoitering. The Confederates, meanwhile, began their own eastward reconnaissance, with a brigade of Maj. Gen. John Pegram's division leading the way. Early in the afternoon Maj. Gen. Samuel W. Crawford's division left V Corps lines and reconnoitered west. At about 2 P.M. the two forces collided near the site of Dabney's steam-powered sawmill.

Crawford pushed the Confederates back at first, but soon Brig. Gen. Clement A. Evans's division counterattacked and stopped the Federal advance. Then two brigades from Brig. Gen. Romeyn B. Ayres's V Corps division reinforced Crawford's left flank and recaptured Dabney's Mill. At 5 P.M., however, Brig. Gen. Joseph Finegan, temporarily commanding Maj. Gen. William Mahone's division, struck the Union center as Crawford's men ran low on ammunition. Crawford's and

Ayres's lines collapsed, and the Federals retreated. The Confederates had won a victory, but it cost the life of John Pegram, felled by a sharpshooter's bullet.

The next morning, Tuesday, February 7, Warren launched an offensive that drove the Confederates back to Dabney's Mill, which merely enabled the Federals to bury their dead from the day before. That night Warren pulled his men back to new trenches at Hatcher's Run.

At a cost of some 1,539 casualties, the Federals had extended their lines still farther west. The Confederates lost about 1,000 men.

Most of the Hatcher's Run battlefield is privately owned, and consists largely of farmland, woods, and scattered residential development. The Civil War Preservation Trust owns fifty acres open to the public. ■

FORT STEDMAN

By late February 1865, Gen. Robert E. Lee's once-vaunted Army of Northern Virginia had been weakened by disease and desertion, and the Union armies grew stronger as they tightened the bands around him. Learning of Lt. Gen. Jubal A. Early's defeat at Waynesboro on March 2 by Maj. Gen. Philip H. Sheridan, Lee realized that Sheridan soon would rejoin the main Federal armies in the east. Lee also knew that Maj. Gen. William T. Sherman was headed north through the Carolinas to unite his forces with Lt. Gen. Ulysses S. Grant's. Lee began to plan for the evacuation of his army from Richmond and Petersburg; on March 7 he furnished Lt. Gen. James Longstreet with detailed instructions.

Grant had 125,000 men at his disposal (not counting Sheridan's force or Sher-

man's 62,000), while Lee estimated he had about 50,000. Facing being outnumbered almost four-to-one should all the Federal armies converge, Lee decided to risk everything on an offensive that he planned with Maj Gen. John B. Gordon, who would lead the attack. Almost half of his army would rendezvous in Colquitt's Salient near City Point, the Federal supply depot and the site of Grant's headquarters. Then Gordon would attack Fort Stedman in the Union works to the east and threaten the landing, causing Grant to contract his lines to protect his base, reversing the recent trend.

Throughout the night of Friday, March 24, Gordon assembled his strike force. Troops marched into the city, rested briefly in the Petersburg streets, and moved quietly into the salient. Across no-

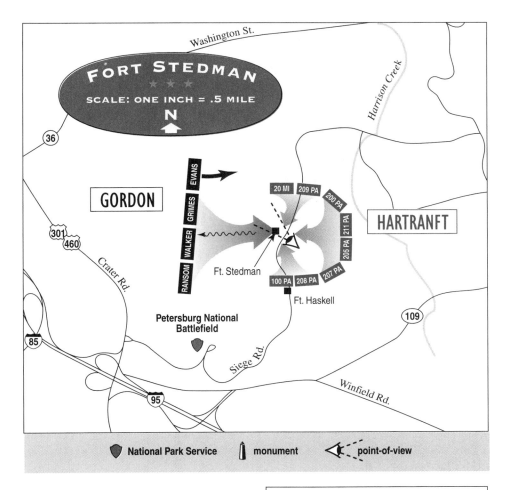

FORT STEDMAN

SCALE: ONE INCH = .5 MILE

N

Washington St.

Harrison Creek

GORDON

EVANS

GRIMES

WALKER

RANSOM

20 MI | 209 PA

200 PA

211 PA

205 PA

207 PA

100 PA | 208 PA

HARTRANFT

Ft. Stedman

Ft. Haskell

Crater Rd.

Petersburg National Battlefield

Siege Rd.

Winfield Rd.

National Park Service | monument | point-of-view

---

man's-land, the Federals grew suspicious at the ominous silence. At about 2 A.M. armed Confederate "deserters" walked into Union picket outposts holding their weapons reversed in surrender, then suddenly flipped them business end first and captured the Federals without a struggle.

Gordon knew that success depended on stealth and surprise: Clear Confederate obstructions, capture Union pickets, open lanes of attack through abatis, and chop openings through the fraises (sharpened stakes) projecting from the Federal earthworks—all without bringing firepower down on Confederate heads. If these preliminaries were successful, then Gordon

DIRECTIONS: I-95 Exit 52 (Washington St., Wythe St., from n.; Bank St. from s.), e. on Wythe St. and follow signs about 2.5 miles to Petersburg National Park entrance. From I-85 Exit 69 (U.S. Rte. 301 South, Wythe St./ State Rte. 36), e. on U.S. 301 South, Wythe St., about 2.4 miles to Petersburg National Park entrance. Walking and driving tour information available at park visitor center. Visit the National Park Service Web site at nps.gov/parks.html for a virtual tour of this and other national parks.

would send storming parties to capture the forts and fieldworks as well as special forces to seize certain strongholds believed to exist just behind the Union lines. Next, the infantry would widen the breach to enable the cavalry to charge through to

Interior of Fort Stedman with bombproof munitions store on right. VIRGINIA DEPARTMENT OF HISTORIC RESOURCES, JOHN S. SALMON

the Federal rear, to cut communication lines and wreak havoc generally. It was a bold and complicated plan with many opportunities for failure. Nevertheless, it was up to Gordon to carry it out.

Opposite Colquitt's Salient, Maj. Gen. John G. Parke's IX Corps occupied the Federal works, which included (at that point in the line) Battery X, Fort Stedman, and Batteries XI and XII. Artillerymen manned the fortifications, with some infantrymen in support. Behind the line, in reserve, was Brig. Gen. John F. Hartranft and his infantry division.

At 4:15 A.M. on Saturday, March 25, Gordon launched his attack, and it seemed that enough obstacles had been cleared to ensure success. Battery X fell after some initial cannon and small-arms fire, Fort Stedman after a dozen cannon rounds, and Battery XI without a shot. Battery XII remained in Union hands, and Battery XI was briefly retaken, but soon the Confederate onslaught overwhelmed them all, and by 4:45 the breakthrough had been accomplished, and Gordon himself stood in Fort Stedman.

Yet the Federals to north and south did not panic or run for the rear, where Hartranft had his division assembling within fifteen minutes of the attack. Instead, the soldiers fought hard to contain the breach and prevent its widening, buying time for Hartranft to organize a counterattack. Knowing that no Federals remained in the fort or the batteries opposite Colquitt's Salient, nearby artillerymen trained their cannons on them and opened fire. Soon the pocket became a trap for the Confederates.

Unknown to most of the soldiers, the tide already had turned. A crucial phase of Gordon's plan had failed because his special forces had not penetrated to the Union rear. Furthermore, the railroad trains that were supposed to rush additional troops to Gordon's aid had broken down; no help was imminent. Instead, Hartranft was encapsulating the pocket. Soon a semicircle had been formed that blocked every potential Confederate route of advance and repulsed a drive on a Federal depot on the U.S. Military Railroad. By 7:45 A.M. Hartranft took the offensive and attacked the Fort Stedman pocket.

Gordon, meanwhile, had received orders from Lee to withdraw, and for many Confederates the morning's combat turned into a race across no-man's-land to the safety of the lines at Colquitt's Salient before being shot down or captured. Many failed to make it as Hartranft's men recaptured Fort Stedman and Batteries X, XI, and XII, and poured fire into their retreating foes. By 8 A.M. the Union line had been restored.

So concluded the attack on Fort Stedman—as well as any hope Lee had of compelling Grant to contract his lines. Evacuation was now only a matter of time.

The attack cost the Confederates 2,681 casualties, including 1,949 prisoners, while the Federals lost 1,017. Fort Stedman and the adjoining batteries are preserved in Petersburg National Battlefield. ■

APPOMATTOX CAMPAIGN, 1865

The first half of the nineteenth century was a period of rapid growth in Virginia's "internal improvements": turnpikes, plank roads, canals, and railroads. By the Civil War, the Southside Virginia Piedmont was rich in these resources. Canals aided commerce on the James and Appomattox Rivers above the falls at Richmond and Petersburg. The Richmond & Danville Railroad linked those two cities and passed through Chesterfield, Amelia, and Nottoway Counties to the southwest. Petersburg was joined to Lynchburg by the South Side Railroad, which ran westerly through Dinwiddie, Nottoway, Prince Edward, and Appomattox Counties. Another rail line, the Petersburg Railroad (also called the Weldon Railroad), ran almost directly south from the city to Weldon, North Carolina. The Boydton Plank Road extended to the southwest from Petersburg through Dinwiddie County to Mecklenburg County, and the Jerusalem Plank Road connected the city with the Southampton County seat made notorious by Nat Turner a generation earlier. During peacetime, all these transportation routes were important farm-to-market avenues. During wartime, the railroads in particular became strategically important lines of communication, supply, and escape.

Lt. Gen. Ulysses S. Grant's Overland campaign of May–June 1864 forced Gen. Robert E. Lee's Army of Northern Virginia to maneuver from the Wilderness in Spotsylvania County southward, eventually into a complex network of fortifications around Richmond and Petersburg. The railroads became lifelines for both sides in the conflict. Grant's force consisted of two combined armies, the Army of the Potomac commanded by Maj. Gen. George G. Meade, and the Army of the James, which was commanded first by Maj. Gen. Benjamin F. Butler and then, after Butler was relieved on January 8, 1865, by Maj. Gen. Edward O. C. Ord. Federal assaults failed to penetrate the lines, so the Union and Confederate armies settled into what became a ten-month-long siege. Lee protected Richmond with Lt. Gen. Richard S. Ewell's and Lt. Gen. James Longstreet's corps and secured Petersburg with Gen. P. G. T. Beauregard's command and Lt. Gens. A. P. Hill's and Richard H. Anderson's corps; he already had dispatched Lt. Gen. Jubal A. Early's command to the Shenandoah Valley in June to protect the Confederacy's breadbasket and threaten Washington. Grant kept up probing attacks against Lee's thin defenses and sent his own army south around Petersburg and then westward to turn the Confederate right flank and sever Lee's lines of communication, particularly the rail lines.

By the end of August 1864, Grant's strategy had secured the Petersburg Railroad for the Union and cut Lee's most direct route to North Carolina. In the meantime, Beauregard had been reassigned and his troops incorporated into the Army of Northern Virginia. Late in September Grant captured Fort Harrison near Richmond, forcing Lee to defend the capital city

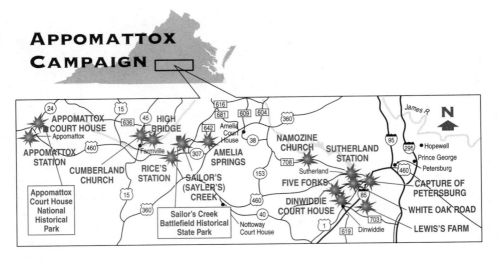

aggressively. Lee thwarted Grant's efforts to some extent by shifting his troops continuously to meet Union threats, but this tactic required an irreplaceable expenditure of men, matériel, and energy. The Confederates suffered during the winter, while the Union army extended its lines ever westward and bombarded Petersburg. By March 1865 Lee was defending some twenty-eight miles of fortifications around Richmond and Petersburg with an army daily shrinking from death, illness, and desertion.

Grant attacked Lee's supply line along the Boydton Plank Road southwest of Petersburg early in February 1865. Lee successfully defended the position, but the Union army retained most of the gained ground. Then on March 2, Maj. Gen. Philip H. Sheridan defeated the remnants of Lt. Gen. Jubal A. Early's command, the Army of the Shenandoah, in the battle of Waynesboro, leaving Sheridan's sizeable force free to join Grant at Petersburg. On March 25 Lee launched a desperate assault on Fort Stedman, hoping to break through Grant's lines and force the Union commander to shorten them, thereby enabling the Confederates to escape to North Carolina and join the army led by

Gen. Joseph E. Johnston. The tactic failed. The Confederates retreated to their own lines, and Grant prepared for what would be the final campaign of the war in Virginia.

The campaign opened on Wednesday, March 29, when a force of about 50,000 troops—the II Corps under Maj. Gen. Andrew A. Humphreys, the V Corps under Maj. Gen. Gouverneur K. Warren, and the cavalry commanded by Maj. Gen. Philip H. Sheridan—marched around the Confederate right flank west of Petersburg to seize the South Side Railroad. Grant reseaoned that the rupture of this last major supply line from the west to Petersburg would force Lee to withdraw from the defenses of Petersburg and the Confederate capital at Richmond. Grant's plan ultimately succeeded, but it took several days to execute.

Lee, realizing the importance of protecting the railroad, dispatched a force of 10,000 infantry and cavalry under Maj. Gen. George E. Pickett to hold a strategic crossroads called Five Forks, just two miles south of the rail line. In a series of sharp engagements over three days, the Union army maneuvered into position to attack Pickett on April 1.

The final week of March brought heavy rains to the Petersburg area. Consequently, creeks and rivulets were swollen beyond their banks. Leading Grant's offensive, Warren's V Corps moved up Quaker Road on March 29. At the Lewis farm Union forces led by Brig. Gen. Joshua L. Chamberlain engaged Confederates under Maj. Gen. Bushrod R. Johnson. After hard fighting the Union troops entrenched nearby along the Boydton Plank Road while the Confederates withdrew to their lines on White Oak Road. Thus the engagement at Quaker Road (Lewis farm) ended with the Union army straddling both the Quaker Road and the Boydton Plank Road, severing two important highways. Meanwhile, Sheridan's cavalry pushed on to Dinwiddie Court House on the Boydton Plank Road, where they could head northward toward the railroad. The distance between Dinwiddie Court House and Five Forks was only six miles.

Heavy rains began in the evening of March 29 and continued the next day, limiting operations. Humphreys's and Warren's corps edged closer to Sheridan and threatened the Confederate right flank. When the rain stopped on Friday morning, March 31, Sheridan advanced toward Five Forks from Dinwiddie Court House. About three miles from the village, Sheridan's left came under attack from Pickett, who had sallied forth from Five Forks in an attempt to drive Sheridan away. Sheridan's advance was halted, and he fell back to a position just north of the county seat. However, Pickett, threatened from the east by Humphreys's and Warren's corps, could not keep his force exposed and so withdrew to Five Forks.

As Pickett and Sheridan struggled, to the east Warren confronted Confederate earthworks on White Oak Road near the intersection of Claiborne Road and sought to sever the line of communication with

Pickett's detachment near Five Forks, four miles west. Lee personally supervised the counterattack to Gravelly Run by Lt. Gen. Richard H. Anderson's corps. After a brief success, the Confederates were forced back into their entrenchments as Warren's men gained the important roadway. Warren also sent a force west to threaten Pickett's left and rear. Seeing his predicament, Pickett fell back from near Dinwiddie Court House to his original position of that morning. He then received a dispatch from Lee to hold Five Forks at any cost to prevent Union forces from striking the South Side Railroad.

As a result of the fighting at Dinwiddie Court House and White Oak Road on March 31, the thin Confederate defenses had been weakened further by battle losses. Pickett had relinquished his hard-won ground, while Warren and Sheridan moved closer to the Confederate works.

Saturday, April 1, found Pickett's men building entrenchments parallel to the White Oak Road that extended almost two miles east and west from Five Forks. A considerable gap existed between the eastern end of the Five Forks earthworks and those near the White Oak Road–Claiborne Road intersection, which left Pickett's left flank exposed. Partly to mitigate this defensive shortcoming, Pickett "returned" his left flank; that is, he ordered the earthwork there constructed at a right angle to the rest, bending away from the road to the north for about 150 yards, for better protection. By noon all seemed quiet in front of the works, so some of the high command rode north to the rear and partook in a fish bake.

Because the area was heavily wooded, Pickett's 10,000 infantry and cavalry could not see or hear except for short distances. They were unaware that Sheridan had left Dinwiddie Court House with 3,000 cavalry augmented by the 12,000 infantry of

Warren's corps. By late afternoon Sheridan's horse soldiers were in position to assault Pickett's front, while Warren was moving into position to attack his left. Finally, at about 4:15 P.M., the crash of small arms was heard as Warren's infantry appeared. Warren did not know that Pickett's flank was exposed, so at first his own left was subjected to a raking fire from the return. Warren's corps quickly wheeled to face the threat and soon got in the rear of Pickett's defenses. Resistance was savage at first, then weakened as the Confederates fell back toward the forks. Simultaneously, Brig. Gen. George A. Custer's cavalry rode down on Pickett's right flank. By the time Pickett left his meal and reached his men, all was lost. Nothing could stop Sheridan's momentum. By dark, the road to the South Side Railroad was open to the Federals, while more than 2,000 Confederates had surrendered and the rest had scattered. That night, on receiving news of this victory, Grant issued orders for an all-out assault the next day at selected points along the Petersburg lines.

At dawn on Sunday, April 2, the Union army launched its attack, and the VI Corps under Maj. Gen. Horatio G. Wright broke through southwest of the city on the Boydton Plank Road. Southeast of Petersburg, Maj. Gen. John G. Parke's IX Corps attacked along the Jerusalem Plank Road and captured the outer works but could not puncture the inner. Back on Wright's front, the Confederate Third Corps commander, Lt. Gen. A. P. Hill, was killed in a confrontation with two Federal soldiers. Wright's breakthrough enabled Ord's Army of the James to capture Forts Gregg and Whitworth, two outposts protecting Petersburg's western approaches, after overcoming a stubborn defense.

Ten miles west of Petersburg, a Confederate detachment fought a symbolic stand at Sutherland Station on the South Side Railroad. Maj. Gen. Nelson A. Miles's division of Humphrey's II Corps attacked the Confederate line there, which was held by Maj. Gen. Henry Heth's division. After holding off three assaults, the Confederates finally yielded their position, losing a thousand prisoners and two cannons in the process. With the Federals in control of Lee's lifeline to the west, he had no alternative but to retreat from both Petersburg and Richmond. He sent word to Pres. Jefferson Davis in Richmond, who was informed during worship services at St. Paul's Episcopal Church.

When Lee ordered the Army of Northern Virginia to evacuate the two cities, he intended the separate contingents, totaling between 55,000 and 58,000 men, to rendezvous about forty miles west at the Richmond & Danville Railroad depot at Amelia Court House. There he would resupply his army, march to Danville, then head into North Carolina to join Johnston.

At the beginning of its departure from Richmond and Petersburg, Lee's army—infantry, cavalry, and artillery—included more than a thousand baggage and supply wagons. The logistics of moving so many men and supplies meant that the Confederates retreated, and the Federals followed, along several different routes. Lt. Gen. Richard S. Ewell's Reserve Corps, Maj. Gen. Joseph B. Kershaw's division, and Brig. Gen. Martin W. Gary's cavalry brigade left Richmond over Mayo's Bridge. The division commanded by Maj. Gen. G. W. Custis Lee crossed the James River on a pontoon bridge to Drewry's Bluff. The departing Confederates set fire to downtown warehouses and also burned the bridges behind them.

Maj. Gen. William Mahone led his division from the Bermuda Hundred front west through Chester and Chesterfield

Court House. Eventually his column joined Maj. Gen. John B. Gordon's and Longstreet's corps.

Most of the Confederates in Petersburg crossed to the north side of the Appomattox River over four bridges: one railroad, two vehicle, and one pontoon. All but the pontoon bridge were burned, and the various corps and divisions then marched west on several roads.

The Union armies pursued with about 76,000 men as well as their own lengthy wagon trains. Grant's objective was to prevent Lee from uniting his army with Johnston's and surround and defeat it. His strategy to accomplish this objective was to send the infantry in pursuit while his cavalry rode to get ahead of Lee. Part of the infantry and cavalry followed in Lee's rear while the remainder marched on parallel roads to the south, keeping between the Confederates and North Carolina.

Lee's army marched some twenty miles on April 2–3, its progress hampered by swollen watercourses and washed-out bridges that forced changes in the assigned routes of march. By the evening of April 3, most of the Army of Northern Virginia bivouacked just a few miles short of Amelia Court House.

On bringing his army together at the county seat on April 4, Lee found to his dismay that a mix-up in communications caused no subsistence to be sent there. By remaining in the area while his army foraged, he allowed the Federals to eliminate the one-day lead that he enjoyed. Consequently, hard riding by Sheridan's cavalry, despite the occasional skirmish such as the one at Namozine Church on April 3, enabled Grant's army to get in front of the Confederate army and cut the intended path of Lee's retreat along the railroad at Jetersville, the next station down the line. On April 5, when the Southerners marched

out of Amelia Court House, they found not only Federal cavalry blocking their way but fast-marching Union infantry arriving in support. Lee, deciding not to bring on a battle then, ordered a night march around the entrenched Union left flank. His destination was Farmville, where his men could find rations at the South Side Railroad depot.

A Federal cavalry raid that day destroyed a Confederate wagon train near Paineville. The engagement was significant as the only documented instance of the war in Virginia in which uniformed black Confederate soldiers saw action. The Federal cavalrymen quickly overwhelmed the inexperienced recruits. Returning to Jetersville from their attack, the Union horse soldiers encountered part of Maj. Gen. Fitzhugh Lee's cavalry corps near Amelia Springs, and the Confederates pursued them back to Jetersville.

On April 6 the opposing armies fought several significant actions. Riding along roads parallel to those on which Lee's column was moving, Sheridan's cavalry intercepted the Confederate line of march near Little Sailor's (Sayler's) Creek. Custer's troopers drove into a gap between Longstreet's and Anderson's corps, blocking two-thirds of the column. With the II and VI Corps closing in from behind, the Confederates had to make a stand. In three separate engagements—at the Hillsman farm, the Lockett farm, and Marshall's Crossroads (the Harper farm)—the Federal infantry and cavalry were able to put 7,700 men hors de combat, mainly as prisoners, almost one-fifth of Lee's army. Eight Confederate generals, including Ewell, were among those captured. Those who escaped continued on another night march to Farmville, on the south bank of the Appomattox River, or crossed to the north bank over High Bridge with Gordon.

Before the action at Little Sailor's Creek, Ord directed a body of infantry and cavalry from the Army of the James to destroy High Bridge so that the Confederates could not use it in their retreat. High Bridge, an enormous South Side Railroad trestle, spanned the Appomattox River about four miles east of Farmville. Confederate cavalry discovered the raid and overtook the Union force near the bridge. In the fight that ensued, most of the Federals were either killed or captured, while Confederate brigadier general James Dearing was mortally wounded. During the night, Gordon and Mahone crossed the bridge and in the morning made a failed attempt to burn it as well as the nearby wagon bridge so that the Federals could not follow.

Longstreet, meanwhile, continued his march westward. Learning that High Bridge—a few miles north of his route—was threatened, he entrenched at Rice's Station on the South Side Railroad to block the Union advance. That night, while the bridge remained in Confederate hands, Gordon's corps and Mahone's division crossed to an illusory safety. Infantry from Maj. Gen. John Gibbon's XXIV Corps, the advance of Ord's column, approached Longstreet's position. There was heavy skirmishing, but Longstreet held Gibbon at bay long enough to escape.

Arriving in Farmville on the morning of April 7, the ravenous Confederates found some 40,000 rations of bread and 80,000 of meal aboard the trains at the depot. As rations were being issued, word came that the Federals not only were approaching the town on the south side of the river but also were pressing Gordon and Mahone on the north side. Lee had to entrench his army around Cumberland Church, about three miles north of the town and within sight of the Blue Ridge, to protect his wagon train. Federal attempts to break the Confederate line that afternoon failed but held most of

the Southern army at bay until dark. The Confederates were compelled to make their third night march in a row. That evening Grant sent the first of a series of dispatches to Lee requesting the surrender of his army.

From Cumberland Church Lee planned to march his army west to Campbell Court House, just east of Lynchburg. En route he hoped to resupply his men at Appomattox Station on the South Side Railroad, about three miles southwest of Appomattox Court House. The Confederates faced a thirty-eight-mile march to the station, but south of the river, the route was eight miles shorter and provided an opportunity for the Union armies to get around them.

Lee's army was relatively unmolested on this final day of the march, April 8, although two Federal corps (II and VI) pursued it north of the river. To the south, with Sheridan's cavalry leading, the V Corps and the Army of the James were taking advantage of their situation. Arriving at Appomattox Station ahead of the van of Lee's column, the cavalry captured the supply trains and supplies that awaited the famished Confederates and, later that evening, a portion of the artillery and wagon train. This action placed part of the Union force directly in front of Lee's army gathering around Appomattox Court House. With the Federal infantry behind him and Union cavalry across his line of march, Lee decided to attempt a breakout through the horsemen early the next morning.

At daybreak on April 9, a combined force of infantry and cavalry under Gordon and Fitzhugh Lee attacked the Federal troopers, forcing them to give ground. As the cavalrymen fell back, however, infantry from the Army of the James began arriving in support. It became apparent to Lee that he was about to be surrounded, especially when the V Corps appeared on his flank. The Southerners carried forward flags of truce, and that afternoon—Palm Sunday—Lee met with Grant in Wilmer McLean's parlor to discuss and accept surrender terms.

The casualties for the Appomattox campaign totaled approximately 9,000 for the Federal army and 28,000, including desertions, for the Confederate. Lee surrendered more than 28,000 men at Appomattox, and they were all paroled and allowed to go home. After four years of bloodshed, the fighting in Virginia had ended. ▩

LEWIS'S FARM

With the approach of spring in 1865, Lt. Gen. Ulysses S. Grant became concerned that Gen. Robert E. Lee might evacuate the Army of Northern Virginia from Richmond and Petersburg, march into North Carolina, and join forces with Gen. Joseph E. Johnston. Grant planned to strike before that could happen.

For his part, Lee needed to keep his last lines of communication open to evacuate the cities and move south. The South Side Railroad had to be held at all costs. That task had fallen to Lt. Gen. Richard H. Anderson's understrength corps, which consisted of Maj. Gen. Bushrod R. Johnson's reinforced division.

Grant launched his offensive on Wednesday, March 29, in a driving rain that continued for two days. Maj. Gen. Gouverneur K. Warren's V Corps and Maj. Gen. Andrew A. Humphreys's II Corps were to drive the Confederates from the Boydton Plank Road (present-day U.S. Rte. 1) preparatory to cutting the South Side Railroad. Maj. Gen. Philip H. Sheridan, meanwhile, was directed to occupy Dinwiddie Court House and then attack the Confederate right flank and rear. If the offensive did not succeed, Sheridan could either return to Grant's army or join Maj. Gen. William T. Sherman's army group in North Carolina.

Brig. Gen. Joshua L. Chamberlain's brigade of Brig. Gen. Charles Griffin's division formed the vanguard of Warren's

View north on Quaker Road in vicinity of Chamberlain's position. VIRGINIA DEPARTMENT OF HISTORIC RESOURCES, JOHN S. SALMON

corps. It marched southwest on Vaughan Road (Rte. 675), forded Rowanty Creek, then turned north on Quaker Road (Rte. 660). The Confederate works that were the Federals' first objective extended along the southeast side of the Boydton Plank Road, and Brig. Gen. Henry A. Wise's and Brig. Gen. William H. Wallace's brigades defended it. Wise's brigade had moved out of its works toward the Federals and engaged them in a field on the Lewis farm.

Chamberlain pushed Wise's brigade back toward the intersection of the Quaker Road and the Boydton Plank Road as he awaited reinforcements. Wise counterattacked, however, reinforced by Wallace, and Chamberlain's left flank weakened. Anderson ordered forward two of his remaining brigades to support Wise and Wallace. Chamberlain, wounded, called on Griffin for assistance, and four brigades and a four-gun battery were rushed to his

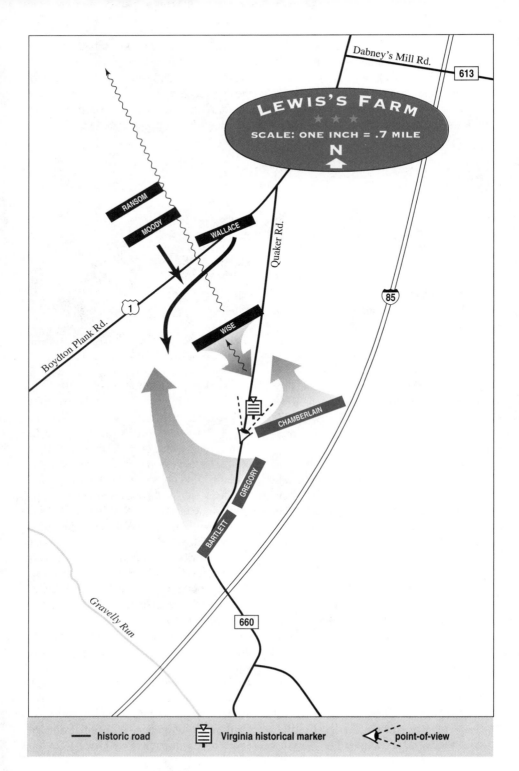

LEWIS'S FARM
★ ★ ★
SCALE: ONE INCH = .7 MILE
N

Dabney's Mill Rd.

613

RANSOM

MOODY

WALLACE

Quaker Rd.

85

Boydton Plank Rd.

1

WISE

CHAMBERLAIN

GREGORY

BARTLETT

Gravelly Run

660

—— historic road   Virginia historical marker   point-of-view

aid. Anderson, realizing that his undermanned brigades were in danger of being overwhelmed, recalled them to their prepared fortification on White Oak Road and abandoned the Boydton Plank Road.

Griffin's division surged forward and entrenched across the plank road. The Federals, after months of effort, finally occupied the Boydton Plank Road, thereby severing one of Lee's principal lines of communication. The casualties for the two sides were about even: 381 Federals and 371 Confederates.

The Lewis farm battlefield retains good integrity despite some light residential development. The Lewis farmhouse, which stood in deteriorated condition a few years ago, has since collapsed. ■

DINWIDDIE COURT HOUSE

As the Federal infantry marched toward the Boydton Plank Road on Wednesday, March 29, 1865, Maj. Gen. Philip H. Sheridan led more than 9,000 cavalrymen to Dinwiddie Court House. Sheridan's force consisted of three cavalry divisions headed by Maj. Gen. George Crook, Brig. Gen. Thomas C. Devin, and Maj. Gen. George A. Custer. Brevet (temporary) Maj. Gen. Wesley Merritt commanded the latter two divisions.

The next day Sheridan reconnoitered from the county seat toward Five Forks, an intersection en route to the South Side Railroad. Sheridan's men encountered elements of Maj. Gen. Fitzhugh Lee's cavalry corps, which was protecting the intersection. Maj. Gen. George E. Pickett's division of Lt. Gen. James Longstreet's corps arrived at the Five Forks junction at about 4:30 P.M., and the remainder of the Confederate cavalry joined Lee in the evening. Meanwhile, the Federal infantry was advancing, with Maj. Gen. Gouverneur K. Warren's V Corps moving to within three miles of Dinwiddie Court House and Maj.

Chamberlain's Bed, across which Lee and Rosser attacked Smith. VIRGINIA DEPARTMENT OF HISTORIC RESOURCES, JOHN S. SALMON

Gen. Andrew A. Humphreys's II Corps probing west of Hatcher's Run.

On Friday, March 31, the rain ended, and Sheridan immediately sent his force north toward Five Forks. Devin led the

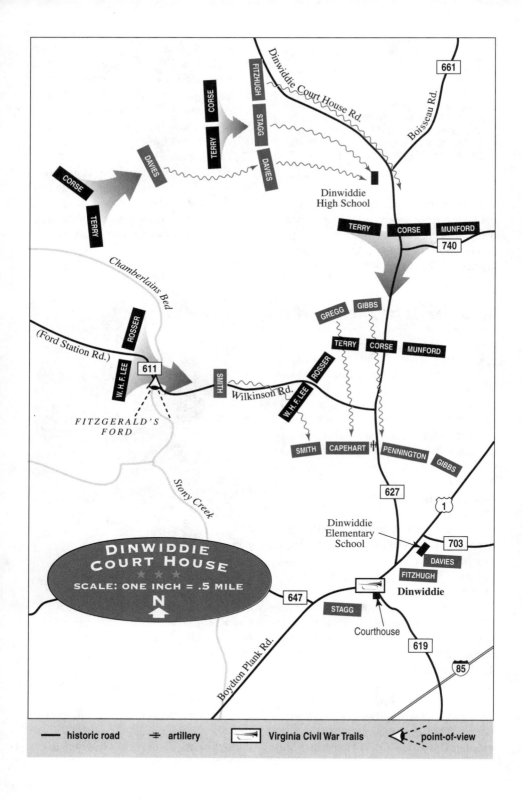

661

Dinwiddie Court House Rd.

Boisseau Rd.

FITZHUGH

CORSE

TERRY

STAGG

DAVIES

DAVIES

Dinwiddie
High School

CORSE

TERRY

TERRY   CORSE   MUNFORD

740

Chamberlains Bed

(Ford Station Rd.)

ROSSER

GREGG   GIBBS

W.H.F. LEE

611

SMITH

TERRY   CORSE   MUNFORD

FITZGERALD'S
FORD

Wilkinson Rd.

W.H.F. LEE

ROSSER

Stony Creek

SMITH   CAPEHART   PENNINGTON   GIBBS

627

1

Dinwiddie
Elementary
School

703

DAVIES

DINWIDDIE
COURT HOUSE
★ ★ ★
SCALE: ONE INCH = .5 MILE
N

FITZHUGH

Dinwiddie

647

STAGG

Courthouse

619

Boydton Plank Rd.

85

— historic road   ⟊ artillery   [ ] Virginia Civil War Trails   ◁ ⋯ point-of-view

DIRECTIONS: I-85 Exit 53 (Rte. 703, Dinwiddie); w. on Rte. 703 (Carson Rd.) about 1 mile to U.S. Rte. 1 (Boydton Plank Rd.); s.w. (left) on U.S. Rte. 1 .4 mile to Dinwiddie Court House (courthouse on left); return n.e. .2 mile on U.S. Rte. 1 to Rte. 627 (Courthouse Rd.); n. (left) on Rte. 627 .9 mile to Rte. 611 (Wilkinson Rd.); w. (left) on Rte. 611 1.2 miles to Chamberlain's Bed (watercourse); continue on Rte. 611 .4 mile to Confederate position on high ground w. of Chamberlain's Bed; return e. on Rte. 611 1.6 miles to Rte. 627; n. (left) on Rte. 627 1 mile to the Federal position along Rte. 740 (Turkey Egg Rd.); continue n. on Rte. 627 .45 mile to Confederate position along Rte. 661 (Boisseau Rd.); retrace route to I-85.

advance on the Dinwiddie Court House Road (present-day Rte. 627) with Crook following. To protect the left flank, Brig. Gen. Henry E. Davies's and Brig. Gen. Charles H. Smith's brigades of Crook's division were ordered a mile west to guard Danse's and Fitzgerald's Fords across Chamberlain's Bed, a tributary of Stony Creek.

Pickett, his position threatened both by Federal infantry and cavalry, decided to attack Sheridan's column, and at 10 A.M. his cavalry and infantry marched south from Five Forks on Scott's Road (Rte. 645). A Confederate cavalry division attacked two Federal brigades as they approached Five Forks and drove them south. Two of Pickett's infantry brigades forced a crossing at Danse's Ford, pushing back Davies's brigade. Two cavalry divisions rode on to Fitzgerald's Ford, where

they attacked Smith and likewise pushed him eastward on the Ford Station Road (Rte. 611).

Gradually, the Federal cavalry fell back in good order toward Dinwiddie Court House. Two brigades of Crook's division helped slow the Confederate attack. Shortly before 5:30 P.M. Custer sent two brigades to a point about half a mile north of the village to construct fieldworks of fence rails. The cavalrymen were joined by four cannons of Company A, Second U.S. Artillery. By nightfall the Federals were behind their works, having prevented Pickett's infantry and cavalry from reuniting and dealing a serious defeat to the Union horse soldiers.

A costly tactical victory for the Confederates—354 Federal casualties and 760 for the Confederates—the battle had no effect on Sheridan's plans to capture Five Forks. He was pleased that he had drawn Pickett's infantry division out of the Petersburg lines, and he was determined to crush it the next day. Pickett also understood his own precarious position when Maj. Gen. Gouverneur K. Warren positioned an infantry brigade near his left flank. He withdrew to Five Forks at 5 A.M. the following morning and entrenched, having received a message from Gen. Robert E. Lee: "Hold Five Forks at all hazards."

The Dinwiddie Court House battlefield remains partly agricultural today, with encroaching residential development. ■

WHITE OAK ROAD

While the Federal cavalry fought north of Dinwiddie Court House on Friday, March 31, 1864, Maj. Gen. Gouverneur K. Warren's V Corps sought to seize the lightly defended Confederate fieldworks protecting White Oak Road

(present-day Rte. 613). The day before, Maj. Gen. George E. Pickett's division had been observed marching west on the road to Five Forks. If the Federals secured the road, Warren could prevent reinforcements from reaching Pickett, thereby isolating

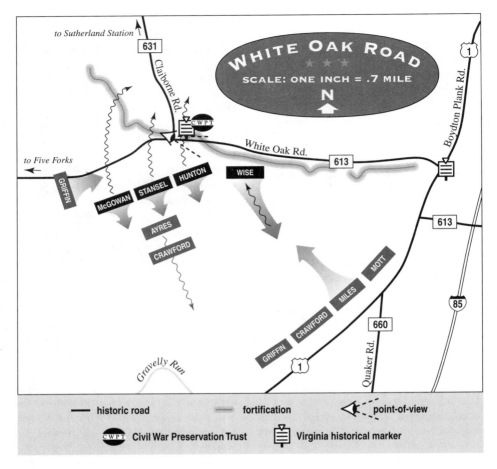

WHITE OAK ROAD

SCALE: ONE INCH = .7 MILE

N

to Sutherland Station

631

Claiborne Rd.

1

Boydton Plank Rd.

CWPT

White Oak Rd.

613

to Five Forks

GRIFFIN

McGOWAN STANSEL HUNTON

WISE

AYRES

CRAWFORD

MOTT

MILES

CRAWFORD

GRIFFIN

660

Quaker Rd.

85

613

Gravelly Run

1

——— historic road   ———— fortification   ◀ ‹‹ ‹ point-of-view

CWPT Civil War Preservation Trust   Virginia historical marker

---

DIRECTIONS: I-85 Exit 61 (Sutherland), e. on U.S. Rte. 460 about .3 mile to U.S. Rte. 1; s.w. (right) on U.S. Rte. 1 2.1 miles to Rte. 613 (White Oak Rd.) and state historical marker S-52, White Oak Road; w. (right) on Rte. 613 1.7 miles to Rte. 631 (Claiborne Rd.), state historical marker S-81, White Oak Road Engagement, and Civil War Preservation Trust White Oak Road Battlefield Civil War Site. You may return to I-85 by same route or proceed n. on Rte. 631 3.6 miles to U.S. Rte. 460 and Sutherland Station; right on U.S. Rte. 460 4.1 miles to I-85. If you wish to drive to Five Forks, continue w. on Rte. 613 4.4 miles.

him from the left flank of the main Confederate army.

Lt. Gen. Ulysses S. Grant and Maj. Gen. George G. Meade, the commander of the Army of the Potomac, both approved Warren's plan. At midmorning Warren

proceeded. He was expecting to strike a line of fieldworks lightly defended by Lt. Gen. Richard H. Anderson's undermanned corps.

Gen. Robert E. Lee, meanwhile, had anticipated Warren's movement and acted to counter it. He thinned the Petersburg and White Oak Road lines to assemble three brigades and posted them in woods north of White Oak Road. This force, led by Maj. Gen. Bushrod R. Johnson of Anderson's corps, numbered about 3,800.

Brig. Gen. Romeyn B. Ayres's division, some 4,000 men, led the Federal advance. Brig. Gen. Samuel W. Crawford's division came next, followed by Brig. Gen. Charles Griffin's division. Ayres's and Crawford's divisions deployed in the Butler farm fields south of the intersection of White Oak Road and present-day Rte. 631. Just as Ayres's men stepped off to attack at about 11 A.M., the Confederates marched out of the woods and unleashed a volley that sent the Federals streaming to the rear through Crawford's division, which was flanked by the oncoming gray line and likewise retreated. By noon the two Union divisions had fallen back a mile across a branch of Gravelly Run.

Brig. Gen. Joshua L. Chamberlain's brigade of Griffin's division was thrust forward to fend off the Confederate advance, which already had stalled as Lee's men hastily dug rifle pits in the open fields in anticipation of a Federal counterattack. There they repelled three assaults by Chamberlain, who was supported by two other brigades. Behind Griffin's division, Ayres's and Crawford's divisions reformed, returned to action, and by late afternoon had helped force the Confederates back.

Meanwhile, on Warren's right, Maj. Gen. Andrew A. Humphreys's II Corps began demonstrating against the Confederate earthworks at the eastern end of White Oak Road and east of the Boydton Plank Road (U.S. Rte. 1) at about 1 P.M. Brig. Gen. Henry A. Wise led his brigade out of the works to challenge Brig. Gen. Nelson A. Miles's division on Humphreys's left flank, but Miles drove him back to the White Oak Road entrenchments and cap-

State historical marker at edge of C.S.A. earthworks, looking east. VIRGINIA DEPARTMENT OF HISTORIC RESOURCES, JOHN S. SALMON

tured about 200 prisoners. When word of this reversal reached Lee, he realized that the Confederate position was untenable and ordered the men to fall back to White Oak Road.

The White Oak Road engagement ended with the Confederates back in their trenches. It cost the Federals 1,781 casualties, while the Confederates lost between 900 and 1,235.

Today most of the battlefield is heavily wooded and inaccessible. Some scattered development has occurred on White Oak Road, but most of the site retains very good integrity, and long sections of Confederate and Federal earthworks have survived. The Civil War Preservation Trust owns thirty acres of the battlefield that are open to the public. The tract includes earthworks, a walking trail, and interpretive markers. ■

FIVE FORKS

With his left flank threatened by Federal infantry and his front by a strong cavalry force, Maj. Gen. George E. Pickett withdrew his division to Five Forks. At 5 A.M. on Saturday, April 1, 1865, the Confederates marched north from their positions near Dinwiddie Court House and entrenched at the intersection.

Four roads met there: White Oak Road (present-day Rte. 613), Dinwiddie Court House Road (Rte. 627 southeast of the intersection), Scott's Road (Rte. 645), and Ford's, or Church, Road (Rte. 627 north of the intersection). Pickett spread his 10,000-man force for almost two miles along White Oak Road east and west of

DIRECTIONS: I-85 Exit 61 (Sutherland), e. on U.S. Rte. 460 about .3 mile to U.S. Rte. 1; s.w. (right) on U.S. Rte. 1 2.1 miles to Rte. 613 (White Oak Rd.); right on Rte. 613 8 miles to Five Forks intersection; National Park Service visitor center on right; return to I-85. Visit the National Park Service Web site at nps.gov/parks.html for a virtual tour of this and other national parks.

the junction. Most of the area was wooded except for the farm fields across White Oak Road on the Confederate right.

On the west, Maj. Gen. W. H. F. "Rooney" Lee's cavalry division held the Confederate right flank. Next came Pickett's five infantry brigades, with Brig. Gen. Montgomery D. Corse's brigade and Col. Joseph Mayo's brigade (Mayo commanded in place of the injured Brig. Gen. William R. Terry) west of the intersection. To the east were the brigades of Brig. Gens. George H. Steuart, William H. Wallace, and Matthew W. Ransom. Ransom's men, on the left flank, built earthworks that were "refused"—bent back from the line to provide additional protection. (Pickett's left flank was not linked by infantry with the main Confederate fieldworks on White Oak Road to the east.) A three-mile gap existed that was partially filled by Brig. Gen. William P. Roberts's small cavalry brigade. In addition, Col. Thomas T. Munford's cavalry division reconnoitered the countryside around the intersection of White Oak Road and Gravelly Run Road, about half a mile east of the infantry's left flank. Pickett distributed his artillery among the infantry brigades.

Having deployed his forces and with his front seemingly quiet, Pickett joined several other Confederate officers for a shad planking (fish-bake) lunch, more than a mile north on Ford's Road by Hatcher's Run. The generals neglected to tell their subordinates where they were going, and they also failed to appoint commanders in their absence.

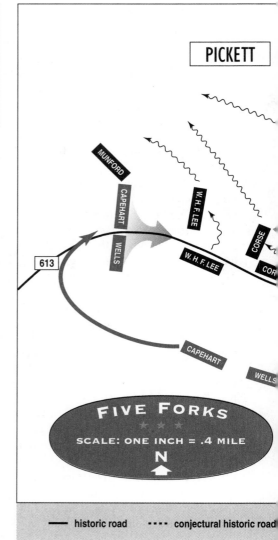

To the south, meanwhile, the Union divisions commanded by Maj. Gen. Philip H. Sheridan and the corps led by Maj. Gen. Gouverneur K. Warren were marching toward Five Forks. The plan called for Sheridan's 6,000–7,000 cavalrymen to attack Pickett's front while Warren's 12,000 infantrymen exploited the gap in the Confederate defenses to crush Pickett's left flank and "roll up" his line.

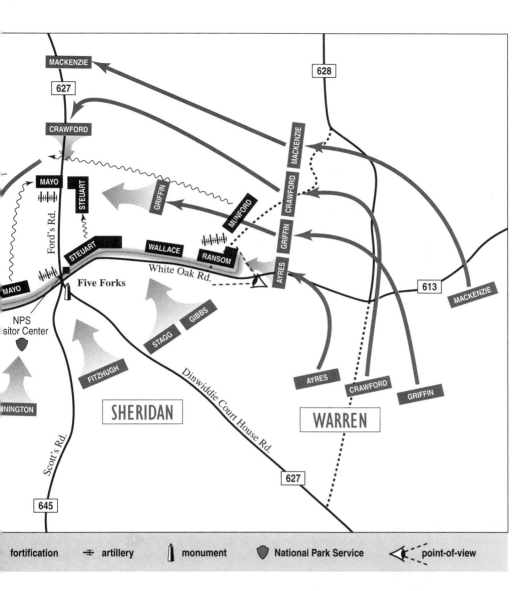

fortification	⫢ artillery	👁 monument	🛡 National Park Service	◀ ⋯ point-of-view

Sheridan sent Maj. Gen. George A. Custer's and Brig. Gen. Thomas C. Devin's cavalry divisions northward to strike the right and left fronts of Pickett's White Oak Road defenses. Maj. Gen. George Crook's division guarded the Federal rear around Dinwiddie Court House. To Sheridan's right, Warren formed V Corps to march northwest to White Oak Road, wheel left, and strike the Confederate left flank. Because of the difficulty of maneuvering

three infantry divisions through the wooded terrain, it was 4 P.M. before Warren was ready to attack. Fifteen minutes later, the Federals marched forward.

Earlier in the day, Brig. Gen. Ranald S. Mackenzie's cavalry division had charged through Roberts's thin skirmish line of North Carolina horse soldiers to seize a stretch of White Oak Road, preventing Pickett from being reinforced from the east. Pickett and his lieutenants, relaxing

Last assault on Pickett's lines at Five Forks. LIBRARY OF CONGRESS

far to the rear after their shad feast, heard none of this.

Because of the thick woods in front of the Confederate troops, most of them also heard little: just muffled sounds that let them know that something was afoot. Shortly after 4:15 P.M., however, the Federals erupted from the woods and struck Pickett's line.

Brig. Gen. Romeyn B. Ayres's division formed the left of Warren's corps and Brig. Gen. Samuel W. Crawford's division was *en echelon* on the right, while Brig. Gen. Charles Griffin's division followed to the right rear of Crawford. When the Federals reached White Oak Road, they found no Confederates but wheeled left and marched on as the plan directed. Due to the thick woods, Ayres's and Crawford's divisions soon lost contact with each other; Ayres guided on the road as he marched west, but Crawford drifted north behind the Confederate lines. Warren himself set off in pursuit of Crawford to lead him south to the battle.

Ayres's division quickly overwhelmed Pickett's refused left flank, capturing about 1,000 Confederates and killing or scattering the rest. The fleeing soldiers fell back on Steuart's position, and Steuart quickly organized another refused line just east of the Five Forks intersection. Griffin's division encountered this new left flank and attacked. Soon Steuart's brigade joined the others fleeing west.

The sounds of battle had finally carried to the rear, and Pickett rode toward the front, barely evading Crawford's division. Pickett sent several regiments from Mayo's brigade to block Crawford, but the Federals soon overwhelmed them and continued west until they found Corse's brigade. As the sun began to set, Warren himself led the assault on this last Confederate position.

While the Union infantry was rolling up the Confederate left, Devin and Custer were attacking the front and right. According to Sheridan's plan, Devin was to assault the eastern half of Pickett's line while Custer feinted against the western portion. Custer instead launched a full-scale attack on the right against Rooney Lee's cavalry. Lee fended off Custer, though, long enough for the fleeing Confederates to escape north to the South Side Railroad some two and a half miles away. By nightfall the rout was complete, and the way to the railroad was open.

The battle of Five Forks was an overwhelming Union victory. At a cost of some 830 Federal casualties, Sheridan had inflicted a loss of 3,000 on Pickett, including between 2,000 and 2,400 men made prisoners. Noted artillerist Willie Pegram was mortally wounded and died on April 2.

Warren himself became a casualty of the battle. Before the engagement began, Grant had sent Sheridan word to use his judgment and relieve Warren if he thought the V Corps should be led by one of the division commanders. Later that evening Sheridan relieved Warren and appointed Griffin in his place. Grant and Meade had lacked confidence in the slow, hesitant Warren for some time and also disliked his leaving his proper position behind the assault line to accompany one division commander, making him difficult to locate on the battlefield. Warren protested his dismissal and sought a court of inquiry. After fourteen years a court finally convened in 1879. Two years later it exonerated Warren of the accusations against him—but handed down its decision three months after the embittered general had died.

The Five Forks battlefield, a National Historic Landmark, is a unit of Petersburg National Battlefield. More than 1,100 well-preserved acres of the battlefield are included in the unit. ■

CAPTURE OF PETERSBURG

L t. Gen. Ulysses S. Grant received word of the Federal victory at Five Forks at about 9 P.M. on Saturday, April 1, 1865. Concerned that Gen. Robert E. Lee might attack Maj. Gen. Philip H. Sheridan in his relatively exposed position, Grant ordered an artillery bombardment of the Confederates around Petersburg, to be followed by a general attack on Confederate lines at dawn on April 2. The end of the siege was at hand.

Federal corps gathered in the darkness for the assault. To the west, Maj. Gen. Charles Griffin's V Corps, together with Sheridan's cavalry corps, had consolidated at Five Forks. To their right, Maj. Gen. Andrew A. Humphreys's II Corps and Maj. Gen. Edward O. C. Ord's Army of the James confronted Lt. Gen. Richard H. Anderson's corps and part of Lt. Gen. A. P. Hill's corps across Hatcher's Run and the Boydton Plank Road (present-day U.S. Rte. 1). Next, Maj. Gen. Horatio G. Wright's 18,000-man VI Corps prepared

DIRECTIONS: The capture of Petersburg came after Union breakthroughs at several points along the Confederate line; some points are preserved, others not. The first breakthrough occurred s.w. of the city and is preserved: I-85 Exit 63A (U.S. Rte. 1 South), s. on U.S. Rte. 1 about 1 mile to state historical marker S-49, Where Hill Fell; then .1 mile to entrance to Pamplin Historical Park and National Museum of the Civil War Soldier; return to U.S. Rte. 1; s. (left) on U.S. Rte. 1. 5 mile to U.S. Rte. 460; w. (right) on U.S. Rte. 460 .2 mile to I-85 Exit 61. Another breakthrough occurred at Confederate Ft. Gregg, in Petersburg National Battlefield: I-95 Exit 52 (Washington St., Wythe St., from n.; Bank St. from s.), e. on Wythe St. and follow signs about 2.5 miles to Petersburg National Park entrance. From I-85 Exit 69 (U.S. Rte. 301 South, Wythe St./ State Rte. 36), e. on U.S. 301 South, Wythe St., about 2.4 miles to Petersburg National Park entrance. Walking and driving tour information available at park visitor center. Visit the National Park Service Web site at nps.gov/parks.html for a virtual tour of this and other national parks. To contrast these preserved sites with another breakthrough point: I-95 Exit 50 (U.S. Rte. 301, Crater Rd.), left on exit road about .1 mile to U.S. Rte. 301; s. (right) on U.S. Rte. 301 .7 mile to Col. George W. Gowen monument on right; return to I-95.

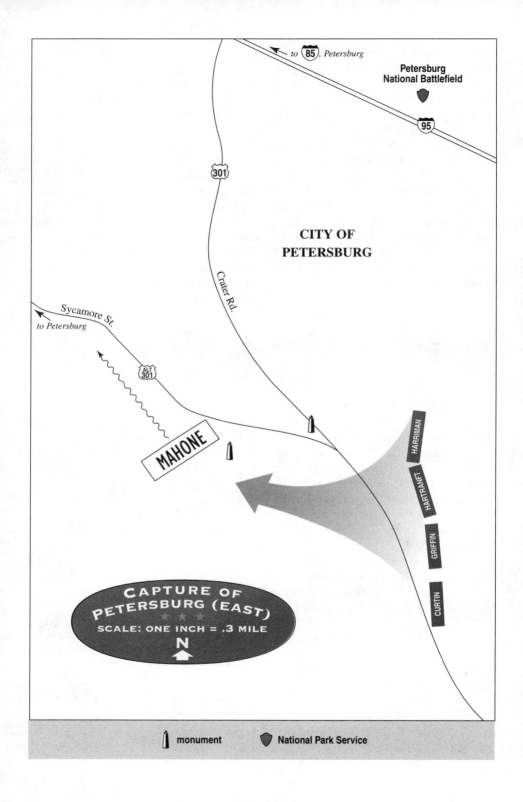

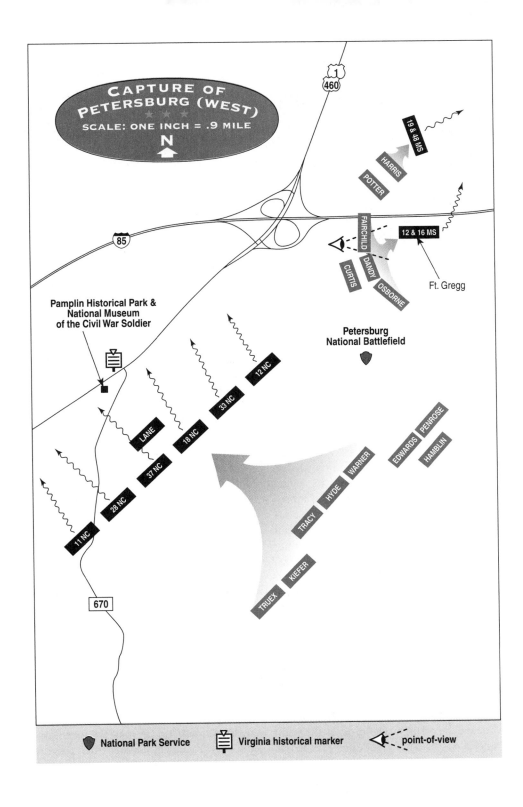

CAPTURE OF PETERSBURG (WEST)
SCALE: ONE INCH = .9 MILE
N

Pamplin Historical Park & National Museum of the Civil War Soldier

Petersburg National Battlefield

Ft. Gregg

National Park Service   Virginia historical marker   point-of-view

Capture of C.S.A. Fort Gregg. LIBRARY OF CONGRESS

to attack the remainder of Hill's line, while on the Union right Maj. Gen. John G. Parke's IX Corps, also 18,000 men strong, faced Maj. Gen. John B. Gordon's corps around Fort Mahone near the present-day intersection of Crater Road and Sycamore Street.

At 4:30 A.M. Parke's corps attacked and captured several batteries in the old Dimmock line. Fort Mahone, however, held firm, preventing a Union breakthrough in the Confederate inner works.

Ten minutes after Parke advanced, Wright's men stepped off in a wedge-shaped formation intended to punch through the opposing lines west of Petersburg. After several minutes of close combat, the Federals swarmed over and through the earthworks, overwhelming Brig. Gen. James H. "Little Jim" Lane's brigade of Maj. Gen. Cadmus M. Wilcox's division, and Lee's heretofore impenetrable works were broken at last. The Federals began to roll up the line both north and south.

Hill rode to Lee's headquarters to consult with him about the breakthrough. He then returned to his lines. Emerging from woods into a clearing, Hill and an aide encountered Federal soldiers. The soldiers opened fire; Hill was struck in the heart and died instantly. His aide escaped to inform Lee.

Farther west, at 6 A.M. Humphreys's II Corps surged north against the Confederate earthworks west of Hatcher's Run. Brig. Gen. William Hays's division captured the Crow House redoubt near the stream at 8 A.M. and set to work reversing the redoubt to support the Federal advance toward the South Side Railroad. Within half an hour the divisions of Hays and Maj. Gen. Gershom Mott occupied the main line of Confederate works in their sector.

By 10 A.M. Lee knew that it was time to order the evacuation of Richmond and Petersburg. He sent a message to Pres. Jefferson Davis, informing him of the decision and advising him to make preparations to leave Richmond that night. He ordered his lieutenants to evacuate the cities that evening and rendezvous at Amelia Court House.

In the afternoon, Maj. Gen. John Gibbon's XXIV Corps marched through the breach opened by Wright's men and wheeled northeast toward Petersburg. Their advance was halted at Forts Gregg and Whitworth, where retreating Confederates made a gallant stand that enabled their comrades to reach the safety of the old Dimmock line near the western edge of Petersburg. The defenders were finally overwhelmed, though nightfall meant that the city remained Confederate for one final evening.

The successful attack on Petersburg resulted in 3,894 Federal casualties and 4,852 Confederate, many of them prisoners. Petersburg escaped the fate of the capital city, where not only were the bridges fired but nearby warehouses, as well. The flames spread, and by morning much of downtown Richmond had been engulfed by the Great Evacuation Fire, as it became known, which took the incoming Federal troops several hours to extinguish.

The location of the Union breakthrough at Petersburg is preserved at Pamplin Historical Park, a privately owned 363-acre park open to the public. The site of the initial Union breakthrough, including Tudor Hall, the headquarters of Brig. Gen. Samuel McGowan, are interpreted in a visitor center and by self-guided walking trails in the park. Many other important parts of the battlefield, such as Fort Gregg, are protected in Petersburg National Battlefield. Some other places, such as Fort Mahone, have been lost to development. ▨

SUTHERLAND STATION

On Sunday, April 2, 1865, the last attempt to keep the South Side Railroad in Confederate hands took place at Sutherland Station, about eight miles west of Petersburg where Maj. Gen. Henry Heth had organized a defense before returning to the main lines near the city. Brig. Gen. John R. Cooke commanded the four brigades in Heth's absence. Cooke's brigade was positioned at the Claiborne Road intersection on the Confederate right, with those of Col. Joseph H. Hyman and Brig. Gen. William MacRae in the center. Brig. Gen. Samuel McGowan's brigade was placed on the left, just east of Ocran Methodist Episcopal Church. Four cannons were located at Sutherland Tavern on the west, two in the center of the line, and one at the church.

At about 10 A.M. Col. Henry J. Madill's brigade, the vanguard of Brig. Gen. Nelson A. Miles's division of Humphreys's corps, approached from the south. An hour later, Madill led an assault on the hastily constructed fieldworks but was repulsed with heavy losses. Madill was wounded, and Col. Clinton MacDougall assumed command.

View northwest to Sutherland Tavern, on C.S.A. right flank. VIRGINIA DEPARTMENT OF HISTORIC RESOURCES, JOHN S. SALMON

Col. Robert Nugent's brigade then arrived on the field and supervised a joint attack that also was repelled, with MacDougall falling wounded. Miles attacked once more at about 2:45 P.M., using the first two brigades again but also having Brig. Gen. John Ramsey's brigade assault the Confederate left flank at the church. Overwhelmed, McGowan's brigade crumbled, as did the rest of the line.

At last Grant's objective had been achieved, and the South Side Railroad lay firmly in Federal hands. Lee's last supply line was severed. Some 366 Federals had been killed or wounded in the Sutherland

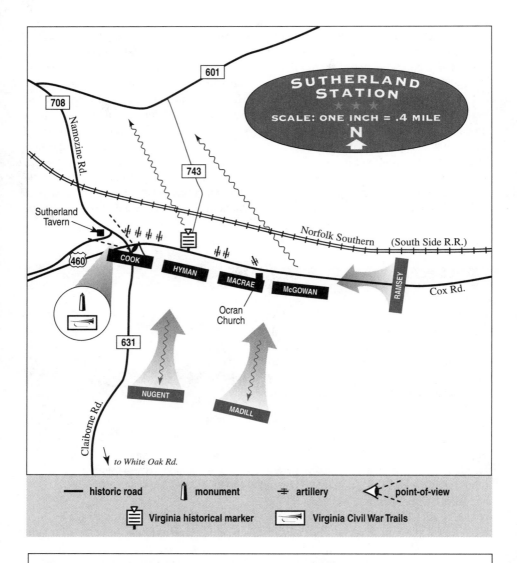

SUTHERLAND STATION

★ ★ ★

SCALE: ONE INCH = .4 MILE

N

601

708

Namozine Rd.

743

Norfolk Southern (South Side R.R.)

Sutherland Tavern

460

COOK

HYMAN

MACRAE

McGOWAN

RAMSEY

Cox Rd.

Ocran Church

631

NUGENT

MADILL

Claiborne Rd.

to White Oak Rd.

—— historic road   🏛 monument   ⚔ artillery   ◄ point-of-view

📋 Virginia historical marker   📯 Virginia Civil War Trails

DIRECTIONS: I-85 Exit 61, w. on U.S. Rte. 460, follow Lee's Retreat signs about 4.1 miles to Rte. 708 (Namozine Rd.); n. (right) on Rte. 708 .1 mile to Lee's Retreat Stop 1 (Sutherland Station) on left; return to I-85.

Station engagement, and the Confederates lost about 600, of whom almost all were made prisoner.

U.S. Rte. 460 has been widened to four lanes, and commercial and residential development lines most of the transportation corridor in the area. South of the high-

way, however, much of the battleground remains open land. The modern Ocran Church occupies the site of the antebellum structure (the original frame building may have been brick-veneered), but Sutherland Tavern (now Fork Inn) stands at the Claiborne Road intersection. ■

After evacuating Richmond and Petersburg on April 2–3, 1865, most of the Army of Northern Virginia marched west on roads north of the Appomattox River. The remnants of Maj. Gen. George E. Pickett's and Maj. Gen. Bushrod R. Johnson's divisions of Lt. Gen. Richard H. Anderson's corps, however, moved along the Namozine Road (present-day Rte. 708), south of the river. Maj. Gen. Fitzhugh Lee's cavalry corps followed, and Maj. Gen. W. H. F. "Rooney" Lee's cavalry division acted as the rear guard. By 2 A.M. on Monday, April 3, the Confederates had crossed from Dinwiddie County to Amelia County over Namozine Creek, and then headed west toward Namozine Presbyterian Church, where Anderson had his headquarters.

To the southeast, Maj. Gen. Philip H. Sheridan started his cavalry corps in pursuit after sunrise. Maj. Gen. George A. Custer's division led the way, and turned west on the Namozine Road.

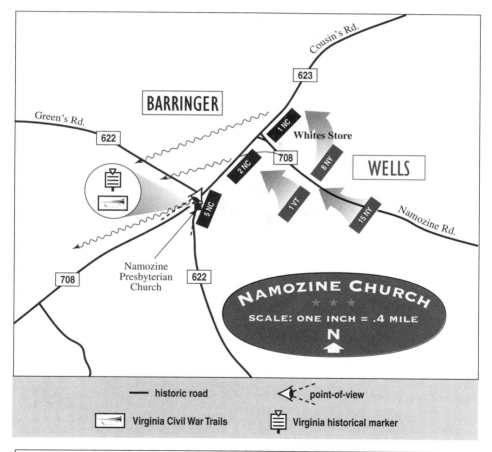

DIRECTIONS: I-85 Exit 61, w. on U.S. Rte. 460, follow Lee's Retreat signs about 4.1 miles to Rte. 708 (Namozine Rd.); n. (right) on Rte. 708, following Lee's Retreat signs 10.7 miles to Lee's Retreat Stop 2 (Namozine Church).

Namozine Presbyterian Church, site of 5th North Carolina Infantry position. VIRGINIA DEPARTMENT OF HISTORIC RESOURCES, JOHN S. SALMON

Namozine Church is located southwest of the intersection of Namozine and Cousin's Roads (Rte. 623/708). Just north of the church, Cousin's Road forked, and Green's Road (Rte. 622) led away to the northwest. Although the land was open around the church and the few houses that stood nearby, there were woods to the south and northwest. Brig. Gen. Rufus Barringer's cavalry brigade guarded the Confederate rear at the church. Behind Barringer, one cannon was stationed on Green's Road.

Sometime after 9 A.M. Maj. Gen.

George A. Custer's division approached Namozine Church on Namozine Road, and the lead regiments charged the Confederates. After an attempt at a counterattack, Barringer's line broke, and those Confederates who did not flee were taken prisoner.

In the confusion, Barringer and his staff became separated from his command and fled several miles southwest on Cousin's Road. Eventually they encountered what they thought were Confederate cavalry pickets but were in reality Federal scouts dressed in Confederate uniforms. Barringer and his men were taken prisoner and escorted to City Point for transportation to Union prisons.

The Namozine Church engagement cost the Federals 81 casualties. The total number of Confederate casualties are not known, but about 350 were captured.

Today, the battlefield retains very good integrity, although it is more heavily wooded than it was in 1865. Namozine Presbyterian Church, a simple and well-preserved rural church built in 1847, is owned by the Amelia County Historical Society. ■

AMELIA SPRINGS

When Gen. Robert E. Lee's Army of Northern Virginia rendezvoused at Amelia Court House on the Richmond & Danville Railroad on April 4, 1865, it found only munitions, not rations, aboard trains from Danville. The day the soldiers spent foraging dissipated the lead Lee had over the pursuing Federals. When the Confederates left Amelia Court House on Wednesday, April 5, the intended route to the southwest was blocked by Union cavalry near Jetersville, the next station southwest of Amelia Court House, with the Federal infantry closing fast. Lee therefore ordered a night march around the Union left flank to Farmville—rations

DIRECTIONS: I-85 Exit 61, w. on U.S. Rte. 460, follow Lee's Retreat signs about 4.1 miles to Rte. 708 (Namozine Rd.); n. (right) on Rte. 708, following Lee's Retreat signs 16.7 miles to Rte. 612 (Richmond Rd.); s.w. (left) on Rte. 612 .1 mile to Rte. 708; w. (right) on Rte. 708 3.8 miles to State Rte. 153 (Military Rd.); n.w. (right) on State Rte. 153 3 miles to State Rte. 38; w. (left) on State Rte. 38 7.1 miles, following Lee's Retreat signs through Amelia Court House to Lee's Retreat Stop 3 (Amelia Court House). From Stop 3, follow Lee's Retreat signs on U.S. Rte. 360 Bus. .3 mile to U.S. Rte. 360; s.w. (left) on U.S. Rte. 360 6 miles to Rte. 671 (Jetersville Rd.); s.w. (left) on Rte. 671 .6 mile to Rte. 642 (Amelia Springs Rd.) and Lee's Retreat Stop 4 (Jetersville) on right. From Stop 4, follow Lee's Retreat signs to left on Rte. 642 .15 mile to U.S. Rte. 360; cross U.S. Rte. 360 and continue n. on Rte. 642 3.2 miles to Lee's Retreat Stop 5 (Amelia Springs).

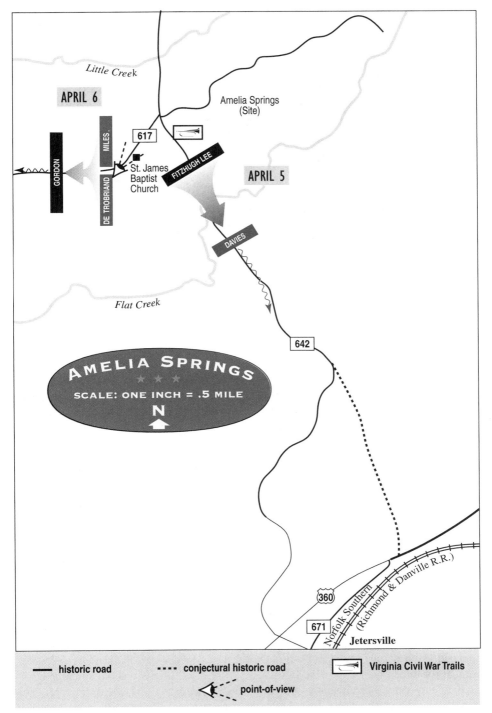

Little Creek

APRIL 6

617

Amelia Springs (Site)

MILES

GORDON

DE TROBRIAND

St. James Baptist Church

FITZHUGH LEE

APRIL 5

DAVIES

Flat Creek

642

AMELIA SPRINGS
★ ★ ★
SCALE: ONE INCH = .5 MILE
N

360

Norfolk Southern
(Richmond & Danville R.R.)

671

Jetersville

— historic road   ···· conjectural historic road   Virginia Civil War Trails

point-of-view

awaited his army there at the South Side Railroad depot—then the army would march south to Keysville and continue to North Carolina.

Maj. Gen. Philip H. Sheridan sent cavalry patrols north of Jetersville to reconnoiter his left flank. The brigade of Brig. Gen. Henry E. Davies, Jr., rode through Amelia

Attack on Gordon's corps (C.S.A. rear guard), Amelia Springs. LIBRARY OF CONGRESS

Springs, then swung north to Paineville. About four miles farther on, Davies attacked a Confederate wagon train, destroying the wagons and capturing equipment, animals, and more than 600 prisoners. Some of the men were armed blacks in Confederate uniforms who successfully repulsed one cavalry charge before being overwhelmed by another. They had been recently recruited in Richmond, armed and quickly trained, and sent along on the retreat. They symbolized the desperate straits of the Confederacy, which long had officially opposed arming blacks and only in February 1865 had finally authorized the raising of black regiments. The Paineville engagement is the only known instance in Virginia of combat involving organized black Confederate soldiers.

Learning of the attack, Gen. Robert E. Lee dispatched two divisions of Maj. Gen. Fitzhugh Lee's cavalry to attack Davies. Fitz Lee found Brig. Gen. Martin Gary's brigade at Paineville; together they engaged Davies's rear guard in a running combat for three miles to Amelia Springs.

Near the springs resort, the Confederates attacked Davies in a mounted combat with drawn sabers. They forced him to retreat, and pursued him almost to Jetersville. When the Confederates encountered additional Federal brigades, however, they retired to Amelia Springs.

That night and the next day, Lee's army marched from Amelia Court House through Amelia Springs toward Farmville. Lt. Gen. James Longstreet's corps led the way, with Lt. Gen. Richard H. Anderson's and Lt. Gen. Richard S. Ewell's corps next, then the wagon train and Maj. Gen. John B. Gordon's corps as rear guard. Two of Maj. Gen. Andrew A. Humphreys's divisions observed the movement and pursued. Brig. Gen. Nelson A. Miles's division marched through the springs and turned west, thrusting after Gordon on the north side of present-day Rte. 617. Maj. Gen. Gershom Mott's division followed suit on the south side of the road; when Mott was wounded, Brig. Gen. Régis de Trobriand took command. Gordon held off his attackers and continued the march west.

The Amelia Springs engagements resulted in about 158 Federal casualties and an unknown, though probably lesser, number of Confederate killed and wounded.

The Amelia Springs battlefield is heavily wooded and difficult to interpret. The springs resort has long since vanished. The property is privately owned, but there appears to be little threat of development. ■

L t. Gen. Ulysses S. Grant joined Maj. Gen. Philip H. Sheridan and Maj. Gen. George G. Meade at Jetersville at about 10:30 P.M. on April 5, 1865. Confident that Lee was heading to Farmville, Grant emphasized the importance of getting ahead of Lee's army, not merely following it. Accordingly, Sheridan's cavalry began riding to Deatonville, five miles to the west. Meanwhile, Maj. Gen. Edward O. C. Ord led the Army of the James toward High Bridge, the South Side Railroad bridge over the Appomattox River about three miles east of Farmville, with orders to burn the structure to prevent the Confederates from escaping to the north side of the river.

As planned, Lee's route of march went west, through Deatonville, then southwest to Rice's Station, and then west to Farmville, on the south side of the Appomattox River, with major river crossings at High Bridge and Farmville. Maj. Gen. John B. Gordon's corps acted as the rear guard and followed the army's wagon

train. Lt. Gen. Richard S. Ewell's corps marched in advance of the train, preceded by Lt. Gen. Richard H. Anderson's corps and with Lt. Gen. James Longstreet's combined corps as the vanguard.

On Thursday, April 6, Maj. Gen. Andrew A. Humphreys's II Corps attacked the rear of Gordon's column near Amelia Springs. Afterwards, Brig. Gen. Régis de Trobriand's and Maj. Gen. Nelson A. Miles's divisions dogged Gordon's every step.

Sheridan's cavalry took roads that paralleled Lee's route. Small units began harassing the Confederate wagon train near Deatonville. Maj. Gen. Horatio G. Wright's VI Corps, after marching from Jetersville to Amelia Court House, reversed course and followed Sheridan. Maj. Gen. Charles Griffin's V Corps marched behind and north of the Confederates.

Late in the morning the vanguard of the Army of Northern Virginia, including Longstreet and Lee, began to arrive at Rice's Station on the South Side Railroad. Unbeknownst to the two commanders, a

Surrender of Ewell's corps, Sailor's Creek. LIBRARY OF CONGRESS

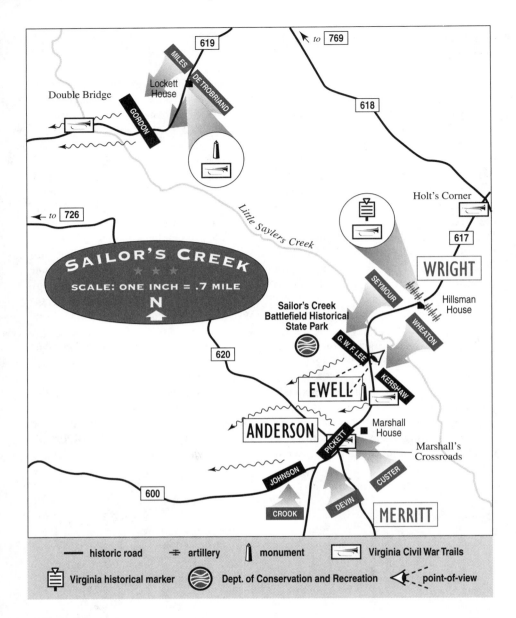

gap had opened in the column between Longstreet's corps and Anderson's when the latter stopped to fight off an attack at Holt's Corner (junction of Rtes. 617 and 618) by Maj. Gen. George Crook's cavalry. Soon Crook retired to join the rest of the Federal cavalry, but meanwhile Maj.

Gen. George A. Custer observed the gap and occupied ground around Marshall's Cross Roads near the Harper farm (intersection of Rtes. 617 and 620).

Anderson continued the march until he crossed Little Sailor's Creek and arrived at Marshall's Cross Roads. Finding not only

DIRECTIONS: From Lee's Retreat Stop 5 (Amelia Springs), continue n. on Rte. 642 (Amelia Springs Rd.) about .25 mile to Rte. 617 (St. James Rd.); w. (left) on Rte. 617 3 miles to Lee's Retreat Stop 6 (Deatonville). From Stop 6, turn left on Rte. 616 (S. Genito Rd.) .5 mile to Rte. 617 (Sayler's Creek Rd.); w. (right) on Rte. 617 4 miles to Lee's Retreat Stop 7 (Holt's Corner) across Rte. 618 (James Town Rd.). From Stop 7, continue on Rte. 617 .9 mile to Lee's Retreat Stop 8 (Hillsman house). From Stop 8, continue on Rte. 617 .8 mile to Confederate position across Sayler's Creek on left, then .5 mile to Lee's Retreat Stop 9 (Marshall's Cross Roads). From Stop 9, retrace Rte. 617 2.2 miles to Rte. 618 (Stop 7 at Holt's Corner); n.w. (left) on Rte. 618 2.1 miles to Rte. 619; s.w. (left) on Rte. 619 .6 mile to Lee's Retreat Stop 10 (Lockett house). From Stop 10, continue s. on Rte. 619 .7 mile to Lee's Retreat Stop 11 (Double Bridges). For more information about the battlefield, visit the Department of Conservation and Recreation's state parks Web site at dcr.state.va.us/parks or call the park at 804-392-3455.

Custer but two additional Federal cavalry divisions in front of him, Anderson informed Maj. Gen. Fitzhugh Lee, who passed the word to Ewell. Ewell decided to send the wagon train and Gordon's corps north from Holt's Corner on the Jamestown Road (Rte. 617) to bypass the roadblock. He then posted his 5,200-man corps on high ground south and west of the creek and stationed infantry and cavalry at the James M. Hillsman house as a rear guard. Soon Wright's VI Corps engaged the rear guard.

At the head of Wright's corps marched Brig. Gen. Truman Seymour's division, followed by Maj. Gen. Frank Wheaton's, then Maj. Gen. George W. Getty's. Sheridan directed operations after Ewell's rear guard fled and instructed Wright to place Maj. Andrew Cowan's twenty-gun artillery brigade atop the ridge at the Hillsman house. Shortly after 5 P.M. the Federal cannons opened up on Ewell's corps, and after half an hour's bombardment the Union infantry attacked.

Sheridan had only parts of Wheaton's and Seymour's divisions available, and at about 6 P.M., the two understrength divisions waded Little Sailor's Creek. The 7,000 Federals then reformed and attacked up the hill toward Ewell's position, but part of the line broke when the Confederates fired into Wheaton's division. Col. Stapleton Crutchfield, commander of artillery, led four of Ewell's battalions in a desperate counterattack and drove some of Wheaton's men into and through the creek. When Crutchfield was killed and canister was fired directly into the Confederates, however, they retreated back up the hill. The Federals then charged in concert and turned Ewell's flanks after savage fighting. Some 3,400 Confederates surrendered, including six generals: Ewell, Maj. Gen. G. W. Custis Lee, Brig. Gen. Seth M. Barton, Maj. Gen. Joseph B. Kershaw, Brig. Gen. Dudley M. DuBose, and Brig. Gen. James P. Simms.

Less than a mile behind Ewell, Anderson's 6,300-man corps faced three Federal cavalry divisions totaling 8,000–9,000 horse soldiers at Marshall's Cross Roads. Crook was to attack Anderson's right flank while Brig. Gen. Thomas C. Devin and Custer assaulted the front. Brig. Gen. J. Irvin Gregg's brigade of Crook's division attacked dismounted and pushed Maj. Gen. Bushrod R. Johnson back on his wagons. Custer led several charges and finally succeeded in routing Maj. Gen. George E. Pickett's division. Anderson's line collapsed, and the men fled through the woods toward Rice's Station. About 2,600 Confederates surrendered, including Brig. Gen. Eppa Hunton and Brig. Gen. Montgomery D. Corse.

Gordon and the wagon train, meanwhile, came under attack from almost every hilltop west of Holt's Corner. This, in turn, slowed the trailing Confederate infantry. At crossings of Little and Big Sailor's Creeks over the Double Bridges, matters reached a crisis when a wagon crashed through the floor of one of the bridges. Gordon was forced to make a stand at the creek when de Trobriand's division appeared atop the hill at the Lockett farm at about 5 P.M. Then Miles's division pressed Gordon's left flank, causing the Confederates to fall back to a hill across the creek. Although many of Gordon's 7,000-man corps escaped as darkness fell, about 1,700 surrendered or were killed.

Lee had ridden toward the sounds of combat from Rice's Station and watched the tattered mob that had once constituted most of his army flee across Big Sailor's Creek. He was heard to exclaim, "My God! Has the army been dissolved?" That night Lee told a courier from Pres. Jefferson Davis, "A few more Sailor's Creeks and it will all be over."

That same night Grant, still at Burke-ville, received a message from Sheridan reporting on the day's successes, concluding, "If the thing is pressed I think that Lee will surrender." Grant transmitted Sheridan's message to Pres. Abraham Lincoln at City Point, who telegraphed back to Grant the next day: "Let the *thing* be pressed."

The total Federal casualties at the three engagements that constituted the battle of Sailor's Creek amounted to 1,148. The number of Confederate dead and wounded are not known, but the number of prisoners alone amounted to about 7,700, including eight generals. About a fifth of Lee's army was now hors de combat.

The Hillsman house and some 317 acres of the battlefield, a National Historic Landmark, are preserved in Sailor's Creek Battlefield State Park and at Marshall's Cross Roads. The remainder of the battlefield is farmland and woods, privately owned but seemingly unthreatened by development. Both the Hillsman house and the Lockett house survive. ▪

HIGH BRIDGE

The only clear-cut Confederate victory on Thursday, April 6, 1865, occurred at High Bridge, the South Side Railroad trestle across the Appomattox River, located about five miles west of Sailor's Creek and three miles east of Farmville. Except for another railroad bridge and wagon bridge at Farmville, High Bridge (and its adjacent small wagon bridge) was the only such river crossing in the area.

Both armies sought control of the bridge, the Federals to deny the Confederates a means of escape, the Confederates to obstruct Federal pursuit. Early in the morning of April 6, Maj. Gen. Edward O. C. Ord's Army of the James was dispatched from Burkeville to march west along the

DIRECTIONS: From Lee's Retreat Stop 15 (Cumberland Church, *see below*), continue left (n.) on State Rte. 45 about .3 mile to Rte. 657 (Jamestown Rd.); e. (right) on Rte. 657 3.5 miles to Rte. 600 (River Rd.); e. (left) on Rte. 600 1.1 miles to Lee's Retreat Stop 16 (High Bridge). **NOTE:** Look to s. (right) .4 mile after turning onto Rte. 600 and observe 1914 metal-truss High Bridge; the brick piers of 1854 High Bridge are beneath it but may not be visible.

South Side Railroad and secure the crossing for the Union. At 4 A.M. Ord sent a combined force of 900 cavalry and infantry across country to the bridge, ahead of his main column. After further reflection, he ordered Col. Theodore Read to catch up with and command the detachment.

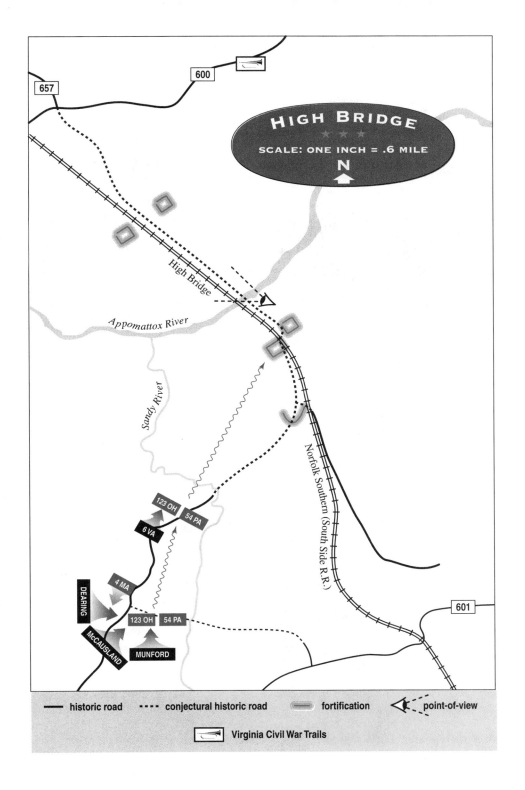

657

600

HIGH BRIDGE
★ ★ ★
SCALE: ONE INCH = .6 MILE

N

High Bridge

Appomattox River

Sandy River

Norfolk Southern (South Side R.R.)

123 OH   54 PA

6 VA

4 MA

DEARING

123 OH   54 PA

McCAUSLAND

MUNFORD

601

—— historic road   •••• conjectural historic road   ⬭ fortification   ◁ ⦙ point-of-view

⬭ Virginia Civil War Trails

Repairing the burned spans at High Bridge shortly after the war. LIBRARY OF CONGRESS

Read's force consisted of two infantry regiments, the 54th Pennsylvania and the 123rd Ohio, some 800 men, and three companies (80 horse soldiers) of the 4th Massachusetts Cavalry. Lt. Col. Horace Kellogg of the 123rd Ohio Infantry commanded the foot soldiers, while Col. Francis Washburn led his own cavalrymen. Read found that four earthen fortifications guarded the bridge's approaches, while a small redoubt defended the northwestern end of the wagon bridge and a larger one had been constructed at the intersection of two roads leading to the bridges.

Lt. Gen. James Longstreet, meanwhile, had learned of the Federal expedition. He ordered some 1,200 horse soldiers under the overall command of Maj. Gen. Fitzhugh Lee to race to the bridge and deny it to the Federals. Word reached Ord, who sent a staff officer to warn Read. The officer never reached Read, however, because the Confederates got between them.

Read and the infantry stopped more than a mile south of the bridge, while Washburn led the cavalry forward to reconnoiter. Finding the bridge well defended, Washburn maneuvered to outflank the Confederates in the larger redoubt at the intersection; they quickly retreated to the railroad bridge and across the river.

The Southern cavalry attacked Read and the Federal infantry between noon and 1 P.M. Hearing the sound of gunfire, Washburn led his troopers back from High Bridge and arrived in time to execute a desperate charge into the onrushing Confederates. The fight was especially bloody among the higher ranks. Washburn and Dearing were mortally wounded, while Read was killed outright.

The Union infantry retreated fighting toward the bridge and made a stand partway there. Col. Reuben B. Boston of the 5th Virginia Cavalry, commanding Brig. Gen. William H. Payne's brigade, joined in a charge of the 6th Virginia Cavalry led by Capt. Frank M. Myers against the Federals. Boston was killed, but the attack succeeded in driving the infantrymen from their position to the bridge, where they surrendered.

The battle for High Bridge cost the Federals 847 casualties, including almost 800 prisoners. About 100 Confederates were killed or wounded, but High Bridge remained in Confederate hands. That evening, the remainder of Lee's army that had escaped the carnage at Sailor's Creek crossed the bridge and then marched west to Farmville. Longstreet's corps kept to the south side of the river and marched to the town.

High Bridge and the battlefield near its southern end are no longer accessible, as the roads have been abandoned and converted to private farm lanes. In addition, the area is now heavily wooded. At least one of the earthworks survives on a farm in Cumberland County, across the river at the northwestern end of the bridge. Many of the brick piers also survive, although the superstructure is gone. A steel bridge constructed in 1914 now carries train traffic across the river. ▪

RICE'S STATION

Lt. Gen. James Longstreet's corps escaped the combat at Sailor's Creek on April 6, 1865, having become separated from the rest of the army when Lt. Gen. Richard H. Anderson's corps, which was following Longstreet's, was forced to stop at Holt's Corner (junction of Rtes. 617 and 618) and to defend itself against Maj. Gen. George Crook's cavalry. Longstreet, accompanied by Lee, continued his march southwest to the South Side Railroad depot at Rice's Station.

When Longstreet learned of the combat at Sailor's Creek and that a small force from Maj. Gen. Edward O. C. Ord's Army of the James was on its way to burn High Bridge, the South Side Railroad trestle across the Appomattox River near Farmville, he entrenched his corps to defend the crossing's approaches.

Early in the afternoon, Maj. Gen. John Gibbon's XXIV Corps, the vanguard of Ord's infantry, neared Rice's Station as it marched west along the railroad from Burkeville. Gibbon deployed Col. Harrison S. Fairchild's brigade of Brig. Gen. Robert S. Foster's division on the right of the Farmville Road (present-day Rte. 600) and Col. Thomas O. Osborn's brigade on

View north toward Wilcox's position, Rice's Station. VIRGINIA DEPARTMENT OF HISTORIC RESOURCES, JOHN S. SALMON

the left, with Col. George B. Dandy's brigade in reserve. Longstreet had posted Maj. Gen. Cadmus M. Wilcox's division and Maj. Gen. Henry Heth's division, both of Lt. Gen. A. P. Hill's former corps, south of the railroad. Maj. Gen. Charles W. Field's division of Longstreet's own corps

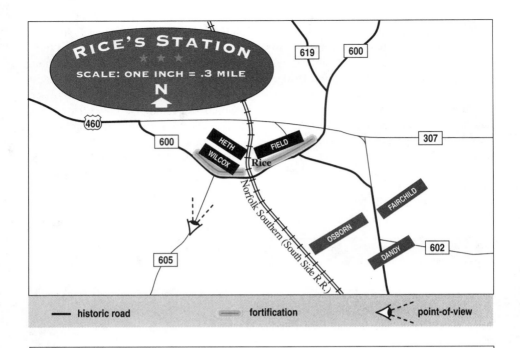

DIRECTIONS: From Lee's Retreat Stop 11 (Double Bridges), continue s. on Rte. 619 about 5 miles to U.S. Rte. 460; cross U.S. Rte. 460 onto Rte. 600 .2 mile to Lee's Retreat Stop 12 (Rice's Depot), just across Rte. 735.

was opposite Osborn and Fairchild. Heavy skirmishing erupted, but Gibbon did not have time before sundown to assault the Confederate position. After dark, assured that Gordon's and Maj. Gen. William Mahone's forces had crossed High Bridge, Longstreet disengaged his corps and marched west to Farmville.

The Federals suffered 66 casualties in the Rice's Station engagement. The Confederate casualties are unknown.

No antebellum structures survive today at Rice, but some late-nineteenth- and early-twentieth-century dwellings occupy the area around the depot site. Otherwise, little has changed in the area. ■

CUMBERLAND CHURCH

During the night of April 6–7, 1865, Gen. Robert E. Lee's Army of Northern Virginia trudged to Farmville, Lt. Gen. James Longstreet's corps by roads on the south side of the Appomattox River and Maj. Gen. John B. Gordon's corps and Maj. Gen. William Mahone's division via High Bridge and then down the South Side

Railroad on the north side. After the last units had passed, elements of Maj. Gen. William Mahone's division remained behind to burn the railroad bridge and the small wagon bridge just downstream.

Maj. Gen. Andrew A. Humphreys's II Corps advanced toward High Bridge at about 5:30 A.M. on Friday, April 7, and the

Cumberland Church, looking west. VIRGINIA DEPARTMENT OF HISTORIC RESOURCES, JOHN S. SALMON

vanguard arrived at 7 A.M. just after Mahone's men had fired the two bridges. While under direct small-arms fire from Mahone's men, Brig. Gen. Francis C. Barlow's 19th Maine Infantry scampered onto the wagon bridge and used their canteens, boxes, and tents to drown and beat out the flames. Despite their best efforts, however, the first several trusses of High Bridge burned, and the fifth span collapsed into the river. Mahone attempted to recapture the wagon bridge at about 9 A.M., but Maj. Gen. Nelson A. Miles's division arrived to support Barlow and drive the Confederates away. Mahone retreated northwest on the Jamestown Road (present-day Rte. 657) and entrenched at Cumberland Presbyterian Church about three miles north of Farmville. Miles's and Brig. Gen. Régis de Trobriand's division followed Mahone, while Barlow pursued Gordon's corps southwest along the railroad toward the town.

Longstreet and Lee arrived in Farmville at about 9 A.M. The soldiers at the head of the column immediately began distributing rations from the waiting trains—the troops were ordered to the north side of the Appomattox River to prepare their breakfasts—while those at the rear fought off harassing attacks by Maj. Gen. George Crook's cavalry division in advance of the

Union infantry. Lee planned to cross over all his men, then burn the railroad and wagon bridges in Farmville to isolate the Federals on the south side of the river, which was not easily fordable there.

Lee himself had finally crossed to the north bank with Longstreet's corps, and the Farmville bridges had been destroyed, when the sound of gunfire was heard to the east. Lee learned that the Federals had crossed at High Bridge after all, and now his army faced a thirty-eight-mile march to the next large depot, Appomattox Station, whereas the Federals would have only thirty miles to cover. In addition, a superior Union force had begun closing in on Mahone near Cumberland Presbyterian Church. Lee would have to stand and fight before he could continue his retreat.

The Confederates constructed a line of earthworks that resembled a fishhook, with Mahone's division occupying the northern part and Gordon the eastern face. Longstreet's corps extended the line to the south. Mahone's division straddled the Cumberland Court House Road (Rte. 45). Lt. Col. William T. Poague's battalion of Brig. Gen. Reuben L. Walker's reserve artillery corps filled the ground between Mahone's right and Gordon's left. Part of Maj. Gen. Fitzhugh Lee's cavalry division protected Mahone's left flank.

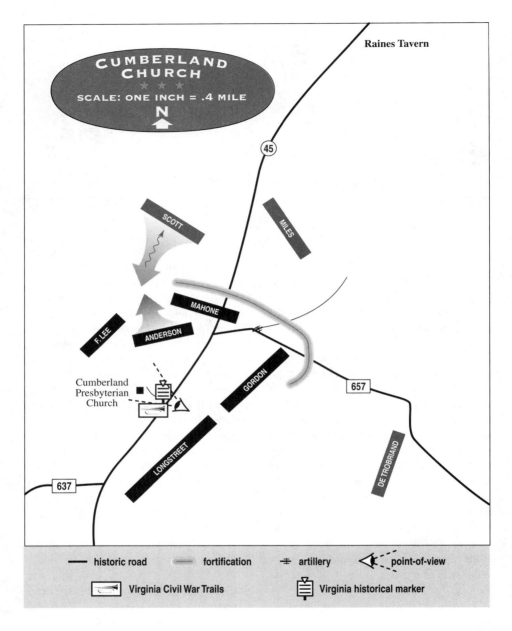

Raines Tavern

CUMBERLAND
CHURCH
★ ★ ★
SCALE: ONE INCH = .4 MILE
N

45

SCOTT

MILES

MAHONE

F. LEE

ANDERSON

Cumberland
Presbyterian
Church

GORDON

657

LONGSTREET

DE TROBRIAND

637

historic road   fortification   artillery   point-of-view

Virginia Civil War Trails   Virginia historical marker

Miles's division faced Mahone, with Humphreys on the field and in command for the Federals. Humphreys did not know that VI Corps had not yet crossed the river at Farmville, still looking for a ford. Hearing gunfire to the southwest, he ordered an attack against Mahone's left, expecting VI Corps to appear momentarily and strike Longstreet from the south.

At about 4:15 P.M. Col. George W. Scott's brigade assaulted Mahone's flank. Some of Scott's men reached Mahone's defenses and got into the rear; a counterattack by Brig. Gen. George T. "Tige"

Anderson's Georgia brigade threw them back to their lines.

The firing to the southwest heard by Humphreys was an attack on part of the Confederate wagon train by Brig. Gen. J. Irvin Gregg's cavalry brigade. Confederate cavalry divisions counterattacked to save the train, drove off the Federals, and captured Gregg. The Union cavalry reformed and charged once more but this time encountered Brig. Gen. William G. Lewis's infantry brigade and Col. William M. Owen's artillery. The Federals abandoned the effort and retired across the river to Farmville.

Nightfall ended the fighting for the day. During the evening, however, VI Corps forded the river and joined II Corps on the north side. Grant, meanwhile, rode into Farmville late in the afternoon and at 5 P.M. sent Lee a message urging the surrender of the Army of Northern Virginia. Lee received it at about 9:30 P.M., read it, and passed it to Longstreet without a comment. Longstreet glanced at it and handed it back to Lee, saying, "Not yet." Lee then wrote a reply to Grant refusing the request but asking what terms he proposed.

At 11 P.M. Lee's army slipped quietly out of its entrenchments on its last night march. Longstreet's corps trudged north about five miles on the Buckingham Plank Road (Rte. 600) to the Curdsville road (Rte. 633). Gordon's corps moved north about two miles before turning west on the Richmond–Lynchburg Stage Road (Rte. 636). Fitzhugh Lee's cavalry followed Gordon as the rear guard. According to Lee's plan, the army would move to Appomattox Court House, then march on toward Campbell Court House (Rustburg).

The Cumberland Church engagement resulted in 571 Federal casualties. The figures for the Confederates are not known.

Much of the battlefield has been affected by development creeping north from Farmville. The site of Scott's attack and repulse is now a junkyard. Cumberland Presbyterian Church, Lee's headquarters during the battle, stands but is much altered and enlarged. ■

APPOMATTOX STATION

It was probably on Saturday, April 8, 1865, that a large part of the Army of Northern Virginia melted away. Sleep deprived and half starved, barely able to walk, they had reached their limits after four long years, and upon seeing a road that might take them home, some took it.

Many hung on nonetheless, driven perhaps by a hopeless determination to be there at the end they saw approaching. On parallel roads, the men of Maj. Gen. John B. Gordon's and Lt. Gen. James Longstreet's corps, with Maj. Gen. Fitzhugh Lee's cavalry division as the rear guard, marched west to New Store and then south toward Appomattox Court House and the supply trains supposedly waiting at Appomattox Station. Resupplied if all went as

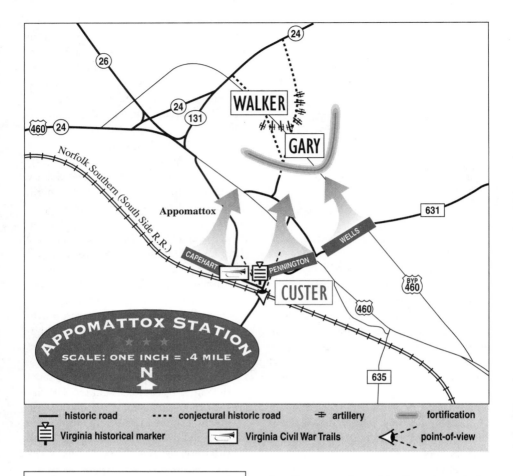

—— historic road	···· conjectural historic road	⚓ artillery	━━ fortification
🏳 Virginia historical marker	🖅 Virginia Civil War Trails	◀⁝ point-of-view

DIRECTIONS: From Lee's Retreat Stop 16 (High Bridge, *see above*), continue n. (right) on Rte. 600 (River Rd.) about 2 miles to Rte. 653 (Cooks Rd.); n.w. (left) on Rte. 653 4.6 miles to Rte. 638 (John Randolph Rd.); w. (left) on Rte. 638 .3 mile to State Rte. 45; s.w. (left) on State Rte. 45 .3 mile to Rte. 636 (Raines Tavern Rd.); w. (right) on Rte. 636 20.5 miles to State Rte. 24; s.w. (left) on State Rte. 24 4 miles to Lee's Retreat Stop 17 (Lee's Rear Guard). Continue s.w. (left) on State Rte. 24 6.2 miles to U.S. Rte. 460 Bus. in Appomattox; s.e. (left) on U.S. Rte. 460 Bus. .2 mile to Rte. 131; right on Rte. 131 and follow Lee's Retreat signs .7 mile to Lee's Retreat Stop 18 (Battle of Appomattox Station) at Appomattox Visitor Center and state historical marker K-159, Battle of Appomattox Station.

planned, the army would march west toward Lynchburg and then south to North Carolina to unite with Gen. Joseph E. Johnston's army.

The Federal II and VI Corps trailed Gordon and Longstreet. To the south, the Army of the James and V Corps marched doggedly toward Appomattox Station, with Maj. Gen. Philip H. Sheridan's cavalry in the lead.

In Farmville, Lt. Gen. Ulysses S. Grant received the message from Gen. Robert E. Lee rejecting Grant's suggestion of surrender but asking what terms he might propose. Grant wrote Lee early in the morning, requesting a meeting to discuss specific conditions for surrender; the letter did not reach Lee until sometime that afternoon. Lee responded that he did not intend to surrender yet but merely wanted to know what terms might be given. He also called for a meeting between the lines at 10 A.M. the next day.

While the generals drafted letters, the Federal cavalry rode west. At Pamplin's Depot, Maj. Gen. George Crook's division captured the Confederate trains sent from Farmville. Learning that additional trains were located near Appomattox Station, Sheridan's divisions galloped on. Maj. Gen. George A. Custer's arrived there first and captured three long trains from Lynchburg loaded with supplies, including 300,000 rations, with hardly a shot being fired. Then he turned northeast toward Appomattox Court House.

Some Confederate troops already were there. Brig. Gen. Reuben L. Walker's reserve artillery corps and wagon train had reached the courthouse village by 10 A.M. and had parked about two miles southwest by early afternoon. Besides the artillerymen, the only combat troops with the corps were some 500 men in Brig. Gen. Martin W. Gary's cavalry brigade.

Suddenly, at 4 P.M., Custer's men charged the artillery park. Walker deployed his guns in an arc about a mile north of the station, with Gary's men dismounted on either end. The Confederate artillery, firing canister, quickly dispersed uncoordinated Federal attacks. Then between 8 and 9 P.M. Custer launched an attack through the woods with three brigades that overwhelmed the thin line of artillerymen and horse soldiers. Custer captured between twenty-four and thirty cannons and about a thousand men.

Wishing to locate the main Confederate force, Custer sent Col. Augustus I. Root's 15th New York Cavalry reconnoitering to Appomattox Court House. At about 3 P.M. Gordon's corps had halted about a mile northeast of the courthouse, and the men bivouacked and began cooking their

Appomattox Station, with destroyed South Side R.R. rolling stock. LIBRARY OF CONGRESS

rations. Pickets were posted in the village, and when the New Yorkers rode in, they opened fire, killing Root.

Now Lee knew that Sheridan's cavalry had gotten in front of his army. He summoned Gordon and Longstreet and Fitzhugh Lee to his tent to discuss the situation. If only Federal cavalry was present, perhaps Fitzhugh Lee's cavalry division and Gordon's infantry corps could punch through and clear the way to Lynchburg. If the Union infantry was present, too, surrender would be the only alternative. The breakout attempt would take place at dawn.

That night, Grant and Maj. Gen. George G. Meade stopped at Clifton, the home of Joseph Crute. Lee's second message to Grant arrived about midnight. Grant was disappointed but the next morning penned a reply agreeing to meet with Lee—reiterating that he could discuss nothing but the surrender of the Confederate army.

Only 48 Federals became casualties during the combat at Appomattox Station. The number of Confederate casualties are not known, but at least 1,000 men were captured.

The Appomattox Station battlefield has been obliterated by residential and commercial development in the town of Appomattox and by the construction of the U.S. Rte. 460 Bypass. ∎

The Army of Northern Virginia bivouacked in and northeast of Appomattox Court House on Saturday, April 8, 1865. Gen. Robert E. Lee arrived at about 9 P.M. and pitched his tent on a low hill a mile northeast of the village, east of the Richmond–Lynchburg Stage Road (present-day Rte. 24). The Appomattox River, but a thin stream at this point, lay between Lee's camp and the village.

Throughout the night and into the next morning, the Union armies converged nearby to surround the Confederates. By dawn, Maj. Gen. Andrew A. Humphreys's II Corps, with Maj. Gen. Horatio G. Wright's VI Corps behind it, faced Lt. Gen. James Longstreet. The cavalry divisions of Maj. Gen. George A. Custer and Brig. Gen. Thomas C. Devin blocked the routes of escape to the southeast confronting Brig. Gen. Martin W. Gary's and Col. T. M. R. Talcott's positions. To the southwest, Brig. Gen. Charles H. Smith's cavalry brigade straddled the Richmond–Lynchburg Stage Road atop a ridge.

Even before Smith took up his position, the battle at Appomattox Station told Lee that Federal cavalry stood athwart the road to Campbell Court House (Rustburg). Lee called a council of war with Maj. Gen. Fitzhugh Lee, Maj. Gen. John B. Gordon, and Longstreet, and decided to attack at 5 A.M. to determine whether the horse soldiers could be brushed aside and the road west opened up.

Lt. Gen. Ulysses S. Grant, meanwhile, spent a restless night at Clifton, an eighteen-mile ride east of Appomattox Court House. In the morning he sent a note to Lee declining Lee's proposal to meet, except to discuss surrender.

At dawn on Palm Sunday, April 9, Lee stood dressed in his best uniform as the Army of Northern Virginia went on the offensive for the last time. He knew that the odds were long and expected that before the day was out, he would probably be Grant's prisoner.

The Confederate line extended across the western end of the village, with Fitzhugh Lee's cavalry on the right and Gordon's infantry on the left. Col. Thomas T. Munford's division was on the Confederate right flank, with Maj. Gen. Thomas L. Rosser's division to Munford's left, then Maj. Gen. W. H. F. "Rooney" Lee's division tying in with the right of the infantry. The center of the Confederate line, its left resting on the Richmond–Lynchburg Stage Road, consisted of Maj. Gen. Bryan Grimes's infantry division in front of the remnants of Maj. Gen. Bushrod R. Johnson's division, commanded by Brig. Gen. William H. Wallace.

Fitzhugh Lee's cavalry pressed forward at dawn, and the Confederate line began to swing like a door, pivoting on the left flank and sweeping south across the Richmond–Lynchburg Stage Road. Lee struck Smith's brigade on the ridge west of the village, capturing two artillery pieces in the process. Smith fell back slowly, buying time for the approaching Union infantry. Maj. Gen. George Crook sent Brig. Gen. Ranald S. Mackenzie's small cavalry division and Col. Samuel B. M. Young's brigade to Smith's aid.

Lee pulled back Munford's and Rosser's divisions and sent them around the Union cavalry's left flank. They encountered Mackenzie's men on the next ridge toward Appomattox Station and pushed them back. Then Young's brigade arrived and was almost overwhelmed by advance regiments of Rooney Lee's division. Just as it seemed that the Confederate

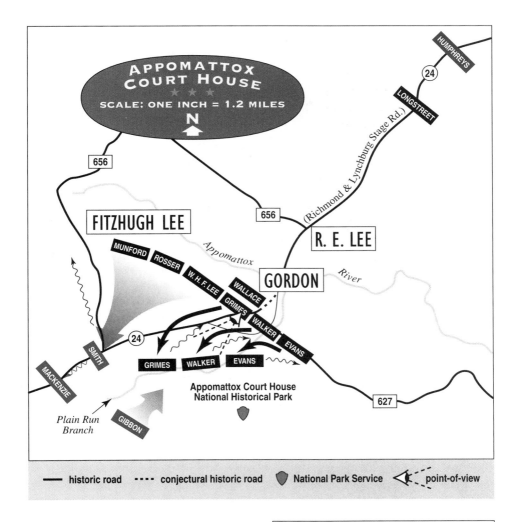

APPOMATTOX COURT HOUSE
★ ★ ★
SCALE: ONE INCH = 1.2 MILES
N

HUMPHREYS

24

LONGSTREET

(Richmond & Lynchburg Stage Rd.)

656

656

FITZHUGH LEE

R. E. LEE

MUNFORD

ROSSER

W. H. F. LEE

Appomattox

WALLACE

GRIMES

GORDON

River

WALKER

24

EVANS

SMITH

GRIMES   WALKER   EVANS

MACKENZIE

**Appomattox Court House
National Historical Park**

627

*Plain Run
Branch*

GIBBON

— historic road   ···· conjectural historic road   🛡 National Park Service   ◀⋯ point-of-view

cavalry would sweep aside their opposition, blue-clad infantry divisions stepped out of the woods to the west: Maj. Gen. John Gibbon's XXIV Corps of Maj. Gen. Edward O. C. Ord's Army of the James and two brigades of United States Colored Troops from XXV Corps.

On the Union right, Devin's division held a ridge against the advancing infantry, thereby separating themselves from the cavalry fight on their right. When Devin turned around and saw Ord's troops passing behind his line to attack from the west, however, he rode west to assist Crook's

DIRECTIONS: From Lee's Retreat Stop 17 (Lee's Rear Guard), s. (left) on State Rte. 24 about 3.9 miles to Appomattox Court House National Historical Park (entrance on right). From U.S. Rte. 460 Bus. and State Rte. 24, n. on State Rte. 24 2.3 miles to park entrance on left. From U.S. Rte. 460 Bypass, n. on State Rte. 24 1.7 miles to park entrance on left. You can visit the National Park Service Web site at nps.gov/parks.html for a virtual tour of this and other national parks.

cavalry, which was engaged with Fitzhugh Lee's.

Parts of Gibbon's division assaulted Brig. Gen. William R. Cox's brigade,

Alfred R. Waud's sketch made as Lee left the McLean house. LIBRARY OF CONGRESS.

which constituted the right flank of the Confederate infantry. The attack was disjointed, composed at different times of various Union brigades. Despite being outnumbered, however, Cox's men held their own and inflicted severe punishment on the Federals.

Gordon realized he could not advance and withdrew his infantry to the ridges on the north side of the Appomattox River, near Lee's bivouac, to avoid being outflanked. On the Confederate right, Fitzhugh Lee's cavalry escaped toward Lynchburg. Gordon sent word back to his commander, who earlier had been informed that the road west was open, that it was now closed. Lee, resplendent in his new uniform, canceled the offensive, saying, "There is nothing left for me to do but to go and see General Grant, and I would rather die a thousand deaths." The last engagement of the Civil War in Virginia cost the Federals 164 casualties, the Confederates about 500.

The battlefield, Lee's headquarters, and the village of Appomattox Court House are preserved in Appomattox Court House National Historical Park. A few modern intrusions have crept toward the park from the town of Appomattox to the southwest, but most of the surrounding area remains agricultural with some residential development. ■

EPILOGUE: THE SURRENDER

On Sunday, April 9, 1865, Lt. Gen. Ulysses S. Grant's reply to Gen. Robert E. Lee's request for a parley passed through Maj. Gen. Andrew A. Humphreys's line and Lt. Gen. James Longstreet's position at about 8:30 A.M. Lee quickly wrote Grant again, specifically requesting a meeting to surrender his army. He sent one message through Humphreys's front, another through Maj. Gen. Philip H. Sheridan's. Truces were called for, and the shooting stopped. Lee sat beside the road in an apple orchard to await Grant's reply.

Just before noon, Lee's note sent through Humphreys reached Grant, whose brain throbbed with a migraine headache. As Grant later wrote, "the instant I saw the contents of the note I was cured." After the letter was read aloud, a staff member proposed three cheers, but the shouts gave way to tears before they were completed. Grant sent a brief reply to Lee by Col. Orville E. Babcock of his own staff, revealing his route to the Confederate commander and asking that he send a messenger to tell Grant where to meet him.

Grant's note reached Lee at the apple orchard at about 1 P.M. Lee responded, then rode with his aides toward Appomattox Court House. Col. Charles Marshall and an orderly, Pvt. Joshua O. Johns, entered the village first, stopped the first white civilian they saw, and explained their mission, which was to find a suitable building for the generals' conference. When they rejected the first place he showed them, the civilian, Wilmer McLean, offered his own dwelling, a modest but commodious brick structure at the western end of the village. McLean had moved to Appomattox Court House to escape the war in Virginia; his former residence was at Manassas.

Marshall approved the choice, and Johns escorted Lee and Babcock to the McLean house, where they went into the parlor to await Grant. A short time later, the Federal commander arrived with a large entourage of officers and went inside. Grant, in contrast to Lee, was wearing a plain field uniform splattered with mud from his long ride and from fording the Appomattox River.

The two commanders made small talk for a few minutes until Lee introduced the subject of the meeting. They each sat at separate tables while Grant wrote out the simple terms: the arms, artillery, and other implements of war to be stacked and surrendered; officers to keep their sidearms and horses; officers and men to be paroled and then return to their homes. When Lee pointed out that Confederate cavalrymen and artillerists supplied their own horses, Grant promised that they could keep them. Marshall wrote a reply to Grant's letter accepting his terms, and Lee signed it. The fighting officially ended.

Grant and Lee discussed rations for the Confederates. When Lee was unable to say how many men remained in his army, Grant offered 25,000 rations, which Lee thought would be sufficient. (The Federal armies were short on rations themselves, but many Union soldiers voluntarily shared their food with their former adversaries.)

The meeting ended at about 3 P.M. Lee walked down the front steps and mounted Traveller, exchanged salutes with Grant, and rode off to face his men. Grant left a few minutes later.

The news of the surrender spread quickly through the ranks of both armies.

Confederate soldiers meeting Lee on the way back to his bivouac had only to look at his face to understand what had happened. Men clustered around their general, patting Traveller and touching Lee's leg, while he told them that he had done all he could for them, and now they must go home and be good citizens. Many wept while some sat stunned by the roadway, unable to believe the news. Soon, however, most of the men would at least be able to feel relief at having survived the war.

Union soldiers were overjoyed, having heard rumors of impending surrender for several days. Lt. Col. Theodore Lyman, an aide to Maj. Gen. George G. Meade, heard the news about 5:00. Meade, who had suffered such a heavy cold that he had ridden in an ambulance for several days, had miraculously recovered. Soon he mounted his horse and galloped down the road shouting: "The war is over, and we are going home!" Grant soon sent word to stop the cannonades and impromptu concerts that had erupted, not wishing to humiliate the Confederates or, as he later wrote, "exult over their downfall."

Lee reached his bivouac in a black mood, and the officers who had to see him on business hastened away as soon as they could. Lee charged Marshall with drafting a farewell message to the Army of Northern Virginia. Constantly interrupted, he did not complete his task until the next morning. Lee edited the text slightly, then approved it to be read to his men:

General Order No. 9
Headquarters, Army of
Northern Virginia
April 10, 1865

After four years of arduous service, marked by unsurpassed courage and fortitude, the Army of Northern Virginia has been compelled to yield to overwhelming numbers and resources.

I need not tell the brave survivors of so many hard fought battles, who have remained steadfast to the last, that I have consented to this result with no distrust of them.

But feeling that valor and devotion could accomplish nothing that would compensate for the loss that must have attended the continuance of the contest, I determined to avoid the useless sacrifice of those whose past services have endeared them to their countrymen.

By the terms of the agreement officers and men can return to their homes and remain until exchanged. You will take with you the satisfaction that proceeds from the consciousness of duty faithfully performed, and I earnestly pray that a Merciful God will extend to you His blessing and protection.

With an increasing admiration of your constancy and devotion to your country, and a grateful remembrance of your kind and generous considerations for myself, I bid you all an affectionate farewell.

R. E. Lee
Genl.

Grant and Lee met again, at 10 A.M. on April 10, to discuss a few of the fine points of the surrender not addressed the day before. Each Confederate soldier would receive a printed pass verifying his status as a paroled prisoner and allowing him to return home unmolested. All those owning horses could keep them, including couriers, and the soldiers could travel through Federal territory for free on government railroads and vessels to reach their homes.

Three officers from each side then met in the village and drew up the protocols for the surrender ceremonies. Lt. Gen. James Longstreet, Maj. Gen. John B. Gordon, and Brig. Gen. William N. Pendleton represented the Confederates, while Maj. Gen. John Gibbon, Maj. Gen. Charles Griffin,

John R. Chapin's rendering of the infantry surrender ceremony as described by Chamberlain.

and Brig. Gen. Wesley Merritt were the Union commissioners. They agreed that the Confederate cavalry would surrender its arms first, that very afternoon, followed by the artillery the next day and the infantry on Wednesday, April 12.

Accordingly, Col. Alexander C. Haskell, 7th South Carolina Cavalry, turned over the horse soldiers' weapons to Brig. Gen. Ranald S. Mackenzie's division. The next day, a rainy morning, Lt. Col. John C. Haskell began surrendering the artillery to Maj. Gen. John W. Turner's Independent Division, which was relieved at noon by Maj. Gen. Joseph J. Bartlett's V Corps division. On Wednesday morning Gordon's corps led the infantry from its bivouacs with Longstreet's corps following, while Brig. Gen. Joshua L. Chamberlain, whose brigade was at the head of Bartlett's division for the ceremony, prepared to receive the surrender.

The rain had stopped by dawn on April 12 when Bartlett's division drew up on both sides of the Richmond–Lynchburg Stage Road through the village. The Federals stood in the early morning dampness, with one end of their line at a place now called the Surrender Triangle, and watched the remnants of Lee's vaunted infantry leave their final bivouac.

As each Confederate division entered the surrender ground, it halted, executed a left face, and dressed its lines as though on parade. The officers took up appropriate positions, commands were issued, bayonets were fixed, and arms were stacked. Cartridge boxes and similar equipment likewise were laid down. Finally, and most reluctantly, the old battle flags were carefully folded and placed on the ground. A few men, weeping, broke ranks to kiss the battle-worn, bloodstained flags. In some cases only empty flagstaffs were turned over, the colors having earlier been cut to pieces and distributed to members of the regiment. Then the division was called to attention and dismissed. And so it went throughout the long day, as the Army of Northern Virginia marched up the hill, laid down its weapons, and slowly passed into history.

For the Union soldiers there would be parades and celebrations: the Grand Review of the armies in Washington late in May followed by more parades and hoopla as the men arrived home. Northern newspapers would trumpet the great victory and extol the heroes, and soldiers of high rank and low would bask in glory real or reflected.

For the Confederates, homecoming would be bittersweet, with only quiet reunions with families and friends. Some would find farms and businesses laid waste, while others would be able to pick up the threads of their lives as though little had changed. Some would join the great migration westward and begin their lives over on the western frontier. Many would remain with their memories on the land that they had striven to defend.

Regardless of the side on which they fought, all the veterans shared common bonds and experiences. On a hundred battlefields boys had become men as they learned to live and die as soldiers. Horrific sights and sounds and smells had seared themselves into the common memory. Some 620,000 lay dead, while many times that number were mangled in body and spirit, overwhelmed by the acts of inhumanity they had suffered or witnessed. Each survivor had a thousand reasons to hoard his own stock of resentments and hatreds and ignore Lee's advice to go home and be good citizens, or Grant's observation that "the Rebels are our countrymen again." For most of them, however, Lee's nobility and Grant's magnanimity had set the tone for the surrender and the days that followed, for by their generous examples each side had sustained the manly pride and dignity of the other.

The standard had been set in Wilmer McLean's parlor, when Lee and Grant first met and the process of reuniting the country had not yet begun. Before the generals sat down to talk, Grant introduced Lee to the other Federal officers present. When Lee shook hands with Lt. Col. Ely Parker, a Seneca Indian who was Grant's military secretary, he said, "I am glad to see one real American here." Parker replied gently, "We are all Americans."

The Americans who had served the Confederacy rather than the Union faced an especially unsettled future. Those who had owned slaves, who had leased them from others, or who had profited from the political, social, and economic systems based on slavery—all of them, in short—had to face the fact that the institution had died with the dream of a separate nation. A new compact had to be negotiated, and a way of life had to be torn apart and sewn anew, following other patterns. Ahead of these men lay—with the murder of Lincoln—the loss of the South's best friend, the humiliating experience of military occupation and Reconstruction, the struggle between Funders and Readjusters, the creation of racial segregation and Jim Crow laws, and a long era of poverty and turmoil, promises and betrayals. But for the moment, in April at Appomattox, despite the crushing disillusionment of defeat, there was at least the hope of spring and renewal, not death and maiming and disease. Unburdened of their weapons, the former soldiers shouldered their packs and bundles and set off on one last march, and every face turned toward home. ▪

GLOSSARY

abatis An obstruction made of trees felled in front of a defensive work, with branches interlocked and pointing toward the enemy

battery Six cannons of the same caliber; (*see also* **section**) also used informally to refer to an earthwork constructed to protect a battery's guns

battle A large military engagement involving armies or major parts of armies

battle flags Flags used to identify units in the smoke and confusion of battle

bivouac A short-term encampment with little or no shelter

brigade A tactical unit consisting of four to six cavalry or infantry regiments (1,000–1,500 men) and commanded by a brigadier general or a colonel

caisson A four-wheeled cart carrying two to three ammunition chests and drawn by six horses

camp A long-term encampment with shelters (tents or huts) and arranged by regiment; often refers to a wintertime encampment

canister An antipersonnel projectile consisting of iron top and bottom plates and a cylinder, or "can," usually filled with forty-eight iron balls; produced a shotgun effect when fired

carbine A short rifle, usually carried by cavalrymen

chevaux-de-frise An obstruction consisting of squared iron or timber six to nine feet long, studded with long sharpened stakes and placed in front of a defensive work

company A tactical unit consisting of fifty to one hundred cavalrymen or infantrymen and commanded by a captain

contraband Technically, supplies or equipment seized because it is useful to the enemy; a term first applied by Maj. Gen. Benjamin F. Butler at Fort Monroe in 1861 to fugitive slaves employed in building Confederate fortifications as a pretext to avoid returning them to their owners

corps A military unit consisting of two to three cavalry or infantry divisions and commanded by a major general (U.S.A.) or a lieutenant general (C.S.A.).

Dahlgren gun Any of three types of naval ordnance developed by Adm. John A. B. Dahlgren, father of Col. Ulric Dahlgren

engagement Generally, a combat of smaller size than a battle; can also refer to any size of armed combat

envelopment An attack on one or both of the enemy's flanks

flank The side or end of a military position

grape shot An antipersonnel projectile consisting of iron top and bottom plates connected by a long bolt around which was stacked nine to twenty-one iron balls wrapped in burlap or held in place by iron bands; produced a shotgun effect when fired

howitzer A usually smoothbore artillery piece with a short tube that lobs shells on a high trajectory

limber A two-wheeled cart bearing an ammunition chest and drawn by three pairs of horses in tandem

Medal of Honor First authorized by U.S. Congress on December 21, 1861; only enlisted men eligible to receive it until World War I

military crest The highest point on an elevation that allows a clear field of fire unobstructed by the slope

minié bullet A hollow-base bullet developed by the French army in the 1840s; standard issue in the Civil War; often called (erroneously) a minié ball

mortar An artillery piece, usually mounted on a heavy bed, designed to throw a shell in a high arc over enemy fortifications; often used in sieges

Napoleon A light howitzer that became the most popular smoothbore field cannon in either army

Parrott Known as Parrott gun or Parrott rifle; developed by Robert P. Parrott; consisted of a rifled tube with a single reinforcing band on the breech

picket A guard post placed in advance of a large force to detect enemy movements

pontoon bridge A floating bridge consisting of interlocked wooden or canvas flat-bottomed boats over which planks and dirt were laid

Quaker guns Cannon-shaped logs painted black and positioned behind fortifications to deceive the enemy; employed mostly by Confederates

regiment A tactical unit consisting of ten cavalry or infantry companies (500–1,000 men) and commanded by a colonel or lieutenant colonel

reverse slope The rear of an elevation out of sight of the enemy; used to conceal troops waiting to enter a battle and also as a defensive position to surprise an attacking enemy

Rodman gun A large smoothbore cannon cast by a process developed by Lt. Thomas J. Rodman in 1844–1845; used primarily for coastal defense

roll of honor A list of officers and soldiers noted for courage in battle that was maintained and published by Confederate authorities beginning in October 1862

salient A part of a defensive work that protrudes toward the enemy beyond the main work

section A two-gun unit of an artillery battery

shell A hollow, gunpowder-filled artillery round exploded by a fuse

shot A solid artillery round

skirmish A small engagement between a limited number of troops, especially when deployed in a skirmish line

skirmish line A spread-out line of soldiers deployed in advance or on the flanks of the main body to draw enemy fire and locate, or "develop," the enemy position

torpedo Today called a mine (especially an underwater mine), the Civil War torpedo consisted of an artillery shell buried in a road to explode when stepped on or a specially constructed device that floated in the water and then exploded on contact with a vessel; employed by both sides, they were considered "infernal machines," outside the bounds of civilized warfare

turning movement A type of envelopment against a point in the rear of the enemy's position; if successful, it compels the enemy to turn away from the front to protect his rear or even to retreat

vedette Also spelled vidette; a mounted soldier, usually a cavalryman, on picket duty

BIBLIOGRAPHY

GENERAL

Civil War Sites Advisory Commission. *Civil War Sites Advisory Commission Report on the Nation's Civil War Battlefields.* Washington, D.C.: National Park Service, 1993.

———. Virginia Battlefield Files and Maps. 1991–1993. Photocopies. Richmond, Va.: Virginia Department of Historic Resources.

Faust, Patricia L., ed. *Historical Times Illustrated Encyclopedia of the Civil War.* New York: Harper and Row, 1986.

Kennedy, Frances H., ed. *The Civil War Battlefield Guide.* 2d ed. Boston: Houghton Mifflin, 1998.

Long, E. B. *The Civil War Day by Day: An Almanac, 1861–1865.* Garden City, N.Y.: Doubleday, 1971.

McPherson, James M. *Battle Cry of Freedom: The Civil War Era.* New York: Oxford University Press, 1988.

Robertson, James I., Jr. *Civil War Sites in Virginia: A Tour Guide.* Charlottesville: University Press of Virginia, 1982.

———. *Stonewall Jackson: The Man, the Soldier, the Legend.* New York: Simon & Shuster Macmillan, 1997.

Thomas, Emory M. *Bold Dragoon: The Life of J. E. B. Stuart.* New York: Harper & Row, 1986.

———. *Robert E. Lee: A Biography.* New York: W. W. Norton, 1995.

———. *Travels to Hallowed Ground: A Historian's Journey to the American Civil War.* Columbia: University of South Carolina Press, 1987.

The War of the Rebellion: A Compilation of the Official Records of the Union and Confederate Armies. Prepared Under the Direction of the Secretary of War by Robert N. Scott. 129 vols. Washington: Government Printing Office, 1880–1901.

MANASSAS CAMPAIGN, 1861

Cooling, Benjamin Franklin, III, and Walton H. Owen II. *Mr. Lincoln's Forts: A Guide to the Civil War Defenses of Washington.* Shippensburg, Pa.: White Mane Publishing, 1988.

Davis, William C. *Battle at Bull Run: A History of the First Major Campaign of the Civil War.* Baton Rouge: Louisiana State University Press, 1977.

Farwell, Byron. *Ball's Bluff: A Small Battle and Its Long Shadow.* McLean, Va.: EPM Publications, 1990.

Hennessy, John. *The First Battle of Manassas: An End to Innocence, July 18–21, 1861.* Lynchburg, Va.: H. E. Howard, 1989.

Holien, Kim Bernard. *Battle at Ball's Bluff.* Orange, Va.: Moss Publications, 1985.

Poland, Charles P. *Dunbarton, Dranesville, Virginia.* Fairfax, Va.: Fairfax County Office of Comprehensive Planning, 1974.

Wheeler, Richard. *A Rising Thunder: From Lincoln's Election to the Battle of Bull Run: An Eyewitness History.* New York, N.Y.: HarperCollins, 1994.

Wills, Mary Alice. *The Confederate Blockade of Washington, D.C., 1861–1862.* Parsons, W.Va.: McClain Printing, 1975.

SHENANDOAH VALLEY CAMPAIGN, 1862

Beck, Brandon H., and Charles S. Grunder. *Jackson's Valley Campaign: The First Battle of Winchester, May 25,*

1862. Lynchburg, Va.: H. E. Howard, 1992.

Collins, Darrell L. *The Battles of Cross Keys and Port Republic*. Lynchburg, Va.: H. E. Howard, 1993.

Hotchkiss, Jedediah. *Make Me a Map of the Valley: The Civil War Journal of Stonewall Jackson's Topographer.* Archie P. McDonald, ed. Dallas: Southern Methodist University Press, 1973.

Krick, Robert K. *Conquering the Valley: Stonewall Jackson at Port Republic*. New York: William Morrow, 1996.

Study of Civil War Sites in the Shenandoah Valley of Virginia, Pursuant to Public Law 101–628. Washington, D.C.: U.S. Department of the Interior, 1992.

Tanner, Robert G. *Stonewall in the Valley: Thomas J. "Stonewall" Jackson's Shenandoah Valley Campaign, Spring 1862*. Garden City, N.Y.: Doubleday, 1976. Updated and revised, Mechanicsburg, Pa.: Stackpole Books, 1996.

PENINSULA AND SEVEN DAYS' CAMPAIGNS

Miller, William J., ed. *The Peninsula Campaign of 1862: Yorktown to the Seven Days*. Campbell, Ca.: Savas Woodbury Publishers, 1993–1995. 2 vols.

Sears, Stephen W. *To the Gates of Richmond: The Peninsula Campaign*. New York: Ticknor & Fields, 1992.

Wheeler, Richard. *Sword Over Richmond: An Eyewitness History of McClellan's Peninsula Campaign*. New York: Harper & Row, 1986.

NORTHERN VIRGINIA CAMPAIGN

Hennessy, John J. *Return to Bull Run: The Campaign and Battle of Second Manassas*. New York: Simon & Schuster, 1993.

Krick, Robert K. *Stonewall Jackson at Cedar Mountain*. Chapel Hill: University of North Carolina Press, 1990.

Stackpole, Edward J. *From Cedar Mountain to Antietam*. 2nd ed. Harrisburg, Pa.: Stackpole Books, 1993.

FREDERICKSBURG AND CHANCELLORSVILLE CAMPAIGNS

Furgurson, Ernest B. *Chancellorsville 1863: The Souls of the Brave*. New York: Alfred A. Knopf, 1992.

Gallagher, Gary W., ed. *The Fredericksburg Campaign: Decision on the Rappahannock*. Chapel Hill: University of North Carolina Press, 1995.

Harrison, Noel G. *Chancellorsville Battlefield Sites*. 2nd ed. Lynchburg, Va.: H. E. Howard, 1990.

Wheeler, Richard. *Lee's Terrible Swift Sword: From Antietam to Chancellorsville, An Eyewitness History*. New York: HarperCollins, 1992.

GETTYSBURG CAMPAIGN

Grunder, Charles S. *The Second Battle of Winchester: June 12–15, 1863*. 2d ed. Lynchburg, Va.: H. E. Howard, 1989.

Coddington, Edwin B. *The Gettysburg Campaign: A Study in Command*. New York: Charles Scribner's Sons, 1968. 2d ed., Dayton, Oh.: Morningside Bookshop, 1979.

BRISTOE STATION AND MINE RUN CAMPAIGNS

Graham, Martin F., and George F. Skoch. *Mine Run: A Campaign of Lost Opportunities, October 21, 1863–May 1, 1864*. 2d ed. Lynchburg, Va.: H. E. Howard, 1987.

Henderson, William D. *The Road to Bristoe Station: Campaigning With Lee and Meade, August 1–October 20, 1863*. Lynchburg, Va.: H. E. Howard, 1987.

OVERLAND CAMPAIGN

Baltz, Louis J., III. *The Battle of Cold Harbor, May 27–June 13, 1864.* 2d ed. Lynchburg, Va.: H. E. Howard, 1994.

Frassanito, William A. *Grant and Lee: The Virginia Campaigns, 1864–1865.* New York: Charles Scribner's Sons, 1983.

Gallagher, Gary W., ed. *The Wilderness Campaign.* Chapel Hill & London: University of North Carolina Press, 1997.

Matter, William D. *If It Takes All Summer: The Battle of Spotsylvania.* Chapel Hill: University of North Carolina Press, 1988.

Miller, J. Michael. *The North Anna Campaign: "Even to Hell Itself," May 21–26, 1864.* 2d ed. Lynchburg, Va.: H. E. Howard, 1989.

Priest, John M. *Nowhere to Run: The Wilderness, May 4th & 5th, 1864.* Shippensburg, Pa.: White Mane Publishing, 1995.

Rhea, Gordon C. *The Battle of the Wilderness, May 5–6, 1864.* Baton Rouge: Louisiana State University Press, 1994.

———. *The Battles for Spotsylvania Court House and the Road to Yellow Tavern, May 7–12 1864.* Baton Rouge: Louisiana State University Press, 1997.

Swank, Walbrook D. *Battle of Trevilian Station.* Shippensburg, Pa.: Burd Street Press, 1994.

Trudeau, Noah A. *Bloody Roads South: The Wilderness to Cold Harbor, May–June 1864.* Boston: Little, Brown, 1989.

BERMUDA HUNDRED CAMPAIGN

Besch, Edwin W. "Action at Wilson's Wharf, 24 May 1864." Richmond, Va.: Virginia Department of Historic Resources, n.d.

Frassanito, William A. *Grant and Lee: The Virginia Campaigns, 1864–1865.* New York: Charles Scribner's Sons, 1983.

Robertson, William Glenn. *Back Door to Richmond: The Bermuda Hundred Campaign, April–June 1864.* Baton Rouge: Louisiana State University Press, 1987.

Schiller, Herbert M. *The Bermuda Hundred Campaign.* Dayton, Oh.: Morningside House, 1988.

SHENANDOAH VALLEY CAMPAIGNS, 1864–1865

Davis, William C. *The Battle of New Market.* Baton Rouge: Louisiana State University Press, 1975.

Duncan, Richard R. *Lee's Endangered Left: The Civil War in Western Virginia, Spring of 1864.* Baton Rouge: Louisiana State University Press, 1998.

Lewis, Thomas A. *The Guns of Cedar Creek.* New York: Harper & Row, 1988.

Morris, George S., and Susan L. Foutz. *Lynchburg in the Civil War: The City—The People—The Battle.* 2d ed. Lynchburg, Va.: H. E. Howard, 1984.

Study of Civil War Sites in the Shenandoah Valley of Virginia, Pursuant to Public Law 101–628. Washington, D.C.: U.S. Department of the Interior, 1992.

Vandiver, Frank E. *Jubal's Raid: General Early's Famous Attack on Washington in 1864.* Lincoln: University of Nebraska Press, 1960, 1988.

Wert, Jeffry D. *From Winchester to Cedar Creek: The Shenandoah Campaign of 1864.* Carlisle, Pa.: South Mountain Press, 1987.

SOUTHWEST VIRGINIA CAMPAIGNS

Duncan, Richard R. *Lee's Endangered Left: The Civil War in Western Virginia, Spring of 1864.* Baton Rouge: Louisiana State University Press, 1998.

Johnson, Patricia G. *The United States Army Invades the New River Valley, May 1864.* Christiansburg, Va.: Walpa Publishing, 1986.

RICHMOND AND PETERSBURG CAMPAIGN

Frassanito, William A. *Grant and Lee: The Virginia Campaigns, 1864–1865.* New York: Charles Scribner's Sons, 1983.

Horn, John. *The Petersburg Campaign. The Destruction of the Weldon Railroad: Deep Bottom, Globe Tavern, and Reams Station, August 14–25, 1864.* Lynchburg, Va.: H. E. Howard, 1991.

Robertson, William G. *The Petersburg Campaign: The Battle of Old Men and Young Boys, June 9, 1864.* Lynchburg, Va.: H. E. Howard, 1989.

Sommers, Richard J. *Richmond Redeemed: The Siege at Petersburg.* Garden City, N.Y.: Doubleday, 1981.

Trudeau, Noah Andre. *The Last Citadel: Petersburg, Virginia, June 1864–April 1865.* Boston: Little, Brown, 1991.

APPOMATTOX CAMPAIGN

Calkins, Christopher M. *The Appomattox Campaign: March 29–April 9, 1865.* Conshohocken, Pa.: Combined Books, 1997.

———. *From Petersburg to Appomattox, April 2–9, 1865.* Farmville, Va.: Farmville Herald Publishing, 1983.

———. *Thirty–Six Hours Before Appomattox, April 6–7, 1865.* Farmville, Va.: Farmville Herald Publishing, 1980 (reprint 1989). ■

Major Preservation Organizations

The organizations listed below are dedicated to the preservation of Virginia battlefields, either directly (as the Civil War Preservation Trust), indirectly (the American Farmland Trust, by helping farmers keep farming, saves land from development), or as part of a larger conservation mission (the Virginia Department of Historic Resources, for instance). Every organization offers some combination of membership, participatory programs, or charitable funds. Contact the Department of Historic Resources for names of battlefield-specific organizations.

American Farmland Trust
1200 18th Street, NW, Suite 800
Washington, DC 20036
Telephone: 202-331-7300
FAX: 202-659-8837
E-mail: info.@farmland.org
www.farmland.org

Central Virginia Battlefields Trust
604A William Street, Suite 1
Fredericksburg, VA 22401
E-mail: webmaster@cvbt.org
www.cvbt.org

Civil War Preservation Trust
E-mail: cwpt@civilwar.org
www.civilwar.org
 Membership:
 11 Public Square, Suite 200
 Hagerstown, MD 21740
 Telephone: 888-606-1400;
  301-665-1400
 FAX: 301-665-1416
 Programs:
 1331 H Street, NW, Suite 1001
 Washington, DC 20005
 Telephone: 202-367-1861
 FAX: 202-367-1865
 Please see page 505 for more
  information.

Commonwealth of Virginia
Department of Historic Resources
2801 Kensington Avenue
Richmond, VA 23221
Telephone: 804-367-2323
FAX: 804-367-2391
www.dhr.state.va.us

Conservation Fund
1800 North Kent Street, Suite 1120
Arlington, VA 22209-2156
Telephone: 703-525-6300
FAX: 703-525-4610
www.conservationfund.org

National Trust for Historic Preservation
1785 Massachusetts Avenue, NW
Washington, DC 20036
Telephone: 202-588-6000
FAX: 202-588-6038
www.nthp.org

The Nature Conservancy
4245 North Fairfax Drive, Suite 100
Arlington, VA 22203-1606
Telephone: 800-628-6860
E-mail: rriordan@tnc.org
www.tnc.org

Virginia Chapter, The Nature Conservancy
490 Westfield Road
Charlottesville, VA 22901
Telephone: 804-295-6106
FAX: 804-979-0370
E-mail: dwhite@tnc.org

Preservation Alliance of Virginia
108 East Grace Street, Suite 1
Richmond VA 23219
Telephone: 804-421-9800
FAX: 804-421-9810
E-mail: pav@vapreservation.org
www.vapreservation.org

Shenandoah Valley Battlefields Foundation
P.O. Box 897
New Market, VA 22844
Telephone: 1-888-689-4545
FAX: 540-740-4509
E-mail: hkittell@shentel.net
www.valleybattlefields.org

Virginia Department of Historic Resources
2801 Kensington Avenue
Richmond, VA 23221
Telephone: 804-367-2323
FAX: 804-367-2391
www.dhr.state.va.us

Virginia Land Conservation Fund
Department of Conservation
  and Recreation
203 Governor Street, Suite 213
Richmond, VA 23219-2094
Telephone: 804-786-1712
E-mail: pco@dcr.state.va.us
www.dcr.state.va.us

Virginia Outdoors Foundation
Department of Conservation
  and Recreation
203 Governor Street, Suite 213
Richmond, VA 23219-2094
Telephone: 804-786-1712
E-mail: pco@dcr.state.va.us
www.dcr.state.va.us ■

INDEX

Cobb, Howell (CSA), 76
Cobb, Thomas R. R. (CSA), 76
Cocke, Philip St. George (CSA), 6–7
Cockpit Point, battle of, 12–14
Cold Harbor, battle of, 107, 294–98
Coleman, Henry E. (CSA), 412
Collis, Charles T. (USA), 229
Colonial National Military Park, 61, 78
Colquitt, Alfred H. (CSA), 304, 319
Colquitt, Peyton H. (CSA), 59, 68
Colston, Raleigh E. (CSA), 174, 179, 182, 188
Cooke, John R. (CSA), 235–36, 471
Cool Spring, battle of, 331, 349–51
Corse, Montgomery D. (CSA), 214, 464, 466, 479
Cosby, George B. (CSA), 390
Couch, Darius N. (USA), 121, 173–77, 183, 186
Coulter, Richard (USA), 144
Cove Mountain, battle of, 377, 385–86
Cowan, Andrew (USA), 479
Cox, William R. (CSA), 491–92
Crater, The, battle of, 398, 418–21
Crawford, Samuel W. (USA), 126, 134, 249, 268, 285, 424, 448, 462–63, 466
Crittenden, Thomas L. (CSA), 285
Crook, George (USA), 251, 329, 332–36, 341, 345–46, 349, 353–55, 362–65, 370, 372, 376–77, 382–83, 385, 459, 461, 465, 478–79, 483, 489–91
Cross Keys, battle of, 45–9
Crutchfield, Stapleton (CSA), 117, 479
CSA units: 1st Md. Inf. Regt., 40; 1st N.C. Inf. Regt., 71, 233; 1st N.C. Cav. Regt., 326; 1st S.C. Rifles Inf. Regt., 284; 1st Va. Cav. Regt., 207–08, 283, 326; 1st Va. Inf. Regt., 15; 2nd Ga. Inf. Batt., 215; 2nd Ga. Inf. Regt., 144–45; 2nd Miss. Inf. Regt., 149; 2nd N.C. Cav. Regt., 326; 2nd S.C. Inf. Regt., 195, 202, 271; 2nd Va. Cav. Regt., 117, 167, 179, 207, 209, 326; 2nd Va. Inf. Regt., 51; 3rd Ga. Inf. Regt., 215; 3rd N.C. Cav. Regt., 326; 3rd S.C. Inf. Regt., 271; 3rd Va. Cav. Regt., 167, 207, 209, 271, 279, 326; 3rd Va. Inf. Regt., 71; 4th N.C. Cav. Regt., 403; 4th S.C. Cav. Regt., 288–89, 298; 4th Va. Cav. Regt., 194, 202, 207, 209, 326; 4th Va. Inf. Regt., 51; 5th N.C. Cav. Regt., 326; 5th N.C. Inf. Regt., 83; 5th S.C. Cav. Regt., 288–89,

326–27; 5th Va. Cav. Regt., 207–9, 282, 326, 482; 5th Va. Inf. Regt., 51; 6th Va. Cav. Regt., 282, 326, 482; 7th Confederate States Cav. Regt., 403; 7th Ga. Regt., 108; 7th La. Inf. Regt., 51–2; 7th S.C. Cav. Regt., 495; 7th Va. Cav. Regt., 134; 8th Ala. Inf. Regt., 190; 8th Ga. Inf. Regt., 108; 9th Ga. Inf. Regt., 144; 9th Va. Cav. Regt., 251; 264; 9th Va. Inf. Regt., 190, 318; 10th Ala. Inf. Regt., 190; 10th Ky. Cav. Batt., 388–89; 11th Ala. Inf. Regt., 190; 11th Ga. Inf. Regt., 138; 11th S.C. Inf. Regt., 313; 11th Va. Inf. Regt., 15; 12th Ga. Inf. Regt., 37, 45; 12th N.C. Inf. Regt., 412; 12th Va. Inf. Regt., 269; 13th Batt. Va. Reserves, 388; 14th Ala. Inf. Regt., 190; 15th Ala. Inf. Regt., 49; 15th Va. Cav. Regt., 282, 326; 17th Va. Inf. Regt., 15, 214–15; 18th Miss. Inf. Regt., 187; 18th N.C. Inf. Regt., 91, 160, 181; 20th Ga. Inf. Regt., 144–45; 21st Ga. Inf. Regt., 141; 21st N.C. Inf. Regt., 141; 21st S.C. Inf. Regt., 308–9, 313; 22nd Ga. Inf. Regt., 215; 23rd Ga. Inf. Regt., 179; 24th Va. Inf. Regt., 83; 25th N.C. Inf. Regt., 98; 25th S.C. Inf. Regt., 309, 313; 26th Va. Inf. Regt., 296; 27th Va. Inf. Regt., 51; 28th N.C. Inf. Regt., 90; 36th Va. Inf. Regt., 382, 384–85, 390; 37th N.C. Inf. Regt., 91; 37th Va. Inf. Regt., 49; 38th Va. Inf. Regt., 318; 43rd Va. Batt., 335; 44th Ala. Inf. Regt., 170; 45th Va. Inf. Regt., 382–84; 48th Ga. Inf. Regt., 215; 49th Ga. Inf. Regt., 154; 50th Ga. Inf. Regt., 417; 53rd Va. Inf. Regt., 318; 54th Ky. Mounted Inf. Regt., 391; 55th N.C. Inf. Regt., 172; 57th Va. Inf. Regt., 318; 60th Va. Inf. Regt., 382, 384; 64th Va. Cav. Regt., 380; African Pioneers, 50; Alexandria Bty., 170; Armory Batt. (Richmond), 264; Army of Northern Virginia, 63, 66, 94–6, 107, 121, 124–25, 131, 142, 173, 183, 197, 203, 217, 219, 223–24, 248–49, 259, 395–96, 400, 451, 454, 473–74, 484, 487, 490, 495; Army of the Valley, 333, 355, 359, 362–63, 370, 372; Beckham Horse Arty., 232; Beckley's Batt., 384; Breathed's Arty., 209; Carpenter's Allegheny Arty., 51; City Light Guards (Columbus, Ga.), 68; Forno's La. Brig., 141; Garnett's Confederates, 134; Ga. Brig., 190; Ga. Legion, 76–7;

Hampton's Legion, 19, 85, 194; Holcombe's Legion, 138; Home Guard (Cloyd's Mt.), 382–4; King and Queen Co. Home Guard, 251; Latham's Bty., 91; Laurel Brig., 366; Light Arty. Blues (Norfolk), 68; La. Brig., 40, 42, 44, 51–53, 106; Miss. Brig., 163, 186; Mosby's Rangers, 154; Norfolk Juniors, 68; Petersburg Bty. 403; Poague's Artillery Batt., 236; Richmond Home Guard, 264; Richmond Howitzers, 260, 262, 286; Ringgold Bty., 382; Rockbridge Arty., 51; S.C. Brig. (Maxcy Gregg's), 103; Stonewall Brig., 30, 35, 42, 51, 132, 134, 147, 206; Stuart's Horse Arty., 198, 219, 233; Tex. Brig., 85, 129, 148, 150, 253, 268; Va. Batt., 71; Wheat's La. Tigers, 40; Wood's Rifles (Norfolk), 68
CSS Patrick Henry, 87; Virginia, 60, 62, 69, 72–5, 86–7
Cullen, Edgar M. (USA), 445
Cumberland Gap: battles of, 375–76, 378–80; National Historical Park, 380
Cumberland Presbyterian Church, battle of, 456, 484–87
Custer, George Armstrong (USA), 220, 224, 237–38, 255, 257–59, 262, 280, 282–83, 289–90, 292, 294, 298–99, 333, 335–37, 357, 367, 372–74, 454–55, 459, 465–66, 474, 489–90
Cutler, Lysander (USA), 219
Cutshaw, Wilfred E. (CSA), 333–35, 367

Dahlgren, John A. B. (USA), 68
Dahlgren, Ulric (USA), 250–51, 262–65
Dam No. 1, battle of, 76–80
Dandy, George B. (USA), 483
Darbytown and New Market Roads, battle of, 400, 436–38
Darbytown Road, battle of, 400, 438–40. See also Fair Oaks and Darbytown Road
Davies, Henry E., Jr. (USA), 237–38, 280, 282, 298, 409–10, 435, 461, 475–76
Davis, Benjamin F. (USA), 199
Davis, Jefferson (CSA), 9, 20, 63, 94–6, 101, 115, 131, 176, 217, 251, 264–65, 306–07, 320–21, 323, 331, 454, 470, 480
Davis, Joseph R. (CSA), 235
Dearing, James (CSA), 304, 456, 482
De Courcy, John F. (USA), 380
Deep Bottom: First battle of, 398, 416–18; Second battle of, 398–99, 421–424

De Trobriand, Régis (USA), 229, 442, 476–77, 480, 485
Devin, Thomas C. (USA), 282–83, 292, 294, 298–99, 333, 357, 459, 465–66, 479, 490–91
Dibrell, George G. (CSA), 388–89
Dickenson, Crispin (CSA), 382
Dimmock, Charles H. (CSA), 395, 401
Dinwiddie Court House, battle of, 453, 459–61
Doubleday, Abner (USA), 147
Dranesville, battle of, 23–5
Drewry's Bluff, battle of, 86–7, 102
DuBose, Dudley M. (CSA), 479
Duffié, Alfred N. A. (USA), 194–96, 198–99, 202, 207, 209–11, 345–47, 349, 385
Duke, Basil W. (CSA), 377, 390
Duncan, Samuel A. (USA), 432
Dunovant, John (CSA), 326–27
Du Pont, Henry A. (USA), 343, 355, 370–71
Duryée, Abram (USA), 69
Duval, Isaac H. (USA), 355
Dwight, William (USA), 334, 362–63

Eagle, Henry (USA), 59, 67–8
Early, Jubal A. (CSA), 6, 16, 20, 62, 82–3, 132, 134–35, 137–38, 141–42, 159–60, 163–64, 174, 176, 178, 184, 187–88, 190–91, 195–96, 204–7, 219, 221–22, 225, 230, 233, 241–42, 244, 249, 257, 259, 274–76, 288, 290–92, 295–96, 331–37, 344–47, 349, 351, 353, 355, 357, 359, 363, 365–68, 371–74, 451–52
Early, William H., 345
Echols, John (CSA), 339, 388
Eltham's Landing, battle of, 83–5
Elzey, Arnold (CSA), 49
Emory, William H. (USA), 333, 363, 365, 370
Evans, Clement A. (CSA), 370–71, 448
Evans, Nathan G. (CSA), 8, 9, 17–9, 21–2
Ewell, Richard S. (CSA), 32, 35–8, 40, 42, 44–5, 49, 50, 54, 104, 109, 127–28, 132, 137, 140–42, 145–48, 195–96, 203–06, 215–16, 218–23, 225–26, 229–30, 232–33, 236–37, 241–42, 249–53, 255–56, 260, 262, 266–68, 270–71, 275–78, 285–86, 288, 416, 431, 451, 454–55, 476–77, 479

Fairchild, Harrison (USA), 445, 483–84
Fair Oaks. See Seven Pines
Fair Oaks and Darbytown Road, battle of, 400, 443–45

Farinholt, Benjamin L. (CSA), 397, 412–13
Farley, Will (CSA), 195
Farnum, J. Egbert (USA), 215–16
Ferguson, Champ (CSA), 377
Ferrero, Edward (USA), 249–51, 420–21
Field, Charles W. (CSA), 249, 286, 400, 423, 433, 436, 438, 440, 443, 483
Finegan, Joseph (CSA), 296, 448
Fisher's Hill, battle of, 334–35, 363–65
Five Forks, battle of, 452–53, 463–67
Flournoy, Thomas S., CSA, 41
Forno, Henry (CSA), 141–42
Forts: Archer, 400, 435; Breckin-ridge, 392–93; Clifton, battle of, 314–16; Darling, 7–8; Early, 345–47; Gilmer, 429, 432; Gregg (Henrico Co.), 429, 432; Gregg (Petersburg), 454, 470–71; Huger, 158, 169–72; Harrison, 399, 400, 416, 429, 431–33, 436, 451; Hatton, 392–93; Johnson, 432; Magruder, 61–2, 81–3; Mahone, 470–71; Milroy, 203–05, 207; Monroe, 28, 58–61, 67, 69, 72–5, 125; Pocahontas, 303–04, 308, 325–28, 429; Powhatan, 303–04, 308, 327; Statham, 392–93; Stedman, battle of, 401, 448–50, 452; Stevens, 322; West, 203–05, 207; Whitworth, 454, 470
Foster, Robert S. (USA), 416, 423, 432, 443, 483
Franklin, William B. (USA), 62, 80, 83–5, 88, 111–12, 117, 119, 155–57, 161–63, 165, 332
Frazer, John W. (CSA), 376, 379
Fredericksburg: First battle of, 156–57, 160–65; Second battle of, 160, 183–88
Fredericksburg and Spotsylvania National Military Park, 164, 184, 188, 192, 270, 279
Frémont, John C. (USA), 31–2, 35–8, 45–50, 54, 126
French, William H. (USA), 197, 215–16, 219, 221–22, 224, 226, 229–31, 235, 239, 241–42, 244
Front Royal, battle of, 38–41
Fulkerson, Samuel (CSA), 31, 34–5, 49
Funsten, Oliver R. (CSA), 222, 227, 232

Gaines's Mill, battle of, 64, 102–08, 164
Gantt, F. Hay (CSA), 313
Garnett, Richard (CSA), 30–1, 34–5, 42
Garnett, Thomas S. (CSA), 132
Garnett's and Golding's Farms, battle of, 64, 107–09

Gary, Martin W. (CSA), 436, 440, 443, 454, 476, 489–90
Geary, John W. (USA), 134
Getty, George W. (USA), 170, 249, 252, 268, 334, 362–63, 371, 479
Gibbon, John (USA), 147, 164, 174, 186, 249, 399, 427–28, 456, 470, 483–84, 491, 494
Gibbs, Alfred (USA), 282
Gillem, Alvan C. (USA), 387–88, 390, 392–93
Gillmore, Quincy A. (USA), 303, 305, 307, 313, 316, 319–24, 395, 401, 403
Giltner, Henry L. (CSA), 388, 390
Glendale, battle of, 112–16
Globe Tavern, battle of, 399, 424–426
Golding's (Gouldin's) Farm, battle of. See Garnett's and Golding's Farm
Gordon, James B. (CSA), 219, 222, 227, 232–33, 280, 282
Gordon, John B. (CSA), 186, 191, 205, 270, 276–77, 279, 334, 336, 345–46, 351, 354–55, 362–63, 370, 372, 401, 448–50, 455–56, 470, 476–77, 479–80, 484–85, 487–90, 492, 494
Gracie, Archibald (CSA), 321
Graham, Charles K. (USA), 314
Graham, Robert (USA), 305, 309
Grant, Ulysses S. (USA), 226, 245, 247–49, 251–59, 266–68, 270, 273–75, 277–79, 284–85, 287–88, 290, 292, 294–95, 298, 303, 306, 308, 316, 318, 329, 332–37, 341, 343, 346, 372, 376, 382, 395–401, 406, 408, 410, 416, 418–19, 421, 424, 429, 433, 441, 443, 448, 450–52, 455–57, 462, 467, 471, 477, 480, 487–90, 492–93, 494, 496
Greene, George S. (USA), 134
Gregg, David M. (USA), 193–96, 198–202, 207–08, 210–13, 219, 221–22, 227, 230, 233, 235, 249, 256, 279–80, 282, 288, 290, 298, 398, 400–01, 408, 421–23, 426, 433, 442, 446
Gregg, J. Irvin (USA), 196–97, 207, 212, 282, 289, 298–99, 410, 479, 487
Gregg, John (CSA), 268, 433, 436, 438
Gregg, Maxcy (CSA), 103–04, 148, 154
Griffin, Charles (USA), 19, 219, 249, 267–68, 292, 426, 435, 457, 459, 462–63, 466–67, 477, 494
Griffin, Thomas (USA), 187
Griffith, Richard (CSA), 112
Grimes, Bryan (CSA), 490
Grover, Cuvier (USA), 98, 334, 362–63
Guard Hill, battle of, 333, 355–57
Gwynn, Walter (CSA), 68